Brassey's Battles

3,500 Years of Conflict, Campaigns and Wars from A-Z

Brassey's Battles

3,500 Years of Conflict, Campaigns and Wars from A-Z

John Laffin

Brassey's
London • Washington

First English Edition 1986
Flexicover Edition 1995

UK editorial offices: Brassey's, 33 John Street, London WC1N 2AT
UK orders: Marston Book Services, PO Box 87, Oxford OX2 0DT

North American Orders: Brassey's Inc., PO Box 960
Herndon, VA 22070, USA

John Laffin has asserted his moral right to be identified as
the author of this work.

Library of Congresss Cataloging in Publication Data
available

British Library Cataloguing in Publication Data
A catalogue record for this book is available from the British Library

ISBN 1 85753 176 0 Flexicover

Printed in Great Britain by BPC Wheatons Ltd

Contents

List of Battles, Campaigns and Wars

In the **List of Battles, Campaigns and Wars,** † *after an entry indicates that there is a corresponding entry in the* **Update Supplement.**

List of Maps

List of Maps in the Update Supplement

Introduction

Brassey's Battles is more comprehensive than any other work of its type in the last century. It is a dictionary in that it lists alphabetically more than 7,000 battles, campaigns and wars, and it is an encyclopaedia in its scope and time span — nearly 3,500 years.

Its preparation had two main difficulties — verification of traditional facts and figures, and decision on precisely what degree of conflict constitutes a "battle".

Wartime statistics are notoriously suspect; each side minimizes its own casualties and other losses while exaggerating those it inflicts on the enemy. Opposing "facts" of a battle can be startlingly different; for instance, some French descriptions of the Battle of Trafalgar make it a decisive French victory. Later historians often fail to do their own research and perpetuate the errors of earlier ones. Ancient recorders speak of millions of men being involved in certain combats, with casualties in the hundreds or thousands. We know that in many cases these figures are grossly incorrect, and where verification is not possible I quote statistics as traditional or as claims.

Dates are another source of difficulty with ancient battles, partly because of changes in calendar systems or because of perpetuated error. In some cases it is possible to give only the year of an action.

A reference book which goes no further than being a dictionary of battles is inadequate as a reference in modern times because many wars and campaigns are fought without a single battle, even of a minor nature. For example, the Northern Ireland conflict is of major political and military importance, but rarely are more than a few men of either side involved in combat; most British casualties are caused by a sniper's bullet or a bomb exploded in a hotel bar. Again, the civil war in Lebanon has had no battles — unless concentrated artillery fire on civilian targets constitutes a "battle". A dictionary reference book which covered nothing but battles would omit mention of the Italian invasion of Abyssinia in 1936, the (Nigerian) Civil War, the American invasion of Grenada in 1983 and the Russian invasion of Afghanistan. In six years, 1979–85, not a single battle occurred in Afghanistan, though there was much guerrilla activity by the Afghan tribesmen against the occupying Soviet armies and helicopter gunship attacks by the Russians against the guerrillas.

In some cases there is only a fine line between a war and a battle. For instance, the war between Israel and the attacking Arab states in 1973 was really a phased battle fought on two fronts.

The difference between a battle and a minor action or a skirmish can also be a fine one. Clearly, a fight involving large numbers of troops, fleets of ships and hundreds of aircraft is a battle. Even here some caution is necessary, for commanders have often manoeuvred large formations without combat being joined, as Marshal Turenne and Marshal Saxe did. Sometimes they achieved decisive political results — and political results are the aim of every war. A campaign of manoeuvre might not produce casualties, but it may be profoundly important. So are some military actions in which not a shot was fired. A classic example is the capture of Sariwond, a heavily fortified stronghold held by the North Koreans in 1950, during the Korean War. In October of that year two company commanders of the Australian 3rd Battalion mounted a tank and drove right up to the forward enemy posts. They told the North Koreans that they were surrounded by an overwhelming force — this was quite untrue — and should give up. No fewer than 1,982 enemy soldiers surrendered, with large quantities of arms, to a few hundred Australians. To omit the capture of Sariwond simply because no shots were fired and nobody was killed would be an historical injustice. (It is not again mentioned in this book.) In a way it was a greater achievement than a conventional battle.

What of a fight involving only a few hundred men or two opposing ships? Tens of thousands of such actions have occurred, particularly during the "great wars". I have included these fights as battles when the result was significant enough to affect the course of a war or campaign, when it had an impact on history, when history itself has in retrospect given an action the status of battle, or when the action was important to one or other of the belligerent nations, regardless of its importance in relative world terms.

In World War I — 1914–18 — many an action, though of some magnitude in itself, was really only a part of a major battle, as was the fight for Fort Douaument in the Battle of Verdun and the fight for High Wood in the Battle of the Somme. Where they meet the requirements set out above, these "sub-battles" are included in the book.

The escape of H.M.S. *Amethyst* along the Yangtse River during the Chinese Civil War of 1949 is held in such importance in Britain that it could hardly be omitted, though, strictly judged, the ship's fight was not a battle at all but an incident of war which showed men's fortitude and endurance.

There is a peculiar vanity among European military historians which blinds them to the importance of battles during the American War of Independence, American Civil War and the American Indian Wars. Many of these actions were major engagements by any standard and they are given due space in this book. Similarly, Australians could well be aggrieved by lack of mention in many war history reference books to the campaign and battles of the Kokoda Trail 1942–3, a name as famous in Australian history as Gallipoli and Tobruk. This applies also to the battles in Papua–New Guinea 1942–3 for Buna, Gona, Gorari and Sanananda, among others.

For the space devoted to each battle, campaign or war I have followed the principle — though not slavishly — of the more recent the event the longer the entry. A naval battle of 435 BC is worth a few lines; the Iran–Iraq (Gulf) War merits 800 words. Recent conflicts deserve greater space if only because it is difficult for the average reader to find adequate consolidated information about events which are still "in the news".

Battle names are derived from the place names in use at the time of the action. Thus, seven battles were fought at what is now Edirne, but the battles are listed under the more famous name of Adrianople. Where wars or battles are known by more than one name, I have listed all. For instance, the term Yom Kippur War for the conflict between Israel and certain Arab countries in 1973 is relevant only to the Israelis; for the Egyptians it was The Great Crossing. Many other people refer to it as the October War. Historians have given some battles the "wrong" names: the fighting which ended in the capture of Damascus in 1918 is often called the Battle of Damascus. But all the fighting took place long before Damascus, and Megiddo is more appropriate as a label, though even this is unsuitable.

Cross-references for battles campaigns and wars are given where this will provide the reader with a fuller understanding of any event.

I have followed the traditional spelling of place names, but some do not easily translate from their original language, especially Arabic.

Preparation of *Brassey's Battles* has been a monumental task spread over many years. In personal acknowledgement I gratefully thank my wife, who is my assistant, for the thousands of hours she has devoted to this book and for the consequential patience she showed during the even longer period I devoted to it. Also, I appreciate the work of my enthusiastic editor, Jenny Shaw, and the labours of Enid Davies, who did much of the typing in the later stages of the book.

For certain pre-1900 entries I have leant on the work of T. H. Harbottle who in 1904 published a dictionary of battles. Harbottle was not a military historian and he made many mistakes. For instance, Bunker Hill he calls Bunker's Hill, a common error which irritates Americans. At Mute (629) he has the Muslims victorious when in fact they were repulsed; at Jassy (1620) he has the Poles defeating the Turks, though in reality they won; at Segesvár (1849) the Russians are "Totally defeated" by the Hungarians; in fact the allied Russians and Austrians beat the Hungarians. Harbottle omits many important battles, such as Lake Trasimeno 271 BC, Verulamium 154 BC, Verulamium II AD 61, Simancas 934, Yellow River 1226, Namur 1692 and 1695, Peking 1900 and all three battles of Savannah. Despite his inadequacies and inaccuracies, Harbottle produced the first quick-reference battles dictionary and students and historians owe him a debt. I acknowledge mine.

Special thanks are due to Martin Gilbert for permission to use his 1948 Israel–Arab war map. The French Revolutionary and Napoleonic Wars map from the *Encyclopedia of Modern War* by Roger Parkinson © 1978 is reproduced by permission of Stein and Day Publishers, New York, and Routledge & Kegan Paul, London. The Tet offensive 1968 map from *The Vietnam War* © 1979 is reproduced by permission of Salamander Books, London. The maps of Neville Cross, Flodden, Edge Hill and Killiecrankie from *The Battlefields of Britain* by John Kinross © 1979 are reproduced by permission of David & Charles, London.

JOHN LAFFIN

Introduction to the New Edition

It might have been expected that the horror and destruction of the Second World War, together with its immense casualties and limitless suffering, would end mankind's appetite for war. On the contrary war, and the threat of war, still affects many countries and, judged by its frequency, is normal — morally deplorable, intellectually grotesque and viciously inhumane, but normal.

The motivating forces for war remain the greed for land and treasure, fear, poverty, the lust for power, religious hatreds and fundamentalism, ideological enmity — and the greatest of these and all other provoking causes is fear. It may be fear of being swallowed up by a larger, stronger neighbour; fear of losing ancient rights; fear of losing national identity; fear of being deprived of basic resources, such as water; or fear of not having enough space — Hitler went to war for *Lebensraum*.

The fears which cause tribes, nations, and alliances to strike pre-emptively or in retaliation are legion, and often they are reciprocal. This is the tragic situation in the former nation of Yugoslavia, which has degenerated into a collection of murderous tribes driven by urges so primitive that they are outrageous in a continent, Europe, that is generally considered cultured.

Towards the end of the 20th century the world is living in a culture of conflict, conflict that flourishes in mistrust, ignorance and envy.

Since *Brassey's Battles* was published in 1986 many new wars have broken out and a few that were described in the 1986 edition have come to an end. Some of them have been major conflicts. In terms of the number of troops deployed and the weight and sophistication of weapons used, the Gulf War of 1991 was the largest conflict since the end of World War II. Wars of genocide now disfigure the international scene, most wickedly in Rwanda. Genocide was actually a military objective in this benighted country, as in Bosnia-Herzegovina, Kashmir and Kurdistan, among other places.

For the new edition of *Brassey's Battles* I have written about all the wars of the world since 1986 and about the campaigns and battles within those wars. Several peace-keeping institutions, notably the United Nations itself, maintain buffer armies in place between belligerents in attempts to stop them from destroying each other, but it is being shown repeatedly that nations and leaders are not interested in moderation or mediation.

Expressed in industrial terms, war is a growth industry and fear is the motor that drives it. As the world's burgeoning population competes for a finite quantity of land and resources, so we will be plagued by wars caused by the *fear of war* itself.

John Laffin, December 1994

By the same Author

Military

Middle East Journey

Return to Glory

One Man's War

The Walking Wounded

Digger (The Story of the Australian Soldier)

Scotland the Brave (The Story of the Scottish Soldier)

Jackboot (The Story of the German Soldier)

Tommy Atkins (The Story of the English Soldier)

Jack Tar (The Story of the English Seaman)

Swifter Than Eagles (Biography of Marshal of the Air Force Sir John Salmond)

The Face of War

British Campaign Medals

Codes and Ciphers

Boys in Battle

Women in Battle

Anzacs at War

Links of Leadership (Thirty Centuries of Command)

Surgeons in the Field

Americans in Battle

Letters From the Front 1914–18

The French Foreign Legion

Damn the Dardanelles! (The Story of Gallipoli)

The Australian Army at War 1899–1975

The Arab Armies of the Middle East Wars 1948–1973

The Israeli Army in the Middle East Wars 1948–1973

Fight For the Falklands!

The War of Desperation: Lebanon 1982–85

The Man the Nazis Couldn't Catch

On the Western Front

Battlefield Archaeology

Western Front 1916–17 — The Price of Honour

Western Front 1917–18 — The Cost of Victory

World War I in Postcards

Greece, Crete & Syria 1941 (The Australian Campaigns)

Secret and Special (Australian Operations)

The World in Conflict: War Annual 1

The World in Conflict: War Annual 2

The World in Conflict: War Annual 3

The World in Conflict: War Annual 4

The World in Conflict: War Annual 5

The World in Conflict: War Annual 6

Western Front Illustrated

Guide to Australian Battlefields of the Western Front 1916–1918

Digging Up the Diggers' War

Panorama of the Western Front

Forever Forward (History of the 2/31st Battalion A.I.F.)

A Western Front Companion 1914–1918

General

The Hunger to Come (Food and Population Crises)

New Geography 1966–67

New Geography 1968–69

New Geography 1970–71

Anatomy of Captivity (Political Prisoners)

Devil's Goad

Fedayeen (The Arab–Israeli Dilemma)

The Arab Mind

The Israeli Mind

The Dagger of Islam

The Arabs as Master Slavers

The PLO Connections

Know the Middle East

Holy War: Islam Fights

Dictionary of Africa Since 1960

Aussie Guide to Britain

Major Wars and Their Battles

The major wars of history are listed chronologically, as are the battles which took place during those wars. A glance at the number of actions during a particular war gives some idea of the conflict's intensity. For instance, 71 battle names appear under *War of the American Revolution* and 166 campaigns and battles are listed for *World War II*; in addition, many more actions appear in the text. The lists of battles are intended as a guide, so that readers may trace the course of a war by its battles. Perhaps for the first time there is a comprehensive list of major sea fights — including a few significant single-ship actions — from 480 BC to AD 1982. In addition, there is a list of airborne assaults in which paratroops actually dropped into battle or where gliders took men into battle. It is important, too, that the codenames of the major operations of World War II should be recorded, as they are here.

Greek–Persian Wars
499–448 BC

Ephesus	499 BC
Lade	494 BC
Marathon	490 BC
Thermopylae	480 BC
Salamis	480 BC
Plataea	479 BC
Mycale	479 BC
Eurymedon River	466 BC

Peloponnesian War
458–447 BC
(sometimes the First Peloponnesian War)

Athens vs. Sparta.

Aegina	458–457 BC
Tanagra-Oenphyta	457 BC
Coronea	447 BC

Great Peloponnesian War
432–404 BC

Plataea	429–427 BC
Naupactus	429 BC
Mytilene	427 BC
Olpae	426 BC
Pylos-Sphacteria (Navarino)	425 BC
Delium	424 BC
Amphipolis	422 BC
Mantinea	418 BC
Syracuse	415–413 BC
Cynossema	411 BC
Cyzicus	410 BC
Notium	407 BC
Ephesus	406 BC
Arginusae Islands	406 BC
Aegospotami	405 BC

Athens surrendered in 404 BC.

Greek City-states Wars
395–362 BC

Haliartus	395 BC
Coronea	394 BC
Cnidus	394 BC
Naxos	376 BC
Leuctra	371 BC
Cynoscephalae	364 BC

1

Mantinea	362 BC

Macedonian Imperial Wars 338–322 BC

These wars would be more correctly called the Conquests of Alexander the Great.

Chaeronea	338 BC
Thebes	335 BC
Granicus River	334 BC
Issus	333 BC
Tyre	332 BC
Gaza	332 BC
Arbela (Gaugamela)	331 BC
Megalopolis	331 BC
Pandosia	331 BC
Hydaspes River	326 BC
Crannon (Athenian revolt)	322 BC

Macedonian–Rome Wars

215–205 BC	No battle
200–106 BC	Cynoscephalae
172–167 BC	Pydna
152–146 BC	A revolt only

Punic Wars 265–146 BC

Rome vs. Carthage.

First Punic War

Messina (Messana)	264 BC
Mylae	260 BC
Liparaean Islands	257 BC
Ecnomus, Cape	256 BC
Tunis (Tunes)	255 BC
Lilybaeum	251 BC
Panormus	251 BC
Drepanum (Trapani)	249 BC
Aegates Islands	241 BC

Second Punic War

Saguntum	219–218 BC
Ticinus River	218 BC
Trebbia River	218 BC
Trasimeno Lake	217 BC
Cannae	216 BC
Nola (three battles)	216–214 BC

Beneventum	214 BC
Syracuse	214–212 BC
Capua	212–211 BC
Herdonea	210 BC
New Carthage	209 BC
Asculum	208 BC
Grumentum	207 BC
Metaurus	207 BC
Ilipa (Silpia)	206 BC
Crotone	204 BC
Utica	203 BC
Zama	202 BC

Third Punic War

Carthage	149–146 BC

The Romans dismantled the city of Carthage stone by stone, slaughtered or enslaved the populace, and it became extinct.

Gallic Wars 58–52 BC

Julius Caesar's Legions vs. the Helvetians, Germans, Gauls of southern France and, in one battle, the Britons.

Bibracte (Mount Beauvay)	58 BC
Vesontio	58 BC
Sambre River (Sabis)	57 BC
Morbihan Gulf	56 BC
Coblenz	55 BC
Tongres (Aduatuca)	54 BC
Verulamium (Britain)	54 BC
Agendicum	52 BC
Alesia (Alise-Ste.-Reine)	52 BC
Avaricum (Bourges)	52 BC
Gergovia	52 BC

Great Roman Civil War or War of the First Triumvirate 50–44 BC

The triumvirs were Julius Caesar, Pompey the Great and Marcus Crassus. When Crassus died during the retreat from the Battle of Carrhae, 54–53 BC, the other two sought dominance. The Senate passed a law which would end Caesar's authority on 1 March 49 BC. In response, he crossed the Rubicon River, thus entering Rome proper and waged war against

Pompey. After twelve actions he was victorious.

Rubicon River	49 BC
Ilerda	49 BC
Utica	49 BC
Bagradas River	49 BC
Illyria	49 BC
Dyrrachium	48 BC
Pharsalus	48 BC
Alexandria	47 BC
Zela	47 BC
Ruspina	46 BC
Thapsus	46 BC
Munda	45 BC

Caesar assassinated 44 BC.

Wars of the Second Triumvirate 43–31 BC

On the death of Julius Caesar a second triumvirate ruled Rome. They were Mark Anthony, Marcus Lepidus and Octavian (Caesar Octavianus). Octavian defeated the others and as Augustus became the first Emperor of Rome.

Mutina	43 BC
Philippi	42 BC
Perusia	41–40 BC
Phraaspa	36 BC
Naulochus	36 BC
Actium	31 BC

Muslim Imperial Conquests 624–982

Muhammad, as the founder of Islam, first commanded the Muslims in battle. For centuries Muslim armies fought against virtually all the races around the Mediterranean and throughout Asia Minor.

Badr	624
Ohod	625
Medina	627
Muta	629
Mecca	630
Hira	633
Ajnadain	634
Pella (Fihl or Gilead)	635
Damascus	635

Yarmuk River	636
Kadisiya (Qadisiya)	637
Jalula	637
Jerusalem	637
Aleppa	638
Babylon	639
Nihawand (Nahavend)	641
al-Fustat	641
Alexandria	642
Tripoli	643
Lycia (Dhat al-Sawari)	655
Basra ("Battle of the Camel")	656
Siffin	657
Cyzicus	668
Constantinople	673–8
Kerbela	680
Sebastopolis	690–2
Carthage	698
Kabul (Maskin)	701
Rio Barbate (Guadalete)	711
Constantinople	717–18
Covadonga	718
Toulouse	721
Tours	732
Kashgar	736
Acroinum	739
Talas	751
Zab al Kabir	806
Heraclea Pontica	838
Amorium	838
Samosata	873
Apulia	875–80
Taormina	902
Erzerum	928
Melitene	934
Simancas	934
Zamora	939
Candia	960–1
Adana	964
Aleppo–Antioch	969
Damascus	976
Crotone	982

Mongol Wars 1190–1402

Genghis Khan's Conquests

Pekin	1214
Khojend	1219
Bukhara	1220
Samarkand	1220
Herat	1220–1

Merv	1221
Bamian	1221
Pirvan	1221
Indus	1221
Kalka River	1223
Yellow River	1226

Genghis died in 1227.

Kiev	1240
Cracow	1241
Liegnitz	1241
Mohi	1241
Baghdad	1258
Ain Jalut	1260
Hakata Bay	1274
Kyushu	1281

Tamerlane's Conquests
(Tamerlane was a Tartar, not a Mongol)

Kandurcha (the Steppes)	1391
Panipat	1398
Delhi	1398
Baghdad	1401
Angora	1402

First Barons' War of England 1215–17

Rochester	1215
Dover	1216–17
Lincoln	1217
Sandwich	1217
Bytham	1220
Bedford	1224

Second Barons' War of England 1264–7

Northampton	1264
Rochester	1264
Lewes	1264
Kenilworth	1265–6
Evesham	1265
Axholme	1265
Newport (holding of Severn River defensive line)	1265
Chesterfield	1266
Ely	1266–7

Hundred Years' War 1337–1457

England vs. France. Portugal and Burgundy were for a time allies of England; Castile supported France. The name of the war is misleading. It lasted 120 years, but was really a series of eight conflicts with a 30-year truce, 1396–1413, and a 5-year truce, 1444–9. The last 4 years of the war consisted mainly of French raids on the English coast.

Sluys	1340
Crécy	1346
Calais	1346–7
Winchelsea	1350
Poitiers	1356
Auray	1364
Navarrette or Najera	1367
La Rochelle	1372
Chateauneuf-de-Randon	1380
Aljubarrotta	1385
Margate	1387
Harfleur	1415
Agincourt	1415
Rouen	1418–19
Beaugé (Baugé)	1421
Cravant	1423
Verneuil	1424
Orleans	1428–9
Rouvray ("the Herrings")	1429
Jargeau	1429
Patay	1429
Rouen	1449
Formigny (Bailleul)	1450
Castillon	1453

Hussite Wars 1419–34

Anti-Catholic revolt against King of Bohemia.

Sudoner	1419
Prague	1420
Kutná Hora (Kuttenberg)	1422
Německý Brod	1422
Ústí nad Labem	1426
Český-Brod	1434

War of the Roses 1455–85

An English civil war fought between

the House of Lancaster (red rose) and House of York (white rose).

Saint Albans	1455
Blore Heath	1459
Ludford	1459
Sandwich	1460
Northampton	1460
Wakefield	1460
Ferrybridge	1461
Mortimer's Cross	1461
Saint Albans	1461
Towton	1461
Hedgeley Moor	1464
Hexham	1464
Banbury (Edgecote)	1469
Lose-coat Field	1470
Ravenspur	1471
Barnet	1471
Tewkesbury	1471
Bosworth Field	1485

Netherlands War of Independence 1567–1648

Revolt of Dutch Protestant provinces against Spanish occupation. In 1585–7 an English expeditionary force supported the Dutch.

Brielle (Brill)	1572
Haarlem	1572–3
Alkmaar	1573
Walcheren	1574
Mookerheide	1574
Leyden	1574
Gembloux (Gemblours)	1578
Maastricht	1579
Antwerp	1584–5
Zutphen	1586
Breda	1590
Turnhout	1597
Nieuwpoort ("Battle of the Dunes")	1600
Oostende	1601–4
The 12-Years' Truce	1609–21
Breda	1624–5
Battle of the Downs	1639

The Spanish defeat in the Battle of Rocroi, during the Thirty Years' War, was the tactical end of the Netherlands War of Independence.

Thirty Years' War 1618–48

Bohemian Phase 1618–25

Religious war between Roman Catholics and Protestants in Germany.

Pilsen	1618
Sablat	1619
White Mountain (Weisser Berg)	1620
Wiesloch	1622
Mingolsheim	1622
Wimpfen	1622
Höchst	1622
Fleurus	1622
Stadtlohn	1623
Breda (Dutch-Spanish War)	1625

Danish Phase: 1625–9

Danish Protestant invasion of Germany.

Dessau Bridge	1626
Lutter am Barenberge	1626
Stralsund	1628
Wolgast	1628

Swedish Phase: 1630–4

A political war of conquest. During this phase the Holy Roman Empire (Ferdinand II, the Hapsburg emperor) and Spain (Philip IV) fought Denmark and Norway (Christian IV) and Sweden (Gustavus Adolphus).

Magdeburg	1630–1
Frankfurt on the Oder	1631
Werben (Havelberg)	1631
Leipzig	1631
Breitenfeld	1631
Rain	1632
Fürth (Alte Veste)	1632
Leck River	1632
Lützen	1632
Nordlingen	1634

French Phase: 1634–48

A mainly political war. The Hapsburg empire fought the allied Swedes and French. Sweden was also fighting Poland and France was at war with Spain. Spain was at war with Protestant Holland and for a time Sweden and Denmark were fighting each other. Throughout the war German princes joined one side or the other.

Wittstock	1636
Breda	1637
Rheinfelden	1638
Breisach	1638
Chemnitz	1639
Breitenfeld	1642
Rocroi	1643
Tuttlingen	1643
Freiburg	1644
Jankau	1645
Mergentheim	1645
Nördlingen (Allerheim)	1645
Zusmarshausen	1648
Prague	1648
Lens	1648

First English Civil War 1642–6

Parliamentarians vs. Royalists.

Edgehill	1642
Brentford	1642
Turnham Green (skirmish)	1642
Grantham	1643
Stratton	1643
Chalgrove Field	1643
Adwalton Moor	1643
Lansdowne	1643
Roundway Down	1643
Newbury I	1643
Nantwich	1644
Cheriton	1644
Selby	1644
Cropredy Bridge	1644
Marston Moor	1644
Tippermuir	1644
Aberdeen	1644
Lostwithiel	1644
Newbury II	1644
Inverlochy	1645
Auldearn	1645
Leicester	1645
Naseby	1645
Alford	1645
Langport	1645
Kilsyth	1645

Philiphaugh	1645
Stow-on-the-Wold	1646

Second English Civil War 1648–51

Preston	1648
Rathmines	1649
Drogheda	1649
Wexford	1649
Carbiesdale	1650
Dunbar	1650
Worcester	1651

War of the Glorious Revolution 1689–92

Followers of the deposed King James II of England vs. forces of William III and Queen Mary.

Londonderry	1689
Killiecrankie	1689
Boyne River	1690
Aughrim	1691
Limerick	1691
Glencoe	1692

Followed by two Jacobite insurrections:

"The '15" (1715)

Sheriffmuir	1715
Preston	1715

"The '45" (1745)

Prestopans	1745
Falkirk	1746
Culloden	1746

War of the Grand Alliance 1688–97

In Europe: War of the League of Augsburg

In America: King William's War (William III of England)

France (Louis XIV) vs. Holy Roman Empire, Sweden, Spain, Netherlands, England, Savoy.

Bantry Bay	1689
Walcourt	1689
Fleurus	1690
Beachy Head	1690
Staffarda	1690
Leuze	1691
La Hogue	1692
Steenkerke	1692
Lagos	1693
Neerwinden (Landen)	1693
Marsaglia	1693
Namur	1695

War of Spanish Succession
1701–14

France vs. England, Holland, Austria, Prussia and most of the German states. French allies were Savoy, Mantua, Cologne and Bavaria. Savoy changed sides.

Chiari	1701
Cremona	1702
Luzzara	1702
Landau	1702
Friedlingen	1702
Vigo Bay	1702
Höchstädt	1703
Spira (Speyer)	1703
Donauworth (the Schellenberg)	1704
Gibraltar	1704
Blenheim	1704
Malaga	1704
Marbella	1705
Cassano d'Adda	1705
Barcelona	1705
Ramillies	1706
Turin	1706
Almansa	1707
Stollhofen	1707
Toulon	1707
Oudenarde	1708
Ghent	1708
Lille	1708
Tournai	1708
Malplaquet	1709
Brihuega	1710
Denain	1712
Barcelona	1714

Great Northern War 1700–21

Sweden vs. Russia, Poland, Denmark.

Denmark sued for peace in the first year, after the Swedes invaded Zealand. Turkey entered the war as an ally of Sweden in 1710.

Humblebeck	1700
Narva	1700
Dunamunde (skirmish)	1701
Klissow	1702
Pultusk	1703
Thorn	1703
Holowczyn	1708
Liesna	1708
Poltava	1709
Gadebesk	1712
Arvenanmaa (Gangut or Hanko)	1714
Stralsund	1715
Frederikshald	1718

War of Austrian Succession
1740–8

Austria, England, The Netherlands and Savoy vs. Prussia, France, Spain and Bavaria. In 1745 Saxony joined Austria while Bavaria withdrew. In 1746 Russia joined Austria. The first two years of the war are sometimes known as the First Silesian War because much fighting took place in Silesia. In North America the entire war was known as King George's War. Some of the actions were part of the colonial conflict known as the War of Jenkins' Ear, 1739–41, which became part of the War of Austrian Succession.

Mollwitz	1741
Chotusitz	1742
Dettingen	1743
Toulon	1744
Velletri	1744
Prague	1744
Cuneo (Madonna del Olmo)	1744
Fontenoy	1745
Hohenfriedeberg	1745
Louisbourg	1745
Soor (Sohr)	1745
Hennersdorf	1745
Kesseldorf	1745
Negapatam	1745
Madras	1746
Rotto Freddo	1746

Rocourt (Raucoux)	1746
Genoa	1746
Finisterre, Cape	1747
Lauffeld	1747
Bergen-op-Zoom	1747
Finisterre, Cape	1747
Maastricht	1747
Havana	1748

French and Indian War 1754–63

This was the American theatre of operations of the Seven Years' War.

Fort Necessity	1754
Beauséjour	1755
Monongahela River	1755
Crown Point Expeditions	1755
Lake George	1755
Oswego	1756
Fort William Henry massacre	1757
Fort Ticonderoga	1758
Louisburg	1758
Fort Duquesne Expedition	1758
Fort Frontenac	1758
Fort St. David	1758
Fort Niagara	1759
Quebec	1759
Plains of Abraham	1759
Quebec	1760
Montreal	1760

Seven Years' War 1756–63

(the land operations are also known as the Third Silesian War)

Prussia, England and Portugal vs. Austria, Russia, France, Sweden, Saxony, Poland. Spain joined this alliance in 1762, while Russia and Sweden withdrew that year.

Minorca	1756
Calcutta	1756
Lobositz (Lovocize)	1756
Prague (Praha)	1757
Kolin	1757
Plassey	1757
Hastenbeck	1757
Gross-Jagersdorf	1757
Rossbach	1757
Breslau	1757

Leuthen	1757
Olmütz	1758
Fort Saint David	1758
Crefeld	1758
Zorndorf	1758
Hochkirch	1758
Negapatam	1758
Madras	1758–9
Bergen	1759
Kay	1759
Minden	1759
Kundersdorf	1759
Lagos	1759
Maxen	1759
Quiberon Bay	1759
Wandiwash	1760
Landeshut	1760
Warburg	1760
Liegnitz	1760
Torgau	1760
Pondicherry	1761
Martinique	1762
Wilhelmstahl	1762
Burkersdorf	1762
Havana	1762
Manila	1762
Freiberg	1762

War of the American Revolution (War of Independence) 1775–83

The British fought all these battles against either the American revolutionary army, the American navy, the French navy or the Dutch navy. Unless otherwise stated, the battles were on land.

Lexington and Concord	1775
Fort Ticonderoga II	1775
Bunker Hill	1775
Boston	1775–6
Great Bridge	1775
Quebec III	1775
Saint Johns	1775
Moores Creek Bridge	1776
Charleston I	1776
Fort Moultrie	1776
Long Island	1776
Valcour Island	1776
White Plains	1776
Harlem Heights	1776
Fort Washington	1776

Trenton	1776
Princeton	1777
Danbury	1777
Fort Ticonderoga III	1777
Hubbardton	1777
Fort Stanwix	1777
Oriskany	1777
Bennington	1777
Cooch's Bridge	1777
Brandywine Creek	1777
Paoli	1777
Germantown	1777
Saratoga	1777
Freeman's Farm	1777
Bemis Heights	1777
Fort Clinton and	
Fort Montgomery	1777
Fort Mercer and Fort Mifflin	1777
Carrickfergus (naval battle)	1778
Monmouth	1778
Ushant I (British–French	
naval battle)	1778
Newport	1778
Savannah I	1778
Port Royal Island	1779
Kettle Creek	1779
Vincennes	1779
Briar Creek	1779
Stono Ferry	1779
Grenada (British–French	
naval battle)	1779
Stony Point	1779
Paulus Hook	1779
Newtown	1779
Savannah	1779
Flamborough Head (British–	
American naval battle)	1779
Gibraltar II (siege by French)	1779–83
Saint Vincent Cape I (British–	
French naval battle)	1780
Charleston II	1780
Waxhaw Creek	1780
Camden	1780
Fishing Creek	1780
Kings Mountain	1780
Cowpens	1781
Guilford Courthouse	1781
Praia (British–French naval battle)	1781
Hobkirk's Hill	1781
Ninety Six	1781
Dogger Bank I (British–Dutch	
naval battle)	1781

Chesapeake Capes (British–	
French naval battle)	1781
Eutaw Springs	1781
Yorktown I	1781
Minorca II (invasion by French)	1782
Madras II (British–French	
naval battle)	1782
Trincomalee I (British–French	
naval battle)	1782
Saintes, Les (British–French	
naval battle)	1782
Cuddalore I (British–French	
naval battle)	1782
Trincomalee II (British–French	
naval battle)	1782
Cuddalore II (British–French	
naval battle)	1783

Wars of the French Revolution 1792–1802

War of the First Coalition 1792–1800

France vs. Austria, Prussia, Russia, Sweden.

Valmy	1792
Jemappes	1792
Valenciennes (minor action)	1793
Neerwinden	1793
Toulon	1793
Hondschoote	1793
Menin (manoeuvre battle)	1793
Wattignies	1793
Geisberg (manoeuvre battle)	1793
Tourcoing	1794
Tournai	1794
Ushant ("Glorious First of	
June")	1794
Hooglede	1794
Fleurus	1794
Quiberon	1795
Genoa	1795
Loano	1795
Montenotte	1796
Dego	1796
Mondovi	1796
Lodi Bridge	1796
Borghetto	1796
Mantua	1796–7
Lonato	1796

Castiglione delle Stiviére	1796
Amberg-Friedberg	1796
Wurzburg	1796
Caliano	1796
Bassano	1796
Caldiero	1796
Arcola	1796
Rivole Veronese	1797
Saint Vincent	1797
Malborghetto	1797
Neuweid	1797
Camperdown	1797

War of the Second Coalition

Russia, England, Austria, Portugal, Naples, the Vatican and Ottoman Empire vs. France.

Pyramids	1798
Nile	1798
Malta	1798–1800
Acre	1799
Mount Tabor	1799
Stockach	1799
Magnano	1799
Cassano d'Adda	1799
Zurich	1799
Trebbia River	1799
Abukir	1799
Novi Ligure	1799
Bergen-op-Zoom — Castricum	1799
Zurich	1799
Alkmaar	1799
Genoa	1800
Stockach	1800
Montebello	1800
Marengo	1800
Hohenlinden	1800

War between Britain and France

Alexandria	1801
Copenhagen	1801

Napoleonic Wars 1803–15

War of the Third Coalition 1803–12

France and Spain vs. England, Austria, Russia, Sweden, Naples. Austria was forced out in 1805 and Prussia joined; Austria rejoined in 1809.

Finisterre, Cape	1805
Ulm	1805
Elchingen	1805
Trafalgar, Cape	1805
Caldiero	1805
Oberhollabrunn	1805
Austerlitz	1805
Cape Town	1806
Buenos Aires	1806–7
Maida	1806
Saalfeld	1806
Jena-Auerstadt	1806
Lubeck	1806
Pultusk	1806
Eylau	1807
Danzig	1807
Heilsberg	1807
Friedland	1807
Copenhagen	1807
Sacile	1809
Abensberg	1809
Landshut	1809
Eckmühl	1809
Ratisbon	1809
Aspern-Essling	1809
Raab	1809
Wagram	1809
Mogilev	1812
Smolensk	1812
Valutino	1812
Borodino (Muscova)	1812
Maloyaroslavets	1812
Krasnaoi (Krasnoye)	1812
Berezina River	1812

War of the Fourth Coalition

France vs. England, Russia, Prussia, Sweden, Spain and various German states.

Lutzen	1813
Bautzen	1813
Grossbeeren	1813
Katzbach	1813
Dresden	1813
Kulm-Priesten	1813
Dennewitz	1813
Leipzig ("Battle of the Nations")	1813
Hanau	1813

Brienne	1814
La Rothiére	1814
Champaubert-Montmirail	1814
Montereau	1814
Bar-sur-Aube	1814
Craonne	1814
Laon	1814
Reims	1814
Arcis-sur-Aube	1814
La Fere Champenoise	1814
Paris	1814

Napoleon's "The Hundred Days" March–June 1815

Tolentino
Ligny
Quatre Bras
Wavre
Waterloo

Peninsular War 1808–14

Part of the Napoleonic Wars, though, in British history, a distinctly separate war. It was fought in Spain, Portugal and south-west France.

France vs. England aided by Spanish irregulars.

Saragossa	1808–9
Bailen (Baylen)	1808
Vimeiro	1808
Corunna	1808
Oporto	1809
Talavera	1809
Busaco	1810
Fuentes d'Onor	1811
Albuhera	1811
Tarragona	1811
Ciudad Rodrigo	1812
Badajoz	1812
Salamanca	1813
Vittorio	1813
San Sebastian	1813
Pyrenees	1813
Nivelle	1813
Nive	1813
Orthez	1814
Bayonne	1814
Toulouse	1814

United States–British War

1812–15 (popularly known as the War of 1812. It was an offshoot of the Napoleonic Wars)

Fort Dearborn	1812
Detroit	1812
Queenston Heights	1812
Frenchtown	1812

Constitution vs. Java 1812

Sackets Harbour	1813

Chesapeake vs. Shannon 1813

Fort George	1813
Stony Creek	1813
Lake Erie	1813
Thames River	1813
Chateaugay River	1813
Chrysler's Farm	1813
Chippewa River	1813
Lundy's Lane	1814
Fort Erie	1814
Bladensburg	1814
Lake Champlain	1814
Plattsburg	1814
Fort McHenry	1814
New Orleans (after peace had been signed)	1815

Italian Wars of Independence 1821–70

The Italian states vs. the occupying Austrians. The patriots of Guiseppe Garibaldi fought several actions during these wars.

Rieti	1821
Custozza	1848
Novara	1849
Rome	1849
Venice	1849
Magenta	1859
Solferino	1859
Calatafimi / Milazzo (Garibaldi vs. the Kingdom of Naples)	1860
Castelfidardo	1860
Ancona	1860

Gaeta	1860–1	Delhi	1857
Aspromonte (Garibaldi		Futteypur (Fatehpur)	1857
vs. Italian regulars)	1862	Goraria	1857
Custozza	1866	Onao	1857
Vis	1866	Lucknow	1857–8
Lissa	1866	Arrah	1857
Mentana (Garibaldi vs.		Cawnpore	1858
Papal troops and		Gaulauli	1858
French regulars)	1867	Jhansi	1858
		Kalpi	1858
		Gwalior	1858

United States–Mexican War 1846–8

Fort Texas	1846
Palo Alto	1846
Resaca de la Palma	1846
Monterrey	1846
San Pasqual	1846
San Gabriel	1847
Buena Vista	1847
Sacremento River	1847
Chihuahua	1847
Vera Cruz	1847
Cerro Gordo	1847
Contreras-Churubusco	1847
Molino del Rey	1847
Chapultepec	1847
Puebla	1847

Crimean War 1853–6

Russia vs. Turkey. England and France entered war as Turkey's allies in 1854, Sardinia in 1855.

Oltenita	1853
Sinope	1853
Silistra	1854
Bomarsund	1854
Alma River	1854
Sebastopol	1854
Balaclava	1854
Inkerman	1854
Eupatoria (minor action)	1855
Chernaya River	1855
Kerch (manoeuvre)	1855
Malakoff	1855
Redan	1855
Sveaborg	1855
Kars	1855

Indian Mutiny Against the British 1857–8

Cawnpore	1857

American Civil War 1861–5

Fort Sumter	1861
Philippi, W. Va.	1861
Big Bethel	1861
Rich Mountain	1861
Bull Run I	1861
Wilson's Creek	1861
Cheat Mountain	1861
Ball's Bluff	1861
Belmont	1861
Mill Springs	1862
Fort Henry	1862
Roanoke Island	1862
Fort Donelson	1862
Pea Ridge	1862
Hampton Roads	1862
Kernstown I	1862
Island No. 10	1862
New Madrid	1862
Shiloh	1862
New Orleans II	1862
Yorktown II	1862
Williamsburg	1862
McDowell	1862
Front Royal	1862
Winchester I	1862
Fair Oaks	1862
Cross Keys–Fort Republic	1862
Seven Days	1862
Mechanicsville	1862
Gaine's Mill	1862
Savage's Station	1862
Frayser's Farm	1862
Malvern Hill	1862
Cedar Mountain	1862
Bull Run II	1862
Groveton	1862
Chantilly	1862
Richmond, Ky.	1862

Harpers Ferry	1862	New Hope Church	1864
Antietam Creek	1862	Monocacy River	1864
South Mountain	1862	Tupelo	1864
Crampton's Gap	1862	Atlanta	1864
Iuka	1862	Peach Tree Creek	1864
Corinth, Miss.	1862	Kernstown II	1864
Perryville	1862	Mobile Bay	1864
Prairie Grove	1862	Winchester III	1864
Fredericksburg	1862	Fisher's Hill	1864
Chickasaw Bluffs	1862	Cedar Creek	1864
Stones River	1862–3	Franklin	1864
Arkansas Post	1863	Spring Hill	1864
Charleston III	1863	Nashville	1864
Fort Wagner	1863	Savannah III	1864
Chancellorsville	1863	Fort Fisher	1865
Salem Church	1863	Bentonville	1865
Port Hudson	1863	Five Forks	1865
Brandy Station	1863	Appomattox River	1865
Winchester II	1863	Sayler's Creek	1865
Gettysburg	1863		
Vicksburg	1863	**French–Prussian War 1870–1**	
Port Gibson	1863		
Jackson	1863	Saarbrucken (skirmish)	1870
Champion's Hill	1863	Weissenburg	1870
Big Black River	1863	Wörth (Froschwiller)	1870
Chickamauga	1863	Spicheren	1870
Bristoe Station	1863	Borny (skirmish)	1870
Chattanooga	1863	Colombey	1870
Orchard Knob-Indian Hill	1863	Mars-la-Tour (Vionville)	1870
Lookout Mountain	1863	Gravelotte-St. Privat	1870
Missionary Ridge	1863	Metz	1870
Knoxville	1863	Sedan	1870
Olustee	1864	Paris	1870–1
Sabine Crossroads–Pleasant Hill	1864	Coulmiers	1870
Alexandria, La.	1864	Orleans (Prussian reoccupation)	1870
Fort Pillow	1864	Hallue	1870
Wilderness	1864	Bapaume	1871
Spotsylvania	1864	Saint Quentin	1871
Yellow Tavern	1864	Le Mans	1871
Drewry's Bluff	1864	Belfort	1871
Resaca	1864		
New Market	1864	**British Egyptian and Sudan**	
North Anna River	1864	**Campaigns 1882–9**	
Cold Harbor	1864		
Piedmont	1864	Alexandria	1882
Brices Cross Roads	1864	Tel-el-Kebir	1882
Trevilian Station	1864	Tamai	1884
Petersburg	1864–5	El Obeid	1884
Crater	1864	El Teb (Trinkitat)	1884
Fort Stedman	1865	Abu Klea	1885
Lynchburg	1864	Kirkeban	1885
Kenesaw Mountain	1864	Tofrek	1885

South African Wars

British vs. Boers

First "Boer War" 1880–1

Laing's Nek	1881
Majuba Hill	1881

Second "Boer War" 1899–1902

Mafeking	1899–1900
Kimberley	1899–1900
Ladysmith	1899–1900
Talana Hill	1899
Elandslaagte	1899
Nicholson's Nek	1899
Modder River	1899
Stormberg	1899
Magersfontein	1899
Colenso	1899
Spion Kop	1900
Karee	1900
Vaal Krantz	1900
Paardeberg	1900
Bloemfontein	1900
Johannesburg	1900
Guerrilla warfare	1900–2

Balkan War 1912–13

Kirk-Kilissa	1912
Kumanovo	1912
Monastir	1912
Luleburgaz	1912
Catalca	1912
Shkoder	1913
Ioannina	1913
Adrianople	1912–13

World War I 1914–18

Western Front — Germany's war against the Western allies

Liége	1914
Mulhouse	1914
Haelen	1914
Namur	1914
Frontiers of France	1914
Lorraine	1914
Ardennes	1914
Charleroi	1914

Mons	1914
Guise	1914
Le Cateau	1914
Marne River I	1914
Ourcq River	1914
Moselle River	1914
Aisne River I	1914
Artois I	1914
Antwerp	1914
Ypres I	1914
Champagne I	1914–15
Neuve-Chapelle	1915
Ypres II	1915
Artois II	1915
Champagne II	1915
Artois-Loos	1915
Verdun	1916
Fort Douaumont	1916
Fort Vaux	1916
Somme River I	1916
Arras	1917
Vimy Ridge	1917
Aisne River II	1917
Messines	1917
Ypres III	1917
Passchendaele	1917
Cambrai	1917
Somme River II	1918
Lys River (also known as Ypres IV)	1918
Aisne River III	1918
Chateau-Thierry	1918
Cantigny	1918
Belleau Wood	1918
Noyon-Montdidier	1918
Marne River II	1918
Champagne-Marne River	1918
Aisne–Marne rivers	1918
Amiens	1918
Saint-Mihiel	1918
Meuse River–Argonne Forest	1918
Cambrai–Saint Quentin	1918

Eastern Front — Germany's war with Russia

Gumbinnen	1914
Stallupönen	1914
Galicia	1914
Kraśnik	1914
Gnila Lipa River	1914
Lemberg I	1914–15

Rava Russkaya	1914
Przemyśl	1914–15
Tannenberg	1914
Masurian Lakes I	1914
Vistula River–Warsaw	1914
Lódź	1914
Masurian Lakes II	1915
Gorlice-Tarnow	1915
Warsaw	1915
Naroch Lake	1916
Kovel-Stanislav	1916
Lemberg II	1917
Riga	1917

Italian Front

Isonzo River (eleven battles)	1915–17
Asiago	1916
Caporetto	1917
Piave River	1918
Vittorio Veneto	1918

Balkan Front

Jadar River	1914
Rudnik Ridges	1914
Gallipoli	1915–16
Serbia	1915
Salonika	1915–18
Rumania	1916–17

Middle East Front: Britain (and Empire) against Turkey

Sarikamis	1914–15
Kut-al-Imara I	1915
Ctesiphon	1915
Kut-al-Imara II	1915–16
Erzurum-Erzincan	1916
Sinai	1916
Romani	1916
Baghdad	1917
Gaza I	1917
Gaza II	1917
Ramadi	1917
Gaza III	1917
Megiddo	1918
Sharqat	1918
Damascus	1917–18

Africa

Windhoek	1915
Rufiji River	1917

China

Tsingtao	1914

Sea Battles

Heligoland Bight	1914
Coronel	1914
Falkland Islands	1914
Dogger Bank	1915
Atlantic Ocean	1915–17
Dardanelles	1915
Jutland	1916

World War II 1939–45

European Theatre

German offensive — West

Poland	1939
Warsaw V	1939
Finland	1939–40
Suomussalmi	1939–40
Mannerheim Line	1940–4
Norway	1940
Netherlands	1940
Flanders	1940
Dunkirk	1940
France	1940
Britain (Battle of)	1940–1

Southern Europe: German offensive

Yugoslavia	1941
Greece	1940–1
Crete	1941
Dieppe (British–Canadian raid)	1942

Eastern Front

Soviet Union	1941–4
Minsk	1941
Smolensk	1941
Kiev II	1941
Kursk	1943
Leningrad	1941–4

Moscow	1941–2	Germany, West	1945
Vyazma	1941	Ruhr Pocket	1945
Crimea	1941–4		
Sevastopol	1941–4	**Africa and Middle East**	
Caucasus	1942–3		
Stalingrad	1942–3	Dakar	1940
Ukraine	1943–4	East Africa	1941
White Russia	1943–4	Habbaniya	1941
Poland–East Prussia	1944–5	Malta	1941–2
Warsaw	1944		

First British Offensive

Central Front		Sidi Barrani	1940
		Bardia	1941
Balkans	1944–5	Tobruk I	1941
Hungary	1944–5	Beda Fomm	1941
Austria	1945		
Czechoslovakia	1945	*First Axis Offensive*	
Germany, East	1945		
Berlin	1945	Tobruk II	1941
		Sollum-Halfaya Pass	1941

Italian Front

Second British Offensive

Sicily	1943	Sidi-Rezegh	1941
Italy, Southern	1943		
Salerno	1943	*Second Axis Offensive*	
Gustav–Cassino Line	1943–4		
Cassino	1944	Gazala	1942
Anzio	1944	Tobruk III	1942
Gothic Line	1944–5	Mersa Matruh	1942
Po Valley	1945	El Alamein I	1942
		Alam Halfa	1942

Western Front

Third British Offensive

Germany–air bombardment	1942–5		
Normandy	1944	El Alamein II	1942
Cherbourg	1944	Mareth Line	1943
German V-bomb bombardment	1944–5	Medenine	1943
Saint-Lô breakthrough	1944		
Falaise-Argentan pocket	1944		
France, northern	1944	*Anglo–American Offensive*	
Paris	1944		
France, southern	1944	Northwest Africa	1942
Siegfried Line	1944	Tunisia	1942–3
Arnhem	1944	Kasserine Pass	1943
Aachen	1944		
Hürtgen Forest	1944	**Atlantic and Mediterranean**	
Ardennes	1944–5		
Saint-Vith	1944	*Graf Spee* sunk	1939
Bastogne	1944	Atlantic Ocean II	1940–4
Celles	1944	Oran II	1940
Rhineland	1945	Taranto	1940
Remagen	1945	Matapan	1941

Bismarck sunk	1941
Dodecanese Islands	1943

Pacific

Japanese Offensive

Pearl Harbor	1941
Hong Kong	1941
Malaya	1941–2
Wake Island	1941
Philippine Islands	1941–2
China	1941–5
Prince of Wales — Repulse sunk	1941
Guam I	1941
Dutch East Indies	1941–2
Bataan–Corregidor	1942
Burma I	1942
Singapore	1942
Darwin	1942
Java Sea	1942
Ceylon Raid	1942
"Shangri-La Operation"; bombing of Japan	1942
Madagascar	1942
Coral Sea	1942

Allied (American–Australian) *Offensive — South Pacific*

Midway	1942
Solomon Islands	1942–4
New Georgia	1943
Kula Gulf	1943
Vella Gulf	1943
Vella Lavella	1943
Bougainville	1943–4
Guadalcanal	1942–3
Guadalcanal — naval action	1942
Savo Island	1942
Eastern Solomons	1942
Esperance Cape	1942
Santa Cruz Islands	1942
Tassafaronga	1942
New Guinea	1942–4
Owen Stanley Mountains	1942
Milne Bay	1942
Markham Valley	1943
Aitape	1944
Huon Peninsula	1944
Wewak	1944
Hollandia	1944
Wake Island	1944

Biak Island	1944
Morotai	1944
Bismarck Sea	1943
Rabaul	1943–4
Gloucester Cape	1943
Admiralty Islands	1944
Leyte	1944
Leyte Gulf	1944
Surigao Strait	1944
Engano Cape	1944
Samar	1944
Luzon	1945
Southern Philippines–Borneo	1945

Allied (American) *Offensive– Central Pacific*

Tarawa-Makin	1943
Truk	1944
Kwajalein-Eniwetok	1944
Mariana Islands	1944
Saipan	1944
Guam II	1944
Tinian	1944
Philippine Sea	1944
Peleliu-Angaur	1944
Iwo Jima	1945
Okinawa	1945

Allied (American) *Offensive– Northern Pacific*

Aleutian Islands	1943
Attu	1943

Allied (British–American) *Offensive–Asia*

Burma II	1943–5
Arakan	1943
Myitkyina	1944
Imphal	1944
Kohima	1944
Meiktila	1945
Mandalay	1945
Japan–air bombardment	1944–5

World War II: Codenames for Battles and Campaigns

Before World War II codenames were rarely used. When they were employed they were designated by some letter and numeral. In any case, they were rarely known to press and public even after an operation was complete. During World War II codenames were used for security reasons by all the belligerents, and staff officers, in documents and speech, never referred to an operation by any other name.

Allied

Accolade: British attack on Dodecanese Islands, 1944.

Acrobat: Projected British advance into Libya, 1941.

Anakim: Plan for the recapture of Burma, 1944.

Anvil: Early name for Dragoon, q.v.

Argument: Air attack on German war factories, February 1944.

Avalanche: Allied landing at Salerno, September 1943.

Battleaxe: British offensive in North African Western Desert, November 1941.

Baytown: Crossing of Straits of Messina to Italian mainland, September 1943.

Bertram: British Eighth Army deceptions to deceive Rommel, 1942.

Bolero: Build-up of American forces in Britain, 1942.

Brevity: British offensive in Western Desert, May 1941.

Brimstone: Projected Allied invasion of Sardinia, 1941.

Buttress: Attack at Reggio, Italy, September 1943.

Cactus: Recapture of Guadalcanal, 1942–43.

Capital: Recapture of northern Burma, 1944 (see Extended Capital).

Catapult: British destruction of French fleet in North Africa, July 1940.

Catchpole: U.S. operations against Marshall Islands, Pacific, early 1944.

Catherine: Churchill's projected plans for operations in the Baltic, 1940.

Champion: Plans for offensive against Japanese in Burma, 1943.

Clarion: Air attack on German communications in Europe, February 1945.

Claymore: British commando raid on Lofoten Islands, Norway, March 1941.

Cobra: American breakout from Normandy bridgehead, July 1944.

Compass: British–Australian counter-offensive against Italians in Egypt, December 1940.

Corkscrew: Occupation of Pantellaria, June 1943.

Crossbow: Operations against German V-bomb attack on Britain, 1944.

Crusader: British campaign against Rommel, September–November 1941.

Culverin: Projected operation against Japanese in Malaya and Sumatra, 1944.

Demon: British evacuation of Greece, April 1941.

Diadem: Allied operation to capture Rome, 1944.

Diver: Defence against German V-1 bombs, 1944–5.

Dracula: British seaborne attack against Japanese-held Rangoon, May 1945.

Dragoon: Allied invasion of southern France, August 1944.

Dynamo: British evacuation from Dunkirk, May–June 1940.

Epsom: British offensive after landing in Normandy, July 1944.

Exporter: British–Australian campaign against Vichy French in Syria, June–July 1941.

Extended Capital: British advance to Mandalay and operations on the Irrawaddy River, Burma, 1944–5.

Firebrand: Projected invasion of Corsica, 1944.

Flintlock: U.S. operations against Marshall Islands, Pacific, early 1944.

Forager: American operations to capture Mariana Islands, early 1944.

Fortitude: The elaborate deception plan for Overlord, 1944.

Fortune: Allied naval operations in support of Overlord, 1944.

Frantic: Round-the-clock bombing of Germany from Britain, Italy and Soviet Union.

Galvanic: American assault on Gilbert Islands, Pacific, late 1943.

Gomorrah: RAF attack on Hamburg, July 1943.

Goodwood: British armoured offensive after Normandy campaign, July 1944.

Grenade: American offensive in Rhineland, February 1945.

Gymnast: First name for Torch.

Habforce: British expedition to Iraq, May 1941.

Hailstone: Major American naval battle off Turk Islands, 1944.

Harpoon: Malta convoy, June 1942.

Husky: Allied invasion of Sicily, July 1943.

Iceberg: American attack on Okinawa, April 1945.

Imperator: Proposed commando raid on French coast, 1942.

Infatuate: British assault on Walcheren and Antwerp, October 1944.

Ironclad: British capture of Madagascar, September–November 1942.

Jubilee: Canadian raid on Dieppe, August 1942.

Judgement: RAF attack on Italian fleet, Taranto, November 1940.

King II: American liberation of Luzon, Philippines, October 1944.

Lightfoot: Battle of Alamein, October 1942.

Lumberjack: Second phase of battle for Rhineland, March 1945.

Lustre: British military support for Greece, 1945.

Manna: British campaign in Greece, October 1944.

Market Garden: Allied airborne attack at Arnhem, 1944.

Matterhorn: Bombing of Japan from China, 1944.

Menace: Free French campaign in Dakar, September 1940.

Mincemeat: Deception operations for Husky.

Neptune: Codeword within Overlord staff for cross-channel operations.

Noah's Ark: Plan for occupation of Greece when the Germans withdrew, 1944.

Overlord: Allied invasion in Normandy, June 1944.

Plunder: Allied crossing of the Rhine, March 1945.

Pointblank: Allied combined bomber offensives against Germany.

Priceless: Allied invasion of Italy, 1943.

Pugilist: British attack on the Mareth Line, Tunisia, March 1943.

Rainbow: American general codename for anti-Axis operations, 1939–41.

Roundhammer: Early name for Overlord.

Royal Marine: British campaign in Norway, 1940.

Rupert: British Narvik, Norway, expedition, April 1940.

Satin: Allied plans to split the Axis armies in Tunisia, 1942–3.

Shangri-la: American bombing of Tokyo.

Shingle: Allied landing at Anzio, Italy, January 1944.

Sickle: Transport of American air forces to Britain, 1942.

Slapstick: British airborne landing Italy, 9 September 1943.

Stamina: Supply by air of Imphal–Khomima garrisons, Burma 1944.

Strike: Allied operations to capture Tunis, May 1943.

Supercharge: Pursuit of Axis armies after Lightfoot.

Supergymnast: Allied plans to attack Vichy French in Morocco and Algeria, April 1943.

Talon: Capture of Akyab, Burma, December 1944.

Thursday: Second Chindit operation, Burma, 1944.

Tidal Wave: Air attacks on Ploesti, Romania, oilfields, August 1943.

Torch: Allied invasion of French North Africa, November 1942.

Totalize: Canadian attacks in Falaise Gap, Normandy, August 1944.

Undertone: Third part of battle of the Rhineland, March 1945.

Vanguard: British plan to capture Rangoon from the sea, 1944.

Varsity: Allied airborne operations in Rhineland, February 1945.

Veritable: Canadian offensive in Rhineland, February 1945.

Watchtower: American operations in Guadalcanal and Tulagi, August 1942.

Wilfred: Later codename for Royal Marine.

Zipper: British invasion of Malaya, 1945.

In addition, all the Malta convoys had codenames as did numerous projected operations which did not, in the end, take place.

German

Achse (Axis): German disarmament of Italian army on Allied invasion of Italy, September 1943. Also known as Alarich and Konstantin.

Aida: Rommel's advance into Egypt, January 1942.

Anton or **Attila**: Occupation of previously unoccupied part of France, November 1942.

Bär: Plans for Italian campaign in Alsace, June 1940.

Barbarossa: Invasion of Soviet Union, 22 June 1941.

Berlin: Attacks by *Scharnhorst* and *Gneisenau* against British ships, 1941.

Blau: Offensive against Russians by Army Group South, June 1942.

Blau, Fall (Case Blue): Plans for Luftwaffe operations against Britain, 1939.

Blume (Flower): Warning code-signal for Allied invasion against German West Wall.

Bodenplatte (Base plate): Luftwaffe attack on Allied airfields in Holland and Belgium, January 1945.

Braunschweig (Brunswick): Offensives at Stalingrd and in the Caucasus 1942.

Büffel-Bewegung (Buffalo stampede): Campaign on central Russian front, 1943.

Capri: Rommel's campaign in Tunisia, 1943.

Cerberus: Breakout of *Bismarck* and *Prinz Eugen* from Brest, February 1942.

Donnerschlag (Thunderbolt): Planned breakout of Sixth Army from Stalingrad 1942. (Hitler prohibited it.)

Fridericus (Frederick): Campaign in Izyum Salient, Kharkov, 1941–3.

Fritz: First codename for invasion of Soviet Union.

Gelb, Fall (Case Yellow): Invasion of France, Belgium and Holland, 1939.

Haifisch (Shark): Deceptive operations for Barbarossa.

Herbstnebel: Early codename for Ardennes Offensive, 1944.

Herkules: Operations against Malta 1942–3 (Esigenza to the Italians).

Margarethe: Occupation of Hungary, 1944.

Marita: Occupation of Greece and later Yugoslavia, 1941.

Maus (Mouse): Offensive by Army Group South in the Caucasus, 1942.

Merkur (Mercury): Invasion of Crete, May 1941.

Mittelmeer (Mediterranean): Air offensives, 1940–1.

Morgenrote (Dawn): Counter-offensive against Allies at Anzio, 1944.

Nord (North): First codename for invasion of Norway, 1940.

Nordlicht (Northern lights): Campaign against Leningrad, 1942.

Nordwind (North wind): Attack in northern Alsace, December 1944.

Rheinübung (Rhine exercise): Atlantic raid by *Bismarck* and *Prinz Eugen*, may 1941.

Rösselsprung (Knight's move): Attack on Allied Murmansk–Archangel convoy, July 1942.

Rot, Operation (Operation Red): Completion of the battle of France from June 1940.

Seelöwe (Sea Lion): Projected invasion of England, 1940.

Siegfried: Advance by Army Group South to Stalingrad, July 1942.

Silberfuchs (Silver fox): Preparation in Finland for invasion of Soviet Union.

Taifun (Typhoon): Offensive against Moscow, October 1941.

Tiger: Offensive against French army in the Saar, 1940.

Venezia: Desert advance by Rommel, May 1942.

Wacht am Rhein (Guard on the Rhine): Ardennes offensive ("Battle of the Bulge") 1944.

Weiss, Fall (Case White): Invasion of Poland, 1939.

Weserübung (Weser exercise): Invasion of Denmark and Norway, 1940.

Wintergewitter (Winter storm): Campaign to relieve Sixth Army in Stalingrad, 1942–3.

Zitadelle (Citadel): Attack on Kursk Salient, July 1943.

Airborne Assaults

Under this heading are listed only attacks made by paratroops making combat drops, glider-borne combat landings and assault helicopter landings in action. Battles involving paratroops fighting as infantry are *not* airborne operations. The first paratroop drops took place in 1940.

German paratroops drop on Denmark, Operation Weser Exercise, April 1940.

German paratroops drop on Oslo, Sola (Stavanger), and Narvik during campaign in Norway.

German paratroops drop on Holland at The Hague and Rotterdam, 10 May 1940; in Belgium, at Fort Eben Emael. Troop-carrying gliders were also used in Belgium.

German paratroops drop to capture a bridge over Corinth Canal, Greece, 26 April 1941.

German paratroops and glider-borne troops land in Crete during Operation Mercury, May 1941. It is history's only *wholly* airborne combat operation which was successful.

German paratroops drop in the Ardennes, during the Battle of the Bulge, on the night of 16 December 1944.

British and American paratroops drop in Tunisia at Bone, Souk el Arba and Youks les Bains, November 1942.

Japanese paratroops (630) drop behind Australian positions in Dutch Timor, 20 February 1943.

British and American paratroops and glider-borne troops land in Sicily, Operation Husky, in July 1943.

American paratroops with Australian gunners drop at Nadzab, New Guinea, 5 September 1943.

British and American paratroops and glider-borne troops land in Normandy, Operation Overlord, 6 June 1944.

British and American paratroops and glider-borne troops land at Arnhem and other places, Operation Market-Garden, 17 September 1944.

British and American paratroops and glider-borne infantry land east of the Rhine, Operation Varsity, 24 March 1945.

American paratroops drop on Corregidor, Philippines, 16 February 1945.

British glider-borne troops land at "Broadway", Burma, during Operation Thursday, 5 March 1944.

American paratroops drop on Sukchon and Sunchon, Korea, 20 September 1950. For the first time in history large amounts of heavy equipment were also dropped.

American paratroops drop on Munsan, Korea, 23 March 1951.

French paratroops drop on 150 occasions in Indo-China between September 1946 and May 1954. The most notable battle drops were at Dien Bien Phu, 1953–4, Phu Doan, May 1952 and Lang Son, 17 July 1953.

British and French paratroops drop on Suez, 5 November 1956.

American air-mobile (helicopter-borne troops) land in Vietnam on hundreds of occasions 1965–8; the only major combat jump was made by 173rd Airborne Brigade in 1967.

Israeli paratroops drop behind Egyptian artillery lines, 5 June 1967. Helicopter-borne paratroops and commandos were used in assaults in the wars of 1969–71 (War of Attrition), 1973 (Yom Kippur), 1982 (Operation Peace for Galilee).

Main Sea Battles

	BC
Salamis	480
Mycale	479
Cnidus	394

Mylae	260	La Hogue	2 June 1692
Mount Ecnome	256	Lagos	27 June 1693
Drepanum (Trapani)	249	Texel	29 June 1694
Egadian Islands	241	Cadiz	22 August 1702
Syracuse	212	Vigo Bay	22 October 1702
Coryce	191	Gibraltar	4 August 1704
Myonnese	190	Velez-Malaga	22 August 1704
Lemnos	73	Toulon	1707
Morbihan Gulf	56	Beachy Head	13 May 1707
Nauloque	35	The Lizard	21 October 1707
Actium	31	Toulon	11 February 1744
		Finisterre	14 May 1747
	AD	St. Cast	4 September 1758
Sinnigallia	551	Quiberon Bay	20 November 1759
Lycia	655	Cesme	5–7 July 1770
Bravalla	735	The *Belle Poule* and the	
Paris	885	*Arethusa*	17 June 1778
Beirut	7 June 1191	Ushant	23 July 1778
Constantinople	17 July 1203	Grenada	30 June 1779
Constantinople	22 April 1204	The *Serapis* and the	
Damme	31 May 1213	*Poor Richard*	23 September 1779
South Foreland	24 August 1217	The *Surveillante* and the	
Portsmouth	24 March 1338	*Quebec*	6 October 1779
Arnemuiden	23 September 1338	Dominica	17 April 1780
Southampton	6 October 1338	Praia	16 April 1781
Sluys	24 June 1340	Dogger Bank	3 August 1781
Constantinople	1453	Chesapeake Bay	5 September 1781
Brest	10 August 1512	The Saints	12 April 1782
Famagusta	1571	Viborg	3 June 1790
Lepanto	7 October 1571	Svenksund	9 July 1790
Spanish Armada (Plymouth–		The "Glorious First of June"	
Gravelines)	21–29 July 1588		28 May–1 June 1794
Azores	31 August 1591	*Amazon* and *Indefatigable* vs	
Dover	29 May 1652	*Droits de l'Homme*	13 January 1797
Plymouth	26 August 1652	Cape St. Vincent	14 February 1797
Kentish Knock	8 October 1652	The Nile	1 August 1798
Dungeness	10 December 1652	Malta	30 March 1800
Portsmouth	28 February 1653	Copenhagen	2 April 1801
North Foreland	11 June 1653	The "Fifteen-Twenty"	22 July 1805
Scheveningen	10 August 1653	Trafalgar	21 October 1805
Lowestoft	13 June 1665	Finisterre	4 November 1805
The "Four Days' Battle"		Copenhagen	2–5 September 1807
	11–14 June 1666	U.S.S. *Constitution* and H.M.S. *Java*	
Thames Estuary	17–22 June 1667		29 December 1812
Sole Bay	7 June 1672	Lake Erie	10 September 1813
Schoneveldt	14 June 1673	Lake Champlain	11 September 1814
Texel	21 August 1673	Navarino	20 October 1827
Alicuri	8 January 1676	San Juan d'Ulloa	27 November 1838
Augusta	22 April 1676	Sinope	30 November 1853
Palermo	2 June 1676	Hampton Roads	8–9 March 1862
Bantry	9 May 1689	Memphis	6 June 1862
Beachy Head	10 July 1690	Heligoland	9 May 1864
Barfleur	27 May 1692		

The *Alabama* and the
  Kearsarge   19 June 1864
Lissa   20 July 1866
Danube Estuary   25 May 1877
Batoum   20 January 1878
Foochow   23 August 1884
Yellow River 17 September 1894
Manila   30 April 1898
Santiago Cuba   3 July 1898
Port Arthur 8 February 1904
Yellow Sea   10 August 1904
Tsu-Shima   27 May 1905
Penang   28 October 1914
Coronel 1 November 1914
Cocos Islands 9 November 1914
Falkland Islands 8 December 1914
Dogger Bank 24 January 1915
Dardanelles   18 March 1915
Jutland   31 May 1916
River Plate 13 December 1939
Calabria   9 July 1940
Taranto 11 November 1940
Matapan   28 March 1941
Pursuit of the *Bismarck*
        24–27 May 1941
Pearl Harbor 7 December 1941
Kuantan 10 December 1941
Alexandria 19 December 1941

Java Sea 27 February 1942
Coral Sea   6–8 May 1942
(first carrier versus carrier battle;
  opposing ships did not exchange
  fire)
Midway Island   4–6 June 1942
Convoy PQ.17 (Murmansk)
          1–7 July 1942
Savo Island   8 August 1942
Eastern Solomons 23 August 1942
Cape Hope 11 October 1942
Santa Cruz 26 October 1942
Tassafaronga 30 November 1942
Guadalcanal 14 November 1942
North Cape 26 December 1943
Philippines 19–20 June 1944
Leyte Gulf 23–28 October 1944
Iwo Jima   February 1945
Okinawa   April–June 1945
Falkland Islands June–July 1982
(Warships versus aircraft, apart
  from submarine sinking of
  General Belgrano)

Not all these battles appear under the
titles shown in this list; some were part of
wider actions.

Wars Since 1945

Eritrea	1964–92	Liberia Civil War	1989
Falkland Islands	1982	Madagascar Revolt	1947
France–Vietnam	1946–54	Malayan Emergency	1948
Georgia Civil War	1993	Mau Mau War	1952–60
Grenada	1983	Moldavia Uprisings	1990
Guatemala	1954	Morocco–Polisario War	1976–93
Guatemala Civil War	1980–	Mozambique	1964–75
Honduras–El Salvador	1969	Independence War	
Honduras–Nicaragua	1957	Nagorny–Karabakh	1988–
Hungarian Uprising	1956	Civil War	
India's 'caste wars'	1990	Nicaragua Civil War	1979–88
India–Pakistan	1947–	Nigerian Civil War	1966–70
Iran–Iraq (Gulf War)	1980–88	Northern Ireland War	1968–94
Iraq–UN War	1990–91	October (Yom Kippur) War	1973
Israel Intifada War	1987–94	Ogaden War	1977–88
Israeli–Arab War (Six Day War)	1967	Peru's 'Shining Path' War	1980–
Israeli–Arab War of Attrition	1969–70	Philippines 'People's War'	1980–
Israeli–PLO War	1982	Rhodesia Civil War	1964–80
Jordan Civil War	1970	Rwanda Civil Wars	1990 & 1994
Kashmir War I	1947–9	Sinai–Suez	1956
Kashmir War II	1965	Somalia Civil Wars	1974–94
Kirghiz–Uzbek War	1990	Sudan Civil War	1955–72
Korean War	1950–3	Second Sudan Civil War	1982–
Kosovo Albanian–Serbian	1990–	Sri Lanka Civil War	1983–
Civil War		Ukraine Civil War	1990–2
Kurdish Independence War	1975–	Vietnam War	1959–75
Laos Civil War	1953–73	Yemen War	1962–9
Lebanon Civil War	1958	Second Yemen Civil War	1993–4
Lebanon Civil War	1975–90	Yugoslavia Civil Wars	1990–
Lebanon War: Israel v.	1982	Zulu–ANC War	1990–4
PLO & Syria			

List of Battles, Campaigns and Wars

Aachen (*World War II*) *13–20 October 1944*. The encirclement of Aachen, a vital gateway to Germany, was begun in September 1944 and completed on 10 October by the U.S. VII Corps (Major-General J. L. Collins). The German defenders, under General Hermann Balck, defended fiercely for a week. Aachen was the first German city captured by the Allies in World War II; also the German West Wall — the Siegfried Line — was first pierced here. *See* Rhineland.

Abensberg Bavaria (*Napoleonic Wars*) *20 April 1809*. Napoleon's armies were largely occupied in Spain; for the fourth time since 1792 Austria declared war on France and with 200,000 troops the Archduke Charles crossed into Bavaria south of the Danube, hoping to trap Davout's corps at Regensberg (Ratisbon). On 19 April Davout fought his way out to link with Lefèbvre's corps at Abensberg, where Napoleon, hurrying from Paris, took command. As the battle began, Napoleon had 90,000 men, Charles 80,000. On the 20th, Lannes struck at the Austrian centre, dividing the enemy's wings, which were decisively driven back. Casualties: Austrian, 2,800 killed or wounded, 4,000 prisoners; French and Bavarians, 2,000. *See* Landshut; Sacile.

Aberdeen (*English Civil War*) *13 September 1644*. The Marquis of Montrose, with 1,500 Royalists, defeated 3,000 Covenanters (Scottish Presbyterian rebels). No quarter was given and the Covenanters lost heavily before reaching Aberdeen. Royalist losses were slight.

Abu Hamed (*British–Sudan campaigns*) *7 August 1897*. Major-General Hunter led a Sudanese brigade and a small party of British artillery against the Mahdist garrison, commanded by Mahomet Zain, who was captured. Casualties: Sudanese, 80 killed; Madhists, unknown.

Abukir I (*French invasion of Egypt*) *15 July 1799*. Napoleon captured strong positions held by Mustapha Pasha, commanding 18,000 Turks. Two-thirds of the Turkish force was killed or forced into the sea; the Pasha and 6,000 surrendered. French losses were 380. In August Nelson destroyed much of Napoleon's fleet in Abukir Bay. *See* Battle of the Nile.

Abukir II (*British invasion of Egypt*) *8 March 1801*. Sir Ralph Abercromby disembarked 5,000 British troops under heavy fire from the defending French, under General Friant. The British lost 1,100 killed and wounded and the French only 500, but the French were driven from their positions. Abercromby died of wounds.

Abu Klea (*British–Sudan campaigns*) *17 January 1885*. Sir Herbert Stewart, during the attempt to rescue General Gordon from Khartoum, led 1,500 men into the desert from Korti. About 5,000 Mahdists of a total strength of 12,000 forced the British troops to fight in square and broke through. After fierce fighting they were driven off. Casualties: British, 168, including Colonel Frederick Burnaby, a noted adventurer; Mahdists, close to the square 1,100 dead were counted. *See* Atbara; Khartoum.

Abu Kru (*or Gubat*) (*British–Sudan campaigns*) *19 January 1885*. This followed hard on Abu Klea, when a large force of Mahdists attacked Sir Herbert Stewart's troops. Moving in square, the British reached the Nile safely. Casualties: British, 121, including their commander mortally wounded; Mahdists, unknown. *See* Atbara; Khartoum.

Abyssinia (*Italian–Abyssinian War*) *1936*. During January and February 1936, 250,000 Italians (De Bono and Graziani) marched into Abyssinia from Eritrea and another 70,000 moved from Eritrea. In March, Marshal Badoglio became commander-in-chief. Against the well-armed, well-trained Italians, Emperor Haile Selassie could bring only 220,000 ill-armed uncoordinated warriors. Through air attack and use of mustard gas, tanks and heavy artillery, the Italians overwhelmed the Abyssinians, who were never once able to stand and fight, and occupied Addis Ababa on 5 May. The emperor escaped to England. The Italians lost 3,500 men, the Abyssinians an estimated 60,000.

Abyssinian Campaign (*World War II*) *January–May 1941*. Against Italian garrisons of 220,000 troops in Eritrea, Somaliland and Abyssinia the British (Lieutenant-General Sir William Platt, Lieutenant-General Sir Alan Cunningham) mustered about 30,000 men. They depended on naval support along the coast, superior air cover and armour in the interior and an uprising of native tribes to subdue the Italian forces. The British attacked from three directions, converging on Addis Ababa. In Eritrea the British captured the mountain fortress of Keren on 26 March after a 7-week siege and 3,000 casualties. In the south-

east, amphibious forces landed at Berbera, 26 March. The main attack came from Kenya from which Cunningham's armoured forces took Addis Ababa on 4 April. The Duke of Aosta made a last stand at Amba Alagi to prevent British troops from reinforcing those in Libya. Cunningham and Platt overcame all resistance by 19 May. Cunningham's army captured 50,000 prisoners and occupied 360,000 square miles of territory at a cost of 135 men killed, 310 wounded, fifty-two missing and four captured. The 1st South African Brigade had a 5-day battle in Combolcia Pass, losing ten men and taking 8,000 prisoners. Overall, the British had practically destroyed the Italian armies with all their equipment and had occupied an area of 1,000,000 square miles.

Acapulco (*Mexican rising*) *9 August 1885*. Santa Anna, leading the government troops, was routed by Juarez and his liberal rebels. No reliable casualty figures exist, but Juarez claimed that 1,200 government troops died.

Accra I, Ghana (*First British–Ashanti War*) *1824*. A British force of 1,000 under Sir Charles McCarthy was routed by 10,000 Ashantis. Casualties: British, about 200, including the commander, who was killed.

Accra II (*First British–Ashanti War*) *1825*. About 400 British, defending Cape Coast castle with the help of 4,600 native auxiliaries, beat off about 15,000 Ashantis. *See* Amoaful.

Achi Baba. *See* Gallipoli.

Aclea (*Danish invasion of Britain*) *851*. This battle occurred as Ethelwulf, father of Alfred, deployed his Wessex army to meet the Danish Vikings moving south. His victory at Aclea (Oakley), south of the Thames, helped establish Wessex as the principal state among the kingdoms of Britain.

Acragas (*Second Carthaginian invasion of Sicily*) 406 BC. Hannibal and his Carthaginians besieged this fortress, commanded by the Spartan Dexippus. Hannibal became ill and was succeeded by his cousin Himilco. Daphaenus brought a relief force of 35,000 Syracusans, who fought a pitched battle with the Carthaginians under the fortress walls. They held one of the enemy's camps, but the fortress garrison became disaffected, many mercenaries deserted and after 8 months the citizens abandoned Acragas, which the Carthaginians occupied. *See* Selinas; Syracuse.

Acre I (*Third Crusade*) August 1189. The Crusaders tried for two years to take this fortress city from the Saracens. In June 1191 Richard III (Richard "Coeur de Lion") brought a reinforcement English army and the garrison surrendered. Casualties: Crusaders, said to have been 120,000 over the two years, but this is probably exaggerated. In May 1291 Acre was captured from the Christians by the Muslims, under Malek al Aschraf, Sultan of Egypt. This defeat meant that the Christians no longer had a stronghold in the Holy Land. *See* Arsouf; Jerusalem VIII.

Acre II (*Wars of the French Revolution*) 1799. Napoleon had conquered Egypt in 1798, but his fleet had been defeated at the Nile, q.v., by the British navy and he was cut off from France. On 6 February 1799 he set out to march to Europe, with 13,000 soldiers and fifty-two guns. On 18 March he reached Acre, defended by Turks under Ahmed Pasha — "the Butcher". (Two weeks before, Napoleon had himself butchered 1,000 Turks who had broken their parole to defend Jaffa against him.) Because of the presence of two British ships, commanded by Sir Sidney Smith, off Acre, whose guns protected most of the city, Napoleon laid siege to the place. On 16 April Kleber routed a Turkish relief force at Mount Tabor. Unable to break into Acre and with his men struck by plague,

Napoleon withdrew on 20 May; he had lost 2,200 dead. He said of Sir Sidney Smith: "That man caused me to miss my destiny." *See* Abukir; Nile; Pyramids.

Acre III (*Egyptian revolt against Turkey*) 3 November 1840. Admiral Robert Stopford, leading an Allied British–Austrian–Russian fleet, was sent to the Mediterranean to reduce the growing power of the Mehemet Ali of Egypt, who the previous year had destroyed a strong Turkish army at Nizib and captured the Sultan of Turkey's fleet at Alexandria. Stopford bombarded Acre, then landed forces to storm the place. The Egyptians evacuated Acre and before long all Syria. *See* Nizib; Oltenita.

Acroinum (*or Akroinon*) (*Muslim–Byzantine Wars*) 739. The Muslims had been driven from Constantinople 20 years before; now they flooded back to Asia Minor. The Byzantine Emperor, Leo III, blocked the new invasion at Acroinum, in Phrygia, and in a great battle turned it back to Damascus. The Ommiad dynasty, already defeated in France and China, made no further imperialistic ventures. *See* Constantinople IV; Kashgar.

Acs (*or Kamorn*) (*Hungarian uprising against Austria*) 2 July 1849. The Hungarians, 25,000-strong, under Gorgey, were attacked by a greatly superior force of Russians and Austrians under Prince Windischgratz, and were themselves counter-attacked. The result was indecisive. *See* Kapoliná; Sárkány; Schwechat.

Actium, *near the Gulf of Arta, Western Greece* (*Mark Antony's Second Rebellion*) 2 September 31 BC. This remarkable naval battle was fought between Antony, 480 ships, and Octavius, 400 ships, and each with between 35,000 and 40,000 legionaries. Included in Antony's force was Cleopatra's squadron of sixty ships. After about 10 hours' fighting, a large part of Antony's fleet withdrew or surrendered. He signalled to Cleopatra to run for the open sea, which she and her squadron did. Antony's ships were close engaged and fighting was severe, but Antony with about forty ships extricated himself and caught up with Cleopatra. The Octavians had captured 300 galleys and killed 5,000 Antonians. A few days later Antony's large army surrendered.

Morally beaten, Antony yet managed to scatter an Octavian army near Alexandria on 31 July 30 BC, but his troops and ships deserted to the enemy. Hearing that Cleopatra was dead, he stabbed himself and died in Cleopatra's arms; she committed suicide by allowing asps to bite her. Their deaths were a direct result of the defeat at Actium. There has been much dispute as to whether Actium was a fight or flight; Dio and Plutarch, as well as Tarn and Fuller, argue that it was very much a fight. The casualties appear to support this. *See* Phraaspa; Naulochus; Lippe River.

Acultzingo (*French–Mexican War*) *28 April 1862*. General Lorencez, with 7,500 French, advanced upon General Zaragoca's 10,000 troops, who held a strong position in Cumbres Pass, and beat them back to La Puebla, q.v. *See* Calpulalpam.

Adana (*Byzantine–Muslim Wars*) *964*. Nicophorus, Byzantine conqueror of Crete, led an army over the Taurus Mountains to defeat the Muslim garrison of Adana, on the east Mediterranean coast. This was the beginning of the end for the Muslim empire in Syria, for several hundred years.

Aden campaigns *1964–7*. The British, supported by local forces, fought two campaigns. One was in Aden state, against terrorists from three nationalist groups: the National Liberation Front (NLF), a banned organisation, the Front for the Liberation of South Yemen (FLOSY) which was backed by Egypt, and the South Arabian League. The

second campaign was against tribesmen in the hills of the Radfan. In *Operation Nutcracker*, January 1964, the British built a road through Rabwa Pass to Wadi Taym. In May that year *Operation Radforce* restricted the rebels' territory. Fighting continued, though on a reduced scale, until the British withdrawal in 1967. Casualties: British, 57 killed, 651 wounded; local government troops, 17 killed, 58 wounded. Casualties among the terrorists and tribesmen are unknown.

Admagetobriga, *in modern Alsace* (*Gallic Tribal Wars*) *61 BC*. The Sequani under Ariovistus defeated the Haeudi under Eporedorix. *See* Bibracte.

Admiralty Islands (*World War II*) *19 February–18 March 1944*. U.S. troops captured these islands, principally Manus and Los Negros, from the Japanese. *See* New Guinea; Solomon Islands.

Adnatuca (*Rome's Gallic Wars*) *53 BC*. Ambiorix led an unknown number of Eburone troops against 9,000 encamped Romans, led by Titurius Sabinus. When his assault failed, Ambiorex offered the Romans safe conduct to their nearest fort, then attacked them on the march and practically annihilated them. *See* Sabis.

Adowa (*First Italian invasion of Abyssinia*) *1 March 1896*. General Baratieri, with a large force, attacked the Shoan army, strongly positioned in difficult country. The Italians were defeated, with great loss. *See* Agordat.

Adrianople. *General note*. No fewer than seven battles were fought here, 130 miles north-west of Constantinople, the Adrianople region commanded the approaches to that city and the Bosphorus.

Adrianople I (*now Edirne I*) (*War of the Two Roman Empires*) *July 323*. Between Constantine I, ruler of the Roman West, and Licinius, emperor in the east. Constantine marched into Thrace with 50,000 and at Adrianople encountered Licinius' army, of the same strength. On 3 July Constantine manoeuvred the enemy from their trenches and on open plains his disciplined veterans overwhelmed Licinius' inferior troops and pushed them into Byzantium. Total casualties included more than 20,000 dead. *See* Byzantium III.

Adrianople II (*Gothic invasions of the Roman Empire*) *9 August 378*. One of the most decisive battles of history. It established the superiority of cavalry over infantry for 1,000 years and proved that barbarians could defeat even veteran Romans. The barbarians were the Visigoths (Fritigern) whom Valens, Roman emperor in the east, wanted to push out of Thrace. He made his attack on the Visigoth wagon barricade while their cavalry were away foraging. As Valens' Romans drove the Goths back, the Gothic cavalry returned, routed the Roman cavalry and rode down the unsupported legionaries; they killed 20,000 of the 30,000 infantry, including Valens. It was the greatest defeat of the Roman army for 369 years. *See* Aquileia II; Chalons-sur-Marne I; Teutoburger Wald.

Adrianople III (*Wars of the Byzantine Empire*) *972*. Sviatoslav, Duke of Kiev, with 60,000 Russian troops, crossed the Balkan Mountains and moved towards Constantinople, the Byzantine capital. General John I Zimisces marched out with 30,000 infantry and cavalry and near Adrianople blocked the Russian progress. The skilled Byzantine archers demoralised the Russians and then the cavalry charged them from the field. Byzantine ships on the Danube helped John I to drive the Russians right out of Bulgaria. Sviatoslav and many of his survivors were killed by the harassing Pechenegs while returning to Kiev. *See* Antioch; Novgorod.

Adrianople IV (*Bulgarian rising*) *15 April 1205*. Fought between Imperial troops under the Latin Emperor, Baldwin I, and Bulgarian rebels, commanded by Calo-John. The Bulgarian cavalry lured the Latin horsemen into pursuing them, then turned and routed them. After this the Imperialists were completely defeated and the emperor captured. *See* Constantinople V; Philippolis II; Stara Zagora.

Adrianople V (*Byzantine–Bulgarian Wars*) *1254*. The youthful ruler of Bulgaria, Michael Asen, having lost southern Thrace and part of Macedonia to the Nicaean emperor John III, tried to regain these lost territories when John died. At Adrianople, however, he was thoroughly beaten by John's successor, Theodore II Lascaris. The Asen line died out a few years later and in the next century Turkey absorbed the second Bulgarian empire. *See* Constantinople VI; Klokotnitsa.

Adrianople VI (*capture by Ottoman Turks*) *1365*. When the great Serbian leader Stephen Dushan — self-proclaimed emperor of the Serbs, Greeks, Bulgars and Albanians — died in 1355, the Turks took advantage of the lack of a new, dynamic leader. They began to overrun Thrace and in 1365, under Murad I, they attacked and seized Adrianople. *See* Bursa; Maritsa River.

Adrianople VII (*First Balkan War*) *February–March 1913*. The Turkish Government agreed to give up Adrianople during negotiations with the Bulgarians. In Constantinople a *coup d'état* overthrew the government and nationalists, led by Enver Bey, decided to hold on to Adrianople. The Bulgarians invested the city, 3 February, which was forced to surrender, 26 March. Scutari held out under siege by Montenegro troops until the peace treaty of 20 May. Turkey reoccupied and held Adrianople during the Second Balkan War. *See* Ioannina; Shköder II.

Adwalton Moor (*or Atherton Moor, near Bradford*) (*English Civil War*) *30 January 1643*. The Earl of Newcastle, with 10,000 Royalists, defeated Fairfax, who had 4,000 Parliamentarians.

Fairfax himself reached the safety of Hull. *See* Chalgrove Field; Stratton.

Aegates (Egadi) Islands (*First Punic War*) *241 BC*. After the disastrous defeat at Drepanum, Rome had rebuilt and re-trained its fleet for further conflict with the Carthaginians. On 10 March, during a storm, 200 quinqueremes (G. Lutatius Catulus) sank fifty Carthaginian ships and captured seventy. This defeat cost Carthage its claim to Sicily, which Rome made its first province. Hannibal, aged 6, was one of the Carthaginian evacuees from Sicily. *See* Drepanum; Saguntum.

Aegina (Aiyina) (*Third Messenian War*) *458 BC*. Naval battle between Aegina and Athens. Though helped by the Peloponnese States, the Aegina fleet lost the battle and seventy of their ships. The Athenians besieged Aegina and cap-tured it in 457 BC. *See* Tanagra-Oenophyta.

Aegospotami (*Great Peloponnesian War*) *405 BC*. A major naval battle between 170 Athenian triremes under Conon and 180 Peloponnesian ships com-manded by Lysander. The Athenian fleet was at anchor at Aegospotami, opposite Lampsacus, where Lysander was based. On four successive days Conon crossed the straits in vain efforts to bring the enemy to action. On the fifth day Lysan-der, waiting until the Athenians had re-turned to their anchorage, rushed across the straits, caught them by surprise and captured all but twenty ships. He killed all captured Athenians and broke the naval power of Athens. The end of the war soon followed. *See* Cunaxa.

Aerschot (*World War I*) *August–September 1914*. A desultory battle in Belgium between the Allies and the Ger-mans, which ended in German victory. *See* Frontiers of France; Mons.

Afghanistan War *1979–*   In December 1979 the Soviet Union invaded Afghanistan on the pretext that the Afghanistan Government of Hafizullah Amin had asked for Russian help in quell-ing a revolt. In fact, the Soviets were taking another step in a centuries-old strategy to break through to the Indian Ocean. Despite the strength of the occu-pying army — 150,000 in 1984 — the Russians could not defeat the Muslim guerrillas (Mujihadeen) in the hills. In the almost trackless mountains, the Rus-sians found that their fleet of 800 heli-copter gunships was virtually useless.

Armed by the West, the guerrillas con-trolled the countryside and frequently ambushed Russian columns, but they had no chance of winning the war. The Soviet forces built up to a vast military infra-structure, including nine major airfields, from which they could dominate the entire south-east region, including Iran, Pakistan, the Indian Ocean and the Per-sian Gulf. The Afghanistan war has been called "the Soviet Union's Vietnam", but while the American public demanded and achieved an end to their nation's involve-ment in Vietnam, the Russian public could not bring about a change in Krem-lin policy. Soviet casualties amounted to about 3,000 killed. Guerrilla casualty figures are unknown. More than 1.5 million peasants became refugees.†

Agagia *Western Egypt* (*World War I*). A large force of Senussi was defeated by the South Africans (General Lukin). *See* Sinai.

Agendicum,   *present-day   Sens* (*Rome's Gallic Wars*) *52 BC*. A force of Gauls (Camulogenus), sensing victory against the Romans after Caesar's defeat at Gergovia, assembled south of the Seine and cut off Titus Labienus and his four legions from their base at Agendicum. Labienus, undismayed, crossed the river in the face of Camulogenus' much larger army, attacked it skilfully and his vete-ran legionaries cut their way through the Gauls, inflicting heavy casualties. Caesar's legions and Labienus' joined and moved to attack Alesia. *See* Gergovia.

Agincourt (*Hundred Years' War*) 25 October 1415. Henry V, having captured Harfleur with his army of 6,000 (often mistakenly said to number 15,000, crossed the Somme and was confronted by a French army of 50,000 under the Constable d'Albret. The English archers protected their front with a palisade of stakes which broke the charge of the French men-at-arms. Casualties: English, 1,600; French, 10,000 killed, including the Constable and three dukes, and 15,000 prisoners. *See* Harfleur; Rouen II.

Agnadello, *in Cremona province of northern Italy (War of the League of Cambrai)* 14 May 1509. Fought between 30,000 French, under Louis XII and Marshal Trioulzio, and 35,000 Venetians led by General Alviani. The Venetians were defeated, Alviani was captured and Louis XII occupied all the territory assigned to him by the League, up to the River Mincio. Casualties: Venetians, 6,000. The League comprised Ferdinand of Castile, Aragon and Naples, Maximilian I and Pope Julius II. *See* Garigliano River, Ravenna IV.

Agordat (*Sudan campaigns*) 21 December 1893. General Arimondi, with 2,000 Italians and some native troops, defeated 11,500 Mahdists under Ahmed Ali, who had invaded Italian territory. Casualties: Mahdists, 3,000; Italians, about 250. *See* Adowa.

Agra I (*Farokshin's rebellion*) 1713. Farokshin, nephew of the Great Mogul, Jehandar Shah, gave battle to his uncle.

The Mogul's 70,000 troops fought well, but were overwhelmed by the rebels. Farokshin executed his uncle and occupied the throne.

Agra II (*Second British–Mahratta War*) *4–17 October 1803*. The British, led by General Lake, besieged the fortress of Agra, defended by 6,000 of Scinde troops. Lake first attacked and defeated a further enemy force camped in the open town, then on 17 October bombarded the fort, which surrendered the following day. *See* Alighar.

Agra III (*Indian Mutiny*) *August–October 1857*. The British garrison of Agra made a sortie in force on 2 August to attack 10,000 rebels. Some formerly loyal Indian troops with the British now deserted and the British, short of ammunition, were forced back to the fort. In October General Greathead's relief column clashed with 7,000 mutineers, routed them and slaughtered many in the pursuit. *See* Cawnpore I; Delhi V.

Ahmedabad (*First British–Mahratta War*) *15 February 1780*. Strongly held by 8,000 Arabs and Scinde infantry and 2,000 Mahrattas, the fort was taken by bombardment and assault by a much smaller British force under General Goddard. Casualties: British, 106; Arab and Scinde, unknown. *See* Agra II; Bassein; Gwalior.

Ahmedkhel (*Second British–Afghan War*) *1880*. General Stewart was leading 3,500 British troops to Ghazni when his force was attacked by about 15,000 Ghilzis. The tribal leader ordered 3,000 of his fighters to rush the British, who had formed a square. At least 1,000 Ghilzis died around the square and the rest abandoned the fight. British casualties were only 17. *See* Maiwand.

Ahmednugger (*Mogul invasion of the Deccan*) *1599*. Mirza Khan, one of Akbar the Great's generals, besieged the fortress which was actively commanded by Chand Bibi, former Queen of Bijapur. The Moguls breached the walls, but the defenders resisted until a peace was signed.

Aiguillon (*Hundred Years' War*) In May 1346 the Duke of Normandy besieged the fort, held by a small English garrison under Sir Walter Nanny. The defenders repulsed many assaults until the Duke of Normandy was forced by the French defeat at Crécy, q.v., to raise the siege.

Ailette, The (*World War I*) Several actions occurred at this river, March 1917 and October 1918; the only "battle" took place on 20 August 1918 when the French were victorious. *See* Arras.

Ain Jalut, *Palestine* (*Mongol conquest of Western Asia*) *September 1260*. The Mongol army of Hulagu, returning home because of domestic troubles, was caught by a Mameluke army (Bibars I) and its rearguard destroyed by cavalry action. The main Mongol force, turning to fight, was routed. Ain Jalut was the first Mongol defeat in the west. *See* Antioch III; Baghdad I.

Aisne, The (*World War I*). The "Battle of the Aisne" is the generic name given to numerous actions in the vicinity of the Aisne River, northern France. The first battle took place in August 1914 and on 29 August the French retired behind the river. A second battle occurred on 13 September and lasted until the 28th, with the French crossing the river. The third major Aisne battle opened on 6 April, 1917 and by its end on 15 May the French claimed 20,780 prisoners. The third battle was from 27 May to 7 June 1918, but fighting continued at many places until 25 October. Virtually all the actions along the Aisne were running battles and no major fixed action took place.

In more detail:

August 1914. A prelude to the more important Battle of the Marne. The Germans (von Kluck) drove against the French defences of the Aisne River. The battle was really a series of separate engagements.

16 April 1917. Robert Nivelle, new French commander, launched an offensive on the 50-mile front between Soissons and Reims. Army group commander was Micheler, the Sixth Army was under Mangin and the Fifth Mazel. They faced Boehn's Seventh German Army and von Below's First Army. Machine-gun fire pinned down the French infantry and artillery knocked out 150 of the 200 French tanks. The Germans, aware of Nivelle's plans, had vast numbers of reinforcements and French attacks were increasingly costly. The offensive simply died on 9 May; on 15 May Petain succeeded Nivelle and was faced with open mutiny among the demoralized French troops. Of the 23,385 mutineers convicted, fifty-five were shot. Casualties: French, the official figure of 96,000 is one of the most suspect in military history, especially as the Germans admitted a loss of 163,000. The French certainly lost more. *See* Arras II; Messines.

Aisne River, *Third battle* (*World War I*) *1918*. Ludendorff's third offensive of 1918, aimed at the French Sixth Army (Duchene) in the Chemin des Dames area, Aisne River. With forty-one divisions (principal leaders von Below and von Boehn) and a sustained artillery barrage of 4,600 guns the Germans overwhelmed the French on 27 May and made a 13-mile bulge in their lines, the greatest one-day advance in four years. On 30 May the Germans reached the Marne, 37 miles from Paris. The offensive, having gained 36 miles and driven a huge salient into the Allied lines, ended on 6 June. It was during this offensive that the Americans regained Bealleau Wood and won their first victory of the war at Cantigny. *See* Cantigny; Lys River; Noyon-Montdidier.

Aix, Ile d' (*Seven Years' War*) *4 March 1758*. Sir Edward Hawke, commanding a British squadron of seven ships, attacked a French fleet of eleven ships and forty transports preparing to sail to North America and drove many ashore on the Ile d'Aix. The French reverse helped the British to capture Cape Breton.

Aix-la-Chapelle (*now Aachen*) (*Wars of the French Revolution*) *3 March 1793*. The Prince of Saxe-Coburg and his Austrians overwhelmingly defeated a French army under Miranda. Casualties: French, 3,500 and 1,500 prisoners. *See* Fleurus III; Montenotte; Neerwinden II.

Ajnadain (*Muslim conquest of Syria*) *30 July 634*. Muslim cavalry, invading Syria and Persia, were halted at Ajnadain (south-west of Jerusalem) by a Byzantine army (Theodorus). The Muslim General Khalid ibn-al-Walis made a forced march from Hira across the Syrian desert and linking with the cavalry the combined Muslim armies, 45,000 men in all, he routed the 70,000-strong Byzantine army and proceeded with the siege of Damascus. *See* Hira; Pella.

Aladja Dagh (*Russian–Turkish War*) *15 October 1877*. A Russian victory by General Loris Melikoff against the Turks commanded by Mukhtar Pasha. The Turkish army fell back from the Caucasus to the forts of Kars and Erzerum. *See* Plevna.

Alamance Creek (*American Colonial Wars*) *16 May 1771*. The Scots and Irish settlers of western North Carolina were in dispute with those of the east and south. The Scots–Irish objected to discrimination and, calling themselves Regulators, they refused to allow courts to sit in their region. William Tryon, the British governor, marched with thirty cavalry and 1,018 militia to put down the "rebellion". At Alamance Creek they had a two-hour battle with 2,000 settlers. The Royalists killed twenty, wounded many more and hanged six captives. Tryon's victorious army had nine killed and sixty-one wounded. *See* Moore's Creek Bridge.

Alamein (*World War II*) 23 October–4 November 1942. Fought between British and Commonwealth troops under General Montgomery and German and Italian troops under General Rommel, who was absent for part of the battle. Montgomery, whose direct commander was General Alexander, had 150,000 men, 1,114 tanks and 2,182 pieces of artillery, plus the use of 500 fighter aircraft and 200 bombers. At 9.40 p.m. on 23 October nearly 1,000 guns opened fire simultaneously on the Axis lines. The infantry assault was begun by Australians, New Zealanders, South Africans and British. On the 24th, General Stumme, commanding in Rommel's absence, died of a heart attack and General von Thoma assumed command until Rommel's return on the 25th. Despite crippling lack of petrol and artillery ammunition and air cover, the Axis defended the position strongly. Montgomery's combined use of armour and infantry — infantry opening a path for the tanks — resulted in breakthroughs, some of them at great cost. The 9th Armoured Brigade, for example, ran into a formidable tank screen and lost eighty-seven tanks, over 75 per cent of its strength. A fierce tank battle occurred at Tel el Aqqaqir. By nightfall on 4 November the XXth Italian Corps had been destroyed, the Afrika Korps on its left had been broken and General von Thoma captured; a 12-mile gap penetrated the Axis front and Rommel had no reserves and no petrol. However, he was able to withdraw in good order because of Montgomery's reluctance to pursue and to the R.A.F.'s disinclination to engage in low-level attacks. Casualties: figures conflict. According to Rommel, between 23 October and 19 November the Germans and Italians lost 2,300 killed, 5,500 wounded and 27,900 captured — a total of 35,700. Alexander claims that in the shorter period of 23 October–7 November the Axis lost 10,000 killed, 15,000 wounded, 30,000 prisoners — 55,000 in all. British casualties were 13,500 killed or wounded, 500 tanks disabled. *See* Alam Halfa; Mareth Line.

Alam el Halfa 31 August–7 September 1942. The British held Alam el Halfa Ridge in strength, on a plan devised originally by General Auchinleck and adopted by General Montgomery when he took command of the British Commonwealth Eighth Army. In a complex battle plan, General Rommel intended to overrun the Ridge early on 31 August, to cut off the British from their supply depots and then to annihilate them. The British and Axis armies each had about 300 field and medium guns and 400 anti-tank guns. Rommel had 500 medium and light tanks and the British 380 tanks and 230 armoured cars. Rommel achieved no surprise, British minefields impeded his advance and air attacks so disrupted his plans that he had to abandon any major action. He renewed his offensive on 3 September, withdrew and was at once counter-attacked by Montgomery who, having driven Rommel back to the minefields, called off the battle on 7 September. Casualties: Axis, 3,000 killed and wounded, fifty tanks, fifteen guns, thirty-five anti-tank guns and 400 lorries lost; British, 1,640 killed or wounded, sixty-eight tanks and eighteen anti-tank guns disabled.

This battle, not Alamein, was the turning point in the war in North Africa. *See* Alamein; Mersah Matruh.

Alamo (*Texan rising*) February–March 1836. On 23 February General Santa Anna, the Mexican commander, demanded the surrender of the Alamo, a fortified mission station held by only 145 Texans led by Colonel Travis, who fired a cannon as his reply. On 1 March thirty reinforcements reached the station, but Santa Anna had by now 3,000 troops. On 6 March 2,500 Mexicans stormed the Alamo and their third attack broke through. The Americans defended the place room by room, the church being the scene of the survivors' last stand. All the men were killed, but the thirty women and children were spared. Mexican casualties were 1,600 dead in the siege and final assault, with many wounded. "Remember

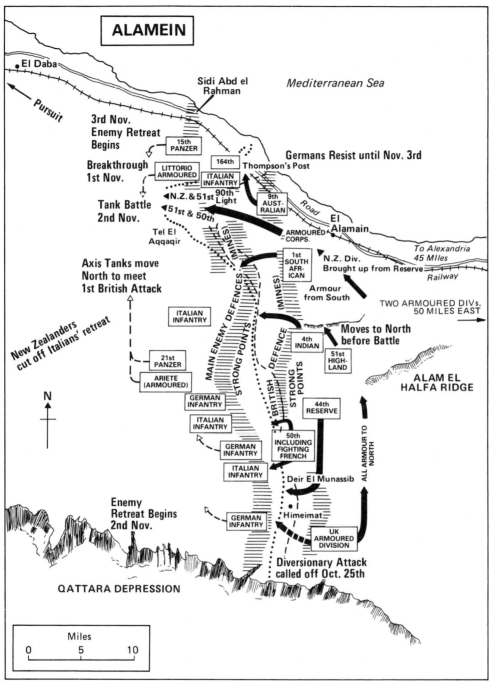

ALAMEIN

El Daba

Sidi Abd el Rahman

Mediterranean Sea

Pursuit

**3rd Nov.
Enemy Retreat
Begins**

15th PANZER

Germans Resist until Nov. 3rd

164th

Thompson's Post

**Breakthrough
1st Nov.**

LITTORIO ARMOURED

ITALIAN INFANTRY

90th Light

9th AUSTRALIAN

Road

El Alamein

**Tank Battle
2nd Nov.**

N.Z. & 51st

51st & 50th

ARMOURED CORPS.

*To Alexandria
45 Miles*

Tel El Aqqaqir

1st SOUTH AFRICAN

N.Z. Div.
Brought up from Reserve

Railway

**Axis Tanks move
North to meet
1st British Attack**

Armour from South

**TWO ARMOURED DIVs.
50 MILES EAST**

ITALIAN INFANTRY

4th INDIAN

**Moves to North
before Battle**

New Zealanders cut off Italians' retreat

21st PANZER

51st HIGHLAND

ARIETE (ARMOURED)

ALAM EL HALFA RIDGE

N

GERMAN INFANTRY

44th RESERVE

ITALIAN INFANTRY

GERMAN INFANTRY

50th INCLUDING FIGHTING FRENCH

ITALIAN INFANTRY

Deir El Munassib

**Enemy
Retreat Begins
2nd Nov.**

GERMAN INFANTRY

Himeimat

UK ARMOURED DIVISION

ALL ARMOUR TO NORTH

**Diversionary Attack
called off Oct. 25th**

MAIN ENEMY DEFENCES. STRONG POINTS

BRITISH DEFENCE STRONG POINTS

(MINES)

(MINES)

QATTARA DEPRESSION

Miles

0   5   10

the Alamo" became the watchword of Texans. *See* San Jacinto River.

Alarcos (*Spanish–Muslim Wars*) *19 July 1195*. The Moors under Yakub el Maasur routed the Spaniards led by Alfonso VIII of Castile. The Moors claimed to have taken 30,000 prisoners, most of whom they massacred. *See* Las Navas de Tolosa; Saragossa I.

Albania, *Battle for* (*World War I*). Operations began with the Italian occupation of Avlona on 25 December 1914. Austrians and Germans entered Albania on 5 December 1915 and much fighting between the Italian–French Allies and the Central Powers followed. The offensive fluctuated, with the Austrians forcing the Osum River and being driven back. The final Italian advance in October 1918 captured, in turn, Elbasan, Alessio, San Giovanni di Medua. Casualties: Italian, 50,000; Austrians–Germans–Bulgarians, 75,000; Serbians, 35,000. *See* Caporetto; Piave River.

Albania, *conquest by Italy* (*World War II*) *1939*. When King Zog I resisted Mussolini's demands on Albania, Italian naval and military forces crossed the Adriatic and on 7 April troops were landed under cover of naval gunfire. There was little resistance and the Albanian royal family fled. *See* Greece.

Albert (*World War I*). Albert, in the Somme region, was a key position on the Western Front and has given its name to a series of complex actions, many of them a long way from Albert. The only real battle of Albert itself took place on 25–29 September 1914, when the French held the town. The final Allied assault of August 1918 was largely concentrated through Albert. *See* Somme; Villers-Bretonneux.

Albuhera (*also Albuera*) (*Peninsular War*) *16 May 1811*. Fought between 46,000 Allied British, Portuguese and Spanish troops under Marshal Beresford

and 33,000 French under Marshal Soult. The effective Allied fighting force were the 7,000 British infantry. The French attacked and would easily have won had it not been for the remarkable steadiness of the British infantry on the ridge — the 57th (Middlesex) Regiment won its nickname "the Diehards" here — and of the Fusilier brigade which drove the French from the field. Only 1,800 British were left standing. The French lost more than 8,000, including five generals. *See* Fuentes de Onõro.

Alcácer do Sol (*Portuguese–Muslim Wars*) *1217*. Alfonso II was trying to push the Moors out of Portugal and in 1217 he sent his army to attack the Moorish stronghold at Alcácer do Sol in the south-west, which the Portuguese captured. With Crusader assistance, Alfonso expanded southwards.

Alcantara I (*Spanish conquest of Portugal*) *25 August 1580*. Following the death in 1580 of King Cardinal Henry, who had no heir, the two main contenders for the throne were Dom Antonio, the prior of Crato, and Philip II of Spain. Philip sent the Duke of Alva and an army to enforce his claim and on 25 August this force met Antonio's hastily conscripted army at Alcantara on the Tagus. The Portuguese were routed; Portugal became a Spanish realm until 1640. *See* Alcazarquivir; Montijo.

Alcantara II (*War of Spanish Succession*) *June 1706*. A force of British and Portuguese (Lord Galway) drove out the Alcantara garrison; ten French battalions surrendered. *See* Ramillies.

Alcazar (*Spanish Civil War*) *July–September 1936*. The Republicans captured Toledo, dominated by the Alcazar, a medieval fortress then used as a military academy. The commander, General Moscardo, had a trained garrison of only 130 Civil Guards and nine cadets, but many civilians volunteered. Before the end of the 72-day siege he had to protect and feed 1,700 people. Before General Franco relieved the fortress on 28 September, 748 of its defenders had been killed or wounded or were missing, and much of the Alcazar was in ruins. *See* Madrid.

Alcazarquivir (*or El Qsae el Kbir*) (*Portuguese invasion of Morocco*) 4 August 1578. Known as the "Battle of the Three Kings", because King Sebastian of Portugal, the King of Fez and the Moorish pretender to the throne of Fez were all killed. Sebastian had attacked the Moorish stronghold, 60 miles south of Tangier, and his defeat ended the Portuguese attempt at Moroccan conquest. Few Portuguese troops survived the slaughter.

Alcolea, *near Cordova (rebellion against Queen Isabella*) 28 September 1868. Between forces of Queen Isabella II and a rebel army under Francisco Serrano. The rebels won decisively and Isabella fled to France next day. King Amadeo came to the throne in 1871, but the search for a royal ruler in the meantime had led to the French–Prussian War. *See* Wissembourg.

Aleppo I (*Muslim invasion of Syria*) 634. Besieged by the Muslims (Abu Obeidah and Khalad) the city surrendered, but the garrison held the citadel where it resisted for 5 months, inflicting heavy loss on the besiegers. Its capture marked the end of serious Syrian resistance to the invading Muslims. (The history of Islam had begun only 17 years earlier.) *See* Jerusalem; Yarmuk River.

Aleppo II, *Antioch* (*Byzantine–Muslim Wars*) 969. The Muslim empire was weakening after 330 years and the Byzantine General Nicephorus II Phocas, an able man, led his veteran army against Aleppo and Antioch, recapturing both. His nephew John I Zimisces murdered Nicephorus and the Muslims briefly regained Aleppo. *See* Adana; Damascus II.

Aleppo III (*Tartar invasion of Syria*) 11 November 1400. The Turks, under their Syrian Emirs, could probably have withstood a siege, but they ventured out to give battle to the Tartars (Tamerlane) and were disastrously defeated, losing many thousands of troops. Tamerlane sacked the city and captured the citadel.

Aleppo IV (*Ottoman War*) 1516. The Turks (Selim I) routed the Egyptians (Tooman Beg, the Mameluke Sultan) and Selim added the whole of Syria to the Ottoman Empire. The battle actually took place at Yaunis Khan near Gaza, but history accepts it as Aleppo. *See* Chaldiran.

Alesia (*or Auxois, near Dijon*) (*Gallic War*). In 52 BC Caesar used 50,000 troops to besiege the town, defended by about 95,000 Gauls (Vercingetorix). An army of Belgi warriors, possibly 180,000 strong, tried to relieve the town but were routed by Labienus with great slaughter. The garrison, losing heart, surrendered. The Gauls were no longer a menace to Rome. *See* Agendicum; Carrhae I; Rubicon River.

Alessandria, *western Po Valley* (*Wars of the French Revolution*) 18 June 1799. About 14,000 French (Moreau) defeated an Austrian–Russian force (Bellegarde) of 20,000; they lost 3,000 and had 900 taken prisoner. The battle is sometimes known as Marengo. *See* Trebbia II.

Aleutian Islands (*World War II*) June 1942–August 1943. A combined operations Japanese attack on Dutch Harbour, on the island of Unalaska, and a landing on the islands of Kiska and Attu were successful. On 11 May 1943 the Americans invaded Attu and in bitter cold and heavy fog squeezed the Japanese into difficult positions from which they launched a desperate counter-attack. Fighting ended on 29 May. Casualties: Japanese, 2,350 killed, 28 prisoners; American, 552 killed, 1,140 wounded. On

15 August 29,000 Americans and 5,300 Canadians landed on Kiska following an air–naval bombardment and found that the Japanese had evacuated. *See* Midway; Tarawa-Makin.

Alexandria I (*Wars of the First Triumvirate*) *48–47* BC. Julius Caesar, with 3,200 men, sailed to Alexandria in pursuit of Pompey the Great after the Battle of Pharsalus. Pompey had been murdered by the time Caesar arrived, but Caesar intervened in the dispute between Ptolemy XII and his sister wife, Cleopatra VII, over the Egyptian crown. Cleopatra was amenable but Ptolemy, aged 13, ordered his general, Achilles, to arrest Caesar. Turning the palace into a fortress, the legionaries held off the 20,000-strong Egyptian army for 5 months. Roman reinforcements then arrived and the Egyptians were routed. Ptolemy was drowned while escaping; Caesar made Cleopatra and her 11-year-old brother Ptolemy XIII joint rulers. *See* Pharsalus; Zela.

Alexandria II (*Muslim invasion of Egypt*) *642*. Then the capital of Egypt, Alexandria was besieged by the Muslims (Amrou) and after a resistance of 11 months Cyrus, Patriarch of Alexandria, surrendered, leaving the Muslims masters of Egypt. Egyptian casualties were 23,000. *See* al-Fustat.

Alexandria III (*British invasion of Egypt*) *21 March 1801*. The French defenders (Menou) were unable to check the British (Abercromby) and after hard fighting were driven against the walls of the city, suffering 3,000 casualties. The British lost 1,400 men including General Abercromby. *See* Abukir; Nile.

Alexandria IV (*Arabi's rebellion or Egyptian rebellion*) *11–12 July 1882*. The British ordered Arabi Pasha to stop work on fortifications — at Alexandria, which could threaten the Suez Canal — and when he refused the fleet of eight battleships and five gunboats (Admiral

Sir Beauchamp Seymour) opened fire. The forts were reduced to rubble and the Canal remained secure. Alexandria was virtually the gateway to Egypt, hence its strategic importance. *See* Tel-el-Kebir.

Alford (*English Civil War*) *2 July 1645*. The Royalists (Montrose) gave the appearance of being in retreat and the Covenanters (General Baillie) crossed the Don to the attack. The Royalists, far from retreating, were actually in ambush and repulsed their enemies with heavy loss. *See* Auldearn; Naseby.

al-Fustat (*Muslim conquest of Egypt*) *641*. Omar I sent an Arabian army (Amr ibn-al-As) into Egypt, held by the Byzantines. Amr, with 4,000 veteran horsemen, took Pelusium and Heliopolis, while the Byzantines prepared for battle at the old Roman settlement of Babylon on the Nile. Camping at al-Fustat (later Cairo), Amr laid siege to Babylon and on 9 April 641 the Byzantines, after heavy losses, surrendered. *See* Alexandria II; Nihawand.

Algeciras (*Spanish–Muslim Wars*) *1344*. Alfonso XI, having defeated the Muslims at Rio Salado in 1340, laid siege to Algeciras which was virtually destroyed before the Muslims surrendered. *See* Nájera; Rio Salado.

Algeciras Bay (*Napoleonic Wars*) *6 and 13–14 July 1801*. The British Admiral Sir James Saumarez, with nine ships, defeated a French squadron of four ships under Admiral Linois, who was helped by Spanish shore batteries and gunboats. On 12 July the French having meanwhile been reinforced by five Spanish ships, Sir James again attacked, capturing one ship and blowing up two others. Casualties: British, 138 killed, 340 wounded; French, 2,306 in all. *See* Alexandria II.

Algheri (*or Alghero*) (*Aragon's conquest of Sardinia*) *1353*. Pedro IV and his Aragonese drove the Genoese out of Sardinia, which became a state of Aragon. *See* Messina II.

Algerian War of Independence *1954– 1962*. The war started when the Front de Libération Nationale (FLN) organized open warfare against the French colonial regime. In June 1958 General de Gaulle offered self-determination by referendum, but it was opposed by the pieds noir (Algerians of French descent). The "Secret Army" or OAS, an extremist group organized by army officers and pieds noir, provoked rioting and terrorism as an excuse for the French army to stay. An uprising of French Rightists in January–February 1960 was suppressed by loyal French troops under General Challe. Later Challe and General Salan headed a mutiny which was suppressed, but Salan inflicted more terrorism from abroad. Fighting between the FLN and the French army and settlers was invariably savage and the insurrection drew half the French army into Algeria. Before the cease-fire on 18 March 1962, 10,200 French soldiers and 70,000 Algerian insurgents had been killed.

Algiers I (*Spanish–Algerian War*) *8 July 1775*. A Spanish force of fifty-one ships and 26,000 men led by Don Pedro de Castijon and Count O'Reilly attacked Algiers, but were beaten off after a bloody fight. Casualties: Spanish, 3,000; Algerians, 5,000.

Algiers II (*bombardment of*) *11 March 1816*. To compel the Bey of Algiers to abolish slavery, Lord Exmouth, commanding nineteen British warships and helped by six Dutch warships, bombarded the massive forts of Algiers, which mounted 500 guns. After 8 hours and great destruction the Bey surrendered. Casualties: British, 885; Algerians, over 6,000.

Alhama (*Spanish–Muslim Wars*) *February–March 1482*. On 28 February Juan de Ortiga led a small party of Spaniards into this fortress, one of several protecting the Moorish capital of Granada. Ortiga opened the gates to admit the Spanish army and bitter street fighting ensued before the Spaniards won the battle. Abul Hassan, King of Granada, besieged the place with 50,000 men, but on 29 March the approach of a large Spanish army forced him to raise the siege. *See* Granada; Loja; Toro.

Alhandega (*or Zamora*) (*Spanish– Muslim Wars*) *939*. The Moors, 100,000 strong and led by the redoubtable Abd-al-Rahman, were besieging Alhandega when they were attacked by Ramiro II of Leon. Caught between this force and a sally by the defenders, the Moors lost 20,000 men in the battle, while 40,000 more are said to have been drowned in the city's moat. No quarter was given by either side.

Aligurh (*or Aligarh*) (*First British– Mahratta War*) *29 August 1803*. This fortress, 43 miles from Agra and the arsenal of Gwalior, was strongly fortified and surrounded by a ditch 100 feet wide and holding 10 feet of water. A battalion of Highlanders under Colonel Monson stormed it and after room-to-room fighting captured it and 281 guns. Casualties: British, 230. *See* Delhi; Laswari.

Ali Musjid (*Second British–Afghan War*) *21 November 1878*. Capture of the fortress by a mixed Anglo–Indian force by Sir Samuel Browne (of "Sam Browne belt" fame). This was the first of six actions in the war, largely caused by Russian intrigue. *See* Peiwar Kotal.

Aliwal (*First British–Sikh War*) *28 January 1846*. 90 miles south-east of Lahore, about 20,000 Sikhs fiercely defended their lines against the attacks of 10,000 British led by Sir Harry Smith. They withstood three British cavalry charges — the 16th Lancers were specially prominent — before breaking. Many Sikhs were drowned in the Sutlej River. Until this battle the Sikhs had been considered virtually undefeatable. *See* Ferozeshah; Sobraon.

Aljubarotta (*Spanish–Portuguese Wars*) *14 August 1385*. This battle was fought 50 miles north of Lisbon between the Castilians under John I, in support of the claim of Beatrix of Castile to the throne of Portugal, and the Portuguese under the Regent John. The Spaniards were decisively beaten and John had to renounce his sister's claim. Many English veterans of the Hundred Years' War fought with the Portuguese. *See* Ceuta; Montiel.

Alkmaar I (*Netherlands War of Independence against Spain***)** *August– October 1573*. On 21 August Don Frederico de Toledo besieged this Dutch city with 16,000 troops. Alkmaar had a defending force of only 800 soldiers and 1,300 armed burghers. The Spaniards lost 1,000 men in a vain assault on 8 September. A Spanish supporting fleet was defeated in the Zuider Zee by Admiral Dirkzoon. The Dutch opened the dykes, making the Spanish military positions untenable and they withdrew on 8 October. The Dutch lost fewer than fifty men. *See* Haarlem; Walcheren.

Alkmaar II (*Wars of the French Revolution***)** *2 October 1799*. Alkmaar and the line of which it was the centre was held by 30,000 French against a comparable force of 30,000 British and Russians under the Duke of York. The Russians drove in the French advanced posts, the British outflanked the enemy line and then attacked the left and centre. The Allies occupied Alkmaar. *See* Bergen-op-Zoom II.

Allia (*First Gaul invasion of Rome***)** *389 BC*. Quintus Sulpiclus and his 40,000 Romans lined the Allia River to check the advance of the barbarian Gauls on Rome. The Gaulish leader, Brennus, attacked the Roman right, where he knew the younger soldiers were stationed, routed it, and then piecemeal demolished the centre and left. Roman losses are unverifiable, but were certainly great. The Gauls sacked and burnt Rome and laid siege to the capitol, which was still holding out when Brennus withdrew. *See* Veii.

Almanza, *60 miles south-west of Valencia* (*War of Spanish Succession*) *25 April 1707*. Lord Galway and the Marquis de Ruvigny led a 15,000-strong English–Dutch–Portuguese force which attacked the French–Spanish led by Marshal Berwick. Disaster followed initial success, for the Portuguese right broke and fled and the British, attacked front and flank, surrendered. The defeat led to the Archduke Charles of Austria losing the whole of Spain except Catalonia. Philip V was left secure in Spain. Galway lost 5,000 killed or wounded and 10,000 prisoners, but the British 6th and 9th Foot behaved with exceptional bravery in this battle. *See* Barcelona I; Stollhofen.

Alma River (*Crimean War***)** *20 September 1854*. The Russians held the heights near the Alma River with 40,000 men under Prince Mentschikoff (Menshikov). They were attacked by a combined British and French army, 26,000-strong, led by Lord Raglan and Marshal St. Arnaud. The British 2nd and Light Divisions carried the heights at bayonet point. Casualties: Russian, 1,200 killed, 4,700 wounded and captured; British, 3,000; French, 1,000. *See* Bomarsund; Sebastopol I; Silistra.

Almenar (*or Almanara***) (***War of Spanish Succession***)** *10 July 1710*. The British part of Archduke Charles' army, under Lord Stanhope, attacked and defeated the Spanish under Philip V. The rout was complete and only the night saved Philip's army from annihilation. *See* Almanza; Lérida; Saragossa.

Almorah (*British–Gurkha War***)** *25 April 1815*. Colonel Nicolls and Colonel Gardiner led 2,000 British troops and some irregulars to capture the mountain fortress of Almorah, leading to the surrender of the province of Kumaon. *See* Jitgurgh; Mukwanpur.

Alnwick I (*or Aln I*) (*English–Scottish Wars*) *13 November 1093*. An English victory against the Scots who had invaded Northumberland. The Scots lost their leader, Malcolm Canmore, and the invasion collapsed. *See* Rochester I.

Alnwick II (*English–Scottish Wars*) *13 June 1174*. William I of Scotland had invaded Northumberland and laid siege to Alnwick Castle. Henry II of England sent a relief army which surprised and routed the besiegers. William was imprisoned in Normandy until he recognised English rule in Scotland. *See* Berwick-upon-Tweed; Wallingford.

Alresford (*English Civil War*) *29 March 1644*. The Parliamentary forces led by Sir William Waller were victorious, but lost so heavily that the Royalists (Earl of Brentford) retreated unmolested. *See* Cropredy Bridge; Marston Moor.

Alsen (*Prussian–Danish War for Schleswig-Holstein*) *29–30 June 1864*. The beaten Danish garrison of Düppel fortress had retreated to Alsen Island. The Prussians crossed to the island by night and under heavy fire forced a final surrender and the end of the war. *See* Düppel.

Altendorf (*Thirty Years' War*) *24 August 1632*. One of the few defeats suffered by Gustavus Adolphus of Sweden. With 40,000 Swedes and Germans, he attacked an equal number of Imperialists (Wallenstein) who held the ruined castle of Altendorf and a hill. Gustavus, having lost 2,300 killed and wounded, withdrew. Imperialist casualties, 2,700. *See* Fürth; Lützen; Rain.

Alte Veste. *See* Fürth.

Alto Pascio *1325*. The Florentine Guelfs were defeated with heavy loss by the Ghibellines (Castruccio Castracane of Lucca).

Amakusa (*revolt of the Japanese Christians*) *1638*. About 30,000 rebels (Masada Shiro) held the castle of Amakusa (Kyushu) which was on the verge of being captured by the troops of the Shogun. Setting fire to the castle, the defenders died to the last man, by flame or sword.

Amanthea (*Napoleonic Wars*) *26 April 1810*. H.M.S. *Thomas*, *Pilot* and *Weazel* fought a decisive action with a number of French gunboats and destroyed some transports off Amanthea, on the toe of Italy.

Amazon, H.M.S. (Captain C. Reynolds) and H.M.S. *Indefatigable* (Captain Sir Edward Pellew) — both frigates — fought the French ship-of-the-line *Droits de l'Homme* on 13 January 1797. The battle started off the south of Ireland and ended 13 hours later with the *Amazon* and *Droits de l'Homme* going ashore on the French coast. More than 900 of the French crew of 1,350 were killed or drowned.

Amberg (*Wars of French Revolution*) *24 August 1796*. In 1795 General Jourdan led the French Army of the Sambre-and-Meuse into Franconia while General Pichegru took the Army of the Rhine and Moselle into Swabia and Bavaria — a twin offensive against the German states of the Holy Roman Empire. The French had much success, but on 24 August the Archduke Charles, the emperor's brother, with 48,000 men, counter-attacked and defeated Jourdan's 45,000-strong army at Amberg, 35 miles east of Nurnberg. Jourdan and Pichegru were unable to unite. *See* Castiglione della Stiviere; Wurzburg.

Ambon (*World War II*) *January 1942*. Principal port of the island of Amboina, Ambon was defended by a small Australian contingent which was overrun by the Japanese. Of the 809 Australians captured, 426 were executed or died of starvation and torture. *See* Timor.

Ambracian Gulf *western Greece (Corinthian–Corcyrean War) 435 BC.* About eighty Corcyrean triremes defeated seventy-five Corinthian ships attempting to relieve Epidamnus.

Ambur I *(Carnatic War) February 1749.* A conflict between the army of Anwar-ud-din, Nawab of Arcot, with 20,000 men and the combined forces of Muzuffor Jung and Chunda Sahib, helped by a French contingent, led by the Marquis de Bussy. The Nawab was defeated and killed.

Ambur II *(First British–Mysore War) November–December 1767.* A strong fortress held by only 500 sepoys in British service, under Captain Calvert, Ambur held out against a major force led by Hyder Ali until relieved on 6 December. *See* Trincomalee II.

American Civil War. *See* List of Battles.

American Revolution. *See* List of Battles.

Amethyst, H.M.S. On 10 November 1808, the *Amethyst* (Captain Michael Seymour) captured the French ship *Thetis* off Lorient, after the French had lost 134 men killed and 102 wounded. On 5 April 1809 the *Amethyst* engaged the French frigate *Niemen*, which surrendered.

Amethyst, H.M.S. *19 April 1949.* A frigate of 1,495 tones with a complement of 170, *Amethyst* was shelled by Chinese shore batteries when on the Yangste River. Her commander was among the killed. After being held in a trap for 3 months, *Amethyst*, now commanded by Lieutenant-Commander Kerans, made a remarkable escape down the river.

Casualties: 21 officers and men killed, 27 seriously wounded.

Amida, *eastern Turkey (Roman–Persian Wars) 359.* This Roman fortress, on the left bank of the Tigris River, withstood a siege of 73 days before being taken by the Persians, who slew everybody in the place. However, the Persians themselves had lost 30,000 men and Sapor (Shapur) II had to abandon his campaigns. In 503 the Persians (Kobad) besieged another Roman garrison. After a 3-month defence, during which the attackers lost 50,000 men, the Persians gained entry by night surprise and massacred 80,000 of the garrison and inhabitants.

Amiens *(French–Prussian War) 27 November 1870.* The French (General Faure) were driven out, but the German victory was indecisive. Casualties: French, 2,383; Prussians, 1,292. *See* Metz; Sedan.

Amiens *(World War I) 8 August–3 September 1918.* The "black day" for the German Army, as Ludendorff called 8 August. The battle was the second Allied offensive of 1918, planned to reduce the enemy salient (won during the great German offensive in March) pointing at Amiens and from which the Germans could shell the Paris–Amiens railway. The main assault was delivered by General Rawlinson's Fourth Army, with seventeen divisions, including one American, four Canadian and the five Australian divisions. Advancing on 8 August on a 10-mile front against twenty weary German divisions (von der Marwitz and von Hutier), the Allies took 16,000 prisoners in 2 hours and had penetrated 9 miles by nightfall, the fiercest fighting falling to the Australians at Villers Bretonneux. On 10 August the French Third Army (Humbert) attacked the southern side of the salient; on 21 August the British Third Army (Byng) and First Army (Horne) also attacked. Ludendorff was forced back to the Hindenberg Line by 3 September. Casualties: German, 75,000 including 30,000 prisoners; British, 22,000; French, 24,000. *See* Marne River II; Saint-Mihiel; Somme.

Amoaful (*Second British–Ashanti War*) *31 January 1874*. A British force (Sir Garnet Wolseley) defeated the Ashantis, who had been raiding British settlements. Most of the British casualties — 190 — were among the 42nd Regiment.

Amorium, *on the Upper Euphrates* (*Muslim invasion of Asia Minor*) *838*. A great battle between the Muslims (Caliph Motassem or al-Mutasim) and the Greeks (Theophilus). A force of 30,000 Persian horsemen, serving with the Greeks, broke the Muslim lines, but the Greeks themselves were beaten. They held out in Amorium for 55 days, during which the Muslims lost 70,000 men. Gaining entry by treachery from within, the Muslims massacred 30,000 Christians. *See* Heraclea Pontica; Samosata.

Ampezzo Valley (*World War I*) *20 June 1917*. The Italians, blowing up a mountain spur in the valley, destroyed an Austrian garrison. *See* Caporetto; Piave.

Amphipolis, *in Macedonia* (*Great Peloponnesian War*) *424–422 BC*. In 424 Sparta invaded the Athenian colonies of north-east Greece, the competent leader Brasidas capturing Amphipolis. In 422 the Athenian leader Cleon moved to attack Amphipolis and was met outside the city by Brasidas and his Spartans. The Athenians were broken. In the close pursuit, Brasidas and Cleon were killed; as a result Sparta and Athens negotiated an uneasy peace, ending the Second Peloponnesian War.

Amritsar *13 April 1919*. Amritsar, holy city of the Sikhs and an important Punjab trading centre, was seriously affected by a civil disobedience campaign. Mobs murdered British bank officials and stoned the police and soldiers. Despite proclamations prohibiting demonstrations, 6,000 people gathered and Brigadier-General Dyer, who had been brought in to take command, ordered fifty Gurkhas to open fire; 400 people were killed and many wounded. His action, severely criticized, showed that a soldier could not presume to take action on matters which were the concern of the government. Not strictly a battle, the action is listed here because of its controversial and political importance.

Amstetten (*Napoleonic Wars: campaign of the Danube*) *5 November 1805*. The Russians retiring on Vienna fought a losing rearguard action against Napoleon's marshals, Murat and Lannes. They lost 1,000 men. *See* Austerlitz.

Anaquito (*Conquest of Peru*) *8 January 1546*. Gonzalo Pizarro convincingly defeated the Spanish Viceroy, Blasco Nunez, and took control of Peru.

Ancona (*Italian Wars of Independence*) *September 1860*. A small Papal garrison (La Moricière) held out for a week against an attack by the Piedmontese fleet of thirteen ships and the army of General Cialdini. *See* Catalafimi.

Ancrum Moor (*English–Scottish Wars*) *17 February 1545*. The English (Sir Ralph Evans) lost to the Scots (the Earl of Angus) because of wholesale desertion.

Ancrya, *in modern central Turkey* (*Syrian Civil War*) *242 BC*. The routing of the Syrians (Seleucus Callincus) by the rebels led by his brother Hierax, reinforced by many Gauls.

Angaur Island (*World War II*) *17–19 September 1944*. Angaur was captured by U.S. troops during the even more important assault on Peleliu Island, q.v. *See* Mariana Islands.

Angolan War of Independence *1961–75*. Portugal, the first European nation to have colonies in Africa, was the last to give up its empire. Three different liberation movements, which often fought against each other, were at war with the occupying Portuguese army. They were: the Communist MPLA (Popular Movement for the Liberation of Angola) led by Agostinio Neto; the UPA (Union of the Population of Angola) which became the FLNA (National Front for the Liberation of Angola) led by Holden Roberto; and, from 1966, UNITA (National Union for the Total Independence of Angola) under Dr. Jonas Savimbi. On 15 March 1961 UPA guerrillas massacred 7,000 Africans and 700 whites in Uige district. Local whites and blacks retaliated so ruthlessly that 30,000 people died. For 14 years sporadic fighting continued, with the United States supporting the FLNA and the Soviet aiding the MPLA. Casualties in the Portuguese Army of 50,000 whites and 10,000 blacks under the command of General Jose Bettancourt Rodriguez amounted to 5,000 dead and 11,000 wounded. Angolan independence was declared on 7 August 1975.

Angolan Civil War *1976–*   . The war, which was in progress before independence, became more violent after the Portuguese withdrawal because of foreign involvement. The FLNA was backed by Zaire and 350 British mercenaries; the MPLA by 13,000 Cuban troops using much Soviet equipment; UNITA by South Africa. South Africa had been drawn into the war because fighters belonging to SWAPO (South-West African People's Organization) used southern Angola as a base for their war against South Africa for the liberation of Namibia.

As American support dwindled, the result of Soviet propaganda, the Cubans moved in more troops and by March 1976 the MPLA nominally held 90 per cent of Angola. With the help of South African advisers, Jonas Savimbi's UNITA troops, by ambush and raid, dominated the more remote regions. In the 12 months between September 1982 and

1983 UNITA killed 3,000 MPLA soldiers and 1,500 Cubans, according to the South Africans' chief adviser, Colonel J. Bock. In August 1983 UNITA besieged the MPLA fortifications of Cangamba for 11 days and then attacked it with waves of infantry; 1,300 MPLA troops were killed. Savimbi's strategy was to demoralize the MPLA, led since 1979 by Jose Eduardo dos Santos. Savimbi's tactics were successful and the Cubans, 20,000-strong by 1984, were afraid to fight in the jungle. Savimbi showed himself to be one of the most successful leaders of irregular troops in history. As a result of their failure to achieve a victory, the Russians and Cubans lost much prestige in Africa.†

Angora (*now Ankara*) (*Tartar invasion of Asia Minor*) 30 June 1402. Fought between the Tartars (Tamerlane) and the Turks (Bajazet I). Traditionally, Tamerlane had 800,000 men, and some historians claim that up to 2 million men were on the field. No documentary evidence supports this extraordinary figure, but both armies were strong in cavalry and the carnage was great. *See* Baghdad II; Nicopolis.

Angora (*Tartar invasion of Anatolia*) 20 July 1402. Tamerlane, leading a vast army of Tartars, defeated the Sultan Bayazid of the Ottoman Turks and captured the Sultan himself. Tamerlane then captured Smyrna from the Knights Hospitalers, over-ran all Anatolia and received tribute from the Sultan of Egypt and the Byzantine emperor. This marked the end of the devastating campaigns of Tamerlane, which had begun in 1381. *See* Baghdad II; Nicopolis; Salonika I.

Angostura, *Mexico* (*American–Mexican War*) 21 February 1847. A total defeat for the Mexicans (Santa Anna) by the Americans (General Winfield Scott). *See* Alamo; Buena Vista.

Angostura–Ypacarai, *Paraguay* (*War of the Triple Alliance or Lopez War*) 22–30 December 1847. North of Angostura, at Ypacarai, the Paraguayan dictator mustered his last 10,000 troops. His enemies' pressure increased and their observation balloons spotted his gun batteries. The Allied flotilla bombarded Lopez's Angostura positions while a Brazilian column threatened his rear at Ypacarai. The Paraguayans repelled a series of assaults at great cost to both sides. On 25 December a general assault broke Lopez's front; only the batteries in Angostura held out. Lopez fled with a cavalry guard, while Angostura surrendered, 30 December. Lopez continued a partisan war until 1870. *See* Humaita; Paso de Patria.

Anholt (*Napoleonic Wars*) 27 March 1801. A large flotilla of Danish gunboats and 1,500 troops attacked the British garrison of 381 (Captain J. Maurice) on the island of Anholt in the Kattegat. British opposition was fierce and many Danes surrendered and 520 were killed. Two Royal Navy ships chased the fleeing expedition and captured four ships and many prisoners. (The British garrison was observing the Danish navy for infringements of British orders forbidding help to Napoleon.) *See* Copenhagen.

An Lao Valley (*Vietnam War*) January–February 1966. To clear the Binh Dinh plains of Viet Cong, the Americans and South Vietnamese launched a major offensive, with An Lao Valley the centre of the battle. An Allied force of 19,000 troops, in a 3-week pincers battle movement (Operation Double Eagle), killed 1,800 enemy and suffered 800 casualties themselves. The bulk of the Viet Cong forces escaped. *See* Vietnam.

Anse La Barque 18 December 1809. A squadron of British ships chased French warships and transports under the guns of Anse la Barque, Brittany, and captured both the ships and the battery.

Antietam (*American Civil War*) 17 September 1862. "The bloodiest day of the war." Fought between the Confederates (General Lee) and the Federals (General McClellan). Lee had only 35,000 men to McClellan's 95,000 at the start of the battle and his left flank was driven back. When reinforcements arrived Lee began an offensive, but by the following day a stalemate developed and the battle came to an indecisive halt. Casualties: Federals, 12,140, including 2,108 killed; Confederates, 13,724, including 2,700 killed. *See* Bull Run II; Harpers Ferry.

Antioch I (*Aurelian's expedition to Palmyra*) 272 BC. Spiritedly led by their queen, Zenobia, the Palmyrenian cavalry drove from the field at Immae the Roman horse, but the queen's infantry could not repel the charge of Aurelian's infantry and she suffered a total defeat. *See* Emesa.

Antioch II 244 BC. The Syrians (Seleucus Callincus) were defeated by the Egyptians (Ptolemy Energetes). *See* Raphia.

Antioch III (*Byzantine–Persian War*) 611. The Byzantine Army, having suffered several defeats and rotten with corruption, was easily defeated by the Persians of Chosroes II. It was the first of many Persian victories in Syria and Anatolia. *See* Damascus; Jerusalem.

Antioch IV (*First Crusade*) 20 October 1097–28 June 1098. Bohemond of Taranto and Raymond IV of Toulouse besieged Antioch, held by a Turkish garrison under Yaghi-Siyan. Both sides became desperate and on 29 December the Turks sallied out to fight, only to be driven back by the Christian knights. On 9 February 1098 a strong Turkish relief army arrived from Aleppo; Bohemond led 750 knights in a charge that routed the Turks. Then he bribed a traitor in the garrison to open a gate on the night of 2–3 June. The crusaders rampaged through the city, slaughtering the Muslims, including Yaghi-Siyan, but they could not capture the citadel. Kerboga of Mosul reached Antioch with a big Turkish army and fierce fighting developed. On 28 June 1098 Bohemond led his whole army against Kerboga's army, which broke up. The crusaders slaughtered the Turks by the thousand and prepared for further combat. *See* Dorylaeum I; Jerusalem VII; Tarsus.

Antioch V (*Crusader–Turkish Wars*) *1119*. In the spring the Turkish lord of Aleppo, Ilghazi, marched on the Christian state of Antioch, commanded by Roger of Salerno. Sending for help, Roger rode out with his troops to intercept the Turks. On the morning of 29 June the Norman knights awoke to find themselves ringed by mounted enemy bowmen. Nearly all Roger's force — knights, infantry, camp followers — were killed or captured. Ilghazi, instead of moving on to capture Antioch, returned to Aleppo where he tortured his Christian captives to death. The French called the battle Ager Sanguinis (Field of Blood). *See* Dyrrachium III; Edessa II; Ramleh I.

Antioch VI (*Crusader–Turkish Wars*) *18 May 1268*. The Mameluke leader Baybars (Bibars) I in 1265 captured Caesarea and Arsouf, in 1268 Jaffa and Saint Simeon. On 18 May, having collected a great army, he assaulted Antioch, held by the Christians since 1098, overwhelmed the Frankish defenders and reduced the great fortress to rubble. It was never rebuilt. *See* Ain Jalut; El Mansura; Tripoli (Syria); Tunis II.

Antium (*now Anzio*) (*War of Chiozza*) *30 May 1378*. A Venetian fleet (Vittorio Pisani) defeated the Genoese fleet (Fieschi). *See* Chioggia.

Antwerp I (*Netherlands War of Independence*) *4 November 1576*. This battle is known as "the Spanish Fury", because the 5,600 Spaniards (Sancho d'Avila) massacred 8,000 civilian inhabitants after having overcome weak resistance by the 6,000 Walloon defenders. *See* Maastricht; Zutphen.

Antwerp II (*Liberation of Belgium*) *November–December 1832*. Holland refused to recognize the London Protocol creating Belgium as an independent state, so the French laid siege to Antwerp in November. It held out until 23 December when, with its citadel in ruins, surrender was unavoidable.

Antwerp III (*World War I*) *August–October 1914*. The main Belgian army of 150,000 fell back from their front line to a second line based at Antwerp, which the Germans needed to protect their rear. On 1 October von Beseler's heavy siege guns began to smash Antwerp's forts one by one. On 6 October King Albert I evacuated his army from the city, linked with Rawlinson's British forces, but continued to fall back, finally taking up positions on the extreme left of the Allied line. Antwerp's inner forts fell on 8 October and the Germans (van Falkenhayn) entered next day, to impose a levy of £20 million. *See* Aisne I; Frontiers of France; Ypres I.

Antwerp IV (*World War II*) *September–November 1944*. Having liberated France from the Germans, the Allies moved north. Hitler ordered General Student's First Parachute Army to block further Allied advance across the Albert Canal, while General von Zangen's Fifteenth Army held the Scheldt Estuary. This meant that the Allies could not use Antwerp as a port and clearing the city became the main mission of the British Second Army (General Dempsey). After heavy assaults the British captured South Beveland on 31 October and Walcheren Island on 8 November. Antwerp was not clear for use until 27 November. *See* Ardennes; Arnhem.

Anual (*Spanish–Riff War*) *21 July 1921*. Rebelling against Spanish rule, the Moorish Riffs (Abd-el-Krim) surrounded a Spanish force of 20,000 at Anual and killed 12,000 of them. The Spanish commander, Silvestre, committed suicide. By the end of 1924 Abd-el-Krim had forced the Spaniards out of the interior, but made the mistake of attacking French forces in the west. Marshal Petain, with an Allied French–Spanish army, subdued the Riffs and captured Abd-el-Krim, 26 May 1926.

Anzac. *See* Gallipoli.

Anzio (*formerly Antium*) *30 miles south of Rome* (*World War II*) *23 January–May 1944*. A daring attempt — codename SHINGLE — by British and American allies to outflank the German Gustav Line, built from the Adriatic to the Ligurian Sea. A pet project of Winston Churchill's, the attack was commanded by General Alexander, who had 85,000 men of the American Fifth and British Eighth Armies under his command. Landing from 253 ships by midnight on D-Day, 36,000 men were ashore with 3000 vehicles — without resistance except minor air attacks. Field Marshal Kesselring, commanding the German forces, took advantage of Allied slowness and desperately threw a cordon around Anzio by welding odd elements of eight different divisions into a coherent force; a remarkable achievement. Allied attempts to break out were costly; e.g. the American 3rd Battalion Rangers lost all but six of 767 men. By the 7th day 12,350 vehicles had been landed, including 356 tanks; by the 14th day, 21,940 vehicles, supplying a force of 70,000 men. On 8 February General von Mackensen made the first German counter-attack; the others which followed constricted the Allied perimeter. Artillery bombardment and air attacks were incessant and in the confined space almost every shell caused great damage. Many wounded men were killed in the hospital wards. The final German offensive began on 16 February and by the following morning they had driven a bulge 2 miles wide and 2 miles deep in the Allied line. This was despite Allied superiority in artillery; they could fire fifteen or twenty shells to every one the Germans fired. The most savage fighting took place on the 18th and at the end of it the German advance had been checked. The last serious attack was made on 29 February and on 2 March an Allied air fleet — 241 Liberators, 100 Flying Fortresses, 113 Lightnings and 63 Thunderbolts — pulverized the German lines.

For the next 3 months the front line of the beachhead had the look of a 1916 battlefield. For the first and only time in World War II soldiers had to think in terms of communication trenches and barbed wire in no-man's land. The base was remarkably small from which to wage a modern war. It stretched about 16 miles along the coast from the Moletta River in the north-east to the banks of the Mussolini Canal in the south-east, but it was only 7 miles inland to the British forward positions near Nettuno and 9 miles to the American front, Cisterna.

The Allied break-out began on 23 May, with 160,000 Allied soldiers involved, and Rome was entered on 4 June. Due to disagreement between the American commander, General Clark, and the British, General Alexander, the German Tenth Army escaped as a fighting force. Commanders: British, Generals Alexander, Evelegh, Templer, Penney, Gregson-Ellis. Americans: Clark, Lucas, Truscott, Frederick, O'Daniels, Eagels, Harmon. Germans: Field Marshal Kesselring, von Mackensen, Graser, Gruenther, von Pohl, Schlemmer, Westphal. Casualties: Allied, 21,000; Germans, figures unreliable, probably 11,000. *See* Cassino; Salerno.

Aong (*Indian Mutiny*) *15 July 1857*. Rebel sepoys in trenches tried to check the advance of the British force (Havelock) marching to relieve besieged Cawnpore, q.v., but were defeated. *See* Delhi.

Appomattox River (*American Civil War*) *1865*. On the night of 2–3 April General Lee, having been defeated at Five Forks on 1 April, moved his exhausted army of Northern Virginia westward, to join with General J. Johnston's army, retreating before Sherman's thrust. The Federal Commander-in-Chief, Grant, with 125,000 men available, sent

Sheridan to cut Lee's railway route, thus forcing Lee further west. On 6 April General Humphrey's Federal II Corps overwhelmed Lee's rearguard at Sayler's Creek, taking 7,000 prisoners, including six generals. The Federals had 1,180 casualties, including 166 killed. *See* Bentonville; Five Forks; Petersburg.

Apulia (*Muslim–Byzantine Wars*) *875–80*. Under Basil I, the Byzantines became aggressive. Basil sent an expedition from Constantinople to Italy, where the Muslims had taken control of the southern peninsula. In 875 the Byzantines drove the Muslims from their stronghold at Bari and in 880 recovered Taranto (Tarentum). *See* Erzerum; Samosarta; Taormina.

Aquae Sextiae (*now Aix-en-Provence*) (*Gallic attack on Rome*) *102 BC*. The Teutones and the Cimbris, both Gallic peoples, had beaten Roman legions at Arausio, q.v. Now the Cimbris entered Italy through the Brenner Pass while the Teutones (King Teutobod) used the Little Saint Bernard Pass. Gaius Marius and his legion drove the Teutones back through the mountains, caught them at Aquae Sextiae (Aix-en-Provence) and killed most of them. *See* Vercella.

Aquileia I, *at head of the Adriatic* (*German invasion of Italy*) *166–7*. Three German tribes crossed the Alps into north-east Italy — the barbarian Marcomanni (from Bohemia), Quadi (Moravia) and Iazges (Hungary). Repulsed when they attacked Aquileia, they left a siege force and moved on to ravage Opitergium (Oderzo) before Marcus Aurelius defeated them with a scratch army of legionaries. He raised the siege of Aquileia the following year. When the enemy threat along the north-east frontier persisted, Marcus allowed barbarians to settle within the Roman Empire. *See* Philippopolis.

Aquileia II (*Eugenius' Rising*) *6/7 September 394*. A conflict between Theodosius, Emperor of the East, and Eugenius, usurping Emperor of the West, whose army was commanded by Argobastes. Theodosius lost the first day's fighting. During the night Argobastes sent a force to hold the passes in Theodosius' rear, but these men deserted to Theodosius. With their help and that of a dust storm blowing in the faces of Argobastes' men, he won convincingly the following day. *See* Adrianople II; Pollentia.

Aquileia III (*Wars of Western Roman Empire*) *452*. Having been defeated at Chalons-sur-Marne, Attila led his Huns eastward across the Rhine in 451 and in 452 across the Alps and into northern Italy, to storm, sack and burn Aquileia. With Rome and all Italy seriously threatened, Pope Leo I induced Attila to withdraw north of the Alps. The refugees from Aquileia, hiding in the lagoons of the Adriatic coast, founded the city of Venice. *See* Chalons-sur-Marne II.

Arakan Campaign. *See* Burma.

Arar River (*now Saône River*) (*Gallic Wars*) *June 58 BC*. Julius Caesar, leading 34,000 legionaries, made a night march and caught a horde of Helvetians as they were crossing the Arar River towards western Gaul. His legions defeated and annihilated the 32,000 Helvetians still on the east bank. As the other Helvetians continued west towards the Liger (Loire) River, Caesar followed. *See* Bibracte.

Aras (*First British–Mahratta War*) *18 May 1775*. A British force 2,500-strong (Colonel Keating) and 20,000 Mahrattas (Raghunath Rao) fought the 25,000 strong army of the Mahratta chieftains (Hari Pant Phunhay). The untrained Mahrattas broke and gravely endangered their British allies, who rallied and defeated the enemy. Casualties: British, 222; Mahratta chieftains' army, unknown, but heavy. *See* Bassein; Gwalior.

Arausio (*now Orange, Rhone River*) (*Fourth Gallic invasion*) *105 BC*. The Gauls (Boiorix) — of the Teutone and Cimbri people — routed two consular armies under Caepio and Cn. Mallius Maximum. Casualties: the Romans are said to have lost 80,000. *See* Aquae Sextiae; Muthul River.

Arbedo (*Swiss–Milanese Wars*) *30 June 1422*. The Duchy of Milan and the Swiss cantons disputed possession of the city of Bellinzona and war broke out. The Swiss posted 4,000 halberdiers and pikemen at Arbedo, where they faced 6,000 cavalry commanded by Francesco Bussone (also known as Carmagnola). The horsemen's swords and lances wore down the Swiss resistance, but when Carmagnola stopped briefly the badly mauled Swiss were able to withdraw. *See* Näfels; Saint Jacobpen-Birs.

Arbela, *upper Euphrates* (*now the town of Erbil*) (*Alexander's Asiatic campaign*) *331 BC*. A major battle of history between 40,000 Macedonian infantry and 7,000 cavalry (Alexander the Great) and the Persian Army, of at least 200,000 infantry and 45,000 cavalry — several ancient writers speak of a million men — (Darius Codomannus). Alexander himself led the Macedonian right, which included his Agema ("King's Own"), forced a way between the Persian left and centre and attacked the centre on its flank. The Persians hard-pressed the Macedonian left, but the flight of Darius himself — Alexander's tactical target — caused a Persian rout. The victory made Alexander master of Asia. Casualties can hardly be guessed. Diodorus says that 90,000 Persians fell and 500 Macedonians. Other ancient writers give figures for Persian losses that vary between 40,000 and 300,000. *See* Gaza I; Megalopolis.

Arcis-sur-Aube (*Prussian–Austrian invasion of France*) *21 March 1814*. A desperate stand by 23,000 French (Napoleon) against 60,000 Austrians (Prince Karl von Schwarzenberg). In the end, the French, having lost 1,700 men, retreated in good order. The Austrian casualties were at least 2,500, possibly 4,000. *See* Paris I; Reims.

Arcola (*or Arcoli Gorge*) (*Napoleon's Italian campaign*) *15–17 November 1796*. A bloody French–Austrian battle, with Napoleon and his weary, diseased army trying to prevent a junction of two Austrian armies (Alvinczy and Davidovich). He occupied Arcola village, evacuated it at night and failed to retake it the next day. On 17 November, before Davidovich could join Alvinczy, Napoleon attacked from the rear and broke the Austrian defence. Casualties: Austrian, 6,000; French, 6,000. *See* Caldiero I; Mantua.

Arcot (*British–French War in India*) *September–October 1751*. Robert Clive and his "army" of 800 seized this fortress in September; it was then besieged by 10,000 natives and 150 French under Chunda Sahib, French nominee for Nawabship of Arcot. Clive, his garrison weakened by illness, held out for 7 weeks until the approach of a Mahratta relief column forced Chunda Sahib to raise the siege. Casualties of the garrison: 45 Europeans and 30 sepoys killed. *See* Calcutta; Madras I.

Ardennes (*or Battle of the Bulge*) (*World War II*). Originally Operation Christrose to the Germans, but changed by Hitler to "Watch on the Rhine", this remarkable counter-offensive began on 16 December 1944, when 1,900 German heavy guns bombarded the peaceful Ardennes front of 85 miles. The bombardment was followed by the attack of 1,000 tanks and assault guns and 250,000 troops. The plan was so audacious that no Allied commander suspected that it was coming. From Echternach to Monschau, the front was held by only six U.S. Divisions, three of them new to the battle, the other three exhausted and resting. Hitler's intention was to cross the Meuse and head for Antwerp, but by 26 December the battle was static as American and British troops were thrown in to contain the bulge. The British were drawn into the battle on 19 December when General Eisenhower asked Montgomery to take command of the Allied armies on the north side of the Bulge, while Bradley commanded the southern forces.

At one point in the battle, at the Schnee Eifel, nearly 9,000 Americans, facing literal annihilation, surrendered; next to Bataan, this was the greatest mass surrender of Americans in history. Before the battle ended more than a million men were involved. The Ardennes was not an orthodox battle. Lines either did not exist or were bewilderingly fluid. Communications were unreliable; surrounded Americans were, at times, only a few miles from surrounded Germans. The conflict was the greatest pitched battle ever fought by Americans and their only major struggle in the dead of winter.

Part of the German offensive was a last-throw fighter-plane attack of 1,100 Focke-Wulf 190s and Messerschmitts on the morning of 1 January. In four waves, and at tree-top level, the Germans severely damaged twenty-seven Allied bases between Brussels and Eindhoven and destroyed about 300 aircraft. The Germans themselves lost 300 pilots, including fifty-nine leaders and were virtually left without an air force. Casualties: American, 19,000 killed, 47,000 wounded; British, 10,000; Germans, about 100,000. Altogether nearly 80,000 men died during the battle; many froze to death.

Commanders (Major-Generals and above) actively engaged: American: Lieutenant-General Omar Bradley, Lieutenant-General Courtney Hodges, Major-General Level Allen, Major-General R. Barton, General Troy Middleton, Major-General W. Morris, Major-General Alexander Bolling, Major-General J. Lawton Collins; Lieutenant-General George Patton, Major-General M. Ridgway, Major-General Hugh Gaffey, Major-General James Gavin, Major-General Leland Hobbs, Major-General Horace McBride, General Hobart Gay, Major-General Leonard Gerow, Major-General Robert Crow, Major-General Ernest Harmon, Major-General Walter Robertson, Major-General Maurice Rose, Lieutenant-General William Simpson, Major-General Maxwell Taylor. German: Field Marshal Walther Model, General Ernst Brandenberger, General Harmann Balck, General Hasso von Manteuffel, Major-General Fritz Bayerlein, Colonel-General J. "Sepp" Dietrich, Colonel-General Heinz Guderian, Lieutenant-General Walther Kruger, General Heinrich von Luttwitz. British: Field Marshal Sir Bernard Montgomery, Lieutenant-General Sir Brian Horrocks. *See* Rhineland; Siegfried Line.

Argaum (*or Argaon*) (*Second British–Mahratta War*) *November 1803*. After initial setbacks, the British (Wellesley) defeated the forces of the Rajah of Berar (Sindhia of Gwalior). This victory marked the end of the war. Casualties: British, 346. *See* Assaye; Furruckhabad.

Argentoratum I (*now Strasbourg*) (*invasion of the Allemanni*) *May 378*. The Romans (Gratianus) overwhelmed the Allemanni (Priarius) despite their courageous stand. Casualties unknown, but only 5,000 Allemanni escaped from the field. Priarius was killed. *See* Amida I; Mursa.

Argentoratum II (*invasion of the Allemanni*) *August 357*. About 13,000 Romans (Julian) attacked a vastly superior army of Allemanni (Chnodomar) shortly before midnight after a long march. After an early setback, the Romans rallied and routed the Allemanni, taking Chnodomar prisoner. Casualties: Allemanni, at least 6,000; Romans, 247. *See* Amida I; Mursa.

Arges (*World War I*) *1–4 December 1916*. This was one of several battles between the Germans and Romanians early in the war. The Romanian Army was driven back along the Arges River, leaving Bucharest open to the Germans.

Romanian military resistance crumbled by the end of December, with casualties of 400,000.

Arginusae islands (*Peloponnesian War*) 406 BC. The rout of the Peloponnese fleet of 120 triremes (Callicratidas) by the Athenians (Thrasyllus). Because twenty-five Athenian ships were lost, Thrasyllus and all other senior leaders were accused of failing to rescue the men of the disabled triremes. Thrasyllus and six other admirals were executed. *See* Aegospotami; Cyzicus I.

Argonne Forest (*World War I*) 5 October 1915–3 November 1918. For four years many actions occurred in the Argonne area, between the regions of Champagne and Lorraine. The main battle occurred on 26 September 1918, when a combined force of French (General Gouraud) and Americans (General Pershing) attacked on a 40-mile front. The Americans, on the right, advanced 7 miles. General Pershing says of this action: "To call it a battle may be a misnomer, yet it was a battle, the greatest, the most prolonged in American history. Through 47 days we were engaged in a persistent struggle to smash through the enemy's defences." More than 1,200,000 Americans* at one time or another were used, and the attack was driven 32 miles to the north and 14 to the north-east before the armistice. Difficulties of supply and communication and the inexperience of the American troops imposed great strain on Pershing's administration and conduct of the battle. On 2 October a battalion of the 77th Division (Major C. W. Whittlesey) moved more rapidly forward than those on its flanks and was surrounded; it became popularly known as the "Lost Battalion" and with astonishing courage held out until relieved on the 8th.

Between 26 September and 11 November 22 American and 6 French divisions, with an approximate fighting strength of 500,000, engaged forty-three German divisions, with an estimated fighting strength of 470,000. The French and Americans moved in or out of the zone 26 American and 7 French divisions; a total of 173,000 men were evacuated and more than 100,000 replacements were received. The experience of the Argonne battle campaign profoundly influenced American military thinking. Casualties: German, 100,000, 26,000 prisoners, 874 cannon, 3,000 machine guns; French–American, 117,000. *See* Marne River II; Saint Mihiel.

Argos (*Roman invasion of Greece*) 195 BC. 50,000 Romans and Macedonians (Flaminius) routed 15,000 Spartans (Nabis). Nabis was permitted to retain Sparta, but had to surrender all his foreign possessions. *See* Cynoscephalae.

Arikera (or Carigat) (*Second British–Mysore War*) 13 May 1791. After a night march, the British force (Cornwallis) attacked the Mysore army (Tippoo Sahib), but heavy rain made the attack abortive. A frontal assault followed by a flanking movement succeeded and the Mysore soldiers were crushed. Casualties: Mysore, 2,000; British, 500. *See* Laswari.

Arius River, *Iraq* 208 BC. Fought between the Syrians (Antiochus the Great) and the Parthians and Bactrians (Arsaces III) and Eutheydemus. Despite Antiochus being severely wounded, he led his men to complete victory; the Parthians and Bactrians suffered great losses. *See* Raphia.

Arkansas Post (*American Civil War*) 9–13 January 1863. A Federal military–naval attack by General McClernand and Admiral Porter on a Confederate stronghold on the Arkansas River. The attack, though successful, cost 1,061 Federal casualties and when General Grant, commander in the west, heard of

*On 23 October the combat strength of the American Expeditionary Force was 1,256,478.

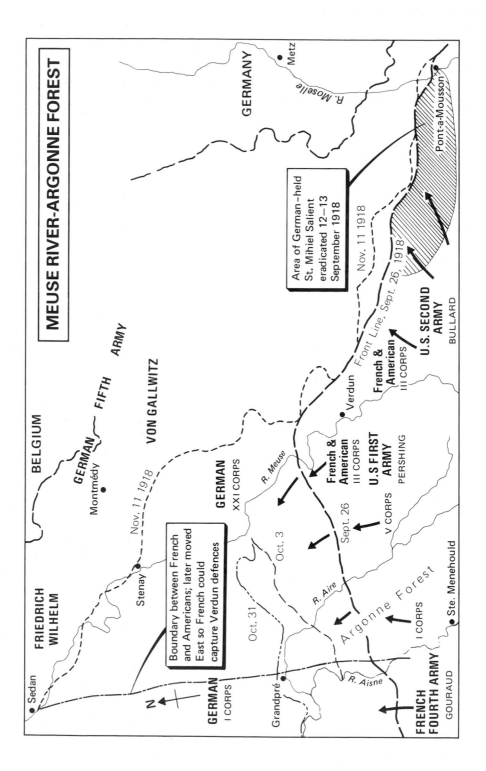

MEUSE RIVER-ARGONNE FOREST

McLernand's operation he ordered a withdrawal so that the troops could be used against the much more important Vicksburg fortress, q.v. *See* Chickasaw Bluffs.

Arkenholm (*Douglas Rebellion*) *12 May 1455*. Rebels led by the three Douglas brothers were decisively beaten by troops of James II of Scotland. Archibald was killed, Hugh captured and James, Earl of Douglas, fled to England. *See* Harlaw.

Arklow (*Irish Rebellion*) *1798*. Father John Murphy led 27,000 rebels in an advance on Dublin, but at Arklow were met and defeated by General Needham with only 1,400 militia and volunteers. Many rebels were slaughtered. *See* New Ross.

Armada, The Spanish *21–30 July 1588*. The Armada consisted of 124 ships, with a total armament of 1,124 guns, and with crews and soldiers, 30,493. The English fleet had 172 ships, 1,972 guns. Medina Sidonia and Don Alonzo de Leyva commanded the Spanish fleet, Howard the English, with Drake as Vice-Admiral. Had de Leyva's advice to attack Drake before he could get out of Plymouth Sound been taken, the English could have suffered a disastrous defeat. The smaller, well-handled English ships harassed the Spanish fleet intermittently. When the Spaniards anchored in Calais Roads, the English sent in eight fireships. They did no damage, but Sidonia ordered the Spanish cables cut and in the darkness many Spanish ships crashed into one another, while others drifted out to sea. Sidonia was unable to rally them and in the morning his Armada was scattered. On this day, 29 July, the main battles occurred and that evening squalls further dispersed the Spanish ships. During a dreadful voyage home, via the North Sea, Scotland and Ireland, the Armada suffered its worst losses. Final accounting: two abandoned to the enemy; three lost off the French coast; two off Holland; two sunk off Gravelines (1,400 casualties in

this battle); nineteen were wrecked off Scotland or Ireland; fate of thirty-five unknown. Thousands of Spaniards died of thirst, starvation, wounds. The English did not lose a ship and probably no more than sixty men. The historical importance of the Armada's defeat is that it laid the cornerstone of the British Empire by endowing England with the prestige that Spain had lost. It founded England as a commercial–imperial power.

Arnee I (*British–French War in India*) *March 1751*. Robert Clive with 900 British troops aided by 600 Mahratta horses (Basin Rao) ambushed a French and native force of 4,800 convoying treasure, which Clive captured after putting the French to flight. *See* Arcot; Madras I.

Arnee II (*First British–Mysore War*) *7 June 1782*. An indecisive action between the British (Sir Eyre Coote) and Mysore troops (Hyder Ali): the British had the greater number of casualties. *See* Aras.

Arnhem, *Holland* (*World War II*) *September 1944*. The military plan for north-west Europe called for an airdrop to seize the bridge across the Rhine at Arnhem and hold it for not less than 24 hours until an army column could arrive. The British 1st Airborne Division (Major General Urquhart) with a Polish Parachute Brigade under command, 10,000 in all, parachuted and glided into the area on 17 September. The Germans, commanded by Field Marshal Model, were present in unexpected strength. Their reaction was powerful and skilful, the British reinforcement and resupply programme was disorganized and the relief column striking from the south could not get through. Under some of the heaviest fire and counter-attacks of the war, the airborne troops held the bridge for 3 days and 4 nights and for 9 days were forced into an ever-shrinking perimeter. Finally, the survivors were called out and fought their way back across the Rhine. When the evacuation had to stop on 26 September, 2,163 men of the Airborne Division and the Glider Pilot Regiment, with 160 Poles and seventy-five British infantry, had reached the south bank; 1,130 airborne troops were killed and more than 6,000 taken prisoner. Of these nearly half were wounded before they were captured. The Germans give their own losses as 3,300 killed or wounded. It was 7 months before British troops captured Arnhem. *See* Ardennes.

Arques, *Normandy (Eighth French Religious War) 21 September 1589*. Henry of Navarre, with 8,000 Huguemot Protestants, lured the Duke of Mayenne, with his army of 24,000 — made up of French Catholics and Spanish Catholics from Flanders — into a defile of the Bethune River. Henry, an excellent tactician, had prepared trenches and gun emplacements behind marshy ground. Mayenne could use only 5,000 troops at a time and he suffered a great defeat. *See* Coutras; Ivry.

Arrah, *near Patna (Indian Mutiny) 25 July–3 August 1857*. Mr Boyle, sixteen Englishmen and sixty Sikh police held a house against repeated attacks by three entire regiments of rebellious sepoys (Kur Singh). The "garrison" was relieved by a force led by Major V. Eyre. *See* Cawnpore I; Lucknow.

Arras I (*Wars of Louis XIV) August 1654*. The Spaniards (The Great Condé) besieged Arras, but on 24 August Marshal Turenne with a relief force attacked the Spanish lines and routed them with a loss of 3,000 men. Condé's fighting retreat to Cambrai prevented an overwhelming French victory. *See* Faubourg St. Antoine; Lens; Valenciennes.

Arras II (*World War I) 1917*. On 4 April Sir Douglas Haig started a massive artillery bombardment (2,800 guns, including gas) on a 20-mile front and on 9 April sent in his infantry, notably the Canadian Corps of Horne's First Army at Vimy Ridge, q.v., and Allenby's Third

Army. They gained $3\frac{1}{2}$ miles, but the German Sixth Army Commander (von Falkenhausen) brought up strong reserves. Gough's Fifth Army in the south could make no impression on the German lines. However, the attack was pressed until 3 May to divert attention from the even greater French attack along the Aisne. Casualties: British, 84,000; German, 70,000. *See* Aisne River II; Somme River I.

Arras III (*World War II) 21 May 1940*. A British force under General Franklyn counter-attacked the German army, which was pushing the British and French defenders back to the French coast. The vigorous fighting of the fifty-eight British tanks (General Martel) and infantry, south and east of Arras, was a factor in Hitler's decision to halt his Panzer groups outside Dunkirk; this gave the British army time to escape. *See* Dunkirk.

Arretium (*now Arezzo), Central Italy (Etruscan–Gaul revolt) 285 BC*. The Etruscans, besieging Arretium, heard that a Roman army (L. Caecilius Metellus) was moving to relieve the fortress. They called on their allies, the Gauls, who in a surprise attack defeated the relief army; 13,000 Romans, including Metellus, were killed, and all the rest were taken prisoner. *See* Asculum; Beneventum.

Arrow, H.M.S. and H.M.S. Acheron. These sloops were protecting a large convoy on 3 February 1805, when attacked by French frigates off the Algerian coast. The British ships were forced to surrender after a 24-hour fight.

Arroyo Dos Molinos (*Peninsular War) 28 October 1811*. At daybreak, General Hill surprised a French division (Girard) at this village, about 40 miles from the Spanish frontier. Of the 2,600 French only 400 escaped. *See* Barrossa; Busaco; Fuentes d'Onor.

Arroyo Grande (*Uruguyan War of Independence) 1842*. The Uruguyans (Ribera) were defeated by the Argentinians (Oribe) who then besieged Montevideo, q.v.

Arsanias River (*Roman Empire Parthian Wars*) 62. In the year 61 Vologesus of Parthia launched a two-pronged attack on Roman Armenia and Syria. Emperor Nero sent Caesennius Paetus to make a counter-offensive. The Roman was outmanoeuvred and surrounded by Parthians on the Armanias River, a tributary of the Euphrates, and surrendered. General G. D. Corbulo, who had been displaced by Paetus, negotiated a peace the following year. *See* Ctesiphon I; Tigranocerta II.

Arsouf (*Third Crusade*) 2 September 1191. A massive conflict between the English Crusaders (Richard Coeur de Lion) and the Saracens (Saladin) who were said to be 300,000 strong. The English had passed Haifa on their way to Jerusalem when attacked. Both English flanks gave way, but the centre, inspired by the king, stood fast and after day-long fighting the Muslims were driven back. Muslim casualties are recorded as 40,000. A 5-year truce was arranged on 2 September the following year. *See* Acre I; Constantinople.

Artaxata (*Roman Empire's Parthian Wars*) 58. Vologesus I of Parthia challenged Roman rule by placing his brother Tiridates I on the Armenian throne. Nero sent General G. D. Corbulo, a veteran commander, to the region. Corbulo wore down sustained guerrilla attacks and captured and destroyed Artaxata. *See* Tigranocerta II.

Artois I (*World War I*) 27 September–10 October 1914. Really part of the first Battle of the Aisne, q.v., in which both the Germans and the French–British attempted to outflank each other by pushing to the north. The fighting was bitter, but both sides failed. *See* Ypres I.

Artois II (*World War I*) 9 May–18 June 1915. A senseless battle of attrition between the French (Joffre) and the Germans (Falkenhayn). On 9 May Joffre began an offensive on a 6-mile front north of Arras and Falkenhayn's troops were pushed back 3 miles; the French gained holds on Vimy Ridge. British troops reinforcing the French were stopped at Festubert on 26 May. Powerful German counter-attacks threw the French back and until 18 June the conflict was merely a steady, purposeless slaughter. Casualties: French, 100,000; German, 75,000. *See* Champagne II; Festubert; Verdun.

Artois III *September–October 1915*. *See* Battle of Loos.

Arvenanmaa (*Russian–Swedish War*) 14 July 1714. With the Swedish king, Charles XII, away in Turkey trying to induce the Muslims to wage war on Russia, a Russian fleet of thirty warships and 180 galleys (Admiral Apraxin) attacked the much smaller Swedish navy off the island of Ahvenanmaa (Aland). The Swedes fought with their customary bravery but were overwhelmed. Russian troops then occupied Aland. This was the first major Russian naval victory. *See* Poltava; Stralsund II.

Asculum I (*Second Punic War*) 208 BC. Hannibal and his 40,000 troops, few of whom were now Carthaginians, held Tarentum as his main base. Marcus Marcellus, Hannibal's opponent in many battles, led a large Roman army to capture Tarentum and a 2-day hard-fought battle took place at Asculum. Hannibal defeated Marcellus, but the victory was in no way decisive. While Hannibal was fighting at Asculum, some of his Italian allies at Tarentum opened the gates to legionaries led by Fabius Cunctator. *See* Capua; Grumentum.

Asculum II *southern Italy (Pyrrhus' invasion of Italy*) 279 BC. 45,000 Romans (Sulpicius Saverrio and P. Decius Mus) tried to force the Epirots and their Italian allies to raise the siege of Asculum. Epirot cavalry and elephants broke the Roman attack. Casualties: Roman, 6,000; Epirots, 3,000. *See* Beneventum; Heraclea.

Asculum III (*War of Rome's allies*) *89 BC*. Some Italian tribes, dissatisfied with rights granted by Rome, revolted and led by the Marsi and Samnites set up a new republic of Italia, with the capital at Corfinium. The Romans — 75,000-strong under Strabo — moving to crush the revolt, besieged Asculum where all Roman citizens had been massacred in 90 BC. The Romans gave battle to Judacilius' 60,000 Italians trying to relieve Asculum and defeated them. Some of the Italians managed to reinforce the garrison, but the Romans captured it. However, the Italians did gain more rights and privileges.

A Shau (*Vietnam War*) *1966*. An attack by 3,000 North Vietnamese regulars on the Special Forces camp in the strategic A Shau valley 360 miles north of Saigon, held by only seventeen U.S. soldiers and 360 others. The fort fell after 30 hours' fighting, but helicopters rescued 200 defenders. About 500 North Vietnamese were killed. *See* Vietnam.

Ashdown (*Danish invasion of Britain*) *871*. A victory of the West Saxons (Ethelred) against the Danes (Bag Secq and Halfdene). Real victor of the battle was Alfred (the Great), whose brilliant handling of one wing caused the repulse of the Danes after a long day's fighting. *See* Hoxne; Reading.

Ash Hollow (*Sioux Wars*) *3 September 1855*. The defeat of Little Thunder's Sioux, west of Fort Kearny, by General W. Harney's 1,200 troops. The Sioux, who had been attacking pioneers on the California Trail, lost 136 warriors. *See* Killdeer Mountain.

Ashingdon (*or Assundun*) *18 October 1016*. A battle between Edmund Ironside of Wessex and Canute of the Danes. Edmund had already won some victories against the Danes and on this occasion success was in his grasp when his brother-in-law, Edric, deserted to the Danes. A negotiated peace resulted, but when Edmund died a month later Wessex accepted Danish rule. *See* Fulford; Pen.

Ashkelon I (*or Ascalon*) (*First Crusade*) *12 August 1099*. Soon after the Crusaders had captured Jerusalem, a Muslim army from Egypt camped at Ashkelon on the Palestine coast. The smaller Crusader force, led by Godfrey of Bouillon, Tancred of Taranto and Robert of Normandy, charged into the enemy camp at dawn on 12 August and routed the Egyptians (Kilidj Arslan) though the Crusaders were unable to take the fort of Ashkelon, gateway to Egypt. It was not captured until 1153. *See* Antioch IV; Jerusalem; Melitene.

Ashkelon II (*Crusader–Turkish Wars*) *1153*. The Egyptian-held fortress was a constant threat to the Jerusalem Christians; Muslim patrols often cut the Jerusalem–Jaffa highway. In 1153 Baldwin III, supported by a force of Knights Templars, forced the Egyptians to surrender, although scores of Knights Templars died in vainglorious charges. Baldwin gave the city to his brother, Almaric — later King Almaric I of Jerusalem. *See* Damascus III; Ramleh II.

Ashtee (*Third British–Mahratta War*) *19 February 1818*. The army of the Peshwa, Baji Rao, which was led by Gokla, charged the British (General Smith), but on Gokla's death his army broke and fled. *See* Kirkee; Sholapur.

Asiago (*World War I*) *1916*. Asiago was the gateway through the Dolomite Alps. On 15 May the Austrian commander-in-chief, von Hotzendorf, put fifteen divisions into an attack against the Italian front along the Trentino, and Asiago fell. The defeat was largely the result of ineptitude by the Italian commander, General Brusati, who had plenty of warnings of the impending Austrian attack. The Italian supreme commander, Cadorna, pushed in reinforcements, but the Austrians had by now to reinforce their Russian front and by 17 June they were virtually back to their starting point. Without final gain for either side, the Austrians and Italians each suffered 100,000 casualties. Relieved of pressure, the Italians reverted to the pointless attacks on the Isonzo line. *See* Caporetto; Isonzo River.

Asirghur (*or* ***Asseerghur***) (***Third British–Mahratta War***) *March 1819*. Sir John Malcom and General Doveton besieged this powerful fortress on 18 March. On the 21st the strong garrison (Jeswunt Rao) was driven by bombardment into the upper fort, where the Mahrattas held out until 7 April. Casualties: British, 313; Mahrattas, less than the British. *See* Ashtee; Kirkee.

Askultisk (***Russian–Turkish Wars***) *August 1828*. 17,000 Russians (General Paskiewitch) routed 30,000 Turks outside Askultisk and captured all their artillery and stores. After a 3-week siege the Russians captured by storm the town of Askultisk, killing many of the 50,000 defenders. *See* Varna.

Aspendus *191 BC*. The wrong name for Eurymedon I, q.v.

Aspern-Essling, *north-east of Vienna* (***Napoleonic Wars: Wagram Campaign***) *21–22 May 1809*. One of the bloodiest battles in history, considering the size of the armies. The French (Napoleon), with 48,000 infantry and 7,000 cavalry, and the Austrians (Archduke Charles), with 90,000. The battle commenced at 4 p.m. when the Austrians attacked the French position; by nightfall they had consolidated in part of the village. Next day, with both armies reinforced, Aspern was taken and retaken at least ten times, while at Essling more fierce fighting took place. That evening the bridge by which Napoleon had crossed the Danube was swept away and he had to retire to Lobau Island. Each side claimed the victory and many his-

torians consider it a drawn battle because the Austrians could not drive the French into the Danube and the French could not break out. Charles called off his attack and used his 264 guns to pound the French bridgehead. Here Napoleon's devoted and capable Marshal Lannes and General St. Hilaire were killed. The French lost 20,000 men in the most severe check Napoleon had then received. The Austrians suffered 23,000 casualties, presumably another reason for considering the battle a drawn one. *See* Eggmuhl; Raab.

Aspromonte (***Italian Wars of Independence: Garibaldi's Rising***) *29 August 1862*. A small force of "Red Shirts", led by Garibaldi himself, was surrounded by Royalist troops (General Pallavicini). After a short fight, during which Garibaldi was wounded, the "Red Shirts" surrendered. *See* Custoza II; Gaeta.

Assaye (***Second British–Mahratta War***) *23 September 1803*. Wellesley (Wellington), with 4,500 British and native troops, routed the 30,000 army of the Sindhia of Gwalior, capturing all the enemy's guns and stores. Wellington always considered this the bloodiest action, for the numbers engaged, that he ever witnessed. British casualties, 1,566 — more than one man in three. *See* Aligurgh; Argaum.

Astraea, H.M.S. (Captain Lord Henry Paulet) captured the French frigate *Gloire* off Brest, 10 April 1795.

Astrakhan I (***conquest by Ivan I***) *1554–6*. Capturing Kazan on the upper Volga, Ivan IV (the Terrible) marched south along the river and in 1554 besieged Astrakhan, a Mongolian–Tartar stronghold at the head of the Volga delta. The garrison resisted fiercely for 2 years; Ivan's eventual victory gave Russia an opening to the east and south-east. *See* Kazan; Polotsk.

Astrakhan II (*Russian–Turkish War*) *1569*. The Turks (Selim II) besieged this town, needed as a base for digging a canal between the Don and Volga rivers, to enable the Turkish fleet to sail from the Black Sea to the Caspian Sea. The small Russian garrison stubbornly defended it and was finally relieved by a Russian army, which routed the Turks. *See* Szigetvár.

Atahualpa (*Spanish conquest of Peru*) *1531*. A butchery rather than a battle, when Pizarro, leading only 160 Spaniards, savagely attacked the Peruvians. First he invited the Inca Manco-Capac to visit him, then he seized him, suddenly attacked the 30,000-strong Peruvian escort and slaughtered 4,000 of them without losing one man of his own. *See* Cuzco; Las Salinas.

Atbara, The (*British–Sudan campaigns*) *8 April 1898*. Between the British and Egyptian army of 14,000 (Sir Herbert Kitchener) and 18,000 Mahdists (Mahmad) who were threatening the flank of a British approach on Omdurman. The Allied force attacked the Mahdists in their zareba — trenches defended by thorn bushes — and decisively defeated them, capturing Mahmad. Casualties: Mahdists, 5,000 killed, 1,000 taken prisoner, British–Egyptians, 570. *See* Abu Klea; Khartoum.

Athenry (*conquest of Ireland*) *1316*. Utter defeat of the O'Connors (Feidlim) at the hands of the English (William de Burgh and Richard de Bermingham). It is said that 11,000 O'Connors fell in the battle.

Athens–Piraeus (*First Mithridatic War*) *86 BC*. Pontus, on the southern shore of the Black Sea, had an able ruler, Mithridates VI, who sent an army to occupy Athens and ordered the death of all Italians in Asia Minor. This roused the Romans, and after fighting a civil war to prove his leadership, L. Cornelius Sulla took an army to Greece, stormed Athens and Piraeus and the larger Pontic Army (Archelaus) was driven out. *See* Chaeronea.

Atlanta (*American Civil War*) *1864*. A Union army under General Sherman was pushing aggressively towards Atlanta, the Confederates' most vital transport, manufacturing and medical centre. On 20 July the Confederates tried to stop the advance in the Battle of Peach Tree Creek, where they lost 2,600 men in 3 hours; the Federals lost 1,600. The forceful Confederate general, John Hood, sent General Hardee and his corps on a 15-mile night march to attack the southern flank of the Federals on 22 July. In a violent struggle the Confederates lost 8,000 men while the Federals suffered 3,700 casualties, including General McPherson. On 28 July the Federals, still forward-moving, were near Ezra Church (near Atlanta) when they were again attacked — this time by Stephen Lee's corps. The Federals held their positions. Sherman now made attacks to cut the railways leading into Atlanta from the south, and though the Confederates were able to hold at Schofield and Utoy Creek, they could not long delay Sherman's envelopment of Atlanta, beginning 20 August. Confederate General Hardee fought the Federals, 31 August–1 September at Jonesboro; that day Hood abandoned Atlanta to join Hardee, losing the city to save the army. Sherman, having advanced 140 miles from Chattanooga, suffered 21,656 casualties to take Atlanta, and inflicted 27,565 on the Confederates. He burnt much of Atlanta and on 15 November marched to the sea at Savannah. *See* Franklin; Kenesaw Mountain.

Atlantic, Battle of (*World War I*) *1915–17*. German submarines and light cruisers fought for 3 years to cut the supply lifeline to Britain. The onslaught reached such proportions that by December 1916 about a hundred U-boats were sinking 300,000 tons of shipping a month; in April 1917 880,000 tons were sunk.

The convoy system, increased numbers of destroyers, Q-ships and the development of the depth charge, cut into German successes. By the end of 1917 the Germans had lost fifty-eight submarines and though 130 were still in operation they were less effective. Nevertheless, they had destroyed 8 million tons of shipping.

Atlantic, Battle of (*World War II*). The Battle of the Atlantic, as the war between German submarines and Allied ships came to be called in 1942, really began on the outbreak of war. The Royal Navy established a blockade of Germany and the Germans retaliated with an undersea counter-blockade. During 1939–40 the British Admiralty reported the loss of 677 merchant ships and total loss of 4,525,288 tones; Britain had an annual shipbuilding capacity of 1.5 million tons. With the fall of France, Germany became an Atlantic power. Acquisition of Scandinavian bases and rapid building of U-boats, in 1941, and training of crews gave Germany great advantages. The German drive reached a new peak in 1941, with sinkings of 3,708,000 tons. Even American shipyards could add only half a million tons in merchantmen, but the United States gave Britain all Axis ships seized in American ports. In February 1941 Germany had only twenty-two ocean-going U-boats, but the fleet increased, by various estimates, to between 180 to 400. They hunted in packs with aerial observers. The British could sink only seventy-one U-boats from the beginning of the war to April 1941.

Because of an increase in British flying patrols and corvettes and bombing of submarine bases, destruction of shipping was cut sharply in the middle of 1941. After the United States entered the war, December 1941, U-boats renewed the Battle of the Atlantic off the American east coast, planning to disrupt the supplies being sent to Britain, Russia and the Middle East. German submarines now had a cruising range of 12,000 miles, and in the first 10 months of 1942 they claimed 498 victims. Intensive countermeasures drove the submarines from inshore waters, but convoys on the high seas were still mauled. Those for Russia were dealt with especially fiercely; 350 bombers attacked convoy PQ17 in the Arctic and sank twenty-three of thirty-four ships. About one-fourth of all ships on the Arctic run were sunk, also two British cruisers and ten destroyers, and as many as seventy-five warships were needed to protect one convoy. Flying Fortresses greatly damaged the German submarine yards at Vegesack in March 1943 and American shipyards launched a growing fleet of destroyer escorts and escort carriers. The German long-range plane, the Condor, caused commensurate losses to Allied shipping. Turning point in the protection of convoys came in May 1943 when at least thirty U-boats were sunk. Between June and October another 120 were sunk. From the beginning of the war until mid-1944 about 500 were destroyed. Between December 1941 and 6 June 1944 American and British naval patrols escorted 7,000 ships across the Atlantic with the loss of only ten while under convoy. Winston Churchill said in Parliament (8 June, 1943): "We British must continue to place the anti-U-boat war first because it is only by conquering the U-boat that we can live and act." This indicates the importance of this war-long battle.

Auchonvillers (*World War I*) commencing 26 March 1918. The New Zealanders, hurried into action, halted a powerful German attack which threatened to break the Allied line. Fighting took place at Mailly-Maillet, Hamel, Rossignol Wood and along the Ancre River. Australians, flanking the New Zealanders, fought at Hebuterne Wood. *See* Albert; Somme.

Auerstadt (*Napoleonic Wars: Jena campaign*) 14 October 1806. Commanding 26,000 men of the French III Corps, Marshal Davout faced 66,000 Prussians. With characteristic attention to detail, he inflicted 12,000 casualties, captured 3,000 men and 115 guns with small loss to his own force. The Battle of Jena q.v., another French victory the same day, has tended to obscure Auerstadt. Together these victories destroyed Prussia as a military power. The lesson was a harsh one and the German armies of 1813, 1870 and 1914 were the results of the remaking of Prussia after the disasters of Auerstadt and Jena. *See* Saalfeld.

Aughrim (*Wars of the Glorious Revolution*) *12 July 1691*. Fought between English troops of William III, under Godert de Ginkel (future Earl of Athlone), and French and Irish allies led by the Marquis Saint-Ruth. Saint-Ruth's lines were protected by a bog and Ginkel's English infantry could make no progress. His cavalry found a way through the bog, turned the French–Irish flank and frightened the Irish into flight. Between 6,000 and 7,000 are said to have been killed by the pursuing English, whose casualties amounted to 700. *See* Boyne, The; Limerick.

Augsberg *910*. German Christians were overwhelmed by invading Hungarian barbarians, the Magyars, whose cavalry won the battle by ambush after first pretending to flee.

Augusta, *Sicily* (*Louis XIV's Dutch War*) *22 April 1676*. The Marquis Duquesne, with twenty-nine ships, gave battle to seventeen Dutch and ten Spanish ships under de Ruyter. The fight, due to incompetent Spanish seamanship, was indecisive, but de Ruyter, one of the greatest naval commanders in history, was mortally wounded. In May the French caught the Dutch–Spanish fleet at anchor in Palermo and smashed it. *See* Mons I; Stromboli.

Auldearn (*English Civil War*) *9 May 1645*. Montrose and his Highlanders defeated a superior force of Covenanters (Sir John Urry) marching north to raid the lands of the Gordon clan. *See* Alford; Inverlochy.

Auray *30 September 1364*. A battle between the forces of John de Montfort and Charles of Blois, rival claimants to the dukedom of Brittany. The English (Sir John Chandos) were besieging Auray when the French (Bertrand du Guesclin) attacked them. The English held fast and counter-attacked the French flank, a move which routed the French. Charles of Blois was killed and du Guesclin captured. Charles V had no alternative but to acknowledge de Montfort as Duke of Brittany. *See* Najéra; Poitiers.

Aussig (*or Usti*), *Czechoslovakia* (*Hussite Civil War*) *September 1426*. The Hussites, considered heretics by most of the Bohemian Catholic population, were led by John Zisca after the execution of John Huss in 1415. Zisca, an able soldier, had a fortified base at Tabor where he taught an offensive–defensive tactical system, built around a *wagenburg* (wagon fortress). When he died before his planned invasion of Moravia could begin, Hussite military command was assumed by Prokob "the Great". The Germans under Emperor Zigismund invaded Hussite territory and Prokop decisively defeated them at Aussig, using *wagenburg* tactics. *See* Prague 1419.

Austerlitz ("*Battle of the Three Emperors*") (*Napoleonic Wars: campaign of the Danube*) *2 December 1805*. Napoleon, with about 75,000 men, after careful reconnaissance, took up his position near and around the Platzen Plateau to meet an attack by the Russian and Austrian Allies — about 95,000 men under Emperor Alexander and Emperor Francis II. Several of Napoleon's marshals were engaged — Davout, Murat, Lannes, Soult, Bernadotte — while the Allies were led by such redoubtable generals as the Princes Bagration and Lichtenstein, and Generals Kollowrath, Buxhowen, Doctorov and Kienmayer. An Allied attempt to turn the French right

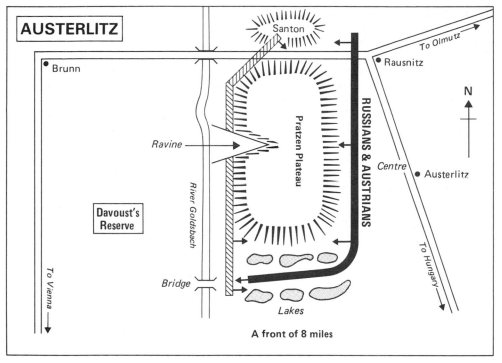

AUSTERLITZ

Santon

To Olmutz

Brunn

Rausnitz

N

Ravine

Pratzen Plateau

RUSSIANS & AUSTRIANS

Centre

Austerlitz

River Goldsbach

Davoust's
Reserve

To Vienna

Bridge

To Hungary

Lakes

A front of 8 miles

flank failed and the Allied left was cut off from its centre. The Allied left and centre were beaten in detail and a large force, fighting now on three sides, was driven in disorder across the partly frozen Lake Menitz, which had been broken by gunfire. Thousands fell through the ice and drowned. The Russian–Austrian army lost 12,000 killed and wounded, 30,000 prisoners, including twenty generals, forty-six standards, 186 cannon, 400 artillery limbers and all their wagons and baggage. About 25,000 demoralized men survived the disaster. The French lost 6,800 men. Legend has it that when William Pitt, Prime Minister of England, heard of the news he had the map of Europe on his wall rolled up, a gesture that meant Napoleon now controlled Europe. This outstanding victory was due to Napoleon's brilliant coordinating of infantry, cavalry and artillery. *See* Oberhollabrun.

Austria (*World War II*) 1945. In March 1945 Malinovsky's Second Ukrainian Army made two powerful thrusts into Austria, one force marching up the Danube to capture Vienna, 8–13 April. The second movement was westward into Upper Austria. The aims were, respectively, to link with the American Seventh Army (Patch) which had invaded Austria from Bavaria late in April and to join the British Eighth Army (McCreery) moving through the Alps from Italy. Germany surrendered before the links were complete.

Austrian Succession. *See* List of Battles.

Avaricum (*now Bourges*) (*Gallic War*) 52 BC. 50,000 Romans (Caesar) besieged Avaricum, headquarters of the rebellious Gauls under Vercingetorix. The defence was spirited, but supplies became desperately low and Vercingetorix attempted to withdraw his troops. This gave the Romans the opening for which Caesar had been waiting; he made a fierce assault, captured the town and massacred the garrison and inhabitants. *See* Gergovia; Tongres.

Avigliana (*French War with Savoy*) June 1630. Montmorency, under the orders of Cardinal Richelieu, defeated the Spanish at Avigliana in the Savoy, thus blocking the main military and logistical route between Spanish Italy and the Spanish Netherlands. The Spanish lost much of their military strength in this battle, a tactical triumph for Montmorency.

Avus (*Second Roman–Macedonian War*) 198 BC. Two Roman legions (T. Quinctius Flaminius) took the initiative in an attack on 20,000 Macedonians (Philip). An assault force of 4,000 legionaries penetrated to the rear of Philip's camp and attacked in conjunction with a frontal attack by Flaminius. The Macedonians, losing 2,000 men, were routed. *See* Cynoscephalae.

Axarquia (*Spanish–Muslim Wars*) 20 March 1483. A Spanish force of 3,000 knights and 2,000 infantry (Marquis of Cadiz) were marching through the defile of Axarquia, en route to attack Malaga, when a Moorish army (Abul Hassan) ambushed and routed them. Spanish casualties: 800 killed, 1,600 prisoners. *See* Granada; Malaga.

Axholme (*Second Barons' War of England*) 1265. Survivors of the defeat at Evesham found refuge at the Isle of Axholme in the Lincolnshire Fens, where the young Simon de Montfort took command. Prince Edward (Edward I) constricted the Montfortians and in December gained their surrender by promising to spare their lives. *See* Chesterfield; Ely II.

Ayacusho (*or Candorcanqui*) (*Peruvian War of Independence*) 9 December 1824. About 9,300 Spaniards (Laserna) met 5,780 Peruvian Patriots (Sucre) in pitched battle. The Patriots' victory practically decided the question of Peruvian and indirectly of South American independence. Casualties: Spanish, 2,100 and 3,500 prisoners, including the commander; Patriots, 979. *See* Junin.

Aylesford, *Buckinghamshire* (*Jute invasion*) 456. Between the Jutes under Hengist and Horsa and the Britons led by Vortigern. Despite Horsa's death, the Jutes were victorious.

Azimghur (*Indian Mutiny*) 15 April 1858. A British column of three infantry regiments and three of Sikh cavalry (Sir Edward Layard) attacked the 5,000 Dinapur mutineers (Kur Singh) and routed them. *See* Delhi; Lucknow.

Azores (*English–Spanish Wars*) 31 August 1591. An English fleet of seven ships (Lord Thomas Howard) was waiting at Flores to intercept a Spanish treasure fleet. They were surprised by news of the approach of a Spanish fighting fleet and all except the *Revenge* (Sir Richard Grenville) cut their cables and ran. Grenville had only a hundred fit men to work and fight the *Revenge*, but for 15 hours she defied fifty-three Spanish galleons and their 10,000 men. The seriously wounded Grenville and the few survivors surrendered at daybreak, Grenville dying on board the Spanish flagship 3 days later. The *Revenge* was hit, according to Raleigh, 800 times. She had defeated fifteen large galleons and sunk some of them. *See* Armada; Cadiz.

Azov (*Russian–Turkish Wars*) 28 July 1696. The fortress of Azov, commanding the entrance to the Black Sea from the Sea of Azov, was held by the Turks. In 1695 Peter the Great led a land assault which the Turks easily defeated. In 1696 Peter made a combined sea and land attack and took the city on 28 July. He lost title to it in 1710 when he surrendered it to save himself from annihilation by a large Turkish army which surrounded his own forces on the Pruth River. In 1739 troops of the Czarina Anna retook Azov, which remained Russian. *See* Crimea.

Azov, Battle of the Sea of (*World War II*) October 1941. This oddly named battle was not fought at sea but in the Crimean Peninsula, q.v.

Babylon (Mesopotamia) (*conquest by Persia*) *539* BC. Babylonia was declining under Nabonidus when Cyrus the Great of Persia led 40,000 men on the city of Babylon. Belshazzar, Nabonidus' son, was forced to withdraw behind the fortress walls of the city. Cyrus diverted the waters of the Euphrates and then entered the city along the dry bed, thus surprising the defenders and conquering decisively. With the fall of Babylon, Persia ruled Asia Minor from the Indus to the Mediterranean. *See* Pelusium; Sardis.

Babylon (Egypt) (*Muslim invasions*) *July 640*. Islam had been founded in 622. The first wave of Islamic Arab warriors swept through Syria and Palestine and then invaded Egypt, held by the Byzantines. Amr ibn al-As defeated the Byzantine army in the sands at the Battle of Babylon, near Heliopolis. This gave the Arabs the necessary base for the siege and capture of the fortress city of Babylon, 641, and Alexandria, 642. *See* Jalula; Nahavend.

Badajoz (*Peninsular War*) *March–April 1812*. Wellington invested this formidable fortress, garrisoned by 5,000 French, Hessians and Spaniards (Phillipon), on 17 March. With great difficulty breaches were made in the walls and the assault was ordered on 6 April. The British lost 3,500 men capturing the town–fortress — they had already lost 1,500 during the siege — and for 2 days they were completely out of hand, committing terrible atrocities against the inhabitants, who were in fact their allies. *See* Ciudad Rodrigo; Salamanca.

Bad Axe (*Black Hawk Indian War*) *2 August 1832*. Several hundred Indians of the Fox and Sauk tribes, led by Black Hawk, crossed the Mississippi to terrorise western Illinois and Wisconsin. On 2 August General Atkinson, with about 1,500 troops, trapped the Indians at the mouth of the Bad Axe River and ended the war with a crushing victory.

Badr (*Muhammad's conquest of Arabia*) *624*. This was Muhammad's first military operation, following his flight from Mecca to Medina. With 300 men he intercepted a caravan guarded by 1,000 Meccans (Abu Sufyan). At Badr, in the Hejaz of western Arabia, Muhammad routed the enemy and captured the caravan. *See* Ohod.

Baduli-Ki-Serai (*Indian Mutiny*) *8 June 1857*. A British force (Sir Henry Barnard) defeated a large body of mutineers barring their advance to the relief of Delhi, q.v.

Baghdad I (*Mongol conquest of Western Asia*) *15 February 1258*. In 1256 Hulagu, grandson of Ghengis Khan, led a great army into the Islamic empire; they annihilated the Assassin sect, which had terrorised the Near East for 150 years. On 15 February 1258 Hulagu stormed Baghdad and sacked it. Mustasim, last of the Abbassid caliphs, was captured and trampled to death by horses. *See* Ain Jalut; Mohi.

Baghdad II (*Tartar invasion of Mesopotamia*) 23 July 1401. Tamerlane led the Tartars in their capture of the city. *See* Angora; Delhi I.

Baghdad III (*Turkish–Persian Wars*) 1534. While the Turk Suleiman I was fighting in the West, the Persians, inspired by Shah Thamasp, recaptured Tabriz in 1526. When Thamasp began negotiations of alliance with Charles V, Holy Roman Emperor Suleiman could not ignore the threat. He turned away from the west, marched a large army into Persia, retook Tabriz and then stormed and captured Baghdad; the Persian revolt was crushed. *See* Tunis III; Vienna I.

Baghdad IV (*World War I*) 1917. On 13 December 1916 General Maude marched from Basra with 50,000 British and Indian soldiers — objective Baghdad, held by the Turks. Eliminating Turkish detachments, he began, on 17 February, to strike at the fortress of Kut-al-Amara, held by 12,000 Turks (General Kara Bay). Maude's operations forced the Turks to evacuate Kut. Moving on, Maude skilfully forced another 11,000 Turks to abandon their defences on the Diyala River. Outmanoeuvred, General Halil Pasha's army withdrew to the north of Baghdad, which Maude entered on 11 March 1917. He took 9,000 prisoners in his brief campaign, one of the most masterly in history. *See* Kut-al-Amara; Ramadi.

Bagradas River, *Tunisia* (*War of the First Triumvirate or civil war of Caesar and Pompey*) 49 BC. A bloody battle between the Caesarians (Curio) and the Numidians (Juba and Saburra) who supported Pompey. The Numidians broke the Roman cavalry, surrounded the legionaries and cut them down to a man. The victory left the Pompeians masters of North Africa. *See* Pharsalas; Ruspina; Utica II.

Bahur (*Seven Years' War*) *August 1752*. A decisive victory for 2,000 British and 4,000 Indian levies (Major Lawrence) against 2,500 French (Kirkjean). The victory induced the wavering Mahrattas to join the British. *See* Calcutta.

Bailen (*Peninsular War*) *19 July 1808*. Spain rebelled against the installation of Joseph Bonaparte as King of Spain. From southern Spain General Comte de l'Etang began to withdraw his 20,000 troops towards Madrid. Harassed by 22,000 Spaniards (Francisco de Castanos), the French were forced to fight for water at Bailen, north of Jaen. General de L'Etang was unable to break away, suffered 2,000 casualties, and surrendered. The report of the astonishing surrender of a Napoleonic army shook Europe, forced the French government to evacuate Madrid and isolated Marshal Junot's army in Portugal. *See* Saragossa II; Vimeiro.

Balaklava (*Crimean War*) *25 October 1854*. Fought between 30,000 Russians (Prince Mentschikov) and the British (nominally, Lord Raglan). There were three phases: (1) The stand by the 93rd Highlanders (Sir Colin Campbell) against the Russian cavalry; they became known as "The thin red streak tipped by a line of steel." (W. H. Russell's phrase. The "thin red line" was a subsequent corruption.) (2) As the Russians fell back the 500-strong British Heavy Brigade (General Scarlett) delivered an audacious attack against a force eight times its own strength and broke the Russians. Had the Light Brigade (Lord Cardigan) charged at this moment the battle might have been decided. (3) The Charge of the Light Brigade (Lord Cardigan). This had no proper purpose or objective and was merely a death ride into the middle of the Russian guns and a fighting retreat. Of the roughly 700 men who took part in the charge, only 195 returned. The 13th Light Dragoons could muster only two officers and eight men. The net result of the whole battle was that the Russians became more firmly established than ever on the British right flank. *See* Sebastopol.

Balathista, *in the Struma River valley* (*Byzantine–Bulgarian Wars*) *1014*. The Byzantine emperor Basil II in 996 began a brutal campaign to curb the growing power of the Bulgarian Empire of Tsar Samuel. After years of fighting, Basil, in 1014, trapped a large Bulgar force at Balathista, took 15,000 prisoners and ordered their eyes put out. A few men were spared one eye to enable them to guide the others back to Samuel, who died of shock. Four years later the Bulgars were incorporated into the Byzantine Empire. *See* Sofia; Stara Zagora.

Balkans Campaign (*World War II*) *1941*. On 6 April the German Second Army and First Panzer Army attacked Yugoslavia (Operation Marita). Yugoslav resistance against the Germans quickly collapsed, then mutinies paralysed the Yugoslav armies. The Germans captured Belgrade on 13 April.

Balkan War. *See* List of Battles.

Balkan Wars *1912–13*. Bulgaria and Serbia formed an alliance against Turkey and soon after Greece and Montenegro joined the league. Fighting began on 8 October 1912 and before it ended on 30 May 1913 the following conflicts occurred — Kirk-Kilissa, Kumanovo, Monastir, Luleburgaz, Catalca, Shkoder, Ioannina, Adrianople. The second Balkan War began on 29 June 1913 with the former anti-Turkish allies, Romania and then Turkey itself at war with Bulgaria. No major battle occurred, but the Allies gained so much ground that on 31 July Bulgaria asked for peace.

Balkans (*World War II*) *1944*. In March 1944 Russian armies from the Ukraine smashed German defences. General Zhukov crossed the Prut and penetrated along the northern border of Romania. General Konev moved through Moldavia and crossed the Prut at Jassy. On 20 August, in a renewed assault on Romania, the Russians (Malinovski and Tolbukhin) attacked south-west and moved on the lower Danube. When the Romanian government capitulated on 23 August many Romanian soldiers turned against their former German allies. With their front collapsing, sixteen divisions of General Freissner's army group were destroyed as a fighting force. On 8 September the Bulgarians changed sides and joined the Russians. The Russians (Tolbukhin) reached the Yugoslav frontier on 6 September and drove back the German South-east Army Group (von Weichs), capturing Belgrade on 20 October. *See* Ukraine.

Balls Bluff (*American Civil War*) *21 October 1861*. A Federal army (General Stone) crossed the Potomac River to attack Confederate positions, but were so violently repulsed that their retreat became a rout. Casualties: Federals, 1,100 killed and wounded, 700 prisoners; Confederates, 155. *See* Bull Run I.

Ballymore (*Irish rebellion*) *3 June 1798*. A force of rebels led by Father Murphy ambushed 500 Royal troops (Colonel Walpole) marching to Enniscorthy and slaughtered most of them. *See* Dunganhill.

Baltimore (*British–American War*) *11 September 1814*. A British ten-ship fleet (Admiral Cochrane) bombarded Baltimore and 3,270 troops (General Ross) landed to assault it. The American army of 17,000 (General Winder) was defeated, but the British retired on the evening of the 13th. Casualties: British, 346; American, 110; 200 taken prisoner. *See* Bladensburg.

Bamian, *Afghanistan* (*Tartar invasion of Kharismia*). Genghis Khan and his Mongols invested the city in 1221, captured it with difficulty after several months. Genghis, angry at the death of a favourite grandson killed in action had killed every man, woman and child in the city. *See* Indus River; Merv.

In numerous fights the French heavy cavalry, supported by Swiss pikemen and Scottish archers, together with efficient artillery, bested the Spanish. Then, at Barletta, Gonzalo de Córdoba, a veteran Spanish captain, reverted to the tactics of the ancient Roman legion. He equipped his well-trained infantry with bucklers and swords, massed them phalanx fashion and used them in close-quarter fighting where the Swiss could not use their long pikes. Barletta is significant: after this battle the Spanish improved until they were the best infantry in Europe. They remained supreme for a century. *See* Cerignola; Fornova.

Barnet (*Wars of the Roses*) 14 April 1471. A conflict between the Yorkists (Edward IV) and the Lancastrians (Earl of Warwick). Warwick prepared to attack the king as he left Barnet, but during the night Edward emerged unseen and took up positions opposite Warwick. The Yorkish left was outflanked and beaten, but their right outflanked and defeated the Lancastrian left and then broke the centre. Warwick was killed. Total casualties are recorded as 1,000. *See* Ravenspur II; Tewkesbury.

Barons' Wars of England 1215–17. The civil war of the nobles against King John of England. The barons wanted Prince Louis of France to succeed John, but John's son, Henry III, took the throne. The main conflicts were Rochester 1215, Dover 1216–17, Lincoln 1217, Sandwich 1217. Louis relinquished his claim in a treaty of 1217, but two other battles were fought on his behalf, Bytham in 1220 and Bedford in 1224. *See* List of Battles.

Barons' Wars 1264–7. Henry III's second civil war was fought against his brother-in-law, Simon de Montfort. The battles were Northampton 1264, Rochester 1264, Lewes 1264, Kenilworth 1265–6, Evesham 1265, Axholme 1265, Chesterfield 1266, Ely 1266–6. *See* Lists of Battles.

Barossa (*Peninsular War*) 5 March 1811. An outstanding victory for the British army of 4,000 (General Graham) which defeated 9,000 French (Marshal Victor). A large Spanish force (La Pena), who were British allies, stood by and took no part in the hard-fought action. Casualties: British, 1,210; French, 2,000, including two generals, 400 prisoners, six guns, two eagles. *See* Albuhera; Badajoz.

Barquisimeto (*Venezuelan War of Independence*) July 1813. Simon Bolivar and his Venezuelan patriots won decisively against the Spanish Royalists in this early battle of Bolivar's campaign for independence.

Bar-Sur-Aube (*Napoleonic Wars*) 27 February 1814. Under Napoleon's pressure, the Austrian commander (von Schwarzenberg) abandoned Troyes on 23 February. Sending Oudinot to pursue the Austrians, Napoleon marched north to cover Paris against Blucher's threat. Schwarzenberg counter-attacked Bar-Sur-Aube and sharply defeated Oudinot, who fell back to Troyes. *See* Craonne; Montereau.

Basra (*or Bassorah*) (*Muslim Civil Wars*) 656. Rebel Arabs seized Basra and on 9 December the Caliph Ali, with 29,000 Muslim troops, outfought the much large rebel force and took the city. Both Arab leaders were killed. This conflict is often called the Battle of the Camel; each of the seventy men who in turn held the bridle of the camel ridden by Aisha, widow of the prophet Muhammed, was killed. *See* Lycia; Siffin.

Bassano (*Napoleon's Italian campaigns*) 8 September 1796. Napoleon, having destroyed the Austrian vanguard at Primolano the previous day, attacked the main army (Wurmser). Augereau and Massena, leading the French, routed the Austrians so completely that 6,000 Austrians surrendered. Wurmser, who had narrowly escaped capture, collected his scattered forces with difficulty and found he had only 16,000 of the 60,000 with which he had commenced the campaign. *See* Caldiero I; Caliano; Mantua.

Bassein (*First British–Mahratta War*) *November–December 1780.* General Goddard besieged this town on 13 November and fought off attempts at relief. At Dugaar, on 10 December, the complete defeat of a relief force so disheartened the defenders that they surrendered next day. *See* Gwalior.

Basseville, *Flanders* (*World War I*) *27–31 July 1917.* New Zealanders captured this strong German position, lost it to a counter-attack and retook it on 31 July. Casualties: New Zealand, 38; German, 112. *See* Arras; Somme.

Bastogne. *See* Battle of the Bulge (Ardennes).

Bataan–Corregidor, *Philippines* (*World War II*) *1942.* On 21 January General MacArthur assembled 15,000 Americans and 65,000 ill-trained Filipinos on the Bataan peninsula and established a defence line of 15 miles from Subic Bay to Manila Bay. MacArthur, with President Quezon, set up his headquarters on the fortified island of Corregidor. The Japanese Fourteenth Army (Homma) began the attack on 14 January and powerful pressure forced MacArthur to retreat on 22 January and again on 26 January. On the night of 11/12 March President Roosevelt ordered MacArthur to leave the Philippines and go to Australia, where he became Supreme Commander Allied Forces, Pacific. Wainwright assumed command in the Philippines. Relentless Japanese attacks, starvation and disease defeated the American–Filipino force by 8 April and on 9 April General King surrendered 76,000 men, including 12,000 Americans; at least 10,000 men died during their march to prison. Wainwright's 13,000 troops on Corregidor held out under devastating artillery fire — 16,000 shells on 4 May alone — until midnight of 6–7 May, when Wainwright, with 2,000 casualties, surrendered. *See* Philippines.

Batavia (*Napoleonic Wars*) *26 August 1811.* The French and Dutch had abandoned the town and occupied the powerful Fort Cornelius nearby. The British, 10,000-strong (Sir Samuel Auchmuty), stormed the entrenchments, inflicted heavy casualties, and forced a surrender. British casualties were 872. A month later the Dutch ceded Timor, Java, Palembang and Macassar to the British.

Batoche (*Riel's Second Rebellion*) *May 1885.* Louis Riel, with a force of half-breeds and Indians, intent on insurrection, between 5 and 9 May fought a running — and losing — battle with General Middleton's Canadians. Casualties: Riel's rebels, 224; Canadian, 54. *See* Red River Campaign; Toronto.

Batowitz, *Poland* (*Polish–Cossack War*) *24 May 1653.* 40,000 Poles (John II) waited to intercept an army of Cossacks (Bogdan). Bogdan led a furious charge, threw the Poles into confusion and almost completely annihilated their army. *See* Beresteczko.

Bautzen (*Napoleonic Wars — Leipzig campaign*) *20–22 May 1813.* A major battle between 150,000 French (Napoleon) and the Prussian and Russian Allies, 100,000 (Blucher and Wittgenstein). The Allies held Bautzen in strength with their front protected by the Spree River. On 20 May Napoleon forced a passage across the Spree and took Bautzen after fierce fighting. On the 22nd he attacked the Allied second line, while Marshal Ney led an attack on their right flank, capturing all their positions. Lack of cavalry prevented Napoleon from exploiting his advantage. Casualties: Allies, 15,000; French, 1,300. *See* Grossbeeren; Lützen II; Vitoria.

Bavay (or Burai) (*Gallic War*) *57 BC.* 50,000 Romans (Caesar) were pitching their camp on the banks of the Sambre when a large force of Gauls, from the Nervii, Viromandui, Atrebates and other tribes, attacked them. Despite the suddenness and violence of the attack the legionaries held their ground and devastated their enemies; the Nervii were practically annihilated as a tribe. *See* Aduatuca; Agendicum.

Bay of Pigs *17–19 April 1964*. The American CIA planned an invasion of Cuba by 1,500 Cuban exiles in the hope of provoking an anti-Castro rising. In the 3-day action the "2506 Brigade" had more than 300 killed and the rest were taken prisoner. The military failure — the result of incompetence — was a profound political humiliation for the United States and President Kennedy. Fidel Castro personally led the Cuban forces and his prestige increased.

Baza (*Spanish–Muslim War*) *June–December 1489*. An outpost of Granada, the fortress of Baza was defended by Moors (Sidi Yahye) and besieged by 95,000 Spaniards (Ferdinand). The Spaniards could make no impression, but the defenders could neither break out nor hope for relief, so in December the fort was surrendered on "honourable terms". *See* Axarquia; Granada; Malaga.

Beachy Head (*War of the League of Augsburg or War of the Grand Alliance*) *30 June 1690*. A combined English and Dutch fleet of seventy-three ships (Earl of Torrington) encountered a French fleet of seventy-eight ships (Comte de Tourville) which had been sent to create a diversion in favour of James II, then in Ireland. The French destroyed six Dutch ships and one British and won the battle. *See* Bantry Bay; Fleurus II; La Hogue.

Beaugé (*Hundred Years' War*) *22 March 1421*. The Armagnacs and their Scottish mercenaries were in well-prepared positions awaiting the advance of the English (Duke of Clarence). The

Duke and his cavalry charged ahead of his main body of troops, became separated from them among the Scottish outposts, and with most of his knights was slain. After this English defeat was inevitable. *See* Cravant; Rouen II.

Beaumont (*French–Prussian War*) *30 August 1870*. The French V Corps (General de Failly) was surprised in cantonments by the German IV and XII Corps (Crown Prince of Saxony) and driven back to Monzon. Casualties: French, 4,800 and 42 guns; German, 3,500. *See* Sedan.

Beaune-La-Rolande (*French–Prussian War*) *28 November 1870*. A notable defensive victory by 9,000 Germans (Grand Duke of Mecklenburg) against 60,000 French (General Crouzat). The Germans beat off massive French attacks, inflicting 8,000 casualties to their own loss of 855. *See* Metz.

Beauséjour (*Seven Years' War*) *June 1755*. A garrison of 460 French (Duchambon de Vergor) held this fort in Nova Scotia against 2,000 Massachusetts volunteers and some regulars (Colonel Monckton) who invested it on 4 June. After two days' continual fire — 14th–16th — the garrison surrendered. *See* Fort Necessity; Lake George; Monongahela River.

Beaver's Dam Creek. *See* Seven Days' Battle.

Beda Fomm, *Libya (World War II)* *5–7 February 1941*. General O'Connor, principally using the 6th Australian Infantry and the 7th British Armoured Divisions, gained the surrender of 20,000 Italians for the loss of nine men killed and fifteen wounded. *See* Bardia; Sollum; Tobruk.

Bedford (*First Barons' War*) *1224*. Hubert de Burgh, for Henry III, took Bedford Castle on 14 August after a 2-month siege and a successful mining. Twenty-four knights were hanged on the walls. *See* Sandwich I.

Bedriacum, *northern Italy* (*Roman Empire's Civil War*) *14 April 69*. A surprising defeat of Emperor Otho's Roman legions by Valens' Vitellians. Driven back to their camp, the Romans surrendered the following day. *See* Cremona I; Jotapata.

Beecher Island, *Republican River* (*Cheyenne and Arapahoe War*) *1868*. Colonel Forsyth and fifty soldiers were attacked, 18 September, by 750 Indians. Holding out on Beecher Island, the Americans were at the point of exhaustion and death from starvation when relieved on 27 September. *See* Fort Phil Kearny; Washita River.

Beersheba, *Palestine* (*World War I*) *31 October 1917*. Part of the third Battle of Gaza and the most outstanding action of the Australian and New Zealand Light Horse during the desert war of 1916–18. In a bold action led by Chauvel, Chaytor and Hodgson, the Anzacs captured Beersheba from the Turks. Fewer than 500 troopers made contact with the enemy, but the victory gave impetus to Allenby's campaign to clear Arabia of the Turks and Germans. *See* Gaza; Megiddo.

Bega (*Turkish War against Austria and Hungary*) *24 April 1696*. A victory by the Turks (Mustapha II) over the Austrian–Hungarians who were trying to absorb Turkey into their empire.

Beirut *1983*. A multi-national peace-keeping force of American marines, French paratroops, British and Italians went to Beirut late in 1982 to give some stability to the city after the Israel–PLO war of 1982. Fighting was frequent between the Christians and the Muslims with their Druze allies. The Syrians were also active, and several Islamic extremist terrorist groups. On 23 October 1983 Islamic *jihad* (holy war) suicide squads drove trucks packed with high explosives into the barracks of the American and French contingents of the multi-national force; 223 Marines and fifty-eight French

paratroops were killed. Because of Syrian involvement in the attacks, U.S. navy ships, notably the battleship *New Jersey*, bombarded Syrian positions. The multi-national units were withdrawn. *See* Lebanon.

Belfort I (*French–Prussian War*) *3 November 1870–15 February 1871*. The French fortress of Belfort, commanded by Colonel Pierre Denfert-Rochereau, was held by 17,600 men, mostly *gardes mobiles* and *gardes nationales*. Denfert-Rochereau developed an outpost ring and kept back the besieging Germans by intelligent shuffling of his defenders. In January the German siege guns were in position and causing much damage, but Denfert-Rochereau held out. On 15 February the French General Assembly, as a body, ordered him to surrender. His garrison marched out under arms and with colours flying and with all baggage. The French had suffered 5,200 casualties, including civilians, the German 2,000. The French Army regards the defence of Belfort as an epic event.

Belfort II (*French–Prussian War*) *15–17 January 1871*. General Bourbaki, with an inexperienced and largely untrained army of 150,000, tried to raise the siege of Belfort fortress. The Germans (General Wilhelm Werder) had only 60,000 men and were forced onto the defensive on the Lisaine River, but the incompetent Bourbaki mismanaged the battle and in 3 days' fighting lost 6,000 men to the Germans' 2,000. Bourbaki tried to commit suicide, failed and was relieved by General Clinchant. When another German army arrived Clinchant, to avoid destruction, marched 85,000 of his men into nearby Switzerland, which interned them.

Belgrade I (*Turkish invasion of Balkans*) *July–September 1456*. A large Turkish army (Muhammad II) besieged the city, which was gallantly defended by Janos Hunyady or Hunyadi. The Turks were compelled to raise the siege on 4 September. Hunyadi, a great hero, died a month later. *See* Constantinople; Negroponte.

Belgrade II (*Turkish conquest of the Balkans*) *1521*. Suleiman the Magnificent, set on westward aggression, marched on Belgrade, which at the confluence of the Danube and Save rivers was the key Christian stronghold in the Balkans. Suleiman and his fine Janisseries mined the city's walls and stormed it. Austria, Hungary and regions beyond were now vulnerable to the Turks. *See* Mohacs; Rhodes.

Belgrade III (*Turkish–Austrian War*) *16 August 1717*. The Grand Vizier of Turkey, Ibrahim Pasha, had consolidated no fewer than 180,000 Turks in and around Belgrade. At night, Prince Eugene launched 40,000 Austrians into an audacious attack. His right wing lost touch and was in danger of being overwhelmed when Eugene extricated them. The whole attack was successful and the Turks were driven out. Casualties: Turks, 20,000, and 166 guns; Austrian, almost as heavy. *See* Peterwardein.

Belgrade IV (*Turkish–Austrian War*) *8 October 1789*. The Turks had gained possession of the city, but surrendered it after a brief siege to an Austrian army (General Laudon) which had already repulsed a Turkish invasion of Bosnia. An armistice was negotiated.

Belgrade V (*World War II*) *April 1941*. Though declared an open city, Belgrade was devastated by German bombers and on 14 April was captured by a pincers movement converging from the borders of Austria, Romania and Bulgaria. The Ukrainian Third Army recaptured the city on 20 October 1944. *See* Austria

Belleau Wood (*World War I*) *6 June–1 July 1918*. At their deepest penetration in the June offensive of 1918, the Germans held Belleau Wood on the Metz–Paris road. On 6 June the American 2nd Division (General Bundy) were committed to the counter-attack of the mile-square forested region, held by four German divisions. The American 3rd Infantry Brigade (General Lewis) and the Marine Brigade (Harbord) bore the brunt of the fighting, which was fierce until the capture of the wood on 1 July. Casualties: American, 9,777, including 1,811 killed; German, uncertain, but 1,600 were taken prisoner. *See* Argonne; St. Mihiel.

Belle Isle* (*or Quiberon Bay*) (*Seven Years' War*) *20 November 1759*. Notable British naval victory. A fleet of thirty-three ships (Sir Edward Hawke) completely defeated twenty-six French ships (Admiral de Conflans). The French lost six ships in action, the British had two run aground.

Belle Isle (*Seven Years' War*) *7 June 1761*. Protected by a fleet under Admiral Keppel, 8,000 British troops (General Hodgson) landed under enemy fire and after difficulty forced the surrender of the garrison of Palais, the main town. British casualties were 700, many more than the French.

Belle Isle (*Wars of French Revolution*) *23 June 1795*. Lord Bridport's seventeen-ship fleet chased a French squadron and captured three ships; 700 Frenchmen became casualties. The action took place 20 miles from Belle Isle, off Ile de Groix.

Bellevue (*French–Prussian War*) *7 October 1870*. Marshal Bazaine tried to break through the Germans besieging the fortress of Metz. At Bellevue he was beaten back into the city. Casualties: French, 2,057; German, 1,778. *See* Metz; Sedan.

Belmont (*American Civil War*) *1861*. On 7 November General Grant landed

---

**Belle Isle commanded the mouth of the Loire and naval ports such as Lorient, Quiberon and St. Nazaire. French and British ships were often in conflict near the island.

about 3,000 men above Belmont, on the Mississippi, and attacked the Confederate camp held by 4,000 troops (Price). The Federals drove the Confederates to the river, but here they came under the protection of their own guns. The Confederates tried to trap Grant, failed, and Grant, having suffered 607 casualties and inflicted 642, re-embarked. *See* Fort Henry; Wilson's Creek.

Belmont (*Second British–Boer War*) 23 November 1890. About 3,000 Boers, in strong positions in hills near Belmont, were frontally attacked and defeated by British infantry and cavalry (Lord Methuen). Casualties: British, 298; Boer, 300, and 500 prisoners. *See* Modder River.

Belorussian campaign (*World War II*) June–July 1944. On 22 June 146 Soviet infantry divisions and forty-three armoured divisions (Generals Bagramyan and Chernyakhovsky) struck General Busch's Army Group North on four fronts. The impetus of the Soviet offensive was so great that the Russians rapidly took Bobruisk, Stolbsty, Minsk, Grodno and the Pripet Marshes. The German defenders were split, with one segment in East Prussia, the other in the Baltic states. Within 24 days the Russians claimed to have killed 38,000 Germans and to have captured 160,000 men, 2,000 tanks, 10,000 guns and 57,000 vehicles.

Bemis Heights (*or Second Battle of Saratoga*) (*American War of Independence*) 7 October 1777. This American victory brought about the surrender of General Burgoyne 10 days later. *See* Saratoga.

Benburb (*Great Irish Rebellion*) 5 June 164 . More than 5,500 Irish rebels (O'Neill) routed a Scottish Roundhead army under Sir George Munroe. The Scots left 3,000 dead on the field; the Irish chased and butchered most of the battle survivors.

Bender (*Russian–Turkish Wars*) August–October 1769. The Russians (Count Panin) besieged this Turkish fort, captured it after 2 months and put the garrison of 3,500 to the sword. *See* Belgrade.

Benevento (*French invasion of Italy*) 26 February 1266. Charles of Anjou led a French army against Mainfroy, usurper of the crown of the Two Sicilies, and commander of a Neapolitan force. Mainfroy was killed in a mauling fight, the Neapolitans were routed; Charles of Anjou retained undisputed possession of the throne. *See* Cortenuova; Tagliacozzi.

Beneventum I, *later Benevento, near Naples* (*Pyrrus' invasion of Italy*) 275 BC. Pyrrus, King of Epirus, with a powerful army of Epirots and Italians, made a night attack on a Roman army (Dentatus) in a fortified camp at Beneventum. The Romans repulsed the attack, then counter-attacked Pyrrus' force on an open plain. At first driven back by war elephants, they rallied, broke the Epirot phalanx and charged their enemies into retreat. Pyrrus made no further major attack and soon left Italy. *See* Asculum I; Messina.

Beneventum II (*Second Punic War*) 214 BC. 20,000 Romans (Tiberius Gracchus) decisively defeated 18,000 Carthaginians (Hanno). Later Hanno was able to re-establish himself, but in 212 BC another Roman army (Fulvius) stormed the enemy camp at daybreak, routed the Carthaginians and captured all the supplies intended for the reprovisioning of Capus. *See* Capua; Syracuse III.

Bennington (*American War of Independence*) 11 August 1777. General Burgoyne sent Colonel Baum with 800 troops, mostly Hessians, to seize the American ammunition and food supply depot at Bennington, but finding the defence too strong Baum sent for reinforcements. While they waited, the English and their Hessian mercenaries found

Bezetha (*Roman Empire's Jewish Wars*) *October 66*. The Jewish population of Jerusalem attacked the Romans (Cestius Gallas), drove them from their camp, killed and wounded 6,000 Romans and captured all their equipment. *See* Jotapata.

Bhurtpore I (*or Bhurtpur*) (*Second British–Mahratta War*) *January–April 1805*. General Lake besieged the city, garrisoned by 8,000 of the Rajah's troops, on 4 January. Lake's Anglo–Indian army made four separate fruitless assaults, lost 3,200 men, and withdrew on 21 April. *See* Farruckhabad.

Bhurtpore II (*Second Siege*) *18 January 1826*. Lord Combermere, after a 2-months' sustained bombardment, took the city by assault. In the desperate fighting the British suffered 1,000 casualties, the Indians 8,000. The battle ended the third British–Mahratta war.

Biak Island (*World War II*) *27 May–20 June 1944*. Australian and American troops captured the island from the Japanese during the New Guinea campaign. *See* Bougainville.

Bialystok–Minsk (*World War II*) *June 1944*. The German Generals Guderian and Hoth trapped a large Soviet army under General Pavlov. The Germans claimed to have killed 30,000 Russians, besides capturing 290,000 others, 2,500 tanks and 1,400 guns. Because of mud and adverse weather, Guderian and Hoth could not complete the encirclement and 300,000 Russians escaped. *See* Kirsk.

Biberac (*French Revolutionary Wars*) *October 1796*. The French (Moreau) were retreating through the Black Forest when the Austrians (Archduke Charles), recently successful against the French at Warzburg, attacked them. In a superbly fought rearguard action Moreau defeated the Austrians. *See* Amberg; Würtzburg.

Bibracte (*Gallic Wars*) *58 BC*. Caesar's Roman army, with only 30,000 legionaries, faced a greatly superior force of Helvetians. Caesar had all officers' horses driven from the camp and gave the order "Win or die." The Romans routed the Helvetians who were compelled to accept Rome's domination. More than 130,000 Helvetians, including women and children, died at Bibracte.

Big Bethel (*American Civil War*) *10 June 1861*. 4,400 men attacked the Confederate fort of Big Bethel, Virginia; the local Confederate commander ordered a counter-attack in which the 1,600 Confederates drove the Federals back to Fort Monroe. They lost only eleven men to the Federals' seventy-six. *See* Bull Run I; Philippi; Virginia.

Big Black River (*American Civil War*) *17 May 1863*. A preliminary action in which a Federal force succeeded in sealing the Confederates in Vicksburg, q.v.

Bilbao I (*First Carlist War*). On 9 November 1836 the Carlist rebels besieged the fortress, held by a small garrison. After several unsuccessful attempts a relief force of Royalists drove off the besiegers on 25 December and relieved the city. The garrison lost about 1,300 men, the relief force 714 killed and wounded during the final action. Carlist losses are unknown. *See* Huesca.

Bilbao II (*Spanish Civil War*) *31 March–18 June 1937*. On 31 March the Nationalist Commander-in-Chief, General Franco, launched an offensive northwest towards Bilbao with 50,000 troops (Mola). The Republican commander in Basque, de la Encomienda, with only 40,000 inferior troops, retreated, abandoning Durango and Guernica on 28 April after devastating air attacks — some of the first dive-bombing. On 11 June the Nationalists bombarded the "Ring of Iron" defences of Bilbao and on 18 June the army survivors abandoned the city. *See* Madrid; Santander.

Bingen (*Gallic Revolt*) 60. The Gauls (Tutor), in camp at Bingen on the Rhine, were surprised by four Roman legions which Petilius Cerualis marched across the Swiss Alps. When many Gauls deserted to the Romans, Tutor's defeat was inevitable.

Bir Hacheim — Gazala, *North Africa 26 May–10 June 1942*. Free French troops held the desert strongpoint of Bir Hacheim, part of the Gazala line where the British blocked General Rommel's advance to the east, the Suez Canal and Cairo. Rommel attacked on 26 May and breached the British line, but the Free French at Bir Hacheim, largely men of the Foreign Legion, bravely resisted against infantry, tank and air onslaughts until 10 June. As the British retreated, Rommel pursued, capturing Tobruk from the South Africans on 14 June. *See* Sidi-Rezegh; Tobruk.

Biruan (*Tartar invasion of Kharismia*) 1221. Jellalladin, Sultan of Kharismia, cleverly leading 60,000 troops, routed 80,000 Tartars (Katuku). *See* Bokhara.

Bismarck (*World War II*) 1941. The German battleship *Bismarck*, 45,000 tons (Admiral Lutjens), was the most powerful ship in service. Moving out to attack Allied shipping, the *Bismarck* was herself attacked on 24 May by a British squadron of four ships, though only the battleships were engaged. Almost at once the *Bismarck* sank H.M.S. *Hood* (only three of the 2,500 crew survived) and badly damaged H.M.S. *Prince of Wales*. Chased for 4 days, *Bismarck* was attacked by British planes and ships — *King George V, Rodney, Norfolk, Dorsetshire* — and was sunk on 27 May, 400 miles from Brest. Lutjens and 2,000 German seamen perished. *See* Atlantic II.

Bismarck Sea (*World War II*) 2–5 March 1943. American and Australian aircraft and American P.T. boats attacked a Japanese fleet taking reinforcements to Lae and Salamaua, New Guinea. They sank four destroyers and all eight transports. About 6,000 of the 7,000 Japanese were killed. *See* New Guinea.

Bithur (*Indian Mutiny*) 16 August 1857. General Havelock attacked 4,000 mutineers who were in strong positions and drove them into the open where 1,100 were killed. *See* Cawnpore II; Delhi.

Bitonto, *Bari, Italy (War of the Polish Throne*) 25 May 1735. Much of this war, though it concerned claims to the Polish throne, took place a long way from Poland. Bitonto was fought between the Austrians of the Holy Roman Empire and a Spanish army under General Mortemar. The Austrians, having already won battles at Parma and Luzzara, q.v., had slightly the better of Bitonto. Nevertheless, the Treaty of Vienna, 1738, gave Charles Bourbon, son of Philip of Spain, the Kingdom of the Two Sicilies.

Bizerta Crisis 1961. In July 1961 President Bourguiba protested to General de Gaulle over the extension of the runway of the French military air base at Bizerta. The Tunisians then blockaded the French naval base. The French sent reinforcements and between 19 and 22 July there was a street battle between French and Tunisian soldiers. The French occupied Tunis, but in October withdrew. Casualties: French, 21 killed; Tunisians, 1,300 killed.

Blackheath (*Flammock's Rebellion*) 22 June 1497. Henry VII attacked rebels led by Flammock and Lord Audley, killed 2,000 of them and captured and executed the two leaders. *See* Bosworth Field.

Black Rock (*Second British–American War*) 1814. 2,000 American Indians occupied a strong position at Black Rock when General Riall attacked and defeated them with 1,400 British troops. He then seized Buffalo. *See* Bladensburg.

Blackwater (*O'Neill's Rebellion*) 1598. The English Marshal, Sir Henry

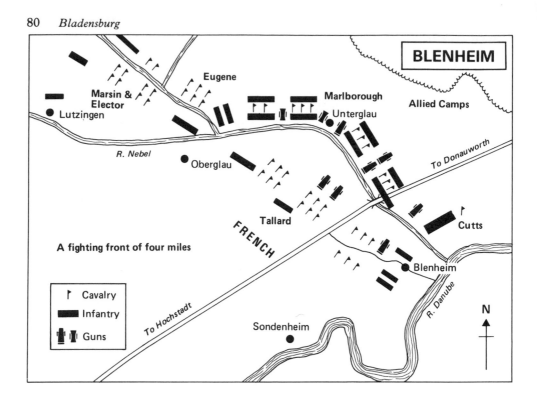

BLENHEIM

Eugene

Marsin & Elector

● Lutzingen

Marlborough

Unterglau

Allied Camps

R. Nebel

● Oberglau

To Donauworth

Tallard

FRENCH

Cutts

A fighting front of four miles

● Blenheim

R. Danube

r Cavalry

Infantry

Guns

To Hochstadt

Sondenheim ●

N

Bagnall, attacked 5,000 Irish rebels led by Hugh O'Neill, but lost 1,500 men, all of his baggage and ammunition, and his own life, being killed by O'Neill. *See* Dunganhill.

Bladensburg (*Second British–American War*) *24 August 1814*. The Americans (General Winder) held the only bridge over the Potomac towards Washington and opposed the British advance. General Ross captured the bridge, forced the Americans from their prepared position, entered the capital and destroyed much of it. Casualties: British, 64 killed, 185 wounded; American, 26 killed, 51 wounded. *See* Fort Henry.

Blanquefort (*Hundred Years' War*) *1 November 1450*. The English force holding Bordeaux made a sally in strength to disperse a marauding band under Amanien. The English cavalry allowed itself to be cut off from the infantry who were slaughtered by Amanien's men. *See* Castillon.

Blenheim (*War of Spanish Succession*) *13 August 1704*. One of the great battles of history. About 56,000 French and Bavarians under Marshals Tallard and Marsin and the Elector of Bavaria faced a roughly equal number of British, German and Dutch led by Marlborough and Prince Eugene; the British contingent numbered about 9,000. Tallard had mistakenly massed 12,000 of his best troops in the village of Blenheim, the key to the 4-mile line across the plain of Höchstadt. The strongpoint resisted for a long time, but Tallard was unable to manoeuvre these troops. French artillery caused many casualties before the Allies attacked with concerted cavalry–infantry action. Late in the afternoon, the issue still in balance, Marlborough's centre was left open to attack; Marsin exploited the opening, but was forced back by Marlborough personally leading a brigade of Eugene's cavalry into action. Eugene, who had himself withstood attacks, now assumed the offensive and the French right and centre were routed. Marlborough's cavalry drove about thirty squadrons of French horse into the Danube and many were drowned. The village was the last point to fall. Casualties: Allies, 6,000 killed, 7,000 wounded; French and Bavarians, 21,000 killed or drowned, 7,000 wounded and 12,000 prisoners. The French lost 200 standards, 50 guns and all their baggage. *See* Donauworth.

Bloemfontein (*Second British–Boer War*) *31 March 1900*. Lord Roberts attacked the Orange Free State capital, drove out the Boers and 12 days later controlled the entire state. *See* Kimberley; Paardeberg.

Blood River (*Boer–Zulu War*) *1838*. The Zulus many times attacked Boer farmers spreading out from Cape Colony. At Blood River the Zulu chief Dingaan led 10,000 warriors in an attack on only 500 Boers commanded by Andries Pretorius, but the Boers killed 3,000 and beat back the others. *See* Boomplaats.

Blore Heath, *Staffordshire* (*Wars of the Roses*) *23 September 1459*. The Lancastrians (Henry VI) had crossed a brook and were re-forming to prepare for an attack on the Yorkists (Earl of Salisbury) when the Yorkists charged them, dispersing them with heavy loss. *See* St. Albans I; Ludford.

Blueberg, *South Africa* (*Napoleonic Wars*) *8 January 1806*. A British force of 6,600 (General Baird) had no sooner landed at Saldanha Bay when the Allied Dutch and French (General Janssens) came out from Cape Town and attacked them. The British victory was decisive and Baird was able to occupy Cape Town. The Allies lost 300 men, the British 152.

Blue Licks (*U.S. Indian Wars*) *August 1782*. On 15 August about 250 Indians and Canadians attacked a small fort at Bryan's Station, near Lexington. Repulsed, they enticed the local militia into pursuit and on 19 August ambushed

them, killing or capturing a hundred and suffering only seventeen casualties themselves. *See* Point Pleasant.

Boadicea, *Defeat of* (*Roman occupation of Britain*) *61*. Suetonius, with 10,000 legionaries, routed a large army of Britons, under Queen Boadicea of the Iceni, who had sacked Camelodunum, in Essex, and taken Londinium (London) and Verulamium (St. Albans). The Britons are said to have lost 80,000 killed and the queen poisoned herself on the battlefield near modern Towcester. *See* Camelodunum.

Bois-le-Duc (*Wars of the French Revolution*) *12 November 1794*. Moreau tried to take his French army across the Meuse into Holland at Fort Crevecoeur, near Bois-le-Duc, but the British and Austrians (Duke of York) prevented the passage and forced Moreau to retire. *See* Fleurus III.

Bokhara (*Tartar invasion of Kharismia*) *March 1220*. Ghengis Khan was proceeding to invest the walled city when the 20,000-strong garrison of Kharismians fled, leaving the Bokhariots no option but to open their gates to the Tartars, although the Governor held out for a short time in the citadel. *See* Biruan.

Bomarsund (*Crimea War*) *16 August 1854*. This Russian fort on Ahvenanmaa Island, Baltic Sea, was bombarded by an English–French fleet and French soldiers then landed and occupied it. This was the extent of the Baltic "campaign", despite two supposedly "offensive" expeditions. *See* Silistra.

Boomplaats (*British annexation of Orange River state*) *29 August 1848*. 1,000 Boers (Commandant Jan Kock) in prepared defences were beaten by 800 British soldiers and 250 Griqua irregulars (Sir Harry Smith). Casualties: British, 22 killed, 38 wounded. Reported Boer casualties, 14. In 1854 the British withdrew. *See* Blood River.

Borgetto (*Napoleon's Italian campaigns*) *30 May 1796*. Napoleon was chasing the Austrians (Beaulieu) after the Battle of Lodi Bridge, q.v. The Austrians had damaged the bridge across the Mincio at Borgetto, but the French repaired it under heavy fire, fought the Austrians out of Pechiara and took 500 prisoners. *See* Lodi; Mantua.

Borneo (*World War II*) *May–August 1945*. An Australian campaign against the Japanese, the major features being the landing at Tarakan Island, 1 May and capture by 18 May; landing and capture of Labuan Island, 10 June; capture of Sarawak, 20 June; capture of Balikpapan, 3 July.

Borneo Campaign, *1965–8*. *See* Brunei–Borneo, 1962–6.

Bornholm, *Danish island in Baltic* (*Danish–Swedish Wars*) *June 1676*. A Dutch and Danish squadron overwhelmed the Swedish fleet (Charles XI). This defeat led to the Swedes losing several fortresses, including Helsingborg and Landscroon. *See* Klöge.

Bornhöved,   *Schleswig–Holstein* (*Waldemar II's campaigns*) *1227*. The province of Dithmarsch rebelled against Danish authority and its insurgent army — Germans led by Henry of Schwerin — defeated the Danish royal troops and Waldemar thus lost the province. Danish domination of the Baltic had ended.

Borodino, *Moskva River* (*Napoleonic Wars; Moscow campaign*) *5–6 September 1812*. Napoleon was ill-advisedly driving towards Moscow, but at Borodino the Russians (Kutuzov) halted his scorched earth retreat and grouped his 120,000 men in strong positions round three hills. The strongest of his positions, the Great Redoubt, was defended by twenty-seven heavy cannon. Napoleon's first move was to capture the hill of Schwardino so as to deploy his army. The battle began with Eugene's troops overruning the village of Borodini and the Great Redoubt, but the Russians (Bagration) retook it, the earthworks disappearing beneath heaps of bodies.

Napoleon had the Redoubt swept by artillery fire, after which Murat threw away all his cuirassiers in a foolhardy attack. The French infantry attacked and foot by foot the Russians gave way, but in good order. Napoleon bombarded them into flight with massed artillery fire. Napoleon's victory was won at frightful cost and was inconclusive; he had captured no prisoners, cannon or flags. He had lost forty-three generals and 110 colonels among the 30,000 dead and wounded French troops. 60,000 Russians lay dead on the hills and in the ravines. Napoleon's marshals and generals criticized his handling of the battle and his failure to pursue the Russians. Before Borodini Napoleon had already lost 150,000 of his troops through various causes; a few months later a winter retreat from Moscow and attacks by the Cossacks destroyed what was left of the army. (In the Soviet Union modern historians claim that Borodino was an outright Russian victory). *See* Smolensk I.

Boroughbridge, *Yorkshire* (*Rebellion of the Marches*) *1322*. Between Royalists (Edward II) and rebels (Hereford and Lancaster). Falling back before Edward, the rebels were surprized by Sir Andrew Hardlay while crossing the bridge at Boroughbridge. Hereford was killed, Lancaster and several hundred knights and barons captured. *See* Byland; Myton.

Borysthenes (*Russian–Polish War*) *1512*. The Poles (Sigismund I) defeated an army of 80,000 Muscovites, who had great numbers killed. Despite this victory Sigismund lost his long war with Basil III of Russia.

Bosra (*Muslim invasion of Syria*) *632*. Serjabil, with 6,000 Muslims, besieged the fortress of Bosra. The Syrians

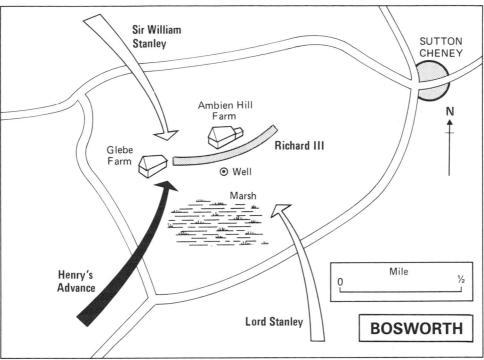

made a spirited sortie and were winning when Khaled arrived with 1,500 Muslim cavalry. The entire garrison emerged and in a pitched battle were defeated by Khaled, who lost only 250 men. *See* Siffin.

Boston (*War of American Independence*). American troops besieged the town from 20 April 1775 until the British, dominated by enemy artillery from heights, evacuated it on 17 March 1776.

Bosworth Field, *Yorkshire* (*Wars of the Roses*) *22 August 1485*. The Duke of Richmond (Henry VII), opposing Richard III, had persuaded Lord Stanley and his uncle, the king's men, to desert Richard during the battle. They went over at a critical time and Richard was routed. He fought to the end and was killed, as were the Duke of Norfolk and Lord Ferrers. *See* East Stoke; Tewkesbury.

Bothwell Bridge, *near Glasgow* (*Scottish Covenanters' Rising*) *22 June 1679*. Royal troops (Duke of Mon-

mouth) defeated the Covenanters — Scottish rebels — who lost 400 killed and 1,200 prisoners. The incident hardly deserves the name of a battle. *See* Drumclog.

Bougainville (*World War II*). Australian and American troops captured this Japanese-held Pacific island during protracted jungle fighting, 1943–4. *See* Soloman Islands.

Boulogne (*English–French Wars*) *July–October 1544*. Henry VIII laid siege to the town, which the French defended with much heroism. After heavy losses they surrendered on 14 September, but Henry allowed the garrison and inhabitants to march out with their arms and property. On 9 October the Dauphin Prince Henry led an attack on Boulogne and nearly took it from the English. Six years later the English sold the place back to the French. *See* Guinegate.

Bourbon, *Indian Ocean* (*Napoleonic Wars*) *8 July 1810*. The British

Commodore Rowley, with five ships, and Colonel Keatinge, with about 1,000 men, captured this French island, losing twenty-two killed, seventy-nine wounded. *See* Blueberg.

Bouvines (*Wars of Philip Augustus*) 26 July 1214. The French (Philip Augustus) defeated an Allied German, Flemish and English army under Otto IV, Holy Roman Emperor. The English army was led by John Lackland. The French victory broke up the coalition, secured Philip Augustus and discredited John, who was forced, the following year, to issue Magna Carta. *See* Damme; Rochester II.

Bovianum, *southern Italy* (*Second Samnite War*) 305 BC. The Romans (Titus Minucius) were besieging Bovianum, which a Samnite force (Statius Gellius) attempted to relieve. Minucius was killed, but the Samnites were heavily defeated, leaving Rome the undisputed major power of Italy. *See* Camerinum; Caudine Forks.

Boyaca (*Colombian War of Independence*) 17 August 1819. Simon Bolivar led Colombian patriots across the mountains to take up positions at Boyaca, cutting the 2,500 Spanish Royalists (Colonel Barreiro) from their base. The Spaniards attacked but were routed, losing 300 killed and nearly all the rest captured. The patriots lost sixty-six killed. *See* Carabobo; Caracha.

Boyne, The, *Ireland* (*War of the Glorious Revolution*) 1 July 1690. James II and his French, Irish and English Jacobites, mostly Catholic, held the line of the Boyne River. William III, leading an army of 40,000, mostly Dutch, Danish and Huguenot Protestants, crossed the river after stiff fighting. One of his commanders, Schomberg the Younger, crossed the river higher up and attacked the Jacobites in flank. The Jacobites were beaten — despite having held the higher ground — but retired in good order. Cas-

ualties: William's forces, 500; Jacobites, 1,500. *See* Aughrim; Londonderry.

Braddock Down (*English Civil War*) 19 January 1643. Parliamentary forces (General Ruthven) crossed the Tamar River, Cornwall, and occupied Liskeard, where the Royalists (Sir Ralph Hopton) sharply defeated them. *See* Stratton.

Bramham Moor (*Northumberland's Rebellion*) 20 February 1408. The Earl of Northumberland was killed in this battle with Sir Thomas Rokeby, High Sheriff of Yorkshire, and the rebellion subsided. *See* Homildon Hill; Shrewsbury.

Brandy Station (*American Civil War*) 9 June 1863. The biggest cavalry battle in American history. Federal cavalry under General Pleasonton surprized General Stuart's cavalry corps of 10,000 men near the Rappahannock River. Recovering rapidly, the Confederate horsemen fought back and battle raged for several hours. Pleasonton withdrew when Confederate infantry arrived. Casualties: Federals, 936; Confederates, 536. *See* Chancellorsville; Winchester II.

Brandywine (*American War of Independence*) 11 September 1777. General Howe, with 18,000 British troops to George Washington's 8,000 Americans, made a flank movement with a large part of his force. Washington frontally attacked the British lines but was driven back. Casualties: British, 590 killed and wounded; American, 900 killed and wounded, 300 prisoners. *See* Cooch's Bridge; Princeton.

Brechin (*Douglas Rebellion*) 1452. The Scottish Douglas clans, led by the Earl of Craufurd, were defeated by Royal troops under the Earl of Huntly.

Breda I (*Netherlands War of Independence against Spain*) May 1590. Maurice of Nassau, son of the assassinated William of Orange, took advantage

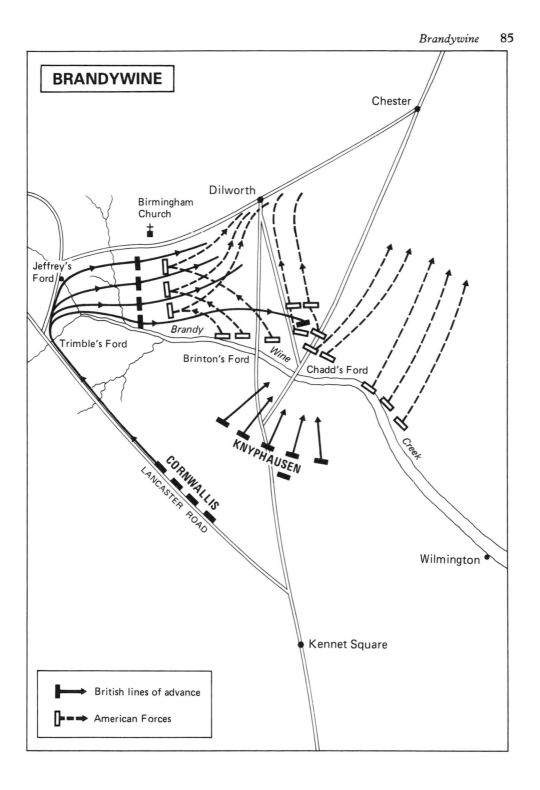

BRANDYWINE

Chester

Dilworth

Birmingham
Church

Jeffrey's
Ford

Trimble's Ford

Brandy

Brinton's Ford

Wine

Chadd's Ford

CORNWALLIS

LANCASTER ROAD

KNYPHAUSEN

Creek

Wilmington

Kennet Square

British lines of advance

American Forces

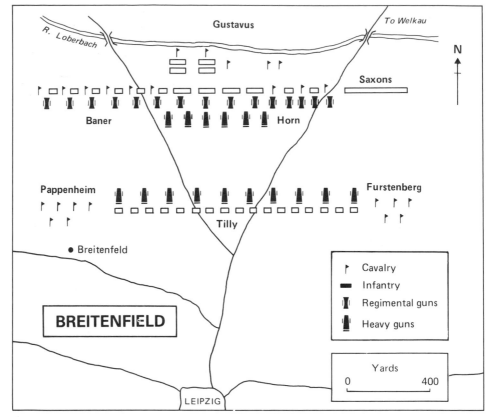

BREITENFIELD

of the absence from Holland of the Spanish commander, the Duke of Parma, and began a military offensive. Packing his soldiers under hatches on commercial barges, he had them poled to Breda's wharves. At night the troops emerged and captured the town from the Spanish garrison. This variation on the Trojan horse was the first of many victories for Maurice. *See* Turnhout.

Breda II (*Netherlands War of Independence*) *January–June 1625.* Spanish troops under Ambrogio de Spinola, failing to take the fortified city, tightly besieged it and drove off a relief force. Six months later, 5 June, the starving garrison surrendered. *See* Fleurus I; Ostend.

Breda III (*Thirty Years' War*) *10 October 1637.* The city and its key fortress, commanding the roads to Utrecht and Amsterdam, had been held by the Spanish for 12 years. Frederick Henry of Orange laid siege to it in 1636 and starved the garrison into a state of low morale. His assault on 10 October 1637 overwhelmed the Spaniards, who were slaughtered. *See* Breda I; Breda II; Wittstock.

Bregenz, *Austria (War of the League Above the Lake) January 1408.* The burghurs of Constance, with their allies, the Swabian nobles, defeated the troops of the League Above the Lake, i.e. Lake Constance. The League was soon dissolved.

Breisach (*Thirty Years' War*) *July–November 1638.* The fortress of Breisach on the Rhine, near Freiberg, was besieged by the Duke of Saxe-Weimar's French–German army — which served Cardinal Richelieu — on 30 July. The siege held fast under two Austrian attempts to relieve the garrison. By November the garrison was starving —

they restorted to cannibalism — and on 17 December the fort surrendered. The French now controlled the Rhine. *See* Chemnitz; Rheinfelden.

Breitenfeld I (*or Leipzig, Germany*) (*Thirty Years' War*) 7 September 1631. A major battle between 40,000 allied Swedes and Saxons and 44,000 Catholic Imperialists. Gustavus Adolphus led the Swedes, John George, Elector of Saxony, the Saxons and Marshal Tilly the Imperialists. In this give-and-take battle the Imperialists routed the Saxons, led in flight by John George. The Swedes meanwhile defeated the Imperialist left (Pappenheim), repulsed Tilly in the centre and when the troops who had chased the Saxons returned they were attacked by the Swedish left. Only four regiments held their ground until nightfall, and Gustavus captured all Tilly's guns. This victory saved the Protestant cause, then precarious in Europe. Casualties: Imperialists, 8,000 killed and wounded, 5,000 prisoners; Allies, 2,700 mostly Saxons. *See* Rain; Werben.

Breitenfeld II (*Thirty Years' War*) 2 November 1642. A remarkable instance of an army, caught at disadvantage, achieving victory. The retreating Swedes (Tortenson) were caught by the pursuing Austrians (Archduke Leopold and Piccolomini), but they held firm, fought their way into line and routed the Austrians, inflicting 10,000 casualties. *See* Breisach; Rocroi.

Brenneville (*or Bremule*) Normandy 20 August 1119. Less than 1,000 men, English under Henry I and French under Louis VI, were engaged and few were killed, but the result was so decisively in favour of Henry that Louis made peace on Henry's terms, i.e. Henry's claim to Normandy was established beyond dispute. *See* Standard; Tinchebray.

Brentford, *Essex* (*English Civil War*) 12 November 1642. Royalists (Prince Rupert) drove three Parliamentary regiments (Denzil Holles) from their entrenchments, taking eleven guns and 1,500 prisoners. *See* Edgehill; Grantham.

Brescia (*Italian Wars of Independence*) 31 March 1849. The Italians, rising in revolt, shut the small Austrian garrison in the citadel. General Haynau, with 4,000 Austrians, fought from barricade to barricade, captured the city and ordered mass executions. The Austrians lost 480 killed. *See* Novara; Venice.

Breslau (*Seven Years' War*) 22 November 1757. An Austrian army of 90,000 (Prince Charles of Lorraine) drove 25,000 Prussians (Prince of Bevern) into Breslau. They evacuated it very soon, leaving a garrison of 6,000 which surrendered on 24 November. Casualties: Prussians, 5,000 killed or wounded, 3,600 prisoners; Austrians, 6,000 killed and wounded. *See* Leuthen; Rossbach.

Brest (*War of the Holy League*) 10 August 1512. An English fleet of 45 ships (Lord Howard) drove a French fleet of thirty-nine (Jean de Thenouenal) into Brest or onto the coast, with heavy loss. Howard lost two ships and 1,600 men.

Brices Cross Roads, *north-east Mississippi* (*American Civil War*) 10 June 1864. A remarkable action in which the Confederate General Nathan Forrest surprized and defeated a force (General Sturgis) twice the size of his own sent out to destroy him. Hearing of the advance of Sturgis's 8,000 troops and eighteen guns, Forrest led 3,500 cavalry rapidly to the crossroads and attacked the Federals before they could deploy, driving their cavalry back against their own infantry. Casualties: Federals, 223 killed, 394 wounded, 1,623 captured, 16 guns and 250 wagons taken; Confederates, 492. *See* Resaca; Tupelo.

Bridge of Dee (*Bishops' Wars*) 18 June 1639. Montrose, leading 2,300 Scottish Covenanters, found the bridge held by Royal troops (Lord Aboyne). By a ruse, Montrose drew off the main enemy body and forced a passage. Casualties were slight.

Brielle (*or Brill*) (*Netherlands War of Independence*) *1 April 1572*. The Dutch patriots, The Beggars of the Sea, about 400-strong (De La Marck and Treslong), captured this fortress from the Spaniards. This first victory of the patriots in their fight against Spanish rule laid the foundation of the Dutch republic. *See* Haarlem.

Brienne, *Troyes* (*Napoleonic Wars: defence of Paris*) *29 January 1814*. About 30,000 Prussians and Russians (Blucher) held Brienne. The 18,000 French (Napoleon) drove the Allies from their positions and occupied the chateau. The Russians (Sachen) made a determined night attack but could not dislodge the French. Casualties: Allies, 4,000; French, 3,000. *See* Hanau; La Rothiere.

Brihuega (*War of Spanish Succession*) *9 December 1710*. The British (Earl of Stanhope), retreating from Madrid to Catalonia, were ambushed and surrounded by the French (Duc de Vendome). Stanhope fought till all his powder was gone, then made a bayonet charge. His force reduced to 500, he surrendered. Stanhope had been trying to replace Philip V with Archduke Charles of Austria on the Spanish throne. *See* Toulon I; Turin.

Bristoe Station (*American Civil War*) *14 October 1863*. Confederates (General Hill) overtook the rearguard of a Federal force withdrawing towards Centreville. Attacking General French's III Corps, Hill came under close-range infantry and artillery fire from another corps whose presence he had not suspected. Casualties: Confederates 1,900 to a Federal loss of 548. The Confederates lost another 2,023 men in a rearguard action, 7 November. *See* Gettysburg; Wilderness.

Britain, Battle of (*World War II*) *10 July–31 October 1940*. The systematic attempt by aerial bombing to so damage British morale, industry and air defences as to make the nation, then standing alone after the Germans had over-run Europe, incapable of continuing the war. To do this the German Luftwaffe (Marshal Goering) had to defeat the R.A.F. (Air Chief Marshal Sir Hugh Dowding was in charge of Fighter Command). The Battle of Britain began on 10 July when 100 German bombers and fighters attacked convoys off the English coast, but attacks switched to ports, fighter airfields, industrial targets and cities. The British had 600 serviceable fighters, including the key No. 11 Group (Air Vice-Marshal Keith Park) with nineteen squadrons of serviceable aircraft for fighting, including six squadrons of 200 aircraft — six of Spitfires and thirteen of Hurricanes. There were 1,253 operationally-fit fighter pilots. German Air Fleets 2 and 3 had 1,130 medium bombers, 320 dive-bombers, 800 single-engined fighters, 250 twin-engined fighters and sixty reconnaissance aircraft. In Norway and Denmark Air Fleet 5 included 130 medium bombers, forty twin-engined fighters. The main German fighter was the Me. 109.

One of the most important days of the battle was 13 August, Eagle Day to the Germans. The plan was to extend the southern fighter defences to their limit; the R.A.F. lost thirteen fighters for the destruction of forty-five enemy aircraft. On 15 August the Luftwaffe flew 1,786 individual sorties, the most for any one day of the battle. In the period 8–18 August Fighter Command lost 183 fighters in battle and about thirty on the ground. Germany lost her chance to win air supremacy in the Battle of Britain by the attack on London on 24 August — "one of the greatest miscalculations in history" — *New York Times*. This attack not only stiffened British resistance but led to retaliation on Berlin. Southampton, Plymouth, Bristol, Liverpool and Birmingham endured many heavy attacks; on the night of 14 November all central

Coventry was virtually destroyed. Civilian casualties amounted to 1,075 killed in August, 6,954 in September, 6,334 in October. The Battle of Britain proved, again, that wars cannot be won by bombardments. The air battle over the south on 15 September was such a victory for the R.A.F. that it put an end to the possibility of invasion; the Germans lost fifty-six aircraft. By 5 October German bombers had ceased daylight operations and by 31 October the Air Ministry considered the battle ended, though enemy bombing persisted until August 1941. Losses: German, 1,733 aircraft (the figure of 2,662 was a propaganda one). The R.A.F. lost 449 pilots and about 600 aircraft.

Battle of Britain, second phase, 15 June 1944–25 April 1945. This was the battle launched by the Germans with the V-bombs, better known as Buzz-bombs. A miniature plane, guided by a magnetic compass, the V-1 travelled at 400 mph and few aircraft could catch it before it plunged to earth with its ton of high explosive. Most of the V-1s were launched in salvos from heavily camouflaged ramps along the Channel coast north of Calais. The barrage lasted 80 days, the Germans firing at London 200 bombs every 24 hours. To the beginning of 5 September 479 people were killed and 15,934 injured. On the various launching sites Allied planes dropped 100,000 tons of bombs, losing nearly 450 aircraft to ground defences. About 1,350 British and American guns were used against the bombs and late in August only one in ten bombs reached London; in all about 2,300 exploded in London. On 8 September the Germans launched their V-2, which was fired at a higher trajectory to great altitudes to reach the earth at a speed greater than sound; 1,050 V-2 rockets reached England up till 25 April 1945, killing 2,754 people and seriously injuring 6,523. All forms of interception were impossible and only the capture of the launching sites stopped the attacks.

British–United States War. *See* List of Battles.

Brittany (*Gallic War*) 56 BC. The first recorded sea fight in the Atlantic. Off the south Brittany coast, the Roman fleet under Brutus defeated the 220-galley fleet of the Veneti. The Veneti land force surrendered as well and the Romans conquered Brittany.

Brody-Lvov (*World War II*) July 1944. On 13 July a Russian army under General Konev began a two-prong offensive to cross the Bug River and to take Lvov. The first trapped 40,000 Germans at Brody after heavy fighting. The Germans evacuated Lvov to evade an outflanking manoeuvre. *See* Kursk; Minsk.

Bronkhorst Spruit (*First British–Boer War*) 20 December 1880. The first engagement of the war. A British party, 259 men under Colonel Anstruther, ambushed by 150 mounted Boers (Joubert), lost 155 killed or wounded. The Boer claim to have lost 2 killed and 50 wounded is probably correct. *See* Majuba Hill.

Broodseinde, *Flanders* (*World War I*) 4 October 1917. A major assault on German positions near Passchendaele by British, New Zealand and Australian forces. German official histories call this battle "the black day". Casualties: German, about 10,000 plus 5,000 prisoners; Australian, 6,432; New Zealand, 892; British, about 300. *See* Flanders; Messines; Passchendaele; Ypres.

Brooklyn (*American War of Independence*) 27 August 1776. A massive defeat for 11,000 Americans (General Putnam) by 30,000 British (Lord Howe). Casualties: American 2,000 killed or wounded; British, 65 killed, 255 wounded. *See* Cape Henry.

Brunanburgh (*Danish invasion of Britain*) 937. Athelstan defeated with much slaughter the combined armies of Anlaf the Dane, Owen of Cumberland and Constantine III of Scotland. *See* Kinloss.

Brunei–Borneo *1962–6*. President Sukarno of Indonesia wanted to bring the Malay Peninsula, Singapore, Sarawak, Sabah and Brunei into a "Greater Indonesia". Tunku Abdul Rahman, Prime Minister of the Malay Federation, stood in his way. Sukarno inspired a rebellion against the Sultan of Brunei, the country which seemed the weakest. British troops and Gurkhas under Major-General W. Walker fought a 6-months' jungle campaign to put down the Brunei revolt. Indonesia declared a "policy of confrontation" against Malaya and on 16 August 1962 a Gurkha unit clashed with Indonesian troops on the Sarawak border. Defending a jungle and swamp border of 900 miles between Indonesia's Kalimantan province and the North Borneo states was difficult. By 1964 troops from Britain, Australia, New Zealand and India numbered 18,000. Operating as company-strength patrols they ventured into Kalimantan and built small "forts" at strategic points. A small battle took place on 27 April 1965 when Indonesian troops attacked a British base at Plaman Mapu. Gurkhas were then extensively used in aggressive raids. The undeclared war ended on 11 August 1966. Total Commonwealth losses were 114 killed and 180 wounded. The Indonesians admitted to having lost 680 killed. The British Minister of Defence told the House of Commons that the Borneo campaign was "one of the most efficient uses of military force" in world history.

Brunete (*Spanish Civil War*) *6–25 July 1937*. Republicans attacked the Nationalists besieging Madrid and suffered about 11,000 casualties for no gain whatever. *See* Madrid.

Brunkeberg, *Stockholm* (*Norwegian/Danish–Swedish Wars*) *10 October 1471*. A decisive Swedish victory; Sten Sure, for Charles VIII, defeated the invading Danes and Swedes led by Christian I of Denmark and Norway.

Bryansk–Vyazma, *Russia* (*World War II*) *October 1941*. The fighting which comprised this battle was a prelude to the German assault on the Moscow front. The Germans (Guderian, Hoepner, Khige, Reinhardt, Hoth) divided and encircled the Red Armies, which adopted a hedgehog defence and made ferocious efforts to break out. After nearly 3 weeks of continuous fighting the Nazis claimed the destruction of eight armies with the capture of 648,196 prisoners. But the Russians had abandoned Bryansk and Vyazma several days before (12 October) and many divisions fell back to guard Moscow, q.v.

Bucharest (*Russian–Turkish Wars*) *1771*. The Russians (General Romanzov) heavily defeated the Turks (Mousson Oglou). The Turks retreated behind the Danube. *See* Focsani.

Budapest (*World War II*) *20 October 1944–18 February 1945*. The Germans under Friessner and later Woehler fought desperately against the Russians (Tolnulkin and Malinovsky) to hold a pocket protecting Budapest and the Lake Balaton oilfields. By 24 December, with another Russian army through the Carpathian passes and in rear of Budapest, the Hungarian capital was encircled. Hitler ordered much of the army's reserve into a counter-attack, but Pest, on the Danube's east bank, fell on 18 January and Buda, west bank, on 18 February. The Russians claim to have killed 49,000 Germans and captured 110,000 during the Budapest fighting. *See* Austria; Ukraine.

Buena Vista (*American–Mexican War*) *22 February 1847*. General Zachary Taylor's 4,500 Americans occupied a series of heights dominating the Angostura Pass. General Santa Anna's 18,000 Mexicans could not dislodge them and retired next day. Casualties: American, 746; Mexican, at least 1,500 killed.

Buenos Aires I (*Napoleonic Wars*) *27 June 1806*. General Beresford, helped by Admiral Sir Home Popham, occupied the city by a *coup de main*. With only 1,700 men Beresford could not hold until reinforcements arrived and was defeated and forced to surrender by the Spanish defenders. (General Liniers) after losing 250 killed or wounded. *See* Cape Finisterre; Cape Town.

Buenos Aires II (*Napoleonic Wars*) 5 July 1807. General Whitelocke, in an ill-conceived attack on the city, committed his 9,000 British troops to movement through the streets. They came under heavy fire from windows and rooftops and suffered serious losses. The force surrendered and the British evacuated the River Plate region. *See* Cape Finisterre; Cape Town.

Buenos Aires III (*Mitre's Rebellion*) 6 November 1874. Argentine government troops (Sarmiento) defeated the rebels Mitre and Aredondo. The rebels were massacred.

Bulawayo, *Rhodesia (British–Matabele Wars) 23 October 1893*. The Matabele chief, Lobengula, was defeated when he gave battle to the British who then occupied his capital. *See* Doornkop.

Bullecourt I, *Somme (World War I) 10–11 April 1917*. The Australian 4th Division, without an artillery barrage, failed by the tanks, and attacking against uncut wire, yet broke the Hindenberg Line. Left without support, the force withdrew and lost 3,000, including 28 officers and 1,142 men captured. *See* Bullecourt II.

Bullecourt II, *3–26 May 1917*. One of the great battles of World War I. Units of three Australian divisions (Gellibrand) took and held a 2-mile section of the Hindenberg Line, beating off seven violent counter-attacks and a dozen smaller ones. The Australians had 7,000 casualties. *See* Arras.

Bull Run I (*American Civil War*) 21 July 1861. A major Confederate victory. General Beauregard's 30,000 Confederates (southerners) held 9 miles of the Bull Run river. General McDowell, with 40,000 Federals, attempted to turn their left flank, but the Confederates went on the offensive and routed the northerners in this first major battle of the war. Casualties: Federals, 1,492 killed or wounded, 1,600 prisoners; Confederates, 1,982. *See* Ball's Bluff; Philippi; Rich Mountain.

Bull Run II (*American Civil War*) 30 August 1862. Another Confederate victory. The Federals (Pope) attacked the Confederates (Stonewall Jackson). Jackson waited until evening and when the Federal left weakened he advanced, driving the Federals from the field; 7,000 were taken prisoner. *See* Cedar Mountain.

Buna, Gona and Sanananda, *New Guinea (World War II) late 1942, early 1943*. Australians and Americans against the Japanese. In the general area of these three beaches the Japanese built a maze of earthworks able to stand even a direct hit from a 25-pounder. The main Australian assault occurred on 19 November. Gona was captured on 1 December; then followed the battle for Gona Mission, for its size the most severe of the campaign. It was captured on 9 December, the Japanese losing 800 dead. Australians captured Cape Endaidere, and Buna fell on 28 December. Sanananda, the most difficult position, held out until 23 January. Outnumbered 2 to 1 the Australians, and in the last part of the campaigns, the Americans, wiped out a Japanese force of 16,000. *See* Kokoda Trail; New Guinea.

Bunker Hill (*American War of Independence*) 17 June 1775. The Americans were holding Breed's Hill and Bunker Hill on the outskirts of Boston. The 2,000 British finally dislodged the Americans but lost 800 men. The battle polarized the conflict and estabished "sides".

See Lexington and Concord; Long Island.

Burgau, *Germany* (*Thirty Years' War*) *1631*. A cavalry action in which a small force under Gustavus Adolphus defeated 4,000 Croats (Colonel Spar). *See* Magdeburg.

Burkersdorf, *Silesma* (*Seven Years' War*) *1762*. Between Frederick the Great and the Holy Roman Empire's army of Marshal von Daun. The Prussians drove back the Austrians, but gained no decisive victory and casualties were low. *See* Frieburg; Torgau.

Burlington Heights (*Second British–American War*) 5 *May 1813*. General Proctor, who had only 1,000 British troops and some Indian auxiliaries, was engaged with an American force holding Burlington Heights, when he was attacked by 1,300 more Americans (General Clay). The British lost their guns, but, rallying, routed Clay, who lost 1,000 men killed, wounded or captured. *See* Lake Erie.

Burma Campaign (*World War II*) *January 1942–July 1945*. The Japanese invaded lower Burma from Thailand early in the Malaya campaign; the British (General Alexander) prepared to defend upper Burma on the line of the Salween River, 31 January. The Japanese drove the defenders west to Sittang and the loss of Rangoon cut the supply lines of the British and Chinese forces in Burma. The British escaped over jungle trails to Imphal, India, the Chinese retreated north. By the end of May the Japanese held all Burma. Even India was threatened by Japanese ships. Nearly 2 years elapsed before the Allies could undertake a major counter-offensive. British airborne infantry (the Chindits) organized by Major-General Orde Wingate first invaded the jungle of northern Burma in March 1943. A similar American force was Merrill's Marauders. At the southern end of the front at Akyab the Japanese launched a tactical offensive against assembling British troops now commanded by General Sir William Slim. They penetrated the Mavu Mountains and enveloped the 7th Indian Division. The renewed British attack was carried as far as Buthudaung, 6 April 1944, but this was evacuated 6 May. The contest moved northwards to the Manipur front, where the Japanese tried to cut the Assam–Bengal railway. Three Japanese divisions cut off the 17th Indian Division at Imphal and fierce fighting developed, especially at Kohima, which was encircled and captured. Later the Japanese dug into Kohima and made it the "Cassino" of Burma. Here they were worn down by constant assault and after 2 months of bitter fighting Anglo–Indian troops recaptured Kohima and raised the siege of Imphal Plain. About 13,000 Japanese were killed in this campaign.

The most successful campaign in Burma in the spring of 1944 was fought in the north by Chinese and American troops under General Stilwell who were covering the extension of the Ledo Road, pushing towards China. After the capture of Myitkyina, 3 August 1945, Chinese and American forces in northern Burma pressed on towards the important road junction of Bhamo, Lieutenant-General David Sultan now being the American commander. The first American truck convoy reached Kunming on 4 February 1945, thus regaining contact with China.

General Slim's Fourteenth Army attacked. They had first to drive the Japanese across the Chindwin and then to cross in force themselves; in the path of their advance were the fierce actions of Fort White, Kennedy Peak and Kalemyo. They captured Katha on 16 December 1944 and Shwebo on 9 January 1945. On 2 March Meiktila was captured, cutting Japanese communications with the south. The Japanese contested Mandalay street by street, 8–22 March. On this date Indian troops captured Fort Dufferin, the main enemy strongpoint. Rangoon fell to the British IV Corps 2–4 May. Admiral Lord Mountbatten, supreme commander

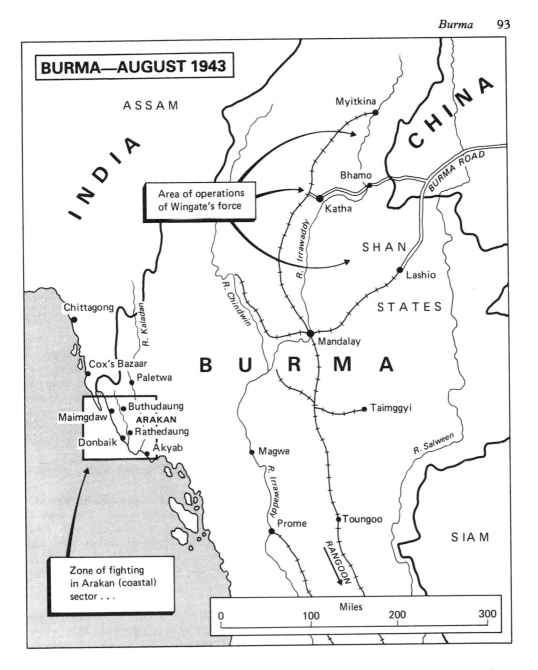

BURMA—AUGUST 1943

ASSAM

INDIA

CHINA

Myitkina

Bhamo

BURMA ROAD

Area of operations
of Wingate's force

Katha

R. Irrawaddy

SHAN

Lashio

R. Chindwin

STATES

Chittagong

R. Kaladan

Cox's Bazaar

Paletwa

BURMA

Mandalay

Maimgdaw

Buthudaung

ARAKAN

Rathedaung

Donbaik

Akyab

Taimggyi

Magwe

R. Salween

R. Irrawaddy

Prome

Toungoo

SIAM

RANGOON

Zone of fighting
in Arakan (coastal)
sector . . .

Miles

0   100   200   300

since 1943, announced on 4 May that the Japanese had suffered 347,000 casualties of which 97,000 were counted dead and that the campaign was at an end, but fighting went on.

Within a week of entry into Rangoon, troops from the Arakan front had made contact with those of the Fourteenth Army and the Japanese were trapped west of the Irrawaddy. The British (General Stopford) captured Moulmein and blocked their escape. Towards the end of July 1945 the Japanese made a determined effort to break through; this matured into hard fighting on 20 July and the Japanese lost 6,000 killed. Throughout the campaign Slim's generalship had been highly skilful.

Burns Hill (*British–Kaffir Wars*) *1847*. A British force, sent to arrest the Kaffir chief, Sandilli, were outnumbered and forced to retreat after losing nearly all the officers.

Bursa (*or Brusa*) (*Rise of Ottoman Turks*) *1317–26*. In 1317 Osman I (otherwise Othman) laid siege to Bursa, a Byzantine outpost near the sea of Marmara. The garrison, often under attack, held out for 9 years until starved into surrender by Osman's son, Orkhan I. Until 1336 Bursa was the Ottoman capital (then Adrianople). *See* Adrianople; Erzincan.

Busaco (*Peninsular War*) *27 September 1810*. A notable British victory in Spain. The 25,000 British (with 25,000 Portuguese) occupied the heights of Busaco in the face of 40,000 French (Massena). The corps led by Ney and Reynier assaulted the British lines and after a particularly bloody and stubborn battle were beaten off. Casualties: French, 4,500; British, 1,500. *See* Fuentes d'Onor; Talavera.

Bushire, *Persia* (*British–Persian War*) *18 January 1857*. An engagement in which the 3rd Bombay Light Cavalry charged a well-formed Persian square and broke it. The British held Persia to keep Russia from the Arabian Gulf.

Bushy Run (*Pontiac's Rebellion*) *5–6 August 1763*. Pontiac, an Ottawa Indian chief, led rebellious warriors in a series of attacks, 16 May–20 June, that destroyed every British post west of Niagara except Detroit and Fort Pitt, which were besieged. Colonel Henry Bouquet, a Swiss serving the British, hurried to relieve Fort Pitt and at Bushy Run, 30 miles to the south-east, met a large force of Indians. Though heavily outnumbered, Bouquet defeated the Indians in a 2-day battle and 4 days later relieved Fort Pitt. Pontiac himself remained undefeated and not until 24 July 1766 did he agree to a treaty.

Buxar, *Bengal* (*British reconquest of Bengal*) *23 October 1764*. A remarkable victory for 7,000 British troops and sepoys, led by Major H. Monro, against the rebellious army of Oude, 40,000, under Surajah Dowlah and the Great Mogul, Shah Allum. The Indians lost 4,000 men and 130 guns; the British, 847 men. *See* Panipat II.

Buzenval (*or Battle of Mont Valerian*) (*French–German War*) *19 January 1871*. General Trochu led a sortie from besieged Paris and established positions in the Park of Buzenval, but the following day, because of failure at other points, the occupied positions were abandoned. Casualties: German, 40 officers, 570 men; French, 189 officers, 3,881 men. *See* Sedan Metz.

Byland (*English–Scottish Wars*) *14 October 1322*. Following the invasion of England by Robert the Bruce, Edward II marched into Scotland. The Scots pushed him back and brought him to battle at Byland, north of York. His army routed, Edward escaped capture but was forced to accept Scottish independence. *See* Boroughbridge; Dupplin Moor; Myton.

Bytham, *Lincolnshire* (*First Baron's War of England*) *1220*. The Earl of Aumale refused to give up two royal castles he had held for King John and now held for Henry III. Hubert de Burgh besieged the castle of Bytham and then stormed it. *See* Bedford; Sandwich I.

Byzantium I *later Constantinople* *381 BC*. The Macedonian fleet (Antigonus) surprized the Asiatics (Clytus) at anchor and destroyed or captured the entire fleet, though Clytus escaped.

Byzantium II (*Wars of Byzantine Empire*) *55*. A mass of Huns and Slavs (Zabergan) crossed the Danube and burning and plundering reached Constantinople, whose outer walls they quickly subdued; Sergius, commander of the militia, fell into their hands. Belisarius, the great commander, now retired, quickly gathered 300 of his demobilized veteran horsemen. At Chettus, by bluff, tactical movements and discipline, he put the 7,000 barbarians to flight. Closely pursuing, Belisarius so cleverly deceived the invaders into believing that he had a powerful force that they abandoned their campaign and withdrew to the Danube.

Byzantium III (*Roman Empire's Civil Wars*) *194–6*. On the assassination of Emperor Publius Helvius Pertinax, several men claimed the throne, notably Clodius Albinus, commanding in England, Septimus Severus, commander in Pannonia, and Pescennius Niger of Egypt. Severus marched to Rome, assumed emperorship, then besieged Niger's large army in Byzantium in 194. Niger's troops were also driven out of Cyzicus, Nicaea and Issus, near where Niger himself was executed. In the spring of 196 Septimus' men stormed Byzantium and sacked it. Meanwhile, Albinus had been raising an army in Gaul. *See* Lugdunum.

Byzantium IV (*War of the Two Empires*) *323*. Constantine the Great, having defeated Licinius at Adrianopolis, besieged Byzantium. Licinius crossed to Asia to find reinforcements to raise the siege, but was defeated at Chrysopolis and Byzantium surrendered. Constantine was proclaimed emperor and Byzantium, under the name of Constantinople, was made his capital. For other battles at the site of Byzantium, *see* Constantinople.

Cabala (*Second Carthaginian invasion of Sicily*) *379* BC. The Syracusans (Dionysius) defeated the Carthaginians and killed their leader, Mago.

Cabira (*Third Mithridatic War*) *72* BC. Three Roman legions (Lucullus and Fabius Hadrianus) defeated the Pontic Army (Diophantus and Taxiles) and King Mithridates was driven out of Pontus, Asia Minor, which became a Roman province. *See* Syracuse.

Cadesia (*Muslim invasion of Persia*) *636*. Between 30,000 Muslims under Said, the Caliph Omar's lieutenant, and 120,000 Persians under Rustam. On the first day the Persians, by virtue of numbers, could only check the fierce Muslim attacks, but next day Rustam was killed and the Persians, losing morale, were driven from the field with great slaughter. The Muslims lost 7,500. *See* Aleppo; Jerusalem; Yarmuk.

Cadiz *19 April 1587*. Sir Francis Drake, with between thirty and forty ships, destroyed over forty-five Spanish vessels in Cadiz Bay without loss to himself. Drake described the exploit as "Singeing the King of Spain's beard". *See* Armada; Zutphen.

Cadsand (*Hundred Years' War*) *10 November 1357*. A force of 2,500 English (Earl of Derby) defeated 5,000 Flemings in French service, the Flemings losing 1,000 men. *See* Auray.

Caesarea (*Roman Empire's Jewish Wars*) *135*. In 132 the Jews began to expel Roman forces from Judea. Rome sent the veteran General Sextus Julius Severus to command the legionaries and he crushed the revolt. His reconquest became complete in 135 when he captured the port of Caesarea (Qisarya) and killed the Jewish leader, Bar Kokhba. *See* Jerusalem.

Cairo (*Turkish invasion of Egypt*) *29 January–3 February 1517*. Selim I and his Turks captured Cairo, routing the Egyptians and slaughtering 50,000 inhabitants. The Turks hanged the Mameluke Sultan, Toomaan Bey, and Egypt became part of the Ottoman empire. *See* Marj-Dabik; Rhodes.

Cajamarca (*Spanish conquest of Peru*) *16 November 1532*. Marching into the interior with only 102 infantry and sixty-two horsemen, Francisco Pizarro encountered a great Inca army led by Atahualpa. By a trick Pizarro captured the Inca chief, which demoralized his followers. Pizarro received a huge ransom for Atahualpa, but murdered him nevertheless. *See* Tenochtitlan.

Cajwah (*Mogul Delhi Civil War*) *8 January 1659*. Aurungzebe, the Great Mogul, confronted an army raised by his brother, Shuja, who supported Dara, rightful heir to the throne which Aurungzebe claimed. After a day-long battle Shuja, having lost many troops and 114 guns, withdrew.

Calafat (*Crimean War*) *14 February–mid-May 1854*. The Turks, 30,000-strong, under Ahmed Pasha, held strong entrenchments at Calafat. The Russians made one frontal attack after another, had no success and lost 20,000 men through wounds, disease and privation. The Turks lost 12,000. *See* Kars.

Calais I (*Hundred Years' War*) *1346–7*. Edward III besieged the fortress in August and the garrison and citizens held out until the following August before privations forced surrender. *See* Crécy.

Calais II *8 January 1558*. By this time Calais was the last English stronghold in France. The Duc de Guise captured it after a 7-day siege. Queen Mary of England is said to have exclaimed that at her death the word "Calais" would be found engraved on her heart. *See* Boulogne; St. Quentin I.

Calais (*World War II*) *1940*. *See* Dunkirk; France.

Calatafimi, *Sicily* (*Italian Wars of Independence: Garibaldi's Rising*) *15 May 1860*. Garibaldi's "Thousand Volunteers" aided by some Sicilians gave battle to General Landi's 4,000 Neapolitans, driving them back with heavy loss to Palermo. Garibaldi lost eighteen killed and 128 wounded among his famous thousand. *See* Solferino.

Calcutta (*Seven years' War*) *June 1756*. Surajah Dowlah, Nawab of Bengal, on 16 June besieged the city, which had a garrison of only 514 regular soldiers and 1,000 others. Abandoning the city to defend the fort, the garrison beat off an attack, losing ninety-four killed or wounded, but surrendered on 20 June. The 146 survivors were put in a small room — the Black Hole, a military punishment cell — and only twenty-three survived until morning. Robert Clive recaptured Calcutta in January 1757 and in March took Chandernager. *See* Arcot; Plassey.

Calderon Bridge, *Guadalajara* (*Mexican War of Independence*) *17 January 1811*. General Calleja, the Spanish General, pursuing a force of revolutionaries led by a Creole priest, Miguel Hidalgo, caught them at Calderon Bridge. Hidalgo and his chief aides survived the bloody defeat, but were summarily executed. *See* Calupulalpam.

Caldiero I (*Napoleon's Italian campaign*) *12 November 1796*. Napoleon attacked Alvinzi's Austrians and, for the first time in this campaign, was beaten. After severe fighting and loss of 3,000 men he retired. (His victory at Arcola followed within the week.) *See* Arcola; Bassano.

Caldiero II (*Napoleonic Wars*) *30 October 1805*. A major strategic battle between Massena with 50,000 French and the Archduke Charles, whose 80,000 Austrians held the village and heights of Caldiero. Massena attacked and carried the heights. That night Charles withdrew his artillery and supplies from the village, leaving General Hillinger and 5,000 men to cover his retreat. This force was captured en bloc. The battle was indecisive, but the strategic victory went to the French, who lost 4,000 killed or wounded. Austrian casualties: 3,000 killed or wounded and another 3,000 prisoners. *See* Oberhollabrun; Ulm.

Caliano, *north Italy* (*Wars of French Revolution*) *4–6 September 1796*. Napoleon, learning that Marshal Wurmser had divided his Austrian army, sent Massena to drive Davidovich's 20,000-strong advance guard out of Marco. Next day, 5 September Napoleon directed the 10-mile advance on Caliano, shelled the Austrians and then drove them out at bayonet point. Wheeling his army east, Napoleon pursued Wurmser's main body. The Austrians had lost 6,000 men. *See* Castigliano della Stiviere.

Calicut (*Second British–Mysore War*) *10 December 1790*. A remarkable victory by Colonel Hartly with 3,000 men (one British regiment, two native) over Hussein Ali's 9,000 Mysore troops. Casualties: British, 52; enemy, 1,000 killed or wounded, 2,400 prisoners including the commander. *See* Seringapatam.

Callao I (*Peruvian War of Independence*) 5 November 1820. Lord Cochrane, British commander of the Chilean navy, was blockading the Spaniards in Callao. Rowing into the harbour by night with 240 seamen and marines, he cut out the Spanish frigate, *Esmerelda*, from under the 300 guns of the shore batteries. He lost forty-one men and captured or killed the entire crew of the *Esmerelda*. *See* Ayacucho; Junin.

Callao II (*Peruvian Revolution*) 2 May 1866. A duel between a Spanish fleet of eleven ships and the Peruvian shore batteries. The Spaniards lost 300 men and were driven off, while the Peruvians lost 1,000 killed or wounded. *See* Ayacucho; Callao I; Junin.

Callinicum, *east bank of the Euphrates* (*Byzantine–Persian War*) 531. The Persian ruler, Kavadh I, routed the Byzantine army at Callinicum, but Belisarius saved most of his army by taking refuge on islands in the river. At Sura he resisted the Persian efforts to crush his beaten but spirited army and the action, though indecisive, ended the war. *See* Dara.

Calpulalpam (*Mexican Rising*) 20 December 1860. Liberals under Benito Juarez won a notable victory against the Government troops (Miramon); it caused the downfall of Miramon's administration. *See* Puebla II.

Calven (*Swiss–Swabian War*) 22 March 1499. Benedict Fontana led 6,000 Swiss from the Grisons against strong entrenchments held by 15,000 Austrians, mostly from the Duchy of Swabia, under Maximilian I and drove them out with heavy loss. *See* Dornach; Frastenz.

Cambodia–North Vietnam War *1971–*. The North Vietnamese backed the pro-communist Prince Nordom Sihanouk and the extreme left Khmer Rouge movement against the government of General Lon Nol. When the Khmer Rouge troops captured the capital, Phnom Penh, on 17 April 1975 they drove the entire population of 2 million into the countryside. Under the brutal regime of Pol Pot, which ended in 1979, about 3 million people died. In December 1978 Vietnam invaded Cambodia and captured Phnom Penh; Cambodia was renamed Kampuchea. Pol Pot and his Khmer Rouge, now a resistance army, fought the Vietnamese. Total military casualties are estimated at 500,000.

Cambrai (*World War I*) 20 November–4 December 1917. The first great tank battle. The British Commander-in-Chief, Sir Douglas Haig, used 324 tanks, under the command of General Elles, as the striking force and without an artillery barrage to break enemy wire, to strike at the German lines in an effort to break through before massive German reinforcements from the collapsing Russian front could reach the Western Front. Though the tanks could move only at walking pace, they punched a 6-mile hole in the lines of German Second Army (von der Marwitz). Infantry made the gap into a salient, but failure to exploit, lack of knowledge about infantry–tank co-operation and rapid German defensive reaction prevented the British from making the most of the initial success. When Haig ordered a withdrawal, 4 December, there had been no overall gain of territory. Casualties: British, 43,000 including 6,000 prisoners taken on the first day, 30 November, of the German counter-offensive; Germans, 41,000, including 11,000 captured. *See* Arras.

Cambuskenneth. *See* Stirling.

Camden (*American Revolution*) 16 August 1780. Cornwallis had concentrated about 2,000 British troops at

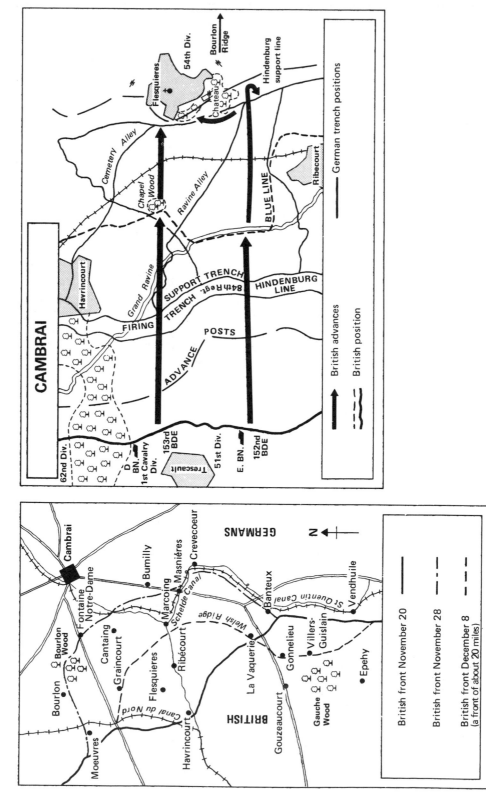

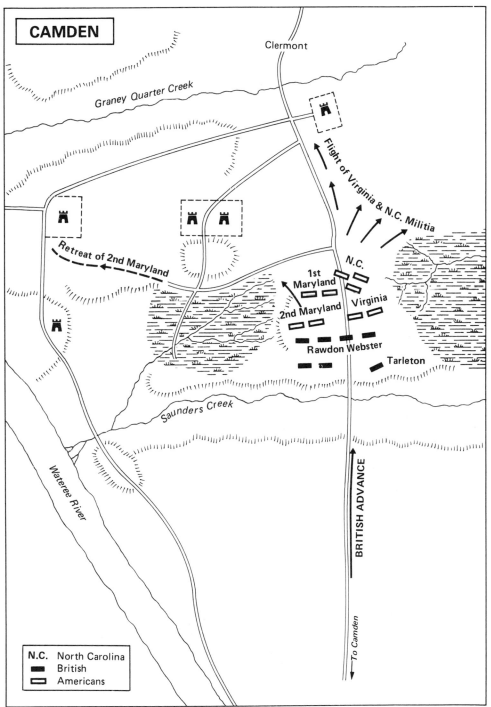

Camden against 5,000 untrained Americans led by Gates and de Kalb. The British drove in the American outposts and their steadiness demoralized the Americans, who fled after suffering heavy loss; de Kalb was killed. Cornwallis lost 312. *See* Kings Mountain; Waxhaw Creek.

Camelodunum (*now Colchester*) (*Second Roman invasion of Britain*) *43*. The Romans (Emperor Claudius) routed the Britons under Caractacus and his capital, Camelodunum, was taken. *See* Boadicea.

Camerinum, *Umbria, Italy* (*Third Roman–Samnite War*) *298* BC. Fought between two Roman legions under Lucius Scipio and the Samnites led by Gellius Equatius, who was aided by a force of Gauls. Scipio, stationed near Camerinum to watch the pass through which the Gauls were expected to cross the Apennines, could not prevent the union of Samnites and Gauls and was defeated, one of his legions being destroyed. *See* Bovianum; Sentinum.

Campaldino, *Arno River*, *11 June 1289*. The Ghibellines, who had been expelled from the city, tried to regain it but were beaten by the Guelfs and lost their power in Florence. (Dante fought with the Guelfs.) *See* Curzola; Messina.

Campen (*Seven Years' War*) *18 October 1759*. The French (de Castries) defeated the Prussians (Prince of Brunswick) who lost 1,600 men. *See* Bergen; Crefeld.

Camperdown (*Wars of French Revolution*) *11 October 1797*. A major English–Dutch naval battle. Admiral de Winter was taking sixteen ships to join a French fleet in a landing in Ireland. Admiral Duncan, also with sixteen ships, intercepted the Dutch, broke the Dutch line and captured eight ships including the flagship, *Vrijheid*. Casualties: British, 1,040; Dutch, 1,160 and 6,000 prisoners. *See* Cape St. Vincent.

Campo Santa (*War of Austrian Succession*) *8 February 1743*. The Spaniards under Count John de Gages were trying to join with the army of Prince de Conti but the Austrians (Marshal Traun) prevented this. The battle was tactically indecisive, but a strategic victory for the Austrians, as they forced the Spaniards to retreat to Naples. *See* Dettingen.

Campus Castorum (*Revolt of Vitellius*) *69*. 70,000 legionaries under Valens and Caecina had revolted and were attacked by the Imperial troops of Emperor Otho under Suetonius Paulinus. The Imperial troops had an initial advantage, but Suetonius did not exploit it and Otho deposed him from command. *See* Bedriacum.

Candia I (*Byzantine reconquest of Crete*) *960–1*. The Byzantines sent an expedition (Phocas) to Crete, then held by the Muslims. Phocas, who had 3,000 ships, began his campaign with an attack on Candia (Heraklion). After 6 months' continual fighting all Crete was in Byzantine hands by March 961. All Muslims were converted to Christianity, expelled or killed. *See* Adana; Melitine.

Candia II (*or Heraklion, Crete*) (*Canadian War*) *1648–69*. A remarkable 21-year defence. A small garrison of Venetians under Francesco Morosini defended the place so vigorously that the Turkish enemy lost 20,000 men in the first 6 months. From time to time the French and Venetians reinforced and reprovisioned Candia, but finally beaten by the relentless Turks, Morosini surrendered it on 27 September 1669. *See* Khotin I; Szentgotthárd.

Cannae, *Apulia, Italy* (*Second Punic War*) *2 August 216* BC. A major battle, between 90,000 Romans under Varro and 50,000 Carthaginians under Hannibal. The Romans were drawn up with the sea to their rear, but were broken by the

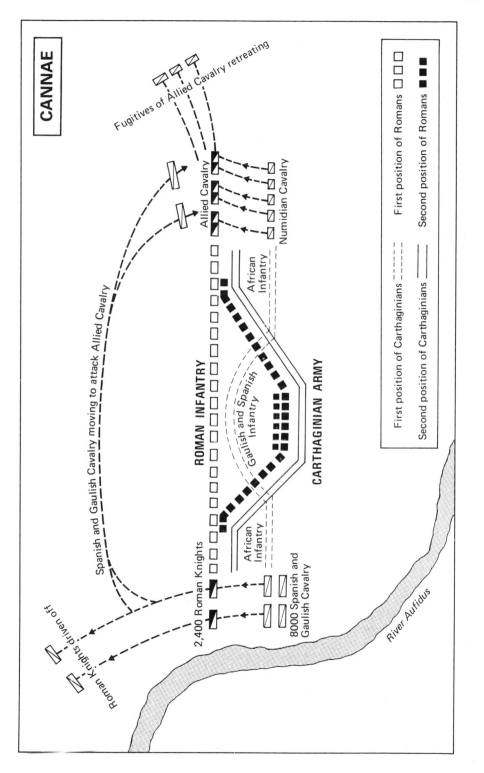

superior Carthaginian cavalry and over-whelmed by the infantry. The Romans, encircled and unable to flee, were savagely attacked and 50,000 were killed. The Carthaginians lost 6,000. The victory was a classic example of envelopment and of the principle of using masses of an army against fractions of the enemy. Cannae was Rome's greatest defeat. *See* Lake Trasimeno; Nola.

Cantigny (World War I) 28 May 1918. On the second day of the great German offensive along the Aisne the American 1st Division (Bullard) captured Cantigny, held by elements of the German Eighteenth Army (Hutier), and held against fierce counter-attacks. The Americans lost 1,607. *See* Belleau Wood.

Cape Bona (or Bon) (invasion of the Vandals) 468. The Roman fleet of 1,100 galleys and transports under Basilicus was lying at anchor when Genseric sent in a fleet of Vandal fireships and followed up with an attack. More than half the Roman ships were destroyed. *See* Hippo.

Cape Esperance (World War II) 11 October 1942. This naval engagement was the first time in the Pacific war that the Americans successfully attacked the Japanese navy. In a confused action, Rear Admiral Scott sank one cruiser and a destroyer and damaged others. Two U.S. ships were damaged, mostly by fire from other American vessels. The battle was not the "great victory" claimed by the Americans at the time. *See* Guadalcanal.

Cape Finisterre I (War of Austrian Succession) 3 May 1747. A British fleet of sixteen ships commanded by Admiral Anson soundly defeated a French fleet of thirty-eight under Admiral de la Jonquiere; the French lost ten ships and 3,000 prisoners. *See* Louisburg I; Toulon II.

Cape Finisterre II 14 October 1747. Admiral Hawke's ships attacked a French fleet of nine (Admiral de Letendeur). The

British lost 598 men, the French four ships and about 2,500 men. *See* Finisterre I; Maastricht III.

Cape Finisterre III (Napoleonic Wars) 22 July 1805. Admiral Villeneuve was bringing a combined Franco–Spanish fleet of twenty from the West Indies. Sir Robert Calder attacked him and captured two ships, but fogs and weak winds prevented him from following up. Tried by court-martial, he was unjustly censured. Casualties: British, 183; French, 149 killed, 327 wounded. *See* Copenhagen; Trafalgar.

Cape Henry (American War of Independence) 16 March 1781. An indecisive battle between a British fleet, eleven ships, under Vice-Admiral Arbuthnot and a French squadron of twelve. *See* Brooklyn.

Cape Passaro (or Battle of Messina Straits) (War of Quadruple Independence) 31 July 1718. Admiral Sir George Byng with twenty-one ships attacked the Spanish fleet, twenty-nine ships, of Don Antonio Casteneta. In a severe fight Byng captured or destroyed fifteen Spanish ships and Casteneta was killed. This naval engagement was the only battle of the war.

Cape St. Vincent (Wars of French Revolution) 14 February 1797. Sir John Jervis with his fifteen ships of the line and five frigates gave battle to twenty-six Spanish ships of the line and twelve frigates. The Spaniards were badly beaten, losing four ships and having most of the others battered. Losses in men were heavy; 3,000 were captured. The British lost 74 killed and 227 wounded. Jervis was created Lord St. Vincent. *See* Camperdown.

Cape Town I (French Revolutionary Wars) June 1795. Holland owned the Cape of Good Hope but Holland was under French occupation so Britain considered Dutch possessions as hostile.

Major-General Craig captured Cape Town and thus the whole Cape. *See* Buenos Aires.

Cape Town II (*Napoleonic Wars*) 8 January 1806. Cape Town had been restored to the Dutch by the Treaty of Amiens. In 1805, on renewal of war against France and with The Netherlands under French control, Britain sent Sir David Baird and 6,000 troops to South Africa. Landing at Saldanha Bay on 8 January, Baird beat back French and Dutch troops and pressed on to capture Cape Town.

Caporetto, Italy (*World War I*) 24 October–12 November 1917. The pivot battle of the whole Austrian–Italian campaign, fought between the Austrians (von Bojna, von Hotzendorf, von Straussenberg) and the Italians (Cadorna, Capello, Caviglia who were later replaced by Diaz and Badoglio). The first 3 weeks, on a front of 180 miles, was all disaster and confusion for the Italians until, on 10 November, they made a stand on the Piave. British and French corps were now supporting them against the Austrian–German forces of fifty-five divisions with 4,000 guns and 500 aircraft. The Italian strength was thirty divisions, with another twenty being reformed in the rear. Hardly any artillery had been brought into action and the Italian air force had been driven out of the skies. The front was now 75 miles.

On 12 November the Austrian–German forces began a new offensive, with aid from an Austrian fleet which bombarded Italian batteries and drove Italian warships from Venice. In the month to 20 November the Italians lost 400,000 men, including 350,000 taken prisoner; further major losses occurred in the so-called "Christmas Battle". French counter-attacks stemmed the enemy advance. On 15 June the Austrians launched another major attack and much confused fighting followed, including multiple infantry raids — eight by the British. All this culminated in the Battle of Vittorio Veneto,

q.v. The casualties for Caporetto, one of the heaviest defeats of the war, are unreliable, but each side probably suffered something like 400,000 casualties excluding prisoners. *See* Piave.

Caprysema (*First Messenian War*) 743 BC. The Spartans and Corinthians against the Messenians and their allies from other Peloponnesian states under Cristomenes. The Spartans were routed. *See* Cecryphalae.

Capua (*Second Punic War*) 212 BC. Fulvius and Appius Claudius besieged Carthaginian-held Capua with 60,000 Romans, who formed a double wall or circumvallation round the city. The garrison vainly attacked the Romans from within and Hannibal attacked from without. Hannibal marched on Rome in an attempt to draw the besiegers away, and when this failed the city soon surrendered. *See* Metaurus.

Carabobo, *Venezuela* (*Colombian War of Independence*) 14 June 1821. Simon Bolivar led 8,000 Colombian patriots to victory against 4,000 Spanish Royalists (La Torre). Only 400 Royalists reached Porto Cabello, and the battle determined the independence of Colombia. *See* Boyacá.

Caracas (*Colombian War of Independence*) 6 August 1813. A victory for the Colombian patriots (Bolivar) against the Spanish Royalists.

Caraguatay (*War of the Triple Alliance or Lopez War*) 10 August 1869. After another bloody fight the Brazilians (a member of the alliance) defeated the Paraguayans led by their dictator, Francisco Lopez).

Carberry Hill (*Scottish Rebellion against Mary*) 15 June 1567. A rebel force led by Scottish nobles who objected to Mary's third marriage (to Bothwell) met and defeated the royal army at Carberry Hill, east of Edinburgh. Mary was taken prisoner, forced to dismiss Bothwell and to agree to abdicate in favour of her son, the future James VI. *See* Langside; Pink.

Carbiesdale, *north Scotland* (*English Civil War*) *27 April 1650*. An allied force of 1,000 Orkney Royalists and 500 Swedish mercenaries (Duke of Montrose) met a small Parliamentary force (Colonel Strachan). The Parliamentary cavalry broke the Royalist lines, only the Swedes standing firm. The Parliamentarians killed or wounded 396 for a loss of only two men wounded. This was Montrose's last fight; he was captured soon after. *See* Dunbar II; Philiphaugh.

Carchemich (*Babylonian–Egyptian Wars*) *605 BC*. The beginning of the military career of Nebuchadnezzar. With his Chaldean army he crushingly defeated the Egyptians on the banks of the Euphrates. *See* Jerusalem; Megiddo.

Carenage Bay, *St. Lucia* (*American War of Independence*) *4 June 1778*. An English combined force (Admiral Barrington and General Meadows) defeated the French (Comte d'Estaing) and captured the island.

Carham (*Scottish Nationalist Wars*) *1016*. Malcolm II of Scotland, having already beaten Danish invaders, came into conflict with the Northumbrians and defeated their army (Uhtred) on the Tweed River. The victory ensured Scottish possession of the Central Lowlands. *See* Dunsinane; Mortlack.

Carigat. *See* Arikera.

Carlisle (*1745 Rebellion*) *November 1745*. The Young Pretender and his Jacobites besieged the town on 9 November and attacked it on 13 November. The defenders — the Cumberland and Westmoreland militia under Colonel Durand — surrendered the following day. *See* Culloden; Prestopans.

Carnoul, *near Delhi* (*Persian invasion of India*) *1739*. The Persians (Nadir Shah) attacked the Mogul army of levies led by Emperor Mohammed Shah and his grand vizier, Nizam-ul-Mulk, defeating them completely and sacking Delhi; it was said that the Persians took away jewels and coin valued at £30,000,000. *See* Panipat III.

Carpi (*War of Spanish Succession*) *July 1701*. A notable victory by the Imperialists (Prince Eugene) over the French Army of Lombardy (Marshal Catinat). *See* Cremona III.

Carrhae I, *northern Mesopotamia* (*Wars of the First Triumvirate*) *53 BC*. Crassus, one of the three triumvirs (the others were Julius Caesar and Pompey), was called to intervene in a major quarrel among the Parthians. At Carrhae (Haran) Crassus with 6,000 men gave battle to a Parthian army of 25,000, under Orodes I. The Parthian horsemen harassed the Roman legionaries until they pursued the cavalry and thus lost formation — their principal defence against cavalry. The Parthians cut the Romans to pieces, killing 5,500 of them. Crassus was captured and executed. Pompey became virtual dictator of Rome. *See* Alesia; Rubicon River.

Carrhae II (*Roman Empire's Persian Wars*) *296*. With Persia belligerent, the Emperor Diocletian sent Galerius to the east. His legions met the Persians (Narses) in battle at Carrhae and suffered a severe defeat. Galerius survived, built up his army, and the following year in a surprise night attack virtually wiped out Narses' Persians. *See* Edessa I; Singara; Verona.

Carrical (*or Nogapatam*) *east coast of India* (*Seven Years' War*) *3 August 1758*. A British squadron (Admiral Pococke) forced a French fleet (Comte d'Ache) to withdraw, but could not pursue and the French escaped to Pondicherry, q.v.

Carrickfergus, *northern Ireland* (*American Revolution*) *24 April 1778*. The first defeat of a British warship by an American naval vessel. Captain John Paul Jones, in *Ranger*, defeated H.M.S. *Drake* off Carrickfergus. *See* Flamborough Head.

Carrizal (*American expedition in Mexico*) *21 June 1916*. An American column under General Pershing was sent into Mexico to bring to justice the guerrilla leader Francisco (Pancho) Villa who had raided towns in New Mexico. At Carrizal, 85 miles south of Ciudad Juarez, Pershing routed a force of Mexican regulars and continuing his advance broke up Villa's bandit army. *See* Columbus.

Carso Plateau (*World War I*) *2 May 1915–10 September 1917*. Italian and Austrian forces attacked and counterattacked each other many times in and around the Carso, but throughout the fighting the Italians made the greater gains, taking nearly 50,000 prisoners. The most important features of the protracted, intermittent battle were the Italian capture of Carso Plateau, 19 July 1915; San Michele, 26 July 1915; defeat of the last Austrian counter-attack, 10 September 1917. *See* Assiago; Isonzo; Piave.

Carthage I, *North Africa* (*Third Punic War*) *149–146 BC*. A Roman consular army (Manius Manilius) besieged the city with the help of a fleet (Censorinus). The Carthaginian army (Hasdrubal, Hannibal's brother) camped outside the walls and prevent the Roman siege from being effective until Scipio Aemilianus, then a military tribune, was given some authority. In 148 BC Scipio was made consul, appointed to command and completely blockaded the city. Two years later it was captured and burnt. *See* Numantia; Zama.

Carthage II (*or Ad Decium*) (*reconquest of North Africa from the Vandals*) *14 September 533*. Fought outside Carthage between 30,000 Vandals (Gelimer) and about 16,000 Romans (Belisarius). Gelimer, dividing his army into three, led one division in an attack on the main Roman force, but the Vandal vanguard (Ammatus) attacked prematurely and was routed. Gelimer attacked the Romans who took up the pursuit, but Belisarius arrived and drove off the Vandals, who were defeated. *See* Constantinople; Rome.

Carthage III (*Muslim conquest of North Africa*) *698*. A fierce assault by Arab Muslims (Hasan ibn No'man) overwhelmed the Byzantine garrison of the great city of Carthage and with this victory virtually gained control of all North Africa. *See* Rio Barbate; Tripoli I.

Carthage IV (*Charles's expedition to Tunisia*) *1280*. Charles I of the Two Sicilies — Naples and Sicily — to expand his empire and authority engaged the Moors then occupying Carthage. After pretending flight he defeated them in a brilliant cavalry manoeuvre. *See* Messina; Tunis.

Carthagena, *Colombia* (*War of Austrian Succession*) *March–April 1741*. A British fleet under Admiral Vernon blockaded the port on 9 March and later attacked the forts but was unsuccessful, and having lost 3,000 men withdrew on 9 April.

Casale, *Piedmont* (*Wars of Louis XIV*) *April 1640*. 20,000 Spaniards were besieging Casale, when 10,000 French (Harcourt) broke their lines and routed them. The Spaniards lost 3,000 killed or wounded, 800 prisoners and 18 guns.

Casilinum, *modern Capua* (*Second Frank invasion of Italy*) *554*. 30,000 Franks and Allemanni under Buccelin attacked 18,000 Byzantine–Roman troops led by Narses, who is said to have exterminated the Franks while losing only 80 of his own men. *See* Taginae.

Cassano d'Adda, *near Milan (War of Spanish Succession) 16 August 1705.* Eugene of Savoy, with assistance from Victor Amadeus II, Duke of Savoy, struck at the French lines at Cassano on the Adda River. They made some initial gains, but Marshal Louis Joseph, Duc de Vendôme, arrived hurriedly to take over command of the French from his less able brother, Philippe de Vendôme. Each side lost several thousand men in this drawn conflict. *See* Blenheim; Luzzara; Turin.

Cassel, *northern France (French–Flemish Wars) August 1328.* A battle between the French mounted knights and the Flemish pikemen and infantry, who could not stand their ground against the furious cavalry attacks; thousands were ridden down and killed, including the Flemish leader, Nicolas Zannequin. *See* Mons-en-Pévèle.

Cassino *(or Monastery Hill) (World War II) January–May 1944.* Monte Cassino, the key point of the Gustav Line, was a mountain feature of 1,700 feet, crowned by a Benedictine monastery and dominating the 7-mile wide Liri Valley through which ran Route 6, the only practicable highway leading to Rome and its airfields. The Germans (Field Marshal Kesselring and General von Senger) had made it into an immensely strong fortress, which the Allied commanders — Generals Alexander (British) and Clark (U.S.) — were compelled to take. The first Allied shells fell on Cassino on 15 January 1944; the main battle opened when the 36th (Texas) Division of the U.S. Army splashed through flooded meadows, thickly sown with mines to the Rapido River. According to an American estimate it was "the biggest disaster to American arms since Pearl Harbour". In an action of less than 48 hours the 36th had 1,681 casualties. Other American assaults, helped by French troops (General Juin), gained little ground, though the American 34th Division fought with remarkable gallantry, losing

2,200 men. The Americans made their last attempts on 8–11 February. The 1st New Zealand Corps — comprising the New Zealand Division and the 4th Indian Division — under General Freyberg took up the assault. Two of the finest fighting divisions of the war, they were facing the 1st Parachute Division, possibly the outstanding formation of the German army (Lieutenant-General Richard Heidrich). The 15th and 90th Panzer Grenadier Divisions, the 5th Mountain and 71st Infantry, all took their turn defending Cassino. The hill was air-bombed and the first New Zealand–Indian attack, which began on 15 February, was beaten back. The next operation — sometimes called the second New Zealand Battle of Cassino — began on 15 March after a massive air and artillery bombardment. Substantial gains were made, but the Germans still held Monastery Hill and the New Zealanders were withdrawn by 13 April, having lost 206 men killed, 1,085 wounded and 101 missing. The fourth and last battle of Cassino was General Alexander's masterpiece, and he fought it with much greater numbers, using the Fifth and Eighth Armies and much deception as to his intentions. American units, two Canadian Divisions, the French Corps and the Polish Corps (General Anders) were also involved. With this powerful force Alexander began the battle on 11 May, having available 1,600 guns, 2,000 tanks and the entire strength of the Mediterranean air forces of more than 3,000 aircraft. By the morning of 18 May, after ferocious infantry fighting, the Germans had been pushed out; the II Polish Corps finally took Cassino Hill. The Gustav Line was smashed and the Allies moved on to the Adolph Hitler Line (later the Dora), the last chain of German defences before Rome.

Overall, in 24 days of fighting, impregnable Cassino fell, two German armies were defeated, 20,000 prisoners were taken, three defence lines were smashed and vast quantities of German material were destroyed. But Allied casualties in the four battles amounted to about

21,000, including 4,100 killed in action. *See* Anzio; Gothic Line; Salerno.

Castalla I (*Peninsular War*) *21 June 1812*. Part of a larger action between the British (Wellington) and the French (Marmont). The British won, but the tactical advantage lay with the French. *See* Salamanca.

Castalla II (*Peninsular War*) *13 April 1813*. An Allied force of 17,000 (Sir John Murray) defeated 15,000 French (Suchet). Casualties: Allies, 600; Murray claimed 3,000 enemy casualties, but the French admitted only 800. *See* Vittoria.

Castelfidardo (*Italian Wars of Independence*) *18 September 1860*. A one-sided battle between the Sardinians, 40,000 strong under Cialdini, and 4,000 Papal troops (General La Moriciere). After the action La Moriciere had only 300 men. *See* Gaeta; Milazza.

Castelnaudry, *southern France* (*French Civil Wars*) *1 September 1632*. Louis XIII's defeat of rebel nobles under Duc de Montmorenci, who was captured. *See* La Rochelle.

Castiglione delle Stiviere, *north Italy* I (*War of Spanish Succession*) *8 September 1706*. The Prince of Hesse, besieging Castiglione, was attacked by the French (General de Medavi) and lost 8,000 men killed, wounded or missing. *See* Turin.

Castiglione della Stiviere II (*Napoleon's Italian campaigns*) *5 August 1796*. Napoleon, with 25,000 men, advanced on Lonato while Augereau moved on Castiglione, both held by the Austrians (Wurmser). The Austrian army was cut in two. One part retreated to the Mincio, but the other was roughly handled by Guyeaux and Junot and lost 3,000 prisoners. Napoleon inflicted 2,000 casualties on the Austrians near Castiglione and was driven back towards Mantua. At Lonato next day the Aus-

trians urged Napoleon, who had only 12,000 troops, to surrender, but he deceived the Austrians into thinking he was in the middle of the main French army and *they* surrendered. *See* Lonato; Mantua.

Castillejos (*Spanish–Moroccan War*) *1 January 1860*. The advance guard of the Spanish army (General Prim) opened the way to Tetuan by defeating, in a savage fight, a strong force of Moors. *See* Guad-el-Ras.

Castillon (*Hundred Years' War*) *17 July 1453*. The last battle of the war. The English under the Earl of Shrewsbury attacked the French besieging Castillon, but the French made a successful flank attack and broke the English formations, Shrewsbury being killed. In effect, this English reverse gave Bordeaux to the French. *See* Formigny; Guinegate.

Catalca Line (*First Balkan War*) *17–18 November 1912*. This Turkish defensive line, from the Black Sea to the Sea of Marmara, held firm against the Bulgarian attack designed to capture the Turkish city of Constantinople. *See* Lüleburgaz.

Catana (*Second Carthaginian invasion of Sicily*) *387 BC*. A vast Carthaginian fleet overwhelmed 200 Syracusan galleys, an inevitable defeat aggravated by poor admiralship of Leptines. The Carthaginians laid siege to Syracuse, q.v.

Caucasus Campaign (*World War II*) *1942–3*. The attempt by Hitler to reach Stalingrad and the Caucusus oilfields, although the first move came from the Russians, on 12 May, when Timoshenko attacked Kharkov. By 31 May the Germans had recovered all lost ground and had taken 80,000 prisoners. The main German thrust was launched by von Kleist from near Kharkov; it crossed the Don on 22 July, Rostov falling on 27 July. Three Panzer columns broke out to the south, one advancing 200 miles, the others 150. Supply problems slowed the advance, and the demands for men and material to be sent to Stalingrad weakened Kleist. The Russians stabilized the front by 18 November and in January, with large forces in danger of being cut off, the Germans began their retreat. Successfully managed, it left few Germans in Russian hands. Kharkov fell to the Russians on 16 February 1943, but on 15 March the Germans again took it. Neither side could make progress on the thawing icy steppes, and this ended the campaign. *See* Crimea; Stalingrad; Ukraine.

Caudine Forks *later Forchia d'Arpaia (Second Samnite War) 322 BC.* Four Roman legions (Calvinus and Postumius) were trapped by the Sabines (Pontius) in a narrow pass at Caudium. They fought till nightfall, but next day, facing annihilation, the survivors surrendered. *See* Bovanium; Trifanum.

Cawnpore I *(Indian Mutiny) June 1857.* The mutineers (Nana Sahib) invested Cawnpore Residency on 6 June. The tiny garrison, nominally under General Wheeler but effectively under Captain Moore, held out until 24 June. Promised safe conduct to Allahabad, Wheeler surrendered his people, who were fired on as they took to the boats on the Ganges. The survivors, mostly women and children, were butchered on the orders of Nana Sahib. Despite widespread search after the mutiny, this man was never found. *See* Delhi II.

Cawnpore II *(Indian Mutiny) 6 December 1857.* Sir Colin Campbell routed the 25,000 mutineers and British cavalry pursued them for 14 miles, taking thirty-two of their thirty-six guns and inflicting heavy casualties. The British lost 99. *See* Jhansi; Lucknow.

Cecryphalea *(Third messenian War) 458 BC.* A naval action in which the Athenians beat the Peloponnesians by setting fire to most of their ships.

Cedar Creek *(American Civil War)*

17 October 1864. General Early led 10,000 Confederates, under cover of a fog, in an attack on General Sheridan's 40,000 Federals. He turned Sheridan's right flank and captured 18 guns, but Sheridan rallied his right wing and counter-attacked the Confederates as they were plundering the Federals' camp. The Federals lost 5,685 men to the Confederates' 3,000, but Sheridan won the battle and took twenty-two guns, and regained his own lost eighteen. *See* Fisher's Hill; Petersburg.

Cedar Mountain *(American Civil War) 9 August 1862.* 20,000 Federals (General Pope) attacked strong Confederate positions (Jackson) and were repeatedly repulsed, until at night they withdrew, having lost 2,800 killed, wounded or missing. The Confederates lost 900. *See* Bull Run II; Cross Keys; Port Republic.

Cepeda *(Argentine Civil War) 23 October 1859.* Troops of the Argentine Confederation under Urquiza attacked those of the state of Buenos Aires, under Mitre. Urquiza's victory led to Buenos Aires joining the Confederation. *See* Monte Caseros.

Cephisus, *Thessaly 1397.* 9,500 Catalans — known as the "Great Band" — protected their camp by flooding the country around it. Walter de Brienne, Duke of Athens, had 15,000 men and sent his cavalry in to the attack. Caught in the morass, they were hacked to pieces, de Brienne himself being killed.

Cerignola, *near Naples (French–Spanish War over Naples) 26 April 1503.* After the Battle of Barletta, q.v., the Spanish under Gonsalvo de Cordóba had been reinforced by 6,000 men. Cordóba marched out of Barletta and took a hillside position behind a ditch and palisade. The French heavy cavalry and Swiss pikemen attacked, but were repulsed in confusion by the accurate fire of the Spanish arquebusiers behind the palisade. The Spanish infantry counter-attacked and the French were routed; their leader, Duc de Nemours, was killed. This was probably the first battle in history won by gunpowder small arms. *See* Garigliano River.

Cerisolles (*Wars of Charles V*) 25 May 1544. The French (Francois de Bourbon) defeated the Imperialists (de Gast). *See* Pavia IV; Rebec.

Cerro-Gordo (*American–Mexican War*) 18 April 1847. In the mountain pass of Cerro Gordo, General Winfield Scott with his 8,500 Americans found his advance blocked by General Santa Anna, who commanded 12,000 Mexican regulars. Scott had planned an enveloping attack, but another general made a premature attack on 17 April and Scott was forced to make his own attack next day. In vicious fighting the Americans forced the pass. Casualties: American, 63 killed, 337 wounded; Mexican, 204 officers and 2,837 taken prisoner and about 700 casualties. In August Scott took Churubusco, another strongpoint. *See* Contreras-Churubusco; Vera Cruz.

Český-Brod (*or Lipan*) near Prague (*Hussite Civil Wars*) 30 May 1434. The decisive battle between the Hussites and the Taborite–Ultraquist allies for control of Bohemia. At least 18,000 dead were left on the field and Bohemia, having lost so heavily, had to accept domination by Sigismund, who also ruled the Holy Roman Empire and Hungary. *See* Usti nad Laben.

Ceşme (*Turkish–Russian Wars*) 5 July 1770. When Turkey declared war on Russia, Catherine the Great sent fifty ships (Orlov) into the Mediterranean where, at Ceşme, west of Smyrna, they destroyed the larger Turkish fleet. The battle is notable for the brilliant naval leadership of Sir Samuel Greig, a Scot in Russian service. *See* Focsani.

Ceuta (*Portuguese African campaign*) 24 August 1415. John I led an expedition against the Muslim trading centre of Ceuta, on the south side of Gibraltar. Its capture encouraged John to build an empire in Africa. *See* Aljubarrota.

Ceylon (*World War II*) 1942. On 5 April Japanese aircraft bombed Colombo, causing damage but losing twenty-one aircraft; the British lost twenty-five aircraft. The same day H.M.S. *Dorsetshire* and *Cornwall* were sunk south of Ceylon. On 6 April the Japanese lost fifteen aircraft in bombing Trincomalee and sinking two ships. *See* Burma; Java Sea; Madagascar.

Chacabuco (*Chilean War of Independence*) 12 February 1817. A complete victory for the Chileans (San Martin) against the Spanish royalists. *See* Maipo River; Rancagua.

Chad Civil War 1968–84. This war was fought between Arab guerrillas of the Chad National Liberation Front (FROLINAT) against the dominantly negro government in the south. About 2,500 French troops became involved in 1968 following a request for help by the Chad government. In 1977 Libya began to aid the rebels. Civil war broke out afresh in March 1980 between the armed forces of the north (Hussein Habre) and the popular armed forces (Goukouni Queddei). Libyan troops captured the capital, N'Djamena, for Goukouni in December 1980. Fighting reached its peak in summer 1983, with Libya heavily aiding the rebels and France and the United States backing the government. More than 18,000 Chadian fighters were killed between 1968 and 1984, 50 French troops and 250 Libyans.

Chaeronea I (*Macedonian conquests*) 338 BC. A major battle between 32,000 Macedonians (Philip) and 31,000 Athenians and Thebans (Chares and Theagenes, respectively). Philip's horsemen were led by Alexander (the Great), then only 18. Philip, reinforcing his troops facing the

Athenians, considered the Thebans the weaker part of the allied force and sent his heavy cavalry against them. The horsemen broke the Theban ranks and then attacked the Athenians in flank and rear. The rout was complete, except for the fight to the death of the Theban "Sacred Band". Casualties: Athenians, 6,000 killed, 2,000 prisoners; Thebans, virtually annihilated. *See* Mantinea; Thebes.

Chaeronea II (*First Mithridatic War*) 86 BC. The Roman General Lucius Sulla with about 30,000 men faced a battle against two Mithridatic–Greek armies of 110,000 men and 90 chariots under Archelaus and Aristion. Sulla dug trenches to protect his flanks against envelopment and erected palisades along his front. The Mithridatic cavalry charged and were easily repulsed by the Roman legions, formed into squares. Then the chariots were sent against Sulla. The chariot horses, maddened by arrows and javelins, bolted back through the Greek phalanx, causing confusion. Sulla's instant counter-attack routed the Greek armies. Chaeronea is the first known offensive use of field fortifications. *See* Orchomenus.

Chalcedon, *opposite Byzantium* (*Third Mithridatic War*) 74 BC. A victory for the Pontic fleet, which first drove the Roman fleet (Rutilius Nudo) into harbour and then broke the harbour boom protecting them. *See* Cabria.

Chalchuapa, *near Santiago* (*Chilean War of Independence*) 12 February 1817. After a march across the Andes with 6,000 men, San Martin and O'Higgins defeated the Spanish army in a battle as clever as it was courageous. The victory led directly to Chilean independence.

Chaldiran, *east of the Euphrates* (*Turkish invasion of Persia*) 23 August 1514. The Turks, led by Selim the Grim, Sultan of the Ottoman Turks, overwhelmed the massive Persian cavalry of Shah Ismail I with heavy fire from weapons then new to the Turks — cannons and handguns. Selim occupied much territory. *See* Marj-Dabik.

Chalgrove Field, *Oxford* (*English Civil War*) 18 June 1643. A cavalry skirmish between the Royalists (Prince Rupert) and Parliamentarians, in which their leader, John Hampden, was killed. *See* Adwalton Moor; Stratton.

Chalons-sur-Marne I (*Revolt of the Legions of Aquitaine*) 271. Tetricus, having led certain legions into revolt, came to private terms with the Emperor Aurelian and betrayed his followers, so disposing his units that Aurelian had every advantage. Tetricus then deserted, leaving the rebels to be cut to pieces. *See* Argentoratum.

Chalons-sur-Marne II (*invasion of the Alemanni*) July 366. After a day-long engagement the Romans (Jovinus) routed the Alemanni, who lost 6,000 killed and 4,000 prisoners. The Romans lost 1,200. *See* Argentoratum.

Chalons-sur-Marne III (*invasion of the Huns*) 451. Between the Huns (Attila) and the Romans and Visigoths (Actius and Theodoric, respectively). The allies' right and centre held firm under Attila's attack while their left, in a remarkable charge, routed the Huns' right, though Theodoric was killed. Attila withdrew and Actius failed to pursue him. *See* Hippo Regius; Rome.

Chalons-sur-Marne IV, *often called The "Little" Battle of Chalons* 1274. During a tournament the life of Edward I of England was in danger following foul play. This led to a serious fight between the British and French knights, many of whom were killed.

Champagne Campaigns (*World War I*). Between 20 December and 17 March 1915 the French lost many soldiers in vain attacks against German machine-guns. On 25 September 1915 Joffre launched another attack under Petain and de Cary and by 6 November had captured 25,000 Germans and 150 guns — at a cost to themselves of 145,000 casualties. Both sides held their original positions. Between 15 and 17 July 1918 the Germans went on the offensive, crossing the Marne. *See* Artois-Loos; Marne River II.

Champ-aubert-Montmirail (*Napoleonic Wars*) 10 February 1814. Blucher was advancing on Paris with three divisions when Napoleon, by an astonishing forced march, attacked the second section (Alsusieff), dispersing it and taking 2,000 prisoners and all its guns. Next day he defeated Sachen's advance guard, 20,000 men, at Montmirail, inflicting 6,000 casualties and forcing him to retire. On 13 February he encountered General Yorck with 30,000 Russians and Prussians at Chateau Thierry, took 3,000 prisoners and stopped Yorck. On 14 February Napoleon turned on Blucher, who lost 3,000 killed, wounded and prisoners but retired in good order. This three-fold victory by a flank march was one of Napoleon's greatest achievements. *See* La Rothière; Montereau.

Champlain, Lake (*British–American War of 1812–14*) 11 September 1814. A remarkable battle won by ships at anchor. The American naval commander on Lake Champlain (Captain Macdonough) had deployed his fourteen ships in a narrow channel into which sailed the sixteen British ships commanded by Captain Downie. After a battle of 2 hours Macdonough up-anchored his flagship, *Saratoga*, and gave battle to Downie's flagship, *Confiance*. Downie struck his flag and four British ships were captured or destroyed. *See* Bladensburg; Fort McHenry.

Chancellorsville (*American Civil War*) 2–4 May 1863. Between 120,000 Federals (Hooker) and 53,000 Confederates (Lee). On 2 May Lee sent half his force under Jackson to turn Hooker's

right and he routed the Federal XI Corps. In the dark a South Carolina regiment (Confederates) fired by mistake at Jackson's staff and Jackson himself was mortally wounded. On 3 May the Confederates had further success and on 4 May the Federals were driven off, Hooker being forced to cross the Rappahannock River. Casualties: Confederates, 10,000; Federals, about 18,000, including 7,650 prisoners. Considering the disparity of numbers, the Confederate success was startling. *See* Brandy Station; Fredericksburg.

Chanda (*Third British–Mahratta War*) 9–11 May 1818. Colonel Adams besieged Chanda, chief stronghold of the Rajah of Nagpur, on 9 May. After a 2-day bombardment the fort was taken by storm, the garrison of 3,000 losing 500 killed. *See* Kirkee.

Chandernagore (*Seven Years' War*) March 1757. Robert Clive, with 2,000 East India Company troops, besieged the fort on 14 March. On 19 March three British ships (Admiral Watson) arrived and on 25 March a combined attack resulted in the capture of the fort and its garrison — 600 French and 300 sepoys. *See* Arcot; Madras.

Chantilly (*American Civil War*) 1 September 1862. The last action of the second Battle of Bull Run; Lee drove the Federals back to Washington. *See* Bull Run II.

Chapultepec (*American–Mexican War*) 13 September 1847. The capture of Mexico City by General Winfield Scott. With 7,200 men he outmanoeuvred and outfought Santa Anna's 16,000 troops. The American troops had to fight their way up steep slopes and then to smash through the city's walls with picks. American casualties were 159 killed, 703 wounded. *See* Contreras-Churubusco; Molino del Rey.

Charasia (*Second British–Afghan War*) 6 October 1879. Sir Frederick

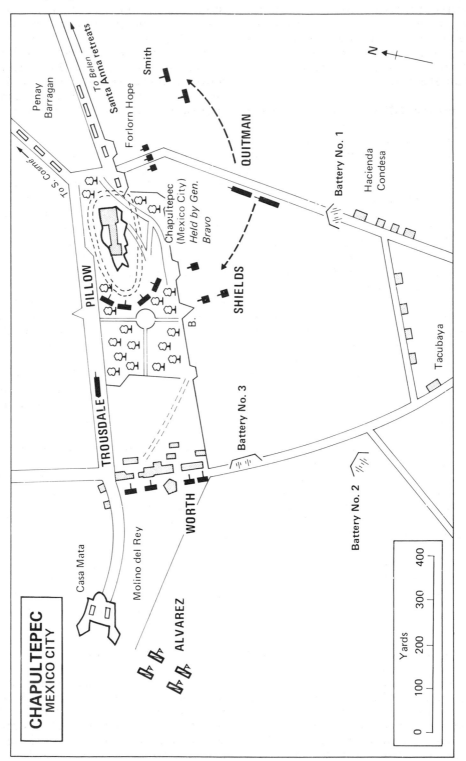

CHAPULTEPEC
MEXICO CITY

Roberts with 7,500 men and twenty-two guns defeated a force of Afghans and Ghilzais, 8,000-strong, who were threatening an approaching convoy. He then occupied Kabul. *See* Kandahar; Maiwand; Sherpur.

Charenton (*War of the Fronde*) 8 February 1649. A victory for the Great Conde, whose 8,000 Royal troops defeated those of the Paris Parliament, the Frondeurs (Clauleu). The Frondeurs lost many killed, including their commander and 100 other officers. *See* Palais Gallien; Porte St. Antoine.

Charleston I (*American Revolution*) 28 June 1776. The attack by Admiral Sir Peter Parker to knock out an island fort (Colonel Moultrie) which protected Charleston, South Carolina. In a day-long duel with the fort's twenty-one guns, Parker had three of his nine ships crippled and suffered 195 casualties to the Americans thirty-seven. The ships withdrew at night. *See* Morres Creek Bridge; Savannah I.

Charleston II (*American Revolution*) 14 April–12 May 1780. General Benjamin Lincoln had 5,250 men to hold the 3 miles of fortified lines protecting Charleston. On 14 April a British cavalry–infantry assault (Tarleton) destroyed the American post covering the line of communications with the north and by 8 May the British totally invested the city. On 12 May the Americans marched out and surrendered, leaving vast quantities of material for the British who had suffered only 265 casualties in winning their greatest victory of the war. *See* Savannah II; Waxhaw Creek.

Charleston III (*American Civil War*) April 1863–February 1865. The Federal fleet of nine iron-clads (Admiral Dupont) attacked Fort Sumter on 7 April but was damaged and repulsed, the defenders losing only two men. On 10–11 July a Federal land force attacked Fort Wagner and was beaten off. On 18 July

three brigades (General Seymour) suffered heavily in another abortive attack. On 5 September heavy bombardment drove the Confederates from Fort Wagner and Morris Island, but Fort Sumter proved impregnable and was blockaded. On 18 February 1865, as Sherman's army approached, the 9,000 garrison evacuated the city. *See* Fort Sumter.

Chateau Gaillard (*English–French Wars*) 1203–4. The chateau was a military fortress built by Richard I of England at Les Andelys on the Seine to protect his hold on Rouen. In September 1203 Philip II laid siege to the fort and in March 1204 it fell, leaving the British hold on Normandy very vulnerable. It was the outstanding event of the war.

Chateaubeuf-de-Raudon (*Hundred Years' War*) May–July 1380. An English garrison (Ros) stubbornly defended the town against the French led by the remarkable Bertrand du Guesclin, "the Eagle of Brittany". The English surrendered on 4 July, but du Guesclin died from fatigue and privation. *See* Auray; Margate; Montiel; Poitiers.

Chateaugay River (*British–American War*) 26 October 1813. A force of Canadian militia, about 3,500, held strong lines near Chateaugay which 7,000 Americans (General Hampton) stormed. They were repulsed with heavy loss. *See* Chryse.

Chateau Thierry (*World War I*) 1914–18. An intermittent scene of battle throughout the war until the final French capture on 21 July 1918. *See* Aisne River III, Champagne Campaigns.

Chatham. *See* Medway.

Chattanooga, *or Battle of Missionary Ridge* (*American Civil War*) 24–27 November 1863. Between 80,000 Federals (Grant) and the 64,000-strong Confederate Army of the West (Bragg). The Federals attacked Look Out Mountain in thick fog — the "Battle Above the Clouds" — and the next day, 25 November, broke Bragg's centre. Much of the combat on 26th and 27th was rearguard fighting. Casualties: Federals, 753 killed, 4,722 wounded, 349 missing; Confederates, 361 killed, 2,160 wounded, 4,000 prisoners, 40 guns and 7,000 rifles. *See* Chickamauga; Knoxville; Resaca.

Cheat Mountain, West Virginia (*American Civil War*) 10 September 1861. Lee's attack against Federal positions failed because of rough country and incompetent leadership by his brigade commanders. It was Lee's first action of the war. *See* Rich Mountain.

Chemin-des-Dames (*World War I*) 1914–18. Scene of some of the war's most bitter fighting and the arena of several major actions. On 9 September the French attacked and pushed back the Germans. In 1915–16 it was the scene of constant but indecisive fighting, mostly between the French and Germans. In April 1917 it was the area of the ill-fated Nivelle Offensive, in which the French lost 120,000 men in 5 days. On 14 July 1917 a great artillery battle raged over Chemin-des-Dames. On 27 May 1918 the Germans attacked and broke through to the Marne. The Kaiser viewed the battlefield from this place, but by 11 October the Germans had evacuated it. More than 100,000 men are believed to have been killed in and around Chemin-des-Dames. *See* Champagne; Marne River III.

Chemnitz (*Thirty Years' War*) 14 April 1639. The Swedish army of Marshal Baner had been reinforced and now Baner advanced into Saxony, pushing the Austrian Catholic army of General Gallas before him. When he crossed the Elbe, John George, Elector of Saxony, was waiting for him at Chemnitz with a Saxon–Austrian army. With a tactical combination of cavalry, artillery and infantry learnt from the great Gustavus Adolphus, Baner defeated John George and overran western Saxony. *See* Breisach.

Che-mul-Pho (*Russian–Japanese War*) 8 February 1904. A Japanese squadron was convoying troopships towards a landing, which a Russian cruiser and gunboat opposed. The Russians blew up the cruiser to avoid capture and the gunboat was destroyed. *See* Port Arthur.

Cheriton (*English Civil War*) 29 March 1644. The Parliamentarians (Waller) defeated the Royalists (Lord Firth), thus preventing a Royalist incursion into Kent and Sussex. *See* Alresford.

Chernaya River (*Crimean War*) 16 August 1855. Prince Mikhail Gorshakov attacked the Allied line east of Sebastapol, in an attempt to break out of the city. They were repulsed by the British, French and Piedmontese who had 1,200 casualties to the Russians 5,000. *See* Sebastopol.

Chesapeake Capes (*American Revolution*) 30 August 1781. A naval battle which had important military results. The Comte de Grasse, who was assisting Washington, led his fleet of twenty-four ships into Chesapeake Bay on 30 August. When a British fleet (Admiral Graves) arrived off the capes Grasse bested the British in a 2-hour battle. After 3 days of manoeuvring Graves had to withdraw when further French naval units arrived. Lord Cornwallis was now bottled up in Virginia without hope of naval support. *See* Yorktown I.

Chesapeake vs. Shannon (*British–American War of 1812–14*) 1 June 1813. In a 15-minute action, experienced British gunners of H.M.S. *Shannon* (Philip Broke), with a crew of 330 and thirty-eight guns, defeated the U.S.S. *Chesapeake* (James Lawrence), of thirty-eight guns, crew of 379, off Boston. The American ship was taken as a prize into Halifax. Casualties: American, 146 killed or wounded; British, 83.

Chester (*Anglo-Saxon conquest of Britain*) 615. King Aethelfrith, aggressive monarch of the Anglo-Saxon kingdom of Northumbria, was conquering westwards and in 615 reached the River Dee at Chester. Here Solomon, of the Welsh kingdom of Powys, blocked his path with a force of Britons. The Northumbrians attacked and routed Solomon's army and pushed on to the Irish Sea. *See* Degsastan; Dyrham.

Chesterfield, *Derbyshire* (*Second Barons' War*) *15 May 1266*. The Earl of Derby rallied an army of knights in an attempt to impose their power on Henry III despite their defeat at Evesham in 1265. Henry of Amaine, commanding the Royalist army, overwhelmed the knights and the war ended. *See* Ely II; Evesham.

Chetate (*Crimean War*) *6–9 January 1854*. In this bloody battle 6,000 Turks (Ahmed Pasha) attacked an advanced Russian post of 6,000 men (Fischbusch). The Turks lost 1,000 men, but killed or wounded 3,000 Russians, took 1,000 prisoners and drove out the others. The Russians tried desperately to regain the position, General Anrep bringing up 20,000 reinforcements on 9 January; he lost 2,000 before conceding defeat. *See* Almc; Sebastopol.

Chevilly (*French–Prussian War*) *30 September 1870*. General Vinoy, attempting a sortie from besieged Paris, was beaten back by a German corps (von Tumpling). Casualties: French, 3,010; Germans, 441. *See* Sedan.

Chevy Chase. *See* Otterburn.

Chiari, *Lombardy* (*War of Spanish Succession*) *1 September 1701*. Prince Eugene, with 28,000 men, occupied the small town of Chiari, where the Duke of Savoy's French and Spaniards attacked him. The Allies lost 3,000 men in 2 hours' hard fighting, the Austrians only 117. *See* Cremona; Namur I.

Chickahominy (*American Civil War*) *3 June 1864*. Grant, with his Army of the Potomac, attacked Lee's trenches, held by the Confederate Army of Virginia. Successful at first, Grant was steadily forced back and all his further attacks failed. Casualties: Federals, 13,000 killed, wounded or missing; Confederates, about 6,000. *See* Spotsylvania.

Chickamauga (*American Civil War*) *19–20 September 1863*. On 19 September Bragg's Confederate Army of the West attacked General Rosecrans' lines, cutting the Federals off from the river and leaving them waterless. Next day Bragg's further attacks succeeded everywhere except on the right and by nightfall Rosecrans' army was retreating. Casualties: Confederates, 12,000; Federals, 16,351 men and 36 guns. Their losses would have been heavier had Bragg not allowed Rosecrans to retire on Chattanooga unmolested. *See* Chattanooga; Gettysburg; Stones River.

Chickasaw Bluffs (*American Civil War*) *29 December 1862*. A setback for the Federals in their attempt to capture the key Confederate fortified Mississippi River port of Vicksburg, commanded by John Pemberton. Under heavy fire from the bluffs, Sherman, although he had 32,000 men, could make no progress and lost 1,776 of them to the Confederate loss of 207. *See* Corinth; Vicksburg.

Chilianwallah, *near River Jhelum* (*Second British–Sikh War*) *14 January 1849*. Fighting largely in jungle, Lord Gough's 20,000 British and Indian troops drove off 40,000 Sikhs under Shir Singh, but Gough's own position was so insecure that he retired after the action. *See* Gujerat; Ramnagar.

Chiloe (*Chilean War of Independence*) *19 January 1826*. 4,000 Chileans, supported by a few ships, captured a small group of islands held by the Spaniards. *See* Chacabuco.

Chinese Civil War *1945–9*. The civil war in China between Chiang Kai-shek's

Nationalist government and the Communists led by Mao Tse-tung was only partly interrupted by the conflict with Japan. It was renewed after Japan's surrender in 1945 as the Communists moved to take over the territory occupied by the Japanese. In one of the great military transportation feats of history, the Americans moved 500,000 Nationalist troops by sea and air to central and northern China to forestall the Communists. On 15 October 1945 the Communists destroyed five Nationalist divisions (75,000 men) near Tunlui and on 31 October defeated two entire Nationalist armies (more than 250,000 men). The Nationalists had some successes, especially in Shantung between February and August 1947 and in March 1948. The Communists' ninth and final offensive began in Manchuria on 12 September 1948 when they committed to battle 600,000 troops under General Lin Piao. Chiang Kai-shek's forces in this sector totalled 300,000. They lost Manchuria, but other armies inflicted a major defeat on the Communists in north-west China. A major set-piece battle was fought at Kaifeng, Central China, between 30 May and 8 July. The defending Nationalists blocked the Communists' thrusts and counter-attacked so fiercely that the Communists retreated. The Nationalists suffered 90,000 casualties and their "victory" gained them nothing.

The Nationalists evacuated Changchun on 21 October. A week later the retreating nationalist armies were destroyed at the battle of Mukden-Chinchow and the garrison of Mukden surrendered on 1 November. Chiang Kai-shek had lost 300,000 good troops. The Nationalist defeat at Hwai-Hai was the real end of the war, but the Nationalists held Peking until 22 January 1949, Nanking until 22 April and Shanghai until 27 May. In the meantime, Chiang Kai-shek had abandoned mainland China and set up a Nationalist government in Formosa (Taiwan). *See* Kaifeng.

China–India Border War (or Himalayan War) *1959–62*. This war took place on two fronts — in the east on Bhutan Front and in the west in the Ladakh Salient. In Bhutan the first fighting was at Longju on 25 August 1959. Refusing to negotiate on disputed territory, the Indians established forty posts in country claimed by the Chinese. In October 1962 the Indian leader Pandit Neru ordered the army to "free our territory on the North-East Frontier from the Chinese intruders". The Chinese struck first and at dawn on 20 October 20,000 Chinese launched a surprise attack. The Indian positions were over-run. On the Ladakh front the Chinese beat the Indians back onto the capital Leh. An Indian counter-offensive on the Bhutan Front, 14 November, was a disaster. The Chinese, the undisputed victors, ended the war on 1 December by agreeing to allow India to control the disputed Bhutan region in return for Chinese sovereignty over the Ladakh Salient. Casualties: Indian, 1,400 killed, 1,700 wounded; Chinese, 8,000 in all.

Chinese–Vietnam War *1979*. Because Vietnam was interfering in the affairs of Cambodia, a Chinese satellite, a Chinese army of 250,000 invaded Vietnam on 17 February 1979. Opposing the Chinese were 58,000 Vietnam regulars and 10,000 militia. Advancing on six fronts, the Chinese made big initial gains and after major battles captured Dong Dang, Lao Kay, Cao Bang and Ha Giang. The Vietnamese, veterans of the war against the Americans and South Vietnamese, fought well, delayed the Chinese advance, and inflicted heavy casualties on the Chinese before they captured parts of Lang Son. On 5 March the Chinese retreated and again lost many troops to the harassing Vietnamese. The Vietnamese claimed victory in the war and put Chinese losses at 62,500 killed or wounded, with 300 tanks destroyed. The Chinese command said that 20,000 Chinese and 50,000 Vietnamese had been killed or wounded. No independent verification of figures was possible. The Chinese army did not perform as well as foreign analysts expected.

Chingleput (*Seven Years' War*) April 1752. With 700 troops, Robert Clive captured this fortress from a garrison of forty French and 500 native troops. *See* Arcot.

Chioggia (*or Chiozza*) (*Venetian–Genoese conflicts*) 137. The Genoese had captured this city from the Venetians, who then, under Pisani, besieged it. The garrison commander, Doria, was killed, but the fort held out until 24 June. The Venetians captured nineteen Genoese galleys and 4,000 prisoners; their victory broke the power of the Genoese Republic. *See* Pulz.

Chios (*Revolt against Athens*) 357 BC. The island of Chios rose against Athenian rule and Athens sent sixty ships with troops (Chabrias) against it. Chabrias' galley, trying to enter harbour, was encircled by the islanders and Chabrias was killed. The attack was abandoned. *See* Embata; Tolinus.

Chippenham (*Danish invasion of Britain*) 878. King Alfred, from his base in Chippenham, Wiltshire, tried to hold the Danish invaders under Guthrum, but on 6 January a surprise Danish attack wiped out the Wessex army and Alfred himself became a fugitive until his fortunes began to rise in May. *See* Ethandun.

Chippewa River (*British–American War*) 6 July 1814. General Riall with 2,400 British troops attacked General Jacob Brown's 4,000 Americans, who held strong positions, and was repulsed with heavy loss. *See* Chryslers Farm.

Chitor, *India*. This place suffered three sieges and three terrible disasters. About 1390 Ala-ud-Din and his Pathans besieged it and for a time the Rajputs (Lakhsman) held out. When the Pathans overwhelmed the defenders they butchered the survivors; Lakhsman and eleven of his twelve sons died fighting. In 1535 the Rana Bikrmajit defended Chitor gallantly and desperately against Bahadur Shah and his Gujerat troops. The garrison's survivors slew their 13,000 women, then sallied out to die fighting. The only royal child to survive was Udai Singh, during whose reign the third siege occurred, 1568, when Akbar attacked. Jagmal, who defended the place when Udai Singh deserted his capital, had only 8,000 men. Akbar's conduct of the siege was militarily sound and he achieved a breach, but Jagmal exploded a mine in it and 500 of Akbar's men were killed. Jagmal was killed soon after this and Akbar's second assault was successful. The garrison, refusing to surrender, were killed to the last man.

Chitral, *North-West India* (*British Chitral campaign*) 3 March 1895. A remarkable defence. Captain Townshend, commander of the garrison of Chitral fort, had seven British officers, ninety Sikhs and 280 Kashmiris. Shere Afzal, pretender to the Chitral throne, and Umrar Khan of Bajaur attacked with a large force. The garrison not only held out until 18 April, when relieved, but actually made a sortie against the besiegers. A fifth of the garrison was killed or wounded. Townshend later commanded at Kut, q.v.

Chizai (*Hundred Years' War*) July 1372. Du Guesclin, besieging the English-held Chizai, was attacked by another English force equal in size to his own. He defeated it and captured the town. As a consequence Edward III lost part of his French possessions. *See* La Rochelle.

Choczim (*or Chotin*) *Moldavia* (*Russian–Turkish Wars*) June–September 1769. Prince Alexander Galitzin, leading 65,000 men, was ordered by Catherine the Great to capture Choczim, held by the Poles, on the Dniester River. On the way he decisively defeated a Turkish army under Emir Pasha. Galitzin besieged Choczim and the Sultan of Turkey ordered Emir Pasha to encircle the Russians; instead the Emir made a direct attack. He lost and was executed; his

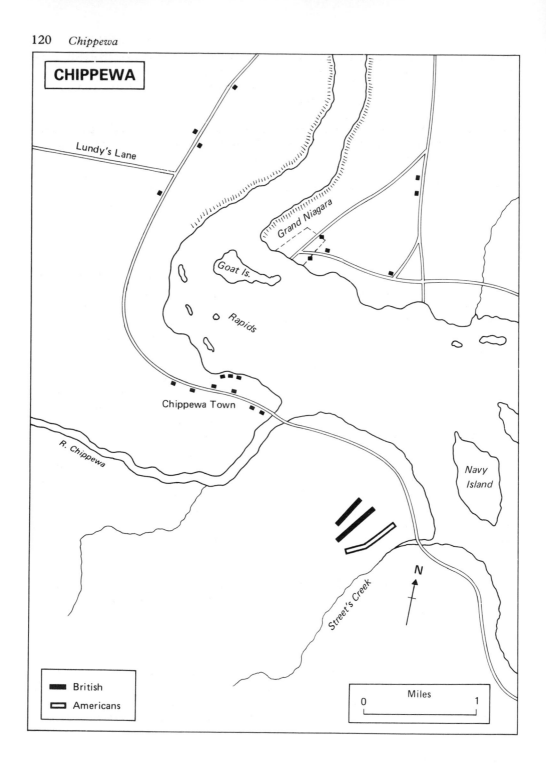

CHIPPEWA

Lundy's Lane

Grand Niagara

Goat Is.

Rapids

Chippewa Town

R. Chippewa

Navy Island

Street's Creek

N

British
Americans

Miles
0   1

replacement, Moldowandji, bridged the Dniester and attacked the Russians. The assault went well until the Turkish soldiers panicked as the river rose in flood. Thousands of Turks drowned and the 6,000 left on the Russian bank were butchered. The Poles evacuated Choczim. *See* Stavrichani.

Chong-Ju (*Russian–Japanese War*) *April 1904*. The advance guard of the Japanese Army made contact with Cossacks (Mitschtchenko), pushed them back and occupied the town. This was the first engagement of the war. *See* Port Arthur.

Chorillos (*Peruvian–Chilean War*) *13 January 1881*. A massive victory for the Chileans (Baquedano). General Caceres' Peruvians lost 9,000 killed or wounded and 2,000 prisoners. The Chileans had 800 killed, 2,500 wounded. Peruvians losses were so high because they made a counter-attack while peace negotiations were in progress. *See* Tacna.

Chotusitz (*War of Austrian Succession*) *17 May 1742*. A drawn battle between the Austrians (Prince Charles of Lorraine) and Prussians (Frederick the Great), in equal numbers. Prussian cavalry made several wild charges and suffered badly, but the steady Prussian infantry wore down the Austrians, who withdrew in good order, leaving eighteen guns and 12,000 prisoners. Each side lost about 7,000 killed or wounded and the Austrians captured 1,000 Prussians. *See* Dettingen; Mollwitz.

Christianople (*Danish–Swedish War*) *September 1611*. Notable as the first military feat of Gustavus Adolphus of Sweden. With 1,500 men he made a night assault, blew in the gate and captured the fort without losing a man. *See* Wimpfen.

Chrysler's Farm, *St. Lawrence River* (*British–American War*) *11 November 1813*. 800 British (Colonel J. W. Morrison) defeated 3,000 Americans (General John Boyd) and gave the British the initiative. Casualties: British, 203; Americans, 249 killed or wounded and 100 prisoners. *See* Chateaugay River; Chippewa River.

Chrysopolis (*War of the Two Empires*) *323*. Constantine, besieging Byzantium (later Constantinople), detached troops and sent them to give battle to Licinius, Emperor of the East, who lost 25,000 of his 50,000 men and surrendered — to be executed. The result was reunion of the whole of the Roman Empire under one head. *See* Adrianople I.

Chunar (*Mogul–Hindu Wars*) *1538*. The Moguls besieged this fortress, held for Shir Khan Sur, Nawab of Bengal. The siege developed into an artillery duel and in the end only hunger forced the garrison's surrender.

Chu Pong-ia Drang River (*Vietnam War*) *14–20 November 1965*. Landed by air near Chu Pong Mountain, a battalion of American troops, the U.S. 1st Cavalry (Airmobile) Division, fought North Vietnamese regulars for 4 days, killing at least 1,000. Crossing the Ia-Pang River another U.S. unit encountered a large North Vietnamese force and in bitter fighting killed 350. The week's fighting cost the Americans 240 dead and 470 wounded. *See* Vietnam.

Cibalis, *later Swilei, Pannonia, near the Danube* (*War of the Two Empires*) *8 October 315*. Constantine the Great, with 20,000 men, was caught in a defile by Licinius, who had 35,000 men. Constantine repulsed the attack and followed the enemy into an open plain, where Licinius rallied and resumed the offensive. He had won the initiative when Constantine personally led a charge which broke Licinius' Illyrians. Having lost 20,000 of his best troops, Licinius abandoned his camp by night and retreated to Sirmium. *See* Heracles.

Ciudad Rodrigo, *Spain* (*Peninsular War*) *19 January 1812*. Wellington invested this walled town, which barred his way to Madrid, on 8 January and carried it by storm 12 days later. The fighting was fierce and bloody, the garrison of 2,000 inflicting heavy casualties on the British — 1,290 killed or wounded, of whom 710, including Generals Craufurd and Mackinnon, died in the storming; French, 300 killed or wounded, 1,500 prisoners and 150 guns. *See* Albuhere; Badajox.

Ciuna, *southern Italy (Second Samnite War) 315 BC*. The Romans (Caius Maenius) defeated the Samnites (Pontius). *See* Bovanium; Caudine Forks.

Civitella (*Norman invasion of Italy*) *1033*. Robert Giuscard with 3,000 Normans routed a German–Italian force under Pope Leo IX. The Allies were cut down to a man and the Pope was captured. *See* Rome.

Clastidium (*conquest of Cisalpine Gaul*) *222 BC*. Roman legions under Gaius Flaminius crossed the Po River in 223 and systematically demolished the Gallic settlements around what is now Milan, the intention being to prevent any Gallic invasion of northern Italy. In 222 the Gauls reacted, concentrated their forces and fought a major battle with the Romans south of the Po at Clastidium. The legionaries won decisively, the Roman General Marcellus killing the Gallic chief, Britomartus, in single combat. The Gauls bowed to Roman rule until Hannibul arrived 4 years later. *See* Telamon; Trebbia River I.

Clermont (*French or Jacquerie Peasant Uprising*) *1358*. The peasants revolted against an order that forced them to repair and fortify castles and chateaux of the nobility. After much trouble the authorities of Clermont, north of Paris, assembled a force and attacked the peasant army of Guillaume Cale. Defeat degenerated into massacre and 800 peasants died. Charles II (the Bad) had thousands more butchered in suppressing the Jacquerie. *See* Poitiers.

Clissau (*Swedish–Polish Wars*) *13 July 1702*. Between 12,000 Swedes (Charles II) and 24,000 Poles and Saxons (Frederick Augustus). The Poles broke and ran at the first Swedish attack and though the Saxons fought bravely the Swedes overwhelmed them; the Swedish cavalry commander, the Duke of Holstein, was killed. *See* Dwina River.

Clontarf (*Norse invasion of Ireland*) *24 April 1014*. Brian Boru, leading the Irish of Munster, Connaught, Ulster and Meath, routed the Scandinavian invaders and killed 6,000 of them. Brian Boru and his son were also killed. *See* Mortlack.

Clusium, *later Ciusi, Etruria (Roman conquest of Cisalpine Gaul*) *225 BC*. The Gauls (Brennus) are said to have inflicted 50,000 casualties on a Roman army.

Cnidus (*or Gnidus*), *later successively Triopia, Pegusa, Stadia 394 BC*. A major naval battle between 120 Spartan triremes (Pisander) and a vastly superior Persian fleet (Pharnabazus and Conon). The Spartan fleet was destroyed, Pisander slain. The maritime power of Sparta vanished and Persia re-established its power in the Greek cities of Asia. *See* Coronea II; Naxos.

Coblenz (*Gallic Wars*) *55 BC*. Julius Caesar marched north to meet the invading Germanic tribes, the Usipetes and Tencteri. His legionaries drove the Germans into the V formed by the Rhine and Moselle; the entire force was either killed in battle or drowned in the rivers. The battle is notable for Caesar's subsequent action. To demonstrate Roman strength he had his engineers build a bridge over the Rhine in 10 days; he manoeuvred his legionaries for about 3 weeks, then recrossed the river and destroyed the bridge. *See* Tongres.

Cocherel (*Hundred Years' War*) *May 1364*. Du Guesclin, executing a strategic retreat with 10,000 French, was attacked by John Joel's English mercenaries, who were serving the Navarrese under Jean de Grailli. Du Guesclin's men surrounded and overpowered the English and killed Joel. When de Grailli came to help them he was captured and his Navarrese surrendered. *See* Auray; Poitiers.

Cold Harbor (*American Civil War*) *1–12 June 1864*. On 1 June the Confederates (Anderson) attacked towards Cold Harbor crossroads, near Richmond, where the Federals (Sheridan) held until reinforced. By mid-morning the Confederate and Federal armies were in confrontation on a 7-mile front; the Federal attack at 6 p.m. failed, having lost 2,200 men. With 108,000 men to the Confederate 59,000, the Federal commander-in-chief, Grant, launched a massive attack at 4.30 a.m. on 3 June. He had massive casualties — 7,000 dead or wounded within an hour. The Confederates lost 1,500. From trenches only 100 yards apart, southern and northern soldiers fought for the next 8 days. Grant then withdrew to change his tactics. *See* North Anna River: Petersburg.

Colenso (*Second British–Boer War*) *15 December 1899*. Sir Redvers Buller, campaigning to relieve Ladysmith, besieged by the Boers, attempted a frontal assault on a strong position on the opposite side of the Tugela. The rash action failed, the British losing seventy-one officers and 1,055 others and ten guns. The action is famous for the attempt by Lieutenant Roberts to save the British guns; he was awarded a posthumous V.C. *See* Ladysmith; Magersfontein; Stormberg.

Colline Gate (*Civil War of Marius and Sulla*) *82 BC*. The Samnites (Pontius) tried to enter Rome, but the Roman Democrats, followers of Sulla, fought stubbornly all night, routed the Samnites and took 4,000 prisoners. The victory ended the civil war. *See* Mount Tifata; Mount Vesuvius.

Cologne (*World War II*) *30 May 1942*. The heaviest of many British air raids on Cologne; 1,000 planes made a saturation attack, dropping 3,000 tons of bombs in 90 minutes, at the rate of one every 6 seconds. About 20,000 people were killed and the chemical and machine-tool industries crippled. The British bomber commander was Air Chief Marshal Sir Arthur Harris. *See* Berlin; Dresden.

Colombey (*French–German War*) *11 August 1870*. The French Army (Bazaine) was retiring on Verdun when the advance guard of the 1st German Army Corps (von Steinmetz) caught it. Two French divisions were scattered and the French retirement was seriously delayed. Casualties: French, about 7,000; German, 5,000. *See* Mars-la-Tour; Spicheren; Wörth.

Colombo (*Wars of the French Revolution*) *July 1796*. A squadron of four British warships (Admiral Rainier) and a small land force (Colonel Stuart) captured the town from the Dutch.

Columbus, *New Mexico 8–9 March 1916*. Pancho Villa, a Mexican bandit leader, led 500 men in a night raid on Columbus. American cavalry drove the invaders off next day, inflicting 190 casualties on them. *See* Carrizal.

Compedion (*or Corupedion*) (*Wars of Alexander's Successors*) *281 BC*. A remarkable battle, in which Lysimachus, commanding the Macedonians, met Seleucus, commander of the Syrians, in single combat in front of their armies. Seleucus, aged 81, slew his former comrade, who was also elderly. In the general battle which followed, the Syrians triumphed. *See* Ipsus.

Concha Rayada (*Chilean War of Independence*) *February 1818*. A victory for the Spaniards, 5,000-strong under Osorio, against the Chileans and Colombians (San Martin). *See* Chacabuco.

Concon (*Chilean Civil War*) *21 August 1891*. Between 10,000 Congressists (del Canto) and 11,000 Balmacedists (Barbosa). The Congressists had landed on 20 August. Supported by naval gunfire, they routed the Balmacedists from their trenches. Casualties: Balmacedists, 1,648 killed or wounded, 1,500 prisoners; Congressists, 869. *See* Tacna.

Concord. *See* Lexington.

Condorcanqui (*French conquest of Algeria*) *1836–7*. The fortified city had resisted French rule for 6 years. In October 7,000 French (Clausel) invested it and, without artillery, stormed it, losing 2,000 men and failing. On 6 October 1837 Damremont besieged the fort with 10,000 men, breached the walls and on 12 October launched his infantry. The attack was virtually complete when Damremont was killed and the French wilted. General Valee, assuming command, captured the fort next day. Algerian casualties were said to be 5,000. *See* Junin.

Congo Civil War *1960–71*. Fighting began immediately after Belgium granted independence to Congo; the native army mutinied and Katanga province seceded. At U.N. request, most Belgian troops were withdrawn and were replaced by a U.N. peace-keeping force, which recaptured Elizabethville, the Katangan capital, in December 1961. A year later the Katangan forces were defeated by the U.N. army, notably Indian and Ethiopian troops. The last U.N. troops were withdrawn on 30 June 1964 after suffering nearly 500 killed or wounded — the largest number ever sustained by a U.N. force. The savage civil war continued and Moise Tshombe, former leader of Katanga, became prime minister. In July 1964 he hired white mercenaries, led by a former British officer, Major Mike Hoare, to defeat the rebels, who were now backed by China. In November the Belgian government lent Tshombe paratroops to retake Stanleyville and release 1,800 hostages held by the cruel Simbas (Lions) of Kivu province. In March 1965 Hoare's mercenaries captured five towns from the rebels. Colonel Joseph Mobotu overthrew Tshombe and in 1972 he changed the country's name to Zaire.

Constantine (*French conquest of Algeria*) *6–12 October 1837*. The French had occupied Algiers but could not subdue the Berber city of Constantine, 200 miles away. In 1836 the Berbers repulsed an attack in which the French lost heavily. On 6 October 1837 the French governor, Clausel, massed 10,000 French and Algerian troops for a siege and the garrison surrendered only a week later. *See* Isly River.

Constantinople I (*Civil War*) *532*. A massacre rather than a battle. The Blues and Greens, factions which had developed among the followers of the city's chariot racing teams, began vicious street fighting against each other. The Byzantine emperor, Justinian I, endured the strife for a week and would have abandoned his throne but for the insistence of his wife, Theodora, that he stay. Justinian ordered the hero Belisarius, now a veteran, to restore order. Leading 2,500 barbarian mercenaries Belisarius allowed 30,000 of the rioters to assemble in the circus to proclaim their own emperor, then sent in his barbarians. Few of the rioters survived the butchery. With new strength Justinian went on to reconquer the Western Roman empire from the barbarians. *See* Callinicum; Carthage.

Constantinople II (*Byzantine–Persian War*) *29 June–10 August 626*. The Byzantine emperor, Heraclius, had left his son Constantine to defend the city, which was close-invested by a Persian army of 100,000 Avars, Slavs, Germans and Bulgarians. Heraclius sent 12,000 veterans by sea to reinforce the garrison. The Avars stormed the city's walls while the Persians tried to cross the Bosporus in a mass of boats and rafts, which the Byzantine navy smashed. After 10 days' incessant fighting Constantine drove off the Avars, who had suffered

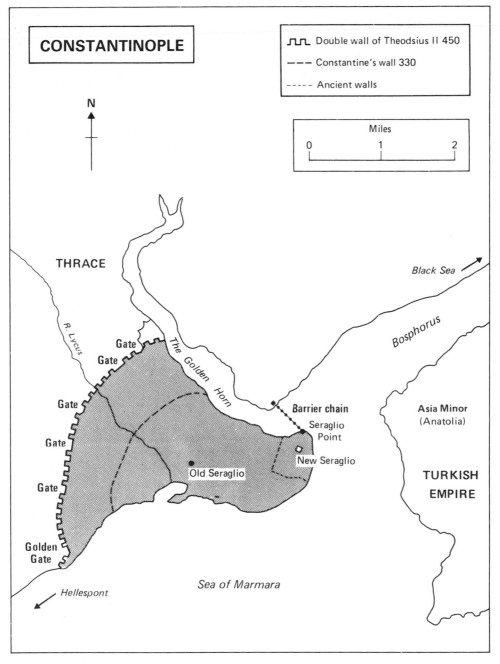

CONSTANTINOPLE

⎍⎍⎍	Double wall of Theodsius II 450
– – –	Constantine's wall 330
- - - - -	Ancient walls

Miles

0   1   2

N

THRACE

R. Lycus

Gate
Gate

Gate

Gate

Gate

Golden
Gate

Hellespont

The Golden Horn

Old Seraglio

Barrier chain

Seraglio
Point

New Seraglio

Black Sea

Bosphorus

Asia Minor
(Anatolia)

TURKISH
EMPIRE

Sea of Marmara

terrible losses. This was one of the great fortress defences of history.

Constantinople III (*Muslim–Byzantine Wars*) *673–8*. Besieging the city by land and sea, April 673, the Muslim Caliph Muawiyah I tried for 5 months to break in, before withdrawing for the winter. Constantine IV's fighting men were skilled and at sea their Greek fire — the equivalent of today's napalm — caused havoc among the Muslim ships.

Every summer for 5 years the Muslims renewed their blockade and assaults. In 677 the Byzantine navy destroyed the Muslim fleet at Syllaeum; this ensured peace for 30 years. During the 5 years the Muslims had lost 30,000 men killed. *See* Lycis.

Constantinople IV (*Muslim–Byzantine Wars*) *717–8*. Assembling 2,000 ships, Maslama, brother of Suleiman, the Ommiad caliph, forced his way into the Sea of Marmara but found his route to the city blocked by a great chain; many ships were destroyed by Greek fire. The Muslim land attack began on 15 August 717 with 50,000 troops storming the walls. Emperor Leo III and his troops fought them off and after a year Maslama had to abandon the siege. Many of his ships were lost in storms and large numbers of this troops perished in Asia Minor. In all the Muslims had lost 40,000 men in a year. *See* Covadonga.

Constantinople V (*Fourth Crusade*) *1203–4*. After sacking the Christian city of Zadar on the Dalmatian coast — and being excommunicated for the outrage — the French–Venetian crusaders (Enrico Dandelo and Boniface III of Montferrat, Italy) moved on to Constantinople, June 1203, deposed the Byzantine Emperor Alexius III and restored Isaac II and Alexius IV. The crusaders — among the most grasping in history — demanded enormous tribute, and Constantinople's citizens revolted, January 1204, killed Alexius IV and Isaac and proclaimed Alexius V as emperor. When Alexius demanded that the crusaders move on they attacked the city, 12 April, sacked it and commited brutal atrocities. Baldwin of Flanders was proclaimed the first Western ruler of the new Latin Empire. For the first time in 900 years Constantinople had fallen to an invader. *See* Adrianople IV; Arsouf.

Constantinople VI (*reconquest by Byzantines*) *25 July 1261*. To reconquer Constantinople, Michael VIII of Nicaea, the state of Asia Minor which perpetuated the glories of the Byzantines, made an alliance with Genoa. On 25 July 1261 Michael, hearing that the Venetian fleet which protected Constantinople was absent, sent Stragopulos across the Bosporus to attack the city. Stragopulos, though he had only a few thousand horsemen, easily captured the place. Michael's line ruled Constantinople for almost two centuries.

Constantinople VII *13 February 1352*. A naval action won by sixty-four Genoese galleys under Doria against the seventy-five Greek and Venetian galleys under Pisani.

Constantinople VIII (*Turkish invasion of Europe*) *1422*. The Greek garrison under Emperor Manuel found itself besieged by 200,000 Turks under Amurath II. In the 2-month siege — June–July 1422 — the Turks lost heavily and Amurath, called home to quell a domestic revolt, raised the siege. *See* Arsouf.

Constantinople IX (*Turkish conquest*) *1453*. The Ottoman Turks' sieges of Constantinople had been voluntarily raised. Then, in April 1453, Sultan Muhammad II, with 80,000 men and much storming equipment, began a serious siege. Constantine XI had only 7,000 troops and no navy; his main asset was John Giustiniani, a great leader, who repulsed violent attacks on 18 April and 7, 12 and 21 May. Muhammad, his navy blocked by the chain across the Golden Horn, had seventy light ships dragged across land and put into the upper end of the Golden Horn. For 50 days the Turks sustained their artillery bombardment — probably the greatest barrage known to that time. On 29 May 12,000 Janissary infantryment — first class shock troops — were thrown into the breaches. In the wild fighting Constantine, Giustiniani and most of the garrison were killed; thousands of civilians were massacred. The Byzantine empire was at an end. *See* Belgrade; Kossovo II.

Constantinople X (*Napoleonic Wars*) February–March *1807*. Because the Ottoman Sultan Selim III was supporting the French, a British fleet (Admiral John Duckworth) forced a passage through the Dardanelles, defeated the Turkish fleet and anchored off Constantinople. Duckworth gave Selim 24 hours to make peace with Russia and dismiss the French ambassador. Sultan Selim defied the ultimatum and within the day the population of Constantinople collected 1,000 guns along the sea wall and opened fire on the British fleet. His ships suffered much damage and Duckworth withdrew, being further mauled as he retreated to the Mediterranean.

Constantinople XI (*military revolt*) *13 April 1909*. The I Army Corps, mostly Albanian, seized control of the city. The violent uprising was put down by troops from Macedonia after a 5-hour battle in the city.

Constantinople XII (*First Balkan War*) *17–18 November 1912*. The Bulgars attempted a siege of Constantinople, but launched a premature assault and the Turks drove them back with heavy loss.

U.S.S. *Constitution* vs. H.M.S. *Java* (*British–American War*) *29 December 1812*. Under the command of Captain William Bainbridge, the *Constitution* — known as "Old Ironsides" — encountered the British frigate *Java* off Bahia, Brazil. After a 2-hour battle the *Constitution*'s forty-four guns and superior handling were too much for the *Java*'s thirty-eight guns. With the *Java* a flaming wreck, the crew surrendered. The *Constitution* had earlier defeated H.M.S. *Guerriere*.

Contreras-Churubasco (*American–Mexican War*) *7 August 1847*. A double battle which left the Americans (Winfield Scott) only 5 miles from Mexico City. The Mexican commander and president, Santa Anna, lost more than a third of his 20,000 troops. Scott lost nearly 200 killed and more than 900 wounded. *See* Cerro Gordo; Chapultepec; Molini del Rey.

Cooch's Bridge (*American Revolution*) *3 September 1777*. A vain attempt by the Americans (Maxwell), acting on Washington's orders, to delay the British advance (Cornwallis) on Philadelphia. *See* Brandywine Creek; Princeton.

Copenhagen I (*Napoleonic Wars*) *2 April 1801*. An over-rated battle with significant results. A British fleet of eighteen ships-of-the-line and thirty-nine smaller craft (Hyde Parker and Nelson) fought ten Danish ships helped by their shore batteries. Nelson attacked with twelve ships but three ran aground. Parker, noticing the Danes' fierce resistance, signalled Nelson to retire; Nelson, telescope to his blind eye, refused to see the signal and continued to fight until the Danes were silenced. The British lost 1,200 men and had six ships badly damaged. The Danes had one ship sunk and all the others damaged. The league of the Northern Powers was dissolved. *See* Alexandria III; Cape Finisterre I.

Copenhagen II (*Napoleonic Wars*) *1–5 September 1807*. The Danes, under a secret clause in the Treaty of Tilsit, planned to put their fleet at Napoleon's disposal. The British navy bombarded the city for 4 days after which Lord Cathcart, with 20,000 troops, easily captured the place. The Danish fleet of eighteen ships surrendered. *See* Friedland.

Coprates, The, *a tributary of the Tigris* (*Wars of Alexander's Successors*) *316 BC*. The Asiatics (Eumenes) attacked the Macedonians (Antigonus) as they were crossing the Copratus River. Both armies were of equal size — 30,000 — and Antigonus, though defeated, retreated in good order. *See* Gaza; Paraetakene Mountains.

Coral Sea (*World War II*) *6–8 May 1942*. The first major engagement in naval history in which surface ships did not fire a shot at one another. A Japanese invasion fleet (Takagi) was heading for Port Moresby, New Guinea, when sighted by aircraft from a U.S. task force. The battle on 7 May and 8 was waged by aircraft from carriers with the opposing fleets. The invasion fleet turned back, but the battle was itself drawn, both sides losing a carrier, the *Shoho* and *Lexington* respectively. The Americans did not claim a victory, as is often supposed. *See* Midway; New Guinea.

Cordova I (*Spanish–Muslim Wars*) *August 1010*. The Moors of Cordova (Almudy) marched out of the city to meet the Berbers (Sulaiman), but were routed, losing 20,000 men. *See* Zamora.

Cordova II (*Spanish–Muslim Wars*) *1236*. Cordova had been the capital of Moorish Spain for five centuries and the Spaniards had coveted it since their victory at Las Navas de Tolosa in 1212. Ferdinand III stormed it in 1236, paving the way for further victories — Seville, 1238; Jaen, 1246; Cadiz, 1262; Valencia, 1238; Mercia, 1266.

Corinth I (*Great Peloponnesus War*) *429 BC*. Phormio, commanding twenty Athenian triremes, allowed Cnemus to take his forty-seven Peloponnesus ships out of the Gulf of Corinth into the open sea, where they were disordered by heavy weather. Phormio attacked, capturing twelve ships and scattering the enemy fleet.

Corinth II (*Corinthian War*) *394 BC*. The Spartan army of only 14,000 defeated 26,000 allied Athenians, Corinthians and Argives, inflicting twice as many casualties as they suffered themselves. However, the Spartans were not strong enough to hold their ground and retired, leaving the isthmus in enemy hands.

Corinth III (*Roman conquest of Greece*) *146 BC*. When the Achaean League attacked Sparta, a Roman satellite since the second century BC, a strong Roman army intervened and began a conquest of the Peloponnesus. The Roman General Lucius Mummius captured the key Achaean city of Corinth, the Greek inhabitants were massacred and the Achaean League broke up. *See* Pydna.

Corinth, *Mississippi* (*American Civil War*) *3–4 October 1862*. The Federals (Rosecrans), strongly entrenched at Corinth, were attacked by the Confederates (Van Dorn) and driven into their inner lines. A renewed attack next day was repulsed and the Federals, taking the offensive, routed the Confederates. Casualties: Confederates, 6,423 killed or wounded, 2,248 prisoners; Federals, 2,359 killed, wounded or missing. *See* Chickasaw Bluffs; Iuca.

Coroneia I (*First Peloponnesian War*) *447 BC*. An Athenian army (Tolmides) had entered Boeotia, north of Attica, to punish certain towns which had rebelled against Athenian rule. A much superior force of Boeotians overwhelmed the Athenians, killed many and captured nearly all the rest; to save their lives, Athens resigned its claims over Boeotia. *See* Plataea II; Tanagra-Oenophyte.

Coroneia II (*Greek city-states' Wars*) *August 394 BC*. Between the Spartans (Agesilaus) and the allied Athenians, Argives, Thebans and Corinthians. The Spartan right was victorious, but the Thebans smashed their left and then turned against the Spartan right. In one of history's most stubborn fights, the Spartans defeated their enemies, but they had suffered so heavily that Agesilaus evacuated Boeotia. *See* Cnidus; Haliartus; Naxos.

Coronel, *Chile* (*World War I*) *1 November 1914*. Five German cruisers, *Gneisenau, Scharnhorst, Nurnberg, Dresden* and *Leipzig* under von Spee, met and destroyed H.M.S. *Good Hope* and H.M.S. *Monmouth*; Admiral Cradock and all 1,600 men of the crews perished. The much smaller H.M.S. *Glasgow* escaped because of her speed, while the lightly armed merchantman, *Otranto*, could only stand off. *See* Falkland Islands I; Heligoland Bight.

Corregidor, *Philippines* (*World War II*) *16–21 February 1945*. The Americans invaded Japanese-defended Corregidor island and after 6 days had practically destroyed the defences; at least 3,300 Japanese were killed. *See* Bataan; Leyte; Luzon.

Cortenuova (*German invasion of Italy*) *27 November 1237*. Frederick II, German Emperor of the Holy Roman Empire, defeated the Lombard Guelfs who had fought for local autonomy. *See* Benevento; Legnano.

Corumba (*Paraguayan–Brazilian War*) *May 1877*. A Brazilian army, trying to enter Paraguay from the north-east, was repulsed and destructively pursued. A corps of women soldiers under Eliza Lynch aided the Paraguayans.

Corunna (*Peninsular War*) *16 January 1809*. Soult's 20,000 French tried to prevent the 14,000-strong British army, after a long and hazardous winter retreat, from embarking at the Spanish port of Corunna. The French were held off and lost 2,000 men; the British lost 800 and their commander, Sir John Moore. *See* Talavera.

Corunna Road (*Spanish Civil War*) *13 December 1936–15 January 1937*. The battle was the result of the Republican attempt to prevent the rebel Nationalists from cutting the road north from Madrid, which the Republicans held. The Nationalists were successful, but at a cost of 1,500 casualties. *See* Madrid.

Coulmiers (*French–German War*) *9 November 1870*. About 20,000 Prussians (Von der Tann) held out for a day against a greatly superior French force (de Paladines), but then gave ground.

Casualties: German, 576 killed or wounded, 800 prisoners; French, 1,500. *See* Bapaume; Paris II; Sedan.

Courtrai (*or Battle of the Spurs*) (*French–Flemish War*) *11 July 1302*. The Flemings (Guy de Namur) routed the French (Robert d'Artois) with great slaughter. After the battle between 4,000 and 7,000 spurs, taken from dead French nobility, were displayed as trophies in Courtrai Cathedral. *See* Mons-en-Pévèle.

Courtras (*French Religious War of the Three Henrys*) *20 October 1587*. The Huguenots (Henry of Navarre) annihilated the Catholic Army (Duc de Joyeuse). The other Henrys were Henry of Valois and Henry I of Lorraine. *See* Arques; Moncontour.

Covadonga (*Muslim invasion of Spain*) *718*. Pelayo, principal chieftain in the Asturian mountains, raised a force to check the Muslims who had over-run the rest of Spain. At Covadonga, near Cangas de Onis, he so decisively defeated the Muslims they never again tried to take Asturias. *See* Rio Barbate; Toulouse.

Covelong (*Seven Years' War*) *24 April 1752*. Robert Clive, with 200 men, captured this fortress from 300 French, after a brief siege, and then ambushed a relief column. *See* Arcot; Coverypank.

Coverypank (*Seven Years' War*) *11 February 1751*. Robert Clive's Anglo–Indian force of 1,700 marched into an ambush set by Rajah Sahib, commanding a Franco–Indian force of 5,000. Clive, leaving his advance guard embattled, circled to the enemy's rear and attacked; the enemy panicked and fled. *See* Arcot; Covelong.

Cowpens, *South Carolina* (*American Revolution*) *17 January 1781*. A remarkable victory for untrained American militia (Daniel Morgan) against 1,100 veteran regular British troops (Colonel Tarleton). Morgan, who had no more

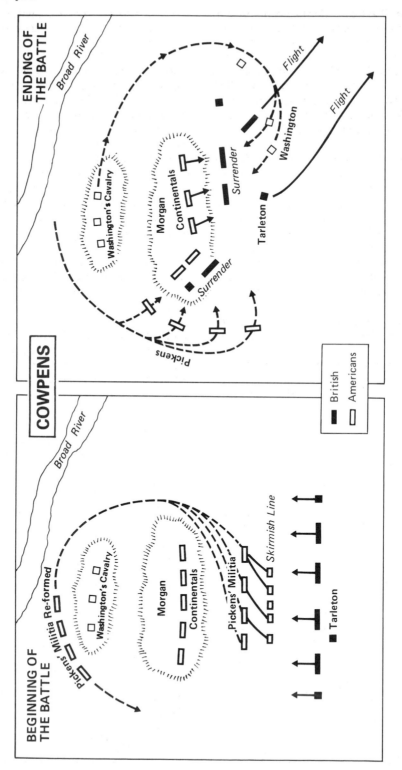

men than Tarleton, deployed his men in four lines, each one of which withdrew after inflicting heavy losses on the charging British; after an hour Morgan counter-attacked with his small cavalry reserve. Casualties: British, 100 killed, 229 wounded, 600 taken prisoner; American, 12 killed, 60 wounded. *See* Guilford Courthouse; Kings Mountain.

Craonne (*Napoleonic Wars*) 7 March 1814. Between Blucher, with 90,000 men, mostly Prussian, and Napoleon, with 37,000. Blucher held strong positions on the heights of Craonne, near Laon, France, and intended to launch a major assault. Napoleon acted first; Ney and Victor took the Prussian positions at bayonet point. Casualties: French, 5,400; Prussians, 5,000. *See* Bar-sur-Aube; Laon.

Crater (*American Civil War*) 30 July 1864. The Federals exploded a 4-ton mine under the Confederate position near Petersburg in an attempt to break through to the town. A vicious hand-to-hand fight took place in and around the crater, but the better-led Confederates held their

line and inflicted 3,793 casualties on the Union troops for 1,182 of their own. *See* Petersburg.

Cravant (*Hundred years' War*) 1 August 1423. A combined French and Scottish force under the Earls of Buchan and Douglas were on their way to capture Cravant near Laon, France, to secure the lines of communication of their leader, the Dauphin Charles (later Charles VIII). Their way was blocked by the Duke of Bedford's English–Burgundian army. The English longbows were devastating and the French were decisively defeated. *See* Beaugé; Verneuil.

Crayford (*Jute invasion of Britain*) 456. The Jutes under Hengest defeated the Britons (Vortigern) and drove them from Kent.

Crécy (*or Cressy*) (*Hundred Years' War*) 26 August 1346. Edward III's small army of 10,000 English defeated Philip VI's French–Genoese army of 24,000. The French losses were eleven princes, 1,200 knights and 8,000 others

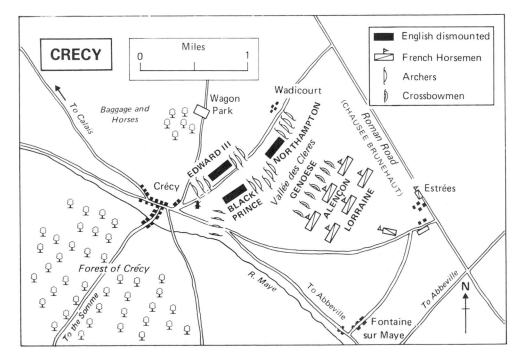

— a total greater than the entire English army. The battle was the first in which an English army was mainly formed of infantry; mounted men were shown to be powerless against English archers. The victory made England a major European military power, while the English longbow became the most deadly weapon of its era. *See* Calais I; Sluys.

Crefeld (*or Krefeld*) (*Seven Years' War*) *23 June 1758*. Prince Ferdinand of Brunswick, with 32,000 veteran and highly disciplined Hanoverians, Hessians and Brunswickers, defeated the Comte de Clermont's 50,000 French. (Ferdinand's king, Frederick the Great, was at this time campaigning against Austria.) *See* Olmnut; Zorndorf.

Cremona I, *west of Mantua, Italy* (*Second Gallic invasion*) *198 BC*. The Romans defeated with heavy slaughter an invading army of Gauls and killed Hamilcar, their Carthaginian leader.

Cremona II (*Roman Empire's Civil Wars*) *December 69*. The Vitellians — followers of Aulus Vitellius, ruler of the Roman Empire — had deposed their leader, Caecina, so were ill-fitted to resist the Flavians, supporters of Titus Flavius Vaspasian for emperor. Led by Antonius Primus, the Flavians attacked the Vitellians in their camp. They fought through-out the night but were routed and the Flavians burnt Cremona. *See* Bedriacum.

Cremona III (*War of Spanish Succession*) *1 February 1702*. Prince Eugene's Austrians entered the French-held fortress town without the alarm being given and took prisoner many senior officers. Part of the garrison held out in the citadel, making Eugene's position precarious and as a relief force approached he withdrew. The French lost 1,000. *See* Chiari; Luzzara.

Crete (*World War II*) *May 1941*. Crete became a battleground following the British defeat in Greece. Crete was held by 7,700 New Zealanders, 6,500 Australians — the chief striking force — and about 18,000 men of British army units, mostly rear echelon troops. All were under the New Zealander General Freyberg, who could do no more than improvize defences. The Germans began systematic large-scale bombing on 13 May; on 20 May the first paratroops and glider-borne Germans attacked, the plan being to take separately the main defended areas — Maleme, Khania, Retimo and Heraklion. The principal German commander was Lohr, the others were von Richthofen (air command), Meindl, Sussman. Sussman was killed in a glider crash, Meindl seriously wounded. The Allied resistance was fiercely stubborn and the

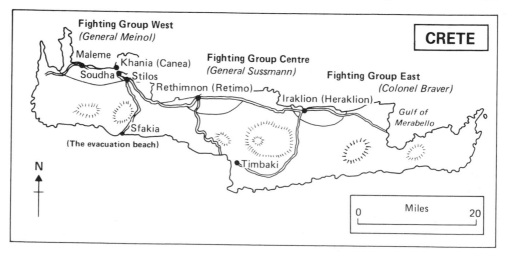

Fighting Group West
(General Meinol)
Maleme
Khania (Canea)
Soudha   Stilos
Rethimnon (Retimo)
Fighting Group Centre
(General Sussmann)
Fighting Group East
(Colonel Braver)
Iraklion (Heraklion)
Gulf of
Merabello
Sfakia
(The evacuation beach)
N
Timbaki
CRETE
Miles
0   20

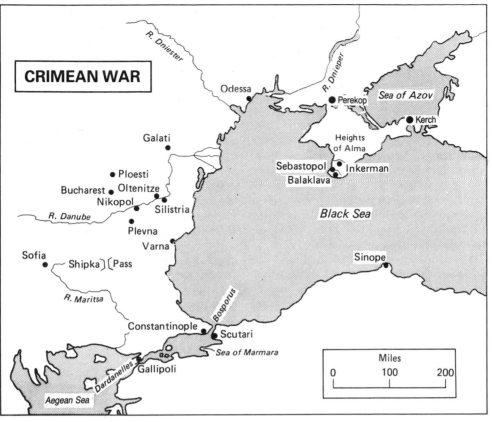

CRIMEAN WAR

Germans suffered heavily. They committed 30,000 men by air and another 10,000 by sea, and used 1,000 aircraft. The New Zealanders made no fewer than twenty-five bayonet charges, but organized resistance ended by 31 May. About 16,000 Allied soldiers were evacuated by the Royal Navy from Sfakia, southern Crete; 4,000 were killed or wounded and another 11,900 captured. The Germans were shocked by their casualties: 6,000 killed or drowned and 11,000 wounded. They lost more than 400 aircraft. Crete was history's first great airborne invasion. *See* Albania; Greece; Yugoslavia.

Crimean War 1853–5 (see map). *See* List of Battles.

Crimean Campaigns (*World War II*) *1941–4*. The fighting between Germans and Russians had several distinct phases:

(1) Following the German invasion of 22 June 1941 Runstedt's army swept through the Ukraine beyond the Crimean Peninsula. On 8 November 1941 Manstein smashed through the Perekop Isthmus and took all the Crimean except Sebastopol. The Kerch Peninsula was also taken, but reoccupied by the Russians. On 7 May 1942 Manstein attacked the Kerch defences and demolished them in 6 days, the Russians suffering 150,000 casualties, including prisoners. On 3 June Manstein attacked Sebastopol and occupied the ruins by 1 July taking 90,000 prisoners. In November 1943 the Russians under Tolbukhin spread along the north shore of the Sea of Azov and trapped many Germans in the Crimea. between 8 and 11 April 1944 Tolbukhin's Russians battered through the Perekop Isthmus defences. The German garrison of Sebastopol surrendered on 9 May 1944. *See* Caucasus; Ukraine.

Crimissus River, *later the Caltabel-lotta, west Sicily* (*Third Carthaginian invasion of Sicily*) *34 BC*. A remarkable victory by 10,000 Sicilians (Timoleon) against 70,000 Carthaginians (Hamilcar and Hasdrubal). Timoleon attacked the Carthaginians while they were crossing the Crimissus River and routed the "Sacred Band" — 2,500 Carthaginians of high birth — before the main army could cross. The Carthaginians were seriously handicapped by heavy rain beating into their faces and the Sicilians forced them to break; they left 10,000 dead and 15,000 prisoners. Many more were drowned trying to recross the river. *See* Himera River; Syracuse II.

Croniun (*Second Carthaginian invasion of Sicily*) *379 BC*. The Carthaginians so badly defeated the Syracusans (Dionysus) that they had to accept most unfavourable peace terms. *See* Syracuse.

Cropredy Bridge (*English Civil War*) *29 June 1644*. Sir William Waller, with Parliamentary troops, crossed the Cherwell near Banbury, hoping to take the Royalists (Charles I) by surprise, but was repulsed. *See* Alresford.

Crosskeys (*American Civil War*) *8–9 June 1862*. The Confederate General Ewell was given 6,500 men and ordered to hold 12,000 Federals (Fremont) while Jackson gave battle to a larger Federal army (Shields) who were trying to link with Fremont. The Confederates lost 664 men, then crossed South Fork River, burning the bridge behind them. Fremont and Shields could not join before Jackson attacked Shields' force and the Confederates had tied down large Federal forces. *See* Fair Oaks; Winchester I.

Crotone I (*Second Punic War*) *204 BC*. Hannibal's brother, Hasdrubal, had fought — and lost — a major battle against the Romans at the Metaurus, q.v., and Hannibal, with inferior troops and inadequate supplies, was under great pressure. The Roman Sempronius led a much larger army against him at Crotone south of Taranto in Bruttium, but under Hannibal's dynamic leadership his troops stood firm and the action was drawn. Under Roman attack at home, the Carthaginians sent messages to Hannibal to return at once to Carthage. *See* Zama.

Crotone II (*German invasion of Italy*) *982*. Emperor Otto II and his Germans had invaded Italy to restore Pope Benedict VII to the papal throne. Benedict asked him to drive the Muslims from southern Italy and Sicily, so by land and sea he attacked their base at Crotone. His spies had been incompetent and to his surprise Otto found himself, when his campaign began on 13 July, confronting an alliance of Byzantines and Muslims led by the Caliph of Egypt. The German knights, though brave, had no tactics to match the dash of their opponents, while Otto's ships were burnt by Greek fire. *See* Lechfield; Sant'Angelo.

Crotoye (*Hundred Years' War*) *1347*. The French fleet tried to relieve Calais, besieged by Edward III, but was defeated with heavy loss by the English fleet. *See* Calais.

Crusader Operation (*World War II*) *1941*. In accordance with a plan by General Auchinleck, on 18 November the British XXX Corps outflanked to the south the German line in the Western Desert of Libya. At the same time the Australian garrison of besieged Tobruk broke out and forced the German commander, General Rommel, to abandon an armoured raid across the Egyptian frontier. XXX Corps smashed the Italian part of the Axis front and on 4 December Rommel withdrew to El Agheila, his starting point 8 months earlier. This campaign was a success for General Ritchie, who succeeded General Cunningham during the battle. *See* Bardia; Tobruk.

Ctesiphon I (*Roman Empire's Parthian Wars*) *165*. Lucius Verus and Avidius Cassius took Roman legions into

Asia Minor to subdue Vologesus III and his Parthian army, which had conquered Armenia. Cassius stormed the Parthian capital, Ctesiphon, on the east bank of the Tigris, and burned it; Verus campaigned through Media, northwards. Beaten, Vologesus submitted and ceded upper Mesopotamia to the Romans. *See* Arsanius River.

Ctesiphon II (*Roman Empire's Parthian Wars***)** *197–8*. Another attempt by the Parthians, under Vologesus IV this time, to drive the Romans from Asia. Septimius Severus, with a large army of legionaries, forced the Parthians to abandon their siege of Nisibis and drove the Parthian army relentlessly ahead of him, taking Ctesiphon without serious check, and sacking it. *See* Ctesiphon I; Lugdunum.

Ctesiphon III (*World War I***)** *22 November 1915*. Having captured Kut-al-Amara, the British (Townshend) headed for Baghdad, but at Ctesiphon, 20 miles from the objective, they ran into strong Turkish positions (Nur-ud-din). Townshend attacked, but the Turks outnumbered his 14,000 British and Indian troops, who suffered 4,500 casualties. Townshend retreated to Kut, q.v.

Cuaspad (*Colombia–Ecuador War***)** *6 December 1862*. Mosquera, who led 4,000 Colombians, routed Flores' 6,000 Ecuadorians, who lost 1,600 killed or wounded, 2,000 prisoners and all their guns.

Cuban Civil War *1953–9*. This was a minor war with only intermittent small-scale fighting, but it brought to power Fidel Castro, one of the most influential national leaders of the century. Castro's first campaign — an attack on a barracks in Santiago de Cuba — was a disaster; seventy-five of his 150 men were killed and he was captured. Released in an amnesty, he went to Mexico but returned as leader of an invasion (20 November 1956) which was also disastrous. During 1957–8 he raised a rebel guerrilla army and forced President Batista to flee the country.

Cuddalore (*War of the American Revolution***)** *20 June 1783*. A naval action fought at long range between seventeen British ships (Sir Edward Hughes) and twelve French (Suffren). Nightfall put an end to the action and left Suffren in command of the approaches to Cuddalore. The British lost 532 men. Hughes and Suffren confronted each other five times without result. *See* Trincomalee.

Cuddalore (*War of the American Revolution***)** *13 June 1784*. The British (General Stewart) attacked the French and drove them from their trenches. Casualties: French, 700 men and 13 guns; British, 1,013 killed or wounded. *See* Trincomalee.

Culloden, *Drummossie Moor* **(***Rebellion of the Forty-Five***)** *16 April 1746*. Between the Royal troops under the Duke of Cumberland and the Highlanders led by the Young Pretender, Prince Charles Edward. The English regular troops routed the rebels then ruthlessly pursued and cut them down; Cumberland became known as "Butcher". The Royalists lost 309 killed or wounded, the Highlanders had 1,000 killed and 1,000 captured; most of the prisoners were killed out of hand or summarily executed. *See* Falkirk II.

Cumae (*Sicilian–Etrurian War***)** *474 BC*. Hiero with the Syracusan fleet of galleys stopped the southward expansion of Etruria in a sustained sea battle. The victory strengthened Syracuse's domination of the central Mediterranean. *See* Himera.

Cunaxa, *near Babylon, Assyria* **(***Greek–Persian Wars***)** *September 401 BC*. Between the Persians, said to be 400,000-strong, under Artaxerxes and an army of 100,000 Asiatics led by his brother Cyrus, aided by 14,000 Greek mercenaries (Clearchus). The Greeks on

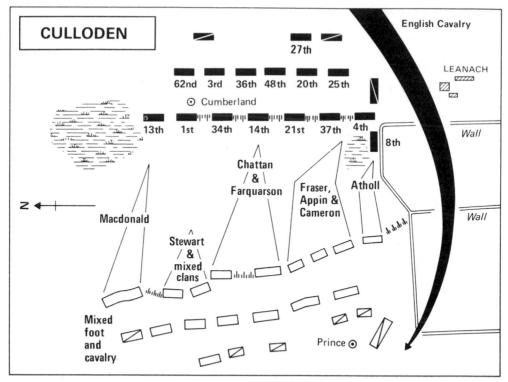

the right drove back the Persian left and Cyrus in the centre broke Artaxerxes' bodyguard, which fled. While pursuing his brother, Cyrus was killed and his troops instantly broke formation and ran. The Greeks, refusing to surrender, were allowed to keep their arms and march to the coast. Cyrus' expedition is the basis of Xenophon's military history, *Anabasis*. Xenophon led 10,000 Greeks on a 5-month 1,000-mile march to safety, which he describes in the *Anabasis*.

Cuneo (*or Coni*) near Genoa (*War of Austrian Succession*) *30 September 1744*. French and Spanish troops, under Prince Louis and Prince Philip respectively, were besieging the Austrian-held Cuneo. Charles Emmanuel I, King of Sardinia, and an Austrian army (Lobkowitz) marched to relieve the city and on 30 September were met and driven back by the French–Spanish force at Madonna del Olmo. However, the French and Spanish lifted the siege on 22 October. *See* Fontenoy; Velletri.

Curicta, *an island off Illyria* (*Great Roman Civil War*) *49 BC*. The Pompeian fleet (Marcus Octavius) destroyed the Caesarian fleet (Dolabella). The Caesarian army on Curicta (Caisu Antonius) was thus cut off and forced to surrender. *See* Pharsalus.

Curupayti (*War of the Triple Alliance or Lopez War*) *22 September 1866*. The Paraguayans (Francisco Lopez) defeated the Allied Brazil–Argentine–Uruguay army (Flores). The Allies lost 9,000 men to the Paraguayans' 54. *See* Aquidaban.

Curzola (*or Korcula*) (*Venetian–Genoese Wars*) *May 1299*. The maritime Genoese, regarding the treaty made between the Venetians and Turks as a trading threat, challenged the Venetian fleet off the Dalmatian coast and soundly defeated it. (Marco Polo was among the many Venetian prisoners.) *See* Campaldino; Pulj.

Custozza I (*Italian Wars of Indepen-dence*) 24 July 1848. An uprising in Milan, 18–22 March, drove out the Austrian army of occupation (Radetsky). Charles Albert, King of Sardinia, declared war on Austria. Italians from Piedmont and Lombardy gave battle to Radetsky's army at Custozza near Verona and were severely mauled; Charles Albert's army was driven out of Lombardy. Rebel casualties amounted to about 7,000. *See* Rieti; Tolentino.

Custozza II (*Seven Weeks' War*) 24 June 1866. A notable victory by 80,000 Austrians (Archduke Albert) over 140,000 Italians (La Marmora). La Marmora crossed the Mincio River to attack Albert, who was covering Verona, but in passing through mountainous country the Italian columns became separated and as they reached the plain of Custozza they were beaten one by one and La Marmora retreated. Casualties: Austrian, 4,650 killed or wounded; Italians, 720 killed, 3,112 wounded, 4,315 taken prisoner. *See* Aspromonte; Vis.

Cuzco (*Spanish conquest of Peru*) September 1536. Juan and Gonzalo Pizarro with only 250 men defended Cuzco against a reported 200,000 Peruvians for 5 months. The Spaniard Almagro, having been assigned certain conquered territories, then arrived, attacked the Peruvians and routed them. But he laid siege to Cuzco on his own account and soon forced Gonzalo Pizarro to surrender, Juan having died during the siege.

Cyme 474 BC. The Etruscan fleet, investing the Greek colony of Cyme, south of Ionia, was routed by the Syracusan fleet (Hiero). The rapid decline of Etruscan power began from this time. *See* Himera.

Cynoessema, *Thrace* (*Peloponnesian War*) 411 BC. Between eighty-six Peloponnesian ships (Mindarus) and seventy-six Athenian triremes (Thrasybulus and Thrasyllus). Mindarus broke the Greek centre, but the Greek wings enveloped and overwhelmed Minarus' ships who saw victory taken from his grasp. *See* Cyzicus; Syracuse.

Cynoscephalae I, *Thessaly* (*Greek city-states' Wars*) July 364 BC. This battle resulted from forced marches made by the Thebans and Thessalonians (Pelopidas) and the army of Alexander, Despot of Pherae (a city of Thessaly), to seize the heights of Cynoscephalae. Both armies reached the spot at the same time. The Theban cavalry drove back Alexander's horsemen, but while they wasted time in pursuit Alexander's infantry consolidated on the heights. They were dislodged after fierce fighting, Alexander was defeated but Pelopidas was killed. *See* Leuctra; Mantinea.

Cynoscephalae II (*Second Macedonian War*) 197 BC. Philip V of Macedonia, intent on empire-building, drove many Greek cities into joining the anti-Macedonian alliance. Even then the Macedonians were dominant. Rome, responding to pleas for help against Philip, sent Flaminius with 20,000 legionaries to Greece. On the heights of Cynoscephalae, south-east Thessaly, the legionaries gave battle to Philip's 20,000 Macedonians and crushingly defeated them, 10,000 Macedonians being killed or wounded. *See* Pania; Pydna; Sellasia; Thermopylae II.

Cyprus (*Turkish conquest*) 1570–1. The Venetians refused a Turkish demand to surrender Cyprus and 50,000 Turks invaded the island, conquering all except the port of Famagusta. Here 7,000 Venetians and Cypriots held out until 3 August 1571 when, having been promised safe conduct, they surrendered. However, most of the leaders were massacred and European feeling against the Turks hardened. *See* Lepanto; Malta.

Cyprus 1954–60. In 1954 demands for Enosis (union with Greece) were pressed by the Greek Cyprian community. After numerous acts of terrorism a compromise solution was evolved (1959) and implemented in August 1960. The British, who had made Cyprus a crown colony in 1925, had a difficult task in controlling the EOKA terrorists led by General Grivas. The British Army, under various commanders but notably General Harding, suffered 320 casualties before U.N. forces assumed responsibility for keeping the peace between Turks and Cypriots.

Cyprus *1963–74*. In December 1963 British troops were called in to deal with serious rioting and the following year a U.N. peacekeeping force was sent. In June 1964 General Grivas returned and was appointed commander of the Greek Cypriot National Guard, which engaged the Turks in violent fighting. The Turkish village of Kokkina was blockaded for 4 years. In 1974 Turkish troops landed near Kyrenia and fighting followed. Following a cease-fire on 16 August the Turks declared the Turkish Federated State of Cyprus.

Cyssus (*Wars of the Hellene Monarchies*) *191 BC*. A Roman fleet of 105 triremes (Caius Livius) defeated the seventy-ship fleet of Antiochus under Polyxenides. *See* Magnesia.

Cyzicus I (*or Cyzicum*) near Armedia, Asia Minor (*Peloponnesian War*) *410 BC*. Mindarus, besieging Cyzicus, was surprised by the Peloponnesian admiral, Alcibiades, whose eighty-six ships practically annihilated the Peloponnesian fleet. Mindarus was killed in action. A land battle took place simultaneously and again Alcibiades forces were successful. *See* Cynossema.

Cyzicus II (*Third Mithridatic War*) *73 BC*. A classic case of piecemeal defeat. The Pontic army of Mithridates VII was besieging Cyzicus when Lucullus, leading a Roman relief force, hemmed in the enemy. Unable, because of inferior numbers, to venture a pitched battle, Lucullus

so wore down the Pontic Army that eventually he destroyed it, causing losses estimated at 200,000. Mithridates himself was lucky to escape. *See* Tigranocerta.

Cyzicus III (*Muslim invasions*) *672*. For more than 50 years Muslim Arabs had warred to overthrow the Byzantine empire and many sea battles took place as the Arabs strove for a foothold west of the Bosporus. In the battle of Cyzicus in the Sea of Marmara the Byzantines destroyed the Arab fleet. Greek fire, an early form of napalm, was used in the battle, apparently for the first time. Greek fire continued to play a major part in destroying Muslim battle ships and in burning invaders away from the walls of Constantinople. *See* Constantinople III.

Czarnovo, Bohemia (*Napoleonic Wars: Friedland campaign*) *24 December 1806*. Napoleon, with Davoust's corps, crossed the Ukra River at night and drove Count Tolstoy's 15,000 Russians from Czarnovo, with a loss of 1,600 men and several guns. The French lost 700. *See* Friedland; Jena.

Czaslau, Bohemia (*War of Austrian Succession*) *17 March 1742*. The Austrians (Charles of Lorraine) drove the Prussians (Frederick the Great) from the field but abandoned the pursuit to plunder the Prussian baggage. Frederick, rallying his army, counter-attacked and broke the main Austrian force, inflicting 4,000 casualties. *See* Chotusitz.

Czechoslovakia (*Soviet invasion*) *1968*. The Czech leadership, under Alexander Dubcek (First Secretary) and General Svoboda (President), had permitted much political freedom in what was known as "the Prague Spring". To "restore order", on the night of 20–21 August about 250,000 Soviet troops invaded Czechslovakia, took over the country and replaced Dubcek with the Soviet puppet, Gustav Husak.

Daegestan *603*. *See* Degsastan

Dakar, *French West Africa (World War II) 23–25 September 1940*. A British naval force (Admiral Cunningham) and Free French troops (de Gaulle) were sent to seize the strategic port and air base of Dakar. The governor, Boisson, loyal to the Vichy (pro-German) government, organized the repulse of this attack. (The Allies secured Dakar, without a fight, in November 1942, following the invasion of French North Africa.) *See* Oran.

Dalmanutha (*Second British–Boer War*) *21–28 August 1900*. The Boers under Botha held a 30-mile position from Belfast to Machadodorp, covering the Delagoa Bay Railway. Lord Roberts attacked on the west and Buller, driving from the south, entered Machadodorp on 28 August. British casualties were 500. *See* Ladysmith.

Damascus I (*Muslim invasion of Syria*) *635*. The Muslims (Khaled) besieged a large garrison of Greeks and Romans, who sent for help to Werdan, a general of the Emperor Heraclius. Werdan's approach drew Khaled away, but the garrison made the mistake of venturing out after him. Khaled inflicted great losses on them, then defeated Werdan and returned to the siege; 2 months later he took Damascus by storm. *See* Yarmuk.

Damascus II (*Byzantine–Muslim Wars*) *976*. Campaigning through Syria to break the Muslim empire, John I Zimisces and his veteran and skilful Byzantine cavalry beat the Muslims in every conflict, their victories culminating in the capture of Damascus. *See* Aleppo–Antioch; Sofia.

Damascus III (*Second Crusade*) *1148*. The few survivors of the Second Crusade joined Baldwin III of Jerusalem in an attack on the Turks, but instead of directly attacking the Turkish leader, Nureddin, they moved on Damascus to cut the road between the chief Muslim centres of Cairo and Baghdad. Assembling at Acre, the knights broke the outer defences of Damascus, 25 July, but then abandoned their siege on hearing that Nureddin was approaching with a large relief army. Retreating to Galilee, 28 July, the Crusaders lost heavily to the Turkish mounted bowmen and their commando-like tactics. *See* Ashkelon; Dorylaeum II.

Damascus IV (*Tartar invasion*) *25 January 1401*. Tamerlane and his Tartars captured the city through treachery by some of its garrison. *See* Aleppo.

Damascus V. *See* Megiddo III.

Damietta, *eastern Nile delta (Fifth Crusade) 1218–21*. In May 1218 Crusaders from Acre and Sicily moved on Damietta as part of a campaign to attack

139

Egypt, believed to be the weak spot of the Muslim world. Divided by dissension, unable to follow a single leader and waiting for the arrival of Frederick II, the King of Germany and Holy Roman Emperor, the Crusaders settled down to a siege. The sultan, Malik al-Kamil, manoeuvred his fine Mameluke troops into position. In November 1219 the Crusaders captured Damietta, but 2 years of extraordinary bickering followed. In July 1221 Cardinal Pelagius assumed command and marched on Cairo with 45,000 men. Blocked by the fort of El Mansura, with his men struggling in flooded ground and the Egyptian fleet sailing downstream to cut him from his base, the cardinal suggested peace. The Egyptian terms were generous: The sultan would allow the crusaders to escape from the trap if they would evacuate Damietta and abandon the campaign. This they did; the crusade had failed. *See* Constantinople.

Damme, *Belgium (English–French Wars) 30 March 1213*. The Earl of Salisbury with, according to report, 500 vessels attacked and dispersed a large fleet of French ships supporting Philip Augustus' invasion of Flanders. The English captured 300 and burnt 100 enemy ships. *See* Bouvines; Muret.

Danbury (*American Revolution*) *26–28 April 1777*. The British General Tryon, landing near Fairfield, Connecticut, marched into Danbury on 26 April and destroyed great quantities of American supplies. General Benedict Arnold raised 700 militiamen and blocked Tryon's retreat; Tryon had 2,000 men so was able to break through the American positions and embarked his men on 28 April. Each side suffered 200 casualties. *See* Fort Ticonderoga; Princeton.

Dan-No-Ura, *Japan (Taira War)* 1189. Between the army of the Shogun, Yorimoto, under his brothers Noriyori and Yoshitsune, and the Taira Clan, under Munemori. The defeat of the Taira broke the clan's power and the Minamoto group became the dominant Japanese faction.

Danzig I (*Thirty Years' War*) *1627–8*. Gustavus Adolphus laid siege to the fort early in 1627, but the Polish garrison held out until the truce of 16 September 1629. In one abortive attack, 27 May 1627, Gustavus was seriously wounded. In October 1627 the Danzig ships sallied out and defeated the Swedish fleet. *See* Dessau.

Danzig II (*War for the Polish throne*) *October 1733–June 1734*. France, Spain and Sardinia supported Leszczynski as new monarch of Poland; Russia and Austria supported Augustus III, son of the previous ruler, Augustus II. In October 1733 the Allies besieged the Polish city of Danzig, where Leszczynski himself commanded the garrison. The French navy tried to relieve Danzig, but it capitulated on 2 June 1734; Leszczynski fled to Paris. The Austrian–Prussian Allies did not have another important victory. *See* Parma III.

Danzig III (*Napoleonic Wars: Campaign of Friedland*) *March–May 1807*. Marshal Lefébvre, with 18,000 French, besieged the city, defended by 14,000 Prussians and 4,000 Russians (Kalkreuth). Lefébvre, commencing operations on 19 March, had too few men for the 17-mile siege trenches and not until 12 April, when he received reinforcements, did he make any progress. On 15 May 8,000 Russians tried *en bloc* to relieve the fortress, but the French inflicted 2,000 casualties to 400 of their own. Lefébvre planned an assault, 21 May, but just before this Kalkreuth offered to parley. He surrendered on 26 May, having then only 7,000 fit men. *See* Eylau; Heilsburg.

Danzig IV (*Napoleonic Wars: Moscow campaign*) *January–November 1813*. After the French retreat from Moscow, General Rapp with 30,000 survivors was besieged in Danzig by 30,000 Allied soldiers under the Duke of Wurtemberg. Rapp's defence was masterly, but his garrison dwindled from starvation and exposure and he surrendered on 29 November. *See* Berezina.

Dara (*Byzantine–Persian Wars*) *530*. Because the Byzantines had built the fort of Dara, northern Mesopotamia, the Persians declared war and sent an army to destroy the place. Not waiting for them to arrive, the great soldier Belisarius moved his forces out to meet the Persian invaders. Attacking frontally with his Byzantines, Belisarius used an aggressive corps of Hun cavalry to attack on the flank. The Persians broke and ran, leaving 8,000 dead on the field. *See* Amida II; Callinicum.

Dardanelles (*World War I*) *19 February–18 March 1915*. The abortive British naval attack, with some French assistance, to force the passage of the Dardanelles and take Constantinople from the Turkish enemy. Gunfire reduced Turkish forts in February and March. On 18 March the British Admiral de Robeck attacked, but new Turkish gun positions on both sides of the narrow waterway were devastatingly accurate. Enemy mines were even more destructive; three heavy ships and several smaller ones were lost and another three big ones crippled. Robeck withdrew. The naval failure led to the equally abortive and far more costly Gallipoli land operation. Winston Churchill had engineered both. *See* Gallipoli.

Dargai (*British–Tirah campaign*) *20 October 1897*. A small-scale but famous British victory. A large force of Afridis held the heights of Dargai and were driven from them by a British brigade, the Gordon Highlanders forming the striking force. They lost 37 killed and 175 wounded. Before the attack the Gordons' colonel, Mathias, addressed them: "Highlanders, the General says the position must be taken at all costs. The Gordons will take it."

Darwin (*World War II*) *19 February 1942*. The only battle of any kind to take place on the Australian mainland. Having swept through south-east Asia and the south-west Pacific, the Japanese bombed the northern Australian port of Darwin; the 200-plane attack sank all seventeen ships in the harbour and caused great damage. Only five Japanese planes were lost to twenty-two Australian and American. *See* New Guinea.

Dazaifu (*Chinese invasion of Japan*) *1281*. Kublai Khan sent Hwan Buako with 100,000 Chinese and 10,000 Koreans to land at Dazaifu. The Japanese held them off for 60 days, when a typhoon dispersed the invasion fleet. The survivors under Chang Pak occupied the island of Takashima where a Japanese army (Shomi Kagasuke) practically annihilated them. It is fairly certain that only 3,000 Chinese returned home.

D-Day, *invasion of Normandy* (*World War II*) *6 June 1944*. This invasion was made by 5,000 ships (including 702 warships) and 4,000 additional ship-to-shore craft, 11,300 aircraft and in the first 5 days sixteen Allied divisions of troops (about 300,000 men). By 20 June 1,000,000 men had been landed. The Allied Supreme Commander was the American, General Dwight Eisenhower, his deputy was Air Chief Marshal Sir Arthur Tedder, R.A.F. Eisenhower's three Commanders-in-Chief were Admiral Sir Bertram Ramsay, naval; Air Chief Marshal Sir Trafford Leigh-Mallory, air; General Bernard Montgomery, land. The Germans were led by Field Marshal von Runstedt, with Field Marshal Rommel commanding Army Group B. In all, von Runstedt had fifty infantry and ten panzer divisions, of which thirty-six infantry and nine panzer were located from Holland to Lorient, Bay of Biscay. He had fourteen divisions immediately available along the 60-mile invasion front of Cotentin Peninsula, the salient attack features being five beaches — Juno, Gold, Omaha, Utah, Sword.

From D-Day to 10 June Allied planes

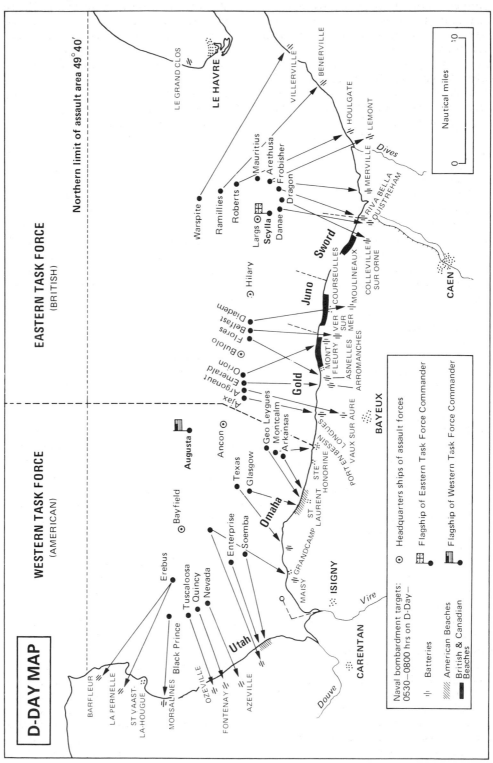

D-DAY MAP

WESTERN TASK FORCE
(AMERICAN)

EASTERN TASK FORCE
(BRITISH)

Northern limit of assault area 49° 40'

Naval bombardment targets:
0530—0800 hrs on D-Day—

⊙ Headquarters ships of assault forces

🏛 Flagship of Eastern Task Force Commander

▦ Flagship of Western Task Force Commander

⦀ Batteries

American Beaches

British & Canadian Beaches

Nautical miles

0   10

dropped 27,000 tons of bombs, many of them in futile obliteration bombing which did very little damage to the Germans but destroyed French town and villages; in Caen alone 5,000 French civilians were killed. Much of the bombing had no effect other than to delay the Allied troops, who were often air-bombed by their own side. The invasion, nevertheless, was competently planned with three airborne divisions being dropped or landed behind enemy lines within 4 hours of the attack commencing.

The German defence was crippled by the compromise evolved by von Rundstedt and Rommel. Rommel had always favoured fighting the enemy on the beaches; von Rundstedt's plan was to let the enemy gain a footing and then counter-attack in great strength. The compromise meant that the German infantry were kept well forward and the armour well back. There was no secondary defensive line so that the whole system was, in effect, a Maginot wall; astonishingly, Hitler and Rommel had the same confidence in it as the French had in the Maginot Line in 1940.

The joining of the Allied beachheads for 80 miles along the Normandy coast and the penetration to a depth of 20 miles at Bayeux marked the end of the first phase of the invasion, but the initiative had been with the Allies since 9 June. On 13 July Stalin said: "The history of wars does not know any such undertaking so broad in conception and so grandiose in scale and so masterly in execution." The execution left much to be desired; the Allies had the weight but not the movement and their overcaution lengthened the war. General Fuller says: "The insistence on attempting to achieve tactical mobility by means of 'colossal cracks' was asinine . . . it was totally unnecessary . . ." (*The Second World War*, 1948).

During the first 2 weeks of fighting in Normandy — 6–20 June 1944 — Allied casualties were 40,549 killed and nearly 100,000 wounded. Of these three-fifths were American, since Americans had struggled for the central beachhead and

had made the drive on Cherbourg. On 19 June General Montgomery reported that German casualties to that date had been 156,000, of which 60,000 were prisoners of war. *See* Falaise–Argentan Pocket.

Dego, *north-west Italy (Wars of the French Revolution) 14–15 April 1796*. Napoleon, with Austrian enemies on his right and Piedmontese on his left, and with his 40,000 men outnumbered by 10,000, attacked the fort at Dego. The garrison of 4,000 surrendered and Napoleon had achieved his aim of keeping the Allies apart. Massena, entrusted with the holding of Dego, incompetently allowed the Austrians to recapture it on 15 April. Napoleon had to counter-attack and recapture the place later the same day. It was a remarkable tactical and strategical performance. *See* Mondovi.

Degsastan (*or Daegestan*) 603. The Northumbrians (King Aethelfrith) defeated the Scots and Picts of Dalriada (King Aidan). The setback was so decisive that for 400 years the Scots could not occupy land south of the Firth of Forth. *See* Chester; Dyrham.

Deig I (*or Deeg*) (*First British–Mahratta War*) *12 November 1780*. General Fraser and 6,000 British routed a much larger force of Mahrattas and captured eighty-seven guns. The British lost 643 men, including the commander. *See* Ahmadabad.

Deig II (*Second British–Mahratta War*) *December 1804*. Lord Lake, a talented cavalry leader, besieged the fortress held by Holkar on 11 December. After 6 days' bombarment the place was taken by storm. *See* Farrukhbad.

Delhi I (*First Mongol invasion of India*) *1297*. Ala-ud-Din gathered 300,000 Delhi Muhammedans, with 2,700 elephants, to repel Kuttugh Khan's 200,000 invading Mongols. The pitched battle pivoted with the Mongols driving in the Indian left and the Indian right overwhelming the Mongol left. Kuttugh Khan lost so heavily that he could not remain in India. *See* Delhi II.

Delhi II (*Second Mongol invasion of India*) *1398*. Tamerlane, leading 700 Mongol horsemen, crossed the Jumna to reconnoitre and was attacked by 5,000 cavalry under Mammud Tughlak, the Muhammadan leader. Tamerlane beat off this attack, brought his army across the river, defeated the Muhammadan forces and plundered Delhi before withdrawing. *See* Meerut.

Delhi III (*Second British–Mahratta War*) *11 September 1803*. About 20,000 Mahrattas (Bourguin) held strong positions with the Jumna River in their rear. Lord Lake, with only 4,000 British, feigned a retreat, drew the Mahrattas from their lines and then turned on them. Driven at bayonet and sword-point into the river the Mahrattas lost heavily. British casualties were 400. *See* Alighar.

Delhi IV (*Second British–Mahratta War*) *1804*. On 7 October 20,000 Mahrattas (Jeswunt Holkar) with 100 guns besieged the fort, held by only a few hundred British. Inexplicably, Holkar withdrew after 9 days.

Delhi V (*Indian Mutiny*) *June–September 1857*. Delhi became the rallying point for the mutineers and on 8 June General Barnard with only 3,500 troops laid partial siege to the place but could not contain the 30,000 mutineers. On 8 September reinforcing British batteries began to breach the walls and on the 14th the city was attacked. The palace held out until 20 September. General John Nicholson, the driving force of the army, was killed during the fighting; the nominal commander was General Archdale Wilson. British casualties during the campaign amounted to 4,000. *See* Delhi; Lucknow.

Delium (*Peloponnesian War*) *424 BC*. Between 17,000 Athenians (Hippocrates) and 18,000 Boeotians (Pagondas). The Athenians, after a stubborn fight, broke and fled when they saw a strong cavalry force on their flank, Hippocrates was killed. *See* Amphipolis; Pylos-Sphacteria.

Delphi (*Third Sacred War*) *355 BC*. The Phocians, 5,000-strong under Philomelus, had seized the sacred city; they attacked the Locrians on the heights above and routed them, driving many over precipices.

Denain, *south-east of Lille* (*War of the Spanish Succession*) *24 July 1712*. A little known Allied British–Dutch defeat at the hands of the French. The Earl of Albemarle, encamped with ten battalions, was attacked by Marshal Villiers leading 130 battalions. Prince Eugene tried to help but was unable to cross the Scheldt and the Allies were overwhelmed. Five generals were killed or captured and only 4,000 men escaped. *See* Brihuega; Malplaquet.

Dennewitz (*Napoleonic Wars: Campaign of Leipzig*) *6 September 1813*. An intended demonstration which became a serious action between the French and the Allied European armies. Marshal Ney detached Bertrand's division to mask Dennewitz while he marched his main army along the road to Berlin. Bertrand was supposed to demonstrate and then move on, but he delayed so long that action was joined and the French lost 10,000 men and 43 guns. *See* Leipzig.

Derna, *Libya* (*World War II*) *27–29 January 1941*. This town, heavily defended by Italians, was captured by a company of the Australian 6th Division at the low cost of twenty-three casualties. *See* Benghazi; Sollum; Tobruk.

Dernancourt, *France* (*World War I*) *28 March–8 April 1918*. A battle of the great German spring offensive. Two Australian brigades held off most of four German divisions. The Australians suffered 1,223 casualties. *See* Somme.

Dessau Bridge (*Thirty Years' War*) 25 April 1626. Between the German Protestants (von Mansfeldt) and the Imperialists (Wallenstein). Mansfeldt was assaulting the fort of Dessau, on the Elbe, when Wallenstein, moving through timbered country, attacked him by surprise on the flank. Three-quarters of Mansfeldt's army was killed or captured — 12,000 in all. *See* Lutter am Barenberge; Stadtlohn.

Detroit (*British–American War of 1812–14*) 16 August 1812. The American General William Hull, with 2,200 men, crossed the Detroit River, 12 July, to invade Canada. Retreating to Detroit, 8 August, Hull for no good reason surrendered, 16 August, to General Brock's 2,000 Canadians who had followed him south. Since Brock had the previous day ambushed and wiped out the garrison of Fort Dearborn (now Chicago) — Hull's fault also — the American setback was decisive. *See* Fort Dearborn; Queenston Heights.

Dettingen (*War of Austrian Succession*) 27 June 1743. Between 40,000 British (George II) and 60,000 French (Duc de Noailles). The British, retiring towards Hanau from Aschaffenburg, were cut off by the French at Dettingen, which was held by de Grammont with 23,000 men. The main French force was on the opposite bank of the Main. de Grammont foolishly left his lines to attack the British; George led in person the charge which drove the French into the river. They left behind 6,000 killed, wounded and taken prisoner. This is the last occasion on which a British sovereign led troops in the field. *See* Mollwitz.

Deutschbrod (*Hussite War*) 1422. John Zisca, leading the Taborite section of the Hussites, defeated the Germans under the Emperor Sigismund. *See* Aussig; Prague.

Devicotta, *Bengal 1749*. A British force of 2,300 (Major Lawrence) bombarded the fortress held by a garrison of the Tanjore army (Pertab Singh) before Robert Clive led the first attack on the breach. This failed, but Lawrence arrived with the main column and the fortress was taken. *See* Arcot.

Dhofar 1965–76. Between the Sultan's Armed Forces (SAE) and the rebel Dhofar Liberation Front (DLF), which was later absorbed by the Communist People's Front for the Liberation of Occupied Arabian Gulf (PFLOAG). By 1970 PFLOAG controlled nearly all Dhofar, and to save the regime Qaboos, son of Sultan Said bin Tamur, deposed his weak father. Sultan Qaboos asked Britain for help and an SAS detachment and engineers were sent. Jordan and Iran despatched infantry units to aid the Sultan. A pitched battle took place at Marbat on 18 July 1972, when 250 well-armed rebels attacked the fort's garrison. It was held by sixty-five men, including ten SAS soldiers of B Squadron under Captain Mike Kealy; two of these men manned a 25-pounder. The desperate battle was turned when eighteen SAS reinforcements arrived by helicopter. Between 1971 and 1975 the Sultan's forces lost 187 men killed and 559 wounded; twenty-four and fifty-five respectively were British. The Dhofar army was commanded (1973–75) by Major-General Tim Creasey and the Dhofar Brigade by Brigadier J. Fletcher (1972–4) and Brigadier J. Akehurst (1974–6). The war is one of the most interesting examples of counter-insurgency operations.

Diamond, *Co. Armagh 21 September 1795*. A faction conflict between the Peep o'Day Boys and the Defenders, who lost forty-eight killed.

Diamond Hill, *near Pretoria (Second British–Boer War*) 11–12 June 1900. Lord Roberts, with 17,000 men and seventy guns, attacked at three points the entrenched lines of General Botha, who had 15,000 men. The British won, but lost 25 officers and 137 men. *See* Ladysmith.

Dien Bien Phu, *North Vietnam (French–Vietnamese War) March– May 1954.* Dien Bien Phu, the French base in the mountains of North Vietnam, was one of the most tenaciously defended fortresses of modern history. It illustrated two methods of waging war, the Western conventional and the Communist improvised, and it showed how Communists employ battles as instruments of political strategy. The French commander-in-chief was General Henri Navarre, the field commander of Dien Bien Phu fortress, Colonel de Castrie. The leader of the Communist Viet Minh forces was General Vo Nguyen Giap. Navarre believed he could smash the Viet Minh by firepower in a pitched battle, but the defences, in a valley bottom, could be plainly seen and were vulnerable to medium artillery. By March 1954 the fortress and its garrison of 10,000 was closely invested by virtually all the Viet Minh army — 50,000 infantry and 150 guns or heavy mortars. On 12 March the Viet Minh took the strongpoint Beatrice, on 14 March Gabrielle. Viet Minh fire closed the airstrip. The Viet Minh had so far lost 2,500 killed.

The second offensive, 30 March–12 April, failed completely. Giap resorted to siege warfare and steadily encroached into the French positions. (At this point the U.S. Government, influenced by British government opinion, refused French requests to intervene). Towards the end of April French fighting strength was about 5,000, against 35,000 Communists. The third assault began on 1 May and by the morning of 7 May only the central area, round de Castrie's command post, held out, to surrender at 4.30 p.m. The 56-day siege cost the Viet Minh 7,000 killed and 15,000 wounded. The French had 1,000 killed, 1,600 missing and 7,000 taken prisoner. Next day, 8 May, the Geneva Conference to discuss Indo-China began; Dien Bien Phu resulted in the Geneva Accords, by which the French army was to evacuate Indo-China; Vietnam was to be partitioned between the Viet Minh in the north and a

pro-Western state in the south. In turn, this led to the American–Viet Cong War. The belief that Dien Bien Phu was a complete French military defeat is ill-founded; had the garrison been entirely formed of Paras and Foreign Legion, it might well have held. *See* Vietnam.

Dieppe *(World War II) 19 August 1942.* An abortive combined operations frontal attack by Canadian troops on German coast defences at Dieppe. A strategic move planned to test the strength of German defences and to discover the problems of invasion, the raid was principally the decision of Lord Louis Mountbatten, adviser on combined operations to the Defence Committee and the Chiefs of Staff, and of Lord Montgomery. The Canadian commander in the field was Major-General J. H. Roberts. A total of 237 ships — many of them small and unarmed — carried 6,100 men; Canadians made up 298 officers and 4,663 men. Other units were British commandos and Royal Marine Commandos and fifty U.S. Rangers. They were supported in attack by the R.C.A.F. The German commander at Dieppe, Colonel-General Hasse, had immensely strong positions very much on the alert. The battle lasted 9 hours and was a debacle. Nearly 1,000 Canadians were unable to land, while only 600 wounded and few unhurt men returned. Nearly 1,000 Canadians died on the beaches; more than 2,000 were taken prisoner. The Royal Regiment of Canada suffered 94.5 per cent casualties.

Yet for all this, Hasse had defended the Dieppe sea front by only one company of infantry. German losses have never been fully detailed, but could not have exceeded 600 dead and wounded. Only three prisoners were taken to England. The Germans are believed to have lost ninety-one aircraft (the Luftwaffe reported only forty-eight) while ninety-eight British and Canadian planes were lost. Mountbatten said of the raid that "it was one of the most vital operations of the war. It gave to the Allies the priceless secret of victory . . .", i.e. the knowledge for the success of the invasion of Europe. *See* D-Day.

Dingaan's Day *16 December 1838*. The Transvaal Boers heavily defeated the Zulus, led by Dingaan. The Boers also defeated the Zulus at Blood River and Magango.

Dipaea (*Arcadian War*) *471 BC*. The Spartans defeated the Arcadian League. Tegea, the head of the League, shortly afterwards submitted to Sparta.

Diu Island I (*Portuguese invasion of India*) *21 February 1509*. The Muslims held the island of Diu, western India. On 2 February Francisco de Almeida's fleet destroyed the Muslim fleet and began a 450-year Portuguese territorial interest in India.

Diu Island II *September 1537*. A garrison of only 600 (Antonio de Silveira), defending a small Portuguese post, were besieged by seventy-six Turkish galleys and 7,000 soldiers (Suleiman, Pasha of Egypt) and by 20,000 Gujeratis (Bahadur Shah and Khojar Zofar). The Portuguese repulsed several assaults but were weakening when the false report of an approaching Portuguese fleet caused Suleiman to withdraw.

Diu Island III *1545*. Again besieged by the Gujeratis (Khojar Zofar), the garrison (Mascarenhas) beat back many assaults and killed Khojar Zofar. Famine was forcing defeat when Diu was relieved by Juan de Castro, who soundly defeated the Gujeratis. *See* Goa.

Dniepr River *August–December 1943*. General Manstein asked Hitler seven times for permission to withdraw to the Dniepr River; in August he was permitted to do so. He had only thirty-seven infantry divisions and seventeen Panzer divisions to protect a 450-mile front and his units had to withdraw from some areas to avoid encirclement. Even so, the Germans made some effective counter-offensives, notably the retaking of Zhitomir. Having captured Kiev, 6 November, the Russians were able to cross the Dniepr. *See* Kursk; Donets.

Dniester (*Turkish–Russian War*) *9 September 1769*. The Turks (Ali Moldovani Pasha) crossed the Dniester River in the face of the Russian army (Prince Galitzin) and were only narrowly beaten off after severe fighting. *See* Ceşme.

Dodecanese Islands (*World War II*) *September–November 1943*. The British needed some of the Dodecanese islands, Aegean Sea, as bases for campaigns in the Balkans. In September 1943 troops were landed on Cos, Leros and Samos. In October and November German paratroops recaptured Cos and Leros and the British evacuated Samos. In their brief, violent attacks the Germans took 3,500 prisoners, sank six destroyers and two submarines. About 1,000 British and Greek troops reached safety. The campaign was a strategic error. *See* Balkans; Crete; Greece.

Dodowah (*First British–Ashanti War*) *March 1826*. The Ashanti army, which was invading the Gold Coast (Ghana), was routed, after courageous fighting, by a British force under Colonel Purdom. *See* Accra; Amoaful.

Dogger Bank I (*War of the American Revolution*) *5 August 1781*. A drawn British–Dutch naval battle. Admiral Hyde Parker with thirteen ships (six of them frigates) forced Admiral Zoutman with the same number of ships (including five frigates) to retreat to port, but the British fleet was too crippled to follow. Hyde Parker was criticized for not using his frigates in the action. *See* Praia.

Dogger Bank II (*World War I*) *24 January 1915*. Admiral Beatty's fleet intercepted Von Hipper's squadron off the Dogger Bank and Hipper, taken by surprise, ran for his base in Heligoland. In the pursuit the British cruisers sank *Blucher* and crippled *Seydlitz* while the British flagship, *Lion*, was damaged. *See* Dardanelles; Falkland Islands I.

Dollar (*Danish invasion of Scotland*) *875*. Danish invaders (Thorstem) defeated the men of Alban (Constantine). This led to the Danes occupying Caithness, Sutherland, Ross and Moray. *See* Kinloss.

Dolni-Dubnik   (*Russian–Turkish War*) *1 November 1877*. Negligible as a battle, but the action made the Russian investment of Plevna complete. General Gourko dislodged the Turks from the redoubt of Dolni-Dubnik. *See* Plevna.

Dominica (*or The Battle of the Saints*) (*a group of islands*) *12 April 1782*. A major British–French naval battle during the war of the American Revolution. Rodney, with Hood as second-in-command and thirty-six ships, gave battle to de Grasse with thirty-three ships. Rodney, departing from the usual tactics of a ship-to-ship action, broke the French line and outmanoeuvred de Grasse; the victory was complete, the British capturing or destroying seven ships. Casualties: British, 261 killed, 837 wounded; French, 3,000 killed or wounded, 8,000 captured. *See* Yorktown.

Domokos (*Greek–Turkish War*) *17 May 1879*. An indecisive battle between five Turkish divisions (Edham Pasha) and 40,000 Greeks (Crown Prince of Greece). Late in the evening the Greek right was outflanked and pulled back, but the Turks did not exploit the advantage. During the night the Greeks withdrew. Casualties: Greeks, 600; Turks, 1,800. *See* Missolonghi.

Donabew (*First British–Burma War*) *7–25 March 1825*. General Cotton with 700 men attacked three strong stockades held by 12,000 Burmese (Maha Bandoola) and carried one of them. Sir Archibald Campbell's arrival with guns on the 25th forced the Burmese, who had lost their leader, to withdraw. *See* Kemendine.

Donauwörth, *sometimes called The Schellenberg*, Germany (*War of Spanish Succession*) *2 July 1704*. The British and Imperialists (Marlborough) attacked the French–Bavarian (Marshal Tallard) trenches at Schellenberg, protecting Donauwörth, and forced the enemy to abandon the town. The British lost 5,374; the French losses were heavier. *See* Blenheim; Hochstädt I.

Donets River (*Russian Front, World War II*) *February 1943*. On 15 February the S.S. Panzer Division holding Kharkov broke under Russian pressure and withdrew in panic. Hitler himself rushed to the scene and ordered the recapture of Kharkov. On 21 February General Hoth attacked, pitting his Tiger tanks with their 88 mm guns against the Soviet T-34 tanks. By 28 February the Germans had the Russians in a pincer grip but were short of infantry to trap them. Nevertheless, they claimed to have taken 9,000 men, 615 tanks and 354 guns. The victory enabled the Germans to reach the Donets. *See* Dniepr.

Doornkop (*Jameson's Raid*) *1895–6*. L. S. Jameson, with 470 men, set off from Mafeking on a 140-mile ill-planned raid on Johannesburg, the intention being to encourage a revolt against the Transvaal president, Kruger. Intercepted and defeated by the Boers (Cronje) at Krugersdorp, 1 January, Jameson with some of his men reached Doornkop where they were captured. The raid was a great political embarrassment and led to Cecil Rhode's resignation as prime minister of Cape Colony. *See* Majuba Hill.

Dormeille, *eastern France* 602. The Austrasians and Burgundians (Theodobert and Thierry) inflicted great slaughter on the Neustrians (Clothaire II).

Dornach (*Swiss–Swabian War*) *22 July 1499*. A decisive battle in Swiss history. The Holy Roman Emperor Maximilian I had long wished to bring the Swiss confederation of cantons within his empire. Beaten several times in 1499 at Hard, Bruderholz, Schwaderloh, Franstenz and Calven, Maximilian's Swabian Germans again gave battle to the Swiss on 22 July at Dornach, near Basle on the Birs River. Once again the Swiss pikes and halberds were invincible and the Germans were routed. Switzerland would not again be attacked for more than 200 years. *See* Giornico; Nancy 1477.

Dorylaeum, *later Eskisehir, Asia Minor (First Crusade) July 1097*. A major Crusade victory. Bohemond of Taranto and Raymond of Toulouse led 70,000 Crusaders against the Sultan Soliman's 250,000 Saracens. The Saracens drove back Bohemond's men on their camp and were busy plundering it when Raymond attacked and routed them, inflicting 30,000 casualties for a loss of 4,000. The victory was tactically good and it enforced Turkish respect of European soldiers. *See* Antioch; Nicaea; Tarsus.

Douai *(War of Spanish Succession) 25 April–26 June 1710*. General d'Albergotti held the town with a garrison of 8,000 when Prince Eugene besieged it on 25 April. The French made many sorties and the Austrians many attacks, but the French were unable to relieve the place and d'Albergotti surrendered on 26 June. Eugene lost more than 8,000 killed or wounded. *See* Denain.

Douro River *(Peninsular War) 12 May 1809*. Wellesley (Wellington) crossed the Douro with 12,000 men and drove the French (Soult) out of Oporto. The French lost 116 during the action and 5,000 of their 24,000 during the pursuit; British casualties amounted to 500. *See* Oporto; Talavera.

Dover I *(First Barons' War of England) 1216–17*. Prince Louis of France, invited by the rebel barons to be their king, landed in May 1216 and rapidly captured all the Cinque ports except Dover, where King John's garrison under de Burgh held out. Next year Louis brought a fleet of eighty ships to the attack, but de Burgh with thirty-six ships sailed out to intercept. Attacking with the wind, the English shipboard archers and lime-throwers so demoralized the French that they were able to destroy or capture most of the enemy ships. The French and the barons abandoned the siege of Dover. *See* Lincoln II; Rochester II.

Dover II *(or Kentish Knock) (First English–Dutch War) 28 September 1652*. With sixty ships the Dutch, under De Witt and de Ruyter, outmanoeuvred an equal number of British vessels commanded by Blake, though in the end the advantage lay with Blake.

Dover Strait *(or The Four Days' Battle) (Second English–Dutch War) 1–4 June 1666*. One of the most sustained naval battles in history, fought between 100 British and 100 Dutch ships. De Ruyter engaged the Duke of Albemarle (George Monck) who had eighty ships — Prince Rupert had another twenty guarding the Channel. Beaten back for 2 days, Monck's ships were reinforced by Rupert's and on day 3 the fighting was even. On 4 June de Ruyter's gunnery drove the British into the shelter of the Thames. They had lost 5,000 men killed, eight ships sunk and nine captured. Dutch losses were 4 ships and 2,000 men. *See* Dover Strait; North Foreland II.

Downs, The *(Netherlands War of Independence against Spain) 21 October 1639*. The Dutch Admiral Maarten Tromp sought and engaged a fleet of Spanish waships and transports, under Antonio de Oquendo, making for Holland. With consummate skill he so manoeuvred his ships that the Spanish could hardly find a target and his heavier guns caused great loss to the Spaniards. The victory gave the Dutch mastery of Europe's narrow seas. *See* Rocroi.

Drepanaum (*or Drepana, west Sicily*) (*First Punic Wars*) *249 BC*. A remarkable naval victory for the Carthaginians (Adherbal) over the Roman fleet of 123 galleys (Publius Claudius). Claudius lost 93 ships, 8,000 men killed and 20,000 prisoners; the Carthaginians did not lose a ship. *See* Aegates Islands; Lilybaeum.

Dresden (*Napoleonic Wars: Campaign of Leipzig*) *27 August 1813*. Between Napoleon, with 130,000 French, and 200,000 Allied Russians, Prussians and Austrians, under, respectively, Wittgenstein, Kleist and Schwartzemberg. Napoleon, holding Dresden, sent Murat to attack the Austrian left which was separated from the centre by the ravine of Planen. Murat was successful, driving the Austrians into the ravine. Napoleon's attacks on the enemy centre and right were also successful and the Allies were defeated. Casualties: French, 10,000; Allies, 10,000 killed or wounded, 15,000 prisoners, 40 guns. *See* Katzbach River; Kulm-Priesten.

Dresden, *Bombing of* (*World War II*) *13–15 February 1945*. 800 R.A.F. bombers made two attacks, dropping 650,000 incendiary bombs and 8,000-lb and 4,000-lb high-explosive bombs on the centre of the city. Next day 1,350 American bombers continued the attack, which was taken up on the 15th by 1,100 American bombers. The city was crowded with scores of thousands of refugees fleeing from Marshal Koniev's Russian armies. At least 100,000 people were killed and 30,000 injured; 6 square miles of the city were totally destroyed.

The reason given for this most destructive bombing in history was that, because Dresden was a rail and road centre, it was essential to prevent the Germans using it to rush troops through to stem the Russian advance. *See* Berlin; Hamburg.

Dreux (*First French Religious War*) *19 December 1562*. Between the Huguenots (Prince de Conde) and the Catholics (Montmorency, Constable of France).

Montmorency, leading a cavalry charge, was beaten and captured. The Catholics fled but the Huguenots, over-pursuing, were charged and routed by de Guise and Conde was captured. The final victory was to the Catholics. *See* Saint-Denis.

Drewry's Bluff (*American Civil War*) *16 May 1864*. General Butler, with 16,000, men was sent to cut the Richmond–Petersburg railway although the Confederates (Beauregard) had 18,000 men. On 12 May Butler moved towards Drewry's Bluff, near Richmond. He procrastinated until 16 May when Beauregard in a surprise attack turned Butler's flank and forced him to retreat. Casualties: Federals, 2,506; Confederates, 4,160. *See* North Anna River; Spotsylvania.

Driefontein (*Second British–Boer War*) *10 March 1900*. The Boers (de Wet) held a 7-mile line covering Bloemfontein. Lord Roberts sent Kelly-Kenny's division to attack frontally and Tucker's division against the left flank. The Boers were driven out but lost only 100 against the British 424. *See* Bloemfontein.

Dristen (*or Drista*) (*Russian invasion of Byzantium*) *972*. The Russians (Duke Swatoslaus) held this post on the Danube against the Greeks under Emperor John Zimisces. After 55 days the Russians surrendered and their invasion of Byzantine territory ended.

Drogheda I (*Irish Rebellion*) *December 1641–February 1642*. Sir Henry Tichborne held the town for 3 months against Irish rebels under Owen Roe O'Neill, who could not sustain the siege.

Drogheda II (*English Civil War*) *3–12 September 1649*. Cromwell and his Parliamentary army laid siege to Drogheda on 3 September. Sir Arthur Alston and his garrison of 2,500 English regulars repulsed an attack on the 10th but were overwhelmed on the 12th and butchered. In all, 4,000 soldiers and inhabitants are said to have perished. The great number of casualties were English and not Irish, as is commonly supposed. *See* Rathmines; Wexford.

Drumclog, *Lanarkshire* (*Scottish Covenanter's Revolt*) *11 June 1679*. To quell the rebellion, Viscount Dundee led a Royalist army to Drumclog, but the attack came from the Covenanters (John Balfour). The royal army was decisively defeated. *See* Bothwell Bridge; Pentland Hills.

Drumossie Moor. *See* Culloden.

Dubba (*British–Scinde campaign*) *24 March 1843*. 20,000 Baluchi troops (Amir Shir Muhammad) held strong positions behind double dried-river beds. Sir Charles Napier's 5,000 British troops, with great gallantry, routed the Baluchis. *See* Hyderabad; Miani (Meeanee).

Dublin (*Irish Easter Rebellion*) *24–29 April 1916*. About 1,500 Sinn Fein republicans led by James Connolly and Patrick Pearse revolted in Dublin, 24 April, and seized the General Post Office and other buildings. British troops quelled the rebellion in 5 days of bitter street fighting; fifteen ringleaders were shot and hundreds of republicans were imprisoned.

Dunbar I (*English–Scottish Wars*) *27 April 1296*. The English (Edward I) inflicted 10,000 casualties on the Scots (Earl of Athol). The victory led to Edward's being proclaimed King of Scotland. *See* Berwick-upon-Tweed; Stirling Bridge.

Dunbar II (*English–Scottish Wars*) *June 1339*. Agnes, Countess of March ("Black Agnes"), defended the town under siege by the Earl of Salisbury, who was compelled to withdraw.

Dunbar III (*English Civil War*) *3 September 1650*. Between 14,000 Parliamentarians (Cromwell, assisted by Monck) and 27,000 Scottish Royalists (David Leslie). Leslie mistakenly left a strong position on high ground to attack Cromwell and was routed, losing 3,000 killed or wounded and 10,000 prisoners. *See* Carbiesdale; Worcester.

Dundalk (*Scottish invasion of Ireland*) *5 October 1318*. Edward Bruce, brother of Robert the Bruce, led 3,000 Scots in an attack on the English and Irish (John de Bermingham) but was killed, together with thirty of his knights and 100 soldiers. The invasion was abortive. *See* Bannockburn; Mytun.

Dundee, South Africa. *See* Talana Hill.

Dungeness (*or The Downs*) (*First English–Dutch War*) *29–30 November 1652*. In a 2-day action Admiral Blake lost six of his forty ships to the superior Dutch fleet, ninety-five ships, of Admiral Tromp, but the action was indecisive.

Dunes, *near Dunkirk* (*Spanish–French Wars*) *14 June 1658*. Between 14,000 Spaniards, under Don Juan of Austria and the Great Conde, and an equal French force — though 6,000 were English troops — under Turenne. Turenne was victorious, inflicting 4,000 casualties on the Spaniards and 10 days later capturing Dunkirk.

Dunganhill (*Great Irish Rebellion*) *8 August 1647*. Colonel Michael Jones routed a large body of Irish rebels, inflicting 6,000 casualties. *See* Ballymore; Benburb; Gibbel Rutts.

Dunkeld (*Jacobite Rising*) *21 August 1689*. The Cameronian Regiment (Colonel Cleland), in the service of the British Government, held a large house in Dunkeld, from which a superior force of Highlanders (Colonel Cannon) could not dislodge them. Cleland was killed, but the Cameronians' remarkable discipline routed the Highlanders. *See* Killiecrankie.

Dunkirk, *Retreat and Evacuation* (*World War II*) *May–June 1940*. In

Belgium the British (Lord Gort) could not hold a defensive triangle based on the Channel against German armour and aircraft. Belgians on the left flank abandoned Antwerp, 18 May. The British moved south to join the French armies, but a German corridor prevented this. The British retreated west to the Lys River, 21 May. When the ports of Boulogne and Calais fell to the Germans only Dunkirk was left. The Belgian Army surrendered, 27 May, and only evacuation could save the British from annihilation. Over 5 nights, 29 May–2 June, 224,585 British and 112,546 French and Belgian soldiers were evacuated to England by a mixed fleet of 887 vessels. The British lost 30,000 men in the campaign, twenty-nine aircraft in the 4 days from 27 May, seven destroyers, a minesweeper and twenty smaller ships. The German commander, von Rundstedt, said later that Hitler had ordered him not to use his panzer divisions against the evacuating British, nor could he send German troops closer than 10 kilometres from Dunkirk. This was not as foolish as it appears; the whole area was one vast tank obstacle. That Hitler wished the British to escape is a myth.

Dunsinane *1054*. Between the Anglo-Saxons under Siward, Earl of Northumberland, who was supporting Malcolm Canmore, son of the murdered Duncan, and Macbeth, the usurper. Macbeth was defeated, losing 10,000 men. The Anglo-Saxons lost 1,500. *See* Alnwick.

Dunsterforce Campaign (*World War I*) *1918*. Named after Major-General L. C. Dunsterforce, the formation was made up of hand-picked soldiers from all the British Empire armies and was sent to Persia and Kurdistan to organize and lead any Russian troops or Trans-Caucasian civilians ready to continue resistance against the Turks after the Russian–German peace of 1917. The force was continually in action.

Dupplin Moor (*Baliol's Rising*) *12 August 1332*. Edward Baliol, and his Scottish barons, defeated David, King of Scotland. *See* Halidon Hill.

Düppel (*or Dybbol*) (*Scheswig–Holstein–Prussian War*) *30 March–17 April 1864*. Prince Frederick Charles with 16,000 Prussians invested this formidable fortress on 30 March. The Danish garrison numbered 22,000. On 17 April the Prussians bombarded the defences then sent in their infantry. The fighting was brief but fierce and the Prussians triumphed. Casualties: Prussians, 70 officers, 1,331 men; Danes, 5,500 including prisoners. *See* Langensalza.

Dürrenstein (*Napoleonic Wars: Campaign of the Danube*) *11 November 1805*. During Napoleon's advance on Vienna, Mortier, with only one French division, was attacked by 30,000 Russians and only the arrival of a reinforcement division saved him. Each side lost about 3,000. *See* Auerstadt–Jena.

Dutch East Indies (*Japanese campaign, World War II*) *1942*. Having captured much of the Philippines, the Japanese swept through the Java and Celebes Seas. They captured Balikpapan, Borneo, on 23 January. The island of Amboina fell on 31 January and Timor was attacked from the air on 3 and 5 February. The Sumatra bases fell in mid-February and on 19 and 20 February the Japanese landed at Bali and Timor. By now General Wavell, the Allied commander, had handed over to the Dutch General ter Poorten. At Bandung the Dutch, stiffened by an Australian commando unit (Brigadier Blackburn), delayed the Japanese advance. At sea Japanese warships had defeated the British, Dutch, American and Australian naval forces. On 8 March General ter Poorten proclaimed that organized resistance in the Dutch East Indies had ended; Dutch, British, Australian and American units were ordered to cease fire. The Japanese took prisoner the entire Allied force in the Dutch East Indies — 100,000 men.

Dwina, The, *the western river, Russia (Swedish–Polish War) May 1701.* Between 15,000 Swedes (Charles XII) and 12,000 Saxons (Marshal von Stenau). Charles, marching on Riga, was blocked at the Dwina River by von Stenau. With the wind at his back, Charles set fire to wet straw and under cover of the smoke crossed the river unseen. He attacked the Saxons and after a stubborn fight drove them out of his way. *See* Kilszow; Narva; Putulsk I.

Dyle (*Norman invasion of France*) *896.* The Germans under Arnulph, Emperor of Germany, routed the Norman invaders. *See* Montfaucon.

Dyrham (or Deorham) (*Teutonic conquest of Britain*) *577.* The Anglo-Saxons (King Ceawlin), expanding westwards, defeated a British army led by three local chiefs. Cwealin then took Bath and thrust through to the English Channel, a major move in the conquest of Britain. *See* Degsaston; Mons Badonicus.

Dyrrachium I (or Durazzo) *modern Durres, Albania (Wars of the First Roman Triumvirate) 48 BC.* Julius Caesar had achieved victories over Pompey's armies in Spain and now, taking 15,000 of his troops, Caesar sailed to Epirus to attack Pompey himself. He occupied Oricum and Apollonia, but at Dyrrachium (the modern Durres) he ran against Pompey, who, despite his 45,000 men, would not attack. Reinforced by troops under Mark Antony, Caesar attacked but lost 1,000 of his finest troops and withdrew to Thessaly. *See* Bagradus River; Ilerde; Pharsalus.

Dyrrachium II (*Norman–Byzantine Wars*) *17 July 1081–February 1082.* The Normans (Robert Guiscard), having already driven the Byzantines out of Italy, besieged Byzantine-held Dyrrachium. The Byzantine Emperor, Alexius I Comnenus, sent from Constantinople an army of 75,000 to relieve the city. On 18 October the vanguard of this army, mostly infantry, launched a wild attack before their cavalry could come up. Guiscard's 18,000 Norman cavalry and archers wiped out the enemy force of 6,000 and deterred the rest of the army from attack. Guiscard took Dyrrachium on 8 February 1082, but his death ended the Norman attempt to invade the Byzantine empire. *See* Nicaea; Rome V.

Dyrrachium III (*Norman–Byzantine Wars*) *1108.* The greatest soldier of the First Crusade, Bohemond of Taranto and Antioch and son of Robert Guiscard, gathered a European army to fight the Byzantines, and in 1107 reached Dyrrachium. But the Emperor, whose troops had been defeated by Bohemond's father, had by now prepared strong lines manned by Turks. Unable after a year to find a way through or around, Bohemond was surrounded in 1108 at Devol and surrendered personally to Alexius. Spared his life, Bohemond returned to Italy where he died in 1111, while planning new expeditions. *See* Melitene; Philomelion.

East Africa (*World War II*). *See* Abyssinian campaigns.

East African Campaign (*World War I*). The British campaign in East Africa, which tied down forces of 140,000, was wholly devoted to countering the activities of the brilliant Colonel (later General) Paul von Lettow-Vorbeck. He repulsed a British landing at Tanga, 3–4 November 1914, and carried on an aggressive guerrilla campaign for 4 years, though he had only 4,000 men. In all, twenty-seven British generals failed to capture von Lettow-Vorbeck or to restrict his activities. He surrendered 12 days after the Armistice. Lettow-Vorbeck's operations had no significance in the war, but they are one of the best examples of guerrilla warfare.

East Prussia (*World War II*) *Summer 1944*. The Russian offensive against Germany. Attacking across the borders of East Prussia and Poland, the Russians encountered stubborn German resistance, but Königsberg (Kaliningrad) fell on 9 April 1945.

Easter Rising *1916*. *See* Dublin.

East Stoke, *Nottinghamshire* (*Yorkist Rebellion*) *15 June 1487*. The Yorkists and a priest named Simon presented a youthful commoner, Lambert Simnel, as the son of the Earl of Warwick, then imprisoned in the Tower of London. The imposture culminated in the "crowning" of Simnel in Dublin as Edward VI. His sponsors crossed to Britain with a large force of Continental mercenaries and Irish and at East Stoke were attacked by Henry VII and a superior force. The chief insurgents were either killed or captured; Lambert Simnel was forced to become a servant to the legitimate king. *See* Bosworth Field.

Eaucourt l'Abbaye, *Somme 1 October 1916*. Notable as the action in which the first New Zealand V.C. of the war was won; recipient, Sergeant Donald Brown, Otago Regiment, posthumously. *See* Somme.

Eben Emael (*World War II*) *10–11 May 1940*. This powerful Belgian fortress, commanding the approaches to the River Meuse and the Albert Canal, was flanked by twenty-four smaller forts scattered over a square mile. The Germans dive-bombed it on 10 May and at dawn on 11 May paratroops, engineers and glider-borne infantry attacked it. It was secured by noon. Casualties: Belgian, 480; German, 360. *See* Maginot Line.

Ebersberg (*Napoleonic Wars: Wagram Campaign*) *3 May 1809*. Massena's corps stormed the bridge and castle of Ebersberg, held by 30,000 Austrians under the Archduke Charles. In ferocious street fighting the Austrians lost 3,000 killed or wounded and 4,000 prisoners and many guns and were driven out. The French claim to have lost only 1,700. *See* Eckmühl.

Ebro River (*Spanish Civil War*) 24 July–18 November 1938. General Juan Modesto, commanding the Republican Army of the Ebro, 100,000 men, including the International Brigade, crossed to the west side of the lower Ebro, 24–25 July, took General de Yague's Nationalist army by surprise and captured 4,000 prisoners. General Lister advanced 25 miles with his corps, but by 1 August Franco's Nationalists had stopped the Republican advance. The battle became semi-static. Nationalist aircraft dropped a reported 10,000 bombs a day, but 200 planes were shot down. The assault pushed the Republicans off some of their captured ground and as the Nationalist build-up continued the Republicans lost more and more ground until, 18 November, Modesto's troops were all back across the Ebro. Casualties: Nationalists, 33,000; Republicans, 30,000 dead, 20,000 wounded, 20,000 captured; the International Brigade had 75 per cent casualties, *See* Barcelona II; Teruel; Vinaroz.

Eckmühl, *near Landshut (Napoleonic Wars: Wagram campaign*) 22 April 1809. Between Napoleon, with 90,000 French — the corps of Davout, Lannes and Lefébvre — and the Archduke Charles, with 76,000 Austrians. Napoleon drove the Austrians from high ground above Eckmühl, but by night Charles was able to retire in fair order, having lost 7,000 killed or wounded, and 5,000 prisoners. French casualties, 5,000. This victory enabled Napoleon to cut the main Austrian army in two. *See* Aspern-Essling; Landshut.

Ecnomus, *southern Sicily (First Punic War*) 256 BC. The Roman fleet of 330 galleys (I. Manlius Valso) defeated 350 Carthaginian ships (Hanno). It is said that 300,000 oarsmen and fighters took part. *See* Mylae; Tunis.

Edessa I *Turkey (Persian Empire's Roman Wars*) 259. The Persians (Sapor I) defeated the Romans, taking prisoner their commander, the Emperor Valerian, who died in captivity. *See* Hormuz.

Edessa II (*Crusader–Turkish Wars*) November 1144. The Christians had held Edessa (Urfa), east of the Euphrates, since 1098 (First Crusade). In November 1144 the Turkish warlord Zangi attacked the fortress when the commander, Joscelin II, was absent and Archbishop High was in charge. Breaking through the walls on Christmas Eve, the Turks killed all the garrison and sold the women and children into slavery. Joscelin's attempt to recapture the city, 1146, was beaten off by Zangi's son and successor, Nureddin. *See* Antioch.

Edgehill (*English Civil War*) 23 October 1642. First battle of the Civil War between the Royalists (Charles I) and the Parliamentarians (Essex), each army being about 20,000-strong. Both sides claimed the victory, but the advantage clearly rested with Charles. The Parliamentarians failed to face Prince Rupert's cavalry and the Royalists were still able to continue their march on London. *See* Brentford; Newbury.

Edgeworth (*Wars of the Roses*) 26 July 1649. Between the Yorkists (Pembroke) and the Lancastrian Nevilles, who so heavily defeated the Yorkists that no fewer than 128 Welsh knights were killed.

Edington. *See* Ethandun.

Egmont-op-Zee (*British North Holland Expedition*) August–September 1799. In August the British (Abercromby) landed on the sand dunes of North Holland, drove back a French–Dutch force and established themselves across the peninsula, thereby securing the surrender of the Dutch fleet at its base. In September the Duke of York arrived as Commander-in-Chief and won the Battle of Egmont-op-Zee in rolling sand-dunes. But the whole campaign was ill-conceived and the British had then to withdraw. *See* Walcheren.

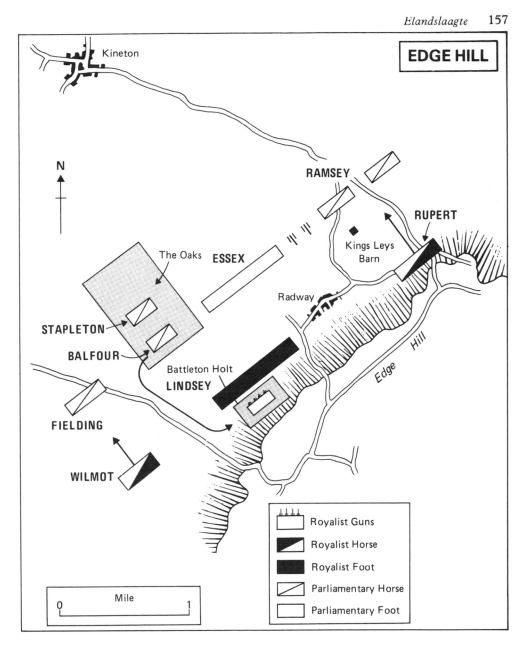

EDGE HILL

Kineton

N

RAMSEY

RUPERT

The Oaks ESSEX

Kings Leys
Barn

Radway

STAPLETON

BALFOUR

Battleton Holt
LINDSEY

Edge Hill

FIELDING

WILMOT

Royalist Guns

Royalist Horse

Royalist Foot

Parliamentary Horse

Parliamentary Foot

Mile

0 1

Egyptian rebellion against the British 1919. This outbreak, which could have been serious, was rapidly quelled by the Australian and New Zealand Light Horse. All regiments except two were in the saddle, their zone of activity extending from Upper Egypt to the Nile Delta.

Egyptian revolt against Turkey 1832–40. Invading Turkish-held Syria,

the Egyptians won three victories — Konya, 1832; Nizib, 1839; Acre, 1840. The European powers intervened to limit Egyptian successes, but Egypt did win its independence from Turkey.

El Alamein. *See* Alamein.

Elandslaagte (*Second British–Boer War*) *21 October 1899*. The Boers

(Koch) occupied a strong position on high ground near the Ladysmith–Dundee railway. General French, commanding the British, dislodged them with his three battalions, five squadrons and twelve guns. Casualties: British, 254; Boer, 450. *See* Ladysmith.

Elands River (*Second British–Boer War*) *4 August 1900*. A force of 400 Australians (Colonel Hore) was surrounded by 2,500 Boers with six guns. Though in an exposed position, into which 1,800 shells fell in 11 days, the Australians held until relieved by Kitchener. They lost seventy-five killed or wounded and nearly all their horses. *See* Spion Kop.

El Caney, *Cuba* (*Spanish–American War*) *1–3 July 1898*. The American commander, General Shafter, sent General Lawton with 6,500 men to capture El Caney, commanding Santiago de Cuba. The 525 Spaniards who held the place inflicted 441 casualties and suffered 355 themselves before being driven out. *See* Las Guasimas; Santiago de Cuba; San Juan Hill.

Elchingen (*Napoleonic Wars: Campaign of Austerlitz*) *14 October 1805*. Ney, after repairing under fire the bridge at Elchingen, led his corps to storm and capture the village and convent, driving out 20,000 Austrians and taking 3,000 prisoners. *See* Ulm.

Elena (*Russian–Turkish War*) *1877*. The Russians (Loris Melikoff) defeated the Turks (Muhktar Pasha). *See* Plevna.

Elinga (*or Silpia*), *Spain* (*Second Punic War*) *206 BC*. Scipio Africanus and his 48,000 Romans in an open-plain battle defeated Hanno's 74,000 Carthaginians. The defeat ended Carthaginian domination in Spain.

Elk Horn. *See* Pea Ridge.

Ellandun *825*. Egbert and the West Saxons defeated Beornwulf's Mercians.

Ellaporous, *Sicily* (*Sicilian–South Italian War*) *389 BC*. Dionysius of Syracuse led 23,000 Sicilians to victory against Heloris' 17,000 Italians, 7,000 of whom were killed. The victory crushed the Italian League; Syracuse dominated the entire central Mediterranean.

El Mansura (*Seventh Crusade*) *8 February–May 1250*. Mansura was the key of the strong Egyptian defensive line preventing the Crusaders from reaching Cairo. King Louis IX of France, leader of the Seventh Crusade, planned a tactically clever attack, but his commanders were too impetuous. The Count of Artois, surprising the Turks, drove many before him, but then the knights rode into El Mansura town, where few survived the arrows fired at close range from the buildings. Elsewhere the Crusaders made some ground, but were too weak now to exploit any advantage. Louis, his communications cut by the Egyptian ships on the Nile, fell back, but his army was so diseased and starving that he surrendered. The Turks killed all the weak and sick; the others bought their freedom by agreeing to hand over the Crusader base of Damietta and to pay a huge ransom. *See* Antioch; La Forbie.

El Obeid (*British Sudan campaigns*) *1–4 November 1883*. The Mahdi, leader of the Dervishes, led a revolt against Egypt. Britain, which then ruled Egypt, sent General William Hicks — known as Hicks Pasha — with 10,000 men, mostly Egyptians, to quell the rebellion. On 1 November 1883 a large force of Mahdists trapped Hicks' force in a gorge at El Obeid, 220 miles south-west of Khartoum. By 4 November the last man had been slaughtered. The defeat induced Gladstone's government to withdraw from the Sudan. *See* El Teb.

El Salvador Civil War *1980*–
Civil war between Government forces and Marxist guerrillas of the Faraibundo Marti National Liberation Front (FMLN) broke out in 1980. The U.S. Administra-

tion backs the government while Cuba, as a Soviet surrogate, supplies arms to the rebels. By 1985 40,000 people, mostly civilians, had been killed by right-wing or left-wing "death-squads" or by government "security units".†

El Teb (*or Trinkitat*) (*British–Sudan campaigns*) *29 March 1884*. The British force of 4,000 (Graham), fighting in square, defeated Osman Digna's 6,000 Mahdist tribesmen after a non-stop 5-hour fight. The British lost 189, the Mahdists 2,200. *See* El Obeid.

Ely I (*Norman Conquest of Britain*) *1071*. Hereward the Wake, the last English leader to resist the Norman conquerors, depended largely on his Danish allies. In 1071 William the Conqueror induced the Danish king, Sweyn, to withdraw from England. Hereward and his followers found refuge in the Isle of Ely — higher ground in the marshy lowlands of Cambridgeshire — which the Normans besieged and captured. Hereward escaped; his subsequent exploits are mostly legendary. *See* Gerberoi; Hastings.

Ely II (*Second Barons' War of England*) *1266–7*. John d'Eyvill, gathering the barons who had survived the wars against the monarchy, made the Isle of Ely into a fortress. In the summer of 1267 Henry III's aggressive son, Prince Edward, subdued the place and the barons who survived submitted to the crown; the barons' war had ended. *See* Axholme; Chesterfield.

Embata, *near Chios, Greece* (*Wars of the Roman Empire*) *356 BC*. The heavily outnumbered Athenians (Chares) were defeated by the Chians. *See* Chios.

Emesa (*Roman War against Palmyra*) *273*. Aurelian's Romans defeated Queen Zenobia's Palmyrenians. Zenobia retired into Palmyra, q.v., to which Aurelian laid siege. *See* Pavia I.

Empingham (*Wars of the Roses*) *12 March 1470*. Edward IV routed the northern rebels under Sir Robert Wells, whose men threw off their coats and fled giving the battle the name "Lose-coat Field". *See* Hexham; Ravenspur II.

Engano Cape (*World War II*) *25 October 1944*. *See* Battle of Leyte Gulf.

Engen, *Black Forest* (*Wars of French Revolution*) *3 May 1800*. Between 75,000 French (Moreau) and 110,000 Austrians (De Kray). There were two distinct actions. Moreau's right, of 25,000 men under Lecourbe, overtook the Austrian rearguard and drove them into and through Stockach, capturing 4,000. Moreau, at another point, was attacked at Engen by 40,000 Austrians led by De Kray. Casualties: French, 2,000; Austrians, 2,000 killed or wounded, 5,000 prisoners. *See* Höchstädt II; Marengo.

Englefield (*Danish invasion of England*) *871*. The first of the battles between the West Saxons (Aethelwulf) and the Danish invaders, who lost. *See* Ashdown; Reading.

English Civil Wars. *See* List of Battles.

Eniwetok, *Marshall Islands* (*World War II*) *18–24 February 1944*. U.S. marines and infantry captured the island from the Japanese. *See* Makin–Tarawa.

Enslin. *See* Graspan.

Entholm (*Danish–Swedish War*) *11 June 1676*. The Danish fleet (van Tromp) heavily defeated the Swedes. *See* Kioge.

Enzheim (*Louis XIV's Dutch Wars*) *4 October 1674*. The great Turenne, following a successful campaign in the Palatinate (*see* Sinzheim), crossed the Rhine westwards in the wake of the army of the Holy Roman Empire, led by Count Montecuccoli, who had bridged the Rhine to invade Alsace. On 4 October Turenne gave battle to the enemy just south of Strasbourg, but withdrew when Brandenburg troops arrived to reinforce Montecuccoli. Turenne went on to defeat Montecuccoli at Turkheim. *See* Sinsheim.

Ephesus I, *Ionia (Persian–Greek Wars)* 499 BC. The Greeks, retreating to the Mediterranean coast after burning Sardis, were overtaken by the Persians (Artaphernes) and badly beaten. The survivors withdrew to their fleet, leaving the Ionian allies to continue the war alone. *See* Lade.

Ephesus II (*Great Pelopponesian War*) 406 BC. The Athenian leader Alcibiades tried to lure the Spartan Lysander into a sea battle at Ephesus, where a new Spartan fleet had been built. Unsuccessful in this, Alcibiades withdrew part of his blockading fleet to collect supplies. Seizing the opportunity, Lysander hurried his ships into combat and defeated the Athenian ships still on station. Alcibiades hastened back to Ephesus, but Lysander, having won a considerable victory, again declined battle. Alcibiades, though the most brilliant of Athenian generals, was relieved of command. *See* Arginusae; Cyzicus.

Ephesus III (*raids of the Gothic Sea Rovers*) 262 BC. The Gallic invaders disastrously defeated the Syrians (Antigonus), and destroyed the famed Temple of Diana, one of the Seven Wonders of the World.

Erbach (*Wars of the French Revolution*) 15 May 1800. The Austrians (De Kray), with 12,000 cavalry among their 36,000 men, vigorously attacked the French (Sainte-Suzanne) who had only 15,000 men. The French, however, held for 12 hours until the arrival of St. Cyr's corps forced the Austrians to retire. Both sides lost heavily. *See* Marengo.

Ereğli I (*First Crusade*) 1101. The Count of Nevers reached Asia Minor in the summer of 1101, with an army of reinforcement Crusaders, to find that an earlier force had not bothered to wait for him but had ridden off into the hostile unknown. They had, in fact, been wiped out at Kizil Irmak. Nevers set off in pursuit. At Ereğli, south-east of Konya, mounted Turkish bowmen ambushed the Crusaders and only a few, after great suffering, reached safety. *See* Mersivan.

Ereğli II (*First Crusade*) 1101. The Dukes of Aquitaine and Bavaria, commanding yet another Crusader army — French and Germans — left Constantinople to bring Christianity by force to the Muslims. Unaware that the two previous armies had been slaughtered, the dukes marched on to Ereğli where they, too, were ambushed by Turkish mounted bowmen. Again, only a few men, including the dukes, reached safety. *See* Ramleh I.

Erie, Lake (*British–American War 1812–14*) 10 September 1813. The British dominated Lake Erie and this gave them strategical land advantage. Captain O. H. Perry was sent to harass the British. With ten small ships (55 guns) Perry gave battle (10 September) to Captain Barclay's six British ships (65 guns). Losing his flagship, Perry fought a 3-hour battle from *Niagara* and captured or destroyed the British squadron: 41 British seamen were killed, 94 wounded. As a result of the defeat British troops evacuated Detroit. *See* Frenchtown.

Erisa (*Paraguayan War of Independence*) 10 December 1814. The 8,000 Spanish royalists (Bover) defeated the patriots and captured their leader, Ribas; he was beheaded in vengeance for Bover, who fell in the battle.

Eritrea War 1964–   . Eritrea became part of Ethiopia in 1952. In 1964 various armed groups affiliated to the Eritrean Liberation Front (ELF) began to fight for independence. The guerrillas had many successes against government troops in

Tigre province as well as Eritrea. By the end of 1977 40,000 ELF fighters were winning the war against 80,000 Ethiopian troops and were besieging Asmara, the only city still to be captured. The tide of war changed in 1978 when the new Ethiopian leader, Colonel Mengistu, accepted Soviet offers of help. With Russian planning and logistical support, the army forced the independence fighters from all the towns. The guerrillas, probably the most skilful irregular fighters in Africa, continued to hold the country. Had the several liberation groups combined under one leader, they almost certainly would have won the war. Casualties: Ethiopian, 22,000 killed, 54,000 wounded. The guerrillas have never disclosed their casualties, but they are believed to be much less than the Ethiopian.

Erzinja (*Wars of the Seljuk Turks*) *1230*. The Seljuks of south-east Turkey, a powerful tribe under Ala-ud-Din Kaikobad, defeated the great Persian army (Jalal-ad-Din) on the western Euphrates river. The victory was the Seljuks' undoing; now that the Persians were beaten, nothing remained to prevent the Mongols from invading the Seljuk regions. The Seljuks never again held power. *See* Baghdad I; Manzikert.

Erzurum, *Armenia* (*Byzantine–Muslim Wars*) *928*. Byzantine cavalry led by John Kurkuas attacked and conquered the Muslim fortress of Erzurum, thus further weakening Muslim power. *See* Melitene II; Samosata.

Erzurum–Erzinjan (*World War I*) *January–August 1916*. A Russian–Turkish conflict. Aware that Turkish troops from the recently ended Gallipoli campaign were being moved against them, the Russians (Yudenich) took the initiative. Capturing Koprukoy on 17 January and Erzurum on 12–16 February, Yudenich by 2 July had driven through the Turkish front and, on 25 July, stormed Erzinjan. Another Russian force had on 17 April, taken Trebizond

the Black Sea port. But while the troops of Abdul Kerim Pasha had everywhere fallen back on the right, Mustafa Kemel's corps held firm and even took Mus and Bitlis on 15 August. Yudenich recaptured these places on 24 August. Following the outbreak of the Russian Revolution the Russian armies lost all cohesion and the Turks gradually recaptured all lost ground. *See* Sarikamis.

Esperance Cape (*World War II*) *11–12 October 1942*. Part of the battle for Guadalcanal, q.v.

Espinosa (*Peninsular War*) *10 November 1808*. 18,000 French veterans (Victor) easily routed Blake's 30,000 Spanish irregulars, but lost 1,100 men. *See* Bailén; Vimeiro.

Essling. *See* Aspern.

Etampes *604*. Queen Brunehilde and her Burgundians totally defeated Clotaire II's Neustrians.

Ethandun, *later Edington* (*Danish invasion of Britain*) *June 878*. Alfred the Great mobilized the Saxon warriors of Wessex and marched on the Danes in camp at Chippenham, Wiltshire, after Guthrum's defeat of Alfred 4 months earlier. Guthrum led his Danes to meet Alfred and the battle took place at Ethandun. Fierce, long and bloody, it was a victory for Alfred who chased and caught Guthrum and forced his surrender. The Peace of Wedmore which followed meant that Wessex survived to be the base for later actions against the Danes. *See* Chippenham.

Eureka Stockade, *Victoria, Australia* *3 December 1854*. Hardly a battle, but a deeply significant event in Australian history and the nearest thing to a land battle ever fought on Australian mainland territory. Peter Lalor led goldminers at Ballarat, Victoria, in an abortive rising against police and troops. The miners were protesting against alleged government and police oppression.

Eurymedon River (*Persian–Greek Wars*) *466* BC. The Athenians and Delians (Cimon) in a counter-offensive against the Persians defeated the Persian fleet and army; the Persians lost 200 ships and probably 30,000 soldiers. The victory brought the south of Asia Minor into the Athenian Confederacy or Delian League. *See* Cunaxa.

Eutaw Springs (*American Revolution*) *8 September 1781*. General Greene, commanding in the American south, prepared a force of 2,200 men and then attacked the British outpost at Orangeburg, South Carolina. The British fell back to Eutaw Springs, where on 8 September, Greene attacked Colonel Stuart and his 2,000 British regulars. After a stubborn resistance the British retreated down the Charleston road, but when the American militiamen stopped to loot the British camp Stuart rallied the British, and beat the Americans from the field. The net result was indecisive, but casualties were heavy. British: 85 killed, 351 wounded, 430 missing (this is an oddly high proportion of missing); American, 139 killed, 375 wounded. *See* Ninety Six; Yorktown I.

Evesham (*Second Barons' War of England*) *4 August 1265*. The Royalists (Prince Edward) defeated the Barons (Simon de Montfort) who were taken by surprise, believing that the approaching force was of reinforcements led by the young de Montfort. Edward's men slaughtered the barons' forces to a man. Simon de Montfort's death virtually ended the war. *See* Axholme; Kenilworth.

Eylau (*Napoleonic Wars: campaign of Friedland*) *8 February 1807*. Napoleon led 46,000 French into battle against Bennigsen's 70,000 Russians. He made no impression in several hours' fighting — much of it in falling snow — until Davout turned the Russian left. Then von Lestocq arrived with a Prussian corps and repulsed the French advance. Bloody fighting lasted until 10 p.m., with both armies standing firm; next day the Russians retired. Casualties: French, 20,000; Russian, higher, including 12,000 dead. The result was indecisive, but Napoleon had blunted the the Russian winter offensive. *See* Danzig II; Pultusk II.

**Faenza (*First Roman–Gothic War*)
541.** The Goths (Totila, King of Italy)
had an easy victory against 20,000 Roman
legionaries, who fled ignomiously. *See*
Rome.

**Fair Oaks (*American Civil War*) *31
May–1 June 1862*.** McClellan's Federal
army, advancing on Richmond, was
attacked by Johnston's Confederates and
driven back 2 miles. He made good this
loss next day, but permitted the outnumbered Confederates to retire unchal-
lenged. Casualties: Federals, 7,000; Confederates, 4,500. *See* Williamsburg.

**Falaise–Argentan Pocket, *France
(World War II) August 1944*.** A thrust
by the Americans (Patton) towards Argentan cut off the rear of the German army
facing the British and Canadians. (The
Germans had been trying to cut off a large
American force.) Patton reached Argentan on 13 August, and moved north while
the Canadians (Crerar) attacked south to
Falaise. Under this threat of encirclement, master-minded by Montgomery,
von Kluge rapidly began to withdraw his
three armies and with desperate skill the
Germans kept open for 5 days a 10-mile
passage to the east. (Kluge, implicated in
the attempt on Hitler's life, committed
suicide.) Model replaced Kluge on 16
August and the Germans, though under
very heavy ground and air attack, filtered
through the gap, which the Allies closed
on 19 August. By 22 August the pocket
was crushed. The Germans lost 10,000

dead, 50,000 prisoners including wounded
and much equipment, including 10,000
vehicles. Allied casualties amounted to
about 800 killed and 1,200 wounded. *See*
D-Day.

**Falkirk I (*English–Scottish Wars*) *23
July 1298*.** Edward I, using his archers
behind a bog to neutralize the advantage
of the Scots (Sir William Wallace), gained
a decisive victory.

**Falkirk II (*The '45 Rebellion*) *11
August 1746*.** 8,000 rebel Highlanders
(the Young Pretender, Prince Charles
Edward) charged General Hawley's 9,000
men, killed or wounded 600, took 700
prisoners, seven guns and all baggage. *See*
Dunbar; Stirling Bridge.

**Falklands, The I (*World War I*) *8
December 1914*.** The revenge of
Coronel. Admiral Sturdee was sent, with
H.M.S. *Invincible, Inflexible, Kent, Cornwall, Glasgow, Bristol, Otranto* and *Macedonia* (also *Canopus*, already in the Falklands) to destroy von Spee's squadron,
*Gneisenau, Scharnhorst, Leipzig, Nurn-
berg* and *Dresden*. The German defeat was
one of the most complete in naval history;
their four warships and two colliers were
destroyed and von Spee and 2,300 men
were killed. Only the *Dresden* escaped,
British casualties were ten men killed and
fifteen wounded. *See* Coronel.

**Falklands Islands War (*Operation
Corporate*) *1982*.** Argentina claimed the

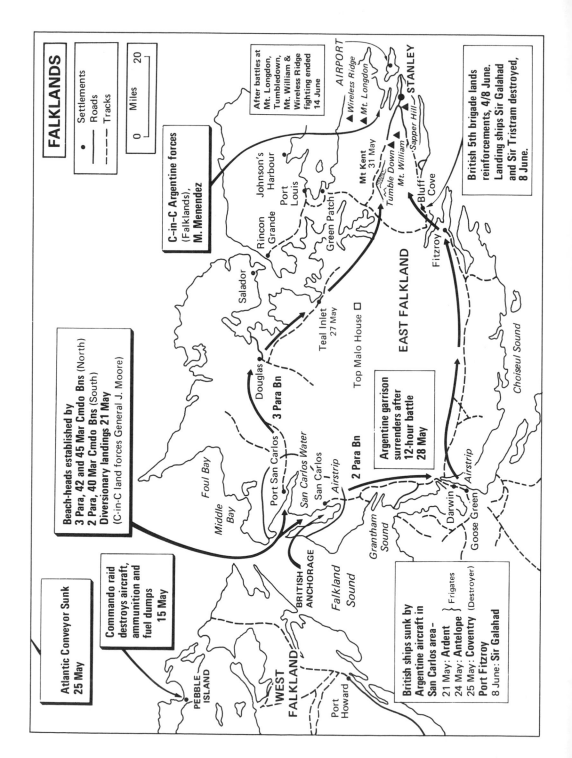

FALKLANDS

- • Settlements
- — Roads
- --- Tracks

0   Miles   20

Atlantic Conveyor Sunk 25 May

Commando raid destroys aircraft, ammunition and fuel dumps 15 May

Beach-heads established by 3 Para, 42 and 45 Mar Cmdo Bns (North) 2 Para, 40 Mar Cmdo Bns (South) Diversionary landings 21 May (C-in-C land forces General J. Moore)

C-in-C Argentine forces (Falklands), M. Menendez

After battles at Mt. Longdon, Tumbledown, Mt. William & Wireless Ridge fighting ended 14 June

British 5th brigade lands reinforcements, 4/8 June. Landing ships Sir Galahad and Sir Tristram destroyed, 8 June.

Argentine garrison surrenders after 12-hour battle 28 May

British ships sunk by Argentine aircraft in San Carlos area –
21 May: **Ardent** } Frigates
24 May: **Antelope**
25 May: **Coventry** (Destroyer)
Port Fitzroy
8 June: **Sir Galahad**

PEBBLE ISLAND

WEST FALKLAND

Port Howard

Falkland Sound

BRITISH ANCHORAGE

Foul Bay

Middle Bay

Port San Carlos

San Carlos Water

San Carlos
Airstrip

Douglas

3 Para Bn

Salador

Rincon Grande

Johnson's Harbour

Port Louis

Green Patch

Teal Inlet
27 May

Top Malo House □

2 Para Bn

Grantham Sound

Darwin

Airstrip

Goose Green

EAST FALKLAND

Mt Kent
31 May

Tumble Down

Mt. William

Bluff Cove

Fitzroy

Sapper Hill

▲ Wireless Ridge
▲ Mt. Longdon

STANLEY

AIRPORT

Choiseul Sound

Falkland Islands, held by Britain since 1833. On 2 April 1982 500 troops captured its capital, Port Stanley, from the British garrison of seventy-nine marines. A day later the Argentinians captured South Georgia. On 5–6 April the British sent a naval task force under Rear Admiral J. F. Woodward to the South Atlantic. A battle group was formed under Brigadier Julian Thompson, though Major-General Jeremy Moore later assumed command of the British land forces. The battle group consisted of 3rd Commando Brigade (40, 42 and 45 Commando), 2nd and 3rd Parachute Battalions, artillery, engineers and eight light tanks from the Blues and Royals, together with Special Air Service and Special Boat Service detachments. The group was reinforced later by 5th Infantry Brigade — Scots Guards, 1st Battalion Welsh Guards, 1st Battalion 7th Gurkha Rifles. Air support was provided by twenty-two Sea Harrier jump-jets. The Argentinian troops on the Falklands were built up to about 15,000 under General Mario Menendez. The main strength of the Argentinians lay in their air force, operating from the mainland. Argentinian planes sank seven British ships and badly damaged six others. About eighty Argentinian planes were shot down and the British submarine *Conqueror* torpedoed the cruiser *General Belgrano*. The Argentinian army surrendered on 24 June. Casualties: British, 255 killed, 777 wounded; Argentinian (speculative), 1,000 killed, including 368 from the *General Belgrano*, 3,000 wounded, 11,400 taken prisoner.

Historically, the war is interesting because it was an imperial nineteenth-century type of conflict, reminiscent of scores of British campaigns in Africa, India and Asia. It is militarily interesting because the British fought the war without a land base at the end of an 8,000-mile sea supply line; they won it as much by logistical competence as by military efficiency.

Fallen Timbers (*American Northwest Indian Wars*) 20 August 1794. The biggest victory won against the Northwest Indians. General Wayne, with 2,000 regulars and 1,000 mounted volunteers, after forcing the Indians back to the Maumee River, north-west Ohio, defeated them in pitched battle. Wayne lost 33 killed and 100 wounded. *See* Fort Recovery.

Famagusta (*Cyprus War*) October 1570–August 1571. A Venetian–Cypriot force of 7,000 (Bragadino) held the town against the Turks (Mustapha Pasha) who lost 50,000 men. On 1 August 1571 the garrison marched out with the honours of war, but Mustapha murdered Bragadino and four of his lieutenants. *See* Lepanto.

Farquhar's Farm (*Second British–Boer War*) 29 October 1899. Between the main Boer army (Joubert) and the garrison of Ladysmith (Sir George White). In an abortive attempt to break the Boer siege, the British suffered 317 killed or wounded and lost 1,068 prisoners. *See* Magersfontein.

Farrington Bridge (*Arundel's Rebellion*) 27 July 1549. Royal troops under Lord Russell defeated a force of Cornish rebels, each side losing about 300. *See* Duffindale.

Faventia, *near Ravenna* (*Civil War of Marius and Sulla*) 82 BC. Norbanus, with his consular army weary after a long march, attacked the Sullans under Metullus and was routed. *See* Mount Tifata.

Fehrbellin (*Swedish–German War*) 28 June 1675. 15,000 Brandenbergers (the Elector, Frederick William) defeated the Swedes (Marshal Wrangel) who were forced to evacuate Brandenberg. Sweden's military prestige suffered severely. *See* Jasmund; Kioge.

Ferkeh (*British–Sudan campaigns*) 7 June 1896. Sir Herbert Kitchener, with 9,500 Egyptian troops and a British horse battery, surprised 4,000 Mahdists

(Emer Hamada) and defeated them. Casualties: British, 101; Mahdists, 1,500 killed, 500 prisoners, including 44 of the 62 Emirs. *See* Khartoum.

Ferozeshah (*First British–Sikh War*) 21 December 1845. Sir Hugh Gough, with 16,700 British and Indian troops, made an unsuccessful night attack on the Sikh camp of 50,000 (Lal Singh). At dawn renewal of the attack brought victory, the Sikhs losing 7,000 men. British losses, 694 killed, 1,721 wounded. *See* Aliwal; Gujerat; Sobraon.

Ferrara (*Napoleon's Hundred Days*) 12 April 1815. Marshal Murat, with 50,000 French and Italians, tried to force the passage of the Po in the face of an Austrian army (Bianchi), but was repulsed with heavy loss. Murat had wanted to aid Napoleon, who was now within 2 months of final defeat at Waterloo.

Ferrybridge (*Wars of the Roses*) 1461. Lancastrian cavalry (Lord Clifford) defeated the Yorkists, under Lord Fitzwalter, who was killed. *See* St. Albans II; Towton.

Finland. *See* Mannerheim Line.

Fish Creek (*Riel's Second Rebellion*) 24 April 1885. Riel was an Indian half-caste who rebelled against British rule in Canada. General Middleton, with 400 Canadians, was repulsed when he attempted to drive the rebels from a strong position near Fish Creek.

Fisher's Hill (*American Civil War*) 21 September 1864. General Sheridan, with 40,000 Federals, proved too strong for General Early's 12,000 Confederates, many of whom were taken prisoner. *See* Cedar Creek; Winchester III.

Fishing Creek (*War of the American Revolution*) 18 August 1780. The British defeat of Thomas Sumter's force in South Carolina during the desperate American retreat from Camden, q.v.

Five Forks (*American Civil War*) 29 March–1 April 1865. Sheridan's Union cavalry struck the Confederate right flank, 29 March; from Dinwiddie Sheridan made for the important crossroads of Five Forks, defended by 19,000 Confederates (Pickett). Sheridan, with only 12,000 men, called up Warren's Corps of 16,000 to support his attack. Pickett's army collapsed under the frontal and flank attack and lost 5,200 prisoners. The defeat forced Lee to evacuate Petersburg, q.v., and Richmond the following night. *See* Appomattox River.

Forbach. *See* Spicheren.

Flamborough Head (*War of American Revolution*) 23 September 1779. The American, John Paul Jones, in *Bonhomme Richard*, gave battle to an English frigate and a sloop. Lashing his ship to H.M.S. *Serapis*, he fought the British for nearly 4 hours, beat them and transferred his crew on the night of 24/25 from his own blazing ship to the *Serapis*. Jones had another frigate and two smaller ships, which stayed out of the fight. *See* Carrickfergus.

Flanders (*World War I*) 1914–18. Flanders is the general name given to the battlefield which stretched from the Lys River in northern France to the Yser River in Belgium. The main point of battle was the city of Ypres (Ieper) — "Wipers" to the British troops. The label "Ypres Salient" is often used to mean Flanders. In this compressed killing ground many local battles took place between the British Empire troops and the Germans, though French troops were sometimes involved and the Belgians held the left part of the line. In 1918 two American divisions were engaged. The main places where local battles occurred, sometimes over and over again, were: Armentieres, Comines, Warneton, Wytschaete, Messines, Zillebeke, Broodseinde, Zonnebeke, Kemmel, Hooge Crater, Pilckem, St. Julien, Langemarcke, Passchendaele, Poelcapelle, Boesinghe, Ploegsteert, Dixmuide, Houthulst Forest, Staden, Veldhoek, Gheluvelt, Hazebrouck, Voormezeeke, Oostaverne, Wieltje, St. Jean, Nieppe, St. Eloi. Many other names were given to various localities by the British armies, such as Hill 60, Polygon Wood, Sanctuary Wood, Hellfire Corner. The British had more than 1 million casualties in Flanders including 150,000 men who died in the 14 weeks of the third Battle of Ypres; during the fourth battle (also known as the Battle of the Lys) there were 240,000 British casualties, while the Germans, the attackers on that occasion, had 348,000. During the preliminary bombardment for Third Ypres the British fired 4,283,550 shells weighing 107,000 tons. These shells turned the low-lying ground into a bog. The British attacks gained little ground and all was lost to the German counter-attacks in March–April 1918. Thousands of battle actions took place in Flanders and the 4-year battle needs a dictionary of its own.

Fleurus I, *near Charleroi (Thirty Years' War) 29 August 1622.* The Palatinate Germans (Count von Mansfeldt), and Christian of Brunswick, were trying to retreat into Holland after their defeat at Hoecht. Intercepted by the Spaniards, the Germans lost all their infantry in trying to cut their way through. *See* Höchst; Stadtlohn.

Fleurus II (*War of the Grand Alliance or War of the League of Augsburg***)** *1 July 1690.* A French army of 45,000 (Duke of Luxembourg) defeated the 37,000-strong English, Spanish and German army of Prince George of Waldeck, inflicting 14,000 casualties and taking forty-nine guns. Luxembourg's manoeuvre of an infantry frontal assault followed by a cavalry double envelopment was classical in conception and deserves to be better known. He suffered relatively low casualties — 2,500. *See* Leuze; Staffarda.

Fleurus III (*Wars of the French Revolution***)** *16 June 1794.* The Austrians

(Duke of Coburg) attacked the French army (Jourdan) and, severely handled, fell back to Brussels to protect the city. Each army had 80,000 men. *See* Tourcoing.

Flodden (*English–Scottish Wars***)** *9 September 1513.* The English (Earl of Surrey) attacked the Scots (James IV) in a strong position on the hill of Flodden. The English left wing (Stanley) turned the Scottish flank and the Scots, losing James and all his chief nobles, were totally defeated. *See* Guinegate; Solway Moss.

Florence (*or Florence-Fiesole***) (***German invasion of Italy***)** *406.* A remarkable double siege. The Germans (Radagaisus) besieged Florence and the garrison was starving when Flavius Stilicho, with a large Roman army, surrounded the German camp and starved them into submission. *See* Pollentia; Rome I.

Flores (*English–Spanish Wars***)** *1591.* Lord Howard, looking for Spanish treasure ships, arrived in the Azores with seven ships and encountered fifteen Spanish warships. The English ship *Revenge* (Sir Richard Grenville) was surrounded for 15 hours against hopeless odds and sank two enemy ships. With Grenville mortally wounded, the *Revenge* surrendered. The battle is one of the most famous in naval history. *See* Armada.

Flushing (*Napoleonic Wars: British Walcheren Expedition***)** *August 1809.* A British expedition of thirty-five warships, escorting 200 transports carrying 40,000 men, was sent to capture Antwerp and thus divert Napoleon's attention from Central Europe. The expedition commander was the Earl of Chatham (the younger Pitt) who wasted time and men in the capture of Flushing on the island of Walcheren. Meanwhile, Louis Bonaparte and Marshal Bernadotte had reinforced Antwerp. Chatham withdrew, leaving a garrison of 15,000 on Walcheren; 5,000 died in a malaria epidemic.

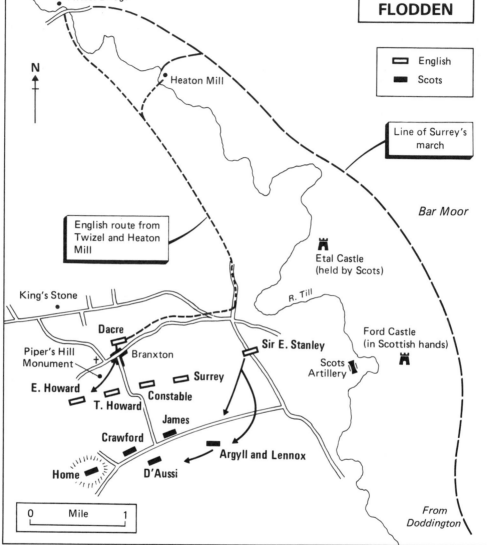

FLODDEN

- English
- Scots

Twizel Bridge

N

Heaton Mill

Line of Surrey's march

Bar Moor

English route from Twizel and Heaton Mill

Etal Castle (held by Scots)

R. Till

King's Stone

Dacre

Ford Castle (in Scottish hands)

Piper's Hill Monument

Branxton

Sir E. Stanley

Scots Artillery

E. Howard

Surrey

Constable

James

T. Howard

Crawford

Argyll and Lennox

Home

D'Aussi

0　Mile　1

From Doddington

Focsani, *in modern Romania (Turkish–Russian Wars) 21 July 1789.* The Russians and Austrians (Suvorov and the Prince of Saxe-Coburg) stormed an entrenched Turkish camp and drove out Yusuf Pasha, who lost 2,000 men. *See* Çeşme; Rimnik.

Fontenoy (*War of Austrian Succession*) 11 May 1745. Marshal Saxe, with 50,000 French, besieged Tournai, a Dutch city on the Schelde River. The Duke of Cumberland led 50,000 English, Hanoverians, Dutch and Austrians to relieve Tournai. They were met by the French at Fontenoy. Saxe had strong defences and after 2 hours' ceaseless battle Cumberland had made no progress. Cumberland then forced 14,000 soldiers into a wedge and marched it straight at the French centre. The wedge had to pass between two French redoubts which kept up a heavy fire. Still, the French line wavered until Saxe counter-attacked the Allied flanks. Cumberland could not induce the Dutch (Prince George of Waldeck) to support him and his men, after gallant fighting, were beaten; Cumberland retreated towards Brussels. The Allies lost more than 7,000 in dead and wounded. Tournai surrendered and Saxe soon took Brussels. *See* Cuneo; Hohenfriedeberg.

Ford of the Biscuits (*Hugh O'Donnell's Revolt*) 7 August 1594. The Irish (Hugh Maguire) were besieging Enniskillen when the English (Sir Henry Duke and Sir Edward Herbert) attempted to raise the siege. Victory went to the Irish who lost only a few men to the English casualties of 125. The name of the ford at which the battle took place was changed to Bel-atha-na-in-Briosgadh (Mount of the Ford of the Biscuits) from the number of biscuits and small cakes left by the beaten British.

Formigny, *near Bailleul* (*Hundred Years' War*) 15 April 1450. The French (Comte de Clermont) attacked and almost annihilated the recently arrived 4,000 reinforcements, led by Sir Thomas Kyriel, for the English army. The defeat virtually ended English domination in northern France. *See* Castillon; Rouen III.

Fornham Saint Geneviève (*Rebellion of the French Princes*) 1173. The forces of Henry II, under the Justiciary Richard de Lucy, defeated the army of the rebel princes led by Robert de Beaumont.

Fornovo (*French Wars in Italy*) 6 July 1495. An army of 34,000 Venetians and Mantuans (Francisco de Gonzaga) attacked Charles VIII's 8,000 French and Swiss as they were retiring, but Charles' leadership and skill were superb and at a cost of only 100 casualties he inflicted 3,500 on the enemy and repulsed them. *See* Barletta; Cerignola; Naples.

Fort Actions of the American Revolution

Fort Clinton and Fort Montgomery 6 October 1777. American forts on the Hudson River captured by Sir Henry Clinton, in a vain attempt to relieve pressure on General Burgoyne at Saratoga.

Fort Mercer 22 October 1777. An attack by 2,000 Hessian mercenaries in British service against Green's 400 Rhode Islanders. The attack was repulsed, but Greene had to abandon the place on 20 November.

Fort Mifflin 10–20 November 1777. A sustained naval bombardment forced the 200 Americans who survived it to evacuate by night.

Fort Moultrie 28 June 1776. The Americans, holding this fort, blocked the first British attack on Charleston.

Fort Stanwix (*upper Mohawk River*) 3–26 August 1777. The British (St. Leger) laid siege to the fort on 3 August, and on 6 August ambushed and routed a relief force. A second relief force (Benedict Arnold) and desertion of his Indian fighters forced St. Leger to abandon the siege.

Fort Ticonderoga 10 May 1775. Surprised and captued by the Americans. On 5 July 1777 Burgoyne, placing guns on commanding heights, forced the garrison out and inflicted heavy casualties.

Fort Washington 16 November 1776. Near the north end of Manhattan Island, the Americans were overwhelmed by 8,000 British and Hessian troops.

Fort Actions of the America–British War 1812–14

Fort Dearborn *August 1812*. Evacuating Fort Dearborn (Chicago) in panic, General Hull ordered the garrison, 15 August, to make for Fort Wayne. A Potawatomi war party ambushed them, killed twenty-four soldiers and fourteen women and children and captured others. The British burnt empty Fort Dearborn.

Fort Erie *2 August–21 September 1814*. The garrison of 2,000 (Gaines) was besieged by 3,500 British (Drummond). Two attacks were repulsed, then an American sortie, 17 September, destroyed the British batteries, forcing Drummond to lift the siege. Casualties: British, 609; American, 511.

Fort McHenry *12–13 September 1812*. A violent sea and land attack by the British on the fort protecting Baltimore. Suffering 346 casualties, including their commander, the British drew off. The American garrison of 1,000 lost 20 killed, 90 wounded and 200 captured.

Fort Actions of the American Civil War

Fort Donelson *6 February 1862*. The Federal capture of Fort Henry forced a realignment of Confederate forces. Johnston sent 12,000 men (Floyd) to reinforce Fort Donelson on the Cumberland River. Grant invested the place, 12 February, with 25,000 men and Federal gunboats bombarded it but were repulsed. The siege succeeded. Casualties: Federals, 724 killed, 2,108 wounded; Confederates, 2,000 killed or wounded, 11,000 captured. Only Nathan Forest's cavalry escaped intact.

Fort Fisher *13–15 January 1865*. Fort Fisher, held by 8,000 Confederates (General Whiting and Hoke), came under attack by 8,000 Federals (Terry). After heavy bombardment, the Federals stormed the fort and captured it. Casualties: Federals, 206 killed, 749 wounded; Confederates, deaths unknown, but 112 officers and 1,971 men captured. The Federals could now use Wilmington Harbour, which Fort Fisher covered.

Fort Henry *6 February 1862*. Facing

large forces of Federal troops (Grant) the Confederate commander of the fort, on the Tennessee River, evacuated most of the garrison to Fort Donelson. The token garrison remaining surrendered after firing on Federal gunboats: 176 casualties in all.

Fort Pillow or Fort Pillow Massacre *12 April 1864*. This Federal fort on the Mississippi was held by 262 negro and 295 white soldiers (Major Booth, then Major Bradford). When Bradford refused a surrender ultimatum Nathan Forrest ordered a Confederate assault. The Confederates lost 14 killed and 86 wounded, but the garrison suffered 231 killed, 100 seriously wounded and 226 captured. The Confederates explained the oddly high casualties by saying that the garrison's defence was exceptionally sustained. There is much evidence, however, that the garrison were killed after surrender because of the many negro soldiers present. *See* Wilderness.

Fort Stedman *25 March 1865*. Lee's last battle in his efforts to break through the Federal siege lines near Petersburg.

Fort Sumter *12–14 April 1861*. The battle which started the Civil War. Held by Major Anderson and only seventy-six men for the Northern States, Sumter, in Charleston Harbour, was surrounded by Confederates (Beauregard). In 36 hours 4,000 shells fell in the fort — without causing casualties. But realizing his hopeless position, Anderson abandoned the fort. *See* Big Bethel; Philippi.

Fort Wagner *11 and 18 July 1863*. In two attacks, the Federals took the fort which covered Charleston. Each side suffered about 1,000 casualties.

Other Fort Actions

Fort Caroline (*Spanish–French War in Florida*) *20 September 1565*. French Huguenots (Laudonniere) built Fort Caroline at the mouth of the Saint

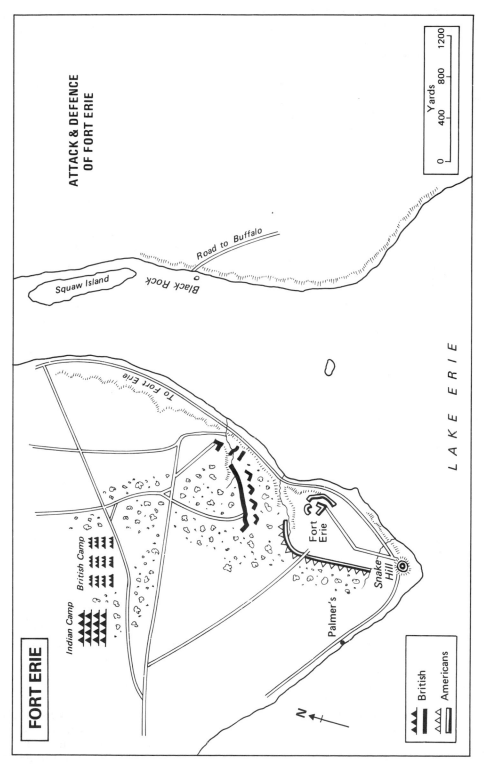

FORT ERIE

ATTACK & DEFENCE
OF FORT ERIE

Squaw Island

Black Rock

Road to Buffalo

To Fort Erie

Indian Camp

British Camp

Fort Erie

Snake Hill

Palmer's

LAKE ERIE

N

British
Americans

Yards

0   400   800   1200

John's River, thus threatening Spanish possessions. A force under Menendez stormed the place, killing 132 defenders in the first hour. Laudonniere was one of the few survivors. Renamed Fort Mateo, the fort came under French attack, 6 April 1568. Capturing it, the French commander, de Gourgues, hanged the Spanish garrison.

Fort St. David (*Seven Years' War*) 14 May–2 June 1758. The French besieged this Indian fort on 14 May. The Anglo–Indian garrison surrendered on the arrival of a French fleet on 2 June.

Fort Douaument (*World War I*) 25 February 1916. A key French position at Verdun. Scene of vicious fighting, the fort was captured by the Germans but regained by the French, 2 November. *See* Verdun.

Fort Frontenac (*Seven Years' War*) 27 August 1758. The third British offensive against the French in North America; others were Ticonderoga and Louisburg. Bradstreet, with 2,000 troops, crossed the eastern end of Lake Ontario, surprised the 110-strong garrison of Fort Frontenac and destroyed supplies and shipping. Their communications cut in the Ohio Valley, the French blew up their Fort Duquesne and retreated into Canada. *See* Fort Louisburg; Ticonderoga.

Fort Necessity (*British–French/Indian War*) 3 July 1754. Notable as an action in which George Washington, then a Lieutenant-Colonel in British service, led 150 Virginia militia towards Fort Duquesne. He routed a small French party, 28 May, and then fell back to a crude position, Fort Necessity (southwest Pennsylvania). Captain de Villiers, with 600 French and 100 Indians, attacked on 3 July; out of ammunition after a day-long fight, Washington surrendered and was parolled. *See* Beauséjour.

Fort Niagara (*Seven Years' War*) 6

June–6 July 1759. The British (Prideaux and Johnson) besieged the French fort — where Niagara River enters Lake Ontario — with 2,000 regulars and 100 Iroquois Indians. A French–Indian force tried to relieve the fort, 24 July, and lost heavily. The survivors of the 600-man garrison surrendered next day.

Fort Phil Kearny (*or the Wagon Box Fight*) (*First Sioux War*) 7 August 1867. The remarkable exploit of Captain James Powell, with thirty-two soldiers and workmen, in beating off six Sioux–Cheyenne attacks by 1,500 warriors (Red Cloud), before help arrived from the fort. Powell's marksmen, using new breech-loading rifles, killed nearly 200 Indians for the loss of 7 soldiers. *See* Massacre Hill.

Fort Recovery (*American–Indian Wars*) 4 November 1791. A major American defeat. General Arthur St. Clair led 2,000 militia from Fort Washington (Cincinatti) against allied Indian tribes in the north-west. Camping at Fort Recovery, Ohio, St. Clair, his force already weakened by desertions, was surprised by an Indian attack under Little Turtle. Within 2 hours 900 Americans were slaughtered. St. Clair, who escaped, had previously been court-martialled (but exonerated) for precipitately abandoning Fort Ticonderoga during the Revolution. *See* Fort Wayne.

Fort Sitabaldi (*Third British–Mahratta War*) 24 November 1817. A garrison of British-officered Madras and Bengal troops, only 1,300-strong, beat off 15,000 Nagpur troops (Nappa Sahib), inflicting immense casualties for a loss of 300. The British victory ended the war. *See* Kirkee.

Fort Texas (*American–Mexican War*) 3–9 May 1846. On the Rio Grande, Fort Texas (Major Brown) was invested by the Mexicans (Arista) but relieved 4 days later by the American commander in the south-west, Zachary Taylor. *See* Palo Alto.

Fort Ticonderoga (*Seven Years' War*) 8 July 1758. Between 12,000 British and American troops (Abercrombie) and 3,000 French and Canadians (Montcalm). Montcalm entrenched his men behind a low ridge in front of the fort. Without any artillery support, the blundering Abercrombie launched five frontal assaults, losing heavily each time. For a total casualty list of 400, the French killed 493 British and wounded 1,117. The French position had all the time been obviously vulnerable to flank attack. Amherst, commanding 11,000 troops, captured the fort on 26 July 1759.

Fort Vaux (*World War I*) 6 June 1916. A French strongpoint near Verdun captured by the Germans despite heroic resistance (Major Raynal). Regained by French, 2 November. *See* Verdun.

Fort Wayne, Indiana (*American–Indian Wars*) 18 October 1790. The battle is misnamed, for no fort existed at this place, which was at the time an Indian town. General Harmer had been sent to break up an Indian confederacy — Miami, Shawnee, Potawatomi and Chippewa under Little Turtle. The Americans were decisively defeated, and on 22 October were again beaten. American humiliation was acute. *See* Fort Recovery.

Fort William Henry (*Seven Years' War*) 4–9 August 1757. Montcalm, with 6,000 French troops, besieged the fort, held by Colonel Monro and 2,200 British and colonial troops, on 4 August. French batteries opened fire on 6 August and on the 9th, Monro, having lost 300 killed or wounded and with nearly all his guns disabled, surrendered. The agreement was that he could retire his force and their women and children unmolested to Fort Edward, but the French could not control their 1,600 Indians who savagely attacked the unarmed British column. Fifty people were killed and 400 carried off as prisoners before the French could — or would — restore order. *See* Fort Ticonderoga; Oswego.

Fort Zelanda, *Formosa* (*Chinese Pirate Wars*) 1661–2. The pirate-general Cheng Ch'eng-kung (Koxinga) laid siege to the Dutch fort, near Tainan. Its surrender the following year ended Dutch rule of Formosa.

Forum Terebronii, *mouth of the Danube* (*First Gothic invasion of Roman Empire*) 251. Gaius Decius, who had won several notable successes against barbarians on both sides of the Danube, trapped Cuiva's Goths at Terebronii. One of his generals, Tribonianus Gallus, failed to push home an attack which would have won the battle. Decius' son was killed at this time. Decius rallied the legionaries and routed two lines of Goths, but the Romans lost formation in swamps and were themselves routed; Decius was killed. *See* Philippopolis.

Four Days' Battle. *See* Dover Strait.

France (*World War II*) 5–22 June 1940. Distinctly a battle rather than a campaign, this conflict followed the German capture of Flanders and Dunkirk in May–June. On 5 June 140 German divisions attacked on a 10-mile front against the demoralized French, who had sixty-five divisions on a line longer than the original front. Von Bock reached the Seine on 9 June and von Reichenau drove down the Oise. As the French Tenth Army collapsed, the Royal Navy evacuated 136,000 British and 20,000 Polish soldiers. The Germans (von Kuechler) reached Paris on 14 June, Dijon on 16 June, and Cherbourg on 18 June. Formal surrender took place on 22 June. *See* Dunkirk.

Frankenhausen (*Peasants' War*) 15 May 1525. The troops of Saxony, Hesse and Brunswick routed the rebellious peasants and summarily hanged their leader, Thomas Munzer. *See* Mühlburg.

Frankfort-on-Oder (*Thirty Years' War*) *2 April 1631*. Gustavus Adolphus, the Swedish king, led 15,000 Swedes in an assault on the town, killing 1,800 of the German–Italian garrison. The Imperialists' leaders, Schaumberg and Montecucculi, escaped with a cavalry escort. *See* Magdeberg; Wolgast.

Franklin, *Tennessee* (*American Civil War*) *30 June 1864*. General Schofield, with 30,000 Northerners, held strong positions covering Nashville, where General Hood, who outnumbered him by 10,000 men, penetrated his lines. Schofield rallied his troops, recaptured lost positions and joined with General Thomas. Neither side could be said to have won, but the Confederates lost 4,500 men to the Federals' 1,500 killed or wounded and 1,000 prisoners. *See* Atlanta.

Frastenz (*Swiss–Swabian War*) *20 April 1499*. The Swiss, under Heinrich Wolleb, gallantly attacked powerful Austrian positions, killed 3,000 of the enemy and drove out the others. Wolleb was killed. *See* Calven; Giornico.

Fraubrunnen (*invasion of the "Guglers"*) *1376*. The Guglers were French and British mercenaries led by Baron Ingelram von Coucy who claimed the Swiss Canton of Aargau for his mother. The Bernese troops routed the Guglers, who fled from the country. *See* Sempach.

Frauenstadt (*Russian–Swedish Wars*) *12 February 1706*. An extraordinary action between 10,000 Swedes (Reinschild) and 20,000 Russians and Saxons (Schulemburg). Within 15 minutes the Allied troops fled. The Swedes claimed to have picked up 7,000 loaded muskets on the battlefield. *See* Pultusk.

Frayser's Farm (*American Civil War*) *30 June 1862*. Part of the Seven Days Battle east of Richmond, q.v.

Fredericksburg (*American Civil War*) *13 December 1862*. A major battle, between General Burnside with 150,000 Federals and General Lee's 80,000 Confederates. Burnside attacked the Confederates, who held a range of heights along the Massaponax River and was repulsed after much hard fighting, losing 13,771 men. Lee lost 1,800, but considered his force too inferior in numbers to exploit his victory and allowed Burnside to evacuate Fredericksburg. *See* Antietam Creek.

Fredrikshald (*Danish–Swedish War*) *December 1718*. Charles XII of Sweden besieged this fortress, the strongest in Norway, early in December. On the 11th, while inspecting his batteries, he was killed by a cannon ball; the Swedes at once raised the siege and withdrew. *See* Stralsund II.

Freeman's Farm (*American Revolution*) *19 September 1777*. Really the first battle of Saratoga, which blocked the British advance (Burgoyne) on Albany. *See* Saratoga.

Freiburg (*Thirty Years' War*) *3–9 August 1644*. Between 20,000 French (the Great Conde and Turenne) and 15,000 Bavarians (Comte de Mercy). Turenne, after making a long flank march, attacked the Bavarians' flank, 3 August, while Conde drove at their front. During the night de Mercy retired to fresh positions where, on 5 August, he held his ground and inflicted twice as many casualties as he suffered. On 8 August he retreated and the following day beat back harassing cavalry, but Conde, coming up, forced the Bavarians into headlong retreat and captured all their equipment. *See* Jankau; Tuttlingen.

French and Indian War. *See* List of Battles.

French–Prussian War. *See* List of Battles.

French Revolutionary Wars. *See* List of Battles.

Frenchtown, *later Monroe, Michigan (American–British War)* **22 January 1813.** The defeat of an American force (Kentuckians under General Winchester) by a British–Canadian unit (Proctor). About 400 Americans were killed in action or massacred by Indians and 500 were captured. The British then tried for 8 days to take Fort Meigs, but were repulsed. *See* Detroit; Erie, Lake.

Freteval *1191*. Richard Coeur de Lion defeated the French under Philip Augustus.

Friedland *(Napoleonic Wars: Friedland campaign)* *14 June 1807*. A major victory for Napoleon, who used 80,000 French against Bennigsen's 70,000 Russians. At 3 a.m., with only Lannes' corps facing him, Bennigsen unaccountably failed to overwhelm the French and contented himself with an artillery duel. When he did attack, at 7 a.m., 26,000 French were in position. They held until the arrival of Napoleon, who launched his fresh troops against the Russian columns massed in a bend of the River Alle. Many Russians were driven into the river and Napoleon, after hard fighting, occupied Friedland at 10 p.m. Casualties: Russian, 15,000 killed or wounded, 10,000 prisoners; French, about 9,500. The victory was followed by the peace of Tilsit. *See* Heilsburg.

Friedlingen *(War of Spanish Succession)* *14 October 1702*. Bavaria declared war against the Allies (England, Holland, Austria, Prussia) and seized Ulm. Louis of Baden, a supporter of the Allies, who had been campaigning in Alsace, recrossed the Rhine to protect his country. Marshal de Catinat sent General de Villers after him with a small army. Villars and Louis clashed at Friedlingen; the French outflanked the Baden troops, many of whom were taken prisoner. Villars was promoted to Marshal. *See* Landau; Luzzara.

Fromelles, *France (World War I)* *19–20 July 1916*. This battle was fought by the 5th Australian Division (Lieutenant-General J. W. McCay) to stop the German command from reinforcing their army on the Somme. The battle was a reckless misconception by the British staff and in 27 hours of close-quarter fighting the Australians lost 5,533 officers and men. *See* Bullecourt; Somme.

Frontiers of France *(World War I)* *20–24 August 1914*. This 5-day battle stretched from the Swiss frontier to Mons, Belgium. The Germans committed seven armies, the French five, the British one of 70,000 men. The segments of the battle consisted of Battles of Lorraine, Ardennes, Sambre (or Charleroi) and Mons. The result was a resounding defeat for the French and their British Allies. The French suffered 300,000 casualties (of 1,250,000 involved), the Germans about the same. At Mons the British had 4,244 casualties in holding up the German advance for 9 hours. The battle established the tactics and strategy — or rather the lack of strategy — of World War I: massive frontal attacks supported by drenching artillery and machine-gun fire. Principal German commanders: von Heeringen, Prince Rupprecht of Bavaria, Crown Prince Freidrich Wilhelm, von Hausen, von Bulow, von Kluck — the whole battle master-minded by von Moltke. French: Joffre, Dubail, de Castelnau, de Cary, Ruffey, Foch, Lanrezac. British: Generals French and Smith. *See* Le Cateau; Marne River I; Namur II.

Front Royal *(American Civil War)* *23 May 1862*. With 16,000 men General (Stonewall) Jackson struck the isolated Federal position at Frontal Royal, east of Strasburg. Because of a spy's information, Jackson knew the enemy's positions and his men swept through the post, killing, wounding or capturing 904 of the 1,063-man garrison. The Confederates lost less than fifty. *See* McDowell; Winchester I.

Fuentes d'Onoro *(Peninsular War)* *5 May 1811*. Wellington, with 34,000 men, held a position behind Fuentes d'Onoro, which Massena attacked in an attempt to relieve the besieged town of Almeida. He had an equal number of troops and guns, and though he could not take Wellington's lines he retired in good order. Each side lost about 1,500 men. *See* Albuhera; Bussaco.

Fulford, *near York* (*Norse invasion*) *1066*. Harold Hardrada, King of Norway, defeated the English under Earls Edwin and Morcar.

Furruckbad (*or* *Farrukhabad*) (*Second British–Mahratta War*) *14 November 1804*. Lord Lake, with a force recorded as 3,000 infantry, defeated Holkar's 60,000 Mahrattas. Holkar lost heavily, but the British claim to have lost only two killed and twenty wounded is suspect. *See* Argaon; Kirkee.

Fürth (*or Alte Veste*) (*Thirty Years' War*) *11 July–18 September 1632*. The Elector of Bavaria, Maximilian I, and Wallenstein, with a Catholic army of 50,000, joined forces at Nürnberg, 11 July. In Nürnberg, Gustavus Adolphus of Sweden faced the desperate choice of starving in the city or attacking the larger Catholic army now occupying a ridge at Fürth, near Nürnberg. Mustering every available man — 40,000 — Adolphus attacked, 3–4 September, and failed. He lost 2,000 men. On 18 September, risking an attack on the march, Gustavus abandoned Nürnberg and retreated southeast. Wallenstein did not pursue. *See* Lützen I; Rain.

Futteypur (*Indian Mutiny*) *12 July 1857*. General Havelock, marching to the relief of Lucknow, defeated a large force of rebels without loss to himself. *See* Cawnpore; Lucknow.

Gadebesk (*Danish–Swedish Wars*) 20 December 1712. The allied Danes and Saxons, though 24,000-strong and protected in strong positions by marshes, were driven out by Steinbock's 12,000 Swedes, and lost heavily. *See* Stralsund.

Gaeta Italian Wars of Independence 3 November 1860–13 February 1861. Francis II of Naples with 12,000 troops made a last stand against Garibaldi's Red-shirts and 10,000 other Italians. Colonel Cialdini, a Piedmontese, directed the siege of Gaeta. Francis was supported by a French fleet but when it withdrew on 19 January Gaeta was bombarded by Pied-montese warships. Defeated, Francis was exiled. *See* Aspromonte; Volturno.

Gallic Wars. *See* List of Battles.

Gallipoli (*World War I*) 25 April 1915–January 1916. Between the Turks (Mustapha Kemel and Liman von Sanders) and the British Allies, English, Scottish, Welsh, Irish, Australian, New Zealand, Indian and French troops, not-ably under Hamilton and Birdwood. Object of the campaign was to take con-trol of the Dardanelles, the narrow strait linking the Aegean Sea with the Sea of Marmara and the Black Sea so that Ger-many could be attacked from the east. The Allies made landings under fire at three points: the Australians, 25 April, at Anzac Cove, British the same day at Cape Helles and British, 6 August, at Suvla Bay. Bitter and arduous fighting took place in several large battles and many small ones. British leadership was inept and lethargic and several extremely wasteful attacks were ordered against notoriously impossible positions. Three fruitless battles were fought at Krithia. The campaign was not only one of the greatest disasters in British history but one of the worst managed. It was relieved only by the remarkable courage of the troops who took part. Turkish–German leadership was exemplary.

The most notable battles were those of Lone Pine, which the Anzacs attacked on 6 August and Sari Bair on 8/9 August — "a battle of valour run waste", says Major-General Fuller.

On 20 December Anzac and Suvla were evacuated and Helles on 16 January 1916. In these remarkably efficient evacuations not a single Allied soldier was lost. But of the 500,000 Allied troops put into the Gallipoli peninsula, 252,000 became cas-ualties. Australia lost 8,587 men killed and 19,367 wounded; New Zealand, with only 200,000 men of military age in the country, lost 2,500 killed and 5,000 wounded. The most reliable estimate of Turkish losses is 251,000 of whom 66,000 were killed. *See* Dardanelles.

Garigliano River I (*French–Spanish Wars in Italy*) 3 November 1503. Fran-cisco de Gonzaga of Mantua, commanding a large French force, built a bridge across the Garigliano and crossed it in the face of Spanish opposition. The Spanish com-mander, Gonsalvo de Cordova, had only

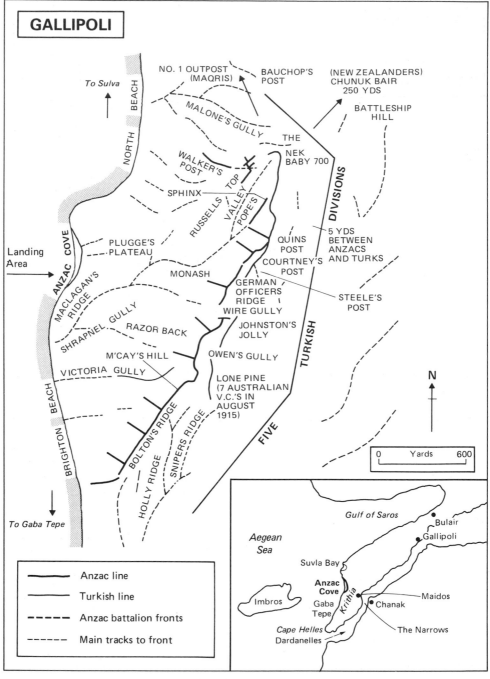

GALLIPOLI

To Sulva

NO. 1 OUTPOST (MAQRIS)

BAUCHOP'S POST

(NEW ZEALANDERS) CHUNUK BAIR 250 YDS

BATTLESHIP HILL

NORTH BEACH

MALONE'S GULLY

THE NEK BABY 700

WALKER'S POST

DIVISIONS

SPHINX

RUSSELLS TOP

VALLEY

POPE'S

5 YDS BETWEEN ANZACS AND TURKS

ANZAC COVE

Landing Area

PLUGGE'S PLATEAU

QUINS POST

COURTNEY'S POST

MONASH

GERMAN OFFICERS RIDGE WIRE GULLY

STEELE'S POST

MACLAGAN'S RIDGE

SHRAPNEL GULLY

RAZOR BACK

JOHNSTON'S JOLLY

TURKISH

M'CAY'S HILL

OWEN'S GULLY

VICTORIA GULLY

LONE PINE (7 AUSTRALIAN V.C.'S IN AUGUST 1915)

FIVE

N

BRIGHTON BEACH

BOLTON'S RIDGE

SNIPERS RIDGE

HOLLY RIDGE

0   Yards   600

To Gaba Tepe

———	Anzac line
———	Turkish line
- - - -	Anzac battalion fronts
- - - - -	Main tracks to front

Gulf of Saros

Bulair

Aegean Sea

Gallipoli

Suvla Bay

Anzac Cove

Maidos

Imbros

Gaba Tepe

Krithia

Chanak

Cape Helles

The Narrows

Dardanelles

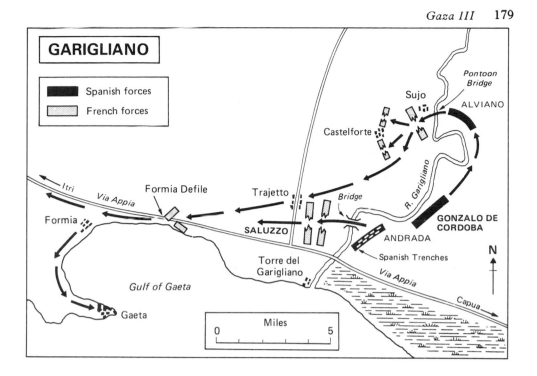

GARIGLIANO

- Spanish forces
- French forces

Pontoon Bridge

Sujo   ALVIANO

Castelforte

R. Garigliano

Itri

Via Appia

Formia Defile   Trajetto   Bridge

Formia   GONZALO DE CORDOBA

SALUZZO   ANDRADA

Torre del Garigliano   Spanish Trenches

N

Gulf of Gaeta   *Via Appia*

Gaeta   Capua

Miles

0   5

12,000 men and could not prevent the crossing. *See* Agnadello; Cerignola.

Garigliano River II (*French–Spanish Wars in Italy*) *29 December 1503*. Gonsalvo de Cordova, chasing the French — 15,000 under Marquis of Saluzzo who were retiring towards Gasta — crossed the river at two points and brought them to battle. The French lost 4,000 killed and all their artillery and baggage. *See* Cerignola; Seminora.

Gate Pah (*Second British–Maori War*) *27 April 1864*. General Cameron, with 1,700 British soldiers and sailors, attacked a Maori stockade, the Gate Pah. About 600 men penetrated the stockade, but 112 became casualties and the others were beaten back. The Maoris, having suffered forty casualties, evacuated the stockade that night.

Gaulauli (*Indian Mutiny*) *22 May 1858*. Sir Hugh Rose's British column caught up with 20,000 rebels (Tantia Topi) and breaking their lines with a bayonet charge routed them. *See* Cawnpore.

Gaza I (*Alexander's Asiatic campaigns*) *October 332 BC*. Alexander the Great besieged the city, defended by a Persian garrison under Batis. His fourth assault was successful. He had the garrison massacred. *See* Tyre II.

Gaza II (*Wars of Alexander's Successors*) *312 BC*. The allied Syrians and Egyptians (Seleucus and Ptolemy Soter) attacked the Macedonians (Demetrius Poliorcetes) who lost 5,000 killed, 8,000 wounded and all their supplies. Each army started with 25,000 men.

Gaza III (*World War I*) *26–27 March and 17–19 April 1917*. The British Army, mostly Australian and New Zealand troops, under Murray, had captured two strong Turkish outposts, Magdhaba and Rafa, in the advance on Turkish-held Palestine. At Gaza the advance was blocked by 17,000 Turks under the German, Kress von Kressenstein. The first

British attack (Dobell) failed because the cavalry mistakenly withdrew, exposing the infantry, who retired. Reinforced, the Turks counter-attacked and in 2 days inflicted 4,000 casualties for a loss of 2,400. The Turks now greatly strengthened their 25-mile Gaza–Beersheba line. Murray and Dobell threw three divisions against the Turks and sustained a hopeless attack for 3 days, losing 6,450 men; Turkish losses, 1,900. Murray sacked Dobell, but was then himself relieved by Allenby, who had been hurried from France. *See* Romani.

Gaza IV (*World War I*) *31 October–7 November 1917*. By now 35,000 Turkish troops held the Gaza–Beersheba line to block the northward advance of Allenby's British Army of 88,000 — still largely Australians and New Zealanders. Allenby attacked at Beersheba on 31 October, from west and east. Then, aided by naval gunfire, he pressed along the coast, forcing the Turkish command to move troops to Gaza from the east. On 6 November Allenby again struck the east end of the line. The Turks fell back and the British reached Jaffa on 16 November. Jerusalem fell, without a battle, on 9 December. *See* Beersheba; Megiddo III.

Gebora, *near Badajoz* (*Peninsular War*) *19 February 1811*. General Mendizabal with 12,000 Spaniards overconfidently attacked Soult's 8,000 French veterans in an attempt to disrupt the French siege of Badajoz, q.v. He lost 850 killed or wounded, 5,000 prisoners and all his guns.

Gelt, The (*English–Scottish Wars*) *February 1570*. Lord Hunsdon and his Royalist troops routed the rebel Borderers (Leonard Dacre).

Gembloux (*Netherlands War of Independence*) *31 January 1578*. General Goignies was leading 20,000 nationalist troops from Namur, pursued by Don John of Austria, who had the same number of Spanish soldiers. He sent in more rapid pursuit a picked force of 1,600 (Gonzaga and Mondragon). This commando-like group savaged and dispersed the rearguard and then surprised the main army. It is reliably recorded that 10,000 Dutch were killed or made prisoner while the Spaniards lost only 100. *See* Leyden; Maastricht I.

Genoa I *6–10 December 1746*. An interesting instance of a successful civil uprising. The Genoese, angered by the behaviour of the Austrian garrison (General Botta), attacked the Austrians on 6 December and in 5 days of street fighting inflicted 5,000 casualties and drove them out.

Genoa II (*Wars of the French Revolution*) *13 March 1795*. Admiral Hotham, with fourteen ships, attacked a French fleet of fifteen, captured two and forced the rest into flight. *See* Fleurus.

Genoa III (*Napoleon's Italian campaigns*) *April–June 1800*. Massena was besieged in Genoa by the Austrians, at first under Melas, later Ott. Since the British fleet was blockading the port Massena could get no provisions. He made several daringly successful sorties, but on 5 June capitulated. Nevertheless, he was permitted to keep his arms. The siege deprived the Austrians of men they might well have used at Marengo, q.v.

Geok Tepe (*Russian conquest of Central Asia*) *1870–81*. The Russians, expanding south and east, besieged Geok Tepe, the stronghold of the Tekke Turcomans, on 9 September 1878. General Lomakine bombarded the walls and tried to storm the fortress, but the 15,000-strong garrison was too strong for him, despite having suffered 4,000 casualties under shellfire. With difficulty he saved his guns and withdrew. In 1881 a much more skilful general, Skobeloff, with 10,000 Russian troops, laid siege to Geok Tepe on 8–17 January and though the garrison now numbered 30,000 he took the place by storm. The Turcomans lost

6,500 during the siege and another 8,000 in the pursuit. *See* Philippopolis.

Gerberoi (*Norman Civil War*) *1080*. Robert, son of William the Conqueror, claimed the Dukedom of Normandy from his father and was aided by Philip I of France, William defeated his son in battle, imprisoned him and forced him to renounce his claim. *See* Hastings.

Gergovia, *central France* (*Gallic Wars*) *52 BC*. Caesar, besieging the town held by Gauls under Vercingetorix, was compelled to withdraw. He made a last assault which the Gauls repulsed, killing 746 Romans. *See* Avaricum.

Germaghah, *central Asia 1193*. The first battle of Genghis Khan. In a narrow pass he surprised the army of his father-in-law, Ung Khan, led by Sankun, and his 6,000 well-trained soldiers inflicted very heavy losses. *See* Bokhara.

Germantown (*American Revolution*) *4 October 1777*. Washington's Americans attacked British trenches and were beaten back with heavy loss by Sir William Howe's veteran regulars. *See* Fort Mercer; Paoli.

Gerona, *Catalonia* (*Peninsular War*) *4 June–10 December 1809*. General Verdier, with 18,000 French veterans, besieged Gerona on 4 June. The commander, Mariano Alvarez, had only 3,000 Spanish troops — regulars of high standard — and was short of everything, but he held out until 10 December, when the French agreed to his marching out with the honours of war. *See* Talavera.

Gettysberg (*American Civil War*) *1–3 July 1863*. A major and bloody battle between the northern army of the Potomac (Meade) and the army of Virginia (Lee). On 1 July General Hills' corps attacked Meade's position in front of Gettysberg and drove the Federals in disorder through the town. Next day Meade took up new positions behind

Gettysberg, where he lost many men repulsing Confederate attacks. On the 3rd he pushed back the Confederate left, but Lee's main attack drove the federals from the ridge. They rallied and recaptured it, but by now had lost 20,000 men and could not continue. Lee, who had also lost 20,000, tried to draw the Federals into battle on 4 July, but when Meade held back Lee withdrew. Great loss of life had resulted in no gain whatever. *See* Bristoe Station; Vicksburg; Winchester II.

Ghent (*War of Spanish Succession*) *12 July 1708*. The British and Austrian Allies, under the Duke of Marlborough and Prince Eugene, had won a great if bloody victory at Oudenarde on 11 July. The next day, Marshal Vendôme, in a superb display of personal leadership, rallied his defeated and retreating troops at Ghent; they stood firm against the pursuing Allies and repulsed them. This battle, so little mentioned, was more decisive than Oudernarde because it enabled the French to keep control of western Flanders. Also, a secure line of communications to France had been regained. *See* Lille; Oudenarde.

Gherain (*British conquest of Bengal*) *2 August 1763*. A 4-hour battle led to a victory for the British (Major Adams) over the army of Mir Cossim, the deposed nawab of Bengal. *See* Buxar; Plassey.

Ghoaine (*First British–Afghan War*) *30 August 1842*. The Afghans (Shems-ud-din) tried to stop the march of General Nott's force from Kandahar to Ghuzni and, defeated, lost all their guns and equipment. *See* Jellalabad.

Ghuzni (*or Ghazni*) (*First British–Afghan War*) *21 January 1839*. A British force, having no artillery to attack the fort, held by 3,000 Afghans, blew in the main gate and then stormed the fort. They captured it at a cost of 182 men, while the Afghans lost 500. *See* Kabul.

Giarabub, *Libya* **(*World War II*)** *19 March 1941*. An Italian oasis fort, Giarabub was captured by the Australian 18th Brigade after a stiff fight in a sandstorm. *See* Bardia; Sollum; Tobruk.

Gibbel Rutts (*Irish Rebellion*) *26 May 1798*. Sir James Duff with English regulars attacked the rebels in their camp on the Curragh and dispersed them at the point of the bayonet. Together, the combatants had 350 killed.

Gibraltar (*War of Spanish Succession*) *24 July 1704*. A combined British and Dutch fleet (Sir George Rooke) captured the fortress from the Spaniards (Marquis de Salinas); the Allies lost 288 men. *See* Blenheim; Vigo Bay.

Gibraltar (*War of American Revolution*) *1779–83*. A combined French–Spanish force laid siege for 4 years; even their powerful floating batteries could make no impression on General Elliot's defences. British fleets several times ran the blockade to reinforce and resupply the garrison. *See* Cape Saint Vincent I; Ushant I.

Gihon, The, *central southern Russia* **(*The Getes Revolt against the Tartars*)** *1362*. The Getes, led by their khan, impressively defeated Tamerlane and his Tartars; the Getes marched on Samarkand, but sickness killed most of their horses and they retired.

Gingi (*Mogul invasion of the Deccan*) *1689–91*. The Moguls spent 3 years besieging Gingi — first under Zulfikar Khan, then Kambaksh, then Zulfikar Khan again. Finally, Aurungzebe took command and, after conniving at the escape of the garrison commander, Rajah Ram, took the place by assault.

Gisikon, *Switzerland* **(*Sonderbund Civil War*)** *23 November 1847*. Troops of the Sonderbund (Colonel Salis-Soglio) were strongly placed at Gisikon, near Lake Zug. General Dufour drove them out and entered Lucerne next day, bringing to an end the 20-day civil war which the Catholic cantons had fought in an effort to avert the dissolution of their Sonderbund — a separate confederation.

Gitschin (*Seven Weeks' War*) *29–30 June 1866*. Prince Frederick Charles with 16,000 Prussians defeated a force of Austrians and Saxons twice as large (Count Gallas). The Allies lost 3,000 killed or wounded and 7,000 prisoners. *See* Müchengratz; Nachdod; Trautenau.

Gladsmuir. *See* Prestonpans.

Glencoe (*William III's Scottish campaigns*) *13 February 1692*. The Highland clans were ordered to take an oath of allegiance to William III before 1 January 1692. When the Macdonald chief was late in doing so troops from the rival Campbell clan were sent into Glencoe, western Scotland. The royalist soldiers attacked on the night of 13 February; most Macdonalds escaped, but thirty-eight were massacred. *See* Killiecrankie; Limerick.

Glen Fruin (*Scottish Civil Wars*) *4 April 1604*. The Macgregors and other Highland clans defeated royal troops under the Duke of Argyll.

Glenlivet (*Huntly's Rebellion*) *4 October 1594*. The rebel Earls of Huntly and Errol, though inferior in numbers to the 10,000 troops of James VI led by the Duke of Argyll, soundly defeated them.

Glen Malone *August 1580*. Irish clansmen, resenting the presence of English settlers (Lord Grey de Wilton), forced them into battle and seriously defeated them.

Glenmarreston *638*. Donald Bree, King of Dalriada, gathered Scottish clansmen and routed the invading Angles.

Glorious First of June. *See* Ushant.

Glorious Revolutionary War. *See* List of Battles.

Gloucester Hill (*or Point 235*) (*Korean War*) *22–25 April 1951*. Part of the greater battle of the Imjin River, the fight at Gloucester Hill, Korea, is notable for the subborn resistance of the British Army's Gloucester Regiment. It was eventually swamped by overwhelming numbers of Chinese; only thirty-nine of the Gloucesters returned to British lines, the others being either killed or captured. *See* Korea.

Goa *May 1511*. General Albuquerque, with a Portuguese garrison, held Goa under an investment by Kumal Khan, the Rajah of Bijapore's general, who had 60,000 troops. After 20 days, Albuquerque found his communication with his fleet threatened and withdrew his garrison. A few months later, having gathered 1,500 soldiers and twenty-three ships, he attacked Goa and took it after fighting so severe that the Indians suffered 6,000 casualties and fled; the Portuguese had only fifty men killed. *See* Diu.

Goits (*Italian War of Independence*) *30 May 1848*. Charles Albert of Savoy, leading the Piedmontese army, completely defeated the Austrians (Radetsky) who at this time ruled Italy, and drove them back across the Adige, where they were able to hold their line. *See* Custozza; Venice.

Golden Rock (*Seven Years' War*) *7 August 1753*. French and Indian troops from Mysore were besieging Trichinopoly when Major Lawrence, with 1,500 British and 5,000 Tanjore troops, took the Golden Rock, a key point, and drove off the enemy in disorder. *See* Calcutta.

Goodwin Sands I (*First English–Dutch War*) *19 May 1652*. A Dutch fleet of forty ships under Admiral Tromp sailed into English waters as a protest against a restrictive English navigation act. Admiral Blake with twenty English ships attacked the Dutch fleet and sank two ships. *See* Dover II.

Goodwin Sands II (*Second English–Dutch War*) *1–4 July 1666*. Admirals Tromp and de Ruyter with 101 vessels fought sixty ships under the Duke of Albemarle. After 2 days' fighting the Dutch were reinforced and Albemarle sailed clear. When he was reinforced by Prince Rupert's squadron on 4 July he returned to the attack, but victory went to the Dutch, who sank ten British ships and disabled most of the others.

Goose Green (*Falkland Islands War*) *28–29 May 1982*. Between 450 men of the 2nd Battalion Parachute Regiment (2 Para) under Lieutenant-Colonel H. Jones and 1,350 Argentinian troops commanded by Air Commodore Pedroza. 2 Para was sent to secure the southern flank of the British advance in East Falkland. Near Darwin Hill Colonel Jones was shot as he rushed an Argentinian post. Assuming command, Major C. Keeble first captured Darwin and then turned to the enemy positions at Goose Green. British Harriers gave support and destroyed gun positions. On 29 May Keeble offered surrender terms which the Argentinians accepted. The Battle of Goose Green was the most famous action of the war. Casualties: British, 17 killed, 31 wounded; Argentinians, 371 in all. *See* Falkland Islands War.

Goraria (*Indian Mutiny*) *23–24 November 1857*. About 5,000 mutineers held strong positions which brigadier Stuart's column of 3,000 attacked. Unable to dislodge the mutineers, Stuart resumed the attack next day and was successful. *See* Cawnpore.

Gorari, *New Guinea* (*World War II*) *9–12 November 1942*. This victory over Japanese forces by the Australian 25th Brigade opened the way for the Australian drive to the northern coast of New Guinea, q.v. The Japanese lost 500 killed. *See* Kokoda.

Gorni-Dubnik   (*Russian–Turkish War***)** *24 October 1877*. The Turks (Achmet Hefzi Pasha) were holding the redoubt of Gorni-Dubnik, which the Russian Guard (Gourko) attacked. After very heavy fighting the Russians dislodged the Turks. Casualties: Russian, 3,300 killed or wounded, including 116 officers of the Guards; Turkish, 1,500 killed or wounded, 2,250 prisoners, including the Pasha. *See* Plevna.

Gorodeczno (*Napoleonic Wars: Moscow campaign***)** *12 August 1812*. Between the French and Austrians (General Raynier and Prince of Schwartzemberg) and the Russians (Tormazoff); both sides had about 36,000 men. The French and Austrians, losing 2,000 men, drove the Russians from their positions and inflicted 4,000 casualties. *See* Borodino.

Gothic Line (*World War II***)** *August– September 1944*. After the defeat of the Germans on the Gustav and Dora Lines, General Alexander had twenty-eight divisions chasing twenty-one German, a third of them reduced to impotence. They should have been pushed back to the Alps, but Generals Eisenhower and Marshall insisted on an invasion of southern France, as decided on at the Teheran Conference the previous year; the striking force would come from the armies in Italy. All the British and American commanders in Italy, and Churchill, protested that destruction of the enemy in Italy was in their grasp, but the American Chiefs of Staff were adamant. The incredulous Germans were thus able to establish the Gothic Line, south of the Po. It should never have taken shape, but now that it was formed there was no point in battering against it. It would have been sufficient to pin down Kesselring. Nevertheless, an assault was opened, 26 August, by the Eighth Army (Leese) and the fighting was bloody.

Pisa was captured, 2 September, and the following thrust reached to within 9 miles of Bologna before a German coun-

ter-offensive stopped it, 20 October. Kesselring had now sealed off the Gothic Line breaches and the coming of winter further helped the Germans to hold firm. From the end of October until 2 April 1945 the only Allied gain was the Eighth Army's drive to Ravenna. The stalemate, the longest in the Italian campaign, proved that Allied weakening of pressure should never have been permitted. *See* Anzio; Cassino; Salerno.

Grampians, The (*Roman invasion of Scotland***)** *84*. The Caledonians, 30,000 strong, led by Galgacus, attacked the Romans under Agricola. Caledonian bravery could not defeat Roman discipline and Galgacus lost 10,000 men. The battlefield was probably on the Moor of Ardoch.

Granada I (*Spanish–Muslim Wars***)** *May 1319*. The Moors, holding Granada, were threatened by a Spanish army under the two regents, Pedro and John of Castile. Said Othman, selecting 5,000 veteran Moor troops, led to a savage sortie into the Spanish lines, inflicting heavy casualties and killing both regents.

Granada II (*Spanish–Muslim Wars***)** *26 April–25 November 1491*. By now Granada was the last stronghold of the Moors in Spain. Ferdinand, with 50,000 Spaniards, maintained a desultory siege and defeated the one serious sortie made by the Moors. Starving, Abdallah, the last king of Granada, surrendered the city on 25 November. Thus ended eight centuries of Muslim power in Spain.

Grand Alliance War. *See* List of Battles.

Grandella (*French Wars in Italy***)** *May 1266*. Charles of Anjou, leading a French army, attacked the troops of the Two Sicilies, under Manfred, son of the Emperor Frederick II. Defeating Manfred, who fell in battle with 4,200 of his troops, Charles usurped the crown of the double kingdom.

Grangram (*Russian–Swedish Wars*) September 1721. A Russian fleet (Admiral Golitshin) captured four large Swedish ships, damaged others and forced the rest to run. *See* Frederikshald.

Granicus, The (*Alexander's Asiatic campaign*) 334 BC. Alexander the Great and his 35,000 Macedonians crossed the Granicus in the face of Memnon of Rhodes' Persian army, 40,000-strong, and their Greek mercenaries. Leading his heavy cavalry, Alexander scattered the Persian light horse, then brought up his phalanx of spearmen and routed the enemy infantry. *See* Issus; Thebes.

Granson (*Swiss–Burgundian War*) 2 March 1476. Charles the Bold, with 36,000 Burgundians, feigned a retreat to entice the Swiss — who had only 18,000 men — on to an open plain. The Swiss responded all too rapidly; they attacked Charles' army. They also took the entire Burgundian baggage train. *See* Hericourt; Morat.

Grant's Hill (*Seven Years' War*) 14 September 1752. Major Grant, with 800 Highlanders and local volunteers, attacked a party of Indians, supporters of the French, near Fort Duquesne. Repulsed by the Indians, Grant found himself attacked by the fort's French garrison of 3,000 (de Ligneris). His little force was overwhelmed, losing a third of its strength.

Graspan (*or Enslin*) (*Second British–Boer War*) 25 November 1899. The Boers, 2,500-strong, occupied a strong position, the key to which was a high kopje. It was attacked by Lord Methuen's division and a naval brigade of 400. The frontal and flank assault failed, Methuen losing 283 men. *See* Kimberley.

Gravelines (*Valois–Hapsburg War*) 13 July 1558. Between 8,500 allied French and Germans (Marshal de Thermes) and 10,000 allied Spanish, Germans and Flemings (Count Egmont). De Thermes' right rested on the sea, but his left was vulnerable and Egmont led a cavalry charge and broke it. In severe hand-to-hand fighting the French lost 1,500 and another 1,500 were driven into the sea and drowned. Many more were ruthlessly cut down in the pursuit and de Thermes was captured. *See* Calais II; Saint-Quentin I.

Gravelotte (*or St. Privat*) (*French–Prussian War*) 18 August 1870. A major battle of the war, the French under Bazaine and the Prussians led by von Moltke. The French held their ground near Gravelotte, but at St. Privat the Germans turned their flank and Bazaine had to retire his army to Metz, where the Germans blockaded them. The casualties were enormous. Prussian, 899 officers and 19,260 men killed or wounded; French, 13,000 killed or wounded and another 5,000 taken prisoner. *See* Mars-la-Tour; Metz; Sedan.

Great Meadows (*Seven Years' War*) 3 July 1752. Washington with only 350 Virginians occupied a square log stockade known as Fort Necessity, where he resisted de Villiers' 700 French for 9 hours before shortage of ammunition forced his surrender; he had lost sixty killed and wounded. *See* Beausejour.

Great Northern War. *See* List of Battles.

Greece (*World War II*) April 1941. British, Australian and New Zealand troops (General Maitland Wilson) had been sent to Greece to strengthen the Greek army's resistance to the German–Italian invaders. On 6 April the German Twelfth Army (Field Marshal List) attacked the Metaxas Line and the Aliakmon Line. After heavy fighting the Greek First Army surrendered on 23 April. The British , heavily outnumbered and outflanked, fought many delaying actions to cover their retreat to the southern ports. The Luftwaffe had a ten to one superiority to the R.A.F. and constantly harassed the British troops. The British evacuated 45,000 men, but their 11,000 casualties were left behind; the Greeks had 30,000 casualties and 270,000 were taken prisoner. The Germans had 5,300 casualties. The Italian invading army lost 30,000 men in their campaign against the Greeks. *See* Crete.

Greek City-States Wars. *See* List of Battles.

Greek Civil War *1943–9*. Long before the occupying German army withdrew from Greece in September 1944 a guerrilla civil war was being fought between the National Popular Liberation Army (ELAS), run by the Greek Communist Party, and various other groups of different political beliefs. Beginning on 3 December, ELAS tried to take over Athens but was defeated by British troops (General W. Scobie) after heavy street fighting. ELAS took to the hills, planning to control the north. When King George II returned to Greece the Communists, with support from Albania, Bulgaria and Yugoslavia, fought the Greek government forces, now known as the Democratic Army of Greece (DSE) led by General Markos Vaphiadis. On 1 January 1948 DSE units relieved Konitsa after a long siege and in heavy fighting gained control of much of the northern border region. In February 1948 the U.S. administration sent General James Van Fleet to command the government forces in counter-guerrilla operations. He instigated wide, vigorous sweeps such as Operation Dawn and Operation Torch, destroying ELAS bases. In January 1949 General N. Zakhariadas replaced Vaphiadis and after 6 months' fighting captured the Mount Grammos region. The war ended on 16 October 1949. The defeat of Communism in Greece was significant, because Greece became a member of NATO. Casualties were heavy. Greek Army, 17,304 killed, 37,732 wounded; Communists, 38,000 killed (accepted figure), 40,000 captured. More than 5,000 civilians were executed by one side or the other. In the 1945 fighting the British had 80 casualties.

Greek–Persian Wars. *See* List of Battles.

Grenada (*American War of Independence*) *3 July 1779*. An abortive attempt by Admiral Byron, with twenty-four ships, to recapture Grenada in the face of Comte d'Estaing's thirty French warships. *See* Porto Praia Bay.

Grenada War (*also known as the American invasion of Grenada*) *October 1983*. Under the orders of General of the Grenada Armed Forces Hudson Austin, Grenadian troops fired into a crowd of several thousand islanders demonstrating in favour of the revolutionary leader, Maurice Bishop. Austin ordered the immediate execution of Bishop and his closest supporters. President Reagan, claiming that Grenada was being developed by the Cubans as an anti-U.S. base for the Soviet bloc, ordered an "invasion of liberation" on 25 October. The task force comprised thirteen ships (Rear Admiral Joseph Metcalf) and 15,000 men, including marines, rangers and infantry. For political purposes four tiny Caribbean states — Antigua and Barbua, St. Lucia, Dominica and St. Vincent and St. Kitts-Nevis and Montserrat — provided 300 policemen and troops. The defending force consisted of 1,000 reasonably well-trained men of the People's Revolutionary Army, 1,000 untrained men of the Grenadian militia and 784 Cubans, most of them airport builders. Colonel Pedro Tortolo commanded the Cubans, who were well armed with Soviet equipment. The defenders put up a fiercer fight than Washington or any outside observer foresaw. The Americans, with tanks, helicopter gunships, artillery and naval bombardment and a landing force of 7,000, needed 2 days to subdue the opposition. Historically the operation is notable for the condemnation it received, even from America's allies. It was said that

President Reagan, after many military and political reverses abroad, needed a war he could win. Militarily, the American invasion showed the qualities of the Marine Corps and the failings of the Army. The troops, improperly organized and equipped, relied on rigid and unimaginative tactics and were weak in combat communication. They failed to gain most of their objectives. In keeping with a minor campaign, the Navy and Marine Corps issued only seventeen medals, all of them Purple Hearts. The Army issued more than 9,000 decorations, 2,000 more than it had soldiers engaged in the war. Casualties: American, 18 killed, 45 wounded; Cuban, 24 killed, 40 wounded; Grenadians, 60 killed, 184 wounded.

Grochow (*Second Polish Rising against Russia*) 25 February 1831. A bloody victory for the Poles, 90,000-strong under Prince Radziwill, over General Dubitsch's 120,000 Russians. The Poles lost 5,000, but killed or wounded 10,000 Russians. *See* Warsaw.

Grossbeeren (*Napoleonic Wars: Leipzig campaign*) 23 August 1813. An allied army of 80,000, under the Crown Prince of Sweden, was covering the road to Berlin which Oudinot's French Army of the North was trying to force. Regnier's corps captured Grossbeeren, which the Prussians (von Bulow) retook. French divisions led by Fournier and Guilleminot recovered the place, but Oudinot, having lost 1,500 men, was not strong enough to follow up his advantage. *See* Bautzen; Dennewitz.

Gross-Jägersdorf, *East Prussia* (*Seven Years' War*) *30 August 1757.* General Apraksin, with 90,000 Russians, defeated von Lehwaldt's 30,000 Prussians, but because of supply difficulties and mutinies failed to exploit his victory and recrossed the frontier. *See* Kolin; Rossbach.

Grozka (*Turkish–Austrian Wars*) 14 September 1739. The Turks, under the Grand Vizier, defeated the Austrians (Count Neipperg) with heavy casualties. Austria's allies, the Turks, fared much better in their battles. *See* Khotin.

Grunnervaldt (*Polish–German Wars*) June 1404. A decisive victory for the Teutonic Knights, under their Grand Master, over the Poles (Vladislas IV). The Polish claim that 50,000 knights were killed is absurd; neither side numbered more than 30,000.

Guadalcanal (*World War II*) 1942–3. Operation Cactus, the American campaign in Guadalcanal, held by the Japanese, was one of the first Allied counteroffensives in the Pacific. On 7 August 1942 16,000 Marines and Raiders (Vandegrift) landed on Guadalcanal and were initially successful before the Japanese brought in powerful army and navy reinforcements. Holding a perimeter around Henderson Field, the Americans repulsed Japanese attacks and American planes were using the airfield by 20 August. Under sustained naval and aerial bombardment and adverse climate, the Americans suffered heavily and by 18 September were outnumbered by the Japanese, now reinforced to 36,000, and savage hand-to-hand fighting was frequent. The initiative passed to the Americans on 15 November, after a major Japanese naval defeat which prevented further infantry reinforcements from arriving. By 2 January 1943 (General Patch now in command) the United States had 50,000 men on Guadalcanal. On the nights of 7–9 February Japanese destroyers evacuated 12,000 troops and the Americans were in control. Casualties: American, 1,600 killed, 4,200 wounded, at least 12,000 disabled by disease; Japanese, 14,000 killed, 9,000 dead of disease or starvation, 1,000 captured, an unknown number wounded. *See* Philippines.

Guadalcanal *naval actions 1942.* **Savo island,** 9 August: The Japanese

(Gunichi Mikawa) sank four heavy cruisers — the U.S.S. *Chicago*, *Quincy*, *Vincennes* and the Australian *Canberra*. **Eastern Solomons**, 24–25 August: The Japanese (Nobutake Kondo), using carriers, badly damaged the U.S. carrier *Enterprise* but lost a cruiser and ninety aircraft. *Loss of* **U.S.S.** *Wasp*, 15 September: Japanese submarines sank the carrier *Wasp* and seven destroyers. **Cape Esperance**, 11–12 October: An attempt by the Americans (Scott) to prevent Japanese ships from bombarding shore positions and from landing reinforcements. **Santa Cruz Islands**, 26 October: Admiral Halsey, having become Supreme Allied Commander, Pacific, used his carriers against a Japanese fleet east of the Solomons. He lost the *Hornet* and seventy-four aircraft and had the *Enterprise* again heavily damaged; the Americans were now without a carrier in the Pacific. The Japanese had three ships damaged and lost 100 aircraft. **Guadalcanal**, 13–15 November: A type of naval pitched battle. On the night of 12–13 November Admiral Kondo, with a powerful force, sank two U.S. cruisers, three destroyers and damaged another cruiser. On the night of 13 November the Japanese heavily shelled Henderson Field but at dawn on 14 November aircraft from the *Enterprise* and land-based bombers destroyed a Japanese cruiser, damaged three others and sank six transports. That night, while Admiral Tanaka protected the disembarkation of troops from the remaining four transports, he lost a battleship and a destroyer, while the Americans had a battleship crippled and lost four destroyers. **Tassafaronga**, 30 November: The Americans sank a Japanese destroyer, crippled another and themselves lost a cruiser. Total losses: Japanese, twenty-four warships; American, twenty-four warships. Overall, the naval battles were an American victory since the Japanese had been unable to drive them out of the Solomons.

Guadeloupe (*Wars of the French Revolution*) *3 July 1794*. Sir John Jervis captured this French island, losing thirty-six killed or wounded. On 10 December the French recaptured it with the loss of about 100, but the British Navy, having destroyed much of the French shipping, held the upper hand.

Guad-el-Ras (*Spanish–Moroccan War*) *23 March 1860*. Marshal O'Donnell, with 25,000 Spanish troops, attacked about 40,000 Moors, strongly entrenched behind the Guad-el-Ras River. The Spanish victory ended the war.

Guam, *Mariana Islands I(World War II*) *11 December 1941*. The U.S. Governor of Guam, Captain G. McMillin, had only 430 marines and sailors to defend this Pacific island when attacked by 5,400 Japanese. After 3 hours McMillin had no option but to surrender; the Americans lost seventeen men, the Japanese one. *See* Philippines; Wake.

Guam II (*World War II*) *21 July–10 August 1944*. The American recapture of the island from the Japanese, who had overwhelmed it in 1941. In combined operations, the Americans suffered about 3,000 casualties but annihilated the Japanese garrison of 12,000. *See* Marianas; Marshall Islands.

Guastalla (*War of the Polish Crown*) *19 September 1734*. The French (de Coligny) defeated the Imperialists (Prince of Wurtemberg); each side lost about 4,000. *See* Bitonto; Danzig; Luzzara.

Guatemalan Invasion *1954*. On 18 June 1954 Colonel Carlos Armas led a force of exiled Guatemalans from Honduras and deposed President Arbenz, who was pro-communist, after a 10-day campaign. The invasion succeeded only because C.I.A. bombers, flown by North American and Nationalist Chinese mercenaries, demoralized the government troops.

Gubat. *See* Abu Klea.

Guilford Court House (*American Revolution*) 16 March 1781. 4,400 Americans (Green) held strong trenches in and around Guilford, North Carolina, when attacked by 1,900 British regulars (Cornwallis). The battle consisted of three relentless British attacks, all of which the British won, driving out the Americans with heavy casualties and loss of all guns and ammunition. But the price was high — 93 dead, 439 wounded: after such losses Cornwallis could not pursue his victory. *See* Cowpens; Hobkirk's Hill.

Guinegate I (*French invasion of Austrian Netherlands*) 7 August 1479. Louis XI, hoping to take advantage of the death of Charles the Bold of Burgundy, sent an army to invade The Netherlands. Maximilian of Hapsburg, son-in-law of Charles, opposed this army. French cavalry defeated the imperial horse, but Flemish infantry held the field with Maximilian fighting on foot in their midst. The French "free archers", a new militia force, fled.

Guinegate II (*English–French Wars*) 16 August 1513. A combined force of English with German reinforcements (Henry VIII) were besieging Therouanne when a large force of French cavalry threatened them. The Allied response in intercepting the French at Guinegate was so aggressive that the French fled without a fight; the haste of the French retreat led to the action being dubbed the "Battle of the Spurs". *See* Flodden; Novara I.

Guise (*World War I*) 29 August 1914. This French counter-attack temporarily checked the German advance into France. *See* Frontiers of France.

Gujerat (*Second British–Sikh War*) 22 February 1849. An army of 50,000 Sikhs (Shir Singh) held strong lines 68 miles north of Lahore when attacked by a British force of 25,000 (Gough). The eighty-four British guns pounded the Sikh lines so heavily that after 2 hours they broke; large numbers were killed and

wounded in the pursuit. British casualties, 92 killed, 682 wounded. *See* Chilianwala; Ramnagar.

Gumbinnen (*or Gusev*) (*World War I*) 20 August 1914. The first major battle between the Germans and Russians on the Eastern Front. The Germans under von Prittwitz had fallen back under the weight of General Rennenkampf's 200,000 men and they deployed in front of Gumbinnen. On 20 August the German infantry and cavalry counter-attacked on the right and broke the Russian right wing. In the centre von Mackensen's XVII Corps jumped off 4 hours late — into a heavy artillery barrage. The corps retreated rapidly and in confusion. On the left von Bülow's I Reserve Corps was 4 hours later still in starting its attack; with his right exposed by XVII's rout, Bülow retreated. The Russian victory was expensive but emphatic. Prittwitz was dismissed and General Hindenburg was called from retirement to take command. *See* Tannenberg II.

Gunzburg (*Napoleonic Wars: Danube campaign*) 9 October 1805. Marshal Ney's corps captured the three bridges over the Danube, at or near Gunzburg, driving off the Austrians, who suffered 1,300 casualties. *See* Ulm.

Gwalior I (*First British–Mahratta War*) 3 August 1780. Gwalior, a powerful fortress, was held by 4,500 Mahrattas when attacked by a force of 2,000 — a small party of English troops supported by sepoys in the British service — under Captain Popham. Scaling the walls, the attacks surprised the Mahrattas who surrendered before they had lost a man. Despite this victory the result of the war was inconclusive.

Gwalior II (*Indian Mutiny*) 17–19 June 1858. A large force of rebels, led by the Ranee of Jhansi, was driven out of the military part of the town on the 17th and in the next 2 days the British (Sir Hugh

Rose) systematically drove them from the town. Rebel losses were very heavy. Gwalior was the last major action of the mutiny. *See* Jhansi.

Haarlem (*Dutch War of Independence against Spain*) *11 December 1572–12 July 1573*. Haarlem was held by 4,000 Dutch troops (Ripperda), including a contingent of women led by Kenau Hasselaer. The Spaniards, 30,000-strong under de Toledo, invested the town on 11 December; the artillery opened up on the 18th and assaults were made on 21 December and 31 January. On 25 March the Dutch sallied out to capture a wagon convoy of enemy provisions. On 28 May a Dutch flotilla of 150 ships (Brand) was beaten by the 100-ship Spanish fleet (Bossu). This made famine inevitable and the place was surrendered on 12 June 1573. The Spaniards, who had lost 12,000 men during the siege, massacred the surviving 1,800 Dutch troops. *See* Alkmaar I; Brielle.

Habbaniya, *Iraq (World War II) 2–19 May 1941*. On 18 April the British landed a brigade at Basra because the Iraqi government had turned pro-German. On 2 May 9,000 Iraqis (Rashid Ali) attacked the British force of 1,000 R.A.F. men, 250 infantry and 1,000 Indian troops (Air Vice-Marshal Smart). Without artillery and having to protect 9,000 civilians, but with dominating air power, the British contained and then pushed back the Iraqis, 6 May. Next day a British counter-attack defeated the Iraqis who retired across the Euphrates. On 9 May the British captured Al Falluja and on 30 May entered Baghdad.

Hadley (*early British–Red Indian Wars) 12 June 1676*. King Philip (or Metacomet) led an uprising against British colonists in western Massachusetts. Major Talcot, 250 settlers and 200 Mohegan Indians, defeated Philip's Indians; he then destroyed an enemy force of 250 at Marlborough. Philip was hunted down and killed in Assowamset Swamp in August.

Hadranum, *Sicily (Sicilian Civil Wars) 344 BC*. Timoleon, deliverer of Sicily, routed Hiketas of Leontini. *See* Himera.

Haelen (*World War I) 12 August 1914*. Hailed as one of the few decisive actions of the war. Belgian Carabiniers under de Witte beat off repeated attacks by German Foot Guards of General Marwitz's command. The Germans withdrew after very heavy losses but the defeat only briefly checked the German advance. Also known as the 'Battle of the Silver Helmets' because of the Belgians' headgear.

Hahozkai (*Tartar invasion of Japan) 1274*. Kublai Khan sent an army, under Ling Fok Hen, to Kyushu where Japanese troops contested their landing. Though the Japanese suffered heavily, they wounded Lin and fought off the invaders who took to their ships, many of which were destroyed in a gale.

Hakata Bay, *Kyushu (Tartar invasion of Japan) 1274*. Mongol weapons and organization (Kublai Khan) were far superior, and the Japanese were defeated.

Halfaya Pass (*World War II*) *15–17 June 1941*. Part of a British counter-attack which failed to check the first Axis offensive in North Africa. The British suffered 400 casualties. *See* Bardia; Capuzzo; Sollum.

Haliartus, *Boeotia (Greek City-states' Wars) 395 BC*. Lysander, leading a Spartan force and so over-confident that he failed to keep a rendezvous with Pausanius' army, attacked the town of Haliartus. The garrison made a sortie and caught the Spartans between themselves and approaching Theban reinforcements. The Spartans were routed and Lysander slain. *See* Cnidus; Leuctra.

Halidon Hill (*English–Scottish Wars*) *1383*. Archibald Douglas led a large force of Scots to relieve Berwick, besieged by England's Edward III. Helpless against the English archers, the Scots are said to have lost 30,000 men. Scotland submitted after this defeat and Edward put his nominee, Balliol, on the Scottish throne. *See* Dupplin Moor; Neville's Cross.

Halleis, *Greece (Greek City-states' Wars) 459 BC*. A defeat for the Athenians against the combined forces of Corinth and Epidamnus.

Hallue, *France (French–Prussian War) 23–24 December 1870*. 22,500 Germans under Manteuffel attacked Faidherbe's 40,000 French and badly mauled their forward lines. Unable to carry the higher French trenches, the Prussians themselves came under a counter-attack. The result was indecisive. Casualties: Prussians, 927 killed or wounded; French, 1,100 besides 1,300 prisoners. *See* Gravelotte; Metz; Sedan.

Hampton Roads (*American Civil War*) *8–9 March 1862*. An interesting battle between the Confederate frigate *Merrimac* supported by five gunboats (Captain Buchanan) and five Federal warships (Captain Marston). On 8 March the *Merrimac* destroyed two enemy ships and

drove one ashore, but next day the turret ship *Monitor* reinforced the Federal squadron and after an indecisive action *Merrimac* drew off. Casualties: Confederates, 10 killed or wounded; Federals, about 260, including 150 on the *Cumberland*.

Hanau (*Napoleonic Wars: Leipzig campaign*) *30–31 October 1813*. Napoleon, beaten at Leipzig, was withdrawing his 80,000 survivors into France when he encountered Wrede's 45,000 Austrians and Bavarians, who barred his path. On the 30th Napoleon attacked Wrede's left, smashed it and continued his retreat, leaving Marmont and Mortier with three divisions to cover the rear. Mortier, 31 October, attacked Hanau and when Wrede was dangerously wounded his successor, Fresnel, retreated. The Allies lost 10,000 men, the French 6,000 in the 2 days. *See* Leipzig.

Hara Castle, *Kyushu (Japanese persecution of Christians) 1637–8*. In 1637 the oppressed Christians of Shimabara, the largest Christian settlement in Japan, revolted against the Shogun Iemitsu. Iemitsu besieged 37,000 Christians in Hara Castle and captured it after 3 months, despite the help they received from a lone Dutch warship. Nearly all the survivors were massacred and Christianity ended in Japan.

Hardenberg (*Dutch War of Independence*) *15 June 1580*. Martin Schenck's Dutch pro-Spanish Royalists, meeting Count Hohenlo's Patriots after a long march, were broken in an hour's fighting and almost annihilated. *See* Maastricht I.

Harfleur (*Hundred Years' War*) *19 August–22 September 1415*. Henry V landed 10,000 men at the mouth of the Seine, mid-August, and laid siege, 19 August, to Harfleur, chief port in north-west France. On its surrender, Henry expelled the French inhabitants and encouraged English immigration. His army reduced to 5,000, Henry marched towards Calais — and the battle of Agincourt, q.v.

Hárkany (*Austrian–Turkish Wars*) *12 August 1687*. Falling back into southern Hungary under pressure from the German–Austrian–Russian–Venetian alliance, the Turks were brought to battle. Routed by Charles V, Duke of Lorraine, the Turkish soldiers fled across the Danube. The battle took place near the site of the battle of Mohacs, q.v., won by Suliman the Magnificent over the Hungarians in 1526. *See* Slankamen; Vienna II.

Harlaw, *near Inverurie* (*Scottish Civil Wars*) *24 July 1411*. Rebel Highlanders under Donald, Lord of the Isles, gave battle to the Lowland Scots, led by the Earl of Mar, together with the Aberdeen militia under their Provost. The Lowlanders were routed in a bloody battle, losing 2,000 men to the Highlanders' 500. *See* Arkenholm.

Harper's Ferry, *Virginia* (*American Civil War*) *16 September 1862*. General "Stonewall" Jackson, with three divisions, surrounded the 11,000-strong Federal garrison of Harper's Ferry and forced a surrender. *See* Antietam; Bull Run II.

Hashin (*British–Sudan campaign*) *20 March 1885*. General Graham, with 8,000 British troops, defeated a portion of Osman Digna's army, killing 1,000 for 48 British killed or wounded. *See* Khartoum.

Haslach, *Black Forest* (*Napoleonic Wars: Danube campaign*) *11 October 1805*. A remarkable action by General Dupont, who was marching to Ulm with only 6,000 French when he ran into 60,000 Austrians in strong positions. Dupont quickly seized and entrenched Hanau village, which he held against 25,000 Austrians (Archduke Ferdinand). Dupont withdrew after nightfall, taking with him 4,100 prisoners who had got into Haslach only to be trapped there. *See* Hanau; Ulm.

Hastenbeck (*Seven Years' War*) *26 July 1757*. The Duke of Cumberland, with 36,000 Hanoverians and others, had positions on the Weser River to protect Hanover. Overpowered by Marshal d'Estrees, who had 80,000 troops, Cumberland fell back to Slade on the Elbe. Ironically, d'Estrees had believed himself beaten. *See* Kolin; Rossbach.

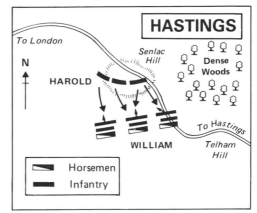

Hastings (*or Senlac*) (*Norman Conquest of England*) *14 October 1066*. A fortnight after the landing of William the Conqueror, the English, under Harold, sought to stop him at Senlac Hill. While fighting defensively, the English were successful, but one wing was lured from the higher ground by a feigned flight of Normans and then routed. Harold was among the killed. Hastings can be considered the most decisive battle ever fought on English soil (apart from the aerial Battle of Britain).

Hatvan (*Hungarian rising against Austria*) *2 April 1849*. The 7th Hungarian Corps, 15,000-strong, held fast to their positions when attacked by Marshal Schlick's 15,000 Austrians and after fierce fighting defeated them. Total casualties were about 5,000. After Russian intervention on the side of the Austrians, the Hungarians' fortunes changed. *See* Temesvar.

Havana I (*War of Austrian Succession*) *12 October 1748*. An indecisive and unpressed battle between seven British ships under (Admiral Knowles) and seven Spanish ships, led by Admiral Reggio. *See* Finisterre II.

Havana II (*Seven years' War*) *1762*. In June British troops and naval units (Earl of Albemarle and Admiral Pococke) laid siege to Havana. They took by storm Moro Castle, key to the defence, and after 2 months captured the city.

Heathfield, *Hatfield Chase* (*Teutonic conquest of Britain*) *633*. The Mercians (Penda) defeated the Northumbrians under Edwin, who was killed. *See* Heavenfield.

Heavenfield (*Teutonic conquest of Britain*) *634*. The Anglo–Saxons (Oswald of Northumbria) defeated the Britons (Cadwallon) near the Roman Wall. This was the last full-scale battle between an exclusively British army and their Saxon conquerors. *See* Heathfield.

Hedgeley Moor, *near Alnwick* (*Wars of the Roses*) *25 April 1464*. The Yorkists or White Roses (Montague) routed the Red-Rose Lancastrians (Margaret of Anjou and Sir Ralph Percy). Percy was killed. *See* Towton.

Heiligerles (*Netherlands War of Independence*) *23 May 1568*. Louis of Nassau, who had about 3,000 men, defeated a small German–Spanish force under John, Duke of Aremberg. Louis held a position on a height, with his front protected by a marsh. Aremberg led his Spanish cavalry in a charge along a causeway and was killed. (The "Sea Beggars" — Dutch privateers encouraged by William of Orange — had no connection with this battle.) *See* Jemmingen; Brill.

Heilsberg (*Napoleonic Wars*) *5–10 June 1807*. The Russians (Bennigsen) attacked the French line while it was forming, but resistance stiffened and the 90,000 Russians fell back. Taking the initiative, Napoleon advanced along the Alle River, driving Bennigsen into his fortified camp at Heilsberg (Lidzbark Warminski). Murat, commanding the French advance guard, precipitately ordered an attack; it was beaten back at a cost of 8,000 casualties on either side. But French pressure was so strong that Bennigsen withdrew. *See* Danzig II; Friedland.

Heligoland Bight (*World War I*) *27–28 August 1914*. The first naval battle of the war. A British squadron (Tyrwhitt) led two light cruisers and two destroyer flotillas on a raid into German waters. A battle-cruiser squadron under Beatty sailed from Scapa Flow in support and in the ensuing battle the Germans lost three light cruisers and a destroyer and had three other cruisers crippled; 1,000 German sailors died. The British, without ship-loss, suffered 33 killed. *See* Coronel.

Helsingborg (*Danish–German Wars*) *1362*. The ships of King Waldemar IV of Denmark decisively defeated a German fleet of the Hanseatic League. *See* Stralsund.

Hennersdorf, *Poland* (*War of Austrian Succession*) *24 November 1745*. An Austrian army (Charles of Lorraine) was moving on Berlin as part of a two-pronged Austrian–Saxon attack. Frederick the Great, with his Prussian troops, surprised the Austrians on the march and scattered them. Leopold I of Anhalt-Dessau dealt with the Saxon thrust. *See* Kesseldorf; Soor.

Heraclea, *Italy* (*Pyrrhus' invasion of Italy*) *280 BC*. Between the Epirots, 30,000-strong under Pyrrhus and 35,000 Romans under P. Laverius Laevinus. The Romans crossed the Siris (Sinni) River in the face of the Epirots, who then attacked. Finally broken by Pyrrhus' elephants, the Romans lost 7,000 men to the Epirots' loss of 4,000. *See* Asculum I; Pandosia.

Heraclea Propontis (*Roman Empire Civil Wars*) *313*. Licinius, leading 30,000 Illyrians to the relief of Heraclea Propontis on the Sea of Marmara, was attacked by Maximinus, the Emperor of the East, with 70,000. At first driven back by weight of numbers, Licinius rallied his veteran troops and overcame Maximinus who suffered heavy casualties. Licinius later became Emperor of the East. *See* Cibalae; Rubra; Saxa.

Heraclea Pontica, *later Erëgli* (*Muslim–Byzantine Wars*) *806*. The forces of Harun al-Rashid (the Caliph of the Arabian Nights) fiercely pushed back the Byzantines of Nicephorus I, stormed into Heraclea Pontica on the Black Sea and captured it. *See* Amorium; Zab al Kabir.

Herat I, *Afghanistan* (*Tartar invasion of Afghanistan*) *1220–1*. The governor, Emin Malek, was unprepared for a siege and surrendered when Sudar Bahadur's 20,000 Tartars appeared before his walls. Shems-ed-din later retook the city and held it until the Mongols (Tuli Khan) besieged it in 1221. When Shems-ed-din was killed, the inhabitants opened the gates to the Mongols, who massacred the garrison. *See* Merv; Samarkand.

Herat II (*Persian–Afghan Wars*) *22 November 1837–9 September 1838*. Muhammad, Shah of Persia, besieged the city held by the Afghans (Yar Muhammad). The only major assault, 24 June 1838, was beaten off and the Persians lost 1,700 men. An armistice was negotiated on 9 September and the Shah, under British pressure, withdrew. *See* Kabul II.

Herdonea, *Affulia* (*Second Punic War*) *210 BC*. The Carthaginians (Hannibal) practically destroyed Cnaeus Fulvius' Roman army of 25,000. *See* Metaurus.

Héricourt, *near Belfort, France* (*Swiss–Burgundian Wars*) *13 November 1474*. 18,000 Swiss, protecting their borders, decisively defeated 10,000 Burgundians and took Hericourt. *See* Granson; Montlhery; Saint Jacob-en-Birs.

Hermannstadt (*Hungarian–Turkish Wars*) *May 1442*. Notable as the first appearance of the Hungarian leader John Huniades in arms against the Turks. He defeated Majid Bey, who was besieging Hermannstadt, inflicted 20,000 casualties on the Turks and relieved the city. Hungarian losses, 3,000. *See* Kossova.

Hernani I, *northern Spain* (*First Carlist War*) *29 August 1836*. The British legion in Spain, under General Evans, were defeated by the Carlists, supporters of Don Carlos, second son of Charles IV. *See* Huesca.

Hernani II (*First Carlist War*) *15–16 March 1837*. The British legion (Evans), supported by a contingent of Cristinos, attacked Don Sebastian's 17,000 Carlists on the Venta heights and after fierce fighting occupied the position. Next day the Carlists were pushed into Hernani but, reinforced, they counter-attacked and Evans retreated. *See* Huesca.

Herrera (*First Carlist War*) *23 August 1837*. Don Carlos, leading a Carlist army on Madrid, was opposed by General Buerens who was trying to join with General Espartero. Before the junction could be effected Carlos attacked Buerens, who lost 50 officers and 2,600 men killed or wounded. Carlos advanced to within 12 miles of Madrid, but retired in the face of Espartero and his 20,000 Cristinos. *See* Huesca.

"Herrings, The" (*or Rouvray*) (*Hundred Years' War*) *12 February 1429*. Sir John Fastolfe commanding a road convoy taking salt fish to the English army covering Orleans occupied Roncray–St. Denis when he heard of the approach of the Bastard of Orleans with a French force. The French attack was severely repulsed, the Bastard being wounded. *See* Jargeau; Orleans.

Charles to turn south towards the Ukraine. Holowczyn was Charles' last great battle. *See* Liesna; Thorn.

Homildon (Humbledon) Hill (*English–Scottish Wars*) September 1402. A Scottish force (Murdoch Stewart), returning from a foray into England, was ambushed by the Percy forces and defeated, losing Stewart and eighty-four other senior leaders.

Honain (*Islamic conquest of Arabia*) 629. A force of 4,000 Arabs lured 12,000 Muslims (Muhammad) into the valley of Honain where slingers and archers caused great destruction. Rallying his demoralized Muslims, Muhammad counterattacked and routed the Arabs. The Islamic conquest swept on. *See* Medina.

Hondschoote (*Wars of the French Revolution*) 6–9 September 1793. General Carnot sent General Houchard with 40,000 troops against an English–Hanoverian army (General Freytag) which was besieging Dunkirk. Unable to use his poorly trained soldiers in any conventional way, Houchard got them to snipe and sharpshoot from the cover of dykes and trees. In 3 days the Allied army had suffered enough and withdrew. Houchard failed to pursue his enemies, was beaten at Courtrai a week later and then guillotined for his incompetence. *See* Neerwinden II; Wattignies.

Honduras–Nicaragua War 1957. On 18 April Nicaraguan troops crossed the Coco River and occupied the town of Morocon to establish Nicaragua's claim to a region under dispute since 1906. On 1 May a Honduran force recaptured Morocon and a cease-fire was signed on 6 May.

Honduras–El Salvador (*The "Football War"*) 1969. This war followed El Salvador's defeat of Honduras in a qualifying round of a World Cup game of soccer. Hondurans were already hostile towards El Salvador, 300,000 of whose

nationals had jobs in Honduras, thus "depriving" Hondurans of employment. In riots after the football match some Salvadorans were killed and 10,000 expelled. On 14 July the Salvador army invaded Honduras and tried to encircle Tegucigalpa. On 30 July, following intervention by the Organization of American States, the Salvadoran army withdrew. More than 4,000 Hondurans, mostly civilians, were killed during the invasion.

Hong Kong (*World War II*) 8–25 December 1941. The Japanese struck at the thinly held British line on the mainland and on the night of 12–13 December the British (Maltby) withdrew to the island where the unequal battle continued for a week before the Hong Kong governor (Young) surrendered the colony. It was the first British possession to fall. Casualties: British, 2,000 plus 11,000 taken prisoner; Japanese, 2,745. *See* Singapore.

Hooghly, The, India (*Seven Years' War*) 24 November 1759. After a 2-hour fight three British ships (Commodore Wilson) defeated a Dutch squadron of seven and captured all the enemy ships. Ashore, Colonel Forde with 1,100 troops defeated a Dutch military force landed from the ships. *See* Madras II.

Hooglede (*French Revolutionary Wars*) 17 June 1794. The French had suffered several sharp reverses in northern France at the hands of the Allied British and Austrians. On the verge of defeat, General Jourdan personally put fire into his men by riding around the battalions and in a fierce attack they forced the Allies to withdraw northward. Jourdan was given command of the combined French armies of the Sambre and Meuse. *See* Fleurus III; Tournai.

Hook, The (*Korean War*) 1951–3. The Hook was a spur south-west of Umdalmal, North Korea, and the scene of much bitter fighting. The first action occurred on the night of 26–27 March 1951, the principal action on 16–17 November 1952, when North Korean and Chinese troops attacked the British positions. After a night of continuous fighting the attack was beaten off. Casualties: British 111; Korean, at least 200 killed. *See* Korea.

Hormuz (*Wars of Sasassian Persia*) 226. Between the Parthian army of Artabanus V and the Persians of Ardashir (Artaxerxes). The Parthians were crushed at Hormuz (Bandar Abbas) and Artabanus was killed. Ardashir's Sassanian dynasty ruled Persia for the next four centuries. *See* Edessa I.

Horseshoe Bend (*or Tohopeka*) (*American–Creek Indian War*) 27 March 1814. The victory by Andrew Jackson over the allied Creek and Cherokee Indians who lost about 900 warriors killed. American casualties, 51 killed and 148 wounded. *See* Talladega.

Hoxne (*Danish invasions of Britain*) 870. Edmund, King of East Anglia, gave battle to the ruthless Danish invaders at Hoxne, Suffolk, but his men were overpowered and Edmund was beheaded. Known as "the Martyr", he was interred at Bury St. Edmund. *See* Ashdown; York.

Hubbardton (*American Revolution*) 7 July 1777. The Americans, retreating after their defeat at Fort Ticerondoga, q.v., fought a rearguard action at this place.

Huesca I (*Spanish–Muslim Wars*) 1096. Pedro I of Aragon and Navarre stormed the fortress city of Huesca, held by the Moors for 300 years, and made it the capital of his kingdom. *See* Saragossa I; Zallaka.

Huesca II (*Spanish–Muslim Wars*) 1105. The Moors (Ali) attacked the Spaniards (Alfonso VI of Castile) besieging Huesca. Ali was routed, losing 10,000 killed in the battle.

Huesca III (*First Carlist War*) 23 May 1837. Between 20,000 Carlists (Don Carlos and Don Sebastian) and 12,000 Cristinos and British (Irribarreu). The soldiers of the British Legion were unsteady and the Cristinos were driven from the field until the Carlist pursuit was checked by a spectacular cavalry charge led by Irribarreu, who was killed. Cristinos casualties were 1,000. *See* Hernani; Herrera.

Humaita I (*War of the Triple Alliance: Lopez War*) May 1866. The Argentinians (Mitre) attacked the Paraguayan trenches (Lopez), but were repulsed with heavy loss. *See* Angostura II; Curupayti.

Humaita II (*War of the Triple Alliance: Lopez War*) August 1867. The allied armies of Brazil, Argentina and Uruguay, outnumbering Lopez's Paraguayans, forced him from his entrenchments and he retired to Tebienari. *See* Angostura; Curupayti.

Humaiti III (*War of the Triple Alliance: Lopez War*) February 1868. A flotilla of Brazilian gunboats trying to force a passage came under fire from Paraguayan batteries and every ship was sunk.

Humblebeck (*Danish–Swedish Wars*) April 1700. Charles XII, with a small force of Swedes, landed in the face of the Danish army, in trenches close to the shore, and drove them headlong from their positions with heavy loss. *See* Narva.

Hundred Years' War. *See* List of Battles.

Hungarian Uprising 1956. In July 1956 the Russians appointed Erno Gero as head of the Workers' Party and therefore leader of Hungary. On 23 October students demonstrated, demanding the reappointment of the popular Imre Nagy as prime minister, and removal of

Soviet troops. Gero asked the Soviet army for help and fighting broke out throughout the country. Nevertheless, Nagy was appointed prime minister on 24 October and the fighting eased, though 10,000 people were killed between 25 and 30 October. On 31 October Cardinal Joszef Mindszenty, liberated from prison, made a triumphal entry into Budapest and the following day Nagy announced Hungary's withdrawal from the Warsaw Pact. On the night of 3–4 November the Soviet army invaded and serious fighting occurred, with about 12,000 deaths. The Russians crushed all resistance by 14 November. Janos Kadar was appointed prime minister and Nagy was shot.

Hürtgen Forest (*World War II*) *November–December 1944*. Part of the Siegfried Line defences won by the American First Army after the capture of Aachen, q.v. The Americans suffered 4,000 casualties in the fierce fighting.

Hussite Wars. *See* List of Battles.

Hwai-Hai (*Chinese Civil War*) *7 November 1948–12 January 1949*. One of the most decisive battles of modern history. Between the 500,000-strong Nationalist Army of Chiang Kai-shek and the Communist People's Liberation Army of Mao Tse-Tung, 750,000. The field commanders for the Nationalists were Liu Chih and Chiang Wei-kuo, Chiang Kai-shek's second son, who commanded the crack Armoured Corps. Ch'en Yi led the P.L.A. Army and methodically isolated the battleground (in east-central China) before crushing the Nationalist units one by one. Chiang's powerful reinforcements, rushed into the battle, could not check the Communists, and in 65 days 550,000 Nationalist troops were annihilated and another 327,000 taken prisoner. *See* Chinese Civil War.

Hydaspes, The (*Alexander's Asiatic campaigns*) *327 BC*. Between Alexander the Great with 65,000 Macedonians and 70,000 Asiatics and the Indian King Porus, who had 30,000 infantry, 200 elephants and 300 war chariots. Crossing the Hydaspes a few miles above Porus' trenches, Alexander routed the enemy, killing 12,000 and taking 9,000 prisoners, including King Porus. Macedonian casualties, 1,000. *See* Arbela–Gaugamela; Crannon.

Hyderabad (*British conquest of Scinde*) *24 March 1843*. Shir Muhammad had 20,000 Baluchi troops in strong positions behind the Fullali River when attacked by Sir Charles Napier and his 6,000 British troops. Demoralized by heavy artillery fire, the Baluchis were overthrown by cavalry charges and routed by following infantry. There was no further resistance from the Scinde emirs. *See* Miani; Mudki (Moodkee).

Hysiae *668 BC*. (traditional date) The Argives routed the Spartans and Argos was left in undisputed supremacy of the Greek Peloponnese.

Ichinotani (*Taira War*) *1189*. The Japanese Taira clan were decisively defeated by the troops of the Shogun Minamoto-no-Yorimoto. Yorimoto had all of his important relatives assassinated and became dictator. He was the first Japanese dictator to hold the title Shogun (generalissimo). *See* Dan-no-ura.

Iclistavisus (*Rome's Germanic Wars*) *16*. A large force of Germans (Arminius) attacked eight Roman Legions (Germanicus) on an open plain, but the superior discipline of the Romans made their ranks impregnable and the Germans were routed with great loss. *See* Teutoburger Wald.

Ilerda (*or Lerida*), *northern Spain* (*Wars of the First Triumvirate*) *49 BC*. In his campaign to conquer Spain, Caesar with 40,000 troops attacked the 70,000 led by Pompey the Great's lieutenants — Lucius Afranius, M. Terentius Varro and Marcus Petreius. From their camp on the Segre River, the Pompeians drove Caesar off, but in a brilliant series of marches and countermarches Caesar manoeuvred his enemy into a weak defensive position, encircled them and forced their surrender. *See* Dyrrachium I; Illyria; Rubicon River; Utica II.

Ilipa (*or Selipia*), *near Seville* (*Second Punic War*) *206 BC*. Scipio, the brilliant Roman, with 48,000 legionaries, took a defensive position against 75,000 Carthaginians under Hasdrubal, Hannibal's brother. Pretending to refuse battle, Scipio made a surprise dawn attack and crushed both Carthaginian wings. His methodical pursuit destroyed the African army. *See* Metaurus; New Carthage; Utica I.

Illyria (*Wars of the First Triumvirate*) *49 BC*. The defeat of a Caesarian fleet (Dolabella) by the Pompeian navy (Marcus Octavius). The sea defeat isolated the Caesarian garrison on the island of Veglia (Krk) and led to its surrender. *See* Bagradas; Dyrrachium I; Ilerda.

Immac (*Syrian revolt against the Romans*) *7 June 218*. An example of the immense moral value of a leader. The Imperial troops and Praetorians, under Emperor Macrinus, with superior discipline and great bravery, broke the Syrian legions (Elagabalus). Victory was in their grasp when Macrinus inexplicably fled; this so demoralized his troops that they were defeated.

Imola (*Napoleon's Italian campaigns*) *3 February 1797*. Marshal Victor, with 8,000 French and Italian troops, took General Colli's papal army of 7,000 in the rear and routed them so rapidly that no stand developed, hence casualties were light. *See* Lodi; Mantua; Rivoli.

Imphal, *Burma* (*World War II*) *30 March–30 June 1944*. The Japanese besieged the British in Imphal and on the Imphal Plain. Encircled, the garrison could only be supplied by air until after the Battle of Kohima (q.v.) It is estimated that 13,000 Japanese were killed in the 3-month siege. *See* Burma.

Inchon (*Korean War*) *13–28 September 1950*. The Battle of Inchon, planned by MacArthur, was the United Nations counter-attack which followed the checking of the Communist conquest of Korea. After a naval bombardment, American marines landed, 16 September, and the U.S. Eighth Army of 140,000 men broke out of the Pusan Perimeter and drove for Seoul, the North Korean capital served by the port of Inchon. It was finally captured on 30 September. U.N. casualties, 6,000; Communist, unknown. *See* Korea.

Indian and French War. *See* List of Battles.

Indian Mutiny. *See* List of Battles.

Indonesian War of Independence *1945–9*. On 31 October 1945 the Indonesian People's Army declared war on the Dutch, who governed Indonesia, and on the British forces in Indonesia, which were disarming Japanese soldiers captured at the end of World War II. Serious fighting occurred throughout October 1945. The British troops were withdrawn by the end of November 1946, but the Dutch army increased to 130,000. Under attack from the Indonesian People's Army, the Dutch reoccupied much of Java and later the entire Republic. After U.N. intervention, the Dutch granted independence to Indonesia. Casualties: British, between September 1945 and August 1946, 49 killed, 134 wounded; British Indian troops, 507 killed, 1,259 wounded; Dutch, throughout the 4-year war, 25,000; Indonesian, 75,000 (estimated).

Indus, The (*Tartar invasion of Kharismia*) *1221*. The Muslim army of Jallalladin, Sultan of Kharismia, 30,000-strong, found itself caught with the river at its back and 40,000 Tartars, led by Genghis Khan, in front. Jallalladin's men fought bravely, but both flanks were enveloped and they were driven across the river, losing 19,000 killed or drowned. The Tartars lost 8,000. *See* Bamian; Kalka River.

Ingavi (*Bolivian–Peruvian War*) *18 November 1841*. 3,800 Bolivians, led by their president, José Ballivián, routed Agustin Gammar's 5,200 invading Peruvians; Gamarra was among the many killed. *See* Yungay.

Ingogo (*First British–Boer War*) *8 February 1881*. A small British column — five infantry companies, four guns — made a frontal attack on Boer positions and was repulsed, losing 139 killed or wounded. *See* Laing's Nek; Majuba Hill.

Inholobane Mountains (*British–Zulu War*) *28 March 1879*. Colonels Buller and Russell, with only 1,300 men, made an ill-advised attack on a strong Zulu kraal and were beaten off with considerable loss. *See* Isandhlwana; Rorke's Drift.

Inkerman (*Crimean War*) *5 November 1854*. 50,000 Russians (Prince Mentschikoff) attacked the British position at Inkerman, held by about 8,000 troops. In dense fog, the fight — a "soldier's battle" — degenerated into a series of hand-to-hand brawls. Chief fighting was around the Sandbag Battery, where the Russians had 1,200 killed. Following the arrival of French reinforcements, the Russians retreated. Total Russian casualties were 12,000; British, 2,500; French, 1,000. *See* Alma; Balaclava; Sebastopol.

Inverary (*English–Scottish Wars*) *May 1310*. A heavy defeat for the English (Mowbray) at the hands of Robert Bruce and his Scots. *See* Bannockburn.

Inverkeithing (*English–Scottish Wars*) *August 1317*. The first onslaught of the English invaders drove the

Scots (Earl of Fife) from their positions. Rallied by Sinclair, Bishop of Dunkeld, the Scots rallied and forced the English to retire to their ships. *See* Bannockburn; Boroughbridge.

Inverlochy (*English Civil War*) 2 February 1645. Montrose, with 1,500 Royalist Highlanders, defeated 3,000 Campbells and Lowland Covenanters, who lost 1,700. The defeat broke the power of the Campbells for many years.

Ioannina (*or Janine*), Albania (*First Balkan War*) 1 December 1912–5 March 1913. Greek troops besieged the Turkish-held town until lack of supplies forced its surrender. Ironically the major belligerents, Bulgaria and Serbia, had earlier agreed to an armistice with Turkey, but Greece and Montenegro fought on against the Turks. *See* Schköder II.

Ipsus, *Phrygia, Asia Minor (Wars of Alexander's Successors)* 302 BC. Seleucus, with 32,000 Syrians, routed Antigonus' 30,000 Macedonians. Poliocetes, assuming command on Antigonus' death, could rally only 8,000 men at the end of a 200-mile retreat. The distribution of spoils after this battle broke Alexander's old empire beyond recovery.

Iran–Iraq War. Generally called the Gulf War, this conflict began on 17 September 1980 when the Iraqi president, Saddam Hussein, attempted to capture Iranian territory which he claimed belonged to Iraq. Ideologically and politically the Iranian leader was Ayatollah Khomeini, but the fighting was organized by the General Staff. Khomeini declared the conflict a holy war or *jihad* of Shi'a Muslims against the Sunni Muslim establishment of Iraq. Iraq has a majority of Shia's and Khomeini hoped that these people would rise against Saddam Hussein.

At the beginning of the war Iraq had a well-equipped army of 200,000 with 100,000 reserves, an air force of 18,000 and a navy of 4,000 men. In material Iraq was formidable, with 2,200 tanks, 3,000 armoured personnel carriers, 800 guns and 1,200 air defence guns. The strength of its air force lay in the 75 MiG-23s and a large fleet of helicopter gunships. Iran had an army of 300,000 with 300,000 reserves, an air force of 100,000 men and navy of 28,000. Much of the material had deteriorated from lack of maintenance after the revolution which deposed the Shah. Even so, the Iranians had more than 2,000 tanks, with 2,000 armoured personnel carriers and many field guns and anti-aircraft guns. Air defence was built around the 188 Phantom F-4s. Because they were considered pro-Shah, at least 250 experienced generals had been replaced by inexperienced officers and military-minded mullahs.

The Iraqi blitz-like invasion achieved tactical surprise and captured some territory, but could not break the Iranian lines. A war of attrition developed and the fighting swung in Iran's favour. In July 1982 Iran launched Operation Ramadan and one of the biggest battles since 1945 was fought. The Iranian command used wave after wave of Revolutionary Guards (the Pasadan), some of whom were as young as 9; they sacrificed themselves to clear safe paths for the tanks. The attack petered out for lack of support.

On 6 February 1983 the Iranians attacked with 200,000 troops along a front of 24 miles in the mud and desert of Ammara, south-east of Baghdad; more than 6,000 Iranians died for minute gains. A similar attack in February 1983 met a similar fate. Another major assault in April 1983, along the axis Mandelei to Baghdad, was also stopped. By the end of 1983 the Iranians had lost 120,000 killed; Iraq's losses were 60,000 dead.

On 22 February 1984 the Iranians launched Operation Dawn V, which reached its climax on 27 February when 500,000 men crossed the marshlands north of Basra. A big battle took place on 29 February and 1 March and more than 19,000 Iranians were killed. The following month, in what the Iraqis call the Battle of Majnoon — fought largely in the

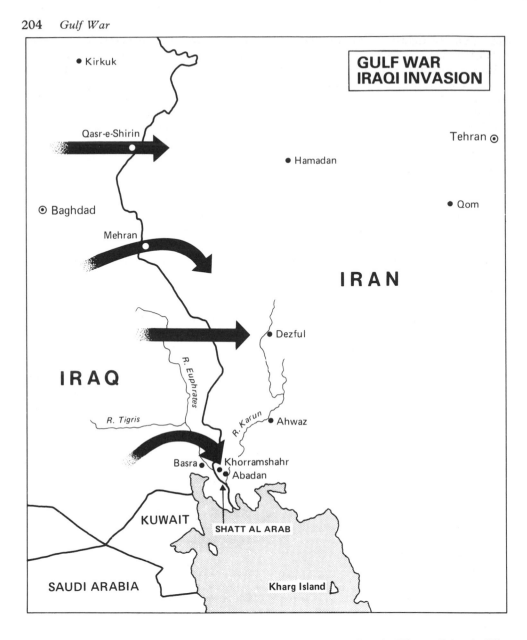

Hawize Marshes — the Iranians sent in tens of thousands of children roped together to swamp the Iraqi defenders. They achieved nothing and the battle of Gzaeil in March was equally fruitless. That month the Iraqis used mustard and nerve gas against Iranian infantry in a desperate effort to induce the Iranians to stop the war. When this failed, Iraq resorted to air attacks, using Exocet missiles, against foreign oil tankers col-

lecting oil at Iran's Kharg Island. The object was to provoke superpower intervention to end the war, but it failed.

Meanwhile, the Iranians went on the offensive on 18 October 1984, attacking on a 12-mile front in the hills overlooking the Tigris Plain. Iranian generalship became more imaginative and professional after the appointment of General Qassemali Zahir Nejad to the Defence Council. His strategy was to take Baghdad, thus bringing about the fall of Saddam Hussein.

Iraqi leadership was little better, but combat engineers were efficiently used to lay mines, develop fortifications and build bridges.

After more than 4 years of fighting Iraq held 270 square miles of Iranian territory while Iran claimed to have captured 386 miles of Iraqi territory. Iranian dead totalled 150,000 and possibly 250,000 and had lost 39,000 men as prisoners. About 60,000 Iraqis had died and 7,000 were prisoners. About 800 Iranian tanks had been destroyed and 600 Iraqi tanks.

China, Israel, Syria and North Korea supplied arms and equipment to Iran, while the Soviet Union, Egypt, Saudi Arabia and Jordan supported and supplied Iraq.

Irun, *Spain (First Carlist War) 18 May 1837*. General Evans, with British Legion troops and 10,000 Cristinos, captured the fortress in an 11-hour assault. *See* Hernani; Huesca.

Isandhlwana (*British–Zulu War*) 22 *January 1879*. One of the British army's most terrible disasters. The Zulus, under Matyana, overwhelmed and massacred six companies of the 24th Regiment with two guns and a small force of Natal volunteers. *See* Rorke's Drift.

Isara, The (*Third Gallic Invasion*) *121 BC*. Between the Arverni and Allobroges (Betuitdus) and the Romans (Q. Fabius Maximus). The Gauls were defeated and suffered further great loss when a bridge crowded with fugitives collapsed.

Isaszcq (*Hungarian rising against Austria*) 6 April 1849. A frontal conflict between 42,000 Hungarians (Gorgey) and the Croats (Jellachich). The Croats beat back the Hungarian Ist Corps, but the other units stood firm and repulsed the Croats. Both armies stood to arms all night, but next morning Jellachich retired. *See* Kapolna; Temesvár.

Island No. 10, *Mississippi River (American Civil War) 7 April 1862*. Virtually a battle without fighting. The Federals (Pope), by superior tactics — they cut a canal through swamps, enabling their gunboats to run past Confederate batteries on Island No. 10 — bottled up 3,500 Confederates (Mackall), who surrendered. Pope became nationally prominent. *See* Fort Donelson; Shiloh.

Isle De France, *later Mauritius (Napoleonic Wars) 3 December 1810*. British Admiral Bertie with nineteen ships and General Abercromby with 10,000 troops captured the island from the French; they captured seventeen warships and twenty-four merchantmen.

Isly, *Morocco (Abd-el-Kader's Rebellion) 14 August 1844*. Marshal Bugeaud, with only 8,000 French, defeated Abd-el-Kader's 45,000 Algerians. Mostly cavalry, the Algerians were stopped by the steady French infantry, shaken by the French artillery and routed by French cavalry. They left 1,500 dead on the field. *See* Constantine.

Ismail (*Russian–Turkish Wars*) 22 *December 1790*. The Russians (Suvorov) captured this fortress at the mouth of the Danube but enraged by their great losses in the attack they massacred the garrison and inhabitants. *See* Focsani; Rimnik.

Israel (*5–10 June 1967*). Though called the Israeli–Arab War or the Six Days War, this conflict was more properly a phased battle. The Israelis took the initiative by air-attacking Egypt, Jordan and Syria and destroying 374 aircraft, chiefly on the ground. Israeli armour made a three-pronged advance towards the Suez Canal. After 3 days the Egyptian army was in rout. A small Israeli naval force captured Sharm el Sheikh on 7 June. On the east, Israeli forces occupied, 7 June, the Old City of Jerusalem and attacked the Jordanian army. Both Israelis and Arabs ceased fire on 10 June. Casualties: Israelis, 679 killed; Arabs, 3,000 dead,

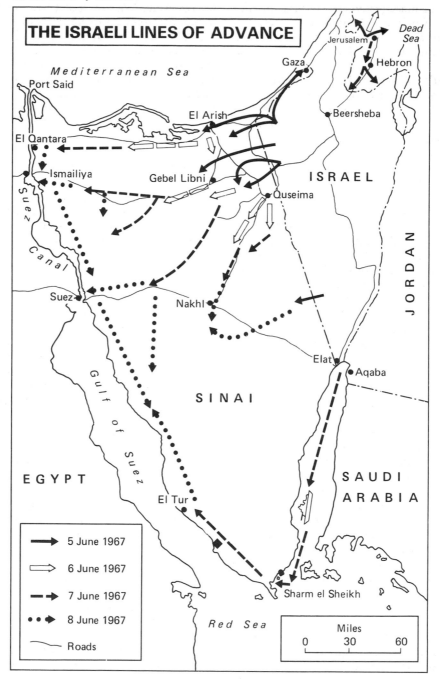

THE ISRAELI LINES OF ADVANCE

Mediterranean Sea

Port Said

El Qantara

Ismailiya

Gebel Libni

El Arish

Gaza

Jerusalem

Dead Sea

Hebron

Beersheba

ISRAEL

Quseima

Suez

Suez Canal

Nakhl

JORDAN

Elat

Aqaba

SINAI

Gulf of Suez

EGYPT

El Tur

SAUDI ARABIA

Sharm el Sheikh

Red Sea

➤	5 June 1967
⇨	6 June 1967
--➤	7 June 1967
•••➤	8 June 1967
‿	Roads

Miles

0   30   60

6,000 wounded (estimated) and 12,000 prisoners. *See* Israel–Arab War of Attrition; Jerusalem IX; Lebanon; October War; Sinai Peninsula; Israel's War of Independence.

Israel's War of Independence (or War of Liberation) 1947–9. This war consisted of phases and operations, but the best known aspect of the war commenced on 14 May 1948. On that date the United Nations approved Israel as an independent state and Egypt, Syria, Jordan, Iraq and Lebanon attacked it. In more detail:

Civil war or communal war phase: December 1947 to 14 May 1948. Arab irregulars and the Arab Liberation Army made many attacks as Israel fought the "Battle of the Roads". Operation Nachshon, 2–20 April 1947; first Jewish attempt at a large-scale break-through besieged Jerusalem. Operation Yiftach, 7 May; Israeli conquest of Safed. Fall of the Etzion bloc: Jordanian capture of a group of kibbutzim.

Invasion phase: Arab nations invade, 15 May–10 June. First truce, 11 June–9 July. Counter-attack phase: the Ten Days' Offensive, 9–18 July. Operation Dani: Jerusalem–Tel Aviv sector. Operation Barosh: Syrian Front. Operation Dekel: Galilee sector. Second truce 18 July–10 October.

Final phase: begins 10 October 1948. Operation Yoav, 15–22 october: Negev and Sinai sectors. Operation Ten Plagues, 15 October–8 November: Sinai, Negev, Hebron. Operation Hiram, 28–31 October: Galilee–Lebanon Front. Operation Lot, 24–25 November: route opened to Dead Sea. Operation Horev, 22 December–7 January 1949: Gaza and Negev sectors. Operation Uvdah, 6–10 March: control of Negev and Judea deserts. Armistices were signed between 24 February and 20 July.

Israel's army of 60,000, under acting chief-of-staff Yigal Yadin, suffered 8,000 casualties. The Arab armies had about 20,000. *See* Israel–Arab War; Israel–Arab War of Attrition; Jerusalem IX; Lebanon; October War; Sinai Peninsular.

Israel–Arab War of Attrition, *sometimes known as the Electronics War March 1969 to 7 August 1970*. This war consisted of almost incessant saturation shelling from the Egyptian side of the Suez Canal and retaliatory raids by the Israelis from their fortifications in the Bar-Lev Line. The war was no less intense on the eastern front (Jordan) and northern front (Syria). The change to static warfare (the three previous Israel–Egypt conflicts had been wars of movement) stimulated the development of electronic devices, including electronic fences, on the eastern front (Jordan) and northern front (Syria). The Israelis made deep-penetration raids; in one 10-hour 40-mile raid commandos destroyed twenty Egyptian installations. On 26 December 1969 paratroopers captured a large radar base on the Gulf of Suez; electronic experts dismantled the equipment and flew it back to Israel by helicopter. Casualties: Israeli, 367 killed, 999 wounded on the Egyptian front; on all fronts the total was 721 killed, 2,659 wounded. The Egyptians lost 300 men a day at the height of the War of Attrition. *See* Israel; Israel–Arab War of Attrition; Jerusalem IX; Lebanon; October War; Sinai Peninsula.

Issus (*Alexander's Asiatic campaign*) *333 BC*. Between Alexander the Great, with 35,000 Macedonians, and a vast force of Asiatics, supported by 30,000 Greek mercenaries, under Darius, king of Persia. The Persians were drawn up on the right bank of the Pinarus, which crosses the plains of Issus. On the left Alexander crossed the river with his heavy horsemen and routed the Persian cavalry. In the centre the Macedonian phalanx, after bitter fighting against the Greek mercenaries, established themselves on the right bank, Alexander with his cavalry attacked Darius' bodyguard, whose flight precipitated the retreat of the whole of Darius' army. Tens of thousands were killed. Macedonian losses were estimated at 450. *See* Granicus River.

Issus (*Ottoman Wars*) *1488*. The

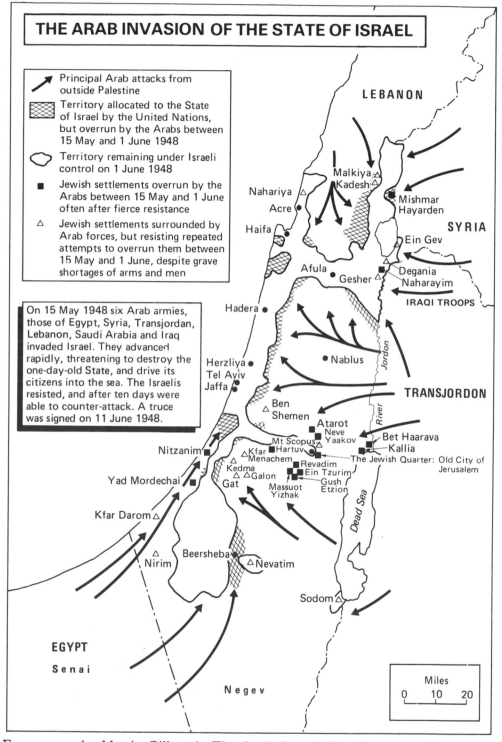

THE ARAB INVASION OF THE STATE OF ISRAEL

↗ Principal Arab attacks from outside Palestine

▨ Territory allocated to the State of Israel by the United Nations, but overrun by the Arabs between 15 May and 1 June 1948

⬡ Territory remaining under Israeli control on 1 June 1948

■ Jewish settlements overrun by the Arabs between 15 May and 1 June often after fierce resistance

△ Jewish settlements surrounded by Arab forces, but resisting repeated attempts to overrun them between 15 May and 1 June, despite grave shortages of arms and men

On 15 May 1948 six Arab armies, those of Egypt, Syria, Transjordan, Lebanon, Saudi Arabia and Iraq invaded Israel. They advanced rapidly, threatening to destroy the one-day-old State, and drive its citizens into the sea. The Israelis resisted, and after ten days were able to counter-attack. A truce was signed on 11 June 1948.

LEBANON

SYRIA

Malkiya △
Kadesh △

Mishmar Hayarden

Nahariya △
Acre ●
Haifa

Ein Gev △

Afula ●
Gesher ● ■ Degania △
Naharayim

IRAQI TROOPS

Hadera ●

● Nablus

Jordan River

TRANSJORDAN

Herzliya ●
Tel Aviv
Jaffa ●

△ Ben Shemen

Atarot ■
Neve Yaakov ■
Mt Scopus △ ● Hartuv ■ Bet Haarava ■
Nitzanim ■   △ Kfar ■   Kallia ■
         Menachem △   The Jewish Quarter: Old City of
Yad Mordechai ■   Kedma ■ Revadim ■   Jerusalem
         △ △ Galon Ein Tzurim ■
Kfar Darom △   Gat   Massuot   Gush
              Yizhak   Etzion

Dead Sea

△ Nirim   Beersheba ▨
          △ Nevatim

Sodom △

EGYPT

S e n a i

N e g e v

Miles
0   10   20

From a map by Martin Gilbert in **The Arab–Israeli Conflict — Its History in Maps**.

Egyptians under the Sultan defeated the Turks (Bajazet II).

Itabitsu *October 740*. The Japanese Emperor Shommu, with only 8,000 troops, attacked Hirotsuke's 13,000 rebels as they were crossing a river and routed them with heavy loss.

Italian Wars of Independence. *See* List of Battles.

Ituzaingó (*Brazil–Argentine War*) *20 February 1827*. Following Argentina's breakaway from Spain and that of Brazil from Portugal, the territory in between was known as Cispalatine Province of Brazil. The people of this area rose under Carlos de Alvear, joined with the Argentinians and soundly defeated the Brazilian army at Ituzaingó. On Britain's intervention, Uruguay became an independent nation in 1828.

Iuka (*American Civil War*) *19 September 1862*. General Rosecrans was close to Iuka with 9,000 troops, trying to cut off an expected Confederate retreat, when the Confederates (Little) made a surprise attack. After a fierce 2-hour fight

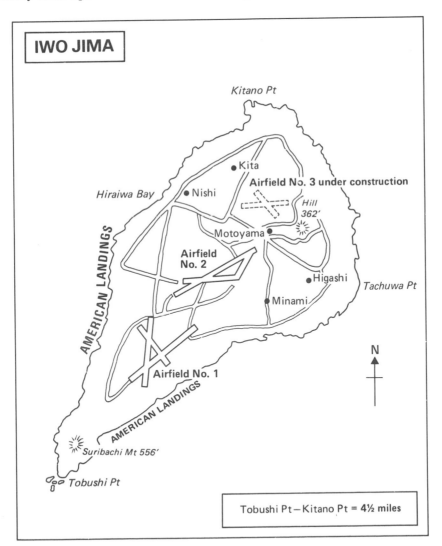

IWO JIMA

Kitano Pt

Kita

Airfield No. 3 under construction

Hiraiwa Bay

Nishi

Hill 362'

Motoyama

AMERICAN LANDINGS

Airfield No. 2

Higashi

Tachuwa Pt

Minami

N

Airfield No. 1

AMERICAN LANDINGS

Suribachi Mt 556'

Tobushi Pt

Tobushi Pt – Kitano Pt = 4½ miles

the attack was stopped. Casualties: Federals, 782; Confederates, 1,156, including their commander.

Ivry (or *Ivry-la-Bataille*) (*French Religious Wars*) *14 March 1590*. Since 1562 France had suffered from eight religious–political wars. Now the Catholic army (Charles of Lorraine, also known as Duc de Mayenne) faced Henry of Navarre's Protestant army, both leaders seeking succession to the throne. At Ivry on the Eure River, 40 miles west of Paris, de Mayenne had 25,000 men and Henry only 13,000, but his cavalrymen were superb. Mayenne's advance was broken and his troops routed; he lost 4,000 men to Henry's 500. This was the decisive battle of the French religious wars; Henry became king 3 years later and, having adopted Catholicism, founded the Bourbon line of kings.

Iwo Jima (*World War II*) *16 February–26 March 1945*. The Japanese General Kuribayashi had 21,000 troops and the heaviest firepower and strongest defences of the Pacific War to defend the 8-square-mile barren island of Iwo Jima. It had 1,500 fortified caves and hundreds of strongpoints. Naval bombardment began on 16 February (after weeks of aerial bombing) and the U.S. Marines (Schmidt) landed on 19 February. Resistance was fanatical and though the American flag was raised on Mount Suribachi on 23 February not until 26 March was the enemy entirely crushed. Casualties were immense. American, 6,821 dead and 18,200 wounded. Only a few Japanese survived. The American high command justified the heavy losses by pointing to the 2,251 Superfortress aircraft which used Iwo Jima's two emergency landing fields to continue the war against Japan.

Jackson (*American Civil War*) *14 May 1863*. Second action of General Grant's Vicksburg campaign, q.v.; he split the Confederate army and defeated Johnston's army.

Jadar River (*World War I*) *12–20 August 1914*. Austria (Oskar Potiorek) attacked Serbia's northern frontier to open the Berlin–Baghdad railway. The battle proper began on 16 August when the Serbs (Radomir Putnik) counterattacked the hinge between two Austrian corps. In the 5-day battle the Serbs outfought four Austrian armies and inflicted 40,000 casualties. *See* Rudnik Ridges.

Jalula (*Muslim invasion of Persia*) *637*. A victory for the Muslims under Said, over the Persians, led by Yezdegerd, whose precipitate flight from the field discouraged his troops and led to their destruction.

Jamaica (*English–Spanish Wars*) *11 May 1655*. A combined operations assault (Admiral Penn and General Venables) which led to the capture of the island from the Spaniards.

Jankau, *near Prague* (*Thirty Years' War*) *6 March 1645*. Between the Swedes (Torstenson) and the Austrians and Bavarians (von Werth). The Imperial Armies of Emperor Ferdinand III and Maximilian I outnumbered the Swedes, but the terrain brought about a series of independent actions, thus preventing the

Allies from using their force. The Bavarian cavalry suffered so heavily that the Imperial army was a generation recovering. *See* Freiburg; Mergentheim.

Japan (*World War II*) *1944–5*. This was a sustained air attack by American bombers. The major attack occurred on 9 March 1945 when 234 B-29 aircraft dropped 1,667 tons of incendiary bombs on Tokyo. The fire-bombing destroyed 16 square miles of city and killed 83,793 people. (This was second only in death and devastation to the bombing of Dresden; it surpassed the Hiroshima and Nagasaki atomic attacks.) Nagoya, Osaka, Kobe and Yokohama were also attacked and largely destroyed. By 1 July 1945 the Americans were making 1,200 bombing sorties a week. These bombings killed 260,000 people and made 9 million homeless. U.S. bomber losses: 343 aircraft, 243 crew members. By 10 July warships were shelling Japanese positions. When Japan rejected an ultimatum to surrender or be destroyed, a B-29 bomber (Enola Gay) from Tinian Island dropped an atomic bomb on Hiroshima, 6 August. Three-fifths of the city was destroyed, 71,379 people died. On 9 August Nagasaki was similarly attacked, with great loss of life. In the sea war against Japan U.S. submarines sank 1,113 ships for a loss of forty-five subs. On 8 August the Soviet declared war on Japan and invaded Manchuria. Still resisting, Japan came under further U.S. sea and air attack — the Third Fleet bombarded Honshu on 9

August and 800 B-29 planes raided the island on 14 August. Japan surrendered on 15 August.

Jarama River (*Spanish Civil War*) *6–28 February 1939*. A Nationalist success south of Madrid; the siege of the capital became more intense. *See* Madrid.

Jargeau (*Hundred Years' War*) *12 June 1429*. The French (Joan of Arc and Comte de Dunois) stormed and captured the English-held fortress of Jargeau, near Orleans. This victory, following that of Orleans, 8 May, gave the French counteroffensive great momentum and other British forts fell. *See* Orleans; Patay.

Jarnac (*Third French Religious War*) *13 March 1569*. A victory for the Catholics (Marshal de Tavannes) over the Huguenots, whose leader, Prince de Conde, was killed. *See* Moncontour; Saint-Denis.

Jasmund, *near Rugen Island* (*Swedish–Danish Wars*) *25 May 1676*. A resounding naval victory for the Danes (Niels Juel).

Jassy (*Polish–Turkish War*) *20 September 1620*. Herman Stanislas Zolkiewski with 10,000 men decisively defeated a much larger Turkish and Tartar army. As a result, the Ottoman Sultan, Osman II, led a large army north from Constantinople and the Poles began to retreat. Osman's Turks caught them at Cecora and annihilated them. *See* Fehrbellin.

Java Sea (*World War II*) *27 February–1 March 1942*. A major naval battle between the Japanese (Sokichi Takagi) and an Allied Australian–British– Dutch–American fleet, under the Dutch Admiral Doorman. Attempting to intercept the superior Japanese fleet, Doorman lost his flagship and his life, the Dutch light cruiser *Java* and two British destroyers, *Electra* and *Jupiter*. Three other ships were badly damaged. The Japanese had only one destroyer crippled. After the 7-hour battle the U.S. heavy cruiser *Houston* and the Australian cruiser *Perth* tried to escape from the Japanese trap, but in a fierce battle both were sunk on the night of 28 February; the two Allied ships sank three enemy cruisers and nine destroyers but the crew loss was 60 per cent. H.M.S. *Exeter*, already badly damaged, and H.M.S. *Encounter* with U.S.S. *Pope* were intercepted in Sunda Strait and sunk on 1 March. Four American destroyers escaped by dangerous navigation through Bali Strait. South of Java the Japanese sank several other ships, thus dominating the area and ensuring their capture of Java itself. *See* Singapore.

Jellalabad (*First British–Afghan War*) *11 March 1842 to 7 April 1843*. The Afghans (Muhammad Akbar Khan), having destroyed a British field force, besieged Jellalabad fortress and its small British garrison (General Sale). Akbar's first assault was beaten. In January 1843 Brigadier Wyld's relief attempt failed when he was defeated in the Khyber Pass. The garrison made several spirited sorties and on 1 April 1843 drove the Afghans from their trenches, captured all their artillery and forced Akbar to raise the siege. General Pollock's arrival with reinforcements prevented any renewal of the siege. *See* Ghazni.

Jemappes, *near Mons* (*Wars of French Revolution*) *6 November 1792*. About 16,600 Austrians (Archduke Albert) held strong positions on heights above Jemappes; the French (Dumouriez), ill-trained but 40,000-strong, drove them out with heavy loss. *See* Neerwinden.

Jemmingen (*Netherlands War of Independence against Spain*) *21 July 1568*. The Spanish Duke of Alva, an able but cruel general, moved his army of 15,000 into the northern Netherlands when Louis of Nassau raised a liberation army, also of 15,000. At Jemmingen, Alva enticed Louis to attack and then overwhelmed him with superior firepower and a crushing counter-attack from the front and flanks. The Dutch lost 7,000 men killed, while the Spanish loss was only 100. The rebel cause in north-eastern Netherlands was crushed for years. *See* Heiligerles; Mookerheyde.

Jena (*Napoleonic Wars: Jena campaign*) *14 October 1806*. The name usually given to two battles fought on the same day at Jena and at Auerstadt by the two wings of the French army commanded by Napoleon. At Auerstadt the Prussian left, 66,000-strong, was beaten after severe fighting by Davout, who had inferior numbers. On the left, at Jena, Napoleon, with 100,000 men, attacked the Prince of Hohenlohe with 70,000 Prussians. The defeated armies, converging on Weimar, were easy prey for the pursuing French cavalry who caused them further heavy losses. Casualties: at Jena: Prussians, 22,000 killed or wounded, 18,000 prisoners and 300 guns; French, 11,000 killed or wounded. *See* Lübeck; Saalfeld.

Jerusalem I (*Babylonian Conquest*) *586 BC*. The battle which ended the kingdom of Judah. Nebuchadnezzar besieged Jerusalem for 16 months until the defenders were starving. The escaping Jewish soldiers were captured and killed and their leader Zedekiah, after being forced to watch the slaying of his sons, had his eyes put out. *See* Carchemish.

Jerusalem II (*Revolt of the Maccabees*) *168–165 BC*. The result of a Jewish revolt against Syrian tyranny. Led by Mattathias and his five sons, the Jews drove off the Syrians. The principal victor was Judas, third son of Mattathias, who took the surname Maccabaeus. Fighting continued intermittently for 25 years. *See* Jerusalem III.

Jerusalem III (*conquest by Rome*) *66–63 BC*. Taking advantage of war among members of the ruling family — the Maccabees — the Roman Pompey the Great laid siege to the city, which surren-

dered 3 years later, to come under the Roman governor of Syria.

Jerusalem IV (*Jewish Wars of the Roman Empire*) March–September *70*. Titus, with 70,000 Romans, besieged the city which was heroically defended by the Jews. After 6 weeks Titus gained possession of Bezetha and then took position after position until, on 8 September, resistance ceased. This was one of history's most bitter battles. The Romans sold 97,000 Jews into slavery. (Josephus says that 1,100,000 people perished in the siege.) *See* Cremona I; Jotapata.

Jerusalem V (*Byzantine–Persian Wars*) *615*. Sweeping all before them, Persian troops under Shahrbaraz stormed Jerusalem, taking 35,000 soldiers and civilians as prisoners and killing another 50,000. *See* Melitene; Nineveh.

Jerusalem VI (*Muslim invasion of Syria*) *637*. The Muslims, under Abu Obeidah and the Khalif Omar, besieged the city for 4 months. After continual fighting, the Patriarch, Sophrinius, surrendered. *See* Aleppo; Yarmuk River.

Jerusalem VII (*First Crusade*) *7–15 July 1099*. The Crusaders, under Godefroi de Bouillon, laid siege to the city and a week later took it by assault; 70,000 Muslims died in the subsequent massacre. *See* Antioch I; Ashkelon I.

Jerusalem VIII *2–16 October 1187*. Saladin and his Saracens besieged the city, repulsed several sorties by the defenders and breached the walls. Guy de Lusignan, the last king of Jerusalem, surrendered. The Christians were given 40 days to evacuate the place.

Jerusalem IX (*Israel–Arab War*) *15 May–17 July 1948*. The new Jewish state came into existence on 15 May as the result of the partition of Palestine by the United Nations. Arab troops from Egypt, Jordan, Syria, Lebanon and Iraq reinforced the Arab irregulars already fighting the Jews and Jerusalem came under Arab siege. The defence was commanded first by Colonel David Shaltiel then by Colonel Moshe Dayan. Jewish defenders of the Old City surrendered on 28 May, to Abdullah el Tel, an Arab Legion commander. On 11 June a cease-fire was arranged, but the battle was resumed on 17 July. The Arabs suffered 5,000 casualties among their force of 25,000 in Israel. A second truce established a boundary between the Old City and the New. The whole of Jerusalem came into Israeli hands during the Six-Day War of 5–10 June 1967. *See* Israel–Arab War.

Jersey *1550*. An English squadron (Sir William Winter) attacked a French fleet blockading St. Helier and after destroying several ships scattered the rest.

Jhansi (*Indian Mutiny*) *March–April 1858*. The mutineers had captured the town and fort in June 1857. Sir Hugh Rose invested it in March 1858 and on 2 April stormed and captured it. *See* Cawnpore II; Gwalior.

Jidballi (*British Somali expedition*) *10 January 1904*. 5,000 Somalis, in camp, were attacked by a small British and Sudanese force (Sir Charles Egerton) and driven out. Pursued by cavalry for 12 miles, the Somalis lost 1,000 killed.

Jidda (*Saudi Arabian Civil War*) *January–December 1925*. The first King of the Hejaz, Ibn-Saud, opposing the powerful Wahabi sect, occupied Mecca on 13 October 1925 and besieged the last Hejaz stronghold, Jidda, on the Red Sea. It surrendered on 23 December. The kingdom acquired the name Saudi Arabia in 1932.

Jiron (*Colombian–Peruvian War*) *28 February 1829*. An indecisive battle between the Peruvians (Lamar) and Colombians (Sucre).

Jitgurgh (*British–Gurkha War*) *14 January 1815*. Between 4,500 British

troops (General Wood) and 1,200 Gurkhas. A treacherous guide led the British into an ambush and though the British fought their way out of it they could not carry the enemy stockade; in fact the Gurkhas had been about to abandon their defences.

Jordan Civil War *1970*. Jordan had become the main base for the Palestinian guerrilla and terrorist organizations. In February 1970 ten of these groups combined to form the Palestine Armed Struggle Command (PASC). PASC fighters clashed with Jordanian troops and King Hussein, desperately trying to keep the peace, agreed to many of the guerrillas' commands. Between 6 and 9 September a terrorist group hijacked and destroyed four foreign airliners; three were blown up in Jordan. By 17 September fighting between the Palestinians and Jordanians was widespread, but was heaviest around the capital Amman. An inter-Arab mission obtained a cease-fire on 25 September; by then the Palestinians had been crushed and scores of thousands fled to Syria and Lebanon. Casualties: Jordanian officials said that their own casualties amounted to 360 and that 700 guerrillas were killed and 1,300 wounded. Palestine Liberation Organization spokesmen repeatedly insisted that 25,000 of their people were killed in the war.

Jotapata (*Jewish War of the Roman Empire*) *December 67–January 68*. The Jewish army under Josephus held out for 47 days against Titus Flavius Vespasian with 60,000 Romans before surrender. The Jews fought with fanatical courage and the campaign was one of the bloodiest in Roman Empire history. *See* Bedriacum; Bezetha; Jerusalem IV.

Jugdulluck (*First British–Afghan War*) *12 January 1842*. Having retreated in winter snow from Kabul, harassed by Afghans and Ghazis, the survivors of General Elphinstone's army made their last stand at Jugdulluck. Of the few who survived only one, Dr.

Brydon, reached Jellalabad, the intended goal. *See* Kabul II.

Julian's Defeat (*Roman–Persian Wars*) *28 June 363*. Julian and his Romans had advanced against Ctesiphon, the Persian capital, only to find it too strong. Withdrawing along the left bank of the Tigris, Julian was attacked by the Persians. Julian was mortally wounded. His successor, Jovian, restored to King Sapor II almost all the Roman conquests in Persia. *See* Amida.

Junin, *95 miles north-west of Lima (Peruvian War of Independence)* *6 August 1824*. The Colombian patriots (Sucre) defeated the Spanish Royalists (Cauterac).

Juno Beach. *See* D-Day.

Jutland (*or Skagerrak to the Germans*) (*World War I*) *31 May–1 June 1916*. The British blockade of Germany provoked the Germans into battle with the British Grand Fleet. The Germans had two divisions — von Hipper with five battle cruisers and the senior commander, Scheer, with sixteen new and eight old battleships; in addition, the Germans had eleven light cruisers and sixty-three destroyers. The British also had two divisions, Beatty with six battle-cruisers and four battleships, Jellicoe with three battle-cruisers and twenty-four battleships; thirty-four light cruisers and eighty destroyers supported. In the first clash Hipper's ships sank Beatty's cruisers *Indefatigable* and *Queen Mary*. The main engagement, between the major divisions, began off the Jutland coast about 6 p.m., with the British holding the initiative since they stood between the German fleet and its base. About 10 p.m. Scheer forced his way through the British light forces and in a 4-hour fight the Germans escaped, losing only the battleship *Pommern* and the already crippled *Lutzow*. Total losses: Britain, three battle-cruisers, three light cruisers, eight destroyers; Germany, four cruisers, five destroyers, apart from the big-ship losses. Germany claimed a victory, but the strategic balance lay with Britain since the German fleet never again sought an open battle.

Kabul I (*Muslim conquest of the East*) *709*. Muhammad-iba-Kasim (or Qasim) took Kabul, a victory which established Muhammadism in what is now Pakistan. *See* Carthage III; Kashgar; Rio Barbate.

Kabul II (*British–Afghan War*) *14 September 1842*. The punitive expedition — under General Pollock — which followed the British disaster at Jugdulluck. Defeating Akbar Khan, Pollock destroyed part of Kabul, but on orders from London withdrew in October. *See* Herat II; Mianee; Peiwar Pass.

Kadesh (*Egyptian–Hittite Wars*) *1288 BC*. Fought on the banks of the Orontes River, Syria, this is the earliest battle of which tactics are known. Pharoah Ramses II led 20,000 men on Kadesh in an attempt to hold his crumbling empire. Muwatallish, the Hittite leader, ambushed the Egyptians, sending in 2,500 chariots, each holding three men. By skilful and courageous personal leadership, Ramses led his men out of the trap, then counter-attacked the Hittites when they stopped to rob the dead. The Egyptian drive reached Kadesh, but the city held out. Combats went on for 17 years. *See* Megiddo I.

Kadisiya, *near Hilla, Iraq* (*Muslim conquest of Persia*) *637*. Between Rustam (regent for Yazdegerd III) and 100,000 men and 30,000 Arabian horsemen led by Sa'ad ibn-Abi Waqqas. The Arabs made several cavalry charges and were then counter-attacked by Persian elephants. After 2 days of bloody and indecisive fighting Sa'ad was reinforced by some veterans of the Syrian campaign who had learned how to fight elephants with arrows and javelins. Stampeded back through the Persian lines, the elephants created gaps through which the Arab horsemen charged. A sandstorm completed the havoc in the Persian lines. Rustam was caught and beheaded. His army, having lost 7,500 men in battle, was practically wiped out by the ruthless Arabs. Yazdegerd tried three times to stop the subsequent Arab advance. Kadisiya was the decisive battle of the war. *See* Hira.

Kagul, *northern Turkey* (*Russian–Turkish Wars*) *3 August 1770*. A remarkable victory for General Roumiantsoff and only 17,000 Russians against Halil Pasha with 150,000 Turks and their 80,000 Tartar allies. His rear threatened by the Tartars, Roumiantsoff attacked the Turkish lines and after severe fighting drove the Turks headlong from their trenches, capturing all their guns and baggage and avoiding conflict with the Tartars. *See* Ceşme.

Kaifeng (*Chinese Civil War*) *19 June 1948*. Defended by 250,000 Nationalist troops loyal to Chiang Kai-shek, Kaifeng was attacked by 200,000 men of the People's Liberation Army (Ch'en Yi, Liu Po-Ch'eng and Ch'en Keng). Weakened by desertions, the garrison gave way before the Communist onslaught. Immense stores of equipment were taken. *See* Chinese Civil War.

Kaiping (*Chinese–Japanese War*) 10 January 1895. A Japanese brigade (Nogi) attacked and drove from their trenches about 3,000 Chinese.

Kakakog, *New Guinea* (*World War II*) September 1943. An Australian victory, at bayonet-point, against the Japanese, who were driven from precipitous jungle-clad slopes. *See* Lae; Wau.

Kalisch (*Russian–Swedish War*) September 1776. A serious defeat for the Swedes whose leader, Mayerfeld, had only 10,000 men to the 30,000 Russians and Poles of Prince Mentschikoff. *See* Thorn.

Kalka River (*or Kalmius*) (*Mongol invasion of Europe*) 1223. A coalition of Russian princes led by Mstislav, Prince of Kiev, scratched together 80,000 soldiers to block the relentless Mongol cavalry led by Genghis Khan's lieutenant, Subotai. Subotai sought peace, but when his envoys were murdered he attacked. Cut down down in swathes by arrows, broken by lance attacks, the Russians were defeated.

Kalpi (*Indian mutiny against the British*) 19–23 May 1858. Sir Hugh Rose invested the town, held by the mutineers, who made two ineffective sorties against the British. The town fell on 23 May. *See* Delhi.

Kalunga (*British–Gurkha War*) October–November 1814. The British (Colonel Gillespie) attacked the fortress town commanded by Bulbuddur Singh and was repulsed with 260 casualties. Guns were brought up a month later; a breach was blown in the walls and a second attack went in, again to be beaten back — with a loss of 680. The fortress was shelled for 3 days; only 70 of the garrison of 600 now survived and they

made their escape before the British infantry took the fort. *See* Jitgurgh.

Kamakura, *Southern Honshu* (*Japanese Civil Wars*) 1333. The Hojo clans, ruling Japan from the great city of Kamakura, were defeated after 2 years of fighting. Their conqueror, Daigo, restored imperial rule.

Kamarut (*First British–Burma War*) 8 July 1824. Sir Archibald Campbell, at the head of a small British force, stormed and captured a series of stockades held by 10,000 Burmese under Tuamba Wangyee, who was killed. *See* Kemendine.

Kambula (*British–Zulu War*) 29 March 1879. The Zulu chief, Cetawayo, launched three impi (fighting divisions) against Colonel Wood's lager, defended by 2,000 British troops and native auxiliaries. Repulsed, the Zulus were pursued for 7 miles. The defeat practically broke Cetawayo's power. The British lost 81. *See* Isandhlwana; Rorkes Drift; Ulundi.

Kampuchea. *See* Cambodia

Kandahar I (*Tartar invasion of Afghanistan*) 1221. The Tartars (Tuli Khan) besieged and took the city and were preparing to overwhelm the citadel when Jellaladin, Sultan of Kharismia, arrived with strong reinforcements and annihilated the Tartar invaders. *See* Biruan.

Kandahar II (*Mogul invasion*) 1545. The Moguls (Humayun) took 5 months to wear down the Afghan garrison (Mirza Askari).

Kandahar III (*Persian–Afghan War*) 1648. In the summer of 1648 the Persians (Abbas II) besieged the city and its Mogul garrison. Aurungzebe, arriving to relieve the fortress, found the Persians had captured it. After a 4 months' siege he retired. Two subsequent attempts at relief also failed.

Kandahar IV (*Afghan Tribal Wars*) 29 July 1834. Shah Sujah, the expelled Amir of Afghanistan, attempted to take the city. His successor as Amir, Dost Muhammad, sallied out and in the following battle defeated Sujah.

Kandahar V (*Second British–Afghan War*) 1 September 1880. Having made a forced march — 313 miles in 22 days — from Kabul, Lord Roberts gave battle to the Afghans (Ayub Khan) and decisively defeated them, inflicting 2,000 casualties. British losses were 248. *See* Maiwand.

Kandurcha (*Tamerlane's Conquests*) 1391. The power of "Timur the Lame" was threatened by his former ally Toktamish, who commanded the fabulous Mongol army known as the Golden Horde. Tamerlane followed Toktamish into Russia and forced him into a mighty cavalry battle, which Tamerlane won decisively. The site of Kandurcha is unknown. *See* Delhi I.

Kápolna (*Hungarian Rising against Austria*) 26–27 February 1849. Four Hungarian divisions (Dembinski) managed to hold firm against the Austrian troops of General Schlick, but on the evening of the second day the Austrians captured the key position of Kápolna, forcing the Hungarians to retire. *See* Schwechat.

Kappel (*Swiss religious rising*) 10 October 1531. The army, 8,000 strong, of the Swiss Catholic Cantons held powerful positions when attacked by General Goldli, whose assault with 1,300 Zurich troops was launched in defiance of orders. It was completely defeated.

Kapyong River (*Korean War*) 22–25 April 1951. A minor action in which U.N. troops, principally Australians and British, held out against a Chinese and North Korean attack. *See* Korean War.

Kara Burur (*Russian–Turkish Wars*) 11 August 1791. The Russian fleet

(Admiral Ouschakoff) defeated the Turks after a long, hard battle. *See* Foksani.

Karaku (*Tartar invasion of Kharismia*) 1218. Another battle of Genghis Khan, said to have had 700,000 troops to the 400,000 Kharismians of the Sultan Muhammad. At nightfall the battle was undecided and the armies withdrew to their camps. Each had lost more than 100,000 men and the battle was not renewed.

Karamuran (*Tartar invasion of Central Asia*) 1225. Genghis Khan, with 300,000 Tartars, was attacked by the Shidasker of Tangat, who had under command 500,000 Turks, Chinese and others. Shidasker was routed with a reported loss of 300,000.

Karee (*Second British–Boer War*) 29 March 1900. General Tucker and his division lost 180 men in driving from their trenches a Boer force holding a line near Bloemfontein. *See* Ladysmith.

Kargaula (*Cossack rising against Russia*) 1774. The Russians (Prince Gallitzin) routed with great slaughter the insurgent Cossacks of the Don, whose leader, Pugatcheff, fled to the mountains.

Kars I (*Crimean War*) March–8 November 1855. Gallantly defended by a Turkish garrison under the British General Williams, Kars surrendered to the Russians when the garrison had reached starvation point. *See* Sebastopol I.

Kars II (*Russian–Turkish War*) 17 November 1877. Hussein Pasha held the fortress with 24,000 Turks, when the Russians (Loris Melikoff) stormed it on the night of 17 November. After severe fighting the Russians captured all the eastern forts. Hussein, isolated, tried to cut his way to the western part, but only he and a few others ran the gauntlet. Casualties: Turks, 2,500 killed, 4,500 wounded,

17,000 prisoners; 303 guns lost; Russians, 2,273 killed or wounded. *See* Plovdiv; Shipka Pass.

Kashgal (*British–Sudan campaigns*) *3 November 1883*. General Hicks (Hicks Pasha), leading 11,000 Egyptian troops, followed a treacherous guide into a defile where the Mahdists ambushed them. After a stubborn 3-day resistance the Egyptians were massacred. *See* Khartoum.

Kashmir War I *1947–9*. The state of Kashmir was uncertain whether to join Pakistan or India when India was partitioned on 15 August 1947. Kashmir Muslims rioted in favour of Pakistan and the Pakistani government declared *jihad* or holy war in their support. When the capital, Srinigar, was threatened, the Maharajah of Kashmir appealed to India for help. In 14 months of fighting the Indian army gained control and the war ended on 1 January 1949. Casualties were heavy, but were never disclosed.

Kashmir War II *1965*. On 5 August 1965 Pakistan invaded Kashmir in another attempt to take it from India. After infantry fighting during August the Pakistani army committed several tank divisions to break the Indian line at Chlamb. In the consequent battle each side lost more than 200 tanks. The Indian forces retaliated with Operation Grand Slam, a three-pronged attack on the West Pakistan capital of Lahore. Another Indian invasion army struck towards Hyderabad, 400 miles further south, in an area where Pakistan had also precipitated conflict over territory. Following U.N. intervention, the war ended on 23 September. Casualties: Indian, 3,712 killed, 7,638 wounded; Pakistani, 13,000 in all.

Kassassin (*Arabi's Rebellion*) *28 August 1882*. Arabi Pasha and his Egyptians attacked British positions commanded by General Graham. After remaining on the defensive all day, Graham in the evening launched his cavalry (Baker Russell) against the enemy who broke and ran. The British lost eleven killed and sixty-eight wounded. *See* Tel-el-Kebir.

Kasserine Pass (*World War II*) *14–22 February 1943*. An action during the battle for Tunisia; American troops met German Panzer units (Rommel) for the first time and were severely mauled. Brilliantly planned and executed, the Panzer attack, extending from Faid to El Guettar, completely smashed several American units. The defeat forced the British and Americans to replan air support for troops. *See* Tunisia.

Katzbach River (*Napoleonic Wars: Leipzig campaign*) *22–26 August 1813*. Initially a decisive victory for Napoleon, whose 130,000 veteran French were too powerful for Blucher's 100,000 Prussians. The previous day Blucher had protected himself behind the Haynau River; now he was driven across the Katzbach. On 26 August Napoleon sent Macdonald and his corps across the Katzbach, but Blucher attacked first and drove the French back. As Macdonald was retiring, his colleague Souham arrived on the field with infantry and cavalry reinforcements, but before he could deploy the Prussians also attacked him, and his men were routed with very heavy loss. The French lost 15,000 killed or wounded and over 100 guns. *See* Dresden; Grossbeeren.

Kay (*Seven Years' War*) *23 July 1759*. Soltykov led 70,000 Russian troops across the Brandenburg border to attack the Prussians of Frederick the Great. The local Prussian commander, von Wedell, had only 26,000 men but impetuously attacked — and suffered defeat and 6,000 casualties. Soltykov moved towards Frankfurt. *See* Korndorf; Kunersdorf.

Kazan I (*Conquest by Ivan IV*) *1552*. The first Russian Czar, Ivan IV (The Terrible), captured the city in his first campaign of imperial expansion.

Kazan II (*Cossack rising against Russia*) *1774*. The Russians (Michelson) overwhelmed the rebel Cossacks (Pugatcheff). *See* Kargaula.

Kemendine (*First British–Burma War*) *10 June 1824*. Sir Archibald Campbell, at the head of 3,000 British, drove the Burmese from a series of stockade forts. *See* Kamarut.

Kenesaw Mountain (*American Civil War*) *27 June 1864*. A frontal attack by the Federals (William Sherman) against the Confederate army of Joseph Johnston. The object was to drive off the Confederates so that the Federals could use the railroad. Only 16,000 men of Sherman's 100,000-strong force could be used and in repeated uphill attacks they suffered 2,000 serious casualties. The Confederates, though outnumbered overall, were in strong positions and had only 270 killed or wounded. It was a clear Confederate victory. *See* Atlanta; Resaca.

Kenilworth (*Second Barons' War of England*) *31 July 1265*. Prince Edward's knights attacked the camp of young Simon de Montfort, capturing most of his troops. Young Simon held out in Kenilworth Castle, but his father was defeated and slain at Evesham in August. Kenilworth Castle held out until 14 December 1266. *See* Axholme; Evesham; Lewes.

Kerbela (*or Karbala*), *near Baghdad* (*Muslim Civil Wars*) *680*. Between Husain, nominee of the Kufans of Iraq as ruler of Islam, and supporters of Yazid I, actual ruler of Islam. Deserted by many of the Kufans at Kerbela, Husain was defeated and killed. Husain's betrayal and death is still commemorated annually by the Shi'a branch of Islam. *See* Siffin; Zab-al-Kebir.

Keresztes, *near Erlau, Hungary* (*Turkish–Austrian Wars*) *24–26 October 1596*. Between the Turks (Muhammad III) and the Imperialists and Transylvanians (Archduke Maximilian and Prince Sigismund of Transylvania). After early setbacks, Muhammad was encouraged by his Grand Vizier and persisted long enough to defeat the Austrians. The battle was part of the so-called Long War — 1593–1610. *See* Khotin I; Lepanto II.

Kernstown I (*American Civil War*) *23 March 1862*. General Thomas (Stonewall) Jackson believed that Kernstown was held only by a small rearguard and stormed it with 4,200 men. In fact, the garrison was 9,000-strong (Shield). Suffering 700 casualties, the Confederates were repulsed, but the vigour of the attack led the Federals to overestimate Jackson's strength and troops were needlessly taken from other areas to reinforce Kernstown. *See* Ball's Bluff; Yorktown II.

Kernstown II (*American Civil War*) *23 July 1864*. The Confederates under Breckinridge attacked lines held by Crook's Federals, inflicted 1,185 casualties and drove them northward across the Potomac. *See* Monocacy River; Winchester III.

Kesseldorf, *near Dresden* (*War of Austrian Succession*) *15 December 1745*. A victory for the Prussians (Leopold I of Anhalt-Dessau) over the Saxons (Rutowski). This victory, following that of Frederick the Great at Hennersdorf, q.v., completely repulsed the forces of the Holy Roman Empire.

Kettle Creek, *Georgia* (*American Revolution*) *14 February 1779*. A partisan combat between 700 pro-English Americans under Colonel Boyd of North Carolina and a patriot militia force of only 300 under Colonel Andrew Pickins. Surprising Boyd's Loyalists in camp, the militia — enraged by their plundering — killed about forty-five, including Boyd, and hanged five others. *See* Port Royal Island.

Kharisme (*Tartar invasion of Kharismia*). Genghis Khan's three sons besieged the capital of Kharismia in 1220, captured it after stubborn 7-month siege and massacred 100,000 inhabitants. *See* Samarkand.

Khartoum (*British–Sudan campaigns*) *26 January 1885*. Defended by an Egyptian garrison under General Charles Gordon, Khartoum was invested by the Mahdi early in 1884 and stormed on 26 January 1885; Gordon was among those killed. A relief force in gunboats arrived off the city 2 days later. *See* Atbara; Tamai.

Khelat-i-Ghilzai (*First British–Afghan War*) *13 November 1839*. 1,000 British troops (Willshire) captured Khelat from its Baluchi garrison (Mahrab Khan) which suffered 4,000 casualties. *See* Ghuzni.

Khirokitia (*Egypt–Cyprus Wars*) *5 July 1426*. Janus de Lusignian led 4,000 infantry and 1,600 cavalry to meet an army of Egyptian invaders. Janus was initially successful, but Cypriot discipline broke and Janus was captured.

Khojah Pass (*First British–Afghan War*) *28 March 1842*. In a desperate effort to relieve General Nott and his troops besieged in Kandahar, General England marched his advance guard of 500 men into the pass where the Afghans ambushed him. Losing 100 killed and wounded, England retired to Quetta. *See* Kabul.

Khojend (*now Leninabad*) (*Mongol conquest of Central Asia*) *February–April 1219*. Juji, eldest son of Genghis Khan, commanding a cavalry force on a sweep through the Tien Shan mountains, encountered a Muslim army under a shah, Muhammad. In a furious battle both sides lost tens of thousands of men and each withdrew. With reinforcements, Juji then attacked Khojend. The garrison commander, Timur Malik, so stoutly continued the defence from an island in the Jaxartes River that the Mongols were held up for a month. Malik was finally the only defender to escape with his life. *See* Bokhara; Pekin I.

Khotin I (*or Hotin*) (*Polish–Turkish Wars*) *May 1621*. Sultan Osman II marched into the Ukraine to quell the rebellious Moldavians. A large Polish army (first under Chodkiewicz, then Lubomirski) met the Turks on the right bank of the Dniester. The Turkish Janissaries were by now decadent; they broke and ran, then murdered Osman before he could rebuild his army. *See* Keresztes.

Khotin II (*Polish–Turkish Wars*) *June 1673*. The Ottoman Turks joined the Cossack revolt against the Polish king, Michael Wisniowiecki. With the tide of war against them, the Poles were rallied by John Sobieski who counter-attacked the Turks at Khotin and routed them. *See* Szentgotthard; Vienna II.

Kiev (*Mongol invasion of Europe*) *6 December 1240*. This battle was the climax of the Mongol second invasion of Russia, led by Subotai and Batu Khan. Without cohesion, the Russian duchies were helpless. The great city of Kiev was stormed, plundered and razed. *See* Cracow; Kalka River; Neva River.

Kiev (*World War II*) *10–26 September 1941*. In this battle the Germans created the largest pocket of their advance into western Russia. About a million Russians (Budenny) were holding the central Ukraine between two German spearheads (Boch and Rundstedt). Hitler ordered his generals to surround Budenny's army group. Halting their advance, Boch and Rundstedt began a great encircling movement which was completed after 2 weeks of desperate fighting. Casualties: Russian, 400,000 killed or wounded, 600,000 prisoners; German, 100,000 in all. The victory so delayed the German's programme that

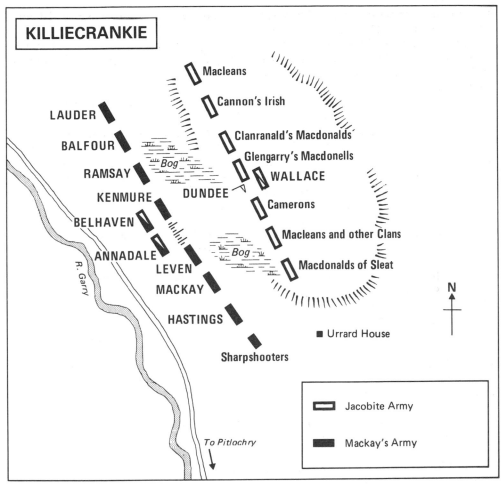

KILLIECRANKIE

Macleans

Cannon's Irish

LAUDER

BALFOUR

Clanranald's Macdonalds

Glengarry's Macdonells

RAMSAY

Bog

WALLACE

KENMURE

DUNDEE

BELHAVEN

Camerons

ANNADALE

Macleans and other Clans

R. Garry

LEVEN

Bog

Macdonalds of Sleat

MACKAY

N

HASTINGS

■ Urrard House

Sharpshooters

Jacobite Army

Mackay's Army

To Pitlochry

winter caught them. *See* Smolensk; Soviet Union.

Kilimanjaro (*World War I*) 3 September 1914 and intermittently to 23 March 1916. The German irregular forces colonel, von Lettow, met the British and South Africans in actions around Kilimanjaro. The major British offensive began on 5 March 1916 and the area was captured by 23 March. von Lettow was never decisively beaten. *See* East Africa.

Killdeer Mountain (*or Tahkahokuty*) (*Sioux Wars*) 28 July 1864. A victory for General Sully's column of 2,200 troops over 5,000 Sioux; casualties were light.

Killiecrankie (*Jacobite Rising*) 27 July 1689. Between General Mackay and 4,500 Royal troops and Dundee with 2,500 Highland Jacobites. Dundee drew Mackay onto the plain below the pass of Killiecrankie and then swept down from the heights, routing the Royalists, who lost 2,000 killed and 500 prisoners. Dundee was among the 900 Jacobites killed. When Mackay reached Stirling he had only 400 men. *See* Boyne; Glencoe.

Kilsyth, *Stirling* (*English Civil War*) 15 August 1645. A notable victory for the Royalists (Montrose) against the Covenanters (Baillie) whose 6,000 infantry were cut down almost to a man. *See* Alford; Langport.

Kimberley (*Second British–Boer War*) *15 October 1899–15 February 1900*. A famous siege. Colonel Kekewich's British garrison of 4,000 was besieged by the Boers (Commandant Wessels, then General Cronje). Under continual and severe bombardment, Kimberley held until relieved by General French's cavalry; casualties were only 181. *See* Ladysmith; Mafeking.

Kineyri (*Second British–Sikh War*) *18 June 1848*. An outstanding junior officer, Lieutenant Edwardes, with 3,000 Sikh irregulars was largely responsible for this victory. The battle began with 8,000 Bhawalpuris (Futteh Muhammad Khan) vainly attacking about 10,000 Sikhs (Rung Ram). Edwardes arrived with his guns and troops and turned the battle for the Bhawalpuris; the Sikhs lost 500 killed in the action. *See* Chilianwala; Gujerat.

King's Mountain (*American Revolution*) *7 October 1780*. Major Patrick Ferguson led 1,100 Loyalists on a raid through the mountains of western Carolina and eastern Tennessee. Under three militia colonels — Shelby, Sevier and Campbell — American frontiersmen surrounded the Loyalists on King's Mountain, killing 157 (including Ferguson), seriously wounding 163 (they were left to die on the field) and capturing 698; 9 were hanged for treason. American losses, 28 killed, 62 wounded. *See* Camden; Cowpens.

Kinloss (*Danish invasion of Scotland*) *1009*. The Danes (Sweyn) were besieging Nairn. The Scots under Malcolm II tried to raise the siege, but were repulsed; Malcolm was wounded. *See* Mortlack.

Kinnesaw Mountain (*American Civil War*) *27 June 1864*. Sherman, leading an army of 90,000 Federals, attacked Johnston who had only 50,000 men but occupied very strong positions. Sherman lost 3,000 men to Johnston's 500. *See* Peach Tree Creek.

Kinsale (*O'Neil's rebellion against Elizabeth I*) *1601*. Juan d'Aguila's Spaniards had seized Kinsale in September 1601, in an attempt to support the rebels. Royal troops (Lord Mountjoy and Earl of Thomond) besieged the Spaniards. On 23 December O'Neil, leader of the rebellion, tried to relieve the place. When he was repulsed d'Aguila surrendered and was allowed to embark his troops for Spain. *See* Flores.

Kirch-Denkern (*Seven Years' War*) *16 July 1761*. The French (Soubise and Duc de Broglei) attacked strong Russian positions in and around Kirch-Denkern and after losing 4,000 killed and wounded were repulsed. *See* Torgau.

Kirkeban (*British–Sudan campaign*) *10 February 1885*. General Earle led 1,000 British troops in a charge against the strong Mahdist force holding the heights of Kirkeban. The vigour and courage of the charge routed the Mahdists, but Earle was among the sixty British killed. *See* Khartoum.

Kirkee (*Third British–Mahratta War*) *5 November 1817*. One British and three native regiments (Colonel Burr) advanced from trenches to defeat the Mahrattas (Bajee Rao) who lost 500.

Kirk-Kilissa (*or Kirklareli*) (*First Balkan War*) *25 October 1912*. A Bulgarian army met an invading Turkish army and threw it back with heavy losses. *See* Kumanovo; Lüleburgaz.

Kirovabad (*Russian–Persian War*) *14 May 1826*. A Russian army under Paskevich (later Count of Erivan and Prince of Warsaw) attacked a large Persian force. He won decisively and began an outstanding military career. The victory gave Russia most of Persian Armenia, another step in the long border conflict. *See* Grochów.

Kiso (*Japanese Taira clan War***) September 1180**. The troops of Taira-no-Kiyomori attacked troops of the Minamoto clan, but were defeated with heavy loss.

Kissingen (*Seven Weeks' War***) 10 July 1866**. A resounding victory for the Prussians (Falkenstein) who drove the Bavarians (Zoller) from the village with heavy loss. *See* Koeniggratz.

Kiu-Lien-Cheng (*Russian–Japanese War***) 1 May 1904**. The Japanese army of Marshal Kuroki crossed the Yalu, 30 April, and next day attacked the Russians (Sassulitch), driving them out with a loss of 4,000 killed or wounded, 530 taken prisoner and 48 guns. The Japanese, who started the battle with 40,000 men to the Russians' 30,000, lost 898 killed or wounded. *See* Tsushima.

Kizil-Tepe (*Russian–Turkish War***) 25 June 1877**. The Russians (Melikov), besieging Kars, were attacked by overwhelming numbers of Turks (Mahktar Pasha) and driven off. *See* Mars; Plevna.

Klausenburg (*Transylvanian–Turkish Wars***) May 1660**. A complete victory for the Turks (Mahomet Koprili) against the Transylvanians (George Ragotski II). *See* Szigeth.

Kliszow, *near Krakow* (*Great Northern War***) 13 July 1702**. Between Charles XII of Sweden with 12,000 veteran Swedes and a Polish–Saxon army of about 30,000, which had halted in its retreat in an effort to block the near-invincible Charles — he had already beaten the Danes and Russians, at Narva. Smashing the Allies, the Swedes pushed on to take Krakow on the Vistula. *See* Narva; Putulsk I.

Klokotnitsa, *on the Maritsa River* (*Bulgarian–Greek Wars***) 1230**. Between Theodore Angelus of Epirus, the aggressor, and John Asen II of Bulgaria. The Bulgarian army was completely victorious and John marched on to conquer western Thrace and Macedonia. *See* Constantinople V; Plovdiv.

Klushino (*Russian–Polish Wars***) September 1610**. A Russian army of 30,000, including 8,000 Swedes, led by Dmitri Shuisky was marching to relieve Smolensk when it was surprised by a Polish force of only 4,000, most of them cavalry, led by Herman Stanislas Zolkiewski. The Russians left 15,000 dead on the battlefield and Shiusky fled. Reinforced to 23,000 by turncoats from the Russian–Swedish army, Zolkiewski marched on to Moscow and to capture Smolensk, q.v.

Knoxville (*American Civil War***) 29 November 1863**. The abortive attack by Longstreet, with 10,000 infantry and 5,000 cavalry (Wheeler), on Knoxville, held for the Federals by Burnside and McLaws. In bitterly cold weather, Longstreet attacked a northern salient known as Fort Sanders, now Loudon. He lost 813 men and withdrew. Federal casualties, 113. *See* Chattanooga; Wilderness.

Koeniggratz (*Seven Weeks' War***) 3 July 1866**. A major and massive battle between 200,000 Austrians with 600 guns under Marshal Benedek and the Prussian armies of Prince Charles Frederick and the Crown Prince, together about the size of the Austrian army. Charles attacked the Austrians early in the morning, but made little impression; the Crown Prince's attack on the Austrian right flank at 2 p.m. made ground. Under heavy artillery fire, the Austrian centre weakened and the Prussians seized the ground which dominated the field. Having lost 20,000 killed or wounded, 20,000 prisoners and 174 guns the Austrians withdrew. The Prussians lost 10,000. The battle made Prussia and not Austria the strongest power in Central Europe.

Koenigswartha (*Napoleonic Wars: Leipzig campaign***) 19 May 1813**. 15,000 Russians (Tolly) attacked Peyr's 8,000 Italians, allies of the French. Ney's

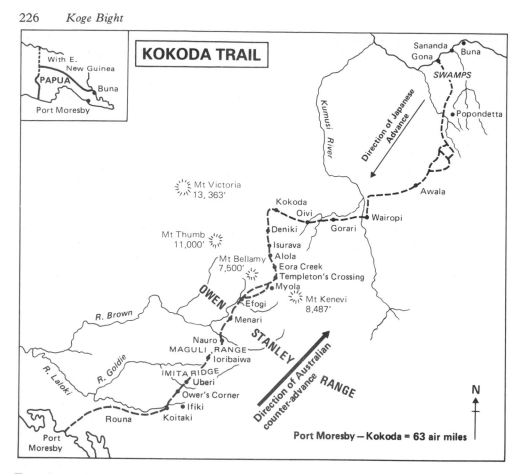

French cavalry was sent in at the gallop and saved the Italians from destruction. *See* Berezina.

Koge Bight, *south of Copenhagen (Swedish–Danish Wars)* ***30 June 1677.*** A clear victory for the Danish fleet (Niels Juel) which sank or captured eleven Swedish ships (Evart Horn). The war was part of the larger conflict between France and Holland, Denmark's ally.

Kogoshima (*Japanese Satsuma Rebellion*) *18 August 1876.* The rebels, who were closely besieged at Enotake, nevertheless infiltrated through the Imperial troops and making a forced march, led by Saige Takamori, seized the city of Kagoshima. The Imperial army (Prince Taruhito) pursued them and the consequent engagement lasted 10 days

before the rebels were driven out; they retired to Shirogama. Both sides lost heavily.

Kohima. *See* Burma Campaign; World War II.

Kokein (*First British–Burmese War***)** *12 December 1824.* Sir Archibald Campbell's 2,000 British stormed and captured two major stockaded forts garrisoned by 20,000 Burmese. *See* Kemendine.

Kokoda Trail, *New Guinea* (*World War II*) *July 1942–January 1943.* The Japanese landing at Buna and Gona, July 1942, found the Australians unprepared. Thrusting south across the high jungle-clad Owen Stanley Mountains, the Japanese moved on Port Moresby, chief Australian base. The first pitched battle occurred at the mission station of Kokoda, 28–29 July; it was a Japanese victory. General Horii, 25 August, having built up his force, overwhelmed after a 4-day fight an Australian post at Isurava. The Australians checked the enemy advance at Imita Ridge and on 25 September Horii ordered a fighting withdrawal. The Australians retook Kokoda on 3 November, and at Gorari they killed 580 Japanese in a bayonet charge. Casualties from disease and wounds were heavy on both sides. The Australians, later helped by the Americans, attacked and captured the Japanese complex of positions around the villages and beaches of Gona, 1 December; Gone Mission, 9 December; Cape Endaidiere, 21 December; Buna, 28 December; Sanananda, 23 January 1943. Outnumbered 2 to 1, the Australians had wiped out 16,000 Japanese. *See* New Guinea.

Kolin (*Seven Years' War*) *18 June 1757*. A Prussian–Austrian bloodbath. Marshal Daun's 50,000 Austrians held heights between Kolin and Chotzewitz where Frederick the Great attacked him, using all his 34,000 troops. (He had left another 26,000 out of battle.) The Austrian right flank was bending when the Prussians at this point uncharacteristically broke and fled. The Prussian cavalry made six valiant charges but the damage could not be made good and Frederick was beaten back after losing 14,000 men and 43 guns. Austrian casualties, 9,000. *See* Gross-Jagersdorf; Hastenbeck; Prague.

Komatsu (*Japanese Nine Years' War*) *5–16 September 1062*. Japanese Imperial troops (Yoriyoshi) besieged the rebel leader, Sadatoki, in his camp. Sadatoki led a desperate sortie of 8,000 men but was beaten back and after days of continual sword combat the rebels were defeated and their leader killed.

Komorn (*Hungarian rebellion against Austria*) *26 April 1849*. The Austrian "masters" of Hungary besieged the rebelling Hungarians holding the key fort of Komorn. In a surprise dawn attack two Hungarian corps (Klapka and Damjanics) hammered the Austrian entrenched camp. Casualties were few, but the demoralized Austrians retired. The Hungarians failed to pursue, but Komorn was relieved.

Koniah (*or Konya*), *in Anatolia (Mehemet Ali's First Rebellion against the Turks*) *21 December 1831*. A total defeat for the Turks (Reschid Pasha) by the Egyptians (Ibrahim Pasha). Mehemet Ali, Viceroy of Egypt, had demanded Syria as the price of supporting the Turks in the Greek War of Independence. Turkish refusal caused Mehemet's rebellion. *See* Navarino; Nizib.

Korean War *1950–3*. When Japan was defeated at the end of World War II (1945) the Japanese troops in Korea surrendered. Those north of the 38th parallel gave themselves up to the Russians, those to the south to the Americans. This artificial line became a political border between the Democratic People's Republic (north) and the Republic of South Korea. U.S. troops withdrew in the summer of 1949. The North Korean Army of 127,000, secretly armed with Russian and Chinese equipment, invaded South Korea on 25 June 1950. The 98,000-strong army of the south was forced back, but U.S. troops from Japan quickly reinforced them. The United Nations supported South Korea, and troops of fifteen nations including Australia and New Zealand, were sent to Korea. This mixed army, first under General Douglas MacArthur and then General Matthew Ridgway, fought the North Koreans and 750,000 Chinese for three years.

Main phases of the war:

1–24 January 1951: Communist offensive. After heavy artillery barrages the Chinese attack forced Ridgway to abandon Inchon and Seoul, 4 January, and Wonju, 10 January. Strong U.N. air support and ground regrouping established a

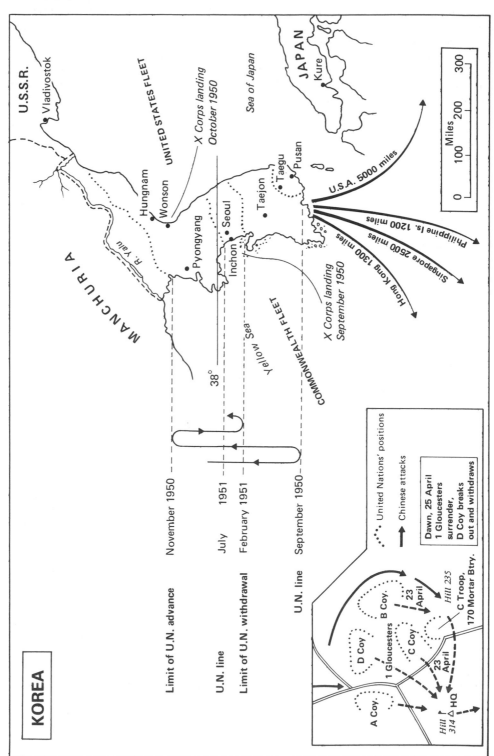

line 75 miles south of the 38th parallel, 24 January.

25 January–11 April 1951: U.N. counter-offensive. In steady assaults the U.N. armies pressed back the Chinese and North Koreans, winning control of the skies and much territory, until they recrossed the parallel, 28 March. Lin Piao lost his command and was replaced by Peng Teh-Huai. MacArthur wanted to attack Chinese bases in Manchuria and President Truman relieved him, 11 April. Ridgway became supreme commander.

2nd Communist offensive: 22 April–20 May. The Communists attacked from the "Iron Triangle" of Chorwon, Kumhwa and Pyongyang, putting 350,000 troops into an offensive against the Seoul area. The blow fell against the American Eighth Army (Van Fleet) which gave ground until a new line was established on 1 May. On 15 May the Communists renewed the offensive, wiping out the South Korean III Corps. U.S. marines and infantry were thrown in to seal the gap and after 5 days of savage fighting the offensive was stopped, 20 May.

2nd U.N. offensive: 21 May–15 June 1951. The American Eighth Army went on to the attack, exploiting the exhaustion of the Communist troops. Gradually the Americans and other U.N. troops retook all their lost territory, reaching the Iron Triangle, 11 June. By 15 June the United Nations held a line about 20 miles north of the 38th parallel.

The attrition period: 20 August 1951–27 July 1953. When peace talks broke down both sides settled down to spasmodic attacks and strengthening of defences by small-scale operations. An armistice was signed on 27 July. No peace treaty was ever negotiated.

The Korean War emphasized the critical importance of air power. The U.N. air forces were initially superior with their F-84s and F-86s, but the Communists brought in Mig-15s, the latest Soviet jet fighters. The training and efficiency of U.N. pilots, who were mostly American, made up for any inferiority in aircraft. They stopped all Communist efforts to establish bases south of the Yalu River. In air-to-air combat 1,108 Communist planes were shot down, 177 were probably destroyed and 1,027 were damaged. The United Nations lost 114 aircraft in aerial combat but another 1,213 to Communist anti-aircraft fire while giving close support to ground troops. Casualties: remarkable variations occur from source to source. The most reliable figures are these: United Nations, 118,515 killed, 264,591 wounded; 92,987 were captured. The great majority of prisoners died of mistreatment or starvation. U.S. casualties, 33,720 killed, 103,284 wounded. Of 10,218 Americans who fell into Communist hands, only 3,746 eventually returned. South Korea, estimated, 70,000 killed, 150,000 wounded, 80,000 captured. About 3 million South Korean civilians died. The Communist armies suffered 1,600,000 battle casualties, of which 60 per cent were Chinese: 171,000 were taken prisoner. *See* Inchon.

Kornspruit. *See* Sanna's Post.

Korygaum (*Third British –Mahratta War*) 1 January 1818. A force of only 1,000 chiefly native troops in British service, under Captain Staunton, was attacked by 25,000 Mahrattas (Baji Rao). The defenders held their ground all day and in the evening the Mahrattas, hearing that strong British reinforcements were approaching, retreated. Five of the eight British officers present were killed.

Kossovo I (*Turkish–Serbian War*) 15 June 1389. Turkish victory over the allied Serbians, Bosnians and Albanians (Lazar) secured Turkish dominion over Serbia and the neighbouring states, though the Turks' leader, Murad I, was killed. *See* Maritsa River; Nicopolis.

Kossovo II (*Turkish–Hungarian Wars*) 17–19 October 1747. In this sustained 3-day battle 80,000 Hungarians and Wallachians (John Huniades) faced a vastly superior number of Turks (Murad II). On the first day the Hungarians, though outnumbered, left their trenches to attack the Turks, the day ending with honours even. On the second day the Wallachians deserted to the Turks and the Hungarians could barely hold. On 19 October they had no option but to withdraw, having lost 17,000 killed and wounded. The Turks admitted a loss of 40,000. *See* Constantinople; Varna I.

Kotah (*Indian Mutiny against the British*) *22–30 March 1858*. General Roberts besieged the town, held by rebelling sepoys. The rajah himself held the citadel with loyal troops and assisted Roberts who bombarded the place and took it by storm on 30 October. *See* Delhi.

Kotzim (*Turkish–Polish Wars*) *22 September 1622*. The Turkish commander, Osman II, had no fewer than 300,000 troops in his attempt to subdue Chodkiewicz's 60,000 Poles. The Poles were faring badly when Chodkiewicz, old and exhausted, was forced to retire to his tent. Command devolved upon Labomirski, who routed the Turks and inflicted 30,000 casualties. *See* Vienna.

Kovel-Stanislav (*World War I*) *4 June–20 September 1916*. This campaign–battle is often called the Brusilov Offensive after the Russian general who engineered it; it was Russia's greatest success of the war. His four-army attack against the Austrian armies in the Ukraine caught the enemy commander, von Hotzendorf, by surprise. Lutz fell on 6 June, then Kovel and Bucovina, 17 June. By the end of June the Austrians and Germans had suffered 700,000 casualties. Hindenburg rushed fifteen German and eight Austrian divisions from other fronts. In the north, after savage fighting, von Linsingen checked the Russian advance in July. In the south Brusilov reached as far as Stanislav before the German–Austrian line held. Russia now had no more men, guns or ammunition to back Brusilov. Results: each side lost a million men, about half as prisoners or deserters. Austria was so weakened

that she submitted to German direction; Romania was encouraged to join the Allies and was overwhelmed by Germany; the Russians blamed the Czar for the check to Brusilov's battle. *See* Lemberg II; Naroch Lake.

Krakovicz (*Turkish–Hungarian Wars*) *17 January 1475*. Suleiman Pasha, in an untenable position near Lake Krakovicz, nevertheless had 100,000 men to oppose 40,000 Moldavian peasants (Stephen of Moldavia) supported by 7,000 Hungarian and Polish regulars. Few Turks escaped drowning or slaughter by sword, the Allies being completely victorious. *See* Scutari.

Krasnaoi (*Napoleonic Wars: Moscow campaign*) *17 November 1812*. The French army, retreating, had been engaged in a series of fights with Kutusov's pursuing Russians. At Krasnaoi Davout held a line which the Russians could not break, but though repulsed they inflicted heavy casualties. In the 3 days French casualties were 5,000 killed or wounded, 8,000 missing.

Krasnik (*World War I*) *23–25 August 1914*. The first Austrian attack in Galicia, fought to check the Russian offensive. *See* Galicia.

Kressenbrun (*Bohemian–Hungarian War*) *July 1260*. The climax to hostility between Ottokar II of Bohemia and Béla IV of Hungary. Béla reached the east bank of the March River, Moravia; Ottokar reached the west bank. Since neither army could cross the river in the face of the other, Ottokar offered to allow the Hungarians to cross unhindered. When they were in position and ready to fight, Ottokar attacked; the Hungarian army was destroyed as a fighting force. Béla escaped, but had to surrender Styria. *See* Marchfeld; Mohi.

Kringellen (*Danish–Swedish Wars*) *29 August 1612*. The mountain ambush and massacre by Norwegians of a Scottish force in Swedish service commanded by Colonel Conclair.

Kronia (*Turkish–Austrian Wars*) *August 1738*. The Austrians under Wallis and Neipperg defeated the Turkish invaders but were so weakened by casualties that they could not save Semendaia, Orsova and other fortresses from falling into Turkish hands.

Krotzka (*Turkish–Austrian Wars*) *23 July 1739*. Another Austrian–Turkish battle. El Hadj Muhammad Pasha had at least 100,000 Turks to the Austrian strength of 56,000. Count Wallis's vanguard was attacked when approaching Kotzin, but the main army held firm under continuous onslaught from 5 a.m. until sunset before retiring. Austrian casualties, 5,700 killed, 4,500 wounded. Turkish casualties unknown. *See* Ceşme.

Kula Gulf, *between New Georgia and Kolombangara Island, south Pacific (World War II)* 6 *July and 12 July 1943*. Battles between ships of the U.S. Third Fleet and the Japanese navy. The Americans lost a cruiser and two destroyers, the Japanese three warships. *See* Solomon Islands.

Kulevcha, *near Varna (Turkish–Russian Wars)*. The Russians (Diebitsch) trapped the Turks (Reschid Pasha) in a defile at Kalevcha and after a struggle killed or wounded 5,000 of their 40,000 strength. The way was now open for a Russian advance deep into Turkey. *See* Konya; Varna II.

Kulm-Priesten (*Napoleonic Wars: Leipzig campaign*) *29–30 August 1813*. The Allied Austrians, Russians and Prussians (commander-in-chief, Schwartzenberg) were retreating after their defeat at Dresden. They occupied Kulm to check their pursuit, but Vandamme drove them out on the 29th. Vandamme had expected reinforcements, but they did not arrive and the Allies sensed that he was now on the defensive. The Austrians and Russians attacked him frontally, the Prussians in the rear, and he was routed, losing 6,000 killed, 7,000 prisoners and 48 guns; Vandamme was wounded and captured. Allied losses, 5,000. *See* Dennewitz; Dresden.

Kulikovo (*Russian Revolt against Mongols*) *8 September 1380*. Dmitri Donskoi, Grand Duke of Moscow, organized other Russian princes in a revolt against the Mongolian Tartars. Near the source of the Don they won an overwhelming victory against an immense Mongolian army; it broke the Mongolian military reputation. Kulikovo is to the Russians what Waterloo is to the British.

Kumai (*Japanese Civil Wars*) *February 1355*. A victory for the Emperor Gomarakami against the rebel troops of Moronishi and Tokiushi.

Kumamoto (*Japanese Satsuma Rebellion*) *22 February–14 April 1876*. Kumamoto castle was held for the Emperor by Tani Tateki against 15,000 Satsuma rebels (Saigo). General Kurodo attacked the rebels in the rear, but the Satsumas maintained their siege. On 14 April, with the garrison starving, Kurodo brought up every available soldier and after great effort drove off the besiegers.

Kumanovo, *near Skiplje (First Balkan War*) *24–26 October 1912*. The second defeat of the Turks; the Serbs beat them back in a 3-day battle and then pressed on to take Monastir (Bitolj) on 18 November. *See* Kirk-Kilissa; Luleburgaz.

Kumasi (*British–Ashanti Wars*) *4 February 1874 and 18 January 1896*. The climax to the Ashanti campaign of General Wolseley who led 2,500 troops against the redoubtable native warriors of Ashanti's king, Kofi (or Koffee) Karikari. The second battle during the fourth Ashanti war 22 years later, was won by General Scott, after which the area became a British protectorate.

Kunersdorf (*Seven Years' War*) *12 August 1759*. A major battle between the Prussians and the Allied Austrians and Russians. Frederick the Great, with 40,000 men, attacked the Russians (Soltykov) in flank and captured 180 guns. Then, against the advice of his brilliant cavalry commander, Seidlitz, he attacked the Austrian position on the Allied left. The Austrians, now deserted by the Russians, held their ground and bringing all their artillery to bear at close range and on selected targets routed the Prussians with a loss of 20,000 men. The Allies lost 24,000, but had 80,000 to start with. *See* Kay; Maxen; Minden.

Kunobitza (*Turkish–Hungarian Wars*) *May 1443*. The Hungarians (John Hunniades) routed the Turks (Amurath II) and gained a 10-year truce.

Kurdlah (*Mahratta–Hyderabad War*) *11 March 1795*. A conflict between the army of the Mahratta Confederacy (Madhao Rao II) and that of the Nizam of Hyderabad. The Hyderabad troops were winning when the Nizam inexplicably left the field; his troops followed him and the Mahrattas turned the retreat into a rout.

Kursk, *known as Operation Citadel to the Germans* (*World War II*) *5–13 July 1943*. The largest tank battle and one of the great conflicts of history. The Russians, under Zhukov and Vassilevsky, held the Kursk salient against Germans under Model and Hoth. No fewer than 6,000 tanks and 4,000 aircraft were involved in the relentless battle; on the first day the Russians claimed to have destroyed 586 German tanks. In the previous 3 months the Russians had brought into the salient 500,000 railway wagons of supplies, making Kursk into a massive strongpoint. The Germans penetrated 30 miles into the salient, but when the battle ended they were still 100 miles from cutting if off. German losses were put at 70,000 killed, 2,900 tanks, 195 mobile guns, 844 field guns, 1,392 aircraft and 5,000 motor vehicles. Any possibility of

the Germans fighting a holding battle was eliminated when the Russians retook the cities of Orel and Belgorod on 5 August. The Russians had suffered at least 160,000 casualties, but by winning Kursk they had, in effect, won the war. *See* Soviet Union.

Kut-al-Amara (*World War I*) *28 September 1915; 8 December 1915 to 29 April 1916 and January–February 1917*. Marching up the Tigris towards Baghdad with 11,000 British and Indian troops, General Townshend encountered a strong Turkish position at Kut-al-Amara. Manoeuvring cleverly, he routed them but most of the Turks escaped north to Ctesiphon. Following, Townshend was repulsed and rather than risk defeat on the march held his ground at Kut, fortifying a tongue of land on the Tigris. Three relief forces tried to get through to him: Aylmer, forced back on 18–21 January with a loss of 6,000 men; Aylmer, on 8 March, a loss of 3,000; Gorringe, beaten back on 22 April. With his 10,000 survivors starving and diseased, Townshend surrendered Kut, 29 April. In the third battle of Kut, January–February 1917, General Maude recaptured the city and went on to take Baghdad, q.v.

Kutna Hora (*or Kuttenberg*) (*Hungarian–Austrian War or Hussite War*) *6 January 1422*. Between Sigismund, King of Hungary and Bohemia, and the Holy Roman Emperor with a great army including 50,000 Germans and Jan Zizka, who had only 25,000 men — the Taborite heretics of Bohemia. Zizka was one of the great military minds. The strength of his military organization was his wheeled artillery and his tactical use of baggage wagons as mobile forts. Forty-five miles south-east of Prague Zizka's lagers stopped the baffled enemy with heavy losses. Then his cavalry made fierce dashes into Sigismund's troops, routing them with further heavy losses. Sigismund fell back. Zizka lost his remaining eye at Kutna Hora but retained control of the Hussites. *See* Prague I.

Kwajalein-Eniwetok (*World War II*) *14 February and 18–22 February 1944*. Kwajalein and Eniwetok are island atolls of the Marshall Islands. U.S. marines took Kwajalein and its twin, Roe-Namur. The Japanese (Admiral Kobayashi) fought with their usual ferocity and 7,300 were killed. The marines had 307 killed and 1,547 wounded. The rapid conquest induced the American commander, Admiral Nimitz, to attack Eniwetok, where a further 1,700 Japanese and 333 Americans were killed. *See* Mariana Islands; Tarawa-Makin.

Kyushu (*Mongol invasion of Japan*) *1281*. Seizing the islands of Tsushima and Iki, the 50,000 Mongol invaders of Kublai Khan were checked in northern Kyushu by Japanese forts and at sea the small Japanese ships outfought the lumbering Chinese and Korean ships. After 2 months' fighting only 2,000 Mongols survived.

La Belle Famille. *See* Niagara.

La Bicocca, *near Milan* (*French Wars in Italy*) *27 April 1522*. The French and their Swiss and German mercenaries made a stand against the Spaniards and Italians who were trying to drive them out of Italy. The Swiss–Germans made an extraordinary charge against the Spanish and Italian enemy, who were entrenched behind hedges. The attackers broke through to the main enemy line which was impregnable atop a slope defended by massed pikemen. No fewer than 3,000 Swiss and Germans were killed before the attack faded away. The French and their defeated allies withdrew from Lombardy. *See* Marichano; Pavia V.

Lade (*Ionian War*) *494 BC*. A Persian fleet of 600 ships was blockading Miletus under Artapernes; 353 allied Chian, Lesbian and Samian (both Greek states) ships attempted to raise the siege, but the Samians, bribed by the Persians, deserted at the beginning of the action and the other Greeks were defeated with heavy loss. The Chians fought gallantly. *See* Ephesus; Marathon.

Lade *201 BC*. An indecisive naval battle between the Rhodian fleet (Theophiliscus) and the Macedonians (Heraclides).

Ladysmith (*Second British–Boer War*) *2 November 1899–27 February 1900*. A siege and battle. General Joubert's Boers held 12,000 British troops (Sir George White) in the town. Having plenty of heavy artillery, the Boers bombarded Ladysmith continually until 6 January when a raiding party under de Villiers attempted to force the British lines at Waggon Hill and Caesar's Camp; they were supported by several thousand Boer marksmen posted on the heights. At the end of a day's fighting the Boers withdrew, having lost 800 men. Bombardment was resumed until Buller relieved the town, 27 February. Apart from deaths by disease, the garrison lost 89 officers and 805 men. *See* Kimberley; Mafeking.

La Favorita (*Napoleon's Italian campaigns*) *16 January 1797*. Between the French (Napoleon) and the Austrians (Provers). With Austrian-held Mantua besieged by the French, Provers attempted to drive off the French, who were also attacked by the defenders in a major sortie. Napoleon, recently successful at Rivoli, made a forced march and attacked with such elan that Provers was overwhelmed and surrendered with 5,000 men. *See* Lodi.

La Fère Champenoise (*Allied invasion of France against Napoleon*) *25 March 1814*. An Allied army was marching on Paris when Mortier and Marmont combined forces — 30,000 — to block the advance. Losing 5,000 men and many guns, the French were forced into retreat. This was the last action in the north before Napoleon's abdication.

La Forbie, *near Acre (Sixth Crusade)* 17 October 1244. Between the Frankish Christians and their Syrian–Turks allies against the Egyptian army strengthened by 10,000 savage nomadic Khwarismians from Syria. The Turks bolted and the Frankish Christians were then cut down in thousands. Only sixty-two of the 600 knights reached safety. La Forbie was the only battle of the Sixth Crusade.

Lagos I, *southern Portugal (War of the Grand Alliance)* 17 June 1693. Sir George Rooke, with a squadron of twenty-three Dutch and English ships convoying 400 merchantmen to the Mediterranean, was attacked by a French fleet of seventy-one. The French destroyed ninety-one merchantmen and three warships; only Rooke's skilful manoeuvring saved the rest of the convoy.

Lagos II, *southern Portugal (Seven Years' War)* 7–18 August (intermittently) 1759. A victory for Admiral Boscawen who destroyed the French fleet commanded by De la Clue.

La Hogue (*War of the Grand Alliance*) 19–20 May 1692. A combined Dutch and English fleet (Allemande and Russell respectively) with ninety-six ships gave battle to a French fleet of sixty-four large ships and forty-seven smaller ones (de Tourville). After heavy losses on both sides the French fleet was dispersed; on 20 May Rooke, meeting the French, destroyed 16 warships and several others.

Lahore (*First Tartar invasion of India*) 1296. The Mongols, 100,000-strong under Amir Daood, and the army of Ala-ud-din, King of Delhi, commanded by his brother, Alaf Khan. The Mongols, defeated, lost 12,000 men.

Lake Erie (*British–American War 1812–14*) 10 September 1813. An American squadron under Commodore Perry destroyed the smaller English flotilla of six schooners. Casualties:

British, 134; American, 123. *See* French-town.

Laing's Nek (*First British–Boer War*) 28 January 1881. General Colley, with 1,100 men, made a suicidal frontal attack against strong Boer positions and lost 198 killed or wounded. Boer casualties, 41.

Lake George (*Seven Years' War*) 8 September 1755. Between 1,500 French and Indians (Dieskau) and 2,500 New England militia (Colonel Johnson). Johnson had sent a party to relieve Fort Lyman; the French ambushed it and drove the surviving New Englanders back to camp. Dieskau rashly committed himself to an attack on the camp and was beaten off with a loss of 400. Most of Johnson's 216 killed and 96 wounded fell in the ambush. *See* Beauséjour; Oswego.

Lake Kerguel (*Tartar invasion of Russia*) July 1391. With forces reported to be 300,000 each, the Russians (Tokatmich) and Tartars (Tamerlane) met in a bloody 8-hour battle which left the Tartars victorious.

Lake Regillus 497 BC. Details of this battle are legendary rather than factual. The Tarquinian family, making a last attempt to recover the throne of Rome, were defeated by the Romans (Aulus Postumius). Legend (of Greek origin) claims that the Romans, with the battle at crisis point, found at their head two young men on white horses, said to be the gods Castor and Pollux, who inspired them to victory.

Lake Vadimonian (*Gallic invasion of Italy*) 283 BC. A Roman legion under Publius Dolabella encountered an allied Etruscan–Gaul army as the Etruscans were crossing the Tiber 45 miles from Rome. He annihilated them, then attacked the Gauls, inflicted many casualties and routed them. There was no further resistance to Roman supremacy in central Italy. *See* Heraclea; Sentinum.

Landau (*War of Spanish Succession*) *19 June–10 September 1702*. The Austrians (Prince Louis of Baden) besieged the French-held fortress which, under de Melac, resisted gallantly until 10 September. *See* Höchstadt I; Luzzara.

Landen. *See* Neerwinden.

Landeshut, *Silesia* **(*Seven Years' War*)** *23 June 1760*. Between the Austrians (von Laudon, serving Maria Theresa) and the Prussians (de la Motte-Fouque, a general of Frederick the Great). Laudon enticed Motte-Fouque out of the fortress of Landeshut and occupied it himself. Frederick ordered Motte-Fouque to retake the place. It was too much for 13,000 Prussians against 30,000 Austrians and the Prussian army was destroyed. The defeat took Frederick himself into Silesia. *See* Leignitz II; Maxen.

Landshut, *Germany* **(*Napoleonic Wars: Austrian campaign*)** *21 April 1809*. After their defeat at the hands of the French at Abensberg, the Austrians under Archduke Charles Louis fell back. General Hiller, with 36,000 men, crossed the Isar towards the Danube and took up positions at Landshut. Marshal Lannes smashed the Austrian rearguard, 21 April, then across a burning bridge stormed the city of Landshut. Then Marshal Massena approached Landshut down the right bank of the Isar. Hiller lost 9,000 men and most of his guns and baggage. *See* Eggmühl.

Landskrone (*Danish–Swedish Wars*) *14 July 1676*. Charles XI and his Swedish army decisively defeated the Danes (Christian V).

Langensalza (*Seven Weeks' War*) *27 June 1866*. Between the Prussians (General Flics) and the Hanoverians (George, King of Hanover). Each side had about 12,000 men. The Prussians, attacking the Hanoverian position, were repulsed with a loss of 1,400 killed or wounded and 900 prisoners. However,

Prussian strength in the area was overwhelming and George surrendered on 29 June. Hannover became a sovereign part of Prussia. *See* Dybbol; Münchengratz; Sadowa.

Langport, *Somerset* **(*English Civil War*)** *10 July 1645*. The Parliamentarians (Fairfax) routed the Royalists into Bridgwater with a loss of 300 killed and 1,400 prisoners. *See* Naseby; Stow-on-the-Wold.

Langside, *Glasgow* **(*Scottish rebellion against Mary*)** *13 May 1568*. The forces of the Scottish Regent, Murray, attacked the army of Mary Queen of Scots, 6,000-strong, and dispersed them with a loss of 300. Murray had only one casualty. Mary fled to England. *See* Carberry Hill.

Laos Civil War *1953–73*. The main belligerents in the war were the Royalists and the Pathet Lao Communists who numbered 35,000 at their peak. At times the North Vietnamese Army supported the Pathet Lao while the U.S. Air Force made many bombing raids for the Royalists against the Pathet Lao. In addition, the South Vietnamese forces entered Laos to attack the North Vietnamese. It is said that fighting took place on every day of the 20-year period of the war. By the time a cease-fire was signed on 21 February 1973 Communist troops controlled most of the country; the defeat of South Vietnam by North Vietnam in 1975 brought the Pathet Lao total control. Casualties, both military and civilian, were very heavy, but no records were kept.

La Peubla I (*French–Mexican War*) *5 May 1862*. General Lorencez, with only 7,500 French troops, foolishly tried to take a ridge held by 12,000 Mexicans (Negreti). They were savagely beaten back, losing 456 killed or wounded.

La Peubla II (*French–Mexican War*) *4–17 May 1863*. General Forey, with 25,000 men, laid siege to the city, held by a Mexican garrison (Ortega). Too weak completely to encircle the place, Forey took one fort after another in a deliberate piecemeal campaign. Resistance was bitter and French losses were heavy. On 8 May Marshal Bazaine defeated Comonfort's Mexican relief column of 10,500 men and this resulted in Ortega's surrender.

Larcay (*Chilean Revolution*) December 1829. A victory for the Unitarians (or Pelucones) over the Government party (Zasters).

Largs (*Norse invasion of Scotland*) 2 October 1263. The Norse fleet of 160 ships was driven ashore near Largs by violent storms; Haco, the Norse leader, landed a force to protect the shipwrecked crews. When this force was routed by the Scots, Haco was forced to abandon the invasion.

Larissa (*Third Macedonian War*) 171 BC. Between the Romans, 40,000, under Crassus, and 43,000 Macedonians (Perseus). The Romans were defeated, losing 2,800 killed and 600 prisoners.

Larissus, The (*Wars of the Achaean League*) 209 BC. The allied Aetolians and Eleans were defeated by the Achaeans (Philopoemen).

La Rochelle (*Hundred Years' War*) 22 June 1372. An English fleet (Pembroke), en route to relieve La Rochelle, was intercepted by a Spanish fleet (Becrenegra) and entirely captured or destroyed. *See* Margate; Sluys.

La Rochelle (*Huguenot Rebellion*) 1627–8. The principal Huguenot fortress in France, La Rochelle was besieged by the Royal troops, under Richelieu, in August 1627. The garrison, led by the mayor, Guiton, gallantly defended the place, but the assassination of the Duke of Buckingham prevented the hoped-for arrival of English help and after holding out for 14 months La Rochelle surren-

dered, 28 October 1628. *See* Castelnaudary; Ivry-la-Bataille.

La Rothière, *north-east France* (*Allied campaign in France*) 1 February 1814. Between 32,000 French (Napoleon) and 100,000 Prussians, Russians and Wurtembergers (Blucher). Blucher attacked Napoleon, who held strong positions. Late in the afternoon Blucher captured La Rothière village, but Napoleon with the Young Guard retook it and the battle ended with Napoleon in possession of the field. Casualties: French, 5,000; Allies, 8,000. *See* Brienne; Champaubert-Montmirail; Montereau.

Las Guasimas, *Cuba* (*Spanish–American War*) 24 June 1898. The ridge of Las Guasimas was held by 1,500 Spaniards (General Linares) against 1,000 Americans (Wheeler) aided by 800 Cubans (Garcia). The Spaniards were driven back. Wheeler had 16 killed and 25 wounded. *See* El Caney; Santiago de Cuba.

Las Navas de Tolosa (*Spanish–Muslim Wars*) 16 July 1212. Between an army of Moors (said to number 600,000) under Muhammad al Nasin and the allied armies of the Kings of Castile, Leon, Aragon, Navarre and Portugal. At least 160,000 Moors were killed. *See* Alacos; Cordova; Muret.

Las Salinas (*Spanish conquest of Peru*) 20 April 1538. Almagro's troops were routed by those of Francisco Pizarro, who then executed Almagro.

Laswari (or *Laswaree*) (*Second British–Mahratta War*) 1 November 1803. A violent battle between 10,000 British under General Lake, and Scindhia's army of 9,000 infantry and 5,000 cavalry. Scindhia's veterans made a gallant defence, standing their ground until 7,000 had fallen. The survivors then surrendered. The British, who lost about 800, took 72 guns and vast quantities of stores. *See* Alighar; Assaye; Farrukhbad.

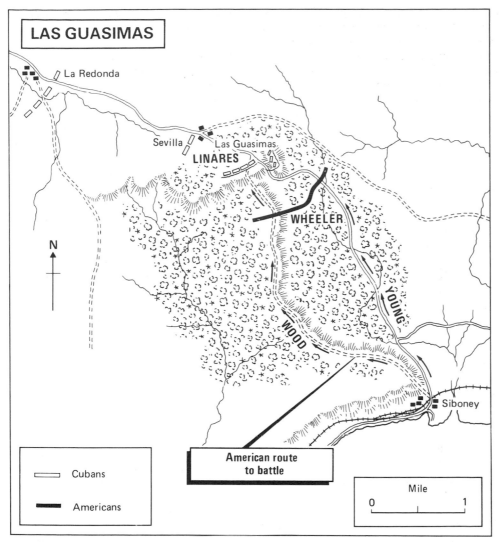

LAS GUASIMAS

La Redonda

Sevilla
Las Guasimas
LINARES

WHEELER

N

YOUNG

WOOD

Siboney

American route to battle

Cubans

Americans

Mile

0   1

Laupen, *near Berne (Swiss–Burgundian Wars) 21 June 1339.* About 15,000 Burgundians (Count Gerard of Vallangin) laid siege to Laupen which the Swiss, calling in volunteers from three cantons, at once began to contest. The Burgundian knights and their infantry supporters were no match for the disciplined halberdiers and pikemen led by Rudolph von Erlach. The Swiss, though outnumbered, even attacked the enemy cavalry — and defeated them. Laupen, together with Bannockburn (1314) and Crécy (1346), showed that mounted knights could not prevail against good infantry. *See* Sempach.

Lautulae (Second Samnite War) 316 BC. The Samnites (Pontius) practically annihilated the Roman army of Fabius Maximus. *See* Caudine Forks; Sentinum.

Lava Beds, *northern California (Modoc Indian Rebellion) 22 January then 14 April–28 May 1873.* Under Chief Jack, the Modoc Indians fought against resettlement in a reservation. Near Tule Lake seventy-five warriors with 150 women and children held the Modoc Line. The Modocs beat off an assault under General Canby, 22 January, inflicting sixty-nine casualties. On 11 April Canby and a missionary were murdered during peace talks. On 14 April General Jefferson Davis, using artillery, began an attack which was to last 6 weeks and cost the Americans another eight-two lives. Chief Jack was executed.

Lawfeldt (or Lauffeld) (War of Spanish Succession) 2 July 1747. Between the Allied Austrians and British (Cumberland) and the French (Saxe). The French three times carried the village of Lawfeldt and the Allies each time recaptured it. At noon the British centre was driven in and defeat was imminent when Sir John Ligonier led a cavalry charge that enabled Cumberland to withdraw in good order. Casualties: Allies, 5,620; French, about 10,000. *See* Bergen op Zoom I; Rocourt.

Lebanon Civil War 1958. The President of Lebanon, the Maronite Christian, Camille Chamoun, was unpopular with both Christian and Muslim Lebanese. They resented his pro-Western policy during the Suez crisis of 1956 and they suspected that he proposed to amend the constitution in order to remain in office. In May 1958 the Muslims of Tripoli rose in armed revolt and the rebellion spread to the Muslim sectors of Beirut and Sidon and to Baalbek. Syrian troops entered the country in support of the Lebanese Muslims. President Chamoun appealed to the United States for military help and American marines landed at Beirut on 14 July. Fighting between the Muslim insurgents and the Lebanese Army, which was Christian-led, continued until General Chehab took over from Chamoun in September. The American troops saw little action, suffered few casualties and withdrew by 25 October. Lebanese casualties amounted to 3,500.

Lebanon Civil War 1975–81. This war is often, but mistakenly, stated to have ended in 1976. In fact, it merely changed direction in 1977 because of the involvement of other belligerents, and hostilities were incessant between 1975 and 1981. Lebanon had been in a state of political tension since 1943 because of the distribution of power between Christians and Muslims. The presence of 250,000 Palestinian refugees, living as a state within a state and dominated by the Palestine Liberation Organization (PLO), increased the tension. In mid-March 1975 fighting broke out between Christians and Muslims in Tripoli and it spread to Beirut in April. On 15 May the government of Rashid Solh resigned and President Franjieh appointed a military government under Brigadier Rifai; it lasted 3 days. On 30 June Rashid Karami formed a government, but he was unable to stop the fighting. When the P.L.O. tried to take control of Beirut the fighting intensified. The Christian forces, the Phalangists, attacked Palestinian refugee camps, and the P.L.O. attacked Christian towns. After a brief cease-fire, fighting continued and the Syrian army occupied the Bekaa Valley against P.L.O. resistance. On 21 October the 56th cease-fire came into effect and the 30,000-strong Arab Deterrent Force, composed mainly of Syrian troops, policed the country. In this phase of the war 45,000 people were killed and 100,000 wounded; about 350,000 Lebanese emigrated.

Fighting broke out again in February 1977 between the Lebanese Forces (actually Phalangists, no connection with the national army) and Palestinians, mostly in the south. Israel supported the Christians. On 16 March the Druze leader Kamal Jumblatt was murdered, provoking Druze attacks on Christian villages. In February 1978 Syrian forces were fighting the Phalangists. Throughout the period the P.L.O. had been making terrorist attacks against Israeli settlements; in retaliation Israel, on 14 March, launched Operation Litani into southern Lebanon to destroy P.L.O. bases. The Israeli Army withdrew when troops of the U.N. Interim Forces in Lebanon (UNIFIL) took over policing of the south. In July Syrian artillery bombarded Beirut in revenge for the murder of Tony Franjieh, son of the former president and a friend of President Assad of Syria. Throughout the period 1978–81 Christians and Muslims were at war against each other; the Syrians, who now backed the P.L.O. against Israel, were also at war against the Lebanese Christians; P.L.O. attacks against Israel continued. Between October 1976 and June 1982 the approximate casualties were: Christians, 20,000; Lebanese Muslims, 18,000; Syrians, 1,300; Israelis, 380.

Lebanon War 1982 (*for the Israelis, Operation Peace for Galilee*). Lebanon was the scene of the war, but was not involved as a combatant. The war was fought between Israel and the allied Syrian and Palestine Liberation Organization (P.L.O.) forces. Israel, having endured P.L.O. terrorist raids from Lebanon for 12 years, moved an army of 60,000 into Lebanon on 6 June 1982. The main objective of the land and sea assault was to drive the P.L.O. (Yasser Arafat) out of southern Lebanon; a secondary aim was to push the Syrians from the Bekaa Valley and to destroy their many missile sites. Opposing the Israelis were about 15,000 P.L.O. fighters and 60,000 Syrians. Both forces were heavily armed with the latest Soviet equipment.

The P.L.O. could not have been expected to withstand the Israeli pressure. Its fighters did best when they used guerrilla tactics and did not attempt to fight as a conventional army. The Syrians did badly because they were unable to read the course of a battle and could not anticipate Israeli moves.

Israel's Chief-of-Staff, General Eitan, planned his advance along three lines — the coast road (Major-General Adam), the ridge and upper western slopes of the Lebanon range (Lieutenant-General Drori), and the Bekaa Valley. On the coast Tyre was captured on 7 June, Sidon on 8 June, Damour on 9 June and Beirut,

the P.L.O. stronghold, was encircled by 14 June. In the centre the Litani River bridges and Beaufort Castle were captured. In the east Israeli and Syrian tank units were embattled from 7 June.

The air battles between the Israeli and Syrian air forces and the destruction of the Syrian missile sites were a remarkable illustration of Israeli military prowess. Within 2 hours on 9 June the Israelis destroyed nineteen missile batteries without loss to themselves. Israelis in U.S.-built F-15s, F-16s and A-4 Skyhawks met Syrian pilots in Russian-made MiG 21s, Mig 23s, Mig 25s and Sukhoi 7s. By the end of 9 June, ninety Syrian planes were destroyed; only one Israeli aircraft was lost. The revolutionary Israeli tank, the Merkava, was used for the first time and mastered the advanced Soviet T-72. The Syrians lost seventy-two tanks in combat in the Bekaa Valley.

The 10,000 P.L.O. fighters besieged in Beirut agreed to an evacuation by sea; this movement began on 28 August and was complete in 10 days.

Hostilities between Israel and the P.L.O.–Syrians ceased at this time, but the Israelis could not withdraw from the south for fear that other P.L.O. fighters from northern Lebanon or the Syrians would occupy the area. They first made a defensive line on the Awali River, then on the Zaharani River and later the Litani River. Casualties to 28 August 1982; Israel, 368 killed, 2,383 wounded; Syrian, 600 killed, 3,800 wounded; P.L.O., between 2,000 and 3,000 killed and as many wounded; 9,000 were captured.

Le Bourget (*French–German War*) *27–30 October 1870*. The French, besieged in Paris, made a determined sortie, carried the village of Le Bourget and held until driven out by the Prussian Guards, leaving 1,200 prisoners with the Prussians, who lost 378. *See* Gravelotte; Metz; Sedan.

Le Cateau (*World War I*) *26 August 1914*. The biggest battle fought by the British Army since Waterloo. General

Smith-Dorrien, commanding XI Corps during the retreat from Mons, blocked the onrushing Germans for 11 hours, thus enabling the B.E.F. to escape the German sweep. The Corps of three and a half divisions lost 8,077 men and thirty-six guns. *See* Frontiers of France; Marne River I.

Lechfeld, *near Augsburg* **(German Internal Wars) 955.** The Germans (Otto the Great) smashed the invading Magyars (from Hungary) in a furious 10-hour battle. The defeated barbarians fell back and never again threatened Germany. *See* Crotone; Riade.

Leck, The **(***Thirty Years' War***) 5 April 1632.** Between the Swedes and German Protestants, 26,000 under Gustavus Adolphus, and Count Tilly's 30,000 Imperialists led by Count Tilly and Maximilian of Bavaria. Gustavus' engineers were placing a bridge to cross the Leck while his artillery kept the Imperialists away. In the artillery duel that followed, Tilly was mortally wounded and his troops retired; the Swedes crossed unmolested and occupied Augsburg, Munich and all south Bavaria. *See* Breitenfeld; Lutzen; Nordlingen.

L'Écluse (*Hundred Years' War***) April 1340.** The English fleet surprised the French in a narrow channel and routed them with a reported loss of ninety ships and 30,000 men. *See* Sluys.

Leghorn *31 March 1653*. A Dutch fleet of sixteen (Van Gelen) destroyed Commodore Appleton's six British ships, but Van Gelen was mortally wounded.

Legnano (*Wars of the Lombard League***) 29 May 1176.** Between the Italian cities organized in the Lombard League aided by Venice and the Pope, and the army of Frederick Barbarossa, King of Germany and Italy. The allied infantry defeated Frederick's feudal cavalry and Frederick fled.

Leicester (*English Civil War***) 31 May 1645.** Charles I marched out of his Oxford headquarters and headed north in an attempt to re-establish himself there. Also, he hoped to divert from Oxford the parliamentary force under General Fairfax. The Royalists stormed Leicester and despite heavy casualties captured and sacked the city. Fairfax and Cromwell hurried to intercept Charles's Royalists. *See* Naseby.

Leipzig I (*Thirty Years' War***) 7 September 1631.** A major battle between Gustavus Adolphus and 20,000 Swedes aided by 20,000 Saxons (John George, Elector of Saxony) and 44,000 Imperialists commanded by Tilly. Tilly's right routed the Saxons, who bolted with the Elector at their head. On the left the Swedes had triumphed and in the centre they repulsed the Imperialists. When the enemy right flank troops returned from chasing the Saxons the Swedes so overwhelmed them that only four regiments held their ground until nightfall. Gustavus captured all the enemy's guns, thus emphasizing his victory, which saved the Protestant cause. Casualties: Imperialists, 8,000 killed and wounded, 5,000 prisoners; Allies, 2,700, of whom only 700 were Swedes. *See* Lützen.

Leipzig II, *the so-called Battle of the Nations* **(***Napoleon's Leipzig campaign***) 16–19 October 1813.** Between the French and the Great Coalition. Napoleon, holding Leipzig with 155,000 men, was faced with 100,000 Austrians and Prussians (Schwartzemberg) and 60,000 Prussians (Blucher). On 16 October Schwartzemberg attacked positions held by 115,000 of Napoleon's men and at nightfall had made no impression. Simultaneously, Blucher attacked Marmont's corps, which, though only 24,000-strong, held fast all day. Casualties were great, the Allies losing 35,000 men, the French 27,000. Both sides were strongly reinforced that night, so that next day the Allies had nearly 300,000, including Bernadotte's Swedes. Napoleon had now

150,000 men. On 18 October Napoleon attacked to open a road of retreat and was repulsed everywhere; driven back into Leipzig, the French retired by the only bridge still serviceable. The corps under Poniatowski, left to cover the retreat, was almost annihilated and its commander killed. The French, beaten but still disciplined, retreated. Casualties: French, 60,000 in the 3 days; Allies, 52,000. *See* Dennewitz; Hanau.

Leitskau (*Napoleonic Wars: Leipzig campaign*) *27 August 1813*. A Prussian division (Hirschberg) helped by Cossacks defeated General Girard's 5,000 French, who ceased to exist as a formation.

Le Mans (*French–German War*) *10–12 January 1870*. The Germans (Prince Charles Frederick), though outnumbered three to one by the French (Chanzy), routed them so completely that they were no longer effective as an army; the Germans took 20,000 prisoners. *See* Bapaume; Paris II; St. Quentin II.

Lemberg (*or Lvov*), *Galicia* (*World War I*) *1914–17*. The Russians captured this city on 3 September 1914 but lost it to a German–Austrian counter-attack on 22 June 1915. General Brusilov, with an army of Finns, Poles and Siberians, tried to retake the place on 1 July but he was counter-attacked on 19 July and his army collapsed. The first Russian advance was known as the Kerensky Offensive.

Leningrad (*World War II*) *1941–4*. The great city of Leningrad was the chief objective of the German northern campaign, summer 1941. Commanded by Field-Marshal von Leeb, the Germans swept through Russian positions while the twelve divisions of Finnish Army (Field-Marshal von Mannerheim) threatened Leningrad from the north. General Voroshilov drew 200,000 troops into Leningrad where Khozin became commandant. German artillery opened fire on 4 September. The Russians attacked at

Lake Ilmen in February 1942, but this attempt to break the siege was fruitless. The Germans were no more successful in breaching the defences, even under Manstein who had been successful in the Crimea. Manstein, Leeb, Busch and Kuechler all tried to take Leningrad. After a siege of 31 months the Russians, attacking along a front of 120 miles in January 1944, opened a road to Leningrad. The Russian advance was not checked until March, when Model stopped it along the Estonian border. However, the Finns were isolated and on 19 September they agreed to Russian armistice terms. German Army Group North held out until the spring of 1945.

Lens (*Thirty Years' War*) *20 August 1648*. The Great Conde, having only 14,000 men and much weaker than the Austrians (Archduke Leopold), feigned retreat, drew the Austrians after him and then turned on them. The Austrian defeat was complete; they lost 4,000 killed, 6,000 prisoners and all artillery and supplies. *See* Arras I; Rocroi; Zusmarshausen.

Leontini (*Second Punic War*) *211 BC*. Three Roman legions (Marcellus) attacked the stronghold of the Nationalist party in Sicily, held by a garrison of Syracusans and Roman deserters. On capturing the place, Marcellus had 2,000 Roman deserters summarily executed by sword.

Lepanto I, *south-west Greece* (*Turkish–Venetian Wars*) *28 July 1499*. The Ottoman fleet defeated the Venetian Navy, thus forcing Venice to give up some of her Grecian trading posts. This was the first major Turkish naval victory.

Lepanto II (*Cyprus War*) *7 October 1571*. The famous battle off Lepanto (Navpaktos) in south-western Greece between Don John of Austria and the Turkish admiral–general Ali Pasha. Selim II's Turks had attacked the Christian Venetian-held island of Cyprus. A specially formed Holy League of Pope Pius V and Philip II of Spain asked Don

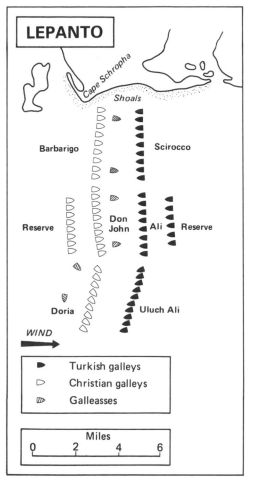

LEPANTO

Cape Schropha

Shoals

Barbarigo

Scirocco

Reserve

Don John

Ali

Reserve

Doria

Uluch Ali

WIND

▶ Turkish galleys
▷ Christian galleys
🝙 Galleasses

Miles
0   2   4   6

John, the 24-year-old half-brother of Philip, to assemble a fleet. Don John brought together 316 ships, including 208 galleys and six double-galleys or galleasses, with 50,000 crew and 30,000 veteran soldiers. The Turks had 250 galleys, manned by 16,000 soldiers and 82,000 crew. The 3-hour ramming and boarding battle was furious and the air was thick with arrows. The Turks lost 130 galleys captured and 80 destroyed; their dead totalled 25,000, including the admiral, and 5,000 were taken prisoner. Don John's fleet suffered 7,500 killed and 17 ships were lost. More than 15,000 Christian slaves were freed from the galleys. Lepanto was the greatest battle since Actium in 31 BC, and the last great sea battle of oared ships.

Lerida I (*Thirty Years' War*) *September 1642*. The French (Lamothe-Houdancourt) defeated the Spanish army (Leganez), the victory giving the French possession of Roussillon. *See* Lens.

Lerida II (*Thirty Years' War*) *12 May–17 June 1647*. The French under Conde besieged the Spanish garrison (Britt) on 12 May. The 4,000 Spaniards made several spirited sorties and about the middle of June the approach of a large Spanish relief army forced Conde either to assault or to raise the siege. He withdrew on 17 September. *See* Lens; Rocroi.

Leucopetra (*Wars of the Achaean League*) *146 BC*. A thrusting Roman Army (Lucius Mummus) overwhelmed the Greeks of the Achaean League (Daicus) and as a result many Greek cities opened their gates to the Roman legions.

Leuctra (*Greek City-states Wars*) *July 371 BC*. A notable victory for the great Theban general, Epaminondas, who had only 6,000 troops to the 11,000 Spartans under Cleomrotus. Epaminondas concentrated his best troops on the left, where they drove back the Spartans, leaving 1,000 dead on the field, and outflanked the Spartan line. The Spartans evacuated Boeotia. *See* Mantinea; Naxos.

Leuthen (*Seven Years' War*) *5 December 1757*. Between 33,000 Prussians (Frederick the Great) and 90,000 Austrians (Prince Charles of Lorraine and Count Daun). Frederick feigned an attack on the Austrian right wing; then, behind high ground, he withdrew the greater part of his force and with it strongly attacked the Austrian left. The Austrians were driven back and overwhelmed, losing 7,000 killed or wounded, 20,000 prisoners and 134 guns. Prussian casualties amounted to 5,000 killed or wounded. Breslau then surrendered to Frederick. Leuthen is one of the great battles of history. *See* Breslau; Rossbach.

Leuze, *near Mons* (*War of the Grand*

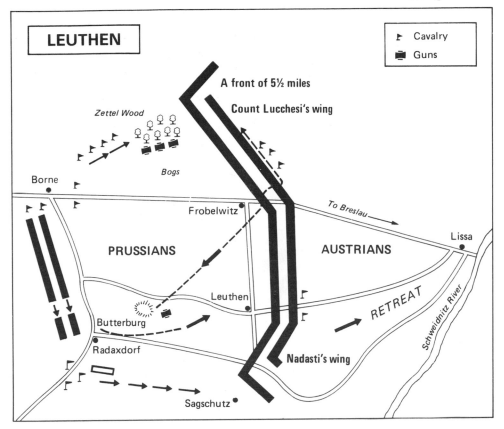

LEUTHEN

A front of 5½ miles

Count Lucchesi's wing

Zettel Wood

Bogs

Borne

To Breslau

Frobelwitz

Lissa

PRUSSIANS

AUSTRIANS

Leuthen

RETREAT

Butterburg

Schweidnitz River

Radaxdorf

Nadasti's wing

Sagschutz

Cavalry

Guns

Alliance) *20 September 1691*. A sharp victory for the clever general, the Duke of Luxembourg, over the Dutch–German army (Prince George of Waldeck) as it was preparing to go into winter quarters. William III of England was now asked to take command of the Alliance armies. *See* Mons; Namur.

Lewes (*Barons' War of England*) *14 May 1264*. Simon de Montfort, leading the Barons, decisively defeated Henry III and Prince Edward. Under an agreement, the Mise of Lewes, the belligerents agreed to submit the points in dispute to arbitration. *See* Kenilworth; Rochester III.

Lexington and Concord (*American Revolution*) *19 April 1775*. The British commander-in-chief in North America, General Gage, sent 700 troops (Lieutenant-Colonel F. Smith) to destroy an American militia depot at Concord, near Boston. At Lexington, 19 April, the British encountered seventy armed minutemen (militia) under Captain John Parker. No official command was given, but the British opened fire, killing eight and wounding ten Americans. This combat started the war. At Concord a British platoon was attacked, suffering fourteen casualties. That afternoon the British column was harassed throughout its return march to Boston. Casualties: British, 99 killed, 174 wounded; American, 100 killed, 41 wounded. *See* Bunker Hill; Ticonderoga II.

Lexington (*American Civil War*) *18–20 September 1861*. 8,000 Confederates (Prince) invested Lexington and with a loss of only 100 men forced Colonel Mulligan to surrender his garrison of 3,500.

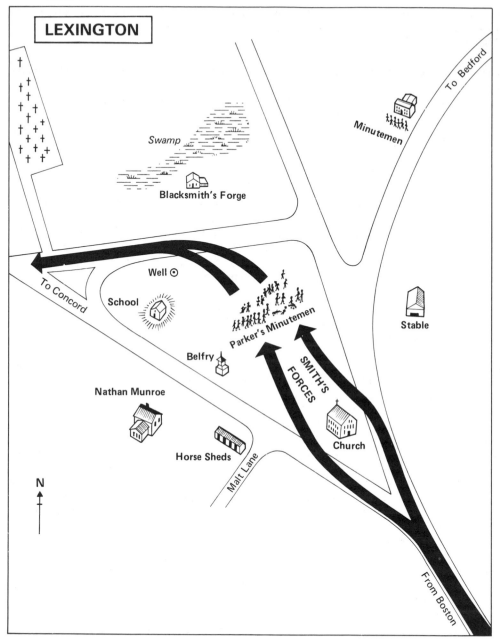

LEXINGTON

To Bedford

Minutemen

Swamp

Blacksmith's Forge

Well ⊙

To Concord

School

Parker's Minutemen

Belfry

Stable

SMITH'S FORCES

Nathan Munroe

Church

Horse Sheds

Malt Lane

N

From Boston

Leyden (*Netherlands War of Independence*) *26 May–3 October 1574*. Valdez, the Spanish commander, placed 8,000 Walloons and Germans and sixty-two gun batteries around Leyden which had no garrison except a burgher guard and a few freebooters, all under Jan van der Does. Nevertheless, Leyden held out. On 3 August the Prince of Orange had the dykes at Schieham and Rotterdam opened to make the investment more difficult for the enemy. The city was starving and 8,000 inhabitants had died of disease by the time Admiral Boisot broke through with some relief. The Spaniards and their allies were driven out of one redoubt after another and, 3 October, Valdez was forced to raise the siege. *See* Alkmaar; Gembloux.

Leyte (*World War II*) *17 October–25 December 1944*. In the centre of the Philippines Leyte was strongly held by the Japanese (Suziki). On 17–18 October U.S. Rangers captured small islands guarding Leyte Gulf; on 20 October the U.S. fleet bombarded Japanese positions and four infantry divisions were landed on the east side. The supreme Japanese commander in the Philippines sent in 45,000 reinforcements. The battle proper lasted until 25 December, but another 4 months were needed to wipe out all pockets of resistance. Casualties: American, 15,584 including 3,584 killed; Japanese, exact figures unknown, but more than 70,000 were killed, wounded or captured. *See* Leyte Gulf; Luzon; New Guinea; Philippines.

Leyte Gulf (*World War II*) *23–26 October 1944*. One of the largest and most complex of naval battles. Three Japanese fleets converged on the Philippines; one of them, with four carriers and two battleships, was to draw the U.S. Third Fleet from Leyte Gulf. The others were to drive off the U.S. Seventh Fleet so that the American land forces could be dealt with. Together these two Japanese fleets comprised 4 carriers, 7 battleships, 16 cruisers, 23 destroyers. The Americans had 32 carriers, 12 battleships, 26 cruisers and 144 destroyers, but the command was not unified; the Seventh Fleet was part of General MacArthur's command. The Japanese had intended to take the initiative, but American submarines and planes attacked first. Losses were considerable. The Japanese sank the American carrier *Princeton* — but at a cost of fifty-six planes. By 25 October the battle was in three parts — in Surigao Strait, off Cape Engano and at Samar. The battle overall cost the Japanese three battleships, four carriers, ten cruisers and nine destroyers — 300,000 tons in all. The Americans lost three carriers, two

destroyers and a destroyer escort — 37,000 tons. The way was now open for the Allied advance. *See* Luzon.

Liaoyang, *near Mukden (Russian–Japanese War*) *25 August–3 September 1904*. A battle of attrition between armies both 100,000 strong. In the end the Russians retreated, but they had inflicted 23,500 casualties to their own 16,500. *See* Shaho River; Yalu River.

Libyan Campaign I (*World War II*) *September 1940–February 1941*. The Italians (Grazziani) struck at Egypt, 13 September 1940, the fall of France having secured their rear in Tunisia. They advanced as far as Sidi Barrani and waited there, only to be caught on 9 December by O'Connor, under Wavell. In 60 days Australian and British troops took El Sollum, Bardia, Tobruk, Derna and Benghazi. At a cost of only 604 casualties they captured 133,000 Italians, occupying Cyrenaica as far as El Agheila. *See* Bardia; Derna; Tobruk.

Libyan Campaign II, *March 1941*. Troops and planes were needed in Greece against the impending German invasion and the force at El Agheila was reduced to two weak divisions. Attacking on 24 March, Rommel drove the British back into Egypt, but an Australian division was left to hold Tobruk. An effort to relieve Tobruk, 15–17 June, was defeated. In July the British took advantage of German preoccupation in Russia to build up an army under General Auchinleck, successor to Wavell. *See* Sidi Rezegh; Tobruk.

Liége (*World War I*) *4 August 1914*. The first German attack of the war. The city was entered on 7 August, but eleven of the twelve forts guarding the city held out until 16 August. *See* Frontiers of France; Namur II.

Liegnitz (*or Wahlstatt*) (*Mongol invasion of Europe*) *9 April 1241*. A courageous but ill-fated attempt by

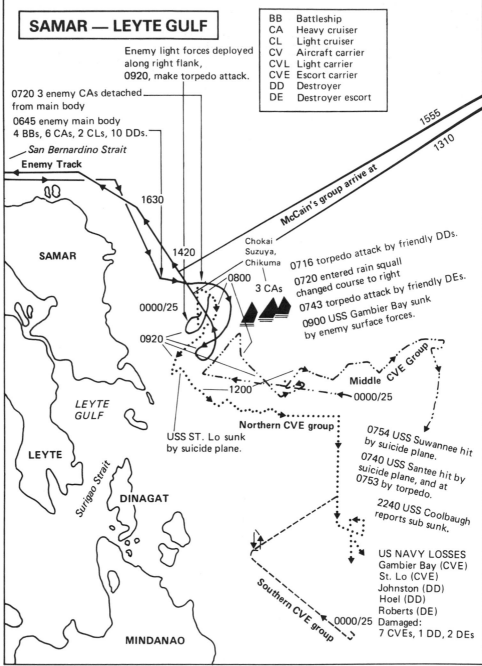

SAMAR — LEYTE GULF

BB   Battleship
CA   Heavy cruiser
CL   Light cruiser
CV   Aircraft carrier
CVL Light carrier
CVE Escort carrier
DD   Destroyer
DE   Destroyer escort

Enemy light forces deployed
along right flank,
0920, make torpedo attack.

0720 3 enemy CAs detached
from main body

0645 enemy main body
4 BBs, 6 CAs, 2 CLs, 10 DDs.

San Bernardino Strait
Enemy Track

1555

1310

McCain's group arrive at

1630

SAMAR

1420

Chokai
Suzuya,
Chikuma

0800

3 CAs

0716 torpedo attack by friendly DDs.
0720 entered rain squall
changed course to right
0743 torpedo attack by friendly DEs.
0900 USS Gambier Bay sunk
by enemy surface forces.

0000/25

0920

1200

Middle CVE Group

0000/25

*LEYTE
GULF*

Northern CVE group

0754 USS Suwannee hit
by suicide plane.

0740 USS Santee hit by
suicide plane, and at
0753 by torpedo.

USS ST. Lo sunk
by suicide plane.

LEYTE

Surigao Strait

2240 USS Coolbaugh
reports sub sunk.

DINAGAT

US NAVY LOSSES
Gambier Bay (CVE)
St. Lo (CVE)
Johnston (DD)
Hoel (DD)
Roberts (DE)
Damaged:
7 CVEs, 1 DD, 2 DEs

Southern CVE group

0000/25

MINDANAO

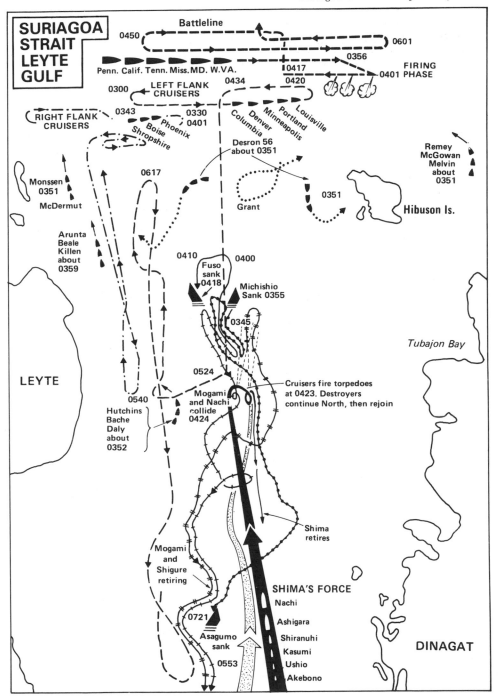

SURIAGOA STRAIT LEYTE GULF

Battleline

0450 0601

0356

Penn. Calif. Tenn. Miss. MD. W.VA.

0417 FIRING
0420 PHASE
0401

0300 0434

LEFT FLANK CRUISERS

RIGHT FLANK CRUISERS 0343 0330
0401

Louisville
Portland
Minneapolis
Denver
Columbia

Phoenix
Boise
Shropshire

Desron 56
about 0351

Remey
McGowan
Melvin
about
0351

Monssen
0351

McDermut

0617

Grant 0351

Hibuson Is.

Arunta
Beale
Killen
about
0359

0410 0400

Fuso
sank
0418

Michishio
Sank 0355

0345

LEYTE

Tubajon Bay

0524

0540

Mogami
and Nachi
collide
0424

Cruisers fire torpedoes
at 0423. Destroyers
continue North, then rejoin

Hutchins
Bache
Daly
about
0352

Shima
retires

Mogami
and
Shigure
retiring

SHIMA'S FORCE

Nachi

0721

Asagumo
sank

Ashigara

Shiranuhi

DINAGAT

Kasumi

0553 Ushio

Akebono

Henry II, Duke of Silesia, to block the Mongol horse-archers of Kaidu, grandson of Genghis Khan. The Mongols hit thousands of enemy with arrows and then charged with the sword. Not one of Henry's force survived. *See* Cracow; Mohi.

Liegnitz (*Seven Years' War*) *15 August 1760*. Frederick the Great, in positions near Liegnitz with 30,000 troops and expecting to be attacked by Count Daun's 90,000 Austrians, commenced a retreat towards Parchwitz. Here he took up a position which his counterpart, Daun, had intended to be occupied by an Austrian corps under Landon. Landon marched straight into Frederick's lines and in a brief but violent battle lost 4,000 killed or wounded, 6,000 prisoners and 82 guns. *See* Landeshut; Torgau.

Liesna (*or Lesno*) (*Great Northern War*) *September–October 1708*. A series of Russian attacks against a Swedish supply column of 8,000 wagons — Lewenhaupt commanding the escort of 11,000 men — marching to support Charles XII in his campaign in the Ukraine. Outnumbered four to one, the Swedes destroyed their artillery and supplies at Liesna, 9 October, and cut their way out; half were killed. The Russians had 10,000 killed. *See* Holoczyn; Poltava.

Ligny (*Napoleon's "Hundred Days"*) *16 June 1815*. The pre-Waterloo battle was fought between Blucher and 84,000 Prussians and Napoleon with 60,000 French. Attacking the Prussian positions, the French met stiff resistance, especially at Ligny. But Blucher used up his reserves and Napoleon, bringing in the Guard and a division of heavy cavalry at sundown, drove them out. Casualties: Prussians, 12,000; French, 8,000. *See* Quatre Bras; Waterloo; Wavre.

Lille (*War of the Spanish Succession*) *12 August–25 October 1708*. Prince Eugene and his Imperialists besieged Lille, but the French com-mander, de Boufflers, repulsed several assaults. Privations forced surrender on 25 October. Casualties: Imperialists, 3,630; French, 7,000. *See* Oudenarde; Tournai.

Lilybaeum (*First Punic War*) *250–241 BC*. Besieged by the Romans (Attilius), defended by the Carthaginians (Himilcon). The Carthaginians' superior seamanship enabled them to supply and reinforce Lilybaeum, and though the Romans took one wall they then encountered another and the siege began anew. Defeating the Romans in the naval battle of Drepanum, the Carthaginians made the place secure from the sea, but military pressure was maintained. In 241, beaten in the naval battle of Aegusae, Carthage sought peace. *See* Aegates Islands; Drepanum; Panormus.

Limerick (*War of the Glorious Revolution*) *June–3 October 1691*. Limerick was the last stronghold held by the Jacobite rebels opposing William III. In 1690 the Earl of Lucan (Patrick Sarsfield) had broken William's siege. In June 1691 General de Ginkel began a new siege for William, and this time Lucan could not break it. The garrison surrendered. *See* Aughrim; Glencoe.

Lincoln (*English anarchy period*) *November 1141*. Stephen of Blois besieged Lincoln Castle during his campaign to hold the English crown against the claims of his cousin Maud. Maud's supporters, led by the Earl of Gloucester, then attacked Stephen, defeated him and took him captive. Maud became monarch.

Lincoln, Fair of, *1217*. The Royalists (Earl of Pembroke) defeated, in the streets of Lincoln, the followers of the Dauphin Louis under the Comte de la Perche, who was killed. The battle was derisively called the "Fair of Lincoln" because in the end half the knights surrendered — but the battle was a bloody one. The event was part of the First Barons' War of England.

Lindley (*Second British–Boer War*) *23–27 May 1900*. Colonel Spragge, with 500 yeomanry, held out for 4 days before surrendering to a superior Boer force. *See* Ladysmith; Mafeking.

Linköping, *Sweden* (*Swedish–Polish Wars*) *June 1598*. Between the Poles (Sigismund III, who was also King of Sweden) and the Swedes (Charles the Regent). The Swedes are said to have lost only 240 men in causing the Poles casualties of 20,000. Sigismund was dethroned and Charles became King of Sweden. *See* Polotsk.

Liparaean Islands (*First Punic War*) *257 BC*. The Roman fleet (Attilius) defeated the Carthaginians.

Lippe River (*Rome's Germanic Wars*) *11 BC*. The barbarian German tribes, Sicambri, Suevi and Cherusii, outnumbered and surrounded Drusus' Roman legions. But the disciplined Romans attacked outwards, routed the barbarians and killed many of them. *See* Teutoburger Wald.

Lisbon (*Portuguese Muslim Wars*) *1147*. A fleet of the Second Crusade, putting in at Oporto, found Alfonso I of Portugal preparing to attack the Moorish stronghold of Lisbon. The Crusaders offered to help, as did English, Flemish and Frisian ships. After a 4-month siege the Moors surrendered, only to be slaughtered. Nearly all the would-be Crusaders settled down in Portugal.

Lissa Island, *Adriatic* (*Seven Weeks' War*) *20 July 1866*. A little known naval action between the Austrian fleet of seven armoured ships (Tegethoff) and some wooden ships and the Italian fleet of ten armoured ships (Persano). Tegethoff, attacking in wedge formation, rammed and sank the Italian flagship; in the confusion which followed the Italians lost three ships and 1,100 men and were forced to raise the siege of Lissa.

Little Bighorn River (*Second Sioux War*) *25–26 June 1876*. Lieutenant-Colonel George Custer, with 600 troopers of the 7th Cavalry, was sent to reconnoitre the Little Bighorn River prior to a planned link up of two army columns. Covering 83 miles in 24 hours, Custer divided his small force in three groups — in the face of up to 3,500 warriors across the river (Sitting Bull, Crazy Horse and Gall). Custer took five troops (211 men), Major Reno three troops, Captain Benteen three troops, and moved to attack the Indian village. Reno was driven back, linked with Benteen and for a day and half held off Indian attacks, losing fifty-three dead and fifty-two wounded. Custer was surrounded and in an hour he and all his men were killed — "Custer's Last Stand". The Americans consider the defeat the worst of the Indian wars. *See* Rosebud River; Wolf Mountain.

Llandilovawr, *Wales 11 December 1282*. Edward I defeated the Welsh, whose leader, Prince Llewellyn, was killed.

Loano, *Italian Riviera* (*French Revolutionary Wars*) *24 November 1795*. Francis II, Holy Roman Emperor, massed his Austrians to drive the French out of Italy, but at Loano the French commander, General Schérer, decisively defeated the Austrians. Schérer was reluctant to go on the offensive so Napoleon hurried from Paris to take command. *See* Fleurus III; Montenott.

Lobositz (or *Lobocize*) (*Seven Years' War*) *1 October 1756*. Frederick the Great, learning that an Austrian army of 50,000 men under Marshal Maximilian von Browne was approaching to relieve their Saxon allies, marched south in equal strength. He defeated Browne's army, inflicted 3,000 casualties and forced Browne to retreat. The victory was important because it led to the surrender of Pirna, with 17,000 Saxons and eighty guns. The Saxon troops were taken into his army and Saxony came into his possession. *See* Prague IV.

Lodi, Bridge of (*Napoleon's Italian campaigns*) *10 May 1796*. Napoleon, pursuing the Austrian–Sardinian army (Baron Beaulieu), reached the bridge of Lodi, over the Adda, which was defended by the Austrian rearguard. Sending cavalry across a ford to attack from the rear, Napoleon, Massena and Berthier led the storming of the bridge. In the fight and pursuit the Austrians lost 2,000 killed or wounded, 1,000 prisoners and all twenty guns; the French had 400 casualties. *See* Loano; Mantua Lonato; Mondovi.

Lodz (*World War I*) *11 November–6 December 1914*. Anticipating a Russian drive into Silesia, the Germans (Mackensen) attacked towards Warsaw and in 4 days of hard fighting advanced 50 miles. Marching 70 miles in 48 hours, the Russian Fifth Army stopped the Germans from encircling the Russian Second Army near Lodz, 19 November. However, the Russians abandoned Lodz on 6 December. *See* Masurian Lakes.

Loftcha (*Russian–Turkish War*) *3 September 1877*. The Russians (Skobelov) made an initial attack on the Turkish positions with 5,000 men, followed it up with 9,000 and drove out the Turks with a loss of 5,200 killed. Russian casualties, 1,500 killed and wounded. *See* Plevna.

Loigny-Pouprey (*French–German War*) *1 December 1870*. Between 34,000 Germans (Grand Duke of Mecklenburg) and 90,000 French, the Army of the Loire (de Paladines). The total German victory broke the aggressive power of the Army of the Loire, the French losing 18,000 killed or wounded. German casualties, 4,850. *See* Gravelotte; Metz; Sedan.

Loja (*Spanish–Muslim Wars*) *4 July 1482*. Ferdinand the Catholic, besieging Loja, had decided to retreat; in doing so he was vigorously attacked by the garrison. After heavy fighting he withdrew, losing most of his baggage and artillery. *See* Alhama de Granada; Málaga I.

Lonata, *Lake Garda* (*French Revolutionary Wars*) *3 August 1796*. His lines of communication threatened by the Austrians, Napoleon attacked the right wing of the advancing Austrian army (Quasdanovitch) and routed it before enemy commander-in-chief, F. M. von Wurmser, could come to support. *See* Castiglione Delle Stiviere; Mantua.

Londonderry (*War of "The Glorious Revolution"*) *19 April–30 July 1689*. 30,000 Ulster Protestants, who had taken refuge in the city, were besieged by James II. Major Henry Baker, assuming command of the defence, had only 7,000 armed citizens. On 30 July Colonel Kirke forced the boom at the head of Lough Foyle and reprovisioned the town. James, who by now had lost 5,000 men, withdrew. The garrison then numbered only 4,000 and it had lost Major Baker. *See* The Boyne.

Long Island (*American Revolution*) *26–29 August 1776*. Between the British, under General William Howe and his brother Admiral Richard Howe, and the Americans led by Washington, Putnam, Sullivan and Stirling. Clever tactics brought British victory and only furious rearguard fighting enabled the American rearguard to reach the defences of Brooklyn Heights. Casualties: American, 1,500, including 200 killed; British, 400. *See* Bunker Hill; White Plains.

Lookout Mountain (*American Civil War*) *24 November 1863*. Part of the battle of Chattanooga, q.v.; the Federals surprisingly pushed Bragg's Confederates from the key height south of the city.

Loos (*or Artois III*) (*World War I*) *25 September–8 October 1915*. One of the fiercest battles of the war and the British part of the Allied offensive in

Artois. In this battle the British used poison gas for the first time. The French attack under d'Urbal in the Vimy Ridge area and the British attack under Haig both gained some ground, but Falkenhayn's counter-attacks blocked the Allies, though the French struggled until 14 October. Casualties: German, 178,000; British, 60,000; French, 190,000. *See* Arras; Artois I; Artois II.

Lostwithiel, *near Plymouth* **(***English Civil War***)** *2 September 1644.* Though badly beaten at Marston Moor, Charles I chased the Roundhead army of the Earl of Essex into Cornwall, attacked it in the rear and surrounded it. Essex and cavalry cut their way out, but all his infantry (8,000) men and guns fell to Charles. *See* Marston Moor; Newbury II.

Loudon Hill (*English–Scottish Wars***)** *10 May 1307.* King Robert Bruce met the attack of the English cavalry (the Regent, Pembroke) with a line of spearmen. Unable to break through, the English withdrew.

Louisburg I, *Cape Breton Island* **(***War of Austrian Succession***)** *30 April–17 June 1745.* The strongest fortress in America, Louisburg was captured by a force of New Englanders (Colonel W. Pepperell) helped by a naval force (Commodore Warren). It was an outstanding combined operation. Loss of the fortress was a great blow to the French, but they regained it by treaty in 1748. *See* Louisburg II.

Louisburg II (*Seven Years' War***)** *3 June–20 July 1758.* Louisburg, having been restored to the French, was invested on 3 June 1758 by 11,600 British troops (General Amherst) and forty-one warships (Boscawen). The Chevalier de Drucour had 3,800 French regulars, and some armed citizens and Indians. In harbour were twelve warships. British siege guns were landed 18 July and on 20 July the infantry stormed the breach. Casual-ties: French, 1,200 killed or died of illness, 5,637 prisoners, 239 guns. *See* Fort Frontenac; Fort Ticonderoga I.

Louvain, *Belgium* **(***Viking Wars in Europe***)** *891.* A victory for Arnulf, the ruler, over the savage Vikings from Scandinavia. After this battle there were no further deep raids into Germany. *See* Montfaucon; Riade.

Löwenberg (*Napoleonic Wars: Leipzig campaigns***)** *21 August 1813.* Napoleon advanced much of his force of 130,000 against Blucher who, with only 80,000, retired behind the Haynau River; he lost 2,000 men in doing so. *See* Dennewitz; Grossbeeren.

Lowestoft (*Second English–Dutch War***)** *13 June 1665.* Between 150 English ships and their 5,000 guns (Duke of York, later James II) and 150 Dutch ships (Admiral Opdam). After furious bombardment the Dutch, having lost their commander during a flagship-to-flagship fight, withdrew. *See* Dover Strait; Texel I.

Lübeck (*Napoleonic Wars: Jena campaign***)** *6–7 November 1806.* The climax to the astonishing series of French victories over the Prussians — Jena-Auerstadt, Berlin, Prenzlau, Stettin. Marshals Soult and Bernadotte pushed Blucher, the ablest surviving Prussian leader, into Lubeck, stormed and captured it on 6 November. Blucher escaped with part of his force to nearby Ratkow but surrendered next day. Prussia was now powerless. *See* Jena-Auerstadt; Pultusk II.

Lucena (*Spanish–Muslim Wars***)** *April 1483.* The Moors (Abdullah) besieging Lucena were attacked by a Spanish force (Comte de Cabra) and the infantry bolted. Ali Atar, leading a cavalry charge to check the Spaniards, was killed, whereupon the whole Moorish army fled; most were cut down on the banks of the Xenil. *See* Malaga.

Lucknow (*Indian Mutiny*) *1 July 1857–21 March 1858*. As the rebel sepoy army approached, the garrison and remaining residents took refuge in the Residency, which had been prepared as a fort. Havelock and Outram left Cawnpore, 19 September, to relieve the garrison and on 23 September defeated 12,000 rebels at the Alumbagh. They forced the Charbagh bridge on 25 September, captured the Secunderbagh and fought street by street into the Residency. By now the garrison had lost 483 killed or wounded and the relief force 535. Sir Colin Campbell and his column, after more heavy fighting, relieved the place on 19 November and escorted the garrison in withdrawal. Conquest of Lucknow began on 1 March 1858 and, after successive assaults, was completed on 21 March. *See* Cawnpore II; Delhi II.

Ludford (*or Ludlow*) (*Wars of the Roses*) *13 October 1459*. A non-battle. The Yorkists fell back to Ludford under Henry VI's Lancastrian thrust and on the night of 12 October the two armies faced each other across the Teme. In the morning Henry found that the Yorkists' morale had broken and their army was in flight. *See* Blore Heath.

Lugdunum, *now Lyons* (*Roman Empire Civil Wars*) *197*. A great combat between the Roman Legions of Britain and Gaul under Albinius and the Pannonian legions of Severus. Winning, Severus beheaded Albinius and returned to Rome in triumph. *See* Byzantium I.

Lüleburgaz (*First Balkan War*) *28–30 October 1912, and 17–18 November 1912*. The Bulgarians routed the Turks in this fierce battle and drove them to Catalca, a fortified line crossing the peninsula protecting Constantinople. Here the Turks held and beat back the Bulgarians. *See* Adrianople VII; Kirk-Kilissa.

Luncarty (*Danish invasion of Scotland*) *980*. The Scots (Kenneth III) repulsed the Danish corsairs who had landed on the Tay to attack Dunkeld and drove them back to their ships.

Lunden (*Danish–Swedish War*) *October 1676*. The Swedes (Charles XI) and the Danes (Christian V) both claimed victory, but since Christian had to fall back on Copenhagen while Charles raised the siege of Malmo, the advantage rested with the Swedes.

Lundy's Lane, *near Niagara* (*British–American War 1812–14*) *25 July 1814*. Sir George Drummond, occupying high ground on either side of Lundy's Lane with 3,000 men, was attacked by 5,000 Americans under Winfield Scott. After a 5-hour fight and a loss on each side of about 850 the Americans retired to Fort Erie. It was the fiercest land battle of the war. *See* Chippewa River; Fort Erie.

Lutter am Barenberge, *Brunswick* (*Thirty Years' War*) *27 August 1626*. Between the Imperialists (Tilly) and the Danes and Germans (Christian IV of Denmark). Tilly, driving the Allies before him, came up with them near the castle of Lutter. Christian had strong lines, but Christian's German troops refused to fight and Tilly overwhelmed the Danes, 4,000 of whom were killed. Tilly took 2,000 prisoners, twenty-two guns. Christian escaped only by slashing his way through the enemy cavalry. *See* Dessau Bridge; Stralsund I; Wolgast.

Lützen I (*Thirty Years' War*) *16 November 1632*. The last battle of Gustavus Adolphus, who had 20,000 Swedes to confront Wallenstein's 30,000 Imperialists. The Swedish right was successful, but Pappenheim drove back the Swedish left; Gustavus, hurrying to rally his troops, was mortally wounded. However, the Swedes charged again and routed the enemy. A heavy fog enabled Wallenstein to make an orderly retreat, though he left all his guns behind. *See* Fürth; Nördlingen I.

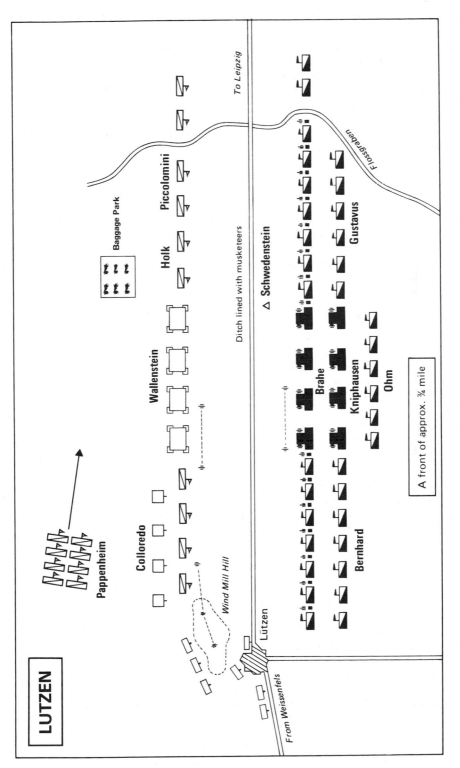

LUTZEN

Pappenheim

Colloredo

Wind Mill Hill

Wallenstein

Baggage Park

Holk

Piccolomini

To Leipzig

Ditch lined with musketeers

△ Schwedenstein

From Weissenfels

Lützen

Bernhard

Brahe

Kniphausen

Ohm

Gustavus

Flossgraben

A front of approx. ¾ mile

Lützen II (*Napoleonic Wars: Leipzig campaign*) *2 May 1813*. Napoleon held five villages in front of Lutzen, but the Russian–Prussian allies (Wittgenstein and Blucher) were only 5,000 fewer than Napoleon's 70,000. The villages changed hands several times during the day, but at 8 p.m. the King of Prussia and the Russian Emperor, despite Blucher's wishes, ordered a retreat. Casualties: Allies, 20,000; French, 18,000. *See* Berezina River; Bautzen.

Luzon (*World War II*) *15 December 1944–4 July 1945*. Luzon, chief island of the Philippines, was held by Yamashita's Fourteenth Army in three main groups of Shobu (140,000 men) in the north, Kembu (30,000) in the centre, and Shimbu (80,000) in the south. On 9 January the Americans landed 68,000 men (Krueger) and penetrated 40 miles by 20 January. Operations were extremely complex. Manila fell, 4 March, after a fanatical 30-day resistance during which 16,000 Japanese were killed. Baguio, the Philippines summer capital, fell on 27 April, Santa Fe, the key Japanese communications centre, on 27 May. By 1 July central Luzon was virtually in American hands. General MacArthur declared Luzon secure on 4 July, but when the war ended, 15 August, more than 50,000 Japanese were still being contained in northern and eastern Luzon. *See* Leyte; Philippines.

Luzzara, *Lombardy* (*War of Spanish Succession*) *15 August 1702*. Prince Eugene, with 25,000 Imperialists to the 35,000 French of the Duke of Vendôme, attacked the French trenches in front of Luzzara and after a stubborn fight drove them out with a reported loss of 27,000. The French lost 4,000. *See* Cremona II; Landau.

Lycia, *off southern Asia Minor* (*Muslim–Byzantine Wars*) *655*. Suc-cessful on land, the Muslims became seafarers and in their dromons — fast galleys — they captured Cyprus and Rhodes. The Constantinople navy of Constans II was sent to drive the Muslims from the sea but was itself soundly beaten. It was the first Arabian sea victory, and it gave the Muslims a taste for maritime conquest. *See* Alexandria II; Basra; Constantinople III.

Lynchburg (*American Civil War*) *18 June 1864*. The Federals (Hunter) attacked Lynchburg, but the Confederates had moved in reinforcements and the Federals were repulsed. Hunter retreated. *See* Monocacy River; Piedmont.

Lynn Haven Bay. *See* Chesapeake Bay.

Lys River (*or Ypres IV*) (*World War I*) *9 April 1918*. A major battle of the war, the key action of Ludendorff's second offensive. Ludendorff used General Quast's Sixth Army to strike from Armentieres: they overwhelmed a Portuguese division in the centre of the British First Army (Horne) and this pushed the entire Allied line back by 5 miles. Next day the German Fourth Army (von Armin) attacked and threw back the British Second Army (Plumer). Messines Ridge, won by the British at great cost in 1917, was lost. On 11 April the German armies linked for a massive drive to the sea, but on 12 April Haig issued his famous "Backs to the Wall", forbidding any further retirement. He rushed in all available units, including some French divisions sent by Marshal Foch, the Allied Commander-in-Chief. The German drive recaptured a great 10-mile strip of land, but it was halted by 17 April. After further attacks and counter-attacks Ludendorff stopped the operation. He had won a tactical victory, but now he had a difficult salient and he had suffered 350,000 casualties. Allied losses were 305,000, nearly all British. *See* Somme II.

Maastricht I (*Dutch War of Indepen-dence against Spain*) *12 March–June 1579*. 20,000 Spaniards (Prince Alexander of Parma) besieged the city, the German gate of The Netherlands, on 12 March. The garrison of only 2,200 (Melchior) beat back two assaults on 8 April and in all inflicted 4,670 casualties. Finally storming the city by surprise, the Spaniards massacred 8,000 civilian inhabitants as "punishment". *See* Antwerp I; Gembloux.

Maastricht II (*Second Dutch War of Independence or War of Devolution*) *16–29 June 1673*. A French force (de Vauban) laid siege to Maastricht, one of the strongest fortresses in Europe, as part of Louis XIV's campaign to crush The Netherlands United Provinces which were supporting Spain. Vauban's engineering genius was too much for the Dutch. With a maze of parallels and approaches, in 13 days he made Maastricht indefensible and the French captured it. *See* Dunes; Sinsheim.

Maastricht III (*War of Austrian Succession*) *March–7 May 1748*. Having conquered the Austrian Netherlands for France, Marshal de Saxe pressed his 1748 offensive by besieging Maastricht with its Dutch–English–Hanoverian–Austrian defenders. Russian reinforcements arrived too late — after the defenders had surrendered. *See* Bergen-op-Zoom I.

Macalo (*Venetian–Milan Wars*) *11 October 1427*. The Venetians (Caemagnola) repulsed the Milanese (Malatesta), counter-attacked and captured the Milanese army of 10,000. Many prisoners were massacred.

Macedonian Imperial Wars. *See* List of Battles.

Madagascar (*World War II*) *1942*. To forestall Japanese seizure of Madagascar and its vital harbour of Diego Suarez, then held by Vichy French troops (General Annet), Britain sent an expeditionary force (Admiral Syfret and General Sturges). The force captured Diego Suarez on 7 May. During negotiations with the French, H.M.S. *Ramillies* was torpedoed in harbour. The British then sent in General Platt with troops from East Africa to occupy the rest of Madagascar. Majunga was taken by amphibious assault on 10 September; Tamatave on 18 September; Tananarive, the capital, fell on 23 September. The French capitulated on 5 November and Free French troops took over the island. British casualties, 500.

Madagascar Revolt *1947*. The Mouvement Democratique de la Renovation Malagache (MDRM) fought the colonial French administration to gain independence. Between March and July MDRM fighters attacked forts at Moramanga, Farafangana, Antsirabe and Diego Suarez. A MDRM force of 4,500 stormed French positions in the capital, Tananarive, but the French Foreign Legion and Senegalese troops held firm. The revolt was over by the end of July. About 10,000 MDRM fighters were killed; the French admitted to 1,000 casualties.

Madeira (*Napoleonic Wars*) 26 December 1807. A British naval–army force (Admiral A. J. Cochrane and General Bowyer) captured the island to prevent the French from using it as an Atlantic base.

Madonna dell Olmo, *north Italy* (*War of Austrian Succession*) 30 September 1744. Between the French and Spaniards (Prince Louis de Conti and Don Philip of Spain) and the Imperialist (King of Sardinia). The Allies, besieging Cuneo, were attacked by the Sardinians, who, though defeated, forced Conti to abandon the siege, 22 October. Conti suffered heavily from famine, flood and battle. *See* Velletri.

Madras I *14–25 September 1746*. The French (Admiral La Bourdonnais) bombarded the fort, which surrendered. Casualties were few. Robert Clive, then a clerk of 21, was one of the defenders who escaped. *See* Arcot.

Madras II (*Seven Years' War*) 16 December–16 February 1758. A French–Indian force of 6,000 (Lally-Tollendal) invested the city, held by a British–Indian force of 4,000 (Colonel Laurence). On 15 February, after continual bombardment since 2 January, the French were about to storm when the arrival of a British fleet forced Lally-Tollendal to retire. Casualties: British, 1,341; French, 1,100. *See* Fort Saint David; Wandiwash.

Madras III (*War of the American Revolution*) 17 February 1782. The French Admiral de Suffren, with twelve warships, sought to land 3,000 troops on India's east coast. He gave battle to a British fleet of nine ships (Edward Hughes) but after 2 hours the fight was broken off without decisive result. The French troops landed near Porto Novo and helped in the capture of Cuddalore, 4 April. *See* Praia; Trincomalee I.

Madrid (*Spanish Civil War*) 1936–9. A long and bloody battle between the Republican (Government) militia defenders and Franco's Nationalist troops, aided by German and Italian forces. There were eight phases.

1. July–August 1936. Nationalists (Escamaz) from Pamplona captured some passes north of Madrid, but with superior artillery the Government troops blocked any further advance.

2. 27 September–23 November. Having taken Toledo, Mola moved his troops in Madrid from the south, south-west and west, and deployed them for assault on 6 November. The defending commander, Miaja, had only poorly armed urban militia and the XI International Brigade with a few Soviet tanks and aircraft. On 7 November Mola sent Verala, with 20,000 Moroccans and Spanish legionaries, Italian armour and German aircraft, to attack west Madrid. Fighting was bitter and by 23 November both sides were so exhausted they dug in. German, Italian and Nationalist aircraft heavily bombed the city.

3. 13 December 1936–15 January 1937. A Nationalist effort to tighten the siege reached its climax when the rebel troops took and held 10 miles of the Corunna Road. In this phase each side lost 15,000 men.

4. February 1937. General Orgaz in a new offensive south-east of Madrid struck for the Valencia road. The Republicans (Pozas) were forced back and lost the line of the Jarama River. The battle died down by the end of the month. The Republicans had held the Valencia road but had lost 20,000 men; the Nationalist losses were 25,000.

5. July 1937. Blocking a Nationalist offensive in March, the Republicans took the initiative on 6 July. Miaja, attempting to isolate the besiegers, captured Brunete and punched a 5-mile salient into

Nationalist lines. But Varela rallied his troops and by 25 July the Republicans were practically back to their starting point. Republican losses, 25,000 men and 100 of their aircraft; Nationalist, about 10,000.

6. *Stalemated siege, August 1937–February 1939*. Franco gradually clawed his way through Spain while Madrid suffered; by early 1939 more than 400 people were dying each week from starvation and disease.

7. *28 February–6 March 1939*. Civil war within the civil war. Colonel Casado, commanding the Republican Army of the Centre, in Madrid, led an anti-Communist revolt against his chief, Miaja, and the government of Juan Negrin. In a savage 6-day fight Republicans fought with Republicans and the Communist faction was defeated.

8. *26 March–31 March*. The final Nationalist attack. Unable to negotiate an unconditional surrender with the defenders, Franco launched an offensive. The Republican defence broke down; 30,000 men surrendered in the south on the first day. Nationalists occupied the capital on 31 March; Valencia had fallen without a fight the day before. The war was over. *See* Barcelona II; Guadalajaram Toledo II; Malaga III.

Mafeking (*Second British–Boer War*) *October 1899–17 May 1900*. General Cronje, with 5,000 Boers, invested the small town of Mafeking, defended by 700 irregulars and armed civilians under Colonel Baden-Powell. Cronje withdrew 3,000 men and left Snyman with the others to continue the siege. On 12 May 1900 Sarel Eloff led 300 men in a spirited raid, but the party was captured. A British cavalry column relieved the town on 17 May. Casualties: British, 273; Boers, about 1,000. *See* Doornkop; Kimberley.

Magdala (*British–Abyssinian War*) *31 April 1868*. Sir Robert Napier led a British–Indian Army of 14,683 to punish the ruthless King Theodore who had imprisoned the British consul and other diplomats. Reinforced by the native forces of dissident chieftains, Napier stormed the fortress of Magdala. Theodore committed suicide, Napier released the prisoners, destroyed the fort and withdrew. The campaign is noteworthy because of the remarkably efficient way Napier led his force of 43,000, including camp followers, for 380 miles over extremely difficult country. This was the first campaign in which British troops were armed with a breech-loading rifle. British casualties, two killed, twenty-seven wounded.

Magdeburg, *Germany (Thirty Years' War) 20 March–May 1631*. Held by a small Swedish garrison under the Hessian professional, von Falkenberg, Magdeburg, with a Protestant civilian population of 30,000, was besieged by Tilly with an army of Imperialists. King Gustavus Adolphus was approaching and Tilly, forced to raise the siege or to storm the city, chose the latter. On 20 May, after a furious 2-hour fight during which Falkenberg was killed, the garrison was overwhelmed. In 3 days of unbridled atrocities Tilly's Walloons and Croats massacred most the civilian population and garrison. *See* Frankfort-on-Oder; Werben.

Magenta, *Italy (Italian War of Independence against Austria) 4 June 1859*. Between the allied Piedmontese and French (Macmahon) and 180,000 Austrians (Clam-Gallas). Macmahon drove the Austrians from Magenta. Casualties: Solferino; Venice.

Magersfontein (*Second British–Boer War*) *11 December 1899*. A major battle of the war between 9,000 Boers (Cronje) and a British division (Methuen). The Highland brigade, attempting to turn the Boer flank by night, lost 57 officers and 700 men. Unable to make any impression on the Boers, the British withdrew, having lost in all 68 officers and 1,011 men. The Boers admitted losses of 320. *See* Colenso; Modder River; Stormberg.

Magnano (*French Revolutionary Wars*) *5 April 1799*. An Austrian army (von Krajowa) inflicted a sharp defeat on the French army (Scherer) defending Magnano, 10 miles south of Verona. When the French troops fell back to the Adda River, Moreau took over command and held the line. *See* Cassano d'Adda II.

Magnesia (*Roman War against Seleucid Syria*) *190 BC*. Between Antiochus the Great (80,000 troops) and Cnaeus Domitius (40,000 Romans). Antiochus drove back the Roman left and nearly captured the Roman camp, but his left flank was routed, his own elephants broke his phalanx and his army disintegrated. It should be noted that the Romans were under the strategic and political direction of the great Scipio Africanus. Reported casualties: Roman, 300; Syrians, 50,000. *See* Thermopylae II.

Maharajpore I (*British–Gwalior War*) *29 December 1843*. The 18,000 Mahrattas of Bhagerat Rao Scindhia with 100 guns held strong, concealed lines into which blundered General Gough's 40,000 British troops. Though inferior in artillery support, the British infantry charged the enemy batteries and routed the enemy. Casualties: British, 787; Mahrattas, 3,000. *See* Punniar.

Maharajpore II (*Indian Mutiny against the British*) *16 July 1857*. General Havelock, moving to re-occupy Cawnpore, found Nana Sahib with 5,000 rebels entrenched across the Grand Trunk Road. Turning their left flank, Havelock defeated the enemy but was left with only 800 fit men. Still, he took Cawnpore the following day. *See* Cawnpore; Delhi.

Mahidput (*Third British–Mahratta War*) *21 December 1817*. The Mahrattas (Holkar of Indore) were strongly posted with 30,000 horse, 5,000 infantry and 100 guns behind the Sipra. Crossing the river under heavy fire, the 5,500 British (Hyslop) inflicted 3,000 casualties for a loss of 778 of their own men and routed the Mahrattas. *See* Bhurtpore II.

Maida, *Calabria* (*Napoleonic Wars: Calabrian campaign*) *4 July 1806*. A British expeditionary force of 5,000 under Sir John Stuart encountered 5,000 French veterans led by General Reynier. A bayonet charge broke the French who lost heavily. Stuart was forced to re-embark his troops in the face of heavy French reinforcements. *See* Austerlitz.

Maidan (*First British–Afghan War*) *14 September 1842*. General Nott's British troops attacked Shems-ud-din's 12,000 Afghans holding heights above the Kabul road and drove them off with heavy loss. *See* Ghazni; Jellalabad.

Maipo River (*Chilean War of Independence against Spain*) *5 April 1818*. The Spanish governor of Peru sent an army of 6,000 (Osorio) to crush the newly established revolutionary government of Chile. On the Maipo River the Spaniards were blocked by 9,000 Chileans (Jose san Martin). In a sustained pitched battle the Spaniards were defeated and Chilean independence was secure. Casualties: Spanish, 1,000 killed, 2,000 captured; Chilean, 1,000 in all. *See* Chacabuco; Junin.

Main River (*Roman–German Wars*) *9 BC*. The Romans (Drusus) attacked and routed the Marcomanni and occupied their territory. Years of guerrilla warfare followed. *See* Teutoburger Wald.

Maiwand (*Second British–Afghan War*) *27 July 1880*. A notable if small-scale battle. A small British force (Burrows) with only six guns was isolated by the Afghan–Ghazi army (Ayub Khan.) The British 66th Regiment (Berkshire) fought with remarkable bravery, but the force was overwhelmed, losing 32 officers and 939 men killed and

17 officers and 151 men wounded. A few men escaped to Kandahar. *See* Kandahar; Peiwar Pass.

Majorca (*War of Spanish Succession*) 25 May 1706. Admiral John Leake's small but well-led British fleet captured the island from the Spaniards, as well as Cartagena on 1 June, Alicante on 24 August and Ibiza on 18 September. *See* Gibraltar.

Majuba (*First British–Boer War*) 27 February 1881. Sir George Colley with only 647 men held the summit of Majuba Hill. Joubert's marksmen pinned down the British while a strong force of young Boers stormed the hill. Forced to retire down the hillside, the British lost 223 killed and wounded, including their commander killed, and fifty prisoners. The disaster led to an armistice and then peace.

Makin Island (*World War II*) 20–23 November 1943. One of the Gilbert Islands taken by American infantry while marines were capturing Tarawa. Makin was defended by only 900 Japanese troops and labourers, but they killed 66 Americans and wounded 152; 450 Japanese were killed. The escort carrier *Liscome Bay* was torpedoed and sunk; 650 of her 900-man crew were drowned. *See* Tarawa.

Málaga I (*Spanish–Muslim War*) 17 April–18 August 1487. Ferdinand the Catholic, with 60,000 Spanish troops, trapped Hamet Zeli's Moor garrison, forced a surrender through privations and sold the inhabitants into slavery. *See* Baza; Loja.

Málaga II (*War of Spanish Succession*) 13 August 1704. A major naval battle, despite no ships being lost, between forty-five English–Dutch ships (Sir George Rooke) and fifty-three French (Thoulouse). The French, trying to join the Spanish fleet blockading Gibraltar, were brought to action off Málaga. In preventing the union Rooke won a strategic victory. Casualties: British, 693 killed, 1,611 wounded; French, 3,139 killed or wounded. *See* Barcelona I; Cassano d'Adda; Gibraltar.

Málaga III (*Spanish Civil War*) 17 January–6 February 1937. Three Nationalist rebel columns aided by nine battalions of mechanized Italian infantry converged on Málaga held by Colonel Villalba with 40,000 poorly organized militiamen. Franco's Nationalists made steady progress, reached the city on 3 February and crushed their opponents 3 days later. Fleeing towards Almeria, the Republicans were harassed by Nationalist–German–Italian aircraft. They suffered 15,000 casualties. *See* Guadalajara; Madrid.

Malakand Pass (*British Chitral campaign*) 3 April 1895. A British expedition (Low) forced the pass in north-west India against 12,000 Chitrali tribesmen.

Malakoff (*Crimean War*) 8 September 1855. General Pelissier's 30,000 French troops surprised the Russian garrison of the fort — part of the great Sebastopol complex — and overwhelmed them. *See* Balaklava; Inkermann; Sebastopol.

Malavilly (*Third British–Mysore War*) 20 March 1799. The British force (Lord Harris) marching to relieve Seringapatam, q.v., was attacked while in camp by the notorious Tippoo Sahib. General Floyd led a cavalry charge, which caused Tippoo's troops 1,000 casualties.

Malaya (*World War II*) 8 December 1941–31 January 1942. On the first day of war in the Pacific Japanese troops of General Yamashita landed at Singora, Patani (Thailand), Kota Bharu (West Malaya) and Penang Island (East Malaya). They rapidly overran airfields and Japanese aircraft soon won control of the skies. The Indian 9th and 11th Divisions (Percival) could fight only delaying actions. By 31 December three Japanese divisions had moved 150 miles to Ipoh, 200 miles from Singapore. Reinforced, the Japanese had to fight stubbornly against resistance by the Australian 8th Division and Indian 18th. Outnumbered and outfought, at the end of January the British forces withdrew over the causeway across Johore Strait to help defend the island of Singapore. They had suffered approximately 5,000 casualties. *See* Hong Kong; Singapore.

Malayan Emergency (*or Communist Insurrection*) *1948–60*. The Malayan Races Liberation Army (MRLA), whose members were Communists, wanted to wreck the federation agreement reached by the British with local Malay, Chinese and Indian leaders. MRLA embarked on a terrorist war and by April 1950 terrorist incidents reached 400 a month. Lieutenant-General Sir Harold Briggs, as Director of Operations, resettled the Chinese rural population of 423,000 in 410 protected "new villages", thus cutting off the terrorists from the sanctuary they had previously found amid the local people. In February 1952 General Sir Gerald Templar developed the Briggs Plan still further and, under pressure from a British force of 45,000, the MRLA terrorists were defeated by 1957, though the Emergency officially continued until 1960. Casualties: British Army, Indian Army and Malayan government forces, 2,384 killed, 2,400 wounded; terrorists, 6,705 killed, 1,286 wounded, 2,696 captured.

Malborghetto (*French Revolutionary Wars*) *23 March 1797*. Having practically conquered northern Italy, Napoleon moved 43,000 troops across the Alps to attack the Austrians. Archduke Charles Louis deployed 35,000 Austrian infantry to hold the mountain passes, but the French momentum was relentless. Massena's division routed the Austrians at Malborghetto in the Carnic Alps. This victory and that at Neuwied (q.v.) resulted in the Treaty of Campo Formio which gave Napoleon the Italian and

Belgian territory he wanted. *See* Pyramids; Rivoli Veronese.

Maldon, East Anglia (*Danish invasion*) *11 August 991*. The Danes (Olaf Triggvason and Guthmund) defeated the Anglo–Saxons and killed their leader, the legendary 6 ft 9 in Brithnoth.

Malegnano (*Italian War of Independence against Austria*) *8 June 1859*. Three divisions of French (d'Hilliers), in 3 hours' hard fighting, drove the five Austrian divisions out of Malegnano with heavy loss, including 1,000 prisoners. French loss, 850. *See* Milazzo; Solferino.

Malo-Jaroslawetz (*or Maloyaroslavets*) (*Napoleonic Wars: Moscow campaign*) *24 October 1812*. A bloody maul between 24,000 Russians (Kutuzov) and about 15,000 French (Eugene de Beauharnais, Napoleon's stepson). The town of Malo-Jaroslawetz was taken and re-taken seven times and tactically the battle was a draw. Strategically the Russians won, for they forced Napoleon to abandon the southerly line of retreat he had chosen. Casualties: French, 5,000 including the commander; Russians, 6,000. *See* Berezina; Borodino.

Malplaquet (*War of Spanish Succession*) *11 September 1709*. Between the British and Imperialists (Marlborough and Prince Eugene) and the French (Marshal Villars). The Allies were besieging Mons when Villars moved into position to threaten them. The Allies, waiting for reinforcements, permitted Villars to dig himself in. Their failure to prevent this resulted in a desperate and costly fight when, finally, they did attack. The French lost 17,000 men; the estimate of Allied casualties ranged from 8,000 to 18,000; the latter figure is more likely. *See* Brihuega; Tournai.

Malta I (*Turkish siege*) *19 May–11 September 1565*. Mustapha Pasha, with 30,000 Turkish troops and 185 ships, besieged the island, defended by

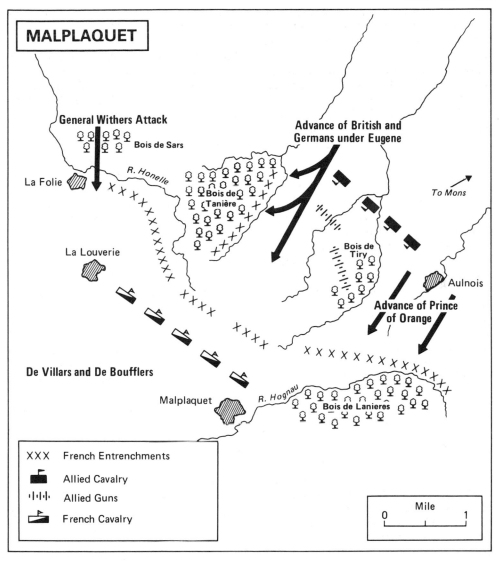

MALPLAQUET

General Withers Attack

Bois de Sars

La Folie

R. Honelle

Bois de Tanière

La Louverie

Advance of British and Germans under Eugene

To Mons

Bois de Tiry

Aulnois

Advance of Prince of Orange

De Villars and De Boufflers

Malplaquet

R. Hognau

Bois de Lanieres

| XXX | French Entrenchments |
| Allied Cavalry |
| Allied Guns |
| French Cavalry |

Mile
0   1

the Knights of Malta under Grand-Master Lavalette. St. Elmo was taken, but Valetta held out against numerous attacks until Mustapha raised the siege. Casualties: Turks, 20,000; garrison, 5,000. *See* Preveza; Rhodes.

Malta II (*French Revolutionary Wars*) *12 June 1798–5 September 1800*. Napoleon, en route to invade Egypt, seized Malta and left General Vaubois with 3,500 troops to hold the island. When the French navy was defeated at the Battle of the Nile, 1

August, the British were able to blockade Malta and land troops who took all the island except Valetta. Only starvation forced the garrison's surrender. *See* Nile River; Pyramids.

Malta III (*World War II*) *1940–2*. This prolonged battle was an epic of the war. With only three modern aircraft — Gladiators named Faith, Hope and Charity — Malta managed to hold out against Italian attacks. Defence of the island was vital for the war in the Western Desert; from Malta, aircraft and submarines attacked Italian convoys carrying supplies to North Africa. Early in 1941 large numbers of German aircraft moved into Sicily and throughout 1941 the battle for the island raged with increasing fury. Air Vice-Marshal Lloyd commanded the R.A.F.; General Dobbie and later Lord Gort governed the island. In April 1941 Malta was awarded the George Cross for bravery. Continually bombed, the island suffered heavily. Relief convoys for the starving island came under heavy attack; in June 1941 a total of seventeen ships set out from Alexandria and Gibraltar — only two reached Malta. Later five out of fourteen — Operation Pedestal — ran the gauntlet. Pressure eased in the autumn of 1942, with the war moving away from Africa into southern Europe. By May 1942 there had been 2,470 air raids on Malta.

Malvern Hill, *American Civil War*. *See* Seven Days' Battles.

Mangalore (*First British–Mysore War*) *20 June 1762–26 January 1763*. After a remarkably stubborn defence the small British garrison, under Colonel Campbell, starving and without ammunition, surrendered to Tippoo Sahib's overwhelming army of about 80,000.

Manila I (*Seven Years' War*) *5 October 1762*. Spain, entering the war as France's ally, was gambling its Philippine possessions. Sailing from India, a combined British force (Admiral Cornish and General Draper) entered the harbour and forced a rapid surrender. The following year a peace treaty restored Manila to Spain. *See* Havana.

Manila and Manila Bay II (*Spanish–American War*) *1 May–13 August 1898*. Commodore Dewey, sailing from China, brought his squadron of four cruisers and two gunboats into Manila Bay, 30 April. At daybreak next morning Dewey moved on the ten-ship Spanish fleet anchored off Cavite Point and in a 7-hour battle destroyed it, sinking, cap-

turing or putting out of action every ship. Most were small and several unarmoured. The Spaniards lost 381 killed, the Americans had eight men wounded, without damage to their ships. Dewey then blockaded Manila and waited for troops to arrive from the United States. By 25 July General Merritt had 10,700 men in position and could call on 10,000 Filipino rebels. When the governor refused to surrender the city — it had a garrison of 13,000 — the American infantry assault was launched. Victory was rapid and cheap. The rebels, who had gained nothing from all this, commenced an insurrection against American occupation troops; it was to last 3 years. *See* Santiago de Cuba I.

Mannerheim Line Battles (*World War II*) *1939–40, 1941, 1944*. No fewer than twenty-six Red Army divisions (465,000 troops) invaded Finland on 30 November 1939. Along the Mannerheim Line, across the Karelian Isthmus, the Finnish army of nine divisions (130,000) under Field Marshal von Mannerheim fought with stubborn courage and beat back waves of attackers. Between 8 December and 11 January they annihilated two Russian divisions at a loss to themselves of 900 killed and 1,170 wounded. Frustrated, the Russians organized a new offensive under Timoshenko. On 1 February two powerful armies smashed through the Mannerheim Line and captured Viipuri on 11 March. Russian losses were extraordinary — 200,000 in dead alone. The Finns lost 25,000 killed and 44,000 wounded. The victory gave Russia territory to defend Leningrad.

On 22 June 1941 Germany invaded the Soviet Union and 4 days later Finland launched its own attack, quickly recapturing the lost Finnish territory. Mannerheim's army then helped the Germans in their long siege of Leningrad. In June 1944 the Russian armies mounted a tremendous Europe-wide offensive. The Mannerheim Line was breached and the Finns accepted a humiliating peace —

though they declared war on the crumbling Germany on 3 March 1945.

Mansfield (*American Civil War*) 8 April 1864. General Banks, with about 20,000 Federals, was marching through difficult country when ambushed by General Taylor with only 8,000 Confederates. The Federals were routed with heavy casualties; they also lost 3,500 prisoners, 22 guns and 220 wagons of stores and ammunition. *See* Port Hudson.

Mantineia I (*Greek City-states Wars*) 418 BC. Between 10,000 Spartans and Tegeans (Agis) and 10,000 Athenians (Laches and Nicostratus). The Athenians pushed back the Spartan left, but their own centre and left gave ground so much that the Spartans were victorious. Both Greek leaders were killed. *See* Chaeronea I; Cynoscephalae I; Leuctra.

Mantineia II (*Greek City-states Wars*) 362 BC. The last fight of the great Boeotian leader, Epaminondas, who gave battle to the combined forces of Athens, Sparta and Mantineia. Epaminondas attacked strongly with his left, drove back the Mantineians, and then knocked out the Spartans who formed the enemy centre. The Athenians on the allied left were barely engaged, but withdrew. The Boeotians pursued, but at this point lost their leader, became disheartened and allowed the pursuit to lapse. *See* Leuctra.

Mantineia III (*First Macedonian War*) 207 BC. The Achaeans (Philipoemen) drove the Spartans (Machanidas) into a ravine where, completely disordered, 4,000 of them were killed. Machanidas, an able king and general, was among the dead. *See* Larissus.

Mantua (*Napoleon's Italian campaigns*) 4 June 1796–2 February 1797. Napoleon invested the city, held by General Canto-d'Iries with 14,000 Austrians, and harassed the defenders until 31 July when an Austrian relief force (Wurmser) approached. Napoleon dispersed this force, drove Wurmser and part of his army into Mantua, and reinvested the place on 19 September. On 2 February the following year Wurmser, with provisions exhausted, 27,000 soldiers and civilians dead and with only 8,000 men fit for service, surrendered. *See* Lodi Bridge; Malborghetto; Rivoli Veronese.

Manzikert (*or Malazkirt*) (*Byzantine–Turkish Wars*) 1071. Between 40,000 veteran Byzantine troops (Romanus IV) and 70,000 mounted Turks (Sultan Alp Arslan). The Byzantines had gone to relieve Manzikert, besieged by raiding Turks. Romanus led a furious charge into the Turkish centre and forced the enemy back until dusk, when he called off the attack. The instant the Byzantine withdrawal commenced, the Turks counterattacked and surrounded the Byzantines. Despite heroic fighting, the Byzantine army was destroyed and Romanus captured. The victory was a decisive one; there was now nothing to stop the Turks from taking Antioch, Damascus and Jerusalem, q.v. Also, the Byzantine army could no longer draw its best troops from the Isaurian and Armenian races. This was the beginning of the end for the Byzantine empire. *See* Dyrrachium II; Nishapur; Philomelion.

Maogamalcha, *Persia* (*Roman–Persian Wars*) 363. The Emperor Julian and his legions besieged this "impregnable" fortress, tunnelled under the ramparts and collapsed the walls. Three cohorts broke through into the streets, the garrison abandoned the walls and the fort fell. After being sacked it was demolished.

Marathon (*Second Persian invasion of Greece*) September 490 BC. One of the great battles of history. The belligerents were the allied Athenians and Plataeans, only 11,000 strong (Miltiades), and the army of the Persian Datis. Possibly 150,000 men had sailed from Persian bases, but Datis had probably

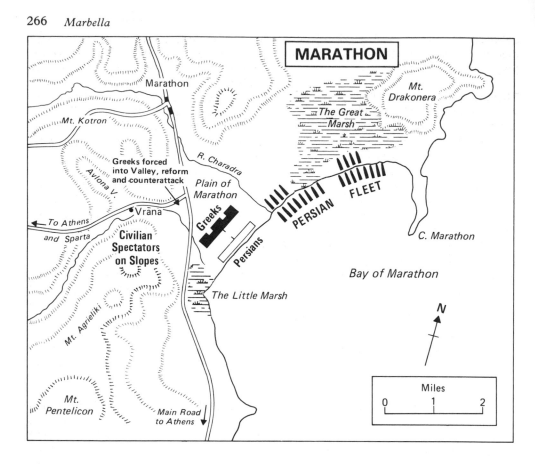

only 20,000 ashore at Marathon. Using his 11,000 men in one phalanx, Miltiades extended his line across a valley to avoid being outflanked. This left his centre weak, but his wings drove back the invaders; then, linking together under Miltiades' direction, they routed the Persian centre. Fleeing in confusion to their ships, the Persians left behind 6,400 dead; the Athenians lost only 192. Until Marathon the Persians had been considered invincible; their defeat started a chain reaction which was to inspire the Greeks to beat back Xerxes and lead on men such as Xenophon, Agesilaus and Alexander in their Asiatic campaigns. Marathon is traditionally considered the first "great decisive battle" of the world. *See* Lade, Salamis.

Marbella (*War of Spanish Succession*) *10 March 1705*. In this naval action an English squadron under Admiral Sir John Leake destroyed a French squadron under Admiral de Pointis near Gibraltar. The victory enabled the British and Dutch troops to land safely to besiege Barcelona, q.v.

Marchfeld (*or Durnkrut*) (*German–Bohemian Wars*) *26 August 1278*. Between Rudolph I, first Hapsburg ruler of Germany and the Holy Roman Empire, and the Bohemian king, Ottokar II the Great. The armies met on the plain of Marchfeld, north of the Danube from Vienna. In a battle of knights the Bohemians were defeated and Ottakar killed. His son, Wenceslas III, was permitted to take the Bohemian throne under German regency. The Hapsburgs would rule the Danube valley for 560 years. *See* Kressenbrunn.

Marcianopolis (*Gothic invasion of Thrace*) *376*. The Goths (Fritigern) defeated the Romans (Lupicinus) who died where they fought. The Thracians played no part in the battle.

Mardis, *Macedonia (War of the Two Roman Empires) 314*. Between Constantine, Emperor of the West, and Licinius, Emperor of the East. Constantine moved 5,000 men round his enemy's flank and attacked it front and rear. Licinius' Illyrian veterans formed a double front and, though suffering great loss, held their ground until nightfall when Licinius withdrew into the Macedonian hills. Constantine's victory gave him Pannonia, Dalmatia, Dacia, Macedonia and Greece. Licinius retained Asia, Egypt and Thrace.

Marengo (*Napoleon's Italian campaigns) 14 June 1800*. Melas, with 31,000 Austrians, attacked Napoleon and his 23,000 French. Overwhelming Marshal Victor, the Austrians seemed certain of victory, but their slow pursuit enabled Napoleon to bring in Desaix's fresh corps and the French reserve to cover his front. He then re-formed his broken divisions. Spearheaded by cavalry under François Kellermann, the French repulsed the Austrians, who fled. Casualties: French, 5,900; Austrian, 9,400. *See* Höchstädt II.

Mareth Line, *Tunisia 6 March–27 March 1943*. The sequel to the Battle of Alamein between British Commonwealth and American troops (Montgomery) and the Afrika Korps (Rommel). The British Eighth Army caught up with Rommel's forces after they had retired into the fortified hills of the old French Mareth Line on 18 February. Rommel lost fifty tanks in a Panzer jab on 6 March, at Montgomery's right. Rommel was recalled to Germany on 13 March.

With the Americans at Maknassy and the French south of them around Ksar Rhilane, Montgomery broke the Mareth Line. After heavy artillery preparaton, 21–22 March, the 50th Division bridged an anti-tank ditch and got tanks across the waterlogged Wadi Zigzaou, but was then hit by the counter-attack of two Panzer divisions. Pinning the enemy in front, Montgomery turned the Mareth Line by a left hook delivered with all his reserves. On this flank the New Zealand Division (Freyberg) breached the Roman Wall and the 4th Indian circled the enemy's rear through the Matmata Hills. With Americans closing in from Maknassy, the Germans switched troops from front to flank, 26 March, and the British 51st plunged through the weakened Mareth Line, 27 March. In 10 days the Eighth Army had taken 8,000 prisoners. *See* Alamein; Libya, Takrouna.

Margate (*Hundred Years' War) 24 March 1387*. The English fleet (Earls of Arundel and Nottingham) completely defeated the French–Castilian fleet of Louis I, capturing or destroying 110 enemy vessels. This victory, off Margate, eliminated the threat of French invasion. *See* La Rochelle I.

Margus (*Roman Empire Civil Wars between Carinus and Diocletian) May 285*. A Roman battle — on the banks of the Morava River, Yugoslavia — between the legions of the Emperor Carinus and those of Diocletian elected Emperor by his soldiers. These men had been exhausted by wars in Persia and Carinus' fresher legions were winning when one of his generals went over to Diocletian and another officer murdered Carinus. These acts brought victory to Diocletian. *See* Palmyra.

Mariana Islands, *Philippine Sea (World War II) 1944*. The Americans needed the Mariana airfields as bases so that B-29 Superfortress bombers could bomb Japan and the Philippines. The Marianas, also the headquarters of the Japanese Central Pacific Fleet, were held by the Japanese Thirty-first Army (Obata). A distinct battle was fought for each of the three major islands — Saipan, Guam, Tinian.

Saipan. 15 June–9 July 1944. Under General Holland Smith two marine divi-

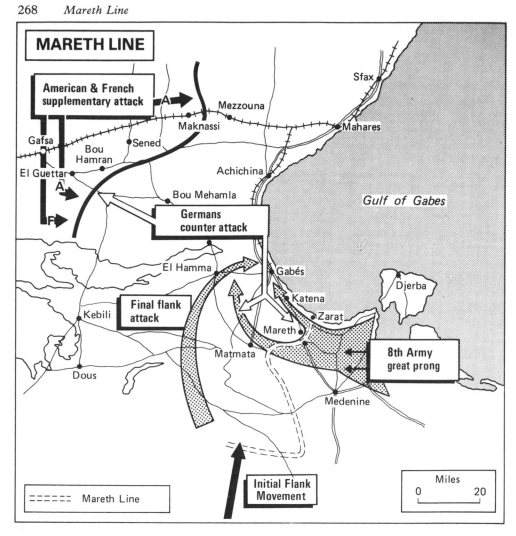

MARETH LINE

American & French supplementary attack

Sfax

A

Mezzouna

Maknassi

Mahares

Gafsa

Sened

Bou
Hamran

El Guettar

Achichina

A

Bou Mehamla

Germans
counter attack

Gulf of Gabes

F

El Hamma

Gabés

Djerba

Katena

Final flank
attack

Kebili

Zarat

Mareth

Dous

Matmata

8th Army
great prong

Medenine

Initial Flank
Movement

Miles

0   20

- - - - - -   Mareth Line

sions, 2nd and 4th, assaulted the island on a 4-mile front, with the 27th Infantry Division joining in on 16 June. Resistance from the 30,000 defenders was savage, but wheeling to the left the American line rolled up the island, the 2nd Marine Division capturing Garapan. On 6 July the Japanese commanders, Nagumo and Saito, committed suicide. In ferocious banzai attacks the Japanese lost 2,500 dead. On 9 July Japanese soldiers and civilians committed mass suicide off Marpi Point. Only 1,000 prisoners survived the Saipan conquest. American casualties, 10,347 marines and 3,674 soldiers, including 3,426 dead.

Guam. 21 July–10 August 1944. Under

General Geiger, the 3rd Marine Division, 77th Infantry Division and other units made two separate attacks on the island's west coast. The 20,000 defenders were commanded by Takashina. It took the marines 4 days of extremely hard fighting to advance a mile and link with the infantry. Ferocious counter-attacks on the night of 25–26 July were narrowly beaten back. The advance then became steady and occupation was complete on 10 August. American casualties, 6,716 marines, 839 soldiers and 245 sailors, including 1,023 dead. Few Japanese survived.

Tinian. 24–31 July 1944. Defended by 9,000 Japanese soldiers and sailors

(Admiral Kakuda), Tinian had the best B-29 bases in the Pacific. General Schmidt made a feint landing with 2nd Marine Division at Tinian Town while the 4th made the real assault. The first night 1,200 Japanese died trying to destroy the American beachhead. The 2nd Marine Division landed next day, captured the island's northern end and advanced with the 4th the length of Tinian. American casualties, 327 killed and 1,771 wounded. Practically all Japanese not killed by the American attack died in hopeless banzai charges or committed suicide.

Making a counter-attack in the Philippine Sea to the west, the Japanese navy was disastrously defeated. *See* Kwajalein–Eniwetok; Tarawa–Makin.

Maria Zell (*Napoleonic Wars: Danube campaign***) 8 November 1805.** The French (Davoust), advancing on Vienna, were confronted by an Austrian corps (von Meerfeld). The French shouldered the Austrians aside, killing many and taking 4,000 prisoners. *See* Austerlitz.

Marignano, *the "Battle of Giants"* (*French wars in Italy***) 13–14 September 1575.** Between 50,000 French (Francis I) and 40,000 Swiss mercenaries employed by Pope Leo X, Maximilian of the Holy Roman Empire and Ferdinand of Spain. The Swiss, attacking the French camp, fought until midnight and resumed the attack at daybreak. On the point of victory, they withdrew when Venetian troops arrived to reinforce the French. Casualties: French, 6,000; Swiss, about 12,000, including 1,200 who died in the flames of a village they were defending. *See* La Bicocca; Novara I.

Maritsa (*or Meric River***) (***Turkish conquest of Balkans***) 26 September 1371.** Three Serbian princes, worried by the growing Ottoman power in the Balkans, marched an army into Turkish territory. The Turks (Murad I) met the Serbs near Cenomen on the Maritsa River. Murad had a fine army of Janissary infantry (highly trained young captives) and spahis (heavy cavalry) and overwhelmed the Serbs; two of the three princes, including the most senior, Lazar, were killed. *See* Kossovo.

Marj-Dabik, *near Aleppo* (*Turkish–Egyptian wars***) 24 August 1516.** Between the Turks (Selim I) and the Mameluke army of Kansu al-Gauri, the Mameluke Sultan of Egypt who had come to the aid of his Persian ally, Shah Ismail I, in the face of Turkish aggression. Turkish tactics and artillery were superior and the Egyptians were beaten; al-Gauri was killed. *See* Cairo.

Marne River I (*World War I***) 6–8 September 1914.** Reaching the Marne on 3 September, von Kluck's German First Army crossed the river only a day behind the retreating French Fifth Army (d'Esperey) and the British Expeditionary Force (General French). Believing the Allies all but beaten, von Kluck was poised for a final thrust when he reached a point directly east of Paris on the evening of 5 September. The Allied Commander-in-Chief, Joffre, faced one of the most crucial battles in history. Chief of the German General Staff, von Moltke, worried about the exposed right of the German advance, ordered von Kluck to withdraw to the north. But that morning, 6 September, the French, under Maunoury (commander of the French Sixth Army) and Gallieni, military governor of Paris, launched a surprise counter-offensive against the German IV Reserve Corps (Gronau) along the Ourcq River. A 30-mile gap had opened between the German First and Second Armies and the French and British moved into it. Also, the French Ninth Army (Foch) attacked the junction between the German Second and Third Armies.

The battle raged along a 300-mile front. The French were barely able to hold their ground and vital reinforcements — 5,000 men from the Moselle front — were rushed into battle by fleets of Paris taxis. On the eastern end of the

French line the First and Second Armies grimly held the fortress cities of Epinal, Charmes, Nancy and Topul, along the Moselle. And in between the two fronts the French Third and Fourth Armies stopped the German drive from Verdun.

Moltke called off the German attack on 9 September, and the entire German line began a 40-mile fighting withdrawal to the Aisne River. Moltke lost his job to von Falkenhayn. Some historians believe that had Sir John French counter-attacked more resolutely the Allied offensive would have pierced the German lines and that such a victory might well have shortened the war. This is unfair and unsound. The British Army was the only Allied force which advanced continuously through 5–8 September, the only army to cross the Marne before the German retreat. The German withdrawal was largely the result of British action. With only 70,000 effective troops — 11,032 had become casualties at Mons and Le Cateau — the British Army achieved more than could be expected of it.

The Germans committed forty-four infantry and seven cavalry divisions — 900,000 men; the Allies fifty-six infantry and nine cavalry divisions — 1,082,000 men. French casualties were about 250,000, German about 200,000; in both cases detailed figures were never published and are not obtainable. British casualties, 1,071. *See* Aisne River I; Frontiers of France; Le Cateau.

Marne River II, or "Champagne–Marne Offensive" (*World War I*) 15 July–6 August 1918. Ludendorff launched a major attack on the Allied line and the German Seventh Army (von Boehn) established a bridgehead 9 miles long and 4 miles deep. The French, with notable assistance from the American 3rd Division, checked the advance in this sector. Statistically, thirty-six Allied divisions — twenty-three French, nine American, two British, two Italian — stopped fifty-two German divisions. This was the last major German attack on the Western Front.

On 18 July Foch, now commander-in-chief, put in a massive counter-attack with four French armies and fourteen Allied divisions — eight American, four British, two Italian, supported by 350 tanks. The Allied thrust threatened to cut German communications along the Soissons–Chateau Thierry road so Ludendorff began to withdraw. He formed a line along the Vesle and Aisne Rivers which was strong enough, 6 August, to beat off an American attack. Allied casualties amounted to 60,000, including 20,000 dead. German casualties were at least 100,000. *See* Amiens.

Marosch, The (*Roman Conquest of Dacia*) 101. The Romans (Trajan) routed the Dacians (Decebalus) and drove them across the river with heavy loss. (Dacia is modern Romania.)

Marsaglia (*War of the Grand Alliance*) 4 October 1693. Between the French (Marshal de Catinat) and the allied Austrians, Spanish and English (Duke of Savoy). The French, after severe fighting, drove the Allies across the river, taking prisoner the Duke of Schomberg and Lord Warwick. Both sides lost about 6,000. *See* Namur I; Staffarda.

Mars-la-Tour (*or Vionville*) (*French–German War*) 18 August 1870. The Germans (von Alvensleben), though hard pressed, held their ground and prevented the French (Bazaine) from breaking through to the west. The German cavalry made desperate charges against the French lines to give the broken German infantry time to reform. Casualties were great — about 16,000 on either side. *See* Colombey; Gravelotte.

Marston Moor (*English Civil War*) 2 July 1644. Between 18,000 Royalists (Prince Rupert) and 27,000 Parliamentarians (Fairfax, Manchester and Leven). For the first time in the war Rupert's dashing cavalry was repulsed by Cromwell's "Ironsides". Fairfax's wing was scattered, but the Parliamentarian left and centre held firm and the Royalists were defeated, losing 4,000 men. The victory gave Parliament control of the north. *See* Cropredy Bridge; Tippermuir.

Martinesti (*Turkish–Austrian War*) 23 September 1789. Osman Pasha led a massive army of 80,000 Turks to drive the Austrians out of Wallachia (Romania). The Russians sent an army under Marshal Suvorov to help the Austrians, led by the Prince of Saxe-Coburg, but together they had only 27,000 men. Suvorov, in supreme command, stormed the Turkish lines and his disciplined troops won a hard fight. The Turks lost 10,000 men killed and 8,000 were drowned trying to cross the Rimnik River. The Allies had 617 casualties.

Martinique I (*Seven Years' War*) 12 February 1762. Admiral Rodney, with veteran British troops from Canada, overwhelmed the French defenders of the island. All the other Windward Islands could then be secured. The Treaty of Paris, 1763, restored Martinique to France. *See* Quiberon Bay.

Martinique II (*Wars of the French Revolution*) 1794. The island was captured from the French by a combined naval and military force under Sir John Jervis and Sir George Grey, with a loss to the victors of six officers and thirty-seven men killed and wounded. The island was later recovered by the French governor, Victor Hugues. *See* Martinique III.

Martinique III (*Napoleonic Wars*) 24 February 1809. Having been restored to France at the Peace of Amines, Martinique was again taken by a British force under Admiral Cochrane and General Beckwith after a stout defence by Admiral Villaret de Joyeuse.

Masada (*Jewish Rebellion against Rome*) 72. At the beginning of the rebellion, 66 AD, a group of Jewish zealots wiped out the Roman garrison and held it throughout a raging 4-year war. The Masada outpost, commanded by Eleazer ben Yair, was the only place to hold out. From here the Jews harried the Romans for 2 years until Flavius Silva marched on Masada with the Tenth Legion. Beaten back, the Romans laid siege, built a siege tower and moved up a battering ram which breached the wall. Knowing that next day Roman conquest was inevitable, the 960 defenders — men, women and children — committed mass suicide. The story was told by the only survivors — two women who preferred to live.

Maserfield, *now Oswestry* (*Teutonic conquest of Britain*) 642. Between the Northumbrians, under Oswald, and the Mercians, under Penda. The Mercians were defeated, and Penda slain. *See* Heavenfield; Winwaed.

Massacre Hill (*First Sioux War*) 21 December 1866. About 2,000 Sioux (Crazy Horse and Red Cloud) attacked a wood train of wagons 5 miles from Fort Phil Kearney (Fort Perilous) on the upper Powder River. To protect the train, Captain W. Fetterman with two other officers and seventy-nine men made a counter-attack. Unaware of the Indians' strength, Fetterman and his men were surrounded on a height later called Massacre Hill where every soldier was killed. The Sioux, who lost sixty, then besieged the fort itself. A veteran scout, "Portugee" Phillips, got through the Indian lines and rode 236 miles to Fort Laramie for help. *See* Fort Phil Kearny; Platte Bridge.

Masulipatam (*Seven Years' War*) March 1759. This fortress, held by a French garrison (Baron Lally), was besieged by the British, about 2,500 strong under Colonel Forde. Forde's objective was to raise the siege of Madras. After a fortnight's bombardment the place was taken by storm. Lally surrendered with his whole force, which greatly outnumbered the British. Forde then relieved Madras, q.v.

Masurian Lakes (*World War I*) *5–13 September 1914*. The Russians, under the direction of General Ivan Jilinsky, had made a vast pincers attack on East Prussia. The Germans defeated one arm at Tannenberg (q.v.). Field Marshal von Hindenberg, with his chief of staff Ludendorff, attacked the second arm, the Russian First Army (Rennenkampf), which had one end anchored on the Masurian Lakes with a cordon thrown out to the Baltic. Threatened by outflanking, Rennenkampf withdrew on 9 September and on 10 September counterattacked. This enabled many Russian units to avoid envelopment, but East Prussia had been cleared of Russians at a cost of 10,000 casualties — a small number in comparison with Russian losses of 125,000. *See* Galicia II; Tannenberg II.

Masurian Lakes, "*The Winter Battle of Masuria*" (*World War I*) *7–21 February 1915*. The Germans struck Baron Siever's Russian Tenth Army during a heavy snowstorm, surprised them and sent them into retreat. Next day the Russians were again hit, this time by the German Tenth Army (von Eichhorn). Only the stubborn resistance of the Russian XX Corps in the forest of Augustow enabled the other three to escape. Nevertheless, the Russians suffered a loss of 200,000, including 100,000 prisoners. German losses were light. The battle was a great tactical victory for Hindenberg and Ludendorff, but it had little strategic value. *See* Gorlice-Tarnów.

Matapan, *off Cape Matapan, Greek Peloponnese* (*World War II*) *28 March 1941*. A decisive victory for a British naval force commanded by Admiral Pridham-Whippell over an Italian fleet (Riccardi). The British had three battleships, four cruisers and an aircraft carrier. They sank three Italian 8-inch cruisers, two smaller cruisers and two destroyers and damaged a battleship. British losses, two naval aircraft. *See* Taranto.

Matchevitz (*First Polish Insurrection against Russia*) *10 October 1794*. Between the Russians (Baron de Fersen) and the Poles (Kosciusko). The outnumbered Poles, after hard fighting, were totally defeated, leaving 6,000 dead. Kosciusko was severely wounded. *See* Warsaw I.

Matchin (*Turkish–Russian Wars*) *10 July 1791*. Between the Turks (Yussuf Pasha) and the Russians (Prince Repnin). The left and centre of the Turkish army held, but a brilliant charge of the Russian left, under General Kutusoff, drove back the Turks who were defeated with heavy loss. *See* Rimnitz.

Maxen (*Seven Years' War*) *21 November 1759*. An army of 42,000 Austrians under Marshal Daun surrounded 12,000 Prussians led by General Finck. Finck attempted to break out, but after comparatively little fighting Daun compelled him to surrender his force, which included seventeen generals. Casualties were light. Frederick the Great imprisoned Finck. *See* Kunersdorf; Landeshut.

Mau Mau War, *also known as Kenyan Emergency, 1952–60*. Through the paramilitary secret society, Mau Mau, the Kikuyu people waged a terrorist war against the British administration. Their atrocity tactics were effective until the British gathered the peaceful Kenyans into protected settlements and then hunted down the Mau Mau. Casualties: British, 63 killed, 465 wounded; African troops in British service, 534 killed, 666 wounded; Mau Mau, 11,500 killed. Mau Mau terrorists killed nearly 2,000 civilians, mostly African.

Maya (*Peninsular War*) *25 July 1813*. A British division (Stewart) of only 6,000 tried to block the French divisions of d'Armagnac, Abbé and Maransin, 26,000 in all. The French, losing 1,500 men, nevertheless forced the pass of Maya, driving back the British with a loss of 1,400 men and four guns. Stewart fell back on Elizonde, which still effectively blocked the French.

Maypo (*Chilean War of Independence*) *5 April 1818*. The Chilean Patriots, 9,000 strong under San Martin, defeated 6,000 Spanish Royalists (Osorio). The Spaniards were defeated with a loss of 1,000 killed and 2,350 prisoners, the Chileans losing over 1,000 killed and wounded. The result of the battle was the establishment of the independence of Chile. *See* Chacabuco.

Mecca (*Muhammad's conquest of Arabia*) *January 630*. Muhammad himself led the attack on Mecca held by rebel factions, and after winning over the inhabitants by sword and speech made the place the Holy City of Islam. *See* Medina.

Mechanicsville (*American Civil War*) *26 June 1862*. The first important action of the Seven Days' Battle, q.v., east of Richmond. The Federals stopped the Confederate attack, which had been marred by inexperienced staff work.

Medellin, *Guadiana River* (*Peninsular War*) *28 March 1809*. Between 17,500 French (Marshal Victor) and 30,000 Spaniards (Cuesta). The Spanish cavalry gave way, thus exposing their infantry who were mercilessly sabred by pursuing French cavalry. The Spanish lost 18,000 killed and wounded. The French lost 1,000.

Medenine. *See* Mareth Line.

Medina (*Muhammad's War with the Koreish Tribe*) *625*. 10,000 Koreish under Abu Sophian besieged Medina, defended by Muhammad with 3,000 Muslims. Several weak-willed assaults were repulsed and Sophian withdrew after a 20-day siege. *See* Mecca; Ohod.

Medola (*Napoleon's Italian campaigns*) *5 August 1796*. Between 23,000 French, under Napoleon, and 25,000 Austrians, under Marshal Wurmser. The Austrians were defeated and driven back to Roveredo, losing 2,000 killed and wounded, 1,000 prisoners and 20 guns. Wurmser had already succeeded in supplying Mantua, but at heavy cost, the Austrian losses during the 3 days' fighting, 3–5 August, being 20,000 men and sixty guns.

Medway River (*Second Roman invasion of Britain*) *43*. The British leader Caractacus blocked the Roman expedition (Aulus Plautius) heading for the Thames. Plautius sent a patrol to kill and cripple the Britons' horses, thus making their war chariots useless. Next day Vespasian (later a Roman emperor) forded the Medway and attacked Caractacus' flank. Roman method was too much for the Britons' courage. The Romans spread to Lincoln and to the Welsh border. *See* Verulamium I.

Meeanee, or Mianee (*British–Scinde War*) *17 February 1843*. Between 2,800 British and native troops under Sir Charles Napier, and about 30,000 Baluchis led by the Amirs of Scinde. The British infantry were almost overpowered, but were rescued by a charge of the 9th Bengal Cavalry. The Baluchis were routed with a loss of 5,000 men and several guns. British casualties: 256 killed and wounded. The 61-year-old Napier, musket in hand, had personally led the British troops. *See* Dubba; Hyderabad.

Meerut (*First Mongol invasion of India*) *1399*. Meerut, besieged by the Tartars under Tamerlane, was considered impregnable. Tamerlane commenced mining, but this was too slow for his followers, who scaled the walls, carried the fortress by storm, and massacred the inhabitants. Tamerlane completed his mines and destroyed the place. *See* Baghdad II; Delhi I.

Megaletaphrus, *Peloponnese* (*Greek City-states Wars*) *740 BC*. Between the Messenians (Aristomenes) and the Spartans. The Messenians were surrounded and cut to pieces, Aristomenes escaping with a few followers.

Megalopolis I, *Arcady* (*Rebellion against the Macedonians*). The Spartans, aided by the Arcadians, Achaeans and Eleians, tried to shake off the Macedonian yoke during Alexander's absence in Asia. The allies, led by Agis, King of Sparta, were besieging Megalopolis, which had declined to join the league, when they were attacked by the Macedonians (Antipater) and routed, Agis falling in the battle. *See* Arbela; Themes.

Megalopolis II (*Greek City-states Wars*) *226 BC*. The Spartans (Cleomenes) defeated the forces of the Achaean League (Aratus). The Achaeans forced the Spartans into flight and pursued with light troops. The Spartans turned and routed them, and then overwhelmed the Achaean hoplites with great slaughter. *See* Megalopolis I.

Megiddo I (*Egyptian invasion of Asia*) *1469 BC*. The first battle of which an account exists. Thutmose III took his Egyptian army around the eastern end of the Mediterranean to quell a rebellion in Palestine. The King of the Syrian city of Kadesh placed his rebel army at Megiddo which commanded the pass leading to the Plain of Esdraelon. Thutmose deployed into three divisions and made a devastating dawn attack. The rebels ran into fortress Megiddo; the Egyptians could have beaten them at this point, but stopped to loot the enemy camp. Thutmose took the place after a 7-month siege. Some historians refer to Megiddo as the site of the Armageddon battlefield mentioned in the Bible. *See* Kadesh.

Megiddo II (*Egyptian conquest of Judah*) *609 BC*. Necho II of Egypt, marching to help the collapsing Assyrian empire, encountered at Megiddo the Judah army under King Josiah and defeated it. He pushed on northwards to the Euphrates. *See* Carchemish; Nineveh I.

Megiddo III (*World War I*) *19 September 1918*. The German general, von Sanders, commanding 30,000 German–Turkish troops, believed that his opponent, General Allenby, would attack on the Turkish left flank. Instead, Allenby hit the enemy right on a 65-mile front. Breaking through in 3 hours, Allenby sent his Australian and New Zealand cavalry through the gap toward Megiddo and cut off the Turkish escape; 25,000 were captured. The relatively few Germans had no opportunity to make a stand. Damascus fell on 2 October, Aleppo on 28 October. The British had 5,600 casualties, but captured 75,000 Turks and Germans. *See* Gaza III.

Melanthias (*Sclavonian invasion*) *559*. Between Roman troops under Belisarius, and the Sclavonians and Bulgarians (Zabergan, Prince of Bulgaria). The barbarians attacked the Roman lines but were repulsed. This was Belisarius' last victory.

Meldorp *1500*. Between 30,000 Danes, under John of Denmark, and the inhabitants of the province of Dithmarsh, which John wished to bring again under Danish rule after two centuries of virtual independence. The advancing Danes assaulted a small fortified outpost but were repulsed and driven in confusion into the surrounding marshes, where over 11,000 died.

Melitene I (*or Malatya*) (*Roman–Sassanid War*) *576*. The Sassanid King of Persia, Chosroes I, was waging war against Byzantine and Tiberius II sent the General Justinian to drive the Persians back. Both sides held their ground in an indecisive hard-fought battle, but Chosroes retired during the night. The following year Justinian invaded Chosroes' territory and forced him to seek peace. *See* Calinicum.

Melitene II (*Byzantine–Muslim Wars*) *934*. John Kurkuas, able general of Constantine VII of Byzantine, took veteran cavalry across the Upper Euphrates and captured the outpost fort of Melitene. The victory gave Constantine control of a vast region. *See* Candia II; Erzerum.

Melitene III (*First Crusade*) *1100*. Bohemond of Taranto, marching to help the trapped garrison of Melitene, was ambushed by a Turkish force. Most of his knights were killed and Bohemond was held for 3 years until his ransom arrived. *See* Ashkelon I; Mersivan.

Memphis I (*Athenian expedition to Egypt*) *459 BC*. The city, capital of Egypt, was captured by an Athenian fleet of 200 ships, which sailed up the Nile to help Inaros, who had revolted against Persia. The citadel, on an island in the Nile, held out until 456 BC when a Persian army (Begabyzus) diverted the course of the river, attacked and annihilated the Athenians.

Memphis II (*Muslim conquest of Egypt*) *638*. In 638 Amron, lieutenant of the Caliph Omar, with 8,000 Muslims, invested the city. After a siege of 7 months, during which the besiegers were nearly trapped by the rising of the Nile, the place was taken by assault. On the site of the Muslim encampment were laid the foundations of Cairo.

Memphis (*American Civil War*) *6 June 1862*. A river action fought between eight Confederate vessels (Commodore Montgomery) and ten Federal gunboats (Commodore Davis). Only one of the Confederate vessels escape destruction, and Memphis fell. Davis's flotilla steamed down to the mouth of the Yazoo River, above Vicksburg, q.v.

Menin Road, *Flanders* (*World War I*) *20–30 September 1917*. The Australian 1st and 2nd Divisions formed the striking centre of eleven divisions of the British Second and Fifth Armies. The Australians suffered 5,013 casualties in the attack, which ousted the Germans from their trenches. *See* Flanders; Ypres.

Mensourah, *Egypt* (*Fifth Crusade*) *1249*. Between the French (Louis IX) and the Muslims. The town of Mensourah was seized by the Comte d'Artois, but Muslims surrounded his party, which was wiped out. The king had taken the Saracen camp, but was unable to hold his ground and was driven back on Damietta. During his retreat his army was surrounded and taken prisoner.

Mentana (*Italian Wars of Independence from France*) *3 November 1867*. Between 10,000 Garibaldians under Garibaldi himself and 5,000 French and Papal troops (Kanzier). Garibaldi was defeated, largely because of the brilliant work of 1,500 Papal Zouaves, who drove the Garibaldians out of position after position. They lost 1,100 killed or wounded, and 1,000 prisoners. Allied losses were 182 killed or wounded.

Mergentheim (*or Mariendhal*) (*Thirty Years' War*) *2 May 1645*. A rare defeat for the French Marshal Turenne. At Mergentheim, on the Tauber River, Turenne had partly dispersed his veterans when surprised by a Bavarian–Austrian army (Mercy and Werth). Turenne lost all his artillery and baggage and with only a third of his force under command he fell back towards the Rhine. Here he was reinforced by an army under the Great Condé. *See* Jankau; Nordlingen.

Merida (*Spanish–Muslim Wars*) *712*. The place was besieged by 18,000 Moors under Musa. After a defeat in the open plain before the city, the Spaniards made a long and obstinate defence, which cost the besiegers many lives. In the end famine forced a Spanish surrender. This was one of the first battles in a conflict which was to last seven centuries.

Mersa Matruh (*World War II*) *26–29 June 1942*. After a long retreat the British Eighth Army under the Commander-in-Chief Middle East, Auchinleck, and Generals Holmes and Gott, took up positions at Mersa Matruh, a base in Egypt. Rommel, with only 2,500 German infantry and sixty tanks, struck at the junction between the two British corps and in 3 days routed four British divisions and 150 tanks. The Eighth Army lost 6,000 prisoners and forty tanks and fell back another 120 miles to El Alamein. German losses were light. *See* Alamein; Gazala; Libya; Tobruk III.

Merseburg (*or Riade*) (*Magyar invasion of Germany*) *934*. During the early tenth century the Magyars ranged unchecked over Italy, France and Germany. The German king, Henry the Fowler, defeated them at Merseberg. The Magyars did not seriously contest the field, apparently because they were surprised by the determination of the Germans. Henry now led raids into the Magyar homeland, Hungary.

Mersivan (*First Crusade*) *1101*. A crusader force of French, German and Lombard knights under Raymond IV of Toulouse reached Asia Minor to reinforce the army of Bohemond. Hearing that Bohemond was held by the Turks, the crusaders, against Raymond's advice, crossed the Halys River and pushed blindly into enemy territory. At Mersivan the Turks ambushed them and cut them down with arrows; the crusaders were never able to get close enough to use sword or lance. Knights, women, children, priests — all were slaughtered. Raymond and a few others cut their way to safety. *See* Melitene III.

Merta (*Mogul invasion of the Indian Deccan*) *1561*. This strong fortress, belonging to the Rajput Rajah of Malwar, was besieged by Sharf-ud-Din Hussein, one of the generals of Akbar, the Great Mogul. The place held out for several months until famine forced capitulation. One Malwar chief refused all terms and cut his way out at the head of 500 men, 250 of whom fell.

Merton (*Danish invasion*) *811*. Between the West Saxons under Alfred and the Danish invaders. After a severe engagement the Danes were victorious.

Merv, *now Mary, in modern Turkmen* (*Mongol conquest of Asia*) *1221*. Tului, youngest son of Genghis Khan, led a cavalry column to Merv whose Muslim garrison easily held off Mongol attacks for 3 weeks. Tului then induced some city elders to open a gate. The Mongols massacred the inhabitants and destroyed the city. *See* Bamian; Herat I.

Mesólongian (*or Missolonghi*) (*Greek rising against the Turks*) *June 1822–April 1826*. A Turkish army quelled all uprisings north of the Gulf of Corinth, but the garrison of Mesólongian under Alexandros Mavrokordatos could not be dislodged. In January 1823 the Turks were even forced back, but factional discord prevented a united Greek effort. Sultan Mahmud called for Egyptian help and in February Ibrahim subdued the peninsula while Reshid freshly invested Mesolongian. On 23 April 1826 the fortress fell. Great Britain, France and Russia now intervened in the war. (Lord Byron died of malaria while helping to defend Mesólongian.) *See* Navarino.

Messina I (*First Punic War*) *264 BC*. Mercenaries from Campania, the Mamertines or "sons of Mars", seized Messina. In 270 BC Carthaginians from western Sicily occupied the city and the Mamertines called for Roman help. In 264 BC a Roman army threw out the Carthaginians. Hiero of Syracuse now attacked the place, but was beaten, pursued and forced to become a Roman ally. *See* Ecnomus; Mylae.

Messina II (*Aragon conquest of Sicily*) 2 October 1284. Between the Sicilian and Catalan fleet, under the Grand Admiral, Roger de Lauria, and the French fleet under Charles of Anjou. The Sicilians, greatly outnumbering the French, burned or destroyed practically the whole of their fleet. Charles of Anjou was captured. *See* Alghero; Tagliacozzo.

Messina III (*French–Dutch War*) 25 March 1676. The French Marshal Louis Victor de Vivonne defeated the Spanish army (allies of the Dutch) in Sicily at the Battle of Messina. This was one of a series of victories for the French. Admiral Marquis Duquesne had repulsed De Ruyter's Spanish–Dutch naval attack on Messina in January. Then, on 22 April, De Ruyter was defeated and mortally wounded by Duquesne in the naval battle of Messina.

Messina 1718. *See* Cape Passaro.

Messines, *Belgium* (*World War I*) 7–14 June 1917. To break out of the Ypres salient, where the British had been contained for 30 months, Haig had first to throw the Germans from Messines Ridge, as it commanded the battlefield. A million pounds of high explosive in 21 great mines was laid under the Germans and 19 exploded on 7 June. Fierce bombardment from 2,266 guns added to the shock. The British Second Army (Plumer), Fifth Army (Gough) and French First Army (Anthoine) were thrown in to exploit the mining and shelling. Prince Rupprecht ordered Arnim to pull back his German Fourth Army and then counter-attack. This blunted the British advance and on 14 June stalemate reigned again, though the British did hold the ridge. The Allies suffered 108,882 casualties. German losses are estimated at 100,000; 10,000 men were blown to pieces or were buried by the enormous mine explosions. *See* Flanders; Passchendaele; Menin Road; Ypres.

Metauras River (*Second Punic War*) 207 BC. Between 50,000 Romans (Claudius Nero and Marcus Livius) and the Carthaginians, in rather smaller force, under Hasdrubal. The Carthaginians were surprised at early dawn as they were trying to find a ford in the Metaurus, and were routed, Hasdrubal being slain. The completeness of the victory was due to Nero, in command of the right wing. The ground prevented his getting to close quarters, and seeing the Roman left hard pressed by Hasdrubal's best troops, he led his force round the Roman rear and attacked Hasdrubal's right. *See* Capua.

Methuen (*English–Scottish Wars*) 19 June 1306. A small Scottish force under Robert Bruce was attacked and defeated by the English in superior force. Bruce returned early the following year to resume the war. *See* Falkirk I; Loudon Hill.

Metz (*French–German War*) 26 October 1870. This fortress was invested by the Germans after Bazaine, defeated at Gravelotte on 18 August, withdrew into it. After several fruitless attempts to break through the German lines Bazaine surrendered to Prince Frederick Charles with three marshals, 6,000 officers and 173,000 men. The Germans took 56 eagles, 622 field guns, 72 miltrailleuses, 876 pieces of fortress artillery and about 300,000 rifles. After the war Bazaine was sentenced to 20 years imprisonment for treason. *See* Gravelotte; Paris II; Sedan.

Meuse River — Argonne Forest (*World War I*) 26 September–11 November 1918. The Allied Commander-in-Chief, Foch, put in operation a gigantic pincers movement as an all-out offensive. French armies attacked from the west, the Americans (Pershing and Bullard) from the south. The Germans had defence in depth to 12 miles under von Gallwitz and Prince Friedrich Wilhelm. In the first 5 days the French drove 9 miles, the Americans 5 along the Meuse heights and 2 more in the difficult

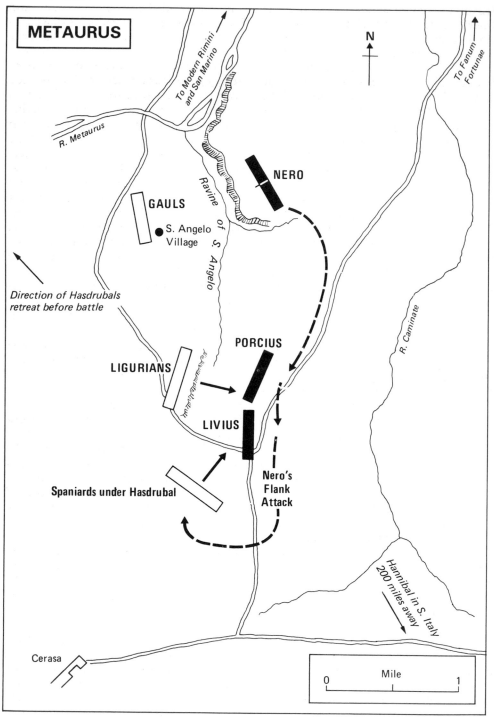

METAURUS

N

To Modern Rimini and San Marino

To Fanum Fortunae

R. Metaurus

Ravine of S. Angelo

GAULS

S. Angelo Village

NERO

Direction of Hasdrubals retreat before battle

LIGURIANS

PORCIUS

R. Caminate

LIVIUS

Nero's Flank Attack

Spaniards under Hasdrubal

Hannibal in S. Italy 200 miles away

Cerasa

0   Mile   1

Argonne. Beginning on 4 October the Americans made several frontal attacks, winning ground at heavy cost. On 31 October the Argonne Forest was cleared — a 10-mile advance. The French Fourth Army, same date, reached the Aisne River, taking 20 miles of country. The grinding advance continued until the armistice, reaching Sedan on the east and Montmédy in the west. Casualties: American, 117,000; French, 70,000; German, 100,000. *See* Marne River II.

Mexico (*Spanish conquest of Mexico*) 20 June 1520. The Spaniards, under Cortez, were evacuating Mexico during the night. Attacked by the Aztecs, the Spaniards suffered heavy loss. The Spaniards called this battle the "Noche Triste" — "night of tears". The site of the battle is unknown.

Michelberg (*Napoleonic Wars: Danube campaign*) 16–17 October 1805. Ney's corps stormed the heights of the Michelberg, Bavaria, at the same time that Lannes carried the Frauenberg, driving the Austrians back into Ulm, where on 17 October General Mack capitulated with 30,000 men. *See* Ulm.

Middelburg (*Netherlands War of Independence against Spain*) 1593–4. This fortress was the last stronghold in Walcheren to hold out for the Spanish king. It was besieged by Dutch patriots in the winter of 1593 and was defended by a garrison under Colonel Mondragon. In spite of a gallant resistance and numerous attempts to relieve him, Mondragon was forced by famine to surrender on 18 February 1594.

Midway (*World War II*) 3–5 June 1942. The turning point of the sea war in the Pacific. The Japanese sent Nagumo, who had led the attack on Pearl Harbour, with eighty-eight ships, including four carriers, to attack Midway island, 1,000 miles west of Hawaii. Anticipating the attack, the U.S. Pacific commander, Admiral Nimitz, assembled two task forces east of Midway (Spruance and Fletcher). The American plans hinged on the heavy carriers *Yorktown*, *Enterprise* and *Hornet*.

The first U.S. air attack on the enemy fleet, 3 June, was unsuccessful. Early on 4 June 108 Japanese planes raided Midway, causing much damage and wrecking fifteen of the twenty-five fighter aircraft there. The Americans made four futile attacks on the Japanese fleet and lost sixty-five aircraft. The fifth — by fifty-four dive bombers from *Enterprise* and *Yorktown* — was vital: The heavy carriers *Akagi*, *Kaga* and *Soryu* were quickly sunk with their aircraft. *Hiryu* was sunk that afternoon, after its own planes had badly damaged *Yorktown*, which a submarine sank on 6 June. The United States lost 150 aircraft, 307 men, the destroyer *Hammann* and *Yorktown*. The Japanese lost 275 aircraft and about 5,000 men as well as the vital carriers. An American–Australian counter-offensive was now possible. *See* Coral Sea; Solomon Islands.

Milazzo, Sicily (*Italian Wars of Independence*) 18 July 1860. Between the Italian Volunteers (Garibaldi) and the Neapolitans, under General Bosco. The Neapolitans occupied a strongly entrenched position, which Garibaldi succeeded in turning. The Neapolitans were defeated and driven out and Garibaldi crossed the straits of Messina.

Miletopolis (*First Mithridatic War*) 86 BC. The Romans under Flavius Fimbria won a complete victory over the Pontic troops under Mithridates by splitting them and defeating them piecemeal.

Millesimo (*or Monte Lezino*) (*Napoleon's Italian campaigns*) 13 April 1796. The divisions of Augereau, Masséna and La Harpe attacked the Austrians, strongly entrenched under General Colli. After severe fighting, the Austrians were driven back, thus cutting Colli's communications with Beaulieu, the Austrian Commander-in-Chief. The

Austrian–Sardinians lost about 6,000 men and thirty guns. *See* Dego.

Mill Springs, *Kentucky* (*American Civil War*) *19 January 1862*. Between 9,000 Federals under Thomas and 8,000 Confederates under Crittenden. The Confederates attacked and at first drove back the Federals, who began the action with only 5,000 men. As reinforcements arrived, Thomas repulsed the Confederates with considerable loss, capturing twelve guns. The Federals lost 246 men. This was the first serious defeat suffered by the Confederates. *See* Fort Henry.

Milne Bay, *Papua* (*World War II*) *August–September 1942*. The first Japanese reverse on land. Intense jungle fighting took place between the Australian defenders of the airstrip and the attacking Japanese. On 7 September, having lost 1,000 highly trained marines, the Japanese abandoned their attempts to take the position. Australian casualties, 300. *See* Kokoda; New Guinea.

Minden I (*Roman Empire's Germanic Wars*) *16*. Emperor Tiberius sent Germanicus Caesar with eight legions to avenge the massacre of Varus' legions in the Teutoburger Wald, q.v., 9 AD. Crossing the Weser near Minden, Germanicus encountered a large force of Germans under Arminius, conqueror of Varus. In open country this time, the Romans were virtually unbeatable and the Germans were routed; Arminius was wounded. He attacked the Roman column on its return march to Italy and was beaten even more thoroughly.

Minden II (*Seven Years' War*) *1 August 1759*. The French, 64,000-strong under the Marquis de Contades, confronted the Hanoverians, British and Prussians, 54,000-strong under Ferdinand of Brunswick. Ferdinand detached a force of 10,000 to threaten de Contades' rear, and then broke the first line of the French. The Allied cavalry failed to advance and the French were able to rally

and carry out an orderly retreat. They lost 7,086 killed, wounded and prisoners, forty-three guns and seventeen standards. The Allies lost 2,762, a half being in the six English regiments. Lord George Sackville, the Allied cavalry commander, was cashiered from George II's army. *See* Bergen; Kunersdorf.

Minqar Qaim, *Libya* (*World War II*) *27 June 1942*. A New Zealand force was encircled by the 21st Panzer Division. After an artillery duel the New Zealanders broke out of the box. Their commander, Freyberg, was wounded. *See* Alamein; Alam Halfa; Libya.

Mingolsheim (*Thirty Years' War*) *27 April 1622*. Count Tilly, commander of the Catholic League's army, was trying to join with a Spanish force from The Netherlands under General de Cordoba. The Protestant military commander, Count Mansfeld, marched towards Tilly, surprised him at Mingolsheim and defeated his army. This delayed the union of the Catholic forces but could not prevent it. *See* Höchst; Wimpfen.

Minorca I (*Seven Years' War*) *20 May 1756*. Garrisoned by 2,800 British troops (General Blakeney) Minorca was invested by the French (Duc de Richelieu). A British squadron of thirteen ships under Admiral Byng attacked Richelieu's blockading squadron of seventeen ships. The attack failed, French ships escaped and Byng took all his reinforcement troops and supplies back to Gibraltar. Blakeney was forced to surrender. Back in England, Byng was tried by court-martial and shot on his own quarter-deck.

Minorca II (*War of the American Revolution*) *July 1781–5 February 1782*. Having been restored to England by the treaty of Paris in 1762, Minorca was recaptured in 1781 by a force of 12,000 French and Spaniards. The garrison of Port Mahon under General Murray was only 900 strong, but held out for six months until disease and casualties forced surrender.

Minsk (*World War II*) *27 June–2 July 1941*. Two German panzer groups, linking east of Minsk, cut off 300,000 Russians who were either killed or captured in bitter fighting. *See* Soviet Union.

Miohosaki *September 764*. Between the Japanese rebels, (Oshikatsu) and the Imperial troops (Saiki-no-Sanya). The rebels were routed and Oshikatsa and his son slain.

Miraflores (*Peruvian–Chilean War*) *15 January 1881*. The Chileans (Baquedano) defeated the Peruvians (Caceres) who lost 3,000 killed or wounded. The Chileans occupied Lima on 17 January, and the war ended.

Missionary Ridge (*American Civil War*) *25 November 1863*. The third action of the battle of Chattanooga, q.v. Grant's Federal troops climbed the ridge — although their officers had ordered them to halt — and captured it.

Mita Caban, *Asia Minor 1362*. The Tartars, under Tamerlane, defeated the Getes, under the Khan Elias. The Getes were never again a threat to Tamerlane.

Mitla Pass, *Sinai* (*Israeli–Arab Six-Day War*) *7 June 1967*. The battle for Mitla Pass was a vital part of the war; the pass is 23 kilometres long and possession gives command of all access to the Suez Canal from the east. The Israelis took it from the Egyptians on 7 June, and held it against attacks by thousands of Egyptians who tried to force it and reach safety. *See* Israel–Arab War.

Miyako I (*Japanese Civil Wars*) *June 1353*. Between the rebelling Moronoshi and his followers and the troops of the Emperor of the South under Yoshinori. Moronoshi's victory was complete and Yoshinori and the Emperor fled into the Eastern provinces.

Miyako II (*Japanese Civil Wars*) *30 December 1391*. Between the troops of the provinces of Idzumo and Idzumi under Mitsuyaki, and those of the Emperor of the South, Gokameyama. A series of engagements took place in and around Miyako; Mitsuyaki was driven off with heavy loss.

Mobile Bay, *Alabama* (*American Civil War*) *3–5 August 1864*. A Federal combined operation to capture the important Confederate port. About 5,500 troops under Granger were landed on Dauphine Island and in 3 weeks reduced the forts of Gaines, Powell and Morgan, capturing 104 guns and 1,464 troops. Running his fleet past the guns, 5 August, Admiral Farragut attacked the Confederate fleet (Buchanan) and forced surrender. Of the 470 Confederates in action, no fewer than 312 were casualties. The Federals lost 319. Despite these successes the city of Mobile held out until 12 April 1865. *See* Atlanta.

Modder River (*Second British–Boer War*) *28 November 1899*. Cronje, with 9,000 Boers, held a strong position on both banks of the river, on which Lord Methuen was marching to the Modder with 1st British Division. His columns came under fire about 7 a.m. and the action lasted till evening, when a turning movement enabled Methuen to drive Cronje from his trenches. British losses were 24 officers and 461 men killed or wounded. Boer casualties, 500. *See* Kimberley; Magersfontein.

Moesia (*Wars of Roman Empire*) *89*. Decebalus, a great leader, united the scattered tribes of Dacia — modern Romania — and crossing the Danube seized the Roman province of Moesia. The first Roman punitive expedition was ineffectual. In 89 Calpurnius Julianus defeated the Dacians, but Decebalus formed a powerful alliance with the Marcomanni and Quadi tribes. The Emperor Domitian negotiated a humiliating peace with Decebalus. *See* Sarmizegetusa.

Mohácz (*Turkish–Hungarian War*) *29 August 1526*. Between 30,000 Hungarians (King Lewis and Tomore, Bishop of Kolocz) and over 100,000 Turks, with 300 guns, under Suleiman the Magnificent. The Hungarians made heroic resistance against overwhelming numbers, but were routed. They left 12,000 dead on the field, including the king, seven bishops and over 500 nobles. This disaster placed Hungary at the mercy of Suleiman and was quickly followed by the fall of Buda-Pesth. *See* Belgrade II; Vienna I.

Mohi (*Mongol invasion of Europe*) *19–11 April 1241*. The Hungarian king, Vela IV, raised an army of 100,000 archers and lancers to face the marauding Mongols under Subotai. The strength of this army induced the Mongols to withdraw eastwards across the Sajo River. Bela overconfidently pursued. That night Subotai sent detachments to recross the Sajo both sides of the Hungarian position at Mohi. At dawn the Mongol bowmen opened fire across the river, hitting the Hungarian centre. This was the signal for the flank forces to attack on the wings and in the rear. Batu Khan led the main Mongol army back across the river and frontally assaulted the Hungarians. By midday the Hungarian Army had lost 70,000 dead. Only Bela and a few others escaped. However, towards the end of 1241 the Mongols heard that Ogadai, son of Genghis, had died and they left for home to elect a new "crown prince". The Mongols never returned to Europe (apart from the Golden Horde on the lower Volga). *See* Leignitz I.

Mohilev (or Mogilev) (*Napoleonic Wars: Moscow campaign*) *23 July 1812*. Between 28,000 French (Davoust) and 60,000 Russians (Prince Bagration). Bagration attacked Davoust in a strong position — at Mohilev on the Dniepr River — which counter-balanced the great disparity of numbers. The Russians lost 4,000 and were repulsed. The French lost 1,000. *See* Smolensk I.

Mohrungen (*Napoleonic Wars: Friedland campaign*) *25 January 1807*. Bernadotte, with 10,000 French, was defeated by Marhof and his 14,000 Russians. They lost about 1,000 killed and wounded. *See* Friedland; Heilsberg.

Molinos del Rey, *Barcelona* (*Peninsular War*) *21 December 1808*. Between 26,000 French (St. Cyr) and the Spaniards, about equal in strength, under Captain-General Vives. The Spaniards were routed with a loss of 3,000 killed, wounded and prisoners, and fifty guns, at slight cost to the victors. The French victory ended the Spanish blockade of Barcelona.

Molino del Rey (*U.S.–Mexican War*) *8 September 1847*. Before attacking the powerful bastion of Chapultepec, near Mexico City, General Winfield Scott sent 3,450 men (Worth) to make a diversionary attack on Molino del Rey. Worth found the place held in force and a day-long battle ensued. The Mexicans suffered 2,700 casualties, but the Americans were so badly mauled — 135 killed, 653 wounded — that Worth withdrew. *See* Chapultepec.

Mollwitz (*War of Austrian Succession*) *8 April 1741*. Between the Prussians, 30,000-strong under Frederick the Great, and an equal number of Austrians, under Neipperg. Frederick surprised the Austrian general, and after severe fighting — the Austrians made five violent charges — drove him from his entrenchments, with a loss of 5,000 killed, wounded and prisoners. The Prussians lost 2,500. *See* Chotusitz.

Monarda (*Spanish–Muslim Wars*) *18 March 1501*. Between the Spaniards, led by Count di Cifuentes and Alonso de Aguilar, and the insurgent Moors. The Spaniards were greatly outnumbered and were overpowered, suffering a disastrous defeat. However, the days of Moor supremacy in Spain were ending.

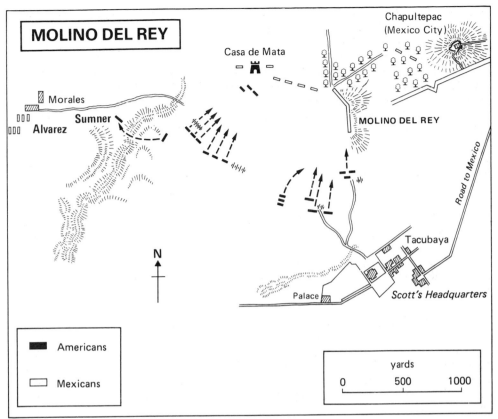

MOLINO DEL REY

Chapultepec
(Mexico City)

Casa de Mata

Morales

Sumner

Alvarez

MOLINO DEL REY

Road to Mexico

N

Tacubaya

Palace

Scott's Headquarters

Americans

Mexicans

yards

0   500   1000

Monastir, *Macedonia (First Balkan War)* 5 *November 1912*. Serbia, Bulgaria and Greece were at war with Turkey. A Serb division stormed high ground and threatened envelopment of the Turkish left. A Turkish counter-attack retook the height and the Serb division was practically wiped out. But the Turks had weakened their centre and a Serb frontal attack now broke through. As Greek units came up from the south, Turkish resistance collapsed. About 20,000 Turks were killed or captured. *See* Kumanovo.

Moncado Fortress (*Castro's Revolt*) 26 *July 1953*. Fidel and Raul Castro with 166 men captured this Santiago fortress inflicting fifty casualties and suffering only seven themselves. Failing to capture the armoury and short of weapons and ammunition, the rebels withdrew. Seventy were killed or captured and the Castros were imprisoned, but the rising marked the end for the dictator Batista. *See* Sierra Maestra.

Moncontour (*Third Huguenot War*) 3 *October 1569*. Between the Huguenot Protestants (Henri le Béarnais) and the Catholics (Duc d'Anjou and Marshal de Tavannes). The Huguenots occupied an untenable position near Poitiers and at the end of half an hour were routed and almost exterminated, only 700 remaining with the colours after the battle. *See* Coutras; Jarnac.

Mondovi (*Napoleon's Italian campaigns*) 21 *April 1796*. Napoleon, with 36,000 French, defeated 50,000 Piedmontese troops, drove them beyond the town and so closely pursued that the enemy army broke up. King Victor Amadeus surrendered, giving Napoleon control of Piedmont. *See* Dego; Lodi Bridge.

Mongol Wars. *See* List of Battles.

Monmouth (*American Revolution*) 28 June 1778. The British commander, Sir William Clinton, evacuated Philadelphia because he anticipated the arrival of the French. Washington started in pursuit and sent Charles Lee, with 6,400 men, to attack the British while on the march. Clinton at once faced his army about and his generalship was so superior that the Americans hurriedly retreated. Washington came up with 7,000 men and managed to hold the British assaults. The fight lasted most of the day, but each side suffered only about 360 casualties. *See* Fort Mercer; Fort Mifflin; Savannah I.

Monocacy River (*American Civil War*) 9 July 1864. A powerful force of Confederates — 10,000 infantry and 4,000 cavalry — was raiding into Maryland when south-east of Frederick it ran into a Federal block of 6,000 men (Wallace). The Confederate commander, Early, made a cross-river flank attack and overwhelmed the Federals who lost 1,880 men. Early, having lost only 700, pressed on to Washington itself, but found it too strong to attack. *See* Kernstown II; Lynchburg.

Monongahela River (*Seven Years' War*) 9 July 1755. Captain Dumas, with 900 French and Indians, attacked about 1,400 British and Virginians under General Braddock. The assault came shortly after the river crossing and though the officers and the Virginians fought gallantly, the British troops, ignorant of Indian warfare, panicked. After 3 hours' fighting they were driven across the Monongahela, losing 877 killed or wounded. The withdrawal was led by George Washington. Of eighty-six officers, sixty-three fell, including Braddock, mortally wounded. The French lost only sixteen, their Indian allies more heavily. *See* Beauséjour; Lake George.

Mons I (*Dutch War of Louis XIV*) 14 August 1678. William III of Orange (later William III of England) attacked the French army near Mons. The French were astonished since they believed, as did everybody else in Europe, that the 6-year war was over. Despite their surprise, they rallied and led by Marshal the Duke of Luxembourg they repulsed William, who lost several thousand men. (William believed he had been betrayed by the Dutch merchants in the truce between Holland and France.) *See* Augusta.

Mons II (*World War I*) 23–24 August 1914. The battle of Mons, part of the Battle of the Frontiers, has perhaps become more famous than it deserves, though it has an important and traditional place in British military history. The German army was attempting to break through the left flank of the Allied armies and envelop them. The initial action was fought along the banks of the Mons–Condé Canal, held for 21 miles by the British 2nd Corps (Smith-Dorrien). French, the British commander-in-chief, was away when the battle started and played no part when he returned. Von Kluck too exercised little control over the Germans, and units stumbled into the British Army one by one.

The British dug in among the slag heaps and houses covering the twenty-one bridges, and it was the infantry's shooting which dominated the day; their rifle fire was so fast and accurate that the Germans believed they were facing massed machine guns. But the German artillery fire was effective and infantry crossed the canal and enveloped a British regiment. The whole line had gradually to be withdrawn 2 to 3 miles south. Then, under an effective rearguard screen, a general retreat began. British casualties were 1,600. German casualties are uncertain, but probably 3,000. *See* Le Cateau.

Mons Badonicus (*Teutonic invasion of Britain*) circa 500. The principal opponent of the invading Angles, Saxons and Jutes was the largely legendary King

Arthur. He is said to have fought twelve battles, the chief being Mons Badonicus (Mount Badon), perhaps near Swinton. His victory checked the Teutonic conquest for 40 years.

Mons-en-Pevèle (*French–Flemish War*) *1304*. The Flemish pikemen were unable to withstand the charge of the French cavalry, and broke and fled, leaving 6,000 dead on the field. Despite the Flemish infantry victory at Courtrai (q.v.) in 1302, it was now apparent that mounted knights were still superior to foot soldiers. *See* Cassel.

Mons Graupius, *Scotland* (*Roman conquest of Britain*) *84*. The Caledonian chief Calgacus led 30,000 rebels against Agricola's legions. At Mons Graupius, possibly Mount Killiecrankie, the disciplined Romans killed 10,000 rebels for a loss of 360 Romans. Organized resistance to Roman rule did not recur for 300 years. *See* Verulamium II.

Monte Aperto (*Guelfs and Ghibellines*) *4 September 1260*. Between the Florentine Guelfs and the Ghibellines, who had been driven from the city, under Manfred of Sicily. The Guelfs were routed; the victors took possession of Florence and re-established their rule.

Montebello I (*Napoleon's Italian campaigns*) *9 June 1800*. Napoleon, ignorant of the fall of Genoa, was marching to the relief of the city, when his advance guard, under Lannes, was attacked by Ott's Austrian army of 17,000. Ott was trying to join his colleague, Melas. Lannes, who had only 6,000 men, held his ground until reinforcements under Victor arrived; he assumed the offensive, and drove the Austrians from the field with heavy loss, capturing 5,000 prisoners. The French lost 500 men. Lannes was made Duc de Montebello. *See* Novi Ligure.

Montebello II (*French–Austrian War*) *20 May 1859*. Between the Aus-

trians (Stadion) and about 7,000 French (Forey). The Austrians were defeated and driven back to Stradella, with a loss of 2,000 killed or wounded, and 200 prisoners. *See* Solferino.

Monte Caseros (*Argentine Civil War or Urquiza's Rising*) *3 February 1852*. Between Argentine Government troops, under President Rosas, the leader of the Gaucho party, 25,000-strong, and 20,000 insurgents under Urquiza. Rosas was defeated and fled to England, thus ending the long domination of the Gauchos in the Argentine Republic. *See* Montevideo.

Montenotte (*Napoleon's Italian campaigns*) *10–12 April 1796*. General d'Argenteau, with the central division of the 50,000-strong Austrian–Sardinian army, attacked the French position at Montenotte, held by General Cervoni's division. Cervoni was driven back, but the key to the position was held throughout the day by Tampon, with 1,500 men. On 12 April d'Argenteau found himself outflanked by Augereau and Masséna, under Napoleon's direction, and fell back with a loss of 1,000 killed, 2,000 prisoners, and some guns. This was Napoleon's first victory, he was 27. *See* Dego; Loano.

Montereau (*Napoleonic Wars: Defence of Paris*) *18 February 1814*. Napoleon checked the Allied advance on Paris at Mortmant. Schwarzenberg, the Allied commander, retreated, but left Prince Eugene of Wurttemburg to hold Montereau at the confluence of Seine and Yonne Rivers. Napoleon shelled the place and then sent in the spirited cavalry general, Gérard. The Allied rout was complete; they lost 2,000 dead and 4,000 prisoners to the French loss of 2,000. *See* Bar-sur-Aube; Champaubert-Montmirail.

Monterrey, *southern California* (*American–Mexican War*) *23–25 September 1846*. This town was captured from the Mexicans by the Americans, under General Zachary Taylor. In hard street and citadel fighting General de Ampûdio lost 367 men to the American loss of 468. *See* San Pascal.

Montevideo I (*Napoleonic Wars*) 3 February 1807. The circumstances which led to this battle are more remarkable than the battle itself. The Argentine was part of the Spanish Empire and Spain was Napoleon's ally. Senior British soldiers and sailors believed that the capture of Buenos Aires would mean immense wealth in prize money and could be justified in the interest of British trade. With 1,500 men Admiral Popham captured the city. The Argentinians soon found only one battalion in garrison, so they revolted and captured the British. To retrieve this disaster Britain sent 5,000 men under Auchmuty, who decided that Buenos Aires was too much of a problem, so he attacked and captured Montevideo on the Uruguayan side of the River Plate. (Uruguay was also part of the Spanish Empire.) British casualties were 400. *See* Buenos Aires.

Montevideo II (*Uruguayan Civil War*) 1843–51. Uruguay had been independent since 1827. Factional troubles developed between the Blancos party (Oribe) and the Colorados (Rivera). Rivera held Montevideo and Oribe marched on it, failed to take it in an attack on 16 February 1843 and laid siege. One of many foreign defenders was Garibaldi, who made a notable sortie with 160 Italians and held out for a day against 12,000 Blancos and Argentinians. A loose siege continued for 8 years until the Argentine rebel leader Urquiza led a combined force of Colorados, Brazilians and Paraguayans, beat off Oribe and his Blancos and relieved the city. *See* Ituzaingo.

Montevideo III (*Uruguayan Civil War*) 11 August 1863. Another fight between the Colorados, under General Venancio Flores, and the Blancos, under General Medina. The Blancos were victorious.

Montfaucon (*Norman invasion of France*) 887. The French, under Eudes, defeated the Norman invaders who lost 19,000 men in the battle and were forced to retire from the walls of Paris, which they were besieging. *See* Saucourt.

Montiel (*Castilian Civil War*) 1369. Between the French (du Guesclin) and the Spaniards (Pedro II of Castile). Pedro was routed and taken prisoner, and Henry of Trastamare placed on the throne of Castile. *See* Nájara.

Montijo (*Spanish–Portuguese Wars*) 26 May 1644. Angered by Spanish intrigue, King John IV who was backed by England and France, sent an army under Albuquerque into Spain. It soundly defeated a Spanish army near Badajos and Spain left Portugal in peace for several years. Portugal became independent in 1688.

Montlhéry (*French–Burgundian War or "War of the Public Good"*) 13 July 1465. Between the forces of the Ligue du Bien Public, under the Comte de Charolais, and the Royal troops under Louis XI. Louis was narrowly defeated after a bloody cavalry battle and driven from the field, but by intrigue he soon broke the terms the Treaty of Conflans imposed on him. *See* Héricourt.

Montmorenci (*Seven years' War*) 31 July 1759. An action during the siege of Quebec, when Wolfe with 5,000 men attacked the entrenched camp of the French, defended by 12,000 men under Montcalm. As the British were landing, thirteen companies of grenadiers advanced to the attack without waiting for the main body. They were repulsed with heavy loss, which so weakened Wolfe that he could not press the attack further. The British loss amounted to 443, mostly grenadiers. French losses were small. *See* Plains of Abraham.

Montreal (*Seven Years' War, also known as the French and Indian

War) *8 September 1760*. After an advance by three British columns the city was surrendered to the British, under General Amherst, by Vaudreuil, Governor-General of Canada. One of the conditions of the surrender was that the whole of the French army in Canada and its dependencies must lay down their arms. Canada thus became a British dominion.

Mont St. Quentin, *Somme (World War I) 30 August–2 September 1918*. The Germans held in strength the key feature of Mont St. Quentin. They — and the British commander, Rawlinson — believed it to be impregnable. The Australian Corps (Monash) and principally the 2nd Division captured it in 3 days, the result of intelligent planning and great individual dash. The capture of Mont St. Quentin is often regarded as the finest feat of the war. Australian casualties, 3,000; German, 15,000. *See* Hindenburg Line; Vimy; Western Front.

Mont Valérien. *See* Buzenval.

Moodkee (or Mudki) (First British–Sikh War) *18 December 1845*. Between the British, 12,000-strong with forty-two guns, under Sir Hugh Gough, and the Sikhs, 30,000-strong with forty guns, under Taj Singh. Gough, at the end of a long march, was surprised by the Sikhs and his force was thrown into some confusion. He rallied then and drove the Sikhs from the field, capturing seventeen guns. The British loss was 872 killed or wounded. *See* Ferozeshah; Hyderabad.

Mook (or Mookerheide) (Netherlands War of Independence) *14 April 1574*. Between the Dutch Patriots, 8,000-strong, under Count Louis of Nassau, and 5,000 Spaniards, under Don Sancho d'Avila. The village of Mook, on the Meuse River, was held by the Dutch infantry, who were driven out by the Spaniards and routed, with a loss of at least 4,000. Among the slain were the Counts Louis and Henry of Nassau. *See* Leyden; Walcheren.

Moore's Creek Bridge (*American Revolution*) *27 February 1776*. Colonel J. Moore, with 1,100 American militia, stopped and routed a force of 1,800 Loyalists, mostly Scots, under General McDonald. Trying to cross the creek under fire, the Loyalists lost 30 killed or wounded and 850 captured. Only two Americans were wounded. *See* Charleston.

Morat, *now Murten (Swiss–Burgundian War) 22 June 1476*. The Burgundians, 35,000 strong under Charles the Bold, expected to overwhelm their 24,000 Swiss opponents under Hans Waldmann. But after a few hours' hard fighting the Burgundian army was split and driven into the plain, where the Swiss utterly routed them. No fewer than 10,000 of the Burgundian army fell, including 6,000 Italian mercenaries, penned against Lake Morat and wiped out. The Swiss suffered only 500 casualties and pursued Charles into Lorraine. *See* Granson; Nancy.

Morawa (or Nish) (*Hungarian–Turkish Wars*) *3 November 1443*. Between the Hungarians under John Hunniades, with 12,000 horse and 20,000 foot, and a greatly superior Turkish army under Murad II. But the Turks were defeated with a loss of 2,000 killed and 4,000 prisoners. *See* Hermannstadt; Semendria; Varna.

Morazzone (*Italian Wars of Independence: Garibaldi's Rising*) *20 May 1848*. Between 1,500 Garibaldian volunteers under Garibaldi himself and 5,000 Austrians under General d'Aspre. After a resistance of 11 hours, Garibaldi, hopelessly outnumbered, withdrew his force and made a skilful retreat to Arona.

Morbihan Gulf (*Gallic Wars*) *56 BC*. The Veneti people of Brittany, rebelling against the Romans, based their strength on their fleet of 200 boats. Caesar quickly built his own fleet at the mouth of the Loire and sent it, under Decimus Brutus, against the Veneti. The Romans, using sickles attached to long poles, cut the rigging on the enemy ships. Boarding the disabled vessels, the Romans systematically killed the crews and burnt the ships. This was probably the first recorded naval battle in the Atlantic. *See* Coblenz; Sambre River.

Morella, *Castile* (*First Carlist War*) *23 May 1840*. This fortress, the last stronghold of the Carlists, was besieged by Espartero, with 20,000 Cristinos. It was defended by a garrison of 4,000 veterans, under Cabrera, who on 30 May attempted to break through the besiegers' lines. His plan had been betrayed, and he was driven back. Most of the garrison surrendered, but Cabrera and a large party made a second and this time a successful attempt to cut his way out. *See* Huesca.

Morgarten (*First Swiss–Austrian War*) *16 November 1315*. The men of Schwyz, 1,400 in number, took post in the Pass of Morgaten and lay in wait for the Archduke Leopold, who, with 8,000 Austrians, was marching into Schwyz to invade Switzerland. Having disordered the Austrian ranks by rolling down boulders, the Swiss then attacked with their halberds, routing the Austrians, who lost 4,500 killed. *See* Laupen; Sempach.

Morotai (*World War II*) *15 September 1944*. This island of the Moluccas was captured by American troops so that its airfields could be used for attacks against Japanese bases. Casualties: American, 45 killed, 95 wounded; Japanese, 325 killed. *See* New Guinea; Philippines.

Morshedabad (*British–Bengal War*) *24 July 1763*. Between the troops of Mir Cossim, the deposed Nawab of Bengal, and a British force of 750 Europeans and large body of native troops, under Major Adams. The British stormed Cossim's entrenchments, drove out his army and followed up their victory by the occupation of Morshedabad.

Mortara (*Italian Wars of Independence*) *21 March 1849*. The Piedmontese, under the Duke of Savoy (Victor Emmanuel) and General Darando, were holding Mortara against the main Austrian army under Radetsky. The Piedmontese had done nothing to make Mortara defensible, and little guard was kept; they were surprised by Radetsky and driven out of the town with a loss of 500 killed or wounded, 2,000 prisoners and five guns. The Austrians lost 300. *See* Novara.

Mortimer's Cross (*Wars of the Roses*) *2 February 1461*. Edward, Duke of York, defeated the Lancastrians (Earls of Pembroke and Wiltshire) and drove them back into Wales, thus preventing a concentration of the Lancastrian forces. Many of the Lancastrians were beheaded. *See* Saint Albans II; Wakefield.

Mortlack (*Danish invasion of Scotland*) *1010*. Between the Danes under Sweyn Forkbeard and the Scots under Malcolm II. After a long and desperate engagement the Danes were defeated and ran to their ships. A victory for the Danes would probably have given them a permanent stay in Scotland as Malcolm had his last available man in the field.

Mortmant (*Napoleonic Wars: Defence of Paris*) *17 February 1814*. The Russian advance guard of the Allied armies under the Count de Pahlen were blocked by the French rearguard (Victor) and repulsed with a loss of 3,000 killed or wounded, and eleven guns. *See* Craonne; Montereau.

Moscow (*World War II*) *1941–2*. This battle really began 200 miles from Moscow on 2 October with the advance of sixty German divisions (von Bock). On the right the Second Panzer Group (Guderian) took Orel, 8 October, and

Chern, 24 October. In the centre the Third Panzer Group (Hoth) and Fourth Panzer Group (Hoeppner) encircled Vyazma, killing or capturing 600,000 Russians, 2–13 October.

The Third Panzer Group took Kalinin on 15 October. That day the Fourth Army was only 40 miles from Moscow. Russian resistance and winter hardened and by 20 November the Germans could move no further, though on 2 December the Second Panzer Division fought its way to within sight of the Kremlin and an infantry division reached the suburbs. The Germans had by now suffered heavy casualties; the Russians claim to have killed 85,000 between 16 November and 5 December.

Ill-fitted for a Russian winter but unable to withdraw — Hitler's orders — the Germans then came under counter-attack. Zhukov threw in 100 fresh divisions. In the Tula salient, held by Guderian — the furthest German advance — 30,000 German soldiers were killed. The Russians recaptured many places, but along a line between Vyazma and Rzhev von Kluge formed a defence that held against Russian attacks. Bitter cold put many thousands of Germans out of action. The German line held fast until March 1943 when Russian pressure forced a general withdrawal. The Battle of Moscow was the first major defeat for the Germans, but Russia is believed to have lost 500,000 men in the city's defence. *See* Crimea; Leningrad; Ukraine.

Motya (*Syracuse–Carthaginian War*) 398 BC. Motya, chief stronghold of the Carthaginians in Sicily, was besieged by Dionysius of Syracuse, with 83,000 men. Having built a mole to connect the mainland and the island on which Motya stood, he erected his giant wooden catapults, used for the first time in this siege. He also built large wheeled towers on which his men stood to attack the high defences. Having broken in, the Syracusans found that every house was a small fortress; after days of street fighting and heavy casualties the city still resisted. At last by a night surprise Dionysius captured the quarter which still held out. The city's inhabitants were massacred or sold as slaves. *See* Himera; Selinus.

Mount Gaurus, *Appenines* (*First Samnite War*) 342 BC. The Romans under Valerius Corvus defeated the Samnites.

Mount Lactarius (*Second Gothic War*) March 553. Between the troops of the Emperor Justinian, under Narses, and the Goths, under Teias, the last Gothic king of Italy. The Roman victory was decisive and Teias was slain; the Goths accepted the rule of Justinian.

Mount Panium (*Syrian–Egyptian War*) 198 BC. Between the Syrians (Antiochus the Great) and the allied Greeks and Egyptians under (Scopas). Scopas was routed, and Antiochus took possession of all the territory held by Egypt in Asia up to the frontier of Egypt, a vast area.

Mount Seleucus (*Roman Empire Civil Wars*) 10 August 353. Rebel legions under Magnentius held out against the Imperial legions under Constantius. Constantius forced the passage of the Cottian Alps, and defeated Magnentius in a no-quarter battle. This broke Magnentius' power and Gaul and Italy were again brought under Roman rule.

Mount Tabor (*French campaign in Egypt 1798–1800*) 15 April 1799. Isolated in Egypt because of the Battle of the Nile, q.v., Napoleon took the offensive and marched into Syria with 8,000 men. He besieged British-held Acre, which a Turkish army under Achmed Pasha (the "Butcher") attempted to relieve. Achmed surrounded General Kleber's division, which was formed in hollow squares, but Napoleon with the rest of his troops then surrounded the Turks. Under a combined attack, the

Turks were defeated and driven across the Jordan. *See* Aboukir; Acre.

Mount Taurus (*Muslim invasion of Asia Minor*) *804*. Between the Muslims, under Harroun-al-Raschid, and the Greeks, under the Emperor Nicephorus I. The Greeks were defeated, losing 40,000 men, but Nicephorus, thrice wounded, escaped from the field.

Mount Tifata, *southern Italy* (*Civil War of Marius and Sulla*) *83* BC. The legions of Sulla defeated the army of the Consul, Norbanus, with heavy loss, and drove them to take refuge in Capua. *See* Colline Gate; Orchmenus.

Mount Vesuvius (*Third Servile War*) *73–71* BC. The Thracian slave and gladiator Spartacus seized Mount Vesuvius and rallied 40,000 fugitive slaves. From his base he controlled most of Campania and twice won pitched battles against the Roman legions. He was defeated by Licinius Crassus and the revolt was finally stamped out by Pompey, just back from Spain. Spartacus was killed in battle and his followers were executed.

Mouscron, *Flanders* (*French Revolutionary Wars*) *11 June 1794*. The French army under Generals Souham and Bertin was advancing into Austrian-held Flanders where the French were already besieging Menin. The Prince of Saxe-Coburg ordered the Austrian Count Clerfayt to relieve Menin and block the advancing French column. Generals Souham and Bertin were more aggressive; they attacked the Austrian column front and flank at Mouscron, inflicted 2,000 casualties and captured eleven guns. The Austrians were routed. *See* Fleurus.

Mozambique War of Independence *1964–75*. This desultory and largely jungle war was fought between the Imperial Portuguese forces and the Front for the Liberation of Mozambique (FRELIMO), which was heavily supplied by China. While no major battle was fought, the Portuguese suffered 3,900 casualties and FRELIMO 11,500. More than 50,000 civilians were killed during the fighting. Mozambique became independent on 25 July 1975.

Mühlberg, *near Leipzig* (*Wars of Charles V or German Reformation Wars*) *24 April 1547*. Between 9,000 German Protestants under the Elector Frederick of Saxony and the Landgrave of Hesse, and the Imperial army allied with 3,500 Papal troops, 13,000 in all, under Charles V. The Protestants were defeated and their two leaders taken prisoner. The Imperialists lost only fifty. *See* Frankenhausen; Sieverhausen.

Mühldorf, *near Munich* (*Holy Roman Empire Civil War*) *1322*. The Imperial troops under the Emperor Louis the Bavarian defeated the German rebels under Frederick, Duke of Austria, who also claimed to be Holy Roman Emperor. Louis' victory ended resistance to his rule. *See* Morgarten.

Mühlhausen, *now Mulhouse* (*Gallic War*) *58* BC. A battle between the Romans, 36,000-strong, under Julius Caesar, and the Sequani led by Ariovistus. The Romans occupied two camps, one of which was held by two legions against a determined Gaullish attack. Caesar then united his forces and led them against the Sequani, whom he routed with great loss. *See* Bibracte.

Mukden I (*Russian–Japanese War*) *21 February–10 March 1905*. A massive battle of attrition between 300,000 Japanese (Oyama) and 300,000 Russians (Kuropatkin). On 6 March Oyama completed an encirclement, but Kuropatkin had already withdrawn most of his troops. Mukden cost the Japanese 50,000 casualties, the Russians, 100,000. Strategically, possession of the city meant little. *See* Shaho River.

Mukden II (*Chinese Civil War*) *December 1947–1 November 1948.* Mao Tse-tung used 200,000 troops — commanded by Lin Piao — of the Communist People's Liberation Army to encircle Mukden, held for the Nationalists by Wei Li-huang. The PLA grip was unbreakable and in October 1948 Liao Yao-haiang led three Nationalist armies in a massive breakout. Within 2 weeks the entire force was dead or captured. The surviving garrison, principally the 207th (Youth) Division, surrendered on 1 November. Mao now controlled all Manchuria. *See* Chinese Civil War.

Mukwanpur (*British–Gurkha War*) *27 February 1816.* A village forming part of Sir David Ochterlony's position was attacked by 2,000 Gurkhas. It was defended by 300 sepoys and 40 men of the 87th Regiment. The arrival of reinforcements enabled the garrison to beat off the Gurkhas.

Mulhouse (*World War I*) *7–9 August 1914.* The French easily took the Alsation centres Altkirch and Mulhouse, but were unprepared for the German counterattack. Under the onslaught General Bonneau held Mulhouse for only 24 hours before withdrawing. He was relieved of command. *See* Frontiers of France; Liege.

Multan (*Second British–Sikh War*) *July 1848–22 January 1849.* This fortress, defended by the Sikhs under Mulraj, was besieged by Lieutenant Edwardes with about 1,200 men in July 1848. After an ineffectual bombardment, the siege was raised on 22 September, but was renewed on 27 December by General Whish, with 17,000 men and sixty-four guns. After a heavy bombardment the place was stormed on 2 January 1849, and on the 22nd of the same month Mulraj surrendered the citadel. British losses during the siege were 210 killed and 910 wounded.

Münchengrätz (*Seven Weeks' War*) *28 June 1866.* Between the advanced guard of Prince Frederick Charles army, and the Austrians, under Count Clam-Gallas. The Austrians were defeated with a loss of about 300 killed and wounded, and 1,000 prisoners. Prussian losses were small. *See* Langensalza; Sadowa.

Munda, *southern Spain* (*Civil War of Caesar and Pompey*) *46 BC.* The Caesareans, under Julius Caesar, defeated the army of Cnaeus Pompeius, son of Pompey the Great. The Pompeians lost 30,000 men, including Labienus and Varro, while the Caesareans lost 1,000. Cnaeus was wounded, captured and executed. This defeat ended the resistance of the Pompeian faction in Spain. The action was Caesar's last battle; he was assassinated the following year. *See* Thapsus.

Muret (*Crusade against the Albigensians*) *1213.* Pope Innocent III called for a crusade against the Albigensians or Catharist heretics led by the Count of Toulouse, aided by Pedro II of Aragon. The main leader of the crusading armies was the half-English Simon de Montfort, whose brilliant and daring tactics defeated the Albigensians. They had besieged de Montfort's stronghold, Muret, but by sortie, stratagem and ambush he routed them. Pedro was killed and the Albigensians organized resistance ended. *See* Bouvines.

Murfreesboro (*or Stones River*) (*American Civil War*) *31 December–2 January 1862.* Between 35,000 Confederates (Bragg) and 40,000 Federals (Rosecrans). Bragg attacked and drove back the Federal right, but the centre and left held and prevented the defeat degenerating into a rout. Both sides lost heavily, but the Confederates captured a large number of prisoners and over twenty guns. The following day the Federal right retook the ground it had lost and at nightfall both armies occupied their original positions. Early on 2 January Bragg retired in good order. Each side lost about 8,000 killed, wounded or missing, in the 2 days' fighting. *See* Chickamauga; Perryville.

Mursa (*Roman Empire Civil Wars or Revolt of Magnentius*) *28 September 351*. The usurper Magnentius raised 100,000 troops to do battle with the 80,000 of the Emperor Constantius. The battle was long and savage, but finally the legions of Magnentius were driven from the field with a loss of 24,000. The victors lost 30,000. Deserted by his troops, Magnentius commited suicide.

Musa Bagh (*Indian Mutiny against the British*) *19 March 1858*. A British force (Outram) routed a body of mutineers, 7,000-strong, under Huzrat Mahul, Begum of Oude, which was holding the Musa Bagh, a fortified palace in the outskirts of Lucknow, q.v.

Muslim Imperial Conquests. *See* List of Battles.

Muta (*Muslim invasion of Byzantine Palestine*) *629*. This was the first Muslim raid into Byzantium and the first battle between the Muhammadan Arabs and a foreign enemy. The Muslims were led by Zaid, Jaafar and Abdullah, all of whom were slain by the soldiers of the Byzantine Emperor Heraclius. Khaled led the surviving Muslims from the field. *See* Aiznadin; Aleppo; Bakr; Medina.

Muthul River (*Roman Conquest of Numidia or Jugurthine War*) *108 BC*. Between the Numidians of North Africa under Jugurtha, and the Romans (Metellus Numidicus). The Numidians had been successful against the Romans and were now strongly posted on the heights above the river, but were driven out by the legionaries with heavy loss. Jugurtha did not again face the Romans in the field, and turned to guerrilla warfare. He was captured 3 years later and died in prison. *See* Numantia.

Mutina, *or* Modena (*Wars of the Second Triumvirate*) *21 April 43 BC*. Between Antony's army and three Consular armies, under Hirtius, Octavius and Vibius Pansa. Antony, who was besieging Mutina, 200 miles north of Rome, was attacked simultaneously by the three armies. That of Pansa was routed, and Pansa slain, but Octavius and Hirtius made ground. Antony was undefeated and continued the siege. Ten days later Octavius and Hirtius made a combined attack on his lines and forced their way through into the town, though Hirtius fell in the action. Antony fled to Gaul and later he and Octavius became allies. *See* Munda; Philippi.

Mycale (*Third Persian invasion of Greece*) *479 BC*. Between the Greeks (Leotychides the Spartan) and a large Persian army. The Greeks landed near Cape Mycale and drove the Persians back on their entrenchments, which they then carried. The Persian auxiliaries fled. The fugitives were slaughtered by the rebelling Ionians, and the whole Persian army destroyed. *See* Eurymedon River; Plataea; Salamis.

Mylae (*First Punic War*) *260 BC*. The Roman Fleet (Caius Duilius) defeated the Carthaginians, under Hannibal, with loss of 50 ships, 3,000 killed and 7,000 prisoners. Duilius had introduced the boarding bridge, which was lowered on to the deck of the opposing galley. The Romans, outstanding as close-quarter fighters, quickly overcame the Carthaginians. This was Rome's first sea victory. *See* Ecnomus; Messina I.

Mylex (*Civil War of Caesar and Pompey*) *36 BC*. The Pompeian fleet (Sextus Pompeius) was destroyed by the fleet of the Triumvirs fleet commanded by Agrippa. *See* Actium.

Mynydd Carn (*Welsh Civil War*) *1081*. In an attempt to secure unity, the leaders Gruffydd ap Cyan of Gwynedd and Rhys ap Tewdwr of Deheubarth joined forces and near St. Davids completely defeated the numerically larger army put together by several princes. Wales became more stable for two centuries.

Myonnesus, *in Ionia (Wars of Antiochus the Great) 190 BC*. Between the Roman fleet (Lucius Regillus) and the fleet of Antiochus, under Polyxenides, who had an advantage of nine ships. He was defeated by the superior seamanship of the Romans, with a loss of forty-two vessels. *See* Thermopylae II.

Myriocephalon, *in ancient Phrygia (Byzantine–Turkish Wars) 17 September 1176*. Manuel I and his Byzantine army were ambushed in a defile and surrounded by a large force of Turkish bowmen under Kilij Arslan I. The Byzantines were almost annihilated and Byzantine prestige was seriously damaged. *See* Erzincan; Philomelion.

Mytilene I, *Lesbos (Great Peloponnesian War) May 427 BC*. This city, which had revolted against Athens, was besieged in the autumn of 428 BC by the Athenians, under Paches, with 1,000 hoplites and a fleet of triremes. A Spartan squadron (Alcidas) unsuccessfully tried to relieve Mytilene. In May 427 the city surrendered and all the male inhabitants were condemned to death. However, only the leaders of the revolt were executed. *See* Phylos-Sphacteria; Plataea;

Mytilene II *(Peloponnesian War) 406 BC*. A naval action between 140 Peloponnesian vessels (Callicratidas) and 70 Athenian triremes (Conon). Conon was defeated with the loss of thirty ships and the rest of his fleet was driven into Mytilene where it was blockaded. In a desperate and amazing effort Athens, though impoverished, raised a new fleet which was sent to raise the blockade. Callicratidas was drowned in this engagement, which was successful. *See* Aegospotami; Ephesus.

Myton *(English–Scottish Wars) 20 September 1319*. Edward II was besieging Berwick so Robert the Bruce sent a large raiding party under James Douglas southward into Yorkshire. At Myton, near the Swale River, the Scots encountered an English army hastily raised by the Archbishop of York. The English were defeated and Edward II, fearful of a victorious enemy in his rear, raised the siege of Berwick. *See* Bannockburn; Boroughbridge.

Nachod (*Seven Weeks' War*) *27 June 1866*. Between the 5th Prussian Corps (Steinmetz) and the Austrians (Ramming). The Austrian cavalry, though superior in numbers, was defeated by the Prussian Uhlans and the Austrians retreated with great loss in killed and wounded. The Prussians, who lost 900, captured 2,000 prisoners and five guns. *See* Munchengratz.

Naefels (*Swiss–Austrian War*) *9 April 1388*. 6,000 Austrians under Tockenburg faced only 500 men of Glarus. The Swiss were driven from their first position at the entrance to a valley. They hurried to the heights of the Rauhberg and demoralized the advancing columns by rolling boulders on them. Then they attacked the Austrians and routed them. The Austrians lost 80 knights and 2,000 soldiers. *See* Sempach.

Nagy-Sarlo (*Hungarian Rising against Austria*) *19 April 1849*. The Hungarians, 25,000-strong, under Görgey, were trying to bridge the Gran River and were opposed by the Austrians. The Austrians were defeated, and the river successfully bridged. *See* Kapolna.

Nairn (*Danish invasion of Scotland*) *1009*. The Scots under Malcolm II marched to Nairn to raise the siege imposed by the Danish raiders led by Sweyn I, the Forkbeard. The formidable Danes drove back the relief force and Malcolm was wounded. The Danes withdrew as winter set in, but returned the following year. *See* Mortlack.

Naissus (*or Nisch*) (*Gothic invasion of the Roman Empire*) *269*. Between the Imperial troops under Emperor Claudius and the invading Goths in the Morava Valley of the Balkan Mountains. The Romans were hard pressed, but the Gothic lines were then attacked in rear by 5,000 men Claudius had concealed in the neighbouring mountains. The Goths were routed; 50,000 are said to have fallen. Claudius received the honorary title Gothicus for his victory. *See* Philippopolis; Placentia.

Najara (*Najera*). *See* Navarrete.

Naklo (*Rise of Poland*) *1109*. Seeking access to the Baltic, the Polish leader Boleslav III attacked the Pomeranians and routed them. The Polish state, newly risen, held its gain for only a century before the aggressive Teutonic knights again blocked Poland's access to the sea. *See* Cracow.

Nam Dong (*Vietnam War*) *6 July 1964*. An armed camp near the Laos border, Nam Dong was held by 300 South Vietnamese troops, 60 Nung soldiers and 12 Americans. They beat off attacks by 900 Viet Cong troops. The action is notable in the United States for the first award of the Congressional Medal of Honor in Vietnam — to Captain R. Donlon. *See* Vietnam.

Namur I (*War of the Grand Alliance*) *1 June–5 June 1692, and 8 July–1 September 1695*. Cleverly fortified, Namur was a key point in control of the Spanish Netherlands. The French under de Vauban took it after a siege of 36 days in which the Dutch defenders suffered 5,500 casualties and the French 2,600. In May 1695 William III of England (formerly William of Orange) besieged the French in Namur. He had the assistance of van Coehoorn, who had built the fortress, and finally he took it — at a cost of 18,000 casualties. The French suffered 9,000. It was one of the costliest sieges in history for an attacking army. *See* Chiari; Marsaglia; Neerwinden I.

Namur II (*World War I*) *20–25 August 1914*. Under the German onslaught, Namur became the last fortress city to block the advance into France. It was held by 37,000 Belgians, but the Germans had 100,000 men and 540 guns, some of them firing 2-ton shells. They battered Namur into surrender, though by then only 5,000 Belgians remained in the place to be taken prisoner. German casualties, 1,000. *See* Frontiers of France.

Nancy (*Swiss–Burgundian Wars*) *5 January 1477*. Charles the Bold of Burgundy, having been driven out of Switzerland (*see* Morat), established himself strongly in Nancy. But the invincible Swiss infantry advanced into Burgundy and launched a frontal and flank attack together. Their pikes and halberds destroyed the Burgundian army and Charles was killed. Burgundy was finished as a power and became part of France. *See* Giornico.

Nanking I (*Defeat of Mongols*) *1356*. The turning point of the Chinese revolution against the Mongols. A monk-warrior, Chu Yuan-chang (later Hung Wu), stormed and took Nanking, establishing the Ming dynasty. *See* Peking I.

Nanking II, *better known as the Rape of Nanking* (*Chinese–Japanese War*) *13 December 1937*. Nanking was then the capital of China and Chiang Kai-shek had his headquarters here until the Japanese invaders marched up the Yangtze River to attack it. Nanking was mercilessly bombed and when the city fell the Japanese slaughtered at least 40,000 civilians and raped thousands of women. The "rape of Nanking" outraged world opinion. The Japanese sank the U.S. river boat *Panay* on the Yangtze the day before Nanking fell. *See* Chinese Civil War.

Nanking III (*Chinese Civil War*) *22 April 1949*. The Communists stormed and captured the city from Chiang Kai-shek's Nationalists, but Chiang had already left for Chungking. The fall of Nanking, in which 60,000 Chinese soldiers died, meant the end of Nationalist resistance, for Shanghai fell, 27 May, without difficulty. Chiang and his government fled to Formosa. *See* Chinese Civil War.

Nanshan Hill (*Russian–Japanese War*) *26 May 1904*. Three Japanese divisions (Oku) faced a Russian division with strong artillery support (Stoessel). The Russians held a powerful position on the heights of Nanshan. After artillery preparation, the Japanese eight times tried to storm the heights, each time failing before concentrated enemy gunfire. After a further bombardment, aided by the Japanese fleet in Kiuchau Bay, the whole Japanese force attacked simultaneously, penetrated the defences on the Russian left and drove out the Russians. The Japanese lost 4,304 killed or wounded but took 78 guns and penned the Russians in Port Arthur, q.v. *See* Liaoyang; Sandepu; Shaho; Ulsan.

Nantwich (*English Civil War*) *25 January 1644*. A minor battle in which the Parliamentarians (Fairfax) defeated the Irish Royalists, aided by local troops. Half the defeated Irish then joined Fairfax's army. *See* Marston Moor.

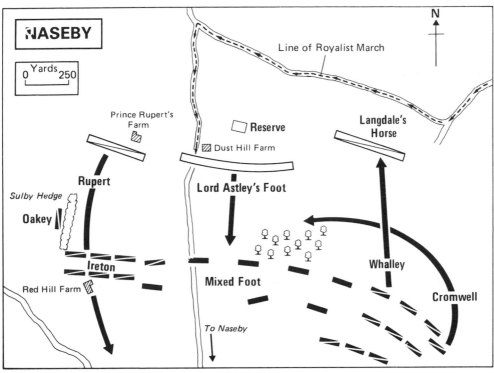

N

NASEBY

0 Yards 250

Line of Royalist March

Prince Rupert's Farm

Reserve

Dust Hill Farm

Langdale's Horse

Rupert

Sulby Hedge

Oakey

Lord Astley's Foot

Rupert

Ireton

Red Hill Farm

Mixed Foot

Whalley

Cromwell

To Naseby

Naples (*French invasion of Italy*) 22 February 1495. Charles VIII took a well-organized army of 30,000 across the Alps and after brushing aside resistance in north Italy drove the Spanish holders of Naples from the city. Later that year, with Charles absent, an army raised by the Holy League (Milan, Venice, Pope Alexander VI, Ferdinand V of Castile, Maximilian I of the Holy Roman Empire) easily pushed out the French garrison. *See* Fornovo.

Napoleonic Wars. *See* map *and* List of Battles.

Naroch Lake (*World War I*) 18–26 March 1916. A disastrous attempt by Czar Nicholas II of Russia to divert German forces from the Western Front. In personal command of the Russian armies he used his Tenth Army to attack the Germans north of the Pripet Marshes. Hindenberg's artillery and machine guns devastated the Russians who then became bogged in the mud of a spring thaw. They suffered 100,000 casualties and gained nothing. *See* Gorlice-Tarnów.

Narva (*Great Northern War*) 30 November 1700. General Dolgorouky had 80,000 Russians besieging Narva. Charles XII of Sweden had only 8,000 men, but after driving in two advanced positions he attacked the entrenched enemy camp. After 3 hours' hard fighting in the snow the defenders were driven out in disorder, leaving 10,000 men in the trenches and losing many more in the fight. The Swedes lost only 600 — a remarkable victory for the 17-year-old Charles. *See* Klissow.

Narvik. *See* Norway.

Naseby (*English Civil War*) 14 June 1645. Between 14,000 Parliamentarians (Fairfax) and 7,500 Royalists under Charles I, with Prince Rupert in actual command. Rupert's first charge broke the

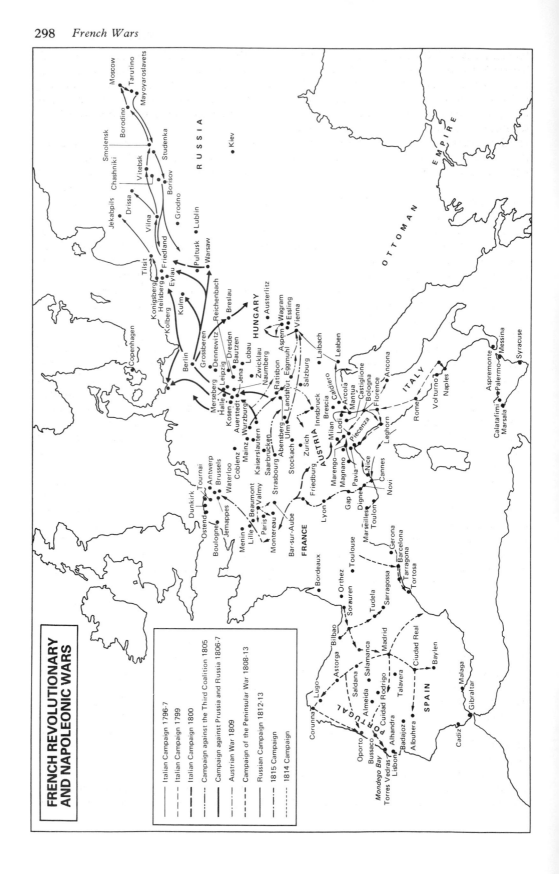

FRENCH REVOLUTIONARY
AND NAPOLEONIC WARS

Italian Campaign 1796-7
Italian Campaign 1799
Italian Campaign 1800
Campaign against the Third Coalition 1805
Campaign against Prussia and Russia 1806-7
Austrian War 1809
Campaign of the Peninsular War 1808-13
Russian Campaign 1812-13
1815 Campaign
1814 Campaign

Parliamentary left wing, but, as usual, Rupert's pursuit was carried too far. Before the cavalry could return, Cromwell on the right had turned the scale, and the battle was over. The Royalist infantry was overwhelmed and 3,500 were taken prisoner. In their first real test the New Model Army had been eminently successful. *See* Alford; Marston Moor; Newbury II.

Nashville (*American Civil War*) *15–16 December 1863*. The Confederate General Hood had approached Nashville and here deployed 31,000 troops — the Army of Tennessee — and virtually invited the Federals (George Thomas) to do battle. Thomas, with 41,000 men, launched the attack in his own good time. He first made a secondary attack against Hood's right, drew some Confederate units in that direction, and then hit very hard at Hood's left. The Confederate lines buckled, but the early winter night gave Hood time to reorganize his lines.

About 3.30 a.m., 16 December, the Federals, having close pressed the Confederates during the night, unleashed a violent attack. On the far right Federal dismounted cavalry (Wilson) reached Hood's rear and threatened to cut his line of retreat. The entire Confederate position collapsed. Again night and heavy rain saved the Confederates from being flooded by pursuit, but they had already lost 1,500 killed or wounded and 4,462 captured. Federal losses, 499 killed, 2,562 wounded. *See* Franklin; Savannah III.

Naulochus. *See* Mylex.

Naupactus (*Great Peloponnesian War*) *429 BC*. Twenty Athenian ships (Phormio) were trapped by Cnemas who had 77 Peloponnese ships at the entrance to the bay of Naupactus (modern Taranto). Nine Athenian vessels were driven ashore and the remaining eleven fled towards Naupactus, closely pursued by the Peloponnesians. The rearmost of the flying Athenians suddenly turned and rammed the leading ship of Cnemas'

squadron. When the pursuers hesitated, the rest of the Athenians returned to the attack. The Athenians were victorious, capturing six ships and recovering their own which had run ashore. *See* Mytilene.

Navarino (*Greek War of Independence*) *20 October 1827*. The Allied fleets of Great Britain, France and Russia under Codrington, de Rigny, and Heiden respectively — twenty-four ships in all — destroyed the Turkish and Egyptian fleets, sixty vessels being burnt or sunk and the remainder driven ashore. The Allies lost 272 killed and wounded; the Turks over 4,000. The battle was the last general action fought between wooden sailing ships. *See* Mesolongion; Varna II.

Navarrette (*or Najéra*) (*Hundred Years' War*) *3 April 1367*. A remarkable but little known battle of Edward the Black Prince of England. Edward led an army of 20,000, including 5,000 English archers, across the Pyrenees to restore Pedro of Castile to his throne. Outmanoeuvring his enemies, Henry of Trastamara and the French General du Guesclin, Henry crossed the Ebro and faced a French–Spanish army of more than 40,000. In a ferocious fight, in which the English archers were dominant, the Spanish were driven off and the French surrendered. The Spanish lost 7,000 dead, including 700 heavy cavalry, with an equal number wounded. A quarter of the 2,000 French heavy cavalry were also killed. The English army lost no more than 100 dead.

Naxos (*Greek City-states Wars*) *September 376 BC*. Between eighty Athenian triremes (Chabrias) and sixty Spartan ships (Pollio) who were endeavouring to waylay Athenian grain ships from the Euxine. Pollio was defeated with a loss of forty-nine triremes. *See* Cnidus; Coronea II; Leuctra.

Nechtan's Mere (*Northumbrian invasion of Scotland*) *20 May 685*. The

Picts under Brude defeated the Northumbrians under Ecgfrith. With this victory the Picts freed themselves from the Northumbrian domination.

Neerwinden I (*War of the Grand Alliance*) *29 July 1693*. Near Liege, William III of England and Holland took up position with about 30,000 English, Dutch, German and Spanish troops to face the Duke of Luxembourg's 40,000 veteran French soldiers. William had a good position with both flanks protected by small streams, but the French pressure on his centre forced him to take men from the flanks. As this happened Luxembourg launched a double flank attack. Under the threatened envelopment, the Allied line broke. William suffered 18,000 casualties in killed, drowned, wounded or captured and 104 guns. French casualties, 10,000. Luxembourg, though the victor, could not pursue. *See* Marsaglia; Steenkirke.

Neerwinden II (*Wars of the French Revolution*) *18 March 1793*. Between the French (Dumouriez) and the Austrians (Prince of Coburg). The Austrians won a decisive victory and Dumouriez was compelled to evacuate Belgium. He went over to the Austrians and their allies. *See* Hondschoote; Jemappes.

Negapatam I (*War of Austrian Succession*) *25 July 1746*. Off the Coromandel coast a British squadron of six ships (Captain Peyton) encountered nine French ships (Labourdonnais). The fight was at long range and was indecisive, but after the action Peyton sheered off and made for Trincomalee. He thus practically admitted defeat, though the French had suffered the heavier loss. *See* Madras.

Negapatam II (*Seven Years' War*) *3 August 1758*. In the Bay of Bengal, off the Coromandel coast, Admiral Sir George Pocock encountered the French fleet of Count Antoine d'Aché. D'Aché had been trying to avoid the British since April when Pocock had stopped him from landing reinforcements for Pondicherry.

Now the British ships so badly damaged the French fleet that d'Aché could no longer support the army. *See* Pondicherry.

Negapatam III (*Second British-Mysore War*) *21 October–3 November 1781*. Siege was laid by a British force of 4,000 under Colonel Braithwaite. The garrison, partly Dutch and partly Mysore troops, were 8,000-strong, but surrendered on 3 November.

Negapatam IV (*War of the American Revolution*) *4 October 1782*. A naval action fought between a British squadron (Edward Hughes) and a French squadron (Suffren). The opposing forces were about equal in strength, and the action was indecisive, but the French designs on Negapatam were frustrated and Suffren drew off. *See* Trincomalee IV.

Negroponte (*or Euboae*) (*Venetian-Turkish Wars*) *1470*. The Ottoman Turks stormed and captured Negroponte Island, probably the most valuable Aegean commercial outpost possessed by the city-state of Venice. It was the first Turkish naval victory in history.

Nehavend (*Muslim invasion of Persia*) *637*. A huge Muslim army under Said, the lieutenant of the Caliph Omar, defeated a Persian army, 150,000-strong. This was the last stand made against the conquering Muslims. *See* Tripoli.

Nemecky Brod. *See* Deutschbrod.

Neon (*Third Sacred War*) *354 BC*. The Phocians, aided by mercenary troops, 10,000 in all, under Philomelus, faced the Thebans and Locrians. They were convincingly defeated. Philomelus, wounded and driven fighting to the edge of a precipice, leapt off the cliff. Called the Sacred War because Philomelus had plundered the temple of Delphi.

Netherlands War of Independence. *See* List of Battles.

Netherlands (*World War II*) *10–14 May 1940*. The German offensive against the West (after the conquest of Norway) began with von Bock's Army Group B crashing across the Dutch and Belgian borders, 10 May. General Student put 16,000 airborne troops, including 4,000 paratroops, into Rotterdam and other key places. On 12 May the German Eighteenth Army covered 100 miles to link with the airborne troops, preventing French and Dutch troops from joining. On 14 May the Luftwaffe bombed Rotterdam; 32,000 civilians were killed or wounded. The Dutch Army (Winkelman) surrendered that day. Dutch military casualties, 10,000; German, no more than 3,000. *See* Norway.

Neuve-Chapelle (*World War I*) *10–13 March 1915*. After a massive artillery barrage Sir John French sent the British First Army (Haig) against the German-held village of Neuve-Chapelle in an attempt to gain a vital ridge. The British took the village, but von Falkenhayn rushed 16,000 reserves into the battle and stopped any possibility of a breakthrough. British casualties, 13,000; German, 14,000. *See* Artois II; Ypres I; Ypres II.

Neuwied (*War of the French Revolution*) *18 April 1797*. Between the French, 80,000-strong under Hoche, and the Austrians under Werneck. Hoche won a decisive victory, driving the Austrians beyond the Lahn with a loss of 8,000 men and eighty guns. *See* Malborghetto.

Neva River (*Russian–Swedish War*) *1240*. Alexander, Prince of Novogorod, decisively defeated the Swedish invaders near what is now Leningrad. It was a great victory and the victor took the name Alexander Nevski to commemorate it. *See* Novogorod.

Neville's Cross, Co. Durham (*English–Scottish Wars*) *17 October 1346*. The Scottish invading army (David II) were routed by the northern levies under Henry Percy and Ralph Neville. The Scots lost 15,000 men and David and many of his nobles were captured. David himself was held for 10 years while 100,000 marks' ransom was paid in instalments over 10 years. *See* Halidon Hill; Otterburn.

Newark (*English Civil War*) *21 March 1644*. Newark was a vital town as it protected the York–Oxford road. It was held by Sir Richard Byron for King Charles. Parliament sent 6,500 men (Meldrum) to take the place while Charles sent Prince Rupert to relieve it. Rupert had the novel idea of ferrying his troops down the Severn to Bridgnorth where his cavalry met them. Meldrum had his headquarters on an island in the Trent, but soon had to withdraw much of his force to the island under heavy Roundhead attack. When one of his regiments mutinied, Meldrum surrendered. It was a decisive and welcome victory for the Royalists who held Newark for the king in a long siege, not capitulating until May 1646.

Newburn (*English–Scottish Wars or British Bishops' Wars*) *28 August 1640*. Between 4,500 English (Lord Conway) and the Scottish army of 22,500 (Leslie). Conway tried to hold the ford of Newburn, near Newcastle, but his raw levies, after a cannonade of 3 hours, fled in confusion. Conway then evacuated Newcastle, which was occupied by the Scots. Losses on both sides were small. (The Scots had rejected the Church of England, hence "Bishops' Wars".)

Newbury I (*English Civil War*) *20 September 1643*. Fought between 14,000 Royalists, under Charles I, and 14,000 Parliamentarians, under Essex. Charles's object was to stop Essex's march on London. His troops held their ground, but during the night he abandoned his position. *See* Cheriton; Roundway Down.

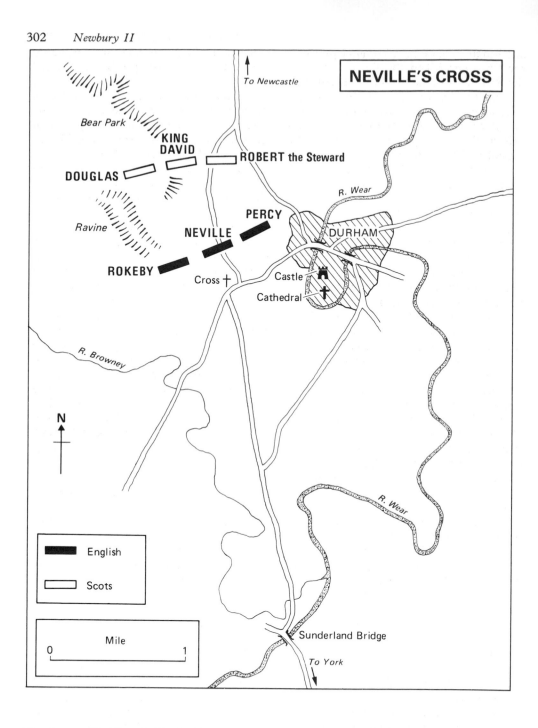

NEVILLE'S CROSS

To Newcastle

Bear Park

KING DAVID

ROBERT the Steward

DOUGLAS

R. Wear

Ravine

PERCY

NEVILLE

DURHAM

ROKEBY

Cross †

Castle

Cathedral

R. Browney

N

█ English

▢ Scots

Mile

0   1

Sunderland Bridge

To York

R. Wear

Newbury II (*English Civil War*) 27 October 1644. A second indecisive battle when 9,000 Royalists (Charles I) again held firm against the attacks of the Parliamentary army, 17,500-strong under Waller, Manchester and others. But again they retired to Oxford during the night. *See* Naseby.

New Carthage, *later Cartagena, Spain (Second Punic War) 209 BC.* In 212 BC Hannibal's brothers, Hasdrubal and Mago, defeated the Roman legions on the Ebro and killed the Roman leaders, the Scipio brothers, Publius and Gnaeus. In 209 BC the younger Publius Scipio, later famous as Africanus Scipio and one of the greatest generals in history, surprised the Cathaginians, stormed the capital and took it. It was a triumphant revenge for the death of his father and uncle. *See* Ilipa; Trebbia River I.

New Guinea (*World War II*) *1942–4*. The Japanese had to capture the great island of Papua–New Guinea if they were to conquer Australia to the south. Here and in the neighbouring islands of the south-west Pacific — New Britain and the Solomons — Australian troops fought many campaign-battles. The Australians, with American support, cleared Papua of Japanese by January 1943. Those on New Guinea's northern coast and mountains defended their positions with fanatical stubbornness and the Australian–American drive, though steady, was slow. Salamaua fell on 12 September 1943, Lae on 16 September, Finschhafen on 2 October, Wareo on 8 December. After fighting on the Huon peninsula, the Australians captured Bogadjim, Madang and Alexishafen, 24–26 April 1944.

The American battle for Hollandia, 22–27 April 1944, was one of the most superbly executed of the war. Through competent co-ordination of air, sea and land operations an entire Japanese army was surrounded and ineffective. For the loss of 100 dead and 1,000 wounded, the Americans killed 5,000 Japanese and wounded 7,000; another 6,000 fled into the jungle.

American landings bottled up 45,000 Japanese in Wewak, where Australians fought them for most of 1944. Meanwhile the Americans were fighting at Aitape, Maffin Bay, Wake Island and Biak Island, where the Japanese held out until August 1944. The New Guinea campaign was considered ended with the capture of Morotai Island, in the Moluccas, late in September.

The two-year campaign, which was predominantly Australian, was arguably the most arduous fought by any Allied troops during World War II. From 3 September 1943 General Sir Thomas Blamey, the senior Australian, commanded the New Guinea Force; principal American generals under General Douglas MacArthur were Eichelberger and Krueger. The Japanese commander in Western New Guinea was Lieutenant-General Jo Imura. Allied air support came from General Kenney's American–Australian Fifth Air Force and naval support from Admiral Kinkaid's Seventh Fleet. Casualties: to 26 August 1944, Australian Army battle casualties totalled 57,046, including 12,161 killed. American casualties in 1943–4 amounted to about 19,000, a small number compared to their heavy losses on the islands north and east of New Guinea. About 13,000 Japanese had died in Papua by January 1943; another 35,000 were killed during the northern New Guinea campaign. Tens of thousands were bypassed or taken prisoner. *See* Bougainville; Coral Sea; Gorari; Kokoda Trail; Milne Bay; Rabaul; Sattelburg; Scarlet Beach; Shaggy Ridge; Solomon Islands; Wau.

New Hope Church (*American Civil War*) *25–28 May 1864*. The Federals (Sherman) and the Confederates (Johnston) were engaged in desultory hit-and-run skirmishing, each side losing 2,000 casualties for no particular gain. *See* Kenesaw Mountain.

New Madrid and Island No. 10 (*American Civil War*) *February–March 1862*. The Federal advance down the Mississippi started as an amphibious operation. General John Pope, with 23,000 men, attacked new Madrid and Island No. 10; Flag Officer Foote supported the operation with his gunboats. Pope drove the Confederate garrison out of New Madrid on 13 March. Two gunboats steamed through fire from the heavy guns on Island No. 10 and escorted Pope's soldiers across the river. They cut land communication with the island which surrendered on 8 April. *See* Memphis; Murfreesboro.

Newmarket (*American Civil War*) *13 May 1864*. Between 5,150 Federals (Sigel) and 3,500 Confederates (Breckenridge). The Confederates, by a rapid flank movement, attacked Sigel's force on the march, and drove them into a wood behind their artillery. The guns were then gallantly attacked and taken by 247 cadets of the Virginia Military Institute who lost 10 killed and 47 wounded. Sigel retired, having suffered 831 casualties, and leaving six guns in the enemy's hands. *See* Piedmont; Spotsylvania.

New Orleans I (*American–British War of 1812*) *December 1814–January 1815*. The city, held by a garrison of 12,000 Americans under General Jackson, was attacked by a British force of 6,000 under General Keane, aided by the fleet. On 13 December the American warships in the Mississippi were captured and by 21 December the troops had been disembarked. After a few skirmishes, Sir Edward Pakenham arrived to take command on the 25th, and on 1 January 1815 he launched a determined attack on the American position. This failed, and short of supplies, the British retired. On 7 January the British made another attack and were again repulsed, losing 1,500, including Pakenham. The expedition then withdrew. Peace had already been concluded, but neither side knew of it. *See* Fort McHenry.

New Orleans II (*American–English War of 1812*) *14 December 1814*. A remarkable action carried out by boats from ships of the Royal Navy. Before the capture of the town of New Orleans could be attempted the guardships had to be destroyed. Admiral Cochrane sent a fleet of ships' boats, and about 1,000 men, all under Captain Lockyer. By capturing one enemy ship and using it against the others the party destroyed them all.

New Orleans III (*American Civil War*) *28 April 1862*. On 16 April the Federal fleet of thirty armed steamers and twenty-one mortar vessels (Commodore Farragut) began the bombardment of Fort Jackson and Fort Mary. After 9 days of shelling Farragut forced the passage. When he anchored off New Orleans the city surrendered. *See* Chicasaw Bluffs; Shiloh.

Newport (*American Revolution*) *5–28 August 1778*. An abortive attempt by Washington, using twelve French warships (Comte d'Estaing) and 10,000 American troops (Sullivan), to take the British base at Newport, Rhode Island, held by Sir Robert Pigot with 3,000 British troops. A British relief fleet of eight ships (Richard Howe) arrived on 7 May and the rival fleets manoeuvred vainly for 2 days before both fleets were badly damaged by storms. The French ships left for repairs and, unsupported, the American troops deserted in large numbers. In the end Sullivan had to fight his way out. British casualties, 260; American, 311.

New Ross (*Irish Rebellion against the British*) *5 June 1798*. Between 30,000 rebels under Father Roche and Bagnal Harvey, and about 1,400 British regulars (General Johnstone). The rebels attacked the garrison of New Ross, and penetrated into the centre of the town, but were driven back with the bayonet and routed. They lost 2,600 killed.

Newtown (*American Revolution*) *29 August 1779*. To deter further Indian attacks — encouraged by the British and American Loyalists — Washington sent 1,400 troops (Sullivan and Clinton) to destroy Indian villages and crops. Indians and Loyalists, under Mohawk chief Joseph Brant and Captain Butler with 1,500 men, made a stand but were routed. *See* Paulus Hook.

Newtown Butler (*War of the Glorious Revolution*) *2 August 1689*. Between 5,000 Catholics (MacCarthy) and 3,000 Protestants, under Colonel Wolseley, who was defending Enniskillen. The Catholics were routed, losing 1,500 in the action, and 500 drowned in Lough Erne during their flight. *See* Boyne; Londonderry.

Nez Perće War *1877*. The Nez Perće Indian tribe, under their young chief Joseph, refused to leave their homeland in Oregon. An army detachment tried to herd the 700 Nez Perćes into a reservation, but Joseph defeated them in White Bird Canyon, 17 June. Moving eastwards, the Nez Perćes were pursued by a force of regular soldiers under Brigadier O. Howard. At the Clearwater River Joseph repulsed the troops. After minor engagements, the tribe reached the Big Hole Basin, where Colonel J. Gibbon and another army force surprised and besieged them. Joseph and his 300 warriors surrounded the besiegers. As the army brought up reinforcements, Joseph took his people northwards to Canada. On Eagle Creek, after a 2,000-mile trek, two generals and 3,000 troops blocked the Nez Perćes path. Joseph fought for 4 days against odds of ten to one and then surrendered. He was a remarkable military leader.

Niagara (*Seven Years' War*) *June–July 1759*. This French fort was besieged on 3 June by 2,500 British with 900 Indians, under General Prideaux. The garrison of 600 French was commanded by Captain Pouchot. Prideaux was killed in the accidental explosion of a shell and Sir William Johnson assumed command. On 24 July 1,300 French and Indians (Ligneris) tried to relieve the fort, but were repulsed at La Belle Famille, and Pouchot surrendered.

Nicaea (*now Iznik*) (*First Crusade*) *May–June 1097*. This city on Lake Ascaria was besieged by the Crusaders under Godefroi de Bouillon. The Saracen defenders were aided by possession of Lake Ascanius, but with great effort the Crusaders transported boats from the Sea of Marmara to the lake and thus completed the investment of the place. Sultan Soliman made two determined attempts to relieve Nicaea, but both were repulsed, Nicaea surrendered on 18 June, not to the crusaders, but to Byzantine Emperor Alexis I Comnenus, virtually a neutral. *See* Dorylaeum.

Nicaragua Civil War *1979–* . The warring groups are: Frente Sandinista de Liberacion Nacional (FSLN), generally known as Sandinistas; Nicaraguan Democratic Front (FDN), usually referred to as the Contras; Democratic Revolutionary Front (ARDE). In July 1979 the Sandinistas defeated the National Guard and the president, Anastasio Somoza, fled the country. From Honduras the National Guard, with American help, began to raid Sandanista posts. Both FDN and ARDE back the war against the Sandanistas, who are numerically powerful. In 1985 they had 25,000 regular troops, 25,000 reserves, 80,000 in the militia and 10,000 in paramilitary units. Cuba provided 3,000 advisers and much equipment.†

Nicholson's Nek. *See* Farquhar's Farm.

Nicopolis I (*Third Mithridatic War*) *66 BC*. Between the Romans under Pompey and the army of Mithridates. The Romans had occupied the heights in front of the retreating Asiatics and Mithridates was foolish enough to camp under their position. The Romans rushed the enemy camp by night and annihilated Mithridates' army. This was the last battle Mithridates fought against the Roman legions. *See* Tigranocerta.

Nicopolis II (*Rome's Pontic campaign*) *48 BC*. Domitius Calvinus, with one Roman legion and a contingent of Pontic and other Asiatic troops, encountered the Bosporans, under Pharnaces. Calvinus' Asiatic troops fled at the first setback and he was defeated, but the steadiness of the Romans prevented disaster.

Nicopolis III (*Turkish–Hungarian War*) 28 September 139. 50,000 Hungarian, Polish, German, Italian and English "crusaders" plus 3,000 French knights, all under the Duke of Nevers and Sigismund of Hungary, faced the Turkish army of Bajazet I. The Allies had no battle plan and the French charged the Turkish lines without waiting for their allies. They penetrated the two first lines, killing 1,500 Turks, but they were then overpowered by the Janissaries in the third line and all were killed. Bajazet then turned on the rest of the Allied army who fled without striking a blow. Thousands were killed in the field and Bajazet massacred another 10,000 prisoners, except for twenty-five nobles. The "crusade", inspired by Pope Boniface IX, was a disaster. *See* Kossovo I; Prague I.

Nicopolis IV (*Russian–Turkish War*) 16 July 1877. The town, now known as Nikopol, was captured by the 9th Russian Army Corps (Krudener) after 2 days' bombardment, when the garrison of 7,000 Turks surrendered. The Russians lost 1,300 killed and wounded. *See* Plevna.

Nicosia (*Venetian–Turkish War*) 25 July–9 September 1570. Lala Mustafa, commanding the armies of Sultan Selim II, wanted to capture the Cyprus capital and expel the Venetians from the island. He had a force of 50,000 infantry and 20,000 seamen against the 8,000 — 3,000 Venetians, 5,000 Cypriots — mustered by Nicolo Dandolo, Governor of Nicosia. The garrison had a reported 900 guns — but little powder or shot. The Venetians fought with great gallantry and on 15 August made a spirited sortie which threw back the Turks, but Dandolo refused to commit his reserves. Finally an all-out day-long assault won Nicosia for the Turks. The garrison's casualties were heavy. The Turks massacred most of the civil population and all surviving members of the garrison. *See* Lepanto.

Nieuwpoort (*Netherlands War of Independence*) 2 July 1600. Between the Dutch (Maurice of Orange) and the Spaniards (Archduke Albert of Austria). Prince Maurice's force was surprised in its positions among sand dunes but stood firm and after a long engagement defeated the Spaniards with heavy loss. *See* Oostende; Turnhout.

Nigerian Civil War (*also known as Biafran War*) 1966–70. After much tribal fighting and several massacres in 1966 the Supreme Commander and Head of Military Government, General Yabuku Gowon, declared (27 May 1967) that Nigeria would be divided into twelve states under a Federal government. Lieutenant-Colonel Odemegu Ojukwu, military governor of the eastern region, declared unilateral independence for "The Republic of Biafra" and its oppressed Ibo people. Federal forces blockaded Biafra, though the Biafran fighters received supplies from France, Portugal and the Vatican. Count Carl-Gustav von Rosen, a Swedish pilot, formed a small but effective air force using Minicon planes armed with rockets. Britain, the United States and the Soviet Union supplied the Federal forces. The Biafrans held out longer than anybody expected, but 200,000 of them died. Their forces finally succumbed to overwhelming force, using Russian-supplied MiG fighters and armour. The war ended on 9 January 1970 when the Biafran 12th Division could no longer hold Owerri. Nigerian casualties were not disclosed, but unofficial sources put the figure at 10,000 dead.

Nihawand, *near Hamadan, Iran* (*Muslim conquest of Persia*) 641. Building up an army of 100,000, Yazdegerd III and his son Firuz tried to make a determined stand against the Arabian Muslims led by Sa'd ibn Abi-Waqqas. But the fast, daring Muslim horsemen were invincible and destroyed the Persian army; Yazdegerd fled to the mountains. The Muslim conquest of Persia was complete. *See* Jalula.

Nijmegen. *See* Arnhem.

Nikko (*Japanese Revolution*) May 1868. Between the followers of the Shogun (Otori Keisuke) and the Imperial army (Saigo Takamori). The rebels were defeated, and fled to the castle of Wakamatsu.

Nile (*or Abukir*) (*French invasion of Egypt*) 1 August 1798. Admiral Brueys, with thirteen French ships of the line and four frigates, was anchored in Abukir Bay. Nelson, with thirteen line-of-battle-ships and one fifty-gun ship, penetrated with half his squadron between the French line and the shore, while his remaining ships engaged them on the outside. Caught between two fires the French were routed, only two of their vessels escaping capture or destruction. Admiral Brueys was killed, and his ship *L'Orient* blown up. The English victory cut Napoleon's communications with France and doomed his projected conquest of the Middle East. *See* Acre; Mount Tabor.

Ninety Six (*American Revolution*) 22 May–18 June 1781. At Ninety Six, western South Carolina, Colonel Cruger with 550 Loyalists held a British post against 2,000 Americans (Greene). Hearing that 2,000 British regulars were marching to relieve Ninety Six, Greene switched from siege to attack, but was beaten off with 147 casualties. However, the British evacuated the fort. *See* Eutaw Springs; Hobkirk's Hill.

Nineveh I (*Fall of Assyria*) 612 BC. The allied Medians and Chaldeans attacked the Assyrian capital on the Tigris River. The Assyrian resistance, inspired by Sin-shar-ishkun, was stubborn, but the king was killed and his people overwhelmed. The victors demolished Nineveh. *See* Megiddo II; Samaria.

Nineveh II (*Byzantine–Persian Wars*) 1 December 627. This was the decisive battle of the last war between the Eastern Roman empire and the Sassanid empire. The Emperor Heraclius led the imperial troops while Rhazates, the general of Chosroes II, commanded the Persians, who outnumbered the Romans. During the hard-fought battle Heraclius was in the midst of the fighting, as always, and was wounded; nevertheless, he led the final charge and personally killed Rhazates. The Persian army was beaten and the remnants retreated. Despite his own losses, Heraclius pursued the Persians and broke them completely. *See* Jerusalem V; Viminacium.

Niquitas (*Colombian War of Independence*) 3 February 1813. The Colombian Patriots under Bolivar completely defeated the Spanish Royalists.

Nishapur (*Rise of the Seljuk Turks*) 1038. The Turkish tribe of Seljuks — named after their first chief — defeated the Muslims of Ma'sud, of the Ghaznevid dynasty, in a one-sided battle that followed an ambush. The victory gave the Turks — under Tughril Beg and Chagar Beg — control of the Iranian plateau. *See* Manzikert.

Nisibis (*or Nusaybi*) (*Byzantine–Persian Wars*). This Roman fortress, known as the Bulwark of the East, was besieged in 338, 346 and 350 by Sapor II, King of Persia. In the two former years he was compelled to retire after a siege of 60 and 80 days respectively. In 350 the city was defended by a garrison under Lucilianus. Sapor, desperate to break through the defences, diverted the Mygdonius River and built dams to form a large lake. He put a fleet of vessels on it and from them his troops attacked the city almost from the level of the ramparts. Under pressure of the water, part of the wall gave way and many Persians attacked through it. They died to a man. By the following day the garrison had rebuilt the wall. At the end of about 3 months, Sapor, having lost 20,000 men, raised the siege. He did not attack Nisibis again.

Nissa *1064*. A naval action, fought at the mouth of the Nissa in 1064 between the Danish fleet (Sweyn II) and the Norwegians under Harold Hardrada. Sweyn was defeated, and his fleet destroyed; he escaped with difficulty to Zealand.

Nissa. *See* Morawa.

Nive (*Peninsular War*) *13 December 1813*. Between 35,000 French, (Soult) and 14,000 British and Portuguese under Wellington. Having crossed the Nive on 10 December, Wellington took up a strong position on the heights near the village of St. Pierre. Here he was attacked by Soult, but repulsed him, and occupied the French position in front of the Adour. French losses in this battle and the combats which preceded it exceeded 10,000 men. British losses, 5,019 killed or wounded. *See* Orthez.

Nivelle (*Peninsular War*) *10 November 1813*. The French (Soult) were driven from a strong position by the British (Wellington) and retired behind the Nivelle. The French lost 4,265, including about 1,200 prisoners, 51 guns, and all their field magazines. British losses, 2,694 killed and wounded. *See* Nive; Vitoria.

Nizib, *northern Syria* (*Mehemet Ali's Second Rebellion against Turkey*) *23–24 June 1839*. Between 30,000 Turks (Hafiz Pasha) and the Mehemet Ali's Syrian–Egyptian army, under his son Ibrahim. Ibrahim was far the stronger in artillery, and his fire so shattered the Turks that when he advanced his infantry, the enemy fled. Von Moltke, later the mastermind of the German Army, was under fire in this action for the first time; he was a military adviser in Constantinople. *See* Konya.

Noisseville (*French–German War*) *31 August–1 September 1870*. A French sortie under Marshal Bazaine, from Metz, in an attempt to break through the investing line of the Germans (Prince Frederick Charles). The French had some success at first and maintained the ground they had won during the day. Next day their efforts to advance were fruitless and they were driven back into Metz with a loss of 145 officers and 3,379 men. German losses, 126 officers and 2,850 men. *See* Gravelotte; Metz; Sedan.

Nola (*Second Punic War*) *216–214 BC*. Rome had suffered a crushing defeat at Cannae, q.v., at the hands of the great Carthaginian, Hannibal. Many Italian towns considered joining Hannibal, but the proconsul Marcus Marcellus held the walled town of Nola and repulsed Hannibal. In the following year the Romans, rebuilding their strength, avoided open battle and again Marcellus repulsed Hannibal at Nola. In 214 BC Hannibal, in desperate need of an adequate defensible base, again tried to storm Nola. Once more Marcellus fought him off. Hannibal turned elsewhere. Marcellus was the first commander to defeat Hannibal. *See* Cannae; Capua; Tarentum.

Nördlingen I (*Thirty Years' War*) *6 September 1634*. Between 40,000 Imperialists (Ferdinand of Hungary) and a numerically inferior force of Germans and Swedes (Duke of Weimar and Count Horn). The action was fought to relieve Nördlingen, which Ferdinand was besieging, and resulted in the defeat of the Allies, who lost 17,000 killed, 6,000 prisoners, including Horne, and 80 guns, *See* Lützen I; Wittstock.

Nördlingen II (*Thirty Years' War*) *3 August 1645*. 12,000 French and Weimar troops under Condé and Turenne attacked the village of Allersheim, where Baron Mercy's 14,000-strong Bavarian–Austrian army was strongly entrenched. After severe fighting the left wing under Turenne succeeded in pushing out Mercy's troops with a loss of 6,000 killed, wounded and prisoners, and almost all their guns. General Mercy was killed. The French loss amounted to about 4,000. *See* Mergentheim; Zusmarshausen.

Normandy. *See* D-Day; Invasion of Normandy.

Northallerton *1138.* *See* The Standard.

Northampton I (*Second Barons' War of England*) 6–7 April 1264. Raising a Royalist force at Oxford, Henry III and his son Edward (Edward I) attacked Northampton Castle, held by young Simon de Montfort. The elder Montfort, hurrying from London with reinforcements, was too late. *See* Evesham; Lewes; Newport.

Northampton II (*Wars of the Roses*) 18 July 1460. Henry VI, marching on London with a Royalist army, held good entrenchements, but they were betrayed to the Earls of Warwick and March by Lord Grey de Ruthyn. On top of this, a rainstorm drenched the Lancastrians' gunpowder. In the battle the Lancastrians lost 300 killed, including the Duke of Buckingham and the Earls of Shrewsbury and Egremont. The king was captured. *See* Blore Heath; Mortimer's Cross; Wakefield.

North Anna River (*American Civil War*) 20–26 May 1864. Aware that his right flank was threatened, General Lee deployed 50,000 Confederates behind the North Anna River and was in position when General Grant's 100,000 Federals arrived opposite him. Grant's probing manoeuvres gave him initial gains, but split his force into three widely separated groups, thus making him vulnerable to counter-attack. The attack never came: Lee and his generals Hill and Ewell were ill, Longstreet was wounded and out of action and Anderson, though in a strong position, was inexperienced. Grant, however, could not move the Confederates and marched on; the Confederates also moved, keeping between the Federals and the Confederate capital, Richmond. Total casualties, about 3,000. *See* Cold Harbour; Spotsylvania.

North Foreland I (*First English–Dutch War*) 2–3 June 1653. An indecisive, stand-off fight with Monck (Duke of Albemarle) commanding the British fleet and Maarten Tromp the Dutch.

North Foreland II (*Second English–Dutch War*) 25 July 1666. Between the English fleet, under the Duke of Albemarle and Prince Rupert, and the Dutch under Van Tromp and de Ruyter. The English were victorious, capturing or burning twenty ships. The Dutch had 4,000 men killed or drowned.

North Ireland Community War (*also known as the Terrorist War, the Ulster Crisis or the Northern Ireland Troubles*) 1968– . The Protestant "Loyalist" majority and the Roman Catholic minority have been in a state of tension, if not conflict, for generations. The Protestant organizations, notably the Civil Rights Association (CRA), wants eternal union with Britain. The Catholic organizations, notably the Provisional Irish Republican Army (IRA) — generally known as the Provos — wants union with Eire. The troubles began on 5 October 1968 when the CRA staged an illegal march in Londonderry; eighty-eight people were injured in the riots which followed. To keep the warring factions apart, British troops moved into Londonderry on 14 August 1969 and Belfast on 16 August. By 31 July 1972 the British Army had 21,000 troops in Ulster. Despite their presence, the level of violence was high. In 1976, for instance, 800 attempted murders were reported and 7,000 terrorist incidents.

The IRA regards its members as active service soldiers and the British troops, members of the Royal Irish Constabulary, and of the Ulster Defence Regiment as foreign enemies and kills them by sniper's bullet, ambush and remotely-fired bomb. Protestant and Roman Catholic extremists kill members of each other's community.†
Deaths in Ulster 1969–1982: RUC, Army and UDR, and civilian:

1969	13	1977	112
1970	25	1978	81
1971	174	1979	113
1972	468	1980	75
1973	250	1981	98
1974	206	1982	85
1975	247	1983	77
1976	297	1984	64

North Korea (*Korean War*) October–December 1950. Several actions made up this great battle. American and South Korean units, under the U.N. Supreme Commander-in-Chief MacArthur, had crossed the 38th parallel and on 20 October captured the North Korean capital, Pyongyang. Other forces reached the Yalu River 26 October. The U.N. advance was relentless, and the North Koreans had suffered 200,000 casualties and lost 135,000 prisoners.

At this point the Chinese Communists intervened and in a fight on the night of 25–26 October drove a South Korean army back to the Chongchon, inflicting 75 per cent casualties. Russian jet fighters joined the battle.

However, the Chinese appeared disinclined to press their advantage and MacArthur, 24 November, launched a counter-offensive along his entire front, the object being to take the U.N. line to the Yalu River. But Chinese intelligence was good and 24 hours later Generals Chin Yi and Lin Piao threw 300,000 men at the Allied line, 180,000 of them at the junction of two American groups — U.S. Eighth Army (Walker) and X Corps (Almond). This assault could not be withstood, and the Allies lost much of their artillery as they retreated.

The Communists ambushed 7,000 men of the U.S. 2nd Infantry Division near the Chongchon River on 1 December killing or wounding 3,000 of them. On 27 November the 1st Marine Division was cut off near Choshin Reservoir by 120,000 Chinese. In a remarkable fighting retreat the marines suffered 7,500 casualties — 50 per cent of them frostbite — but reached Hungnam and safe evacuation. They brought out all their dead and wounded and inflicted, it is believed, 40,000 casualties on the Chinese. By 27 December a line was established near the 38th parallel, but 50 miles of country had been lost. *See* Inchon; Yalu.

North-west Africa, *Operation Torch* (*World War II*) 8–10 November 1942. The Allied forces made three landings — Casablanca (Morocco), Oran and Algiers (Algeria). Eisenhower was in supreme command of 107,000 British and Americans in 650 ships. Their opponents were Vichy French, i.e. French supporting the Nazi regime. General Juin surrendered Algiers on the evening of the invasion; at Oran the French resisted for 2 days before surrendering. At Casablanca French warships battled with the American covering fleet and lost ten vessels. Patton's infantry overcame resistance in 3 days. Admiral Darlan ordered a general cease-fire on 10 November. The Germans reacted to the Allied invasion of Northwest Africa by marching into Vichy — unoccupied — France. The British and Americans hurried towards Tunisia, but strong German and Italian reinforcements reached it first. *See* Mareth Line; Tunisia.

Norway (*World War II*) 9 April–9 June 1940. On the first day of the battle six Nazi battle groups invaded Norway's six major ports — Narvik, Trondheim, Bergen, Stavangar, Kristiansand and Oslo. Surprise was so complete and organization so thorough that Oslo was captured by only 1,500 airborne troops (von Falkenhorst). The English and French counter-invaded on 14–19 April at Namsos and Andalsnes and at Narvik, but only at Narvik was any success achieved. Here 20,000 Allied troops (Admiral Lord Cork and General Auchinleck) besieged the port, held by 6,000 Germans. The Germans were driven into the mountains but the defeat of the Allies in France forced their retreat from Norway. Hitler had achieved his aims: continuation of the flow of Swedish iron ore to Germany (through Narvik) and blocking of any Allied thrust through Scandinavia. Overall German losses: 5,300 killed or wounded; three cruisers, ten destroyers, eight submarines, eleven transports, eleven other ships. Allied ship losses were mostly British: aircraft carrier *Glorious*, two cruisers, nine destroyers, six submarines. *See* Narvik.

Notium (*Great Peloponnesian War*) *407 BC.* Between the Peloponnesian fleet (Lysander) and the Athenian fleet of Alcibiades, which was lying at Notium. Alcibiades was not present during the action, which was the result of a surprise, and the Athenians were defeated with a loss of fifteen ships. *See* Arginusae Islands; Cyzicus.

Novara I (*French–Swiss War in Italy*) *6 June 1513.* The Swiss had established a virtual protectorate over the Duchy of Milan. In May–June a French army under Prince Louis de la Trémoille crossed the Alps, captured Milan and besieged the Swiss garrison at Novara. As a Swiss relief army of 5,000 approached, La Trémoille withdrew from his siege lines and prepared for battle. The Swiss slept only 3 hours then marched all night to attack the unsuspecting French at dawn. They smashed through to the centre of the French camps and cut the infantry to pieces. La Trémoille fled back to France with his shattered army.

Novara II (*Italian Wars of Independence against Austria*) *23 March 1849.* The Austrian army in Lombardy under Marshal Radetsky seized the fortress of Mortara, thus provoking the Piedmontese to battle near Novara. The 50,000 Piedmontese under General Chrzanowski were undisciplined and no match for the three Austrian army corps. Defeated in detail, they were driven from the field in disorder. *See* Custoza I; Rome VII; Venice.

Novgorod (*Rise of Russia*) *862.* The Vikings, or more correctly the Varangians, had embarked on conquest of Slav territory between the Baltic and Black Seas. The mighty chieftain Rurik stormed and took Novgorod, north-west Russia, and founded a royal house whose princes ruled for 700 years. Novgorod became (with Kiev) the great trading base of early Russia. *See* Adrianople III; Neva River.

Novi (*or Novi Ligure*) (*Wars of the French Revolution*) *15 August 1799.* General Joubert, with 35,000 men, attacked the Russian–Austrian army commanded by Marshal Suvarov in southern Italy. But Joubert and four other generals were killed early in the battle and General Moreau, who had been relieved of the command on 5 August, found himself again in command. The French had lost 7,000 killed or wounded, 3,000 prisoners and 37 guns, so Moreau gathered the survivors and escaped into the mountains. The Russian–Austrian army had lost 6,500 killed or wounded and 1,200 prisoners. *See* Abukir; Trebbia River II.

Noyon-Montdidier (*World War I*) *9–13 June 1918.* Ludendorff, launching his fourth offensive of 1918, wanted to link his Amiens salient with the Aisne–Marne salient and so threaten Paris. On 9 June the first attack (Hutier) drove back the French Third Army (Humbert) and on 10 June the second attack (von Boehn) smashed against the French Tenth Army (Mangin). Hutier was able to take 6 miles of country but elsewhere the offensive was blocked and the whole operation stalled. Casualties: German, 35,000; French, 15,000. *See* Aisne River III; Marne River II; Somme River II.

Nujufghur (*Indian Mutiny against the British*) *24 August 1857.* Between 6,000 rebels (Muhammad Bukht Khan) and a small British force under John Nicholson. The rebels were defeated with a loss of over 800 men and all their guns. *See* Cawnpore; Delhi.

**Numantia (*Roman subjugation of*

***Iberia or Lusitanian War*) *133* BC.** This city, defended by the inhabitants under Megaravicus, was besieged 142 BC by a Roman consular army. In the course of 141 BC the Romans were twice defeated under the walls. Negotiations for a surrender were not concluded, and in 139 BC the new Roman commander, Popilius Laenas, refused to ratify the terms. Shortly afterwards he was defeated by the Numantians, as was his successor, Mancius, in 137. It was not till the arrival of Scipio Aemilianus in 134 that resistance was at last overcome. The city fell in the autumn of 133 BC. The Numantian resistance was the most sustained the Romans had experienced. *See* Carthage.

Nyborg (*First Northern War*) *November 1659*. Charles X of Sweden was empire building and was at war with Poland. Denmark declared war against Sweden and in February 1658 Charles led a daring advance over the ice from Jutland to Fyn and then to Zealand. The Dutch intervened and Admiral de Ruyter transported 9,000 Danish troops from Jutland to Fyn where they defeated Philip of Sulzbach and 6,000 Swedish troops. *See* Warsaw 1656.

Nymphe vs. La Cleopatra *18 June 1793*. Capture by the British ship (Pellew) of the French frigate, off Start Point.

Oberhollabrun (*Napoleonic Wars: Danube campaign*) *16 November 1805*. Seizing Vienna from the Austrians, Napoleon turned north to trap the Russian army of 40,000 in Lower Austria. At Oberhollabrun Prince Bagration had positioned a roadblock of 7,000 troops and on 16 November the French cavalry (Murat), with infantry from Lannes' and Soult's corps, assaulted this position. A gallant and clever defence held them off and Bagration moved out after dark, having lost half his force. But the delaying action enabled the main Russian army to withdraw to safety. *See* Austerlitz; Caldiero II; Ulm.

Oberstein (*Polish Wars*) *June 1533*. The Poles (Tarnowski) decisively defeated the Wallachians (Bogden).

Obligado (*Uruguayan War of Independence*) *10 November 1845*. British and French squadrons defeated the Argentine fleet (Oribe) and raised the siege of Montevideo, opening the waters of the Parana to international use.

Ocana (*Peninsular War*) *19 November 1809*. Soult, with 30,000 French, defeated Areizaga's 53,000 Spaniards who lost 5,000 killed or wounded, 26,000 prisoners and all artillery and baggage. French losses, 1,700. *See* Cadiz; Talavera.

Ocean Pond (*or Olustee*) (*American Civil War*) *20 February 1864*. 6,000 Federals (General Truman Seymour) attacked 5,000 Confederates (General Joseph Finnegan) holding a strong position near Lake City, Florida protected by swamps and forests. Repulsed, the Federals lost 1,200 men to the Confederates loss of 700.

Ockley (*Viking invasion of England*) *851*. Ethelwulf and his West Saxons defeated the Vikings after they had sacked London and Canterbury.

October War (*Yom Kippur War or War of Atonement to the Israelis; The Great Crossing to the Egyptians*) *October 1973*. The Arab offensive against Israel began on 6 October, Yom Kippur or the Day of Atonement, the holiest day in the Jewish calendar. It was made on two fronts, with the Egyptian Army attacking across the Suez Canal in the south and the Syrian Army across the Golan Heights in the north. *Commanders: Israel:* Defence Minister, Moshe Dayan; Chief-of-Staff, General David Elazar; G.O.C. Northern Command, General Yitzhak Hofi; G.O.C. Southern Command, General Gonen; Air Force commander, General Benjamin Peled. *Egypt:* Minister of War, General Ahmed Ismail; Commander-in-Chief, General Saad Shazli; Director of Operations, General Abdel Gamasy. *Syria:* Commander-in-Chief, General Moustafa Tlas; Chief-of-Staff, General Yusif Shakkour.

Suez Front: Egyptian troops crossed the canal using pontoon bridges and 1,000 rubber boats. With high-pressure water jets they broke through sand ramparts of Israel's Bar-Lev line and protected by a missile umbrella they spread into Sinai. Taken by surprise, the Israelis lost 150 tanks, mostly to infantry anti-tank missiles, but managed to regroup. The Egyptians failed to rush to the crucial passes in central Sinai, though they had 500 tanks and five divisions in the Sinai by early on 7 October. On the night of 15–16 October Israeli paratroopers and tanks (Major-General Arik Sharon) counter-crossed the Suez Canal between the Egyptian Second and Third Armies. By the time of the first cease-fire on 22 October the Egyptian Third Army was cut off. At the second cease-fire, 24 October, Israel held the initiative.

Golan Front: 700 Syrian tanks, Soviet made T-54s and T-55s, made the first attack near Kuneitra. Israel's weakest tanks were on this front, but yielding ground slowly the Israelis fought the Syrian tank forces to a standstill. Then, bringing in the tank reserves with air protection, they slowly pushed the Syrians back. The Syrians were joined by Iraqi and Jordanian reinforcements, but their attempts to mount a new offensive ended in confusion. As the front stabilized, the Syrians left 867 of their tanks in Israeli hands; the Israelis lost 250. Israeli paratroops recaptured Mount Hermon on 22 October. On the two fronts Israel lost 102 planes, half of them during the first 2 days. The Arab air forces lost 514 planes. Throughout the war giant Soviet Antonov aircraft heavily supplied the Arab forces; U.S. aid for Israel did not begin to arrive until 13 October. Casualties: Israel, 2,412 killed, 5,094 wounded. Syria and Egypt each lost about 9,000 killed and a total of 51,000 wounded.

Oczakov (*or Ochakov*) (*Turkish–Russian–Austrian War*) *1737–8*. The Russians (Count Munnich) stormed the fortress, held by 100,000 Turks and Bosnians, blew up the magazine and routed the garrison. The following year the Russians again besieged the place, but the garrison held out for 6 months.

Taking the fort by storm, 17 December, the Russians massacred 40,000 soldiers and civilians. *See* Khotin.

Odawara (*Hojo Rebellion*) *1590*. The last stronghold of the Hojo family, Odawara Castle was besieged by Japanese Imperial troops (Hideyoshi). With surrender 3 months later the power of the Hojo family ended.

Oenophyta (*First Peloponnesian War*) *457* BC. A defeat for the Thebans and other people from Boeotian states by the Athenians. *See* Tanagra.

Ofen (*Hungarian Rising against Austria*) *4–21 May 1849*. An Austrian garrison held out against the Hungarians (Gorgey) for only a few weeks, mainly because they lost their commander, Hentzi, early in the Hungarian assault. *See* Schwechat.

Ohud (*Muhammad's conquest of Arabia*) *625*. Muhammad, with only 900 soldiers, could not stand against the Koreish tribe led by Abu Sufyan. He lost seventy killed, was himself wounded and withdrew to Medina. *See* Badr; Medina.

Ogaden War (*or Battle for the Horn of Africa*) *1977–* . The war began as a conflict between the Ethiopian Army and the Western Somali Liberation Front (WSLF), which had 5,000 fighters. WSLF claimed the region of Ogaden, which comprises about a third of Ethiopia. At first WSLF captured much territory, but huge shipments of Soviet arms and the help of 10,000 Cuban troops enabled Ethiopia to launch a counter-offensive in February–March 1977. On 12 February the Somalia government of Said Barre threw most of its army into the war to support the guerrillas. The major action was the 2-day battle of Jigjiga, which was won for Ethiopia by the leadership of the Russian General Petrov. On 9 March Somalia withdrew from Ogaden. WSLF continued the war alone, engaging the Ethiopians in open conflict as well as with guerrilla attacks. About two million refugees moved into Somalia from Ogaden.

Okinawa (*World War II*) *1945*. The greatest land battle of the Pacific war. To defend the 794-square-mile island the Japanese commander, Ushijama, had 110,000 troops of the Thirty-second Army dug in behind the Naha–Shuri–Yonabaru Line. The supreme American commander was Admiral Nimitz, and the assault was led by General Buckner, commanding Tenth Army. The amphibious attack began 1 April and by nightfall 50,000 troops held a beach-head 8 miles long by 4 miles deep, but 12 days — 8–20 April — were needed to clear the Motobu Peninsula. The 77th Infantry Division invaded Ie Shima island on 16 April, capturing it in a savage 4-day struggle in which 4,700 Japanese were killed. Fighting on the southern end of Okinawa was even more severe; in 12 days of ruthless fighting the Americans gained less than 2 miles.

On 4–5 May Ushijama launched a heavy counter-attack against the Tenth Army's left flank — and lost 6,227 killed. Japanese positions fell slowly. On 4 June the 6th U.S. Marine Division landed on Oroku Peninsula and took it in 10 days of bitter fighting. On 18 June, Buckner was killed and the Marine General Geiger assumed command. On 21 June the Americans reached the southern coast and then turned back to mop up strong pockets of resistance. Officially, the battle ended on 2 July. Casualties: American, 2,938 marines and 4,675 troops dead, 31,807 wounded; Japanese, 100,000 killed, 10,000 captured.

A sea and air battle was also fought for Okinawa. U.S. carrier planes sank the *Yamata*, the world's most powerful battleship, and 14 other warships. The Japanese made 1,900 kamikaze attacks, sinking 36 American ships and damaging 368; 4,907 American seamen were killed and 4,824 wounded. In the air the Japanese lost no fewer than 7,800 aircraft, the Americans 763. The war ended 6 weeks later. *See* Iwo Jima.

Olmedo (*Civil War of Castilian Succession*) *March 1476*. Henry of Castile defeated the troops of the Archbishop of Toledo, supporting Joan, wife of Alfonso V of Portugal, who claimed the throne. *See* Toro.

Olmutz (*or Olomouc*) (*Seven Years' War*) *May–July 1758*. Frederick the Great besieged the Austrian fortress in Moravia, but his opponent, Count von Daun — acting for the Holy Roman Empress Maria Theresa — managed to keep open supply and communication lines to the city. Austrian irregulars harassed Frederick's 90-mile supply route, destroyed a convoy of 4,000 wagons and forced Frederick to raise the siege, 1 July. *See* Crefeld; Leuthen; Zorndorf.

Olpae (*Second Peloponnesian War*) *426 BC*. With brilliant tactics, Demosthenes with a small force of Athenians ambushed and defeated a Spartan–Ambracio army, killing its commander, Eurylochus. *See* Navarino; Tanagra.

Oltenitza (*Crimean War*) *4 November 1853*. Declaring war on Russia, Turkey sent an army (Omer Pasha) northwards across the Danube. The Turks met the Russian army occupying Wallachia and overwhelmed it. It was the first Turkish victory over Russia in a century of fighting. *See* Sinope. (The British and French were yet to join the war.)

Omdurman (*British–Sudanese campaigns*) *2 September 1898*. Pushing relentlessly along the Nile, the British commander General Kitchener reached Omdurman, opposite Khartoum, held by 45,000 Mahdists under the Khalifa Abdullah et Taaisha. With 26,000 troops, a third of them British, Kitchener attacked and routed the Sudanese who suffered 15,000 casualties to the British 500. The battle completed the reconquest of the Sudan, *See* Atbara.

Onao (*Indian Mutiny against the British*) *28 July 1857*. The British

(Havelock) made a successful frontal assault on a well-protected rebel position killing 300 of the enemy and taking fifteen guns. *See* Cawnpore; Delhi.

Onessant, *French coast (War of the American Revolution) 27 July 1778.* An indecisive battle between thirty British ships (Keppel) and thirty French (d'Estaing). *See* Negapatam.

Ookiep, *South-west Africa (British–Boer War) 4 April–4 May 1902.* A British force of 923 officers and men (Majors Edwards and Dean) held the town and its blockhouses against the Boers until relieved by a land column and reinforcements by sea.

Oondwa Nullah *(British conquest of Bengal) 16 September 1763.* The remarkable victory of 3,000 British and Indian troops (Major Adams) in storming a fort held by Mir Cossim and 60,000 men with 100 guns. The enemy force was so broken it never did re-form. *See* Buxar.

Ooscata, *southern India (First British–Mysore War) 23 August 1768.* The Mahrattas, allies of the British, repulsed an attack by Mysore cavalry, supporting the rebel Hyder Ali.

Opequan Creek *(American Civil War) 19 September 1864.* Part of the third Battle of Winchester. Sheridan's 45,000 Federals were too strong for Early's 13,000 Confederates, though the southerners seemed to be winning until Colonel Custer, leading a charge of 7,000 cavalry, broke their left flank. This routed the Confederates. *See* Franklin; Nashville.

Oporto *(Peninsular War) 12 May 1809.* The British had evacuated Spain under French pressure and their Spanish and Portuguese allies were as yet ineffective. The French (Soult) stormed Oporto, where civilians suffered much more than soldiers. Returning to Portugal in April, Wellesley (Wellington) built up an army

of 30,000 in Lisbon and marched north. Surprising Soult, he took Oporto with slight loss to himself, but the French lost several thousand men in the evacuation and retreat. *See* Corunna; Talavera.

Oran I *(Spanish War against the Moors, in North Africa) 17 May 1509.* Having crushed the Muslims in Spain, the Spaniards, in a crusading mission, carried their war against the Moors into North Africa. Led by Pedro Navarro the Spanish army (organized by Cardinal de Cisneros) captured heights overlooking Oran, climbed the city's walls by using their pikes and then attacked with sword and buckler. The Moors lost 4,000 killed and 8,000 prisoners. *See* Garigliano River; Ravenna IV.

Oran II *(World War II) 3 July 1940.* After the fall of France the great French fleet became a potential threat to Britain, now standing alone against Nazi Germany. A large part of the French fleet, under Admiral Gensoul, lay at Mars-el-Kebir, Oran. It consisted of two battleships, two battle cruisers, and many light cruisers, destroyers, submarines and supply ships. Admiral Somerville, commanding British Task Force H — seventeen ships — moved to Oran and asked Gensoul either to join the Royal Navy, sail to North America or scuttle his ships. Gensoul refused any sort of co-operation. Somerville then destroyed the French fleet in a 10-minute bombardment; only one large French ship escaped destruction. More than 1,000 French sailors died. On 27 November 1942, when the Nazis took over Vichy France, the French scuttled the remainder of their fleet at Toulon. *See* Dakar.

Orchard Knob–Indian Hill *(American Civil War) 23 November 1863.* The opening action of the battle of Chattanooga, q.v. Grant's Federals captured the heights leading to Missionary Ridge.

Orchomenous, *southern Greece (First Mithridatic War) 85 BC.* Archelaus, commander of the Pontic army, had received reinforcements from Mithridates and from his Greek allies (after Chaeronea, q.v.) and again outnumbered Cornelius Sulla's Roman army. The confident Sulla, with careful planning, used field fortifications to assist him in advancing against his less enterprising foes. When Asiatic cavalry drove back part of his line, Sulla personally rallied his troops and routed the Pontic army with great loss. *See* Cyzicus; Tigranocerta.

Ordovici, *North Wales (Roman conquest of Britain)* 50. The Britons (Caractacus) occupied the slope of a hill where they were attacked by the Romans (Scapula) and routed. Caractacus fled to the Brigantes, northern England, who surrendered him to the Romans.

Oriskany (*American Revolution*) 6 *August 1777*. The British defeated an American column trying to relieve Fort Stanwix, q.v.

Orleans (*Hundred Years' War*) 23 *October 1428–7 May 1429*. Orleans guarded the chief passage of the Loire River and was the largest stronghold loyal to the dauphin Charles (Charles VII). The English (Earl of Salisbury) laid siege to the place and though Salisbury was killed the investment proceeded under Duke of Suffolk. Joan of Arc was given command of a relief column and persuaded the Comte de Dunois and others to attack the English bridgehead, and their fortifications on the island of Tourelles. In a fierce fight on 7 May the French drove out the English, killing 300 and capturing 200. The English abandoned the siege. The battle was the turning point of the Hundred Years' War, the tide swinging in France's favour. *See* Jargeau; Rouvray; Verneuil.

Orne River (*World War II*) 6 *June 1944*. A preliminary of the D-Day landing. The British 6th Airborne Division captured German-held bridges to protect the left flank of the invasion. *See* D-Day.

Orthez (*Peninsular War*) 27 *February 1814*. In an amphibious operation, Wellington first besieged Bayonne and then drove the French (Soult) out of Orthez and across the Luy de Bearn. French casualties: 4,000 killed or wounded; Wellington lost 2,000 men. *See* Toulouse.

Oruro (*Bolivian Insurrection*) 2 *August 1862*. A victory for the Bolivian Government troops under the President, General Acha, over the rebels led by General Perez, who had proclaimed himself president.

Ostende (*Netherlands War of Independence*) 5 *July 1601–20 September 1604*. Failing to take Ostende by storm, the Spaniards, under Albert, Archduke of Austria, besieged the place. Despite privations and though completely unsupported — England and France had made peace with Spain — the garrison held out for 3 years and 71 days until a new enemy commander, Spinola, captured the fort. The Spaniards lost 70,000 men during the siege. *See* Breda; Nieuport.

Ostia, *near Rome (French–Spanish Wars)* April 1500. A French garrison (Guerri) held Ostia when besieged by the Spaniards (de Cordova). The defenders endured 5 days' bombardment, but surrendered when caught between Cordova's Spaniards and another force of Spaniards resident in Rome and organized by de la Vega. *See* Cerignola.

Ostroleka I (*Polish Revolt against Russia*) 26 *May 1831*. The Polish army, successful at Grochow (20 February), met a large Russian army on the Narew River, 60 miles north-east of Warsaw. It was commanded by a clever German-born general, von Diebitsch (Count Ivan Ivanovich). His tactics were too much for the Polish General Jan Zigmunt Skrzneki, who was forced to retreat despite the excellent work of his guns under General Bem. The army fell back on Warsaw, q.v.

Ostroleka II (*Crimean War*) 4 December 1853. A victory for the Turks, much superior in numbers and led by Omar Pasha, over the Russians who had invaded the Danubian principalities. *See* Oltenitza; Sinope.

Ostrowno (*Napoleonic Wars: Moscow campaign*) 25–26 July 1812. The Russians (Count Osterman and General Konownitzyn) took the initiative on successive days, but the French corps of Ney and Prince Eugene, with Murat's cavalry, drove them back. Each side lost about 3,000 killed or wounded, the Russians also 800 prisoners. *See* Smolensk.

Oswego (*Seven Years' War, known in America as French and Indian War*) 11–14 August 1756. Montcalm, newly commanding the French in Canada, sent an expedition across the eastern end of Lake Ontario to Oswego, the only British hold on the Great Lakes. After a 3-day siege, in which the commandant was killed, the colonial garrison surrendered. Two years later the British recovered the place. *See* Fort William; Henry; Lake George.

Otrar (*Mongol invasion of Khwarezmian*) 1220. A garrison of 60,000 (Gazer Khan) held out for 5 months against 200,000 Mongols led by Oktai and Zagatai, sons of Genghis Khan. The survivors of about 15,000 were massacred. *See* Bamian.

Otterburn (*English–Scottish Wars*) 15 August 1388. The Scots under James Douglas (2nd Earl of Douglas), aided by some French, invaded northern England. Sir Henry Percy (Hotspur) raised an army of 9,000 Northumberland soldiers, greatly outnumbering the Scots, and made a night assault on the Scottish camp. Douglas was killed but the Scots spearmen could not be broken and inflicted 2,000 casualties on the English. Percy was captured. For 14 years Scottish raiders harassed the borderlands. The ballads *Otterburn* and *Chevy Chase* commemorate the battle. *See* Homildon Hill; Neville's Cross.

Otumba (*Spanish conquest of Mexico*) 8 July 1520. Driven out of Tenochtitlán, the Spanish commander Cortez with only 200 Spaniards aided by 5,000 Indians was intercepted by 20,000 Aztecs. The battle was prolonged and savage, then Cortez led a charge into the middle of the Aztec army. This so demoralized the enemy that they fled, losing a reported 20,000 men. Cortez withdrew to Tlaxcala. *See* Cajamarca; Tenochtitlán.

Oudenarde (*War of Spanish Succession*) 11 July 1708. About 100,000 French (Duke of Burgundy and Marshal Vendome) were besieging Oudenarde when Marlborough and Prince Eugene approached with 78,000 English, Dutch and German troops. Raising the siege, the French gave battle, but could not deploy properly before Eugene on the right and Marshal Overkirk on the left virtually surrounded half the French army. By sundown Marlborough's generalship had decided the battle. Casualties: French, 6,000 killed or wounded, 7,000 prisoners; Allied, 3,000 in all. The victory gave the Allies the initiative. *See* Lille; Malplaquet; Ramillies.

Ourcq River (*World War I*) 6 September 1914. The initial French counter-attack, north-east of Paris, in the first Battle of the Marne, q.v. *See* Frontiers of France.

Ourique (*Rise of Portugal*) September 1139. The crusader knight Henry of Burgundy had been made Count of Portugal (by the Spaniards) in honour of his campaigns against the Moors. His son and successor, Alfonso Henriques, first announced his independence of the kingdom of Castile and Leon and declared war in his own right on the Moors. He attacked their fortress at Ourique in the south-west of Iberia, won decisively and proclaimed himself Alfonso I, king of independent Portugal. *See* Lisbon.

Overlord Operation. *See* D-Day.

Owen Stanley Mountains (*World War II*). *See* Kokoda Trail; Milne Bay; New Guinea.

Paardeberg (*Second British–Boer War*) *18–27 February 1900*. Between 5,000 Boers (Cronje) and four British brigades, with artillery, under Kitchener. Cronje had positions in the bed of the Tugela River. Without cover, the attacking force suffered 1,100 casualties. The Boers were surrounded and on the arrival of Lord Roberts they were pounded by artillery until surrender on 27 February. British losses, 98 officers and 1,437 men; Boer, 1,000 casualties, 4,000 prisoners. *See* Bloemfontein; Kimberley; Ladysmith.

Pabon (*Argentina Civil War*) *17 September 1861*. Between the troops of Buenos Aires (Mitre), aided by an Italian legion (Piloni), and the army of the Argentine Confederation (Urquiza), which was defeated.

Pacific War *1941–5*. *See* map.

Pagahar (*First British–Burmese War*) *18 February 1825*. Sir Archibald Campbell, with 1,300 men, encountered 15,000 Burmese under Zay-ya-Thayan, but the battle was almost bloodless; the Burmese fled, led by their general. *See* Kamarut; Kemendine.

Pagasaean Gulf, *Thessaly* (*Third Sacred War**) *352 BC*. Between the Phocians (Onomarchus) and the Macedonians (Philip). Philip's infantry was about equal in number to that of the Phocians, but his cavalry was superior and in the end the Phocians were defeated, losing a third of their strength. Onomarchus was slain.

Palais Gallien (*War of the Fronde*) *5 September 1649*. Between 8,000 Royal troops (Marshal de la Meilleraic) and 7,000 Bordelais (Dukes of Bouillon and la Rochefoucauld). The Bordelais repulsed five assaults, but by nightfall were driven from their entrenchments into the city, with a loss of about 120. Royalist casualties, 1,000 killed or wounded. *See* Arras I; Lens.

Palermo (*Italian Wars of Independence: Garibaldi's Second Rebellion*) *27 May 1860*. Garibaldi, with 750 of his "Thousand Volunteers", and about 3,000 Sicilian "Picciotti", surprised one of Palermo's gates, which was garrisoned by 18,000 Neapolitans (Lanza). The "Picciotti" fled at the first shot, but Garibaldi fought his way into the city. Joined by citizens, he erected barricades and after severe fighting, in which the Neapolitans suffered heavily, Lanza surrendered. *See* Aspromonte; Novara.

Palestrina (*Italian Wars of Independence: Garibaldi's First Rebellion*) *9 May 1849*. 4,000 Italian Patriots (Gari-

---

*Sacred Wars: The name given to wars declared by the Delphic Amphictiony against one or more of its members on the ground of sacrilege against Apollo.

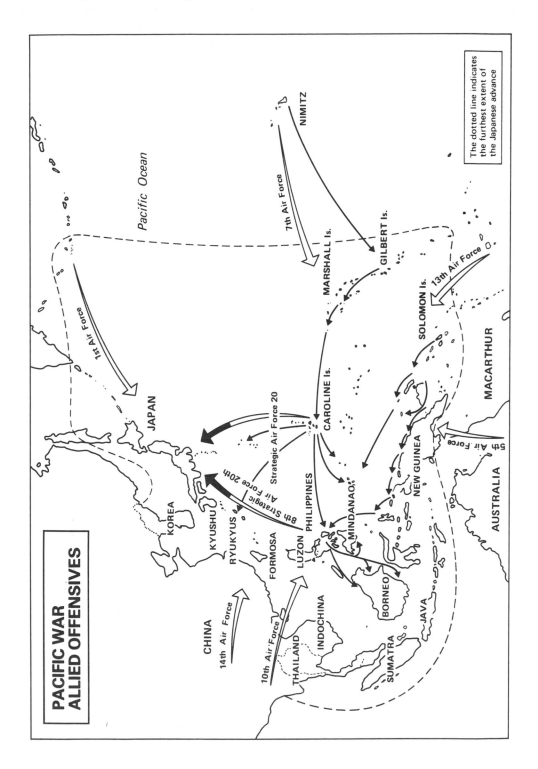

PACIFIC WAR
ALLIED OFFENSIVES

The dotted line indicates the furthest extent of the Japanese advance

Pacific Ocean

NIMITZ

7th Air Force

MARSHALL Is.

GILBERT Is.

13th Air Force

SOLOMON Is.

MACARTHUR

1st Air Force

JAPAN

CAROLINE Is.

NEW GUINEA

5th Air Force

AUSTRALIA

Strategic Air Force 20

Air Force 20th

8th Strategic

PHILIPPINES

MINDANAO

KOREA

KYUSHU

RYUKYUS

FORMOSA

LUZON

BORNEO

JAVA

CHINA

14th Air Force

10th Air Force

THAILAND

INDOCHINA

SUMATRA

baldi) faced 7,000 Neapolitans (King Ferdinand). After 3 hours' fighting, the Neapolitans were routed. Garibaldi was wounded. *See* Rome III.

Palestro (*War of Austria with France and Piedmont*) 30 May 1859. Austria had invaded Piedmont on 29 April and on 30 May the Austrian army under General Stadion attacked the Piedmontese army (Piedmont was part of the Kingdom of Sardinia) while they were crossing the Sesia River. General Cialdini not only forced the passage of the river, but drove the Austrians out of Palestro with heavy loss. The allied forces, under Napoleon III, then invaded Lombardy. *See* Magenta.

Palmyra (*Wars of the Roman Empire*) 272-3. The city was besieged by the Romans (Emperor Aurelian) after the defeat of Queen Zenobia at Emesa in 272. The Queen stubbornly defended the city, but Aurelian was reinforced by Probus early in 273 and Zenobia fled. Palmyra fell. Zenobia was captured and brought to Aurelian's camp. During his return march Aurelian heard that the citizens had risen and massacred his Roman Governor and garrison. He destroyed the city and massacred the inhabitants. *See* Emesa; Margus.

Palo Alto (*American–Mexican War*) 8 May 1846. The Americans (Zachary Taylor) routed the Mexican army of General Arista, inflicting 400 casualties. Taylor then marched on to relieve Fort Texas. *See* Fort Texas; Resaca de la Palma.

Panama I (*Raids of the Buccaneers*) 18 January 1671. On 16 December 1670 Henry Morgan the buccaneer sailed from Hispaniola with thirty-seven ships and about 2,000 men to plunder Panama. Having captured the castle of San Lorenzo at the mouth of the Chagre — an exploit which cost him 170 casualties — Morgan crossed the Isthmus with 1,200 men, 18 January. The garrison of

Panama, 2,400 strong, met him outside the city and were defeated with heavy loss. The buccaneers lost 600 men. Morgan sacked the place and on 24 February withdrew with 175 mule loads of plunder and 600 prisoners.

Panama II (*Raids of the Buccaneers*) 23 April 1680. Between the buccaneers with three ships, under John Coxon, and three Spanish vessels. The Spaniards were defeated after a hard fight in which two Spanish vessels were captured by boarding. The Spanish commander was killed. The buccaneers then captured six merchant vessels.

Pandosia (*Campaigns of Alexander of Epirus*) 331 BC. Between the Italian Greeks (Alexander of Epirus) and the Lucanians. During the battle Alexander (who was the uncle of Alexander of Macedon) was stabbed by a Lucanian exile serving in the Greek army and the Greeks were in the end defeated. *See* Hydaspes; Issus.

Pandu Naddi (*Indian Mutiny*) 15 July 1857. A British relieving force (Havelock) encountered mutineers barring the way to Cawnpore. By a forced march in great heat Havelock seized the bridge over the Pandu Naddi, which the mutineers were mining. The rebels were driven off. A second battle took place on 26 November. *See* Cawnpore.

Panion (*Wars of the Hellenistic Monarchies*) 200 BC. Between the Syrian army of Antiochus III the Great, ruler of the Seleucid Empire, and the Egyptian army under Scopas. Antiochus' complete victory gave him all the Asian territory held by Egypt. Antiochus' daughter, Cleopatra I, was later betrothed to Ptolemy V of Egypt. *See* Raphia; Thermopylae.

Panipat I (*Tamerlane's Conquests*) 17 December 1399. Tamerlane's Mongol armies had invaded India by various routes. Tamerlane himself crossed the Hindu Kush and joined his main force east of the Indus. Plundering and killing indiscriminately, Tamerlane found his way barred at Panipat by an army led by Mahmud Tughluk. His fast-moving veteran Mongols swept over the Indians. Tamerlane massacred 100,000 captured Indian troops and then, with further great slaughter, he destroyed Delhi. *See* Kandurcha; Meerut; Terek.

Panipat II (*Third Mogul invasion of India*) *20 April 1526*. The Delhi Muhammadans, 10,000-strong with 100 elephants, under Ibrahim, confronted the Moguls (Mongols) — 2,000 picked men under Baber, the first of the Great Moguls. Ibrahim was killed and his army defeated. The battle marked the end of the Afghan dynasty of Delhi, and the commencement of the Mogul Empire. *See* Panipat III.

Panipat III (*Mogul–Afghan Wars*) *5 November 1556*. Akbar, the Great Mogul, had 20,000 troops against the 100,000 of the Hindu Rajahs, under Hemu. The Hindus attacked, but their elephants were sent back against them and they were routed. Hemu was wounded and captured. By this victory Akbar recovered Delhi from the rebels. *See* Panipat II; Talikota.

Panipat IV (*Afghan–Maratha Wars*) *14 January 1761*. Ahmad Shah Durrani, angered by incursions of the Maratha tribe into the Indian territory he regarded as his own, went to war when the Marathas took Delhi. From his capital, Kandahar, Ahmad marched east with 70,000 men and met a Maratha–Sikh army of comparable size at Panipat, north of Delhi. The battle was vicious and possibly 50,000 men died. Maratha military power disappeared.

Panormus, *later Palermo (First Punic War*) *254 BC*. Between 25,000 Romans (Metellus) and the Carthaginian army in Sicily (Hasdrubal). Hasdrubal offered battle in front of Panormus and

Metellus sent out his light troops. They ran back into town before a charge of the elephants, which were driven into the ditch where many were killed. Metellus sallied out with his legionaries, took Hasdrubal in flank and routed his troops. All Carthaginian elephants in Sicily were killed or captured in this battle. *See* Lilybaeum; Tunis I.

Paoli (*American Revolution*) *21 September 1777*. West of the Schuykill River, Washington had posted 1,500 men and four guns (Anthony Wayne) to threaten the British flank and rear in its movements around Philadelphia. By night four British regiments (Lord Grey) approached Wayne's division and before daylight made a bayonet charge. The Americans lost 300 killed or wounded and were routed. The British had only eight casualties. The British commander, Howe, was now able to outmanoeuvre Washington. *See* Brandywine Creek; Germantown.

Papua: *See* New Guinea.

Paraetaken Mountains, *Iran (Wars of Alexander's Successors*) *316 BC*. Between 30,000 Macedonians (Antigonus) and an equal force of Asiatics (Eumenes). Eumenes attacked the Macedonian camp, but after a severe engagement, in which the Asiatics held the advantage, Antigonus manoeuvred skilfully to withdraw his army without serious loss. Eumenes was killed the following year by his own men, bribed by Antigonus. *See* Cynoscephalae.

Parana (*War of the Triple Alliance or Lopez War*) *2 May 1866*. Francisco Lopez, having become dictator of Paraguay, warred against the alliance of Brazil, Uruguay and Argentina. Lopez attacked the allied army as it crossed the Parana River but was thrown back. *See* Aquidaban; Humaita.

Paris I (*Napoleonic Wars: Defence of Paris*) *30 March 1814*. Paris, defended only by 20,000 regulars and National Guard (Marmont), was attacked by the Grand Army of the Allies, under Schwartenberg. Three columns assaulted the French positions at Vincennes, Belleville and Montmartre, while a fourth attacked the extreme left of the French line to turn the heights of Montmartre. The first two positions were carried and Montmartre turned. Napoleon's brother, Joseph, had fled; Marmont and Mortier could only surrender. The Allies, though victorious, lost 8,000 men to the French 4,000. *See* Arcis-sur-Aube; Ligny; Toulouse II; Tolentino.

Paris II (*French–Prussian War*) *19 September 1870–28 January 1871*. Paris was invested by the main Prussian army, under Wilhelm I, his sons, and von Moltke, 19 September 1870. The garrison, led by General Trochu, made a good defence with many serious sorties, but no major counter-attack. The Germans gradually mastered the outer defences, and finally the starving city surrendered. Most military analysts believe that Trochu, who had 146,000 troops — rather more than the strength of the Prussians — could have prevented the enemy encirclement; also, that he could have broken the siege.

Paris III (*Revolt of the Paris Commune*) *1 March–28 May 1871*. The National Assembly of the Third Republic had accepted humiliating peace terms after the war with Prussia. The city of Paris, including most members of the National Guard — formed of Parisian working men — rebelled against the Assembly and wanted to continue the war. Troops refused to disarm the rebels; the government fled and the National Guard's Central Committee ruled Paris until it was replaced by a popularly elected Commune. Meanwhile, the French Army was being reorganized from prisoners released by the Germans. On 21 May the army of 130,000, under Comte de MacMahon, assaulted the barricades held by 30,000 National Guardsmen and

citizens. During "Bloody Week" Mac-Mahon lost 83 officers and 790 men, but he took Paris. About 28,000 Communards died — most of them summarily executed. Another 18,000 were captured and some of these were executed after trial. Paris suffered more damage in this battle than in any war. *See* Coulmiers; Metz; Paris III; Sedan.

Paris IV (*World War II*) *23–25 August 1944*. The liberation of Paris from the Germans by Free French inside the city and the French 2nd Armoured Division approaching from the west. Casualties: German, 3,200 killed or wounded, 20,000 prisoners; French, 42 killed, 77 wounded, 841 civilian casualties.

Parkany (*Turkish–Hungarian War*) *8 August–24 September 1663*. Between 200,000 Turks under the Grand Vizier, Achmet Koprili Pasha, and a much smaller Hungarian army under Count Forgacz. The Hungarians were defeated and driven into Neuhäusel. After a brave resistance of 6 weeks the town capitulated. *See* Vienna II.

Parma (*War of the Polish Crown*) *29 June 1734*. Between the French (Marshal de Coigny) and 60,000 Imperialists (de Mercy). The Imperialists were defeated with a loss of 6,000 including de Mercy. The French lost 5,100 troops. *See* Danzig I; Philippsburg.

Paso de Patria (*War of the Triple Alliance or Lopez War*) *24 May 1866*. Enveloped on both flanks by a superior force (45,000 Brazilian, Argentinian and Uruguayan troops) Lopez's army was broken in an all-day battle and suffered 13,000 casualties. The allies did not exploit their success and Lopez regrouped. *See* Humaita; Parana.

Passchendaele (*World War I*) *9 October, 12–14 October and 6 November 1917*. This village in Flanders was a key point in the larger battle for Ypres. Australian and New

Zealand troops were principally involved in the first two attacks, together with Canadians in the third. The Allies suffered 25 per cent casualties; many men were lost in seas of mud. Passchendaele was not taken until the third attack. *See* Flanders; Ypres III.

Passero, Cape (*War of the Quadruple Alliance*) *11 August 1718*. The only battle of the war, which had come about as Britain, France, Holland and Austria tried to preserve the peace settlements after the war of the Spanish Succession, now violated by Philip V of Spain. Admiral Sir George Byng (later Lord Torrington), with a fleet of twenty-one ships, attacked the Spanish fleet of twenty-two ships (Don Castaneta) off Cape Passero, Sicily. In a running fight northward the English destroyed or captured fifteen ships. *See* Denain; Porto Bello.

Patay (*Hundred Years' War*) *18 June 1429*. The French, under Joan of Arc and the Duc d'Alencon, gave battle to the English, under Talbot, Earl of Shrewsbury and Sir John Fastolf. The English were retiring after the siege of Orleans. Their advance guard panicked when attacked by the French cavalry, broke and fled. The main body with Fastolf maintained its formation and retreated to Etampes. Talbot, who was captured, had lost a third of his 5,000 men. *See* Jargeau; Rouen III.

Patila (*Tartar invasion of Persia*) *1394*. Between the Tartars (Tamerlane) and the Persians (Shah Mansur). The Persians violently attacked the Tartar centre and Tamerlane was nearly overwhelmed, but rallying his troops he led a charge which restored the battle and won him victory. Subjugation of Persia followed. *See* Delhi II.

Pavia I (*Ticinum*) (*Rome's War with the Allemanni*) *271*. The Romans, under Emperor Aurelian, practically annihilated the German invaders in northern Italy and they withdrew across the Alps.

Pavia II (*Wars of the Western Roman Empire*) *27–28 August 476*. A victory for Odovacar of the Heruli tribe over Orestes, who had put his son, Romulus Augustulus, on the throne. Orestes was killed and Odovacar deposed Romulus, thus ending the Western Roman Empire. Roman territory was then ruled as a province of Leo II, emperor of the East at Constantinople. *See* Ravenna I; Rome II.

Pavia III (*Lombard conquest of Italy*) *569–72*. The city was besieged by the Lombards of Langobardi (Albion) and after a gallant defence of 3 years was subdued, rather by famine than by force of arms, and surrendered. Pavia then became the capital of the Lombard Kingdom of Italy. *See* Casilinum; Ravenna III.

Pavia IV (*Conquests of Charlemagne*) *773–4*. Charlemagne had outflanked the army of King Desiderius of Lombard in Mont Cenis pass and then besieged the king in the fortress city of Pavia. Losing strength through casualties and starvation, Desiderius surrendered. Charlemagne proclaimed himself "King of the Lombards". *See* Ravenna III; Roncesvalles.

Pavia V (*Venetian–Milanese War*) *22 May 1431*. Fought on the Ticino River near Pavia, between eighty-five Venetian galleys (Nicolas Trevisani) and a superior number of mercenary galleys in the pay of the Milanese. The Venetians were defeated, losing seventy galleys and 3,000 men. *See* Chioggia; Pola.

Pavia VI (*French Wars in Italy*) *25 February 1525*. Francis I of France had fought several battles in pursuit of his claim to Navarre and Naples. His ambitions were opposed by Charles V, the new German emperor, who was also king of Spain. The imperial army of 20,000 was led by the Marquis de Pescara, who got his men into good positions during a stormy winter's night. By dawn the imperials were in line of battle 1 mile north of the main French camp — and on their flank. Francis had been surprised, but he led a cavalry charge to give his infantry time to face north; they failed to do so, and about a third of the French army was never engaged. Francis was badly wounded and captured; his army had 8,000 casualties, mainly from Spanish arquebusiers. The imperialists lost fewer than 1,000 men. *See* La Bicocca; Rome VI.

Peach Tree Creek (*American Civil War*) *22 July 1864*. Fought in the course of the operations around Atlanta, q.v., between the Federals (Sherman) and the Confederates (Hood). Hood attacked the Federal position, and drove off their left wing, capturing thirteen guns and some prisoners. Reinforced, the Federals rallied, and recovered the lost ground. The Confederates, however, claimed the victory. Each side lost about 3,700 men.

Pea Ridge (*or Elk Horn*) (*American Civil War*) *7–8 March 1862*. Between 16,000 Confederates (von Dorn) and the Federals, equally strong (Curtis). The Confederates drove back the Federal right wing but exhausted themselves and lost General McCulloch. Next day the Federals counter-attacked and recovered lost ground. The battle ended without decisive result. Casualties: Confederates, 800; Federals, 1,384. *See* Wilson's Creek.

Pearl Harbour (*World War II*) *7 December 1941*. Admiral Chiuchi Sagumo led a fleet of six aircraft carriers with supporting battleships and cruisers from the Kurile Islands towards Hawaii. Approaching undetected, he launched 360 bombers and fighters on the great American naval base of Pearl Harbour on Oahu Island. They blew up the *Arizona*, capsized the *Oklahoma* and sank the *West Virginia* and *California* at their moorings. The other four battleships were damaged and another eleven ships were sunk or disabled; 247 aircraft were wrecked. Casualties, 2,330 killed, 1,145 wounded. The field commanders, Admiral Kimmel and General Short, were relieved from duty. The attack brought the United States into World War II, 2 years after it had begun. *See* Guam; Philippine Islands; Wake.

Peipus Lake (*Rise of Russia*) *1242*. The Russian city of Novgorod was threatened by the Livonian "Brothers of the Sword", a branch of the Teutonic Knights of Germany. Prince Alexander Nevski met the invaders in battle on the frozen surface of Lake Peipus, defeated them and became the most powerful Russian prince. One of Russia's greatest heroes, Nevski was father of Daniel, founder of Moscow in 1295. *See* Kiev I; Neva River.

Peiwar Kotal (*Second British–Afghan War*) *2 December 1878*. A British force of 3,200-strong under Sir Frederick Roberts, with thirteen guns, was blocked by about 18,000 Afghans, with eleven guns, strongly posted in the Peiwar pass. By an able but difficult turning movement, Roberts crossed the pass and defeated the Afghans with heavy loss; all their guns were captured. British casualties, twenty killed and seventy-eight wounded. *See* Kabul II; Maiwand.

Peking I (*Tartar invasion of China*) *1210–14*. The city was besieged by the Tartars (Genghis Khan). The long and obstinate defence exhausted the besiegers and Genghis Khan is said to have decimated his men into order to feed the rest. Finally, he took the city by bribing some of the defenders. *See* Khojend; Nanking I.

Peking II (*Fall of Ming Dynasty*) *April 1644*. The pirate general Li Tzuch'eng seized the capital. The emperor committed suicide, but General Wu held out, called in the army of the Manchus from Mukden and drove out the pirates. The Manchus set up Shun Chih as the first of the Ch'ing dynasty, rulers of China until 1912. *See* Nanking I.

Peking III (*Boxer Rebellion*) 20 June–14 August 1900. Outbreaks of violence caused an international expedition (Admiral Sir E. H. Seymour) to go to Tientsin. In Peking the so-called Boxers — members of the Society of Harmonious Fists — killed the German minister and laid siege to the foreign legations, 20 June. A six-nation expeditionary force landed at Tientsin, 14 July, fought its way into Peking and relieved the legations, 14 August. *See* Talu.

Pelekanon (*Turkish conquest of Asia Minor*) 1329. Between the Turks (Orkhan) and the forces of Andronicus the Younger, Byzantine Emperor of the East, who was defeated. This was the first Turkish–Byzantine battle. *See* Kossova I.

Peleliu–Anguar (*World War II*) 15 September–25 November 1944. The Japanese held the Palau Islands, western Carolinas, with 10,000 men on Peleliu (Inoue) and 1,400 on Angaur. Despite a heavy naval and air bombardment the Japanese, ably led, fought savagely against the American assault troops (Geiger, Mueller, Julian Smith, Rupertus). Angaur fell in 3 days — 17–19 September. On Peleliu, Bloody Nose Ridge (Umurbrogol Mountain) was reduced yard by yard, notably by 321st and 323rd Infantry Divisions. The Palau conquest cost the highest casualty rate of any amphibious attack in American history. 1st Marine Division lost 6,526 men, including 1,252 killed; 81st Infantry Division 1,393 casualties, including 208 killed. Japanese casualties, including reinforcements from other islands, were 13,600 killed and 400 captured. With the capture of Peleliu–Anguar and Morotai the Allied right flank in the south-west Pacific was secure. *See* Leyte; Mariana Islands; New Guinea.

Pella, *Northern Palestine (Muslim conquest of Syria*) 23 January 635. A victory for the Arabian horsemen of Khalid ibn-al-Walis over the retreating Byzantine army, earlier defeated at Ajnadain, q.v. *See* Damascus I.

Peloponnesian Wars. *See* List of Battles.

Pelusium I, *near Port Said (Persian conquest of Egypt*) 525 BC. The Persians (Cambyses II) crossed the Syrian desert to overthrow the Egyptian army of Psamtik III. Cambyses forced Psamtik's surrender at Memphis soon after and most of Egypt became a Syrian province.

Pelusium II (*War of Alexander's Successors*) 321 BC. Between the Macedonians, under the Regent, Perdiccas, and the Egyptians (Ptolemy Lagus). Perdiccas attacked the fortress, but was driven off with heavy loss, including 1,000 drowned in the Nile. *See* Hydaspes.

Peninsular War. *See* List of Battles.

Penna Cerrada (*First Carlist War*) 21 June 1838. This fortress, held by a Carlist garrison under Gergue, was captured by Espartero with 19,000 Cristinos. After shelling the fort for 7 hours, Espartero attacked the Carlists on the heights outside the town, capturing 600 prisoners and all their guns. The remainder of the garrison then abandoned the fortress. *See* Huesca.

Penobscot Bay (*American Revolution*) 14 July 1779. A British squadron of ten ships under Sir George Collier completely destroyed an American squadron of twenty-four ships and captured the 3,300 men who formed their crews.

Pen (Selwood) *Somersetshire (Danish invasion of England*) 1016. The Saxons, under Edmund Ironside, defeated the Danes (Canute) shortly after Edmund's election as King by the

Witanegemot. This was the first of a series of engagements between the two rivals, which ended with the peace of Olney. *See* Ashingdon; Maldon.

Pentland Hills (*Scottish Covenanters' Revolt*) 28 November 1666. James Wallace led a Covenanter revolt against the Duke of Lauderdale then ruling Scotland as English secretary of state for Scottish affairs. General Dalzell and his Royalists routed the Scots army and quelled the rebellion. *See* Drumclog.

Pered (*Hungarian Rising against Austria*) 21 June 1849. Between 16,000 Hungarians, under Görgey, and the Austrians and Russians led by Prince Windischgrätz. The allies attacked the Hungarian position and after severe fighting drove them out, with a loss of about 3,000. *See* Kapolna.

Perembacum (*First British–Mysore War*) 10 September 1780. A Mysore force of 11,000, under Tippu Sahib, surrounded and cut to pieces a detachment — 3,700 — of Sir Hector Monro's army, under Colonel Baillie. Only a few, including Baillie himself, escaped the massacre. *See* Port Novo.

Pergamum (*Wars of the Hellenistic Monarchies*) 230 BC. A large part of western Asia Minor broke away from the Seleucid dynasty and under Eumenes I set up the kingdom of Pergamum. This brought Eumenes into conflict with another new but better established kingdom, Galatia (capital, Ankara) which demanded tribute. Eumenes paid it, but his successor, Attalus I, refused and destroyed the Galatian army sent against him. *See* Corupedion; Sellasia.

Perisabor (*Roman–Persian War*) May 363. The desert fortress, defended by an Assyrian and Persian garrison, was captured by the Romans under Julian. Having already caused much damage by mining operations, the Romans dismantled the fort and burnt the town.

Perpignan (*French–Spanish Wars*) October 1474–14 March 1475. Perpignan fortress, besieged by 11,000 French under the Seigneur du Lude, was defended by a Spanish garrison. The Spanish army could not relieve the fort, and after holding out with great gallantry the garrison, reduced to 400 men, surrendered. They were allowed to march out with the "honours of war". Capture of Perpignan gave France possession of Rousillon.

Perryville (*American Civil War*) 8 October 1862. An unplanned, confused and bloody battle between 45,000 Federals (Buell) and a smaller Confederate army (Bragg). The Confederates attacked and drove back the Federals, but no decisive result was reached, and during the night Bragg withdrew with a captured artillery train. Casualties: Federals, 4,000; including 845 killed and 515 missing. Confederates, 2,500 killed and wounded. *See* Richmond (Kentucky); Stones River.

Persepolis (*Wars of Alexander's Successors*) 316 BC. Between 31,000 Macedonians with 65 elephants (Antigonus) and 42,000 Asiatics with 114 elephants (Eumenes). A massive elephant–infantry attack overwhelmed Antigonus' infantry, but as they re-formed his cavalry seized the enemy camp and threw Eumenes' phalanx into confusion. The Macedonian infantry now rallied and their disciplined push drove the Asiatics back. Eumenes was captured. *See* Corupedion; Hydaspes.

Persian–Greek Wars. *See* List of Battles.

Perusia (*Wars of Second Triumvirate*) 41–40 BC. Fulvia, wife of Mark Antony, and his brother Lucius led a revolt against Octavian, Mark Antony's colleague. Antony himself was in Egypt

— with Cleopatra. Octavian forces (Agrippa) trapped the rebel force in Perusia and forced surrender. Fulvia died and Mark Antony returned to Italy to marry Octavian's sister. (The third triumvir was Marcus Lepidus.) *See* Naulochus; Philippi; Phraaspa.

Peshawar (*Second Muhammadan invasion of India*) *1001*. Between 10,000 Afghans (Sultan Mahmud of Ghuzni) and 42,000 Punjabis with 300 elephants (Anang-pal, son of the Rajah of Lahore). Anang-pal was defeated and captured, with fifteen of the principal Lahore chiefs. Mahmud made seventeen devastating raids into India. *See* Somnath.

Petersburg I (*American Civil War*) *15–18 June 1864*. An episode in the Federal attack on Richmond. General Beauregard, with only 3,500 men, was responsible for the defence of Petersburg and at the same time had to contain General Butler at Bermuda Hundred. His entrenchments before Peterburg were attacked on 15 June by General Smith, and part of the first line carried. Next day Beauregard withdrew the force masking Bermuda Hundred, and concentrated his troops in front of Petersburg. After holding out till the afternoon, the defenders' morale cracked and they were driven from the first line. Beauregard rallied them, and retook the entrenchments. During the night he withdrew to a second and stronger line of defences and was strongly reinforced by 14,000 men. By 18 June the Federal commander-in-chief, Grant, had 95,000 troops available. Lee was bringing up his Southerners as fast as he could; he started the day with 20,000 and finished with 38,000. Grant's major assault, too late in getting under way, was beaten back. In 3 days he had lost 1,688 killed, 8,513 wounded and 1,185 captured. Confederate casualties are unknown but were certainly less.

Petersburg II (*American Civil War*) *30 June 1864–3 April 1865*. After the abortive Federal attack on Petersburg

siege battle commenced. The Federals blew a mine under the Confederate lines, 30 July, killed or wounded 278 Confederates and left a crater 170 feet long, 80 feet wide and 30 feet deep. About 20,000 Federals attacked to exploit the gap in the enemy line, but Beauregard rapidly covered it and his men slaughtered many Federals trapped in the crater. Federal losses were 3,798, Confederates, 1,500.

Many other Federal attacks were repulsed. On 25 March Lee took the offensive, sending in John Gordon's division against Fort Stedman. The Federals (Parke) lost 2,000 men, but inflicted 4,400 casualties on the Southerners and stopped the attack. Grant had by now amassed 125,000 troops and his line was so long that Lee, with only 57,000 men, could not hope to hold. On 1 April his troops were beaten at Five Forks and next day his lines were pierced. On the night of 2–3 April the Confederates pulled out and withdrew along the Appomattox River. In 10 months the Federals had suffered 42,000 casualties but had broken the southern army, which had lost 28,000 men. *See* Cold Harbor; Five Forks; Monocacy River; Nashville.

Peterwardein (*Austrian–Turkish Wars*) *5 August 1716*. On the Danube in modern Yugoslavia, Prince Eugene of Savoy, with 40,000 Austrians of the Holy Roman Empire, mostly veterans from the Flanders campaign, defeated 150,000 Turks under Darnad Ali Pasha. The Turks lost 30,000 killed, 50 standards and 250 guns. Austrian casualties, 3,000. It was one of the most crushing defeats inflicted on any army during the eighteenth century. *See* Senta.

Petra, Persia (*Rome's Persian Wars*) *549–51*. This powerful fortress, garrisoned by 1,500 Persians, was besieged by 8,000 Romans under Dagisteus. After several assaults the Romans brought down a large part of the outer wall by mining. The garrison had been reduced to 400, but while Dagisteus delayed in storming the fortress, Persian reinforcements brought the garrison up to 3,000. They repaired the walls and the Romans had to undertake a second siege. After severe fighting, the besiegers broke through in 551. 700 Persians fell in the second siege and 1,070 in the attack; only 18 of 700 prisoners were unwounded. 500 retreated to the citadel and perished when it was fired by the Romans.

Pharsalus I (*Civil War of Caesar and Pompey*) 48 BC. Between 60,000 Pompeians under Pompey and 25,000 Caesareans under Caesar. The Pompeian cavalry drove back Caesar's horsemen, but in pursuing were checked by the legionaries. They fled from the field, the infantry followed and the battle became a rout, in which 6,000 Pompeians and only 230 Caesareans fell, according to Caesar himself. Another 20,000 Pompeians surrendered. Pompey escaped to Egypt where he was murdered. *See* Alexandria I; Dyrrachium I.

Pharsalus II (*Greek–Turkish War*) 6 May 1897. Edhem Pasha, with three Turkish divisions, drove the Greeks from their trenches in front of Pharsalus, Thessaly, at a cost to himself of 230 casualties. Throughout the 6-month war Edhem in Thessaly and Epirus, consistently defeated the Greeks.

Philiphaugh (*English Civil War*) 13 September 1645. A Roundhead force of 4,000 veteran Lowland horsemen under David Leslie surprised and cut to pieces Montrose's force of Royalist Highlanders, encamped near Selkirk. Montrose escaped with a few followers. *See* Kilsyth; Langport.

Philippi (*Brutus' Rebellion against the Second Triumvirate*) October 42 BC. Between 100,000 Republicans, under Brutus and Cassius, and the comparable army of the Triumvirs, under Octavius and Mark Antony. Brutus on the right repulsed the legions of Octavius and penetrated into his camp. Cassius, however, was repulsed by Antony and would have been overwhelmed had no aid arrived from the successful right wing. The action was renewed next day, when the Triumvirs were victorious. Brutus committed suicide. (Philippi is 10 miles from the Aegean coast in Macedonia .) *See* Mutina; Perusia.

Philippi, or "the Philippi Races", West Virginia (*American Civil War*) 3 June 1861. The first land battle of the war. A Federal army (McLellan) enveloped and routed 5,000 Confederates of General Garnett, but total casualties were only seventeen. The Confederates left in a hurry, hence "Philippi Races". *See* Fort Sumter; Rich Mountain.

Philippine Islands (*World War II*). *See* Bataan–Corregidor.

Philippine Sea, "The Marianas Turkey Shoot" (*World War II*) 19–20 June 1944. Admiral Toyoda ordered a fleet of nine carriers (Ozawa) and eighteen battleships and cruisers (Ugaki) to attack the U.S. warships protecting the landing on Saipan. Admiral Spruance, commanding the U.S. Fifth Fleet, sent fifteen carriers of Task Force 58 (Mitscher) to intercept the Japanese fleet. The first attack came from Japanese land-based planes from Guam and Truk; thirty-five were shot down. Then 450 American planes battle to 430 Japanese aircraft; only 100 Japanese planes survived. American losses were thirty. This was the most decisive aerial combat in history.

The American submarine *Albacore* sank the *Taiho*, Japan's largest carrier; the submarine *Cavalla* blew up the carrier *Shokaku*. The Japanese fleet fled north-west; on the evening of 20 June 209 American planes destroyed the carrier *Hiyo* and forty aircraft. The Americans lost twenty aircraft in battle and another eighty returning to their carriers after dark, but fifty-one pilots were rescued. The Japanese had lost almost all their trained pilots and about 4,000 seamen. *See* Leyte Gulf; Mariana Islands.

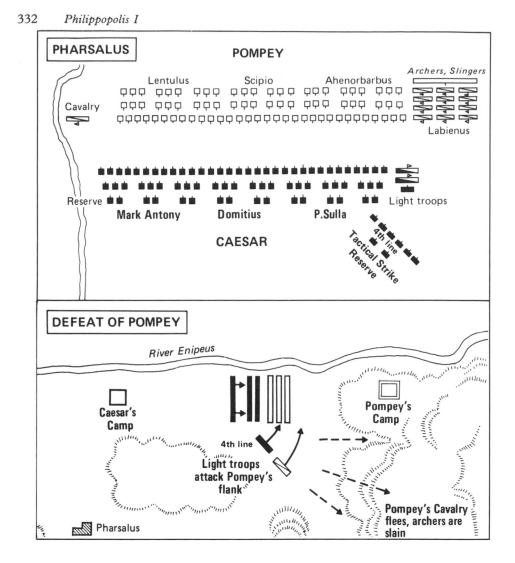

Philippopolis I, *in Thrace, now Bulgaria (First Gothic invasion of the Roman Empire) 25*. The city was besieged by the Goths (Kung Cuiva) and after a gallant defence and the defeat of an attempt by Trajunus Decius to relieve it, it was stormed and sacked. Perhaps 100,000 soldiers and civilians perished in the siege and subsequent massacre. *See* Naissus.

Philippopolis II (*Fourth Crusade*) *April 1208*. The Latin crusaders, under Henry of Flanders, rode up the Maritsa Valley to Philippopolis (later Plovdiv). King Boril's army of Bulgarians could not stand against the knights' charge and Boril, after hiding behind the Balkan Mountains, was forced to make peace with Henry. *See* Adrianople IV; Trnovo.

Philippopolis III (*Russian–Turkish War*) *17 February 1878*. Between the Russians (General Gourko) and the Turks (Fuad and Shakir). The Turks stubbornly defended the approaches to Philippopolis, but were overpowered by superior numbers and forced to retreat. They lost 5,000 killed and wounded, 2,000 prisoners, and 114 guns. Russian casualties, 1,300. *See* Plevna; Schipka Pass.

Philippsburg (*War of the Polish Crown*) *June 1734*. The fortress in Lorraine, held by the Austrian Imperialists, was besieged by the French under the Duke of Berwick. The Duke was killed by a cannon ball while visiting the trenches, but the fort fell on 20 June, despite the efforts of Prince Eugene of Savoy to relieve it. This was the last time that the magnificent Eugene, Marlborough's "military twin", fought in battle. A Frenchman, Eugene had fought all his life for Austria; the Duke of Berwick, an Englishman, had fought all his life for France. *See* Danzig I; Luzzara; Parma.

Philomelion, *central Asia Minor* (*Byzantine–Turkish Wars*) *November 1116*. The great diplomat and general, Alexius I Comnenus of the Byzantines, with a largely mercenary army of cavalry, routed the mounted Seljuk Turk bowmen, who had been ravaging Anatolia. This avenged the great Byzantine defeat at Manzikert, 1071, q.v.

Phraaspa (*Wars of Second Triumvirate*) *36 BC*. Mark Antony, making war on Parthia, attacked the capital, Phraaspa, and was repulsed. The Parthian king, Phraates IV, in the Araxes Valley, had already ambushed and annihilated Antony's siege train, two Roman Legions and his Armenian and Pontine allies. Antony then besieged Phraaspa, a futile action as he had no siege equipment. Winter forced his withdrawal and for 24 days his march was harrassed by Parthian mounted archers. He had lost 30,000 men and then returned to Cleopatra in Alexandria, an action that set Rome against him. (He had married Cleopatra VII, though still wed to Octavia, sister of Octavian.) *See* Actium; Naulochus; Perusia.

Piave River (*World War I*) *15 June–6 July 1918*. The Italians, stubbornly holding a line behind the Piave after their great defeat at Caporetto, built up fifty-seven divisions (General Diaz) against the Austrian's fifty-eight (General von Bojna and Field Marshal von Hotzendorf). The main Austrian attack under von Hotzendorf, 15 June, made gains but was then blocked by the Italians stiffened with British and French divisions. On the lower Piave von Bojna took 3 miles of country and savage and sustained fighting ensued for 8 days. Hotzendorf could not send reinforcements and von Bojna withdrew on 22–23 June. The Italians pressed their advantage until 6 July. Austrian casualties, 150,000 including 24,000 prisoners; Allied, 60,000. The Austrians did not mount another offensive. Some historians consider the Piave one of the world's most decisive battles. It virtually finished Austria's part in the war. *See* Caporetto; Vittorio Veneto.

Pichincha (*Ecuadorian War of Independence*) *24 May 1822*. A victory for the patriot de Sucre, a lieutenant of Simon Bolivar, over a Royalist force. The revolutionaries then occupied Quito and Ecuador accepted Bolivar as president. *See* Carobobo; Junin.

Piedmont (*American Civil War*) *5 June 1864*. In the Shenandoah Valley, Federals under David Hunter moved towards Staunton. At Harrisonburg, Hunter circled to avoid Confederate defences, but General William Jones left his defences and took 5,000 men to intercept Hunter at Piedmont. Hunter struck first in an early morning attack and after some hours the Confederates were overwhelmed; Jones was killed. Casualties: Federals, 600 killed or wounded, 1,000 prisoners; Confederates, 780. *See* Lynchburg; New Market.

Pieter's Hill (*Second British–Boer War*) *19–27 February 1900*. Scene of the most severe fighting during Sir Redvers Buller's final attempt to relieve Ladysmith, q.v. Operations commenced with the capture of Hlangwane on 19 February, This gave the British command of the Tugela, which they crossed on 21 February. Next day a steady advance was made up to the line of Pieter's Hill which was attacked by the Irish Brigade on 3 February. At a cost of nearly 50 percent casualties, they established themselves close to the Boer trenches. On 27 February, when Buller turned the Boer left, a general assault was successful, and the Boers evacuated. British losses, 1,896 killed or wounded.

Pilsen (*Thirty Years' War*) *1 November 1618*. The Protestant army of 20,000 under the German mercenary Count von Mansfeld crossed the Bohemian border to help the Bohemian Protestants and marched on the Catholic stronghold of Pilsen, 52 miles from Prague. After 16 hours of fighting Mansfeld captured the place. *See* Sablat.

Pinkie Cleugh, *Edinburgh* (*English–Scottish Wars*) *10 September 1547*. Between the Scots (Earl of Huntly) and the English under the protector Somerset. The Scots crossed the Esk and attacked the English lines. Successful at first, they were demoralized by a charge of cavalry and fled from the field with heavy loss. The Scots had objected to English policy which demanded that Edward VI of England, aged 10, should marry Mary, Queen of Scots, aged 5. *See* Solway Moss.

Pirot (*Serbian–Bulgarian War*) *26–27 November 1885*. Between 40,000 Serbians (King Milan) and 45,000 Bulgarians (Prince Alexander). After sporadic fighting, the Bulgarians seized the town of Pirot. At dawn on 27 November the Serbians, making a surprise attack, recovered Pirot. It was later retaken by the Bulgarians, though the Serbians continued to hold some positions till nightfall. Franz Joseph of Austria intervened and next morning an armistice was signed. Casualties: Bulgarians, 2,500; Serbians, 2,000. *See* Slivnica.

Pirvan (*Mongol Conquests*) *1221*. Genghis Khan had conquered Bokhara and Samarkand and defeated Muhammad Shah, the Turkish emperor. Jellaluddin, Muhammad's son, gathered an army of 120,000 and struck an advance Mongol force of 30,000 at Pirvan, in the Hindu Kush Mountains near Ghazni. It was a total defeat and Genghis moved swiftly to avenge it. Abandoned by his Afghan allies, Jellaluddin withdrew into the northern Punjab with Genghis in pursuit. *See* Indus.

Placentia, *north Italy* (*Allemanni invasion of the Roman Empire*) *271*. Between the Romans (Emperor Aurelian) and the invading Allemanni. The barbarians attacked the Romans at dusk, after they had made a long and fatiguing march. The Romans were shaken, but Aurelian rallied them. After severe fighting, the Allemanni beat off the Romans — and headed for Rome. Aurelian pursued. *See* Pavia.

Plains of Abraham, *Quebec* (*Seven Years' War or French and Indian War*) *13 September 1759*. General Wolfe, who was aboard ship in the St. Lawrence above Quebec, with 4,000 troops, made a secret night landing and took up strong positions on the Plains of Abraham. Next morning he was attacked by the French (Montcalm) with about equal numbers. Despite desperate fighting, the French could not carry the position and were driven back into Quebec with a loss of about 1,500. British losses, 664. Both Wolfe and Montcalm were mortally wounded. The French immediately evacuated Quebec. The British victory ensured that North America would be an English continent.

Plassey (*Seven Years' War*) *23 June 1757*. Surajah Dowlah, Nawab of Bengal, had sided with France against England. He had an army of 50,000, but his cruelty had sparked rebellion, led by Mir Jafar. Robert Clive, British commander, aligned himself with Mir Jafir, collected an army of 3,000 — one-third British — and marched to Plassey, 80 miles north of

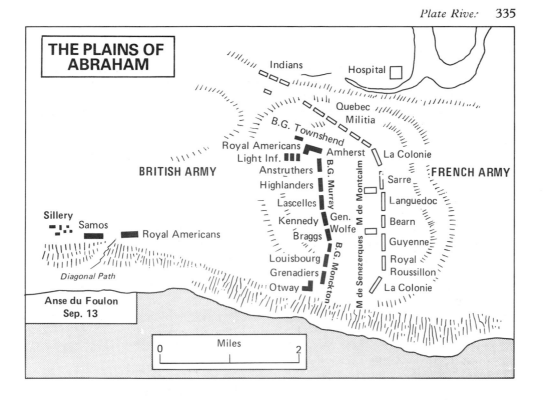

THE PLAINS OF ABRAHAM

Indians
Hospital
Quebec
Militia
B.G. Townshend
Royal Americans
Light Inf.
Amherst
La Colonie
BRITISH ARMY
Anstruthers
B.G. Murray
Sarre
FRENCH ARMY
Highlanders
Languedoc
Lascelles
M de Montcalm
Sillery
Kennedy
Gen.
Bearn
Samos
Wolfe
Royal Americans
Braggs
Guyenne
M de Senezerques
Louisbourg
B.G. Monckton
Royal
Grenadiers
Roussillon
Diagonal Path
Otway
La Colonie
Anse du Foulon
Sep. 13

Miles
0   2

Calcutta, where he established his troops in a mangrove swamp. After a 4-hour cannonade Surajah Dowlah, worried about treachery in his ranks, began to withdraw. Clive at once attacked, inflicted 500 casualties and routed the enemy for a loss of seventy-two of his own troops. This was the real beginning of the British Empire in the East. Surajah Dowlah was murdered and Mir Jafir became ruler of Bengal. *See* Calcutta; Fort Saint David.

Plataea I, *Attica (Persian–Greek Wars)* **479** BC. Between 100,000 Greeks, under Pausanias the Spartan, and 300,000 Persians, with 50,000 Greek auxiliaries, under Mardonius. The Persians fought well but the Greeks' better discipline and superior armour was too much for them. Mardonius fell, the Persians panicked and fled to their entrenched camp. The Athenians stormed it, giving no quarter. 40,000 Persians had left the field early in the battle; otherwise only 3,000 escaped the massacre. *See* Mycale; Salamis.

Plataea II (*Peloponnesian War*) **429–427** BC. The city, held by a garrison of only 400 Plataeans and eighty Athenians, was besieged by 11,000 Spartans (Archidamus). Most non-combatants were sent out of the city, though some volunteer wall-builders remained. The garrison repulsed numerous assaults and the siege soon became a blockade. Provisions were scarce and half the garrison broke through the enemy's lines, with the loss of one man. The remainder held till 427, when, on the verge of starvation, they surrendered. The survivors were tried for "having deserted Boeotia for Athens" and 200 Plataeans and 25 Athenians were executed. *See* Coronea I; Mytilene; Naupactus.

Plate River (*World War II*) **13 December 1940.** The German pocket-battleship *Admiral Graf Spee*, 10,000 tons (Captain Langsdorf), had been sinking merchant shipping in the South Atlantic — nine ships in all. The Royal

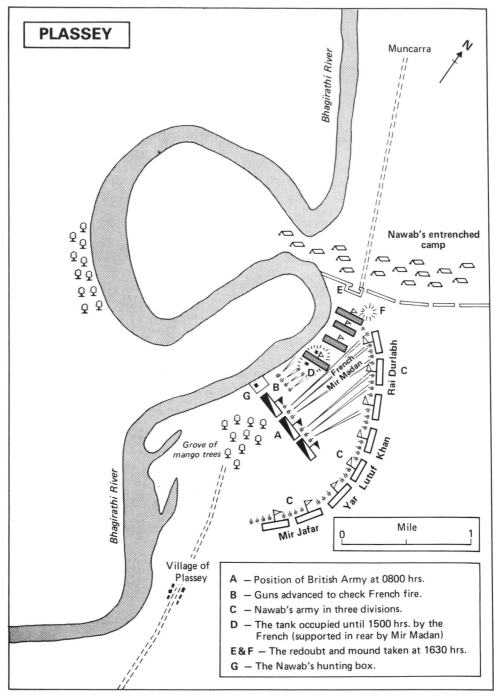

PLASSEY

Muncarra

Bhagirathi River

N

Nawab's entrenched camp

E

F

French
Mir Madan

D

Rai Durlabh

C

B

G

Grove of
mango trees

A

C

Lutuf Khan

Yar

C

Mile

0   1

Mir Jafar

Bhagirathi River

Village of
Plassey

A — Position of British Army at 0800 hrs.

B — Guns advanced to check French fire.

C — Nawab's army in three divisions.

D — The tank occupied until 1500 hrs. by the
        French (supported in rear by Mir Madan)

E & F — The redoubt and mound taken at 1630 hrs.

G — The Nawab's hunting box.

Navy had been hunting *Graf Spee*. Commodore Harwood, with 8-inch cruiser *Exeter* and the 6-inch cruisers *Ajax* and *Achilles*, found the German ship making for the River Plate area. *Graf Spee*, with her armour and six 11-inch guns, had only to keep out of range to deal with the British ships one after the other. Despite severe damage, the British ships pressed the attack to within 7,000 yards, but although Harwood's tactics were excellent, his ships were not strong enough to damage the *Graf Spee*. *Exeter* was ordered to the Falklands for urgent repairs; *Ajax* and *Achilles* kept watch while *Graf Spee* raced into Montevideo harbour. The Uruguayan Government had her inspected, found that the ship had only twenty-seven holes from shellfire and gave Langsdorf 72 hours to repair his ship and leave, or be interned. The British ships *Ark Royal* and *Renown*, with other heavy units, were closing on Montevideo and Langsdorf knew his chances were slim. At 3 a.m. on 17 December Hitler ordered him to scuttle *Graf Spee*, and this was done in the estuary about 6 miles south-west of Montevideo. Langsdorf committed suicide in Montevideo. *See* Atlantic.

Platte Bridge, *now Caspar, Wyoming* **(***First Sioux War***)** *25 July 1864*. Sioux, Cheyenne and Arapahoe warriors under Roman Nose besieged Platte Bridge Station on the Oregon. They ambushed a supply wagon train and Lieutenant Casper Collins took twenty-five troopers to protect it. The Indians surrounded the troop and eleven men, including Collins, were killed. The others, in a 4-hour battle, fought their way to the stockade. *See* Massacre Hill; Sand Creek.

Plattsburg (*American–English War of 1812***)** *6–11 September 1812*. The British occupied the town, but withdrew when the American victory of Lake Champlain, q.v., forced a general British withdrawal.

Plei Me (*Vietnam War***)** *19–28 October 1965*. Plei Me, a fort near the Cambodian border, was held by 400 South Vietnamese troops and twelve U.S. officers and men, when attacked by 6,000 Viet Cong and North Vietnamese regulars, who made numerous assaults in 7 days of fighting. Helicopters brought in 250 Vietnamese Rangers reinforcements, and U.S. aircraft strafed the besiegers. Parts of the U.S. 1st Cavalry Division (Airmobile) landed by helicopter north of the fort and raised the siege. Communist casualties, 850 killed, 1,700 wounded; Allied, 220. *See* Vietnam War.

Plevna (*Russian–Turkish War***)** *July–December 1877*. Four battles were fought during the Russian siege of Turkish-held Plevna. Three were attacks on the defences, the fourth, Osman Pasha's attempt to cut his way through the besiegers' lines. The Russians had 100,000 troops to the Turks' 30,000.

On 20 July 1877 the advance guard of Krüdener's corps attacked the defences north and east of Plevna. They captured some of the advanced trenches, and drove the defenders back to the outskirts of the town. But the Russians' heavy loss and shortage of ammunition had weakened them and the Turks drove them out. The Russians lost two-thirds of their officers and nearly 2,000 men.

In the second battle, 30 July, Krüdener, with 30,000 Russians in two divisions, attacked the Turkish redoubts. Schakofsky commanded the eastern attack, Krüdener himself led the assault on the Gravitza redoubt on the north. Krüdener was unsuccessful. Schakofsky took two redoubts, but before nightfall the Turks retook them and the Russians retired. Their losses were 169 officers and 7,136 men.

On 11–12 September the investing army, now 95,000-strong, under the Grand Duke Michael, assaulted Plevna on three sides. A vain attack on the Omar Tabrija redoubt cost the Russians 6,000 men. On the south-west, Skobelev captured two of the six inner redoubts, but next day they were captured by Skobelev after a terrible struggle. Russian losses in the 2 days' fighting were 20,600, including 2,000 prisoners. The Turks lost 5,000.

On 10 December Osman Pasha, at the head of 25,000 Turks, with 9,000 wounded in carts, tried to cut his way through the Russian army. Crossing the Vid River, Osman charged the Russians on a 2-mile front and broke through the first line of trenches. Russian reinforcements drove the Turks back across the river, Osman being severely wounded. Here the Turks made another stand, but were overpowered and driven into Plevna, which capitulated. In this final engagement the Turks lost 5,000 and the Russians 2,000. Total Russian casualties were about 38,000. The astonishing Turkish defence roused the world's admiration. *See* Kars II; Shipka Pass; Sviśtov.

Plovdiv,   *formerly   Philoppopolis* (*Russian–Turkish War*) *17 January 1878*. The Russians (Gurko) stormed the fortified city and routed the outnumbered defenders (Suleiman Pasha). Casualties: Turks, 5,000 killed or wounded, 2,000 prisoners; Russians, 1,300. The Turks withdrew almost to Constantinople. British intervention led to an armistice. *See* Geok Tepe; Pleona; Shipka Pass.

Podhaic   (or   Podhajce)   (*Polish–Russian Wars*) *July 1667*. Between 10,000 Poles (John Sobieski) and 80,000 Cossacks and Tartars who were besieging Kaminiec. The Cossacks were routed and forced to evacuate Poland.

Podol (*Seven Weeks' War*) *26 June 1866*. Between the advance guard of Prince Frederick Charles' Prussian army, and the Austrians under General Clam-Gallas. The Austrians were defeated and driven out of Podol after severe fighting, in which they lost heavily. The Prussians took 500 prisoners, and moved on to Münchengrätz, q.v.

Point   Pleasant   (*Lord   Dunmore's Indian War*) *9 October 1774*. At the confluence of the Kanawha and Ohio rivers Virginia's governor, Lord Dunmore, had about 2,000 colonial troops ready to put down Indian raids. Chief Cornstalk led a powerful party of Shawnees across the Ohio at dawn and a fierce day-long battle ensued before the beaten indians withdrew by night. The Virginians lost 50 killed, 100 wounded. Indian losses were heavy enough to break their power in the area.

Poitiers   I   (*Gothic   invasion   of France*) *507*. Between the Franks (Clovis) and the Visigoths (Alaric II). Clovis and Alaric met in single combat and Alaric was slain. The demoralised Goths were then routed. This decisive victory added the province of Aquitaine to the Frankish dominions. *See* Tolbiac; Vouillé.

Poitiers II (*Hundred Years' War*) *19 September 1356*. Between 7,000 English, under Edward the Black Prince, and 18,000 French, under King John II of France. The English, who had been deep-raiding, took up a strong position behind lanes and vineyards, in which their archers were posted. The French cavalry, charging up the lanes, were demoralized by showers of arrows from the English archers. They were then charged from the flank by the English knights and men-at-arms and routed with a loss of 8,000 killed and numerous prisoners, including the king. His ransom was £500,000. English losses were light. *See* Auray; Calais.

Pola. *See* Pulj.

Poland (*World War II*) *1–27 September 1939*. The opening conflict of World War II. The Nazi army began its blitzkrieg invasion with five armies comprising fifty-eight divisions, including 14 Panzer. Command: Third Army, von Kueschler; Fourth, von Kluge; Eighth, von Blaskowitz; Tenth, von Reichenau; Fourteenth, List. Von Bock commanded

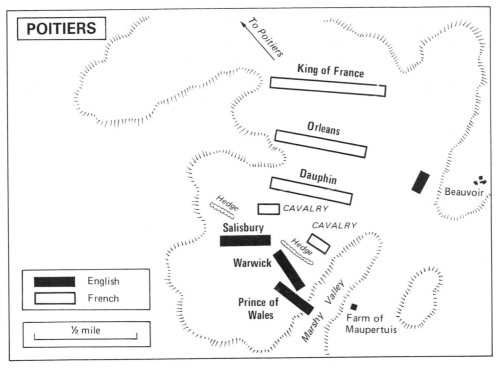

POITIERS

To Poitiers

King of France

Orleans

Dauphin

CAVALRY

Beauvoir

Hedge

Salisbury

CAVALRY

Hedge

Warwick

Prince of
Wales

Marshy Valley

Farm of
Maupertuis

■	English
□	French

½ mile

the northern army group, von Rundstedt the southern. Poland had only thirty divisions and one motorized brigade, under Marshal Smigly-Rydz.

About 1,450 German aircraft destroyed the Polish air force of 900 planes in 2 days, mostly on the ground. Warsaw came under fire, 8 September. The Poles fought well, but were helpless under the enemy speed. On 17 September the Russians joined in the attack from the east. Poland's allies, Britain and France, could do nothing to help and Warsaw surrendered, 27 September, to be partitioned between Germany and Russia. German casualties: 14,000 killed, 30,300 wounded. Polish casualties are believed to exceed 120,000, plus 450,000 prisoners. In June 1941 the Germans, invading Russia, took over eastern Poland. *See* Poland–Russian War 1920.

Poland — East Prussia (*World War II*) *July 1944–April 1945*. This battle was in two sectors:

1. The Fatherland Line between the Baltic and Pripet Marshes. The Third White Russian Army (Chernyakhovski) crossed the Niemen River in three places and moved on East Prussia, where the Germans (Field Marshal Busch) resisted stubbornly. The First White Russian Army (Rokossovski) crossed the Bug, 22 July, to take Brest Litovsk; it reached Warsaw's eastern suburbs on 31 July.

2. Pripet–Carpathian Line. Attacking on 16 July, the First Ukrainian Army (Konev) routed the German armies of Field Marshal Model, 20 July. Petrov, supporting Konev, took Stanislav and Lvov and crossed the San, 28 July. The Ukrainian army had a bridgehead across the Vistula, south of Warsaw by 1 August, but the Germans were able to hold a line for 6 months.

The Russians began a new offensive, along 750 miles of front, on 12 January 1945. Using large numbers of giant Stalin tanks and overwhelming numbers of infantry, Konev smashed the Germans back, taking Krajow, 19 January, and Oppeln, 26 January. Zhukov crossed the Vistula, 14 January, bypassing Warsaw and other fortified centres, all of which soon fell to follow-up troops. By 30 January Zhukov was crossing the Brandenburg frontier, 100 miles from Berlin. He and Konev, their armies now in line, had covered 300 miles in 3 weeks.

Rokossovski led the Second White Russian Army Group to the Baltic west of Danzig, 26 January. This move badly damaged the German front and isolated the German troops in East Prussia, though they kept the Russians out of Danzig until 30 March. In East Prussia the Russians steadily compressed the German defences. The key point of Braunsberg gave way, 20 March, and on 9 April the Königsberg garrison of 90,000 surrendered. *See* Warsaw; White Russia.

Polderhoek Spur, *Flanders (World War I) 3 December 1917.* An attack by New Zealanders on a German strongpoint. *See* Flanders; Messines; Ypres.

Polish–Russian War 1920. (This is sometimes called the Battle of Warsaw, but no battle for the city took place.) On 9 November 1918 Marshal Jozef Pilsudski proclaimed the Republic of Poland and made an alliance, against Russia, with Simon Petlyur of the Ukrainian independence movement. A Polish–Ukrainian force seized Kiev (7 May 1920), but under Leon Trotsky and General Tukhacheveski the Russians recovered from their post-Revolution confusion and crushed the Polish–Ukrainian offensive. Taking immense areas, the Russian army reached the edge of Warsaw. Now, however, the experienced French General Maxime Weygand was advising Pilsudski. With a reorganized Polish army Pilsudski, on 15 August 1920, attacked and broke the Russians near Brest-Litovsk and 10 days later his offensive had gained 200 miles. The Russians suffered a disastrous defeat, with 70,000 soldiers captured. On 12 October an armistice established a Poland–Russia border.

Pollentia *(First Gothic invasion of Italy) 6 April 402.* Between the Goths (Alaric) and the Romans (Stilicho).

Stilicho surprised the Gothic camp while the Goths were celebrating the festival of Easter. Alaric rallied his men and drove off the Romans with heavy loss. Stilicho returned to the attack, forced his way into the Gothic camp and drove out the Goths with enormous slaughter. *See* Verona.

Pollicore *(or Pollilur)* *(Second British–Mysore War) 27 August 1781.* Between 11,000 British (Sir Eyre Coote) and 80,000 Mysore soldiers (Haidar Ali). Coote seized the village of Pollicore, turning Haidar's flank and forcing him to retreat, after an action lasting 8 hours. Casualties: British, 421 killed or wounded; the Mysores, about 3,000. *See* Porto Novo; Trincomalee.

Polotsk I *(Polish–Russian Wars) 14 June 1579.* Stephen Bathory, King of Poland since 1575, rallied his nation against the Russians and in 1579 attacked the enemy holding Polotsk. He regained the city and drove the Russians out of his territory. *See* Linköping.

Polotsk II *(Napoleonic Wars: Moscow campaign) 18 August 1812.* Between 33,000 French and Bavarians (Saint Cyr) and 30,000 Russians (Count Wittgenstein). The Russians were taken by surprise, and after a 2-hour action were driven back with a loss of 3,000 killed, 1,500 prisoners and 14 guns. French casualties, 1,000. *See* Beresina River; Borodino.

Polotsk III *(Napoleonic Wars: Moscow campaign) 18 October 1812.* The "return" battle when Saint Cyr, with 30,000 French and Bavarians, was attacked and defeated by the Russians (Count Wittgenstein) and forced to evacuate Polotsk. *See* Beresina River; Borodino.

Poltava, *Pultowa or Pultava (Great Northern War) 8 July 1709.* One of the decisive battles of history. Charles XII of Sweden, campaigning in Russia, had only 20,000 men after a severe winter. How-

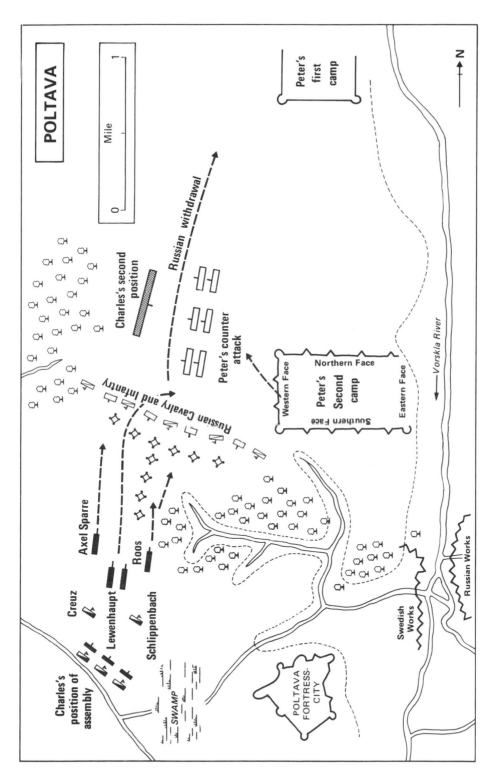

POLTAVA

Mile
0   1

Charles's position of assembly

Creuz

Lewenhaupt

Schlippenbach

SWAMP

POLTAVA FORTRESS-CITY

Axel Sparre

Roos

Charles's second position

Russian Cavalry and Infantry

Russian withdrawal

Peter's counter attack

Peter's Second camp

Western Face

Northern Face

Eastern Face

Southern Face

Swedish Works

Russian Works

Vorskla River

Peter's first camp

N

ever, in May he resumed his offensive by besieging Poltava, 85 miles south-west of Kharkov. Short of artillery and powder, his supply line cut, Charles found himself facing 50,000 Russians in a counter-siege organized by Peter the Great. His position untenable, Charles violently assaulted the Russian lines and for 2 hours his remarkable Swedish soldiers, under galling fire, tried to break the Russian lines. Peter then enveloped the Swedish flanks and Charles's men fell back until squeezed into a small triangle formed by the Vorskla and Dniepr Rivers. Only 1,500 Swedes, including Charles, escaped death or capture. Swedish military power was forever at an end. *See* Ahvenanmaa; Liesna.

Polygon Wood, *Flanders* **(***World War I***)** *25–27 September 1917*. The Australian 4th and 5th Divisions suffered 5,471 casualties in ousting Germans from strong defensive positions. *See* Flanders; Passchendaele; Ypres.

Ponani (*First British–Mysore War***)** *19 November 1780*. A force of 2,500 British and native troops under Colonel Macleod, entrenched near Ponani, were attacked by 18,300 Mysore troops under Tippu Sahib. The Mysores were repulsed at the point of the bayonet, with a loss of 1,100. British losses, 87. *See* Pollicore; Porto Novo.

Pondicherry I (*English–French Wars***)** *30 August 1748*. The port was invested by the British, under Admiral Boscawen, with a fleet of thirty ships and a land force of 6,000 men, and was defended by 5,000 French led by Joseph Dupleix. The siege was mismanaged, and in October Boscawen was forced to withdraw, having lost by sickness or in action nearly a third of his land force. The French lost only 250. *See* Madras.

Pondicherry II (*Seven Years' War***)** *3 August 1760–15 January 1761*. In August 1760 Colonel Coote, with about 8,000 British and native troops, invested the city, held by a French garrison of 3,000 under Lally-Tollendal. Breaching fire opened on 8 December, but on 31 December a hurricane wrecked all land batteries and drove ashore six ships of the blockading squadron. On 10 January 1761 fire was reopened and the town surrendered. Lally-Tollendal was wrongly charged with treason and beheaded. *See* Wandiwash.

Pondicherry III (*English–French War***)** *8 August–16 October 1778*. Having been surrendered to the French by the Peace of Paris, Pondicherry was again besieged by a British force (Hector Monro) in conjunction with a squadron of five ships (Edward Vernon). It was gallantly defended by the French (Bellecombe), but after a month's bombardment the place surrendered. A naval action was fought off Pondicherry, 10 August. A French squadron of five ships (Tronjolly) offered battle to the British ships but was beaten and driven back to their anchrorage. *See* Trincomalee.

Pondicherry IV (*War of American Revolution***)** *20 June 1783*. Between a British squadron of eighteen battleships and twelve frigates (Edward Hughes) and a French squadron of twenty-five ships (de Suffren). The British ships were badly damaged in masts and rigging and were unable to chase when de Suffren sheered off. *See* Cuddalore.

Pontevert (*Caesar's Gallic War***)** *57 BC*. Between 50,000 Romans under Caesar and 300,000 Suevi under Galba. The Suevi attacked the Roman entrenched camp but were repulsed with heavy loss and their army dispersed. *See* Sambre River.

Pont Valain (*Hundred Years' War***)** *1370*. Between the French (du Guesclin) and the English (Granson). The French surprised the English camp, but the English rallied. The fighting was severe and the French attack was at first repulsed. A French flank movement demoralised the English and they were defeated with a

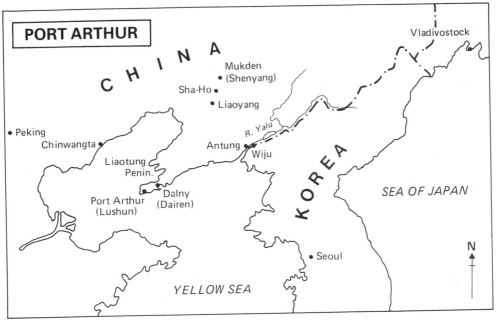

loss of nearly 10,000 in killed, wounded and prisoners. *See* La Rochelle.

Poonah (*Second British–Mahratta War*) 25 October 1802. Between the forces of Jeswunt Rao and the united armies of the Peshwa and Sindhia of Gwalior. After an evenly contested action, Jeswunt Rao triumphed and Sindhia fled, abandoning all his guns and baggage. *See* Alighar; Laswari.

Port Arthur I (*Chinese–Japanese War*) 21 November 1894. The city, held by a Chinese garrison of 9,000, was attacked and stormed by the Japanese after a short bombardment. The Chinese resistance was feeble and the Japanese lost only 270. *See* Yalu River.

Port Arthur II (*Russian–Japanese War*) 8 February–2 May 1904. A Japanese fleet of sixteen warships (Vice-Admiral Togo) attacked the Russian fleet of six battleships and ten cruisers (Vice-Admiral Stark) lying at anchor off Port Arthur. The Japanese struck with torpedo boats and seriously damaged two battleships and a cruiser. Their bombardment damaged a third battleship and four more cruisers. No Japanese ship was damaged.

On 31 April the Japanese torpedo flotilla attacked the Russian squadron (Makaroff). The battleship *Petropavlovsk* was torpedoed and sunk and Makaroff and 700 officers and men were drowned. The battleship *Pobieda* and a destroyer were also torpedoed, but reached harbour. Again, the Japanese suffered no loss.

The Japanese now penned the remainder of the Russian fleet in the harbour by sinking eight merchant ships in the entrance; few members of the volunteer crews survived this exploit. Meanwhile, Japanese troops landed near Port Arthur and surrounded the city; their land-based guns sank the Russians' last four ships. The Russians surrendered on 2 January 1905, but they had exacted a heavy price from the Japanese — 58,000 men killed or wounded and 30,000 sick. *See* Tsushima Strait.

Port Hudson, *Louisiana* (*American Civil War*) 25 May–9 July 1863. The fortress was besieged by five Federal divisions (Banks) and defended by 17,000 Confederates (Gardner). An assault on 27

May was repulsed, and the siege was tightened. A second assault was repulsed on 14 June, but the garrison, with no hope of relief, surrendered. They lost 800 men during the siege. Federal losses were far heavier. *See* Vicksburg.

Port Republic (*American Civil War*) 9 June 1862. Between 12,000 Federals (Shields) and an equal force of Confederates (Thomas Jackson). The Federals were defeated, part of their army being routed with heavy loss. *See* Cross Keys.

Port Royal I, *Nova Scotia* (*King William's War*) April–11 May 1690. Part of the North American sphere of the War of the Grand Alliance. Sir William Phips, with a force mainly composed of Massachusetts militiamen, attacked the French fortress and captured it after a short siege. The French retook the place in 1691. *See* Port Royal II.

Port Royal II (*Queen Anne's War*) 16 October 1710. The North American term for War of Spanish Succession. Port Royal was attacked abortively in 1704 and 1707. In 1710 Colonel Richardson and Sir C. Hobby captured the place, which became Annapolis Royal in honour of the Queen. *See* Port Royal I.

Port Royal Island, *South Carolina* (*American Revolution*) 3 February 1779. Major Thomas Fardiner, with 200 men, was unsuccessful in his attempt — on the orders of General Prevost, British commander in Georgia — to drive General Moultrie and his 300 Americans from this island in the mouth of the Broad River. British losses were heavy; the Americans had eight killed, twenty-two dead. *See* Kettle Creek; Savannah I.

Porte St. Antoine, *Paris* (*Wars of the Fronde*) 2 July 1652. The 8,000 Royal troops (Turenne) held this entrance to Paris against 5,000 attackers led by Condé. Condé had gained a position at the gate and was protected by barricades and fortified houses. Turenne attacked and the barricades were taken and retaken several times. Condé at last abandoned his plan to get into Paris and retired. His losses were heavy, especially in officers. *See* Arras; Lens.

Portland (*First English–Dutch War*) 18–20 February 1653. An English fleet of about seventy ships under Blake, Deane and Monck, attacked a Dutch fleet of seventy-three ships, convoying 240 merchantmen, under Van Tromp, de Ruyter and Evetzen. Early in the severe engagement three English ships were captured by boarding and part of the fleet nearly overwhelmed. The rest of the English ships now engaged, the balance was restored and the captured ships were retaken. On 19 February the battle was renewed off the Isle of Wight; five Dutch ships were captured or destroyed. The Dutch broke off the battle on 20 February. They had lost twelve men-of-war, sixty merchant ships, 1,500 killed or wounded and 700 prisoners. English losses were also heavy. *See* Dover; North Foreland.

Porto Bello I (*Raids of the Buccaneers*) September 1668. The Spanish–American fortress was captured by 460 buccaneers under Captain Morgan. The walls were scaled and the town sacked. The buccaneers were guilty of appalling atrocities, but Charles II knighted Morgan.

Porto Bello II (*War of Jenkins' Ear*) 22 November 1739. The port was captured from the Spaniards by a British fleet of six ships under Admiral Vernon. The British lost only a few men.*

Porto Novo (*Second British–Mysore War*) 1 July 1781. Between 8,500 British troops (Coote) and about 65,000

---

*The war itself was so called because in 1731 an English sailor, Robert Jenkins, allegedly had his ear cut off by a Spanish captain, Fandino. The incident precipitated a war declared *eight years later* — 19 October 1739. This war merged into the major War of the Austrian Succession.

Mysores led by Hyder Ali, the Maharajah of Mysore. Hyder occupied a strongly entrenched camp, blocking the British advance on Cuddalore. Coote, an able general, drove his opponent out and is said to have inflicted 10,000 casualties to the British 306. *See* Madras III; Seringapatam I.

Porto Praya Bay, *Cape Verde Islands* (*American Revolution*) *16 April 1781*. Commodore Johnstone, in command of a British squadron of five warships and five frigates, repulsed a two-prong attack by eleven French ships (Suffren). *See* Minorca.

Portuguese Timor War *1975*. As Portuguese Timor (the eastern half of the island) was about to become independent, the Timor Democratic Union (UDT) on 11 August declared war on the Revolutionary Front for Independence (FREITLIN), which was a Communist organization. UDT was backed by the Timorese Democratic People's Union (APODETI). On 7 December Indonesian paratroops invaded East Timor, defeated FREITLIN and ended the war. Portuguese Timor became part of Indonesia but a guerrilla war continued.

Potidaea *432–429 BC*. This Corinthian colony was besieged by a force of about 3,000 Athenians and was defended by a small garrison of Corinthians under Aristacus. The town held out until the winter of 429 when the garrison surrendered and were permitted to go free.

Po Valley (*World War II*) *9 April–2 May 1945*. The Germans' Gothic Line had held firm through the winter of 1944–5. On 9 April the British, Americans and Poles attacked — spearheaded by British Eighth Army (McCreery) — into the Argentina Gap. The Poles took Imola on 14 April, and the American Fifth Army broke into open country north of Bologna on 20 April. The British and American armies trapped thousands of Germans and the two German armies

— Tenth and Fourteenth, under Vietinghoff-Scheel — retreated across the Po. Under virtually unopposed air attack, the Germans lost most of their equipment and their retreat became a rout. Between 2–8 May Vietinghoff-Scheel surrendered about a million Germans to Field Marshal Alexander. This great victory, though delayed (*see* Gothic Line), largely helped to end the war in Europe. *See* Cassino.

Pozières Ridge, *Somme* (*World War I*) *14 July–31 August 1916*. Pozières was a great buttress on the German flank, narrowing the British offensive on the Somme River. After some of the fiercest, most sustained, fighting of the war, three Australian divisions — 1st, 2nd, 4th — captured the ridge on 4 August. They then held it under artillery barrage and continuous counter-attack. In 7 weeks they suffered 23,000 casualties, 33 per cent of their strength. German casualties, estimated, 40,000. On 26 July the Australians threw 15,000 grenades in possibly the longest bomb fight in war. *See* Somme.

Prague I (*Hussite Wars*) *14 July 1420*. John Zizka, leader of the Taborite or extreme faction of the Hussites, rallied

the Bohemians in their anti-Roman Catholic uprising that followed the execution of John Hus. With a garrison of only 9,000 he repulsed the great army of Sigismund who was King of Hungary and Bohemia and Holy Roman Emperor. *See* Kutná Hora.

Prague II (*Thirty Years' War*) 8 November 1620. The Imperialists, under Maximilian of Bavaria and Count Tilly, forced 22,000 Bohemians (Frederick of Bohemia) up to the walls of Prague and defeated them with a loss of 5,000 men and all their artillery. Frederick took refuge in the city and soon afterwards surrendered. The battle lasted only an hour, and the Imperialists lost no more than 300 men. *See* Lens; Zusmarshausen.

Prague III (*Thirty Years' War*) June–24 October 1648. A Swedish army (von Königsmarck) besieged Prague and demanded surrender. Ferdinand III could send no Holy Roman Empire troops and the defence fell to the townspeople. They resisted fiercely for 3 months; then the Treaty of Westphalia ended the war.

Prague IV (*War of the Austrian Succession*) 2–7 September 1744. Frederick the Great, protecting Silesia from the designs of Maria Therese of Austria, invaded Bohemia and reached Prague with 80,000 soldiers. After a 6-day battle the city surrendered. Frederick's reinforcements did not arrive and pressure by Austrian and Hungarian forces drove him out of Prague with heavy losses. *See* Chotusitz; Dettingen.

Prague V (*Seven Years' War*) 6 May 1757. Between 70,000 Austrians (Charles of Lorraine) and 60,000 Prussians (Frederick the Great). The Austrians occupied strong positions on the Moldau, which Frederick attacked and carried. Charles was driven back into Prague. Casualties: Austrian, 10,000 killed or wounded, including Marshal Browne

killed, 9,000 prisoners; Prussians, 16,000 including Marshal Schwerin. *See* Lobositz.

Prairie Grove, *Arkansas* (*American Civil War*) 7 December 1862. A bloody but indecisive action between 11,000 Confederates (Hindman) and 7,000 Federals (Blunt), later reinforced by 3,000 troops led by Herron. Each side lost about 1,300 men. *See* Pea Ridge.

Preston I (*English Civil War, sometimes Second Civil War*) 17–20 August 1648. The New Model Army of the Parliamentarians held England firmly. James Hamilton (1st Duke of Hamilton) raised an army of 10,000 in Scotland and crossed the border on 8 July. Sir Marmaduke Langdale reinforced him with 3,000 men while another Royalist force landed in Galloway from Ulster. Cromwell and Lambert moved with a well-disciplined Parliamentary army of 8,500 to counter the Royalist moves. Cromwell attacked Langdale, who held a bank overlooking Ribbleton Moor. In a fierce action the Royalists lost many dead and prisoners, though Hamilton, leading his own regiment, held a key bridge, thus allowing some of his Cavaliers to escape. Pursued and confused, the Scots turned at Winwick and in a defile delayed Cromwell for 3 hours, but at least 1,000 Scots were killed and many captured. *See* Preston II; Prestonpans.

Preston II (*Jacobite Rebellion, 1715*) 12 and 14 November 1715. Between 4,000 Jacobites (Forster) and a small force of Royal troops, chiefly dragoons, under General Wills. The Jacobites barricaded the approaches to the town and held their ground throughout the day. With reinforcements arriving, Wills was able to invest the place completely and early next morning Forster surrendered. Many of the rebels had left the town during the night, so Wills took only 1,468 prisoners. *See* Rathmines; Stow-on-the-Wold.

Prestopans (*or Gladsmuir*) (*Jacobite Rebellion 1745*) 21 September 1745.

Between 3,000 Royal troops (Cope) and a slightly superior force of Jacobites led by the Young Pretender, Prince Charles Edward. Cope's infantry could not stand up against the charge of the Highlanders and fled, losing heavily in killed and wounded, and 1,600 prisoners, including seventy officers. The Highlanders lost about 140 killed and wounded. Prince Charles penetrated as far as Derby, where lack of recruits forced him to retrace his steps. *See* Falkirk II; Preston II.

Preveza, *Ambracian Gulf (Christian–Turkish Naval Wars) March 1538*. A sharp fight between the fleet of the Holy League (Holy Roman Emperor Charles V, Pope Paul III and the Venetian Doge), commanded by Andrea Doria, and the Ottoman navy of Suleiman the Magnificent under Barbarossa II. Doria lost seven galleys, could make no impression on the Turks and withdrew. *See* Malta I; Tunis III.

Priesten (*Napoleonic Wars: Dresden campaign***) *30 August 1813*.** Napoleon, having won a battle at Dresden, q.v., sent an army in pursuit of the Russians. The Russians stood firm in good positions in the mountains south of Dresden and beat off the pursuit.

Primolano (*Napoleon's Italian campaigns***) *7 September 1796*.** Napoleon surprised and routed the vanguard of Wurmser's Austrian army and inflicted 4,000 casualties. *See* Lodi; Mantua.

Prince of Wales and Repulse (*World War II***) *10 December 1941*.** The British battleship and battle cruiser (Admiral Phillips) were in the South China Sea to help block the Japanese invasion of the Malay Peninsula. Themselves without air cover, the battleships and their small destroyer escort were attacked by eighty-four bombers and torpedo bombers, flying in nine-plane waves. Both great ships were sunk, Admiral Phillips and 1,000 men being

lost. The Japanese lost only four aircraft. *See* Singapore.

Princeton (*American War of Independence***) *3 January 1777*.** Between the Americans, under Washington, and the British, under Cornwallis. Washington outmanoeuvred his opponent and the British were defeated. The victory enabled Washington to regain possession of New Jersey. *See* Brandywine Creek; Trenton.

Prome, *Burma (World War II) 28 March–2 April 1942*. The Japanese crossed the Irrawaddy River and set up a road block with 5,000 troops 10 miles south of Prome. This was cleared in hard fighting by British troops, but on 1 April the Japanese attacked Prome itself. Fighting lasted throughout the night and next day the British withdrew. *See* Imphal; Kohima.

Prussian–French Wars. *See* List of Battles.

Pruth, The (*Russian–Turkish War***) *2 August 1770*.** The Russians (Romanzov) stormed the triple entrenchments held by the main Turkish army, 120,000-strong, under Halil Bey, and drove out the Turks with a loss of 20,000 killed and wounded. *See* Çeşme.

Przemysl (*World War I***) *24 September–11 October 1914: 6 November 1914–22 March 1915*.** The Austrians and Hungarians held this fortified city against the Russians. Successful in outlasting one siege, the garrison surrendered after a second long siege. In June 1915 the Russians were driven out. Each side lost about 45,000 men. *See* Galicia.

Puebla I (*U.S.–Mexican War***) *14 September–12 October 1847*.** Colonel T. Childs held Puebla with 2,300 men, mostly wounded and sick, when General Joaquin Rea threw a Mexican army around the town. Santa Anna then arrived with another 8,000 Mexicans. Luckily for the Americans, Santa Anna left on 1 October, leaving the Mexicans without aggressive leadership. A relief column (Joseph Lane) raised the siege. *See* Chapultepec.

Puebla II (*French–Mexican War*) 5 May 1862 and 4–17 May 1863. Louis Napoleon III wanted to bring Mexico under French rule. A French army of 7,000 (Comte de Lorencez) attacked Puebla, held by 12,000 Mexicans (Zaragoza), suffered 400 casualties and withdrew. Lorencez was replaced by Elié Forey, who in 1863 launched a new, reinforced drive into Mexico. The garrison of Puebla (Ortega) resisted stubbornly, but on 8 May a Mexican relief column was ambushed and destroyed. Ortega surrendered Puebla and the French pushed on to Mexico City. *See* Calpulalpam.

Puente, *Colombia* (*Colombian War of Independence*) 16 February 1816. The Colombian Patriots (Lorrices) were decisively beaten by the Spanish Royalists (Morillo).

Puente de la Reyna (*Second Carlist War*) 6 October 1873. Between 50,000 Carlists (Ollo) and about 9,000 Republicans (Moriones). The Republicans fought hard, but were at last driven in disorder from the field by a bayonet charge. The Carlists lost only 113; Republican losses were far heavier. *See* Huesca.

Pulj (*or Pola*) (*Venetian–Genoese Wars or War of Chioggia*) October 1379. Between a Genoese fleet of twenty-two galleys (Luciano Doria) and twenty Venetian galleys (Pisano). The Genoese were raiding the Venetian base on the Istrian Peninsula when the Venetians sallied out and captured the enemy flagship, killing Doria. This angered the Genoese who fought back so fiercely that they sank fifteen of the Venetian ships. *See* Chioggia; Curzola.

Pultusk I (*Great Northern War*) 21 April 1703. Between 10,000 Swedes (Charles XII) and an equal force of Saxons (Marshal von Stenau). The Saxons put up practically no fight and fled from the field, losing 600 killed and 1,000 prisoners. *See* Klissow; Thorn.

Pultusk II (*Napoleonic Wars: Friedland campaign*) 26 December 1806. About 37,000 Russians (Bennigsen) blocked 20,000 French (Lannes) from Pultusk. Lannes tried unavailingly to pierce the Russian left and cut them off from the town; in this part of the field the action was indecisive. On the left the French barely held their own, but the Russians retired during the night, having lost 3,000 killed or wounded, 2,000 prisoners, and many guns. The French admitted a loss of 1,500, but the Russians claimed to have inflicted 8,000. *See* Eylau; Lübeck.

Puna (*Raids of the Buccaneers*) 27 April–3 May 1687. Three Buccaneer vessels under Captain Davis engaged two Spanish men-of-war off Puna. The action was entirely one of long-range firing and lasted till 3 May, when the Spanish commander withdrew his ships.

Punic Wars. *See* List of Battles.

Punniar (*British– Gwalior campaign*) 29 December 1843. The left wing of Sir Hugh Gough's army, under General Grey, routed a force of 12,000 Mahrattas, with 40 guns. *See* Maharajpur.

Pusan (*Korean War*) 11 August–31 September 1950. The invasion by the North Koreans of the Republic of Korea in June 1950 had been everywhere successful. American troops were rushed in to help the South Koreans, but despite American dominance by sea and air the defenders fell back. They established a large perimeter around the key port of Pusan. The garrison (Walton Walker) consisted of 91,000 South Korean troops, 87,000 American (Eighth Army) and 1,500 British. The Communists crossed the Naktong in several places, but Walker was easily able to move reserves to crisis points. By the end of September the offensive was thoroughly checked. *See* Inchon; Korea.

Pydna (*Third Macedonian War*) 22 June 168 BC. Between the Romans (Aemilius Paulus) and the Macedonians (Perseus). The Macedonian phalanx attacked the Roman line and drove them back on their camp. When the Macedonians became disordered by the uneven ground, the disciplined legionaries counter-attacked. The result was destruction of the Macedonians, with a loss of 20,000 killed and 11,000 prisoners. At Pydna the Macedonian phalanx fought its last fight and was wiped out. *See* Corinth; Cynoscephalae.

Pylos–Sphacteria (*Great Peloponnesian War*) 425 BC. Pylos is a promontory of the south-west Peloponnese; Sphacteria is a nearby island. When the Athenian General Demosthenes occupied and fortified Pylos, thus threatening Sparta, the Spartans countered the threat by occupying Sphacteria, from where they in turn threatened Pylos. The Athenian Cleon first blockaded Sphacteria and then captured it. He held hostage his Spartan prisoners as insurance against Spartan "aggression", but by now the Athenians had decided to call off the occupation of Pylos. *See* Delium; Mytilene.

Pyongyang, *China (Chinese–Japanese War*) 16 September 1894. The city was held by 12,000 Chinese when attacked by 14,000 Japanese (Nodzu). Much better armed and disciplined, the Japanese routed the Chinese with heavy losses. Japanese casualties, 630. *See* Yalu River I.

Pyramids (*French invasion of Egypt*) 21 July 1798. The Mameluke army (Murad Bey) tried to stop Napoleon's march on Cairo. The 20,000 Mameluke infantry took no part in the fight, but the cavalry, 6,000-strong and perhaps at that time the finest in the world, charged the French squares with the greatest gallantry. They were repulsed time after time and were eventually driven into the Nile, where many drowned. French casualties, 300. *See* Abukir; Acre; Nile River.

Pyrenees (*Peninsular War*) 25 July– 2 August 1813. The engagements fought between Wellington's generals and Soult's army, which was endeavouring to relieve San Sebastian, are collectively the "Battles of the Pyrenees". They include the actions of Soravren, Roncesvalles, Maya, Santarem and Buenzas. The British losses amounted to 7,300, while the French lost 14,000. *See* Bayonne; Nive; Nivelle; Orthez; Toulouse.

Quatre Bras (*Napoleon's Hundred Days*) *16 June 1815*. Returning from exile, Napoleon led the revived French armies into Belgium, his object being to drive a wedge between the Prussian army (Blucher) and the British–Dutch army (Wellington). Napoleon led the attack on Blucher, while Marshal Ney with 25,000 men moved towards Quatre Bras. He smashed against the 36,000 British–Dutch troops of Prince William of Orange and held a clear advantage until Wellington threw in General Picton's division. Even then Ney might have won had he used the French I Corps, but he had a misunderstanding with Napoleon about its use. Wellington's counter-attack decided the issue. Casualties: French, 4,300; Allies, 4,700. *See* Waterloo.

Quebec I (*Seven Years' War*) *27 April–16 May 1759*. The French, beaten out of Quebec by Wolfe (see Plains of Abraham), returned to the attack the following spring. General de Lévis was given 8,500 men and told to retake the city, held by James Murray, British commander in Cananda. Murray, though outnumbered two to one, marched his troops out to meet the French and Indians and lost a third of his force. Hurrying back to Quebec, he held out until a British fleet arrived with reinforcements in May. The British ships destroyed de Lévis' supply ships and he retreated to Montreal, q.v. *See* Fort Niagara; Quebec II.

Quebec II (*American Revolution*) *31 December 1775*. The Americans (Montgomery) had taken Saint Johns (or Saint-Jean) and Montreal in an invasion of British-held Canada. On the Plains of Abraham Montgomery joined forces with Benedict Arnold who had led 600 men for 350 miles through forest from Maine. Together Montgomery and Arnold attacked Quebec, held by 1,800 British (Carleton). It was a rash assault. Montgomery was killed and Arnold wounded, 100 of their men were killed or wounded and 300 taken prisoner. British casualties, five killed, thirteen wounded. After a severe winter the Americans fell back to Lake Champlain in April 1776. *See* Montreal; Quebec I.

Queenston Heights, *Ontario (British–American War of 1812*) *13 October 1812*. About 4,000 British (Brock) held Queenston Heights against the American offensive, commanded on this sector by Van Rensselaer with 5,000 Americans. The Americans carried the heights and Brock — the victor of Detroit — was killed, but 1,000 British troops rallied and after severe fighting practically annihilated the 600 Americans at that time on the heights. Exact losses are unknown, but the British took 1,000 prisoners and Van Rensselaer's army was so broken that he retired from command. *See* Detroit; Frenchtown.

Querétaro (*French–Mexican War*) *14 May 1867*. Under American pressure Napoleon III withdrew his army from

Mexico, 12 March. This left his puppet, Maximilian of Austria, and Miguel Miramón commanding a factional Mexican army. Mariano Escobedo had been organizing a new Mexican army in the United States. He now brought it into action and trapped Maximilian and Miramón in Querétaro, 160 miles northwest of Mexico City, which his troops stormed. Maximilian and Miramon were captured and executed and Benito Juaráz restored order in Mexico. *See* Puebla II.

Quiberon (*French Revolution, sometimes the Vendée Rising*) *16–21 July 1795*. Peasants in the department of Vendée remained Royalist and first rose against the revolutionary National Convention in 1793. A British fleet, 27 June 1795, landed 3,600 French emigrés on the Quiberon Peninsula, Brittany, where they joined thousands of other Royalists. But they had no positive leadership and the Revolutionary army sent to the region destroyed the Vendée "army" in a series of engagements. About 700 rebels were identified as emigrés and summarily executed; 1,800 escaped again to England. *See* Fleurus III; Loano.

Quiberon Bay (*Seven Years' War*) *20 November 1759*. A British fleet of twenty-three warships and ten frigates, (Hawke) gave battle to twenty-one French warships and three frigates (Conflans). The action was fought in a heavy gale on a lee shore and resulted in the French taking refuge in Quiberon Bay, southern Brittany, with a loss of two ships sunk and two captured. Despite the gale, Hawke exploited his advantage and following the French captured or destroyed all but four of the ships which had taken refuge in the bay. Seven others escaped up a small river — and stayed there for 2 years. The gale blew two of Hawke's ships ashore. The British lost only one officer and 270 men killed or wounded. The French gave up their plans to invade Scotland. *See* Lagos II; Martinique.

Quipuaypan (*Peruvian Civil Wars*) *1532*. Between the rival Peruvian chiefs, Atahualpa and Huascar. Huascar was routed and taken prisoner.

Quistello (*War of the Polish Throne*) *18 July 1734*. The Austrians and Russians backed Augustus, son of the former Polish ruler Augustus II, as candidate for the Polish throne. Spain, France and Sardinia supported Stanislaus Leszcznski. The Battle of Quistello brought into confrontation the great Prince Eugene and his Austrians with the Duc de Broglie and a French army. Eugene won yet another victory, though the following year Augustus was installed. *See* Danzig I; Parma; Philippsburg.

Raab (*Napoleonic Wars: Wagram campaign*) *14 June 1809*. Between 44,000 French (Eugène Beauharnais) and about 40,000 Austrians (Archduke John). The French attacked the Austrian position south-east of Vienna, and drove the enemy successively from the villages of Kismegyer and Szabadhegy. Under cover of night, the Archduke retired. Casualties: Austrian, 3,000 killed or wounded 2,500 prisoners; French, 2,500. *See* Aspern-Essling; Eggmühl; Sacile; Wagram.

Rabaul I, *New Britain* (*World War II*) *22 January 1942*. After earlier air and naval bombardment the Japanese sent about 6,000 soldiers in a forty-ship convoy to take this Pacific outpost from its Australian garrison of 1,000 men. Many Australians were massacred after capture, others were lost at sea in a prisoner-of-war ship, Japanese casualties, about 1,000. *See* Guadalcanal; Papua–New Guinea; Solomon Islands.

Rabaul II (*World War II*) *June 1943–September 1945*. Parts of this battle took place far from Rabaul, but all were part of it. The Japanese turned Rabaul (with Kavieng) into a great naval and air base. After the capture of Woodlark and Trobriand Islands in the Solomon Sea, American and Australian aircraft repeatedly raided Rabaul, the plan being to isolate and bypass it, thus reducing its garrison of 60,000 Japanese to impotency. Americans made landings elsewhere in New Britain: 15 December

1943, Arawe; 26 December, Cape Gloucester; 6 March 1944, Talasea. By then the Japanese commander (Matsuda) had lost 5,000 killed and American casualties were 310 killed, 1,083 wounded. On 15 February New Zealand troops occupied the Green Islands; on 1 March the Americans landed at Los Negros, Admiralty Islands; on 20 March, Emirau Island in the Bismarck Islands. In the fighting for the Admiralties another 3,300 Japanese were killed. With complete encirclement, the great bases at Rabaul and Kavieng were no menace and were simply plucked when the war ended. *See* Papua–New Guinea; Rabaul I; Solomon Islands.

Radcot Bridge, *Oxfordshire* (*Revolt against Richard II*) *September 1387*. Between the troops of Richard II, under De Vere, Duke of Ireland, and the forces of the English barons known as the Lords Appellant, under the Earl of Derby (Henry IV). De Vere and his troops fled after a brief fight and Richard was left in the power of the Barons. Twelve years later he lost his crown and his life to Bolingbroke. *See* Margate; Ravenspur I.

Radnor (*English conquest of Wales*) *May 1282*. Edward I marched into Wales to bring to order the Welsh leader Llewelyn ab Gruffyd. He gave battle to the Welsh at Radnor and defeated them. Llewelyn was killed, but the English suffered many casualties from the Welsh longbowmen. Wales came under English administration and Edward's fourth son was named Prince of Wales. *See* Berwick-upon-Tweed; Ely II.

Ragatz, *Switzerland (Armagnac War) March 1446*. Between the Austrians and the Swiss Confederation. The Swiss gained a brilliant victory, which was followed by peace with Austria and the Armagnacs — the inhabitants of the area.

Rain (*Thirty Years' War*) *15 April 1632*. Gustavus Adolphus, victorious at Breitenfeld and commanding the Protestant armies, marched for Bavaria and crossed the Danube on 7 April. His opponent, Field Marshal Tilly, with 20,000 troops of the Holy Roman Empire, retired beyond the Lech River, north of Augsburg. Gustavus with 25,000 Swedes reached the village of Rain, occupied by Tilly, and heavily bombarded it. The Swedes forced a crossing of the river, charged the Imperial positions and routed the Catholic army, which abandoned all its artillery and baggage. Tilly was mortally wounded. Maximilian I collected the broken Imperial army while Gustavus brushed aside opposition and reached Nürnberg. *See* Breitenfeld I; Fürth.

Rajahmundry (*Seven Years' War*) *9 December 1758*. Between 2,500 British troops (Colonel Forde), in conjunction with about 5,000 native levies, and 6,500 French (Conflans). The native troops did little on either side, but Forde's Europeans routed Conflans' Frenchmen. French Madras II; Pondicherry II.

Rakersberg (*Turkish–Austrian Wars*) *September 1416*. Ahmed Bey led 20,000 Turks besieging Rakersberg. With 12,000 Austrians, Duke Ernest of Styria marched to the relief of the city. He routed the Turks who are said to have suffered more casualties than the entire strength of the Austrians. Ahmed Bey was among the slain. *See* Varna I.

Ramadi (*World War I*) *28–29 September 1917*. A clear-cut victory for the British–Indian army (Maude) over the Turkish garrison of Ramadi, holding the right bank of the Euphrates 60 miles west of Baghdad. Most of the Turks were captured. Maude died of cholera in Baghdad, 18 November. *See* Baghdad IV; Kut; Sharqat.

Ramleh I (*First Crusade*) *1101, 1102 and 1105*. The Caliph of Cairo sent an army into Palestine to expel the Crusaders, who had already suffered heavy losses. At Ramleh, a fortress on the road from Jerusalem to the coast, Baldwin I of Jerusalem defeated the invasion. The following year a larger army of Arab horsemen and Sudanese infantry pushed north from Cairo. Baldwin had only 500 knights, but he attacked. Driven back, his group found safety in a castle tower. That night Baldwin evaded the patrolling enemy, scraped together a relief force and routed the Muslims, though on his return he found all his friends in the tower dead. In 1105 the Caliph tried yet another and even larger invasion; again Baldwin defeated it at Ramleh.

Ramleh II (*Crusader–Turkish Wars*) *Autumn 1177*. Saladin, the Turk who had become master of Egypt and of Damascus, brought a powerful army of Mamelukes from Egypt, flicked aside a force of Knights Templar at Gaza and moved on the forces of Baldwin IV, aged 17, part disabled by leprosy, and King of Jerusalem. Baldwin sent a message to the Templars bypassed at Gaza to attack Saladin's army in the rear. Baldwin himself sallied out, cut his way through the besieging Mamelukes, chased Saladin, and charged the rear of the enemy column at Ramleh. The charge broke the Mamelukes' morale and Saladin was lucky to escape. *See* Ashkelon II; Tiberias.

Ramilles, *Spanish Netherlands (Belgium) (War of Spanish Succession) 23 May 1706*. The Duke of Villeroi was moving his 50,000 men eastward to attack, on the order of Louis XIV, from the Dyle River to the Meuse. He was intercepted near Ramillies by Marlborough and his English–Dutch–German army of 50,000, 25,000 of them cavalry. Marlborough feigned an attack on the French left (north), then put in his main attack on the opposite flank. The allied horsemen broke the French cavalry regiments, then wheeled right and rolled up the whole rear of the French line. By this time Marlborough had loosed his infantry on a frontal assault of Ramillies itself. Villeroi's army was broken, 15,000 men being killed, wounded or captured. Marlborough, with only 3,000 casualties, also took most of the French guns. *See* Blenheim; Stollhofen; Turin.

Ramnugger (*or Ramnagar*) *near Lahore* (*Second British–Sikh War*) *22 November 1849*. Lord Gough, with his British–Indian army, attempted to dislodge Shir Singh and 35,000 Sikhs who had occupied a position behind the Chenab River opposite Ramnugger. The attempt failed owing to the strength of the Sikh artillery. *See* Chilianwala; Sobraon.

Raphia (*Rafia*) (*Wars of the Hellenistic Monarchies*) *223 BC*. Between the Egyptians (Ptolemy Philopator) and the Syrians (Antiochus, later the Great). Antiochus held the advantage, but pushed too far in the pursuit, was counterattacked and routed. The Syrians lost 14,000 killed and 4,000 prisoners. *See* Panion; Pergamum; Sellasia.

Rastädt, *Baden* (*French Revolution*) *14 May 1796*. Between the French (Moreau) and the Austrians (Archduke Charles). After a major engagement Moreau seized the heights held by the Austrians, and forced Charles to retreat to the Danube. Total casualties were 11,000. *See* Arcola; Mantua.

Raszyn (*Napoleonic Wars: Wagram campaign*) *19 April 1809*. Between 30,000 Austrians (Archduke Ferdinand) and about 20,000 French and Poles (Poniatowski). The Archduke was marching on Warsaw when Poniatowski came out to give battle. After a vicious fight in the woods and marshes round Raszyn, he was driven back on Warsaw, with a loss of 2,000 killed or wounded. A few days later Poniatowski surrendered the city to the Austrians to save it from bombardment. *See* Abensberg; Eckmuhl.

Rathenow (*Swedish invasion of Brandenburg*) *25 June 1675*. The Brandenburgers, 15,000-strong, under the Elector Frederick William, encountered the Swedes, under Charles XI. The Swedes, exhausted after a long march, were trapped in their camp and most were killed. *See* Fahrbellin.

Rathmines, *Ireland* (*English Civil War*) *2 August 1649*. Between the Royalists (Marquis of Ormonde) and the Parliamentary garrison of Dublin (Colonel Jones). While Ormonde was preparing for a night attack on Dublin, the Parliamentarians made a sortie and drove back the assaulting column. Then they attacked the Royalists in their camp and routed them. The Royalists lost 4,000 killed or wounded and 2,000 prisoners and all their artillery. *See* Drogheda; Preston I.

Ratisbon (*or Regensburg*) (*Napoleonic Wars: Vienna campaign*) *23 April 1809*. After his defeat at the hands of Napoleon and Marshal Davout at Eckmühl on 22 April, the Archduke Charles and his Austrian army hastened to escape northwards across the Danube. Charles posted a strong rearguard in the walled city of Ratisbon, which Napoleon's exhausted troops stormed next day. Most of the Austrian soldiers, having done a competent delaying job, eluded the French net. Napoleon was wounded at Ratisbon, though not seriously. *See* Aspern-Essling; Eckmühl; Landeshut.

Rava Russkaya (*World War I*) *9 September 1914*. This Russian victory opened a 40-mile gap in the Austrian lines, leading to a deep advance into Galicia. On 20 June 1915 the Germans and Austrians retook the place. *See* Galicia.

Ravenna I (*Gothic conquest of Italy*) *491–3*. Theodoric the Great, King of the Ostrogoths, invaded Italy in 489. Odoacer (Odovacar) the Heruli chief, who had deposed Romulus Augustulus in 476, vainly tried to stop the Ostrogoths at Aquileia and Verona, then shut himself in Ravenna. Theodoric besieged the place for 3 years, gained admission under flag of truce and murdered Odoacer. *See* Pavia II.

Ravenna II (*Wars of Byzantine Empire*) *729*. Between the troops of Leo III, the Isaurian, and a force of Italians, raised by Pope Gregory II in defence of image worship — which Leo had outlawed. After a severe struggle, the Greeks were routed; thousands were slaughtered in flight to their ships. The waters of the Po River were so infected with blood, it is said, that for 6 years the inhabitants of Ravenna would not eat fish from the river.

Ravenna III (*Frankish invasion of Italy*) *July 756*. The Lombards under King Aistulf had held Ravenna since 751. Pope Stephen II, disturbed by Aisulf's power, asked Pepin III, the Short, for help. Pepin, King of the Franks, marched across the Alps and quickly beat the Lombards from Ravenna. He presented the conquered territory to the Pope — "the Donation of Pepin". This laid the foundation of the Papal State. *See* Pavia III and IV.

Ravenna IV (*French–Spanish Wars in Italy, sometimes known as the War of the Holy League*) *11 April 1512*. Pope Julius II held Ravenna, which the French army under the Duke of Nemours, nephew of Louis XII, besieged. The Spanish king, Ferdinand, who also ruled Naples, sent the Conde de Alvetto and Marquis de Pescara to break the siege, thus precipitating one of the bloodiest battles of the sixteenth century. For 3 hours, on 11 April, the French infantry held firm under continuous fire from cannon and arquebuses mounted on wheels. Then Nemours got twenty-four French guns into position and enfiladed the Spanish lines. He charged with his cavalry supported by his phalanx of lasquenets — mercenary German pikemen and musketeers. The Spaniards, though veteran troops, were practically wiped out, but Nemours was killed at the end of the battle. The victory did Louis XII little good, for the Austrians and Swiss now came into the war against him. *See* Agnadello; Novara I; Oran I.

Ravenspur I (*Overthrow of Richard III*) *4 July 1399*. Unjustifiably listed by history as a battle. Henry Bolingbroke of Lancaster landed unopposed at Ravenspur, Yorkshire, in his rebellion against Richard III.

Ravenspur II (*Wars of the Roses*) *14 March 1471*. Edward IV landed at Ravenspur with 1,200 Flemish and German mercenaries for his Yorkist (white rose) cause, manoeuvred around his stronger opponent, the Earl of Northumberland, and his Lancastrian (red rose) army and marched to London. Here he put back into the Tower of London Henry VI, freed only a few months earlier by the Lancastrians. *See* Barnet; Lose-Coat Field.

Ré, Ile de, *Bay of Biscay* (*English–French Wars*) *17 July–29 October 1627*. The Duke of Buckingham's troops besieged St. Martin, capital of the island, but the English assault, on 27 October, was repulsed. The landing of the Duke of Schomberg, with 6,000 French, broke the siege. While returning to their ships, the English were attacked and suffered heavily. Their losses during the operations were 4,000. *See* La Rochelle II.

Reading (*Danish invasion*) *871*. Between the Danish invaders and the

West Saxons, under Ethelred and Alfred. The West Saxons charged the Danish camp, but were defeated and driven off with great slaughter. The Vikings went on the offensive. *See* Ashdown; Wilton.

Rebec (*Wars of Charles V*) *1524*. Between the Holy Roman Empire Imperialists (Constable de Bourton) and the French (Bonnivet). The French were defeated with heavy loss; the Chevalier de Bayard was among the dead.

Redan (*Crimean War*) *8 September 1855*. This fort, a strong part of the southern defences of Sebastopol, was attacked by the British Second and Light Divisions. They captured it, but the Russians retook it. However, this battle and the fall of the Malakoff forced the Russians to leave the city 3 days later. British losses, 2,184 killed or wounded. *See* Sebastopol.

Reddersberg (*Second British–Boer War*) *3 April 1900*. 452 British infantry were surrounded by a Boer force with five guns. After holding out for 24 hours lack of water forced a British surrender. They had lost four officers and forty-three men killed or wounded. *See* Kimberley.

Reims (*Napoleonic Wars: Defence of Paris*) *13 March 1814*. Napoleon, with 30,000 French, surprised and routed 13,000 Prussians and Russians (Saint-Priest) with a loss of 6,000 killed, wounded and prisoners. French casualties, 1,000. But Napoleon now stood between two allied armies, each much bigger than his own. *See* Arcis-sur-Aube; Laon.

Remagen (*World War II*) *7 March 1945*. The U.S. 9th Armoured Division captured the only bridge intact across the Rhine, thus opening the way for the Allied advance into Germany. The Germans fell back to the Ruhr. *See* Aachen; Rhineland; Ruhr Pocket.

Resaca, *Georgia* (*American Civil War*) *14 May 1864*. Having been manoeuvred out of Rocky Face Ridge, the Confederates (Johnston) took up good positions at Resaca. The Federals (Sherman) attacked, but Johnston had been reinforced to 60,000 and beat off several assaults. However, Sherman's encircling manoeuvres forced Johnston to retreat. *See* Chattanooga.

Resaca de la Palma (*U.S.–Mexican War*) *9 May 1846*. Zachary Taylor with 1,700 troops was marching to relieve besieged Fort Texas. Only 4 miles from the fort his way was barred by 5,700 Mexicans (Arista). Taylor attacked at once and the Mexicans broke and ran for the Rio Grande, in which many drowned. Other casualties: Mexican, 262 killed, 355 wounded, 150 captured; American, 39 killed, 83 wounded. Taylor recovered Fort Texas that evening. *See* Fort Texas; Monterrey; Palo Alto.

Reval I, *now Tallin* (*Scandinavian Wars*) *1219*. The Danes (Waldemar II), intent on conquering German Baltic territory, had given battle to an army of Germans and were losing ground. According to tradition, Waldemar mysteriously acquired a red and white flag — the Dannebrog, later the national banner of Denmark. Rallying under this symbol, the Danes overwhelmed the Germans and swept over Estonia.

Reval II (*Russian–Swedish Wars*) *29 April 1790*. This port was attacked by the Swedish fleet (Duke of Sudermanland). The Russian batteries aided by the fleet (Admiral Chitchagoff) drove them off with the loss of three ships.

Revolax (*Russian–Swedish War in Finland*) *27 April 1808*. General Klingspoor, with about 8,000 Swedes, surprised an isolated Russian column of 4,000 (Bonlatoff). The Russians tried to cut their way through, but less than 1,000 escaped. General Bonlatoff was killed.

Rheinfelden, *near Basle* (*Thirty Years' War*) *2–3 March 1638*. This battle was a lesson in intelligent tactics. The Duke of Saxe-Weimar and his Protestant German Army (in the pay of France) besieged Rheinfelden on the Rhine, then began a river crossing. With half his force across, he was attacked by the Bavarians (von Werth) emerging from the Black Forest. In a difficult position, Saxe-Weimar managed to get his force over the river by night. He moved along the Rhine a few miles, recrossed the river and next morning returned to Rheinfelden in the Bavarian rear. By then Werth's men were crossing the river and were taken by surprise. All who stayed to fight were captured, including Werth, but Saxe-Weimar lost the noted Huguenot general, de Rohan. *See* Breisach; Wittstock.

Rhineland (*World War II*) *8 February–24 March 1945*. This great battle had several phases.

8 February: Canadian First Army (Crerar) in Operation Veritable thrust from Nijmegen to the Rhine, reaching it 14 February.

16 February: U.S. Ninth Army (Simpson), Operation Grenade, crossed the Roer River 23 February and linked with the Canadians at Geldern, Germany, 3 March.

23 February: U.S. First Army (Hodges) attacked towards Cologne, taking much of the Rhine plain. U.S. Third Army (Patton) breached the Siegfried Line, north of the Moselle.

5 March: Elements of First and Third Army (Bradley), Operation Lumberjack, attacked towards the Rhine, taking Coblenz, Bonn and Cologne, 7 March, and linking with the Canadians.

18 March: Sixth Army Group (Devers), Operation Undertone, made a vast pincers manoeuvre against the German First and Seventh Armies (Hausser).

By 21 March these offensives had eliminated German resistance west of the Rhine. On 22 March the Americans (Patton) crossed the Rhine at Oppenheim, 24 March at Boppard.

Three German army groups under (from north to south) Blaskowitz, Model and Hausser, had been disastrously defeated; 60,000 Germans had been killed or wounded, 250,000 captured, and vast stocks of equipment captured. Allied casualties: American, 6,570 killed; British and Canadian, 1,100.

Rhodes I (*Turkey's Mediterranean Wars*) *23 May–20 August 1480*. This island, defended by the Knights of Saint John of Jerusalem under their Grand Master, Pierre d'Aubusson, was besieged by a Turkish army (Meshid Pasha) and a fleet of 160 ships. The siege was raised after the failure of the second assault, the Turks having by then lost 10,500 killed and wounded.

Rhodes II (*Turkey's Mediterranean Wars*) *28 July–21 December 1522*. Suleiman I, the Magnificent, maintained a ruthless siege. The Knights under Villiers de L'Isle Adam repulsed numerous attacks, but famine compelled surrender. The Turks are believed to have lost 100,000 men by disease and battle. This siege is notable as being the first in which explosive bombs (Turkish) were used. (In 1530 the Knights of Saint John were re-established on Malta.) *See* Baghdad III; Belgrade II; Mohacs.

Rhodesia–Zimbabwe *1964–80*. Three major groups were involved in this guerrilla war. They were (1) the Zimbabwe African People's Party (ZAPU) and its 4,000-strong army, the Zimbabwe People's Revolutionary Army (ZIPRA), led by Joshua Nkomo; (2) the Zimbabwe African National Union (ZANU) and its 14,000-strong army, the Zimbabwe National Liberation Army (ZANLA), led by Robert Mugabe and Ndabaningi Sithole; (3) Rhodesian Security Forces (RSF), consisting of eight battalions, all white; the Rhodesian Light Infantry, 1,000 men; the Rhodesian African Rifles, 700 blacks with white officers; the Selous Scouts, a special force of black and white troops. ZANU and ZAPU were in a state of almost constant friction, but both attacked white settlements. Guerrilla warfare became intensive between 1976 and 1978. By 1980, when the independent Republic of Zimbabwe was proclaimed, 102 white combatants had been killed and about 860 black — the majority in inter-tribal fighting. The post-independence merger of ZIPRA, ZANLA and RSF was not successful; the army's notorious 5th Brigade murdered 1,300 black civilians.

Riachuelo (*Paraguayan–Brazilian War*) *11 June 1865*. Between the fleets of Paraguay and Brazil. After a bloody fight the Brazilians were victorious: two-thirds of the Brazilian fleet were sunk.

Riade (*Wars of the German States*) *933*. Henry I, first Saxon king of Germany, attacked the Magyar barbarians of modern Hungary in a battle designed to pre-empt further Magyar onslaughts. On the Saale River, near Merseberg, his mail-clad German cavalry overwhelmed the lighter enemy horsemen. The Magyars, never before beaten, did not make another raid for 20 years.

Richmond I, *Kentucky* (*American Civil War*) *30 August 1862*. Between 6,000 Confederates (Kirby-Smith) and 8,000 Federals (Manson). The Federals, suffering 1,046 battle casualties, were routed and driven headlong into Richmond, where 5,000 prisoners, nine guns and 10,000 rifles were captured. Confederate losses, 460. *See* Perryville; Shiloh.

Richmond II (*American Civil War*) *8 March 1865*. Around Richmond were fought the final actions of the war, when Lee, with the army of Virginia, vainly tried to break through the ring of Grant's troops. He surrendered on 8 March 1865; by then he had only 10,000 effectives under command.

Rich Mountain, *in Randolph County, West Virginia* (*American Civil War*) *12 July 1861*. To dominate an important area for the Confederates, General Garnett posted Lieutenant-Colonel Pegram and two regiments on Rich Mountain and Laurel Hill. The local Federal commander, McLellan, sent four regiments (Rosecrans) to attack. Rosecrans cut off Pegram's retreat, and after a short battle the badly mauled Confederates surrendered. Garnett, forced to retreat, was killed in action next day. *See* Bull Run I; Cheat Mountain; Philippi.

Rietfontein (*Second British–Boer War*) *24 October 1899*. Between 4,000 British (White) and the Boers who were advancing to harass the retreat of Colonel Yule from Dundee. After an indecisive action, the British retired to Ladysmith, with a loss of 111 killed or wounded. *See* Ladysmith.

Rieti (*Italian Wars of Independence*) *7 March 1821*. Between 12,000 Neapolitans (Pepe) and the Austrian invading army, 80,000-strong, who had come to reinstate the despotic king, Ferdinand IV. Opposing the advance guard, Pepe made resolute resistance, but the Neapolitans were then overpowered by superior numbers. The Austrians restored Ferdinand and banished Pepe. *See* Custoza I; Tolentino.

Riga I (*Thirty Years' War*) *20 August–15 September 1621*. Riga was invested by the Swedes under Gustavus Adolphus and was defended by a tough garrison of 300 Poles. They repulsed several determined assaults, but the Swedes made a large breach on 11 September. The garrison, reduced to a handful, surrendered 4 days later. *See* Frankfort-on-Oder; Khotin I; Kinkoping.

Riga II (*World War I*) *1–3 September 1917*. Kerenski's provisional government in Russia was unstable, the Russian attack on the Germans at Lvov (then Lemberg) had collapsed and Hindenburg believed that one more blow would knock Russia out of the war. He sent his Eighth Army (von Hutier) across the Dvina into Riga and it crushed Russian resistance in

48 hours. The defeated Russian commander, Kornilov, led a counter-revolutionary attack on 8–14 September, and though this was abortive Kerenski was deposed in the so-called October Revolution (7–8 November, new-style calendar). Hostilities on the eastern front ceased on 2 December. Vast numbers of German troops were now available for the Western Front. *See* Lemberg II.

Rimnik (or Rimnitz) (Turkish–Russian Wars) 22 September 1789. The Russian–Austrian army, 25,000-strong, having defeated the Turks at Focsani (q.v), pushed into Moldavia and encountered a much larger Turkish army at Rimnik. The allied commanders, Count Suvorov and Prince of Saxe-Coburg, an able combination, practically wiped out the Turkish troops. Catherine II, the Great, gave Suvorov the title of Count Riminiksy.

Rinya (Turkish–Austrian Wars) 21 July 1556. Between 40,000 Turks (Ali Pasha) and a comparatively small force of Austrians and Hungarians (Thomas Nadasdy). The Turks were defeated with heavy loss, the Christians losing 300 men only.

Rio Barbate (Muslim conquest of Spain) 19 July 711. At Wadi Bekka, on the Barbate River near Cape Trafalgar, King Roderick, with 15,000 Visigoths, tried to stop an invading Muslim force of 7,000 Arab and Berber horsemen, under Tariq. But in an hour's fighting the fast Muslim swordsmen were victorious. Roderick was killed and the Muslims rode on to take Cordova (soon to be the Moor capital) and half Spain. The supreme Arab general Musa ibn-Nusayr followed Tariq and quickly captured other major strongholds — Merida, 1 June 713; Seville, 28 June; then Saragossa. The Visigoths were never again a fighting force. *See* Carthage III; Covadonga.

Rio Salado, near Tarifa, Spain (Spanish–Muslim Wars) 30 October
1340. The war of Christians against Moors had gone on for centuries. Alfonso XI of Castile, threatened by a great army of Muslims from southern Spain and Africa, accepted help from Alfonso IV of Portugal, a relative by marriage. He made a stand, then beat off and pursued the Muslim enemy. *See* Cordova.

Rio Seco (Peninsular War) 14 July 1808. Marshal Bessieres, with about 14,000 French, defeated 26,000 Spaniards (Cuesta). Spanish casualties, 6,000; French, 370. Following this victory, Joseph Bonaparte entered Madrid and proclaimed himself king. *See* Vimeiro.

River Plate 13 December 1939. The British cruiser squadron of *Exeter*, *Ajax* and *Achilles* (Commodore H. Harwood) attacked the powerful German pocket battleship *Admiral Graf Spee* (Captain Langsdorf) in the South Atlantic. The *Graf Spee* inflicted damage on the British squadron, notably *Exeter*, but was herself badly damaged. Langsdorf put into Montevideo on the River Plate for repairs and was given 72 hours to leave. With the British ships waiting for *Graf Spee* to emerge, Langsdorf sailed, but scuttled his ship outside the harbour and later committed suicide in Buenos Aires.

Rivoli Veronese (Napoleon's Italian campaigns) 14 January 1797. The Austrians, 25,000-strong (Alvinczy), made a fourth attempt to relieve Mantua. They attacked French positions on the heights of Rivoli. The position was too strong to be carried and Masséna's superb handling of his troops brought total defeat to the Austrians. An Austrian division which had not taken part in the frontal attack, arrived in the rear of the French position after the battle and, surprised to find the French victorious, laid down its arms. Though outnumbered, the French inflicted 3,500 casualties on the enemy, captured 7,000 prisoners that day and another 6,000 in the pursuit. Masséna became Duke of Rivoli. *See* Arcole; Malborghetto; Mantua.

Roanoke Island (*American Civil War*) *7–8 February 1862*. The island, commanding the entrance to Albemarle Sound, North Carolina, was defended by 3,000 Confederates (Wise). It was attacked by three brigades of Federals (Burnside) aided by nineteen gunboats. The Federals overpowered the garrison and occupied the island, losing 235 killed and wounded. The Confederates lost 91 killed or wounded and 2,500 prisoners.

Rochester I, *Kent (Revolt against "Norman Rufus".) 1088*. The English barons revolted against the strict rule of William II, Rufus, successor to William the Conqueror. Bishop Odo of Bayeux, a leader of the rebellion (and uncle of William Rufus), was captured and agreed to help arrange surrender terms. He rejoined his comrades and fought on, but William took the castle by siege. Odo was exiled.

Rochester II (*First Barons' War of England*) *30 September–30 November 1215*. The rebellious barons occupied Rochester Castle where King John — who had signed Magna Carta on 15 June — besieged them. He successfully mined the castle, 30 November, and the barons surrendered. The war turned against John the following year, but he died on 28 October 1216 and Henry III succeeded. *See* Dover I; Lincoln II.

Rochester III (*Second Barons' War of England*) *April 1264*. The rebel leaders Simon de Montfort and the Earl of Gloucester had captured the town of Rochester and were attacking the castle's outworks when the Royalist army (Henry III and Prince Edward) arrived. Thwarted from near-victory, the rebels retired to London. *See* Lewes; Northampton I.

Rocourt (*or Raucoux*), *near Liege (War of Austrian Succession) 11 October 1746*. Prince Charles of Lorraine took an Austrian army into The Netherlands, but his British army allies had been recalled to put down the Jacobite Rebellion of 1745. Charles, with an Austrian–Dutch force, was no match for the able French General Comte de Saxe, and lost 5,000 men in battle. The victory gave the French the province of Brabant. *See* Cape Finisterre I; Kesseldorf; Lauffeld.

Rocroi, *Belgium (Thirty Years' War) 19 May 1643*. One of the black days in Spanish military history. The 26,000-strong Spanish army (Melo) laid siege to Rocroi, to whose relief hastened the 22-year-old Duke of Enghien (later the Great Condé) with 7,000 cavalry and 15,000 infantry. Both sides had an infantry centre with cavalry wings. Condé charged and routed the Spanish horse on his right, but on the other wing the Spanish cavalry was successful. Condé, with reckless daring, turned left and cut lengthwise through the enemy infantry, separating the veteran Spanish foot from their Italian, Walloon and German rear-line support troops. Going clean through, Condé reached the opposite wing and attacked the rear of the Spanish cavalry as it fought with the other French to their front. The 8,000 élite Spanish infantry, probably the best in the world, surrounded and without hope of relief fought until they perished. Another 7,000 allied infantry were captured. Condé suffered 4,000 casualties. Spanish infantry was never again as fine as the force which fell at Rocroi. *See* Brietenfeld II; Lens; Tuttlingen.

Roliça (*Peninsular War*) *17 August 1808*. Wellington, with 14,000 British and Portuguese (few of whom saw action), attacked Delaborde's 3,000 French. After a half-hearted resistance the French abandoned their position. British casualties, 400. *See* Vimeiro.

Roman Wars. *See* List of Battles.

Romani (*or Rumani*) (*World War I*) *4 August 1916*. After being on the defensive in Palestine for more than a year, the British (Allenby) were ready to take the offensive against the Turks, under the German von Kressenstein. The British force (Murray), principally Australian and New Zealand Light Horse, led by their own generals Chauvel and Haytor, advanced into Palestine. At Romani the Turks tried to turn the British flank, but the Allied commanders had anticipated this; they pivoted their troops to the south and the following day they struck very hard at the Turkish right flank. The victory swung the whole Palestine–Sinai campaign in the British favour. Casualties: British, 1,130; Turkish, 6,000 including 4,000 captured. *See* Beersheba; Gaza.

Rome I (*First invasion of the Gauls*) *387 BC*. In the first siege of Rome by the Gauls (Brennus) the city was burnt by the barbarians. The Capitol, held by the leading patrician families, withstood a siege of 6 months. Brennus then imposed a great ransom and withdrew. *See* Veii.

Rome II (*Second Gothic invasion of Italy*) *408–10*. The city was besieged in 408 by the Goths (Alaric) and after famine had killed thousands the Romans capitulated. They regained their freedom by ransom, and Alaric retired northward. In 409 Alaric seized Ostia, the port of Rome, and again summoned the city to surrender. In the absence of the Emperor Honorius, the populace forced the authorities to yield. Alaric, after deposing Honorius, withdrew his troops. On 24 August 410 Alaric once more appeared stormed through the walls and sacked the city. Thousands of Romans perished. *See* Florence–Fiesole; Hippo Regius.

Rome III (*Wars of Western Roman Empire*) *2–16 June 455*. Rome was torn with conspiracies when Genseric (Gaiseric) the Vandal arrived at the mouth of the Tiber with a great convoy. He reached and took Rome on 2 June, and the city was then ruthlessly plundered and savaged. Alaric's sacking of the place

in 410 had been mild in comparison. *See* Aquileia III; Pavia II.

Rome IV (*Ricimer's Rebellion*) *472*. The rebel Ricimer the Suevian, with a large army of Burgundians, Suevi and other barbarians, laid siege to Rome in 472. After 3 months the besiegers entered the city by storming the Bridge of Hadrian and sacked it.

Rome V (*Wars of Byzantine Empire*) *536–8*. The Ostrogoths held Rome so Justinian I, the Great, sent the able General Belisarius, victor of Carthage, to reconquer the city. First Belisarius, who had only 11,000 troops, all cavalry, took Sicily. Leaving 2,500 men he moved into Italy, took Naples and with great audacity rode into Rome on 10 December 536. The following March the Gothic leader Witiges brought 30,000 men and penned Belisarius in Rome for a year. Then reinforcements from Constantinople enabled Belisarius to break out. In 2 years of continual warfare, Belisarius defeated the Goths, Franks and Burgundians. He ended the war when he captured Witiges in his own capital, Ravenna. *See* Carthage II.

Rome VI (*Second Gothic War*) *546, 549, 552*. The competent General Totila, commanding an army of 30,000 Goths, after several victories on the Italian peninsula laid siege to Rome in May 545. Rome had a garrison of only 3,000 (Claudius Bassus) so the Byzantine Emperor Justinian I sent Belisarius with a relief army. His force was too small and Bassus was too timid to co-operate, so Belisarius withdrew. Totila's Goths stormed Rome on 17 December 546. In 547 Belisarius tricked Totila into leaving the city and then occupied it, but Totila recaptured it in 549 with the help of traitors within. In 552, after Totila was killed in the Battle of Tagina, Narses captured Rome and the Gothic occupation ended.

Rome VII (*Capture by Normans*)

1084. Pope Gregory VIII had refused to recognise Henry IV of Germany as Holy Roman Emperor, so Henry laid siege to Rome in 1082. After a desultory siege, Roman nobles surrendered the city to Henry, March 1084. Gregory was deposed and Pope Clement III was set upon the throne. Gregory called on the Norman adventurer Robert Guiscard to redeem his throne. Guiscard, with an army of both Christians and Muslims, battled the Germans out of Rome but he and his men then sacked the city and Gregory had to leave and live in Salerno.

Rome VIII (*Spanish Sack of Rome*) 6 May 1527. The Spanish troops of the Holy Roman Emperor, Charles V of Spain, led by Charles of Bourbon, stormed and captured the city as a form of punishment on the Pope, Clement VII, who had supported the French, enemies of Spain. In the massacre which followed, 8,000 Roman citizens perished. The Pope retired to the castle of St. Angelo and held out until 26 November. In 1528 a treaty between him and Charles V ended the conflict.

Rome IX (*Italian Wars of Independence: Garibaldi's Rising*) 30 April–2 July 1849. After proclamation of a Roman republic by Garibaldi in 1848, a French army (General Nicolas Oudinot) was sent to restore papal rule. On 30 April 1849 7,000 French attacked the Porta San Pancrazio, where the Republicans (Garibaldi) repulsed them with a loss of 300 killed or wounded and 500 prisoners. The Garibaldians lost 120. On 3 June Oudinot, with 20,000 men, made a night attack which the Garibaldians opposed with 8,000 men. Garibaldi surrendered the city on 2 July and marched out with his 5,000 survivors. They were pursued by an Austrian army who killed, captured or dispersed the Garibaldian army. *See* Novara II; Venice.

Rommerswael (*Netherlands War of Independence*) 29 January 1574. Between the Dutch part-mercenary navy

known as the "Beggars of the Sea" (Admiral Boisot) and a Spanish fleet of seventy-five ships (Julian Romero). The "Beggars" grappled the enemy's ships with hooks and after a savage fight in which the Spaniards lost fifteen vessels and 1,200 men, Romero retreated to Bergen-op-Zoom. *See* Mookerheide.

Roncesvalles I (*Conquests of Charlemagne*) April 778. Between the Franks (Charlemagne) and the Basques and Gascons (Loup II). The army of Charlemagne, retreating from Spain to put down a Saxon revolt, was caught in the defile of Roncesvalles, in the Pyrenees. The large rearguard was annihilated, among those who fell being the famous paladin, Roland. Much medieval literature was written about this defeat, e.g. Chanson de Roland. *See* Pavia IV; Süntelberg.

Roncesvalles II (*Peninsular War*) 25 July 1813. One of the actions known as the "Battle of the Pyrenees". Soult, at the head of Clauset's division, attacked three British brigades (Byng). He was unable to defeat them and after severe fighting was repulsed. Casualties: French, 400; British, 181.

Rorke's Drift, Natal (*British–Zulu War*) 22 January 1879. Triumphant after their victory over the British at Isandhlwana, Chief Cetawayo's 4,000 Zulu warriors marched to Rorke's Drift. At this river ford an outpost was garrisoned by two lieutenants (Bromhead and Chard) and 137 men, mostly from the 24th Regiment. They held out against a night-long attack and beat off the formidable Zulus, who suffered 400 killed. The garrison had 25 men killed or wounded and won the remarkable number of eleven Victoria Crosses and nine Distinguished Conduct Medals. *See* Isandhlwana.

Rosbecque (*or Roosebeke*) (*French–Flemish Wars*) 27 November 1382. Under Philip van Artevelde, the Flemish people rose against despotic French rule and 50,000 of them, ill-trained and poorly armed, massed at Roosebeke. A strong force of French knights (Count of Flanders) attacked them and in repeated cavalry charges cut down the Flemings in swathes. French rule became more severe than ever. *See* Cassel; Clermont.

Rosebud River, *Montana* (*Sioux War II*) *17 June 1876*. Between 1,200 American troops (George Crook) and 1,500 Sioux and Cheyenne warriors (Crazy Horse). The Indians held firm under American attack, killing ten and wounding thirty-four. They then escaped while the American force fell back for supplies. *See* Little Bighorn River.

Roseburgh (*English–Scottish Wars*) *3 August 1460*. This town was besieged by the Scots (James II of Scotland) and was captured and destroyed. This is the first occasion on which the Scots used artillery; during the siege the Scottish king was killed by the bursting of a large gun.

Roses, Wars of. *See* List of Battles.

Rossbach, *Saxony* (*Seven Years' War*) *5 November 1757*. Frederick the Great was encircled by French, Austrian and Russian enemies. An army of 42,000 French and Austrians (Soubise and Prince of Saxe-Hildburghausen) were the greatest threat, so Frederick marched his Prussian veterans 170 miles in 12 days to give battle at Rossbach. Knowing that Frederick had only 21,000 men, the allied commanders planned to crush Frederick by a massive turning movement against his left flank. Frederick expected this. He left a small force to mask his left, sent his 4,000-strong cavalry (Seydlitz) under cover of a range of hills ready to attack with maximum surprise, posted his artillery on commanding heights and so manoeuvred his main force that by mid-afternoon the Austrians were themselves vulnerable to a flank attack. The Prussian attack was so devastating that the action was decided within an hour. Casualties:

Prussian, 165 killed, 376 wounded; Allied, 3,000 killed or wounded, 5,000 prisoners (including eight generals), 67 cannon and vast quantities of baggage. The victory was politically decisive; French military might was discredited and French aggression towards Germany was blunted. *See* Breslau; Cross-Jagersdorf; Hastenbeck; Leuthen.

Rosslavl (*World War II*) *August 1941*. General Guderian, with fourteen divisions, including four armoured, was sent to Roslavl to clear out the remnants of twenty-one Russian divisions which were blocking the German advance on the Central Front and Moscow. Guderian trapped the Russians amid swamps and captured 70,000 of them. *See* Moscow.

Rostock (*Danish–Swedish Wars*) *June 1677*. Between the Danish fleet (Admiral Juel) and the Swedes (Admiral Horn). The Swedes were defeated.

Rostov (*World War II*) *November 1941*. Under the orders of Field Marshal Rundstedt, on 21 November the German First Armoured Army (General Kleist) captured Rostov in a frontal assault. Reacting quickly, Marshal Timoshenko struck back with the Russian Thirty-seventh Army and half the Ninth Army. In violent but brief fighting the Germans were driven out of Rostov. *See* Moscow.

Rotto Freddo, *Lombardy* (*War of Austrian Succession*) *1 July 1746*. The rearguard of the retreating French army (Maillebois) was attacked by the Austrians (Prince Lichtenstein) and after stubborn resistance defeated with heavy loss. The French garrison of Placentia, 4,000, surrendered to the Austrians. *See* Lauffeld.

Rouen I (*English–French Wars*) *24 June 1204*. A sharp attack by the French knights of Philip Augustus II captured the English-held fortress, chief city in Normandy. The English, weaker under King John than under Richard I, Coeur de Lion, now held no territory north of the Loire. *See* Chateau Gaillard; Damme.

Rouen II (*Hundred Years' War*) *1418–19*. Victorious at Agincourt, Henry V took Caen in 1417, Falaise and Cherbourg in 1418, then besieged Rouen, chief city of the area. The garrison (Guy de Boutillier) prepared for a stubborn siege by expelling non-combatants from the city. But the English refused to allow these people through the siege lines and 12,000 of them suffered dreadful hardships, in winter weather, between the opposing forces. An attempt to relieve the fortress was unsuccessful and it surrendered on 19 January 1419. Before long, England controlled all northern France. *See* Agincourt; Beaugé.

Rouen III (*Hundred Years' War*) *1449*. Henry VI, through his English troops in France, held on to Rouen despite reverses which steadily eroded English strength in France. Aided by French troops, the people of Rouen revolted and the English commander (Duke of Somerset) held out in the castle for a time until, 29 October, he surrendered.

Roundway Down, *Wiltshire* (*English Civil War*) *13 July 1643*. The Parliamentarians (Waller and Hazlerigg) attacked the Royalists (Prince Maurice) who were advancing to the relief of Devizes, commanded by Sir Ralph Hopton. The Parliamentarians' attack on Prince Maurice was repulsed and they were taken in the rear by a sortie from the town. Of 1,800 infantry, 600 were killed and the rest taken prisoner. Maurice quickly took Bristol, leaving Gloucester the only Roundhead stronghold between Bristol and York. *See* Lansdowne; Newbury I.

Roveredo (*Napoleon's Italian campaigns*) *4 September 1796*. Between 25,000 Austrians (Davidowich) and the main body of Napoleon's army. Napoleon attacked the Austrian entrenched position and in fierce fighting carried it. Austrian losses included 7,000 prisoners and fifteen guns. This victory enabled Masséna to occupy Trent, and the remnants of the Austrian army were rapidly driven into the Tyrol. *See* Arcole.

Rowton Heath (*English Civil War*) *24 September 1645*. A body of Royalist cavalry (Langdale), trying to save Chester from being besieged, was attacked by the Parliamentary cavalry (Colonel Poyntz). The first attack was repulsed, but Poyntz got infantry support and drove the Royalists from the field. They lost 300 killed or wounded and 1,000 prisoners. *See* Naseby.

Rubicon River (*Wars of First Triumvirate*) *49 BC*. Pompey the Great, with Julius Caesar away fighting the Gauls and the other triumvir, Crassus, killed at Carrhae, became virtual dictator in Rome. On Pompey's insistence, the senate ordered Caesar to disband his army at the end of his successful Gallic campaign. Caesar refused and led his Thirteenth Legion south across the Rubicon River, near Ravenna. The Rubicon marked the limit of Caesar's jurisdiction and in crossing it he was declaring war against Rome. He crushed Pompey's outposts and in 60 days took Rome itself. *See* Alesia; Carrhae I; Ilerda.

Rudnik Ridges (*World War I*) *7–17 September 1914*. Their first invasion of Serbia unsuccessful, the Austrians (Potiorek) attacked again, with two armies. The three Serbian armies (Putnik) fought desperately and on 17 September Potiorek halted his offensive. Putnik withdrew to stronger postions which the Austrians attacked on 5 November. They took Valjevo, 15 November, and occupied undefended Belgrade, 2 December. By now Putnik had his armies along the Rudnik Ridges. Choosing his moment, Putnik made his counter-attack, 3 December. After 5 days of furious fighting, the Austrians fell back, losing all their ground. Casualties:

100,000 dead on each side, wounded unknown. *See* Serbia.

Rufiji River, *East Africa* (*World War I*) *28 November 1917*. This was the only battle which the German guerrilla general, von Lettow-Vorbeck, was forced to fight. The South African General van Deventer, with a force of Nigerians, South Africans, Portuguese, Belgians and Indians, surprised von Lettow-Vorbeck, though he and many of his men evaded capture. *See* East Africa.

Ruhr (*World War II*) *25 March–18 April 1945*. The Ruhr was encircled, 1 April, by the U.S. First Army (Hodges) from the south, near Bonn, and by the XIX Corps of Ninth Army (William Simpson) operating in the north along the Lippe River. Inside the pocket of 4,000 square miles were the German Fifth Panzer and Fifteenth Armies and another 100,000 troops, all under Field Marshal Model. The Germans fought fiercely to slow down the overall Allied advance. They were unsuccessful; the drive continued while the pocket was squeezed tight. On 14 April the Americans made a north–south attack and cut it in two. Resistance ended on 18 April, with the suicide of Model and the capture of 317,000 prisoners, including thirty generals. This was the greatest German surrender of the war. *See* Rhineland.

Rullion Green (*Covenanters' Rising*) *November 1666*. Between the Covenanters (Colonel Wallace) and the Royal troops (Dalziel). The Covenanters were defeated with half their number of 1,100 casualties. *See* Bothwell Bridge.

Rumania (*World War I*) *27 August 1916–7 January 1917*. The Battle of Rumania, which followed Rumania's declaration of war against the Central Powers on 27 August 1916, had three parts:

1. Transylvanian Alps, north-west 28 August–18 September. On a 200-mile front three Rumanian armies advanced 45 miles in 3 weeks against the Austrian First Army (von Straussenburg). But Rumanian communications were poor and the Austrians, with reinforcements arriving from other quieter fronts, stopped the Rumanian attack.

2. Danube–Dobruja, south-east. 6 September–23 October. The Rumanians had hoped that one army (Averescu) would hold the Danube Line against the Bulgarians, but the enemy Army of the Danube was stiffened by Germans and Turks and led by the veteran von Mackensen. Mackensen took Turtucaia, 6 September, Silistra 9 September. A Russian force (Zaoinchovsky) and a division of Serbians had come to help the Rumanians and, 16 September, this allied force, with the Rumanians, stopped Mackensen. Another three Rumanian divisions were rushed from Transylvania, but Mackensen, gathering strength, smashed through, 20 October. Constanta, Rumania's only Black Sea port, fell on 23 October.

3. Transylvanian Alps 2: 18 September–23 November. The Austrians were now backed by the German Ninth Army, whose commander, von Falkenhayn, began counter-attacking on 18 September. He turned back one Rumanian army after another and on 10 November he forced a general Rumanian retreat. On 23 November his troops crossed the Danube and moved on Bucharest.

4. Bucharest. 1 December 1916–7 January 1917. Averescu, rallying the Rumanian troops, tried the only tactic open to him and struck at the gap between Mackensen and Falkenhayn. He was briefly successful, but the Germans threatened his rear and Rumanian morale broke. The Germans took Bucharest on 6 December. The remnants of the Rumanian army retreated behind the Sereth and Pruth Rivers where the Germans and Austrians were content to allow them to rot. A truce was signed on 6 December 1917. Rumania's adventure cost her 400,000 casualties and all her oil and grain production. German–Austrian casualties, 60,000.

Rumersheim (*War of Spanish Succession*) *26 August 1709*. Between the French (Villiers) and the British (Count Mercy). Mercy was forced to withdraw from Alsace and both armies moved west, towards Mons and Malplaquet, q.v.

Ruspina (*Wars of First Triumvirate*) *46 BC*. Titus Labienus, leading an army of Pompey the Great, surrounded Julius Caesar's three legions. With the Pompeian army wholly made up of archers and cavalry, Caesar's infantry were at a disadvantage, but he arranged them in a circle and attacked on a 360-degree "front". With this tactic he broke out and marched his legions towards Thapsus, q.v., in good order.

Russian Civil War *1918–20*. No important battle took place during this war between the Communists (Red) and the White Russians. It was won by the Communists largely by military manoeuvre, political intrigue, the uncoordinated efforts of the Whites, and the sympathy of the majority of Russians for the Red cause. An expeditionary force of American, British and French troops was sent to intervene against the Reds. They landed at Murmansk, north-west, in June 1918 and on 2 August their English commander, General Poole, occupied Archangel. This force was involved in sporadic fighting until withdrawn in November 1919. The White Russians (Yudenich) moved on Petrograd (Leningrad) in 1919, but were beaten back when 10 miles from the city. *See* Vyborg.

Rynemants (*Netherlands War of Independence*) *1 August 1578*. Between 20,000 Dutch Patriots (Count Bossu and Francois de la Noue) and 30,000 Spaniards (Don John of Austria). Don John crossed the Demer, and attacked Bossu in his trenches. He was repulsed, left 1,000 dead on the field, and fell back on Namur.

Saalfeld, *Thuringia (Napoleonic Wars: Auerstadt–Jena campaign)* *10 October 1806*. Prince Louis Frederick, with 9,000 Prussian–Saxon troops, found himself being enveloped by Marshal Lannes' corps of only 6,000 French and steadily crushed against the walls of Saalfeld. Prince Louis Frederick led a cavalry charge and died in the desperate fighting. The Prussians lost 3,000 men and all twenty guns while the French had only 200 casualties. *See* Austerlitz.

Sabine Cross-Roads — Pleasant Hill, *Louisiana (American Civil War)* *8–9 April 1864*. A Confederate force (Taylor) had retreated 200 miles, but now made a stand with 5,300 infantry and 3,000 cavalry. The Union commander, Banks, did not propose to attack Taylor at this point, but his advance guard became committed, and was driven back with heavy losses. Taylor pursued and next day, at Pleasant Hill, he over-confidently attacked the 12,500 Federal troops and was defeated. Casualties: Federals, 3,500; Confederates, 2,500. Both commanders were replaced. *See* Fort Pillow; Fort Hudson.

Sabis River, *northern Gaul (Rome's Gallic Wars)* *53 BC*. With only 7,000 soldiers, Julius Caesar hastened to rescue the Roman camps threatened by the marauding Nervii, led by Ambiorix. With an army of 60,000, Ambiorix met Caesar's force near the Sabis. Caesar feigned indecision, drew Ambiorix into a rash attack, and then counter-attacked. The Gauls broke and ran and Caesar then relieved Cicero, besieged by other Nervii forces. The Sabis River battle was a classic example of Caesar's audacious tactics. *See* Adnatuca.

Sablat *(Thirty Years' War)* *10 June 1619*. The German general Count von Mansfeld was leading his army of Protestant mercenaries from Pilsen (then Plzen) to Budweis. Near Sablat a large part of his force was cut off by a Catholic Bohemian army (Comte de Bucquoy). In a 7-hour fight Mansfeld lost 1,500 dead or captured and all his baggage. *See* Pilsen; White Mountain.

Sabugal *(Peninsular War)* *3 April 1811*. General Reynier held positions on the Coa River where he was attacked by three divisions under Lord Wellington. The British swiftly forced back the French, who lost about 1,500 men to the British 200. *See* Albuhera; Barrossa.

Sacile, *north-east Italy (Napoleonic Wars: Wagram campaign)* *16 April 1809*. Eugene Beauharnais, with a French–Italian army of 36,000, confronted Archduke John's 46,000 Austrians. In a mauling battle neither side won any advantage until Eugene withdrew to protect his line of retreat. Probably 6,000 men fell in the battle. *See* Abensberg; Raab.

Sackets Harbour, *Lake Ontario* *(British–American War of 1812)* *28–29 May 1813.* The Governor-General of Canada, Sir George Prevost, led an expeditionary force to assault the American fort at the eastern end of the lake. The 600-strong garrison (Jacob Brown) beat off the attack. *See* Queenston Heights; Stony Creek.

Sacramento River *(United States–Mexican War)* *28 February 1847.* Near Chihuahua, Colonel Alexander Doniphan, leading 900 Missouri mounted riflemen, confronted a much larger Mexican force. Doniphan's skilled sharpshooters killed or wounded 600 Mexicans and suffered only seven casualties themselves. Doniphan then marched his troops 2,000 miles south to link with the main American force in the west. *See* San Gabriel; San Pasqual.

Sacripontus *(Civil War of Marius and Sulla)* *82 BC.* Between the legions of Sulla and the army of the younger Marius, 40,000-strong. Sulla's veterans were too steady for the newer levies of Marius and routed them. Marius lost more than half his army killed or captured. Sulla occupied Rome.

Sadowa. *See* Köeniggratz.

Sadulapur *(Second British–Sikh War)* *3 December 1848.* After the failure of his suicidal attack on the Sikh position at Ramnugger (Ramnagar) in November, Lord Gough sent a force (Thackwell) to cross the Chenab and turn the Sikh left. The indecisive action which followed Lord Gough claimed as a victory. The Sikhs had retired, but only to take up a fresh position which Thackwell could not attack. *See* Chilianwala; Gujerat.

Sagunto *(Peninsular War)* *23 September–26 October 1811.* Held by a Spanish garrison, Sagunto was besieged by 22,000 French. Built on the heights above Murviedro, the place was access-ible on one side only and an attempt to scale it was repulsed, 28 September. A siege was commenced and a second unsuccessful assault was made, 18 October. A week later General Blake, with 30,000 Spaniards, attempted to relieve the place but was defeated with a loss of 1,000 killed or wounded and 5,000 prisoners. Victory for the French cost 800 men. The garrison surrendered next day.

Saguntum *(Second Punic War)* *219–218 BC.* The Carthaginians had agreed to stay south of the Ebro River while the Romans operated north of it. But in the southern section was the fort of Saguntum, manned by Iberians allied to Rome. Hannibal, his veteran Carthaginian force enlarged by Spanish recruits, attacked the place but was beaten off. It surrendered after an 8-month siege. This started the Second Punic War between Rome and Carthage and led that year to Hannibal's famous winter march across the Alps to attack the Romans in their own land. *See* Aegates Island; Trebbia River.

Saint Albans I *(Wars of the Roses)* *22 May 1455.* About 2,000 Lancastrians (red rose) under Henry VI were attacked in the town by 3,000 Yorkists (white rose) led by the Duke of York. York pierced the Lancastrian centre, and drove them out of St. Albans with heavy loss. Among the killed were the Earls of Somerset and Northumberland. This was the opening battle in the 30-year war. *See* Blore Heath.

Saint Albans II *(Wars of the Roses)* *17 February 1461.* Queen Margaret's army attacked the Yorkists, under Warwick. Warwick had withdrawn his main body, leaving his left unsupported to withstand the Lancastrian attacks. These troops, after a feeble resistance, broke and fled. Henry VI, who was a prisoner in Warwick's camp, escaped and rejoined his Queen, and a rapid advance on London would probably have led to his reinstatement. However, Henry marched north. *See* Ferrybridge; Mortimer's Cross; Wakefield.

Saint Aubin du Cormier, *Central France* (*The Princes War*) *May 1487*. Between the French Royal troops (La Tremouille) and the forces of the rebel Princes (Marshal de Rieux). The rebels were defeated, and a large number of nobles, including the Duc d'Orléans and the Prince of Orange, captured.

Saint Cast, *Brittany* (*Seven Years' War*) *4–10 September 1758*. A diversionary assault by the British to force the French to maintain large garrisons on the Channel Coast and prevent them from being used in the field. Admiral Howe landed an army (Bligh) at Saint Cast, but resistance, organized by the governor of Brittany, Duke d'Aiguillon, was stubborn and having lost 4,000 dead and 800 prisoners the British withdrew.

Saint Charles, *Quebec* (*French–Canadian Rising*) *16 September 1837*. Between the Loyalists (Colonel Wetherall) and the Canadian rebels, who were defeated. *See* Saint Eustache.

Saint Denis (*Second French Religious War*) *10 November 1567*. A narrow victory for the Catholics led by the Constable Montmorenci over the Protestant Huguenots of Prince de Condé. Montmorenci was killed. *See* Dreux; Jarnac.

Saint Denis, *Quebec* (*French–Canadian Rising*) *20 August 1837*. The Canadian rebels defeated a force of British and Canadian troops, but their own defeat the following month ended the war. *See* Saint Charles; Saint Eustache.

Saintes, Les (*American Revolution*) *1782*. *See* Dominica.

Saintes (*English–French Wars*) *21 July 1242*. Henry III of England, trying to win back lands lost during the reign of his father, John, landed at Saintonge, Bay of Biscay. His only real strength lay in his 750 crossbowmen. French help he had counted on did not arrive and Louis IX's army decisively defeated the Englishmen. Henry escaped, retreated into Gascony and abandoned the war. *See* Courtrai.

Saint Eustache, *Quebec* (*French–Canadian Rising*) *30 September 1837*. The rebels, under Paul Girod, were defeated by Government troops (Sir John Colborne). The rebellion was suppressed. *See* Saint Denis.

Saint George (*Turkey's Mediterranean Wars*) *October–December 1500*. Capital of the island of Cephalonia, Saint George was besieged by the Spaniards and Venetians under Gonsalvo de Cordova and Pesaro. The garrison of only 400 Turks resisted for 2 months. Then the attackers stormed from two directions and the eighty survivors surrendered. *See* Lepanto.

Saint Gothard Abbey, *also known as Raab, Hungary* (*Turkey's War against Hapsburg Hungary*) *1 August 1664*. Fazil Koprulu Pasha was making another attempt to advance on Vienna and crossed the Raab River to attack Count Montecuculli's army entrenched at Saint Gothard Abbey. They were beaten off with a loss of 8,000 men. The Austrians were in no state to pursue.

Saint Jacob an der Mirs (*or Saint Jacob-en-birs*) (*Swiss–French Wars*) *24 September 1444*. 15,000 Armagnacs (Orleanists), under the Dauphin, gave battle to 1,300 Confederate Swiss. The outnumbered Swiss fought with extraordinary courage, fierceness and discipline for an entire day, until the last man fell. The Armagnacs, however, had lost 2,000 killed, and the Dauphin abandoned the invasion of Switzerland. The Swiss performance enhanced their reputation for fearlessness. *See* Arbedo; Héricourt.

Saint Johns (*American Revolution*) 2 November 1775. Marching towards Montreal, the American General Richard Montgomery besieged this British fort and took it by storm. *See* Quebec III.

Saint Kitts, *West Indies* (*English–Dutch Wars*) 10 May 1667. Sir John Harman, with twelve frigates, met a Dutch–French fleet of twenty-two under Kruysen and la Barre, off St. Kitts. Despite his inferiority, Harman attacked and gained a notable victory, burning five and sinking several other enemy vessels. The allies took refuge in the harbour of St. Kitts. The English followed and destroyed the rest of the enemy fleet.

Saint-Lo, *Operation Cobra* (*World War II*) 25 July–8 August 1944. Despite great advances after the Normandy invasion, the Allies were stopped by von Kluge along a line from Caen to Lessay through Saint-Lo. The breakout was planned by Montgomery and Omar Bradley. Chronologically, the steps in the fierce battle were these:

25 July: Allied aircraft dropped 4,200 tons of bombs in an area 6,000 yards by 2,500, inflicting 558 American infantry casualties with misplaced bombs. The U.S. First Army (Lawton Collins) suffered 1,000 casualties in that day's attack.

26–27 July: Collins put in two mobile columns, one to contain violent German counter-attacks, the other to drive through German defences.

28 July: The Americans reached Avranches, creating a gap.

1 August: U.S. Third Army (Patton) exploited this gap. Some formations captured much of Brittany while others moved to cut off German Seventh Army (Hausser).

6 August: German armour counter-attacked towards Avranches in an effort to cut off Patton's army.

7–8 August: U.S. First Army blocked the German thrust in particularly heavy fighting.

8 August: Patton struck northward to Argentan, seriously threatening von Kluge's main army group, and ending the battle. The Germans, however, still held much of eastern Normandy. *See* D-Day; Falaise–Argentan Pocket.

Saint Lucia (*French Revolution*) 4 April 1794. This West Indian island was captured from the French by a British squadron under Sir John Jervis.

Saint Mary's Clyst (*Arundel's Rebellion*) 4 August 1549. Lord Russell, marching with the Royal army to the relief of Exeter, was attacked by 6,000 rebels. The rebels were defeated and lost 1,000 killed. Arundel was forced to raise the siege of Exeter.

Saint Mihiel (*World War I*) 12–13 September 1918. The Germans had held the Saint Mihiel salient south-east of Verdun since 1914. With the Allies now pressing hard along the Western Front, the Germans planned a withdrawal from the salient. But it could not get under way before the American First Army (Pershing) struck the salient, supported by French artillery and some French colonial infantry. Casualties: German, about 5,000 killed or wounded and 15,000 prisoners; American, 7,000. Foch moved Pershing's Americans to the Argonne Forest, q.v. *See* Amiens; Marne River II.

Saint Nazaire (*World War II*) 28 March 1942. The Germans, having occupied France, had turned the port of St. Nazaire, on the Loire River estuary, into a major naval base. At St. Nazaire existed the only dock facilities on the Atlantic coast of Europe big enough to take the German battleship *Tirpitz*. Also, St. Nazaire had fourteen U-boat pens with overhead cover impervious to aerial bombardment. A British commando and naval force, under the command of Lieutenant-Colonel A. C. Newman and Commander R. E. D. Ryder raided St. Nazaire. The raid, the first of its kind in World War II, was a success; the dock was not rebuilt even by the end of the war. Of the 611 British who took part in the

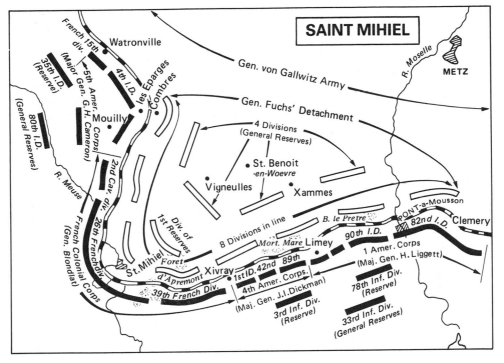

raid, 169 were killed and most of the others were taken prisoner; the Germans lost more than 200. *See* Dieppe.

Saint Privat (*French–Prussian War*). *See* Gravelotte.

Saint Quentin I, *Somme* (*Spanish–French Wars*) *10 August 1557*. Philip II of Spain sent an army of about 13,000 under the Flemish Comte d'Egmont into northern France because Henry II of France had seized three bishoprics — Toul, Metz, Verdun. A French army of 20,000 (Duke of Montmorency) hurried to block the Spanish army, but the French were intercepted in a cutting and lost 14,000 men killed, wounded or captured. *See* Calais; Gravelines; Pavia V.

Saint Quentin II (*French–German War*) *19 January 1871*. Between 40,000 French (General Faidherbe) and 33,000 Germans (Von Göben). The French, who had been trying to relieve besieged Paris, were decisively defeated, with a loss of 3,500 killed and wounded,

9,000 prisoners, and six guns. The Germans lost 96 officers and 2,304 men. *See* Bapaume; Le Mans.

Saint Thomas, *West Indies* (*Napoleonic Wars*) *21 December 1807*. This island was captured from the French by a combined British naval and military force under Admiral A. J. Cochrane and General Bowyer. They also took Saint Croix, without much opposition.

Saipan (*World War II*). *See* Mariana Islands.

Sakarya River (*Greek–Turkish War II*) *24 August–16 September 1921*. The Greeks, with Allied encouragement, had invaded Turkey to fight the Turkish nationalist movement led by Mustafa Kemal (Kemal Ataturk). After a temporary check at Ismet Pass the Greeks reached the Sakarya River where desperate fighting continued for 3 weeks before the Turks were victorious. Within a year the Greeks were pushed out of mainland Turkey. Mustafa Kemal became

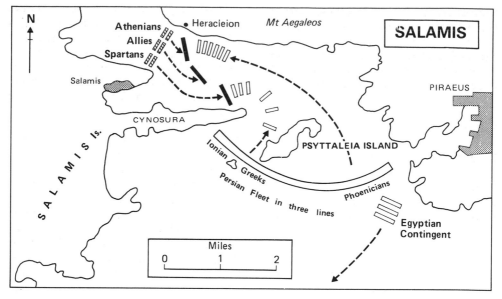

the first president of the Republic of Turkey on the abdication of Muhammad VI. Battle casualties are unreliable.

Salado (*Spanish–Muslim Wars*) 30 October 1344. Between the Portuguese and Castilians, under Alfonso IV of Portugal and Alfonso XI of Castile, and the Moors, under Abu Hamed, Emir of Morocco. The Christians won decisively.

Salamanca (*Peninsular War*) 22 July 1812. Wellington had captured the French-held fortresses of Ciudad Rodrigo and Badajoz and was now moving in northern Spain, manoeuvring for an advantage over the French army, also 40,000-strong, of Marshal Marmont. Marmont himself brought on the clash at Salamanca, but he was seriously wounded and Clausel assumed command. The French were badly mauled, suffering 12,000 casualties before Clausel could withdraw his army. Wellington, who lost 5,000 men, marched for Madrid, but French pressure pushed him back to the Portuguese frontier. *See* Badajoz; Vittoria.

Salamanca, Mexico (*Mexican Liberals' Rebellion*) 10–11 March 1858. Between the Government troops (Mira-

mon) and the Liberals under Doblado. Doblado's levies could not face Miramon's trained troops and were routed.

Salamis I (*Persian–Greek Wars*) 480 BC. Xerxes and his Persian invading army had conquered much of Greece and in the Saronic Gulf his great navy of 1,000 galleys bottled up the 370 Greek triremes. The Greek commander Themistocles then lured the Persian ships into the cramped waters of Salamis, where they could not readily manoeuvre. The Spartan Eurybiades led spirited Greek attacks against the Persian galleys. By ramming some and boarding others, the Greeks sank 300 Persian ships and lost only forty of their own. The rest of the enemy fleet was scattered. Xerxes and his army watched the battle from the shore. The year-long delay imposed on Xerxes by this naval defeat gave the Greek city-states time to unite against him. This was the first great naval battle recorded. *See* Mycale; Plataea I; Thermopylae I.

Salamis II (*Wars of Alexander's Successors*) 307 BC. The Macedonian fleet (Demetrius Poliorcetes) defeated the Egyptians (Ptolemy Soter), who had 100 ships captured and the rest sunk.

Salankemen (*Turkish–Austrian Wars*) *19 August 1691*. Between 100,000 Turks (the Grand Vizier, Mustapha Köpriali) and 45,000 Austrians under the Margrave Louis. The Turks were defeated and Köpriali slain.

Salano (*Spanish–Muslim Wars*) *1340*. Between the Spaniards (Alfonso XI of Castile) and the Moors led by Abu Hasan of Granada, who were besieging Tarifa. They were attacked by the Spaniards, who were commanded personally by Alfonso XI. Abu Hasan fled to Africa and Alfonso recovered Algeciras.

Saldanha Bay, *Cape of Good Hope* (*French Revolution*) *17 August 1796*. Admiral Elphinstone's British squadron captured a Dutch warship in the harbour, then landed a force which captured the fort.

Salerno, *Operation Avalanche* (*World War II*) *9–16 September 1943*. The Allies wanted the key port of Naples and the first step was the capture of Salerno. The Allied Fifth Army (Mark Clark, U.S.) made the amphibious assault with the U.S. VI Corps (Dawley, later Lucas) on the right and the British X Corps (McCreery) on the left or north. Initial advances were good, but on 12 September the Germans mounted a violent counter-attack which recaptured most of their lost ground. Allied warships and bombers pounded German positions; Alexander, commanding Allied ground troops in Italy, hurried support divisions into the battle. By the night of 15 September the German supreme commander, Kesselring, began to pull back his now vulnerable units. Salerno became secure with the arrival next day of the British Eighth Army (Montgomery) from the campaign in southern Italy. Breaking out of the Salerno beachhead, American forces took Naples on 1 October.

Salo. *See* Castiglione.

Salonika I (*Turkish–Venetian Wars*) *1 March 1430*. A victory for the Turks (Murad II) in capturing the fortress of Salonika, giving them access to the Vardar Valley and thus into Europe. The Venetian garrison of 1,500 was overwhelmed, to be butchered or sold into slavery. *See* Angora; Varna I.

Salonika II (*World War I*) *3 December 1915–29 September 1918*. A British and a French division were moved from Salonika towards Serbia, but the armies of the Central Powers were too strong. Serbia fell and the Allies withdrew to Salonika which soon became choked with troops, who labelled it the "Bird Cage". The front erupted occasionally, as when the French commander (Sarrail) mounted an offensive by British, French, Russian, Italian and Serbian troops which took Bitolj (Monastir). This cost 60,000 dead and wounded. In December 1917 another French general, Guillaumat, took over in Salonika, then, in July 1918, d'Esperey. The Allied army now numbered 375,000. The final battle began on 17 September 1918, when the Bulgarians were overwhelmed and the Allied troops rolled through the Balkans. By holding on to Salonika for so long the Allies merely tied up men and supplies they needed elsewhere. Disease caused great losses; the British had 481,000 cases of illness, 18,000 wounded. *See* Serbia.

Salt River, *Arizona* (*Apache Wars*) *26 December 1872*. In a canyon on Salt River Colonel George Crook destroyed a force of outlaw Apaches, the survivors being returned to their reservations. Further hostilities in 1885 ended when the Apache chief, Geronimo, surrendered.

Samaghar, *near Agra* (*Rebellion of Aurungzebe*) *June 1658*. Between the army of the Great Mogul, Shah Jehan, under Dara, and the forces of his rebellious sons, Aurungzebe and Marad. Dara was defeated, and his army dispersed; 3

days later the rebels occupied Agra. Shah Jehan was imprisoned (and later killed) and Aurungzebe seized the crown.

Samaria (*Fall of Israel*) 724–722 BC. At this time Israel was a kingdom in northern Palestine. When King Hoshea withheld the traditional monetary tribute to Assyria, Shalmaneser V besieged Israel's capital, Samaria, 36 miles north-west of Jerusalem. The inhabitants held out for more than 2 years. Then Sargon II, successor to Shalmaneser, stormed and sacked Samaria. Hoshea and about 30,000 others were exiled to Media. *See* Jerusalem; Nineveh I.

Samarkand (*Mongol invasion of Central Asia*) June 1220. Defended by 110,000 Turks and Kharismians, under the Governor Alub Khan, Samarkand was besieged by the Mongols under Genghis Khan. The garrison harassed the Mongols by numerous sorties and the Mongols made little progress, but some inhabitants, hoping to save the city from pillage, opened the gates. After heroic efforts to defend the city, Alub Khan cut his way out at the head of 1,000 picked horsemen. The 30,000 survivors of the garrison were butchered. *See* Bukhara; Herat I; Khojend.

Sambre River (*Caesar's Gallic Wars*) 57 BC. Several Gallic tribes, headed by the Nervii, resisted further Roman advances into what is now northern France and Belgium. Caesar, holding the south bank of the Sambre, sent cavalry to reconnoitre the Gauls' positions. The Gauls put the Roman horsemen to flight and then 50,000 crossed the Sambre. The Roman left and centre held firm, but the onslaught so shook the legions on the right that they faced destruction. Caesar took personal charge of the fight, rallied his legionaries and counter-attacked the Gauls. Fewer than 600 survived. A second battle was fought near Namur, where Caesar defeated the Aduatuci tribe. When the Aduatucis feigned surrender the Romans killed 4,000 and sold many others into slavery. *See* Morbihan Gulf; Vesontio.

Samosata, *Upper Euphrates River* (*Byzantine–Muslim Wars*) May 873. This victory by the Byzantine army of Basil I of Macedonia over the Muslims was the beginning of a Byzantine military resurgence.

Sampford Courtney (*Arundel's Rebellion*) 17 August 1549. The final battle with the rebels when Arundel was defeated by the Royal troops (Lord Russell) with a loss of 700 killed and many prisoners.

Sand Creek, *Colorado* (*Cheyenne and Arapahoe War*) 29 November 1864. More a massacre than a battle. Militia colonel Colonel J. M. Chivington, an Indian-hater, led 900 men against an Indian village, many of whose leading warriors were absent on peace talks with the U.S. government. Chivington's men, all militia or irregulars, killed 300 Indians including 225 women and children. Not surprisingly, the Plains Indians embarked on a long, ruthless war against the Army and the white settlers.

Sandwich I, *Kent* (*First Barons' War*) 24 August 1217. English Royalist ships (Hubert de Burgh) intercepted a French fleet (Eustace the Monk) bringing aid to the rebel barons. The troopships escaped, but the supply ships were captured, also Eustace, who was immediately executed.

Sandwich II (*Wars of the Roses*) 20 June 1460. The Earl of Warwick, arriving from France with his Yorkist (white rose) army, defeated the Lancastrians confronting him. This "cancelled" the Yorkist defeat at Ludford the previous year and Warwick marched north-west. *See* Ludford; Northampton II.

San Gabriel (*United States–Mexican War*) 9 January 1847. Brigadier General Stephen Kearny, having established control over New Mexico, went on to south-eastern California and after a battle at San Pasqual marched on, with a combined army–naval force, to San Gabriel. Here he defeated the main Mexican force covering Los Angeles. This ended Mexican–Californian resistance to the Americans' western campaign. *See* Sacramento River; San Pasqual.

San Giovanni (*French Revolutionary Wars*) *17 June 1799*. Between the French (Macdonald) and the Russians (Suvarov). After 3 days the French retreated, having lost 6,000 killed and wounded and 9,000 prisoners. The Russian losses were about 6,000. *See* Marengo.

San Isidoro (*War of the Triple Alliance or Lopez War*) *10 April 1870*. Between the Paraguayans (Lopez) and the allied army of Brazil, Argentina and Uruguay, under General Camera. Camera attacked Lopez's entrenchments and drove him into the mountains with the few survivors of his troops. *See* Aquidaban; Parana.

San Jacinto River I (*Texan War of Independence*) *2 April 1836*. The 1,200-strong Mexican army of Santa Anna was routed and almost destroyed by a smaller force of Texans (General Houston). The survivors, with Santa Anna and his staff, were taken prisoner. Santa Anna, who had stormed the Alamo the previous month, recognized Texan independence. *See* Alamo; Fort Texas.

San Jacinto River II (*Maximilian's War in Mexico*) *12 February 1867*. Between the followers of the Emperor Maximilian, under Miramon, and the Mexican Constitutionalists, under Escobedo. Miramon was defeated and his army surrendered; Miramon himself escaped. *See* Puebla.

San Juan Hill (*Spanish–American War*) *1–3 July 1898*. The Americans (Shafter and Lawton) were moving on Santiago de Cuba, the major assault being against San Juan Hill where the Spanish (Linares) had 10,400 troops. A smaller American attack against El Caney, q.v., was checked for a day, thus keeping 6,500 Americans out of the major fight. Shafter put 8,400 into the attack on San Juan and 1,572 became casualties before the Spaniards were dislodged. The whole campaign swung the Americans' way when the U.S. fleet (Sampson) destroyed the Spanish fleet outside Santiago on 3 July. *See* Las Guásimas; Manila II; Santiago de Cuba I.

San Lazaro (*War of Austrian Succession*) *14 June 1746*. Between 40,000 Austrians (Prince Lichtenstein) and the French and Spaniards (Marshal Maillebois). The allies attacked the Austrian entrenched camp, and after a bitter 9-hour conflict were repulsed with a loss of 10,000 killed and wounded. *See* Roucoux.

Sanna's Post (*or Kornspruit*) (*Second British–Boer War*) *31 March 1900*. A British force of cavalry and artillery with a large convoy (Colonel Broadwood) was ambushed by Boers (De Wet) while crossing a donga. Broadwood extricated his force at a cost of nineteen officers and 136 men killed or wounded, 426 prisoners, seven guns and the whole of his convoy. *See* Vaalkranz.

San Pasqual, *near San Diego* (*U.S.–Mexican War*) *6 December 1846*. The U.S. "Army of the West" (Colonel Kearny) defeated a Mexican–Californian force blocking the way into the California region. California became part of the United States in the treaty which ended the war in 1848. *See* Buena Vista; Chihuahua; Monterrey.

San Sebastian I (*Peninsular War*) *10 July–9 September 1813*. The town was besieged by the British (Graham) and was defended by a French garrison (Rey). An assault on 25 July was repulsed. Graham sent to England for heavy guns and the siege turned into a blockade. Operations were resumed and on 31 July the town was taken by storm. Rey still held out in the citadel, but after bombardment surrendered on 9 September. The British lost 2,500 killed or wounded. *See* Nivelle; Vittoria.

San Sebastian II (*First Carlist War*) *February–June 1836*. The Carlists, under Sagastibelza, besieged the fortress, which was defended by a Cristinos garrison. About 250 men of the British Legion led by Colonel Wylde was moved from outpost to outpost to repel Carlist attacks. The besiegers were driven off by an army of 10,000 Spanish and British troops under General Evans. *See* Huesca.

Sant 'Angelo (*German invasion of Italy*) *September 998*. The Roman Duke Crescantius had deposed Pope Gregory V — the first German Pope — and installed John XVI. The German Emperor Otto III drove the duke and his forces into their castle on the Garigliano River near Cassino. He took the place by storm, executed Crescentius and restored Gregory. *See* Crotone; Rome.

Santa Clara-Santiago (*Castro's Cuban Revolt*) *28 December 1958–1 January 1959*. Castro forces (Guevara and Cienfuegos) surrounded Santa Clara then captured it as part of Castro's plan to cut Cuba in two. Fidel Castro and his brother Raul took Santiago from the army of Batista, the dictator, 2 January. By 8 January Castro held the whole of Cuba, q.v.

Santa Cruz de Tenerife (*English–Spanish Wars*) *20 April 1657*. Admiral of the Commonwealth Robert Blake sailed a fleet into the Canary Islands, attacked a Spanish fleet of sixteen ships defending the strongly fortified city of Santa Cruz and sank every one of them. Then he destroyed the city. Blake lost one ship and fifty seamen in this, his last battle. *See* Jamaica; The Dunes.

Santa Cruz Islands (*World War II*)

25–26 October 1942. This naval battle took place when two small American task forces (Rear Admirals Lee and Kinkaid) tried to stop a Japanese fleet of five aircraft carriers, two battleships and thirty-six destroyers (Admiral Nagumo) from reaching Guadalcanal, Philippines. The Americans lost the carrier *Hornet* but put out of action two Japanese ships. Victory went to the Japanese, but they had lost many pilots in the air battles above the fleet. *See* Coral Sea; Midway.

Santa Lucia (*Rio Grande or Brazilian Rising*) *September 1842*. Between the Brazilian Government troops (Caxias) and 6,000 rebels (Feliciano) who were defeated.

Santander, *Bay of Biscay* (*Spanish Civil War*) *14–15 August 1937*. Santander was held by 50,000 poorly trained and armed Republicans (Ulíbarri). They fell back before the onslaught of the Nationalist Army of the North (Dávila) and suffered heavily under air and artillery bombardment. Most of the Basque Republicans surrendered to the Italian General Bastico, 23 August, and Dávila occupied Santander. *See* Bilbao; Saragossa III.

Santarem I, *on the Tagus* (*Portuguese–Muslim Wars*) *1171 (month unknown)*. In his long campaign to drive out the Moors, Alfonso I fought the enemy out of their stronghold of Santarem and brought in Christian settlers. The Muslims tried to retake Santarem in 1184 but were beaten back. *See* Lisbon.

Santarem II (*Portuguese Civil War*) *18 February 1834*. Portuguese Government troops, under Marshal Saldanha, defeated the "Miguelists", under Dom Miguel.

Santa Vittoria (*War of Spanish Succession*) *26 July 1702*. Four regiments of Prince Eugene's Austrian army, under General Visconti, were attacked by

15,000 French and Spaniards led by the Duc de Vendome. The Austrians abandoned their camp and baggage. They lost 500 men, while the Allies' "victory" cost them nearly 2,000 killed or wounded. *See* Landau; Luzzara; Saragossa II.

Santiago de Cuba (*Spanish–American War*) 3 July 1898. The Spanish fleet of four cruisers and three destroyers (Cervera) was trapped in the harbour of Santiago de Cuba, where the Americans (Sampson) blockaded them. Trying to break out, 3 July, the Spanish ships were forced to run the gauntlet of the American fleet's guns; all were sunk or ran ashore in flames. Casualties: American, three; Spanish, 323 killed, 151 wounded, 1,813 captured. *See* El Caney; Las Guasimas; Manila II; San Juan Hill.

Sapienza (*Turkey's Wars in the Mediterranean*) May 1490. Between the Turkish fleet (Kemal Reis) and the Venetians; the Venetians lost most of their 90 ships. This was the first naval victory of the Turks in the Mediterranean. *See* Lepanto; Rhodes.

Saragossa I (*Spanish–Muslim Wars*) October 1118. Striking out from Huesca, capital of Aragon and Navarre, Alfonso I took a bold step against the Muslims, storming and capturing Saragossa. It became the Aragonese capital. *See* Alarcos; Huesca.

Saragossa II, *Ebro River* (*War of Spanish Succession*) 20 August 1700. Between 25,000 Spaniards and a force of Austrians, British, Dutch and Portuguese troops, 23,000 in all, under the Archduke Charles of Austria. The Portuguese on the right wing gave way, leading a large force of Spaniards in pursuit, but the left and centre stood their ground and finally repulsed the enemy. The Spaniards lost 4,000 prisoners, besides killed and wounded.

Saragossa III (*Napoleonic Wars*) June–July 1808, December 1808–20 February 1809. Having induced Charles IV into abdicating the Spanish throne, Napoleon made his brother, Joseph, King of Spain. Saragossa refused to accept Joseph and the French (Lefébvre) laid siege. A French defeat at Bailén forced Levébvre to raise the siege, but in December the French returned, this time under Moncey and Mortier. The Spanish garrison (Palafox y Melzi) resisted gallantly under great privations. A notable defender was the Maid of Saragossa, whose part-legendary exploits in taking her wounded lover's place on the ramparts are described in Byron's *Childe Harold*. Lannés took command of the siege in January and on 20 February French troops stormed and captured the city. *See* Bailén.

Saragossa IV (*Spanish Civil War*) 24 August–27 September 1937. The Republican Army of the East (Pozas) advanced on a wide front from the French border and had some initial gains along the Ebro. The area Nationalist commander, Ponte, outmanoeuvred his opponent along a line from Huesca through Saragossa to Teruel. The Republican attack, having cost 70,000 casualties, faltered to a stop. The Nationalists lost 30,000 killed or wounded. *See* Gijón; Santander.

Saratoga (*American Revolution*) 19 September and 9 October 1777. En route to Albany, N.Y., a British army of 6,000 (Burgoyne) encountered an American army entrenched on Bemis Heights, south of Saratoga. The American commander, Gates, had 7,200 troops and a steady flow of reinforcements. Burgoyne sent 2,000 troops (Fraser) to outflank the American left commanded by Benedict Arnold, but in fierce fighting around Freeman's Farm they were driven back. The British had 600 casualties, the Americans 320.

Burgoyne was in a desperate position. On 7 October he sent Fraser with 1,700 picked men to make a reconnaissance in force against the American left and if possible to turn it. But the Americans were too strong; they not only drove back the British but then launched a spirited counter-attack under Benedict Arnold. Their capture of a key redoubt exposed Burgoyne's left flank and forced him to withdraw 8 miles to Saratoga Heights. Here, by 13 October, the British were surrounded. Burgoyne surrendered on 17 October and 5,728 men laid down their arms. This victory was decisive. It encouraged the Americans and it drew France, then Spain and Holland, into the war on the Americans' side.

The second phase of the battle has various labels: Bemis Heights; second battle of Freeman's Farm; Stillwater. *See* Bennington; Fort Ticonderoga III.

Sardis I (*Persian conquest of Lydia*) *546 BC*. Cyrus the Great, with 20,000 men, invaded Lydia, Asia Minor, the kingdom of Croesus, and after a winter march surprised his enemy outside the walls of Sardis, the Lydian capital. Cyrus' brilliantly coordinated attack by armoured spearmen, javelin throwers and archers demoralized the Lydians and the survivors ran into the fortress. After a short siege Cyrus got his men through breaches in the walls and captured the city. Lydia ceased to exist as a kingdom. *See* Babylon; Tyre I.

Sardis II (*War of Alexander's Successors*) *280 BC*. Between the troops of Pergamus, under Eumenes, and the Syrians, under Antigonus Soter. After his decisive victory Eumenes annexed a large part of the dominions of Antigonus. *See* Sentinum.

Sárkány (*Hungarian Rising against Austria*) *30 December 1848*. Between the Austrians (Windischgrätz) and the Hungarians (Perczel). Perczel had been ordered to hold the Sárkány defile, but when attacked by the Austrians, his division performed poorly and fled. The whole Hungarian line had to fall back. *See* Kapolna; Schwechat.

Sarikamis, *Caucasus* (*World War I*) *29 December 1914–2 January 1915*. The Turkish General Ahmet Pasa, with 95,000 troops, cleverly drew the Russian army of the Caucasus away from its bases so as to destroy it in the icy wastes of Asia Minor. But when he fell on the 60,000 Russians under Myshlayevski at Sarikamis, they defeated him so badly that in 5 days' fighting and a 14-day retreat the Turks lost 77,000 men. Two lesser conflicts occurred on this front, the Russians losing at Malazgirt (formerly Manzikert) 22 October 1915, and winning at Karakilisse, 2 November. *See* Erzerum-Erzincan.

Sarmizegetusa (*Dacian Wars of the Roman Empire*) *June 102 and summer 105*. The Emperor Trajan took seven legions across the Danube to quell the revolt by the Dacians (Decebalus). North of the Danube's "Iron Gate" the disciplined, veteran legions ground the Dacians to defeat in a fierce battle. Decebalus made peace, but rebuilt his army and it became a threat to Rome. Trajan this time fought his way to Sarmizetetusa, the Dacian capital. His country broken, Decebalus committed suicide. Dacia became a Roman province.

Sasbach (*Dutch War of Louis XIV*) *27 July 1675*. The last battle of the great French commander, Marshal Turenne. By clever manoeuvring, Turenne trapped his old enemy, Count Montecuccoli, commander of the army of Leopold I's Holy Roman Empire. In a hopeless position east of the Rhine near the Swiss border the Austrians faced annihilation, but when a cannon ball killed Turenne his generals lost control of the situation. French casualties were only half those of the Austrians, but they were driven back to Alsace. Montecuccoli vigorously pursued and Louis called the elderly Great Condé from retirement to check the threatened invasion. Condé drove back the Imperials, but the loss of Turenne was irreparable. *See* Mons I; Stromboli; Turckheim.

Sattelberg, *New Guinea (World War II)* *17–25 November 1943.* A major action of the Australian Finschhafen campaign against the Japanese. The natural defensive position, 2,400 ft high, was so strongly defended that orders were given, 24 November, to break off the action. However, on the very narrow front, a single Australian NCO, Sergeant T. Derrick, led an attack which opened the way to the summit and won the battle for the Australians (Brigadier Whitehead). Casualties: Australians, 167; Japanese, about 500. *See* Lae; Wau.

Sauchie Burn (*Rebellion of the Barons***)** *18 June 1488.* Between the rebel barons, under Angus "Bell-the-Cat", and the troops of James III of Scotland, under the king. The royal army was defeated and James slain.

Saucourt (*Norse invasion of France***)** *861.* Between the Neustrians, under Louis III, and the invading Norsemen. Louis gained a decisive victory.

Sauroren, *Pyrenees (Peninsular War)* *28 and 30 July 1813.* Soult, with 25,000 troops, confronted Wellington, with 12,000 British. Soult tried to turn the British left to drive them from a strong position, but after severe fighting he was repulsed with a loss of 3,000. British losses, 2,600. Soult renewed his attack on 30 July, but was again repulsed, with a loss of 2,000 killed or wounded and 3,000 prisoners. British losses, 1,900. *See* Nive; Nivelle; Pyrenees.

Savandroog (*Second British–Mysore War***)** *10 December 1791.* This fort, with a Mysore garrison of more than 3,500, was considered impregnable. With 4,000 troops Lord Cornwallis besieged it on 10 December, breached the walls a week later and stormed it on 21 December. The British did not lose a single soldier. *See* Seringapatam.

Savannah I (*American Revolution***)** *29 December 1778.* A force of 3,500 British troops (Colonel A. Campbell) landed at the mouth of the Savannah River and moved towards Savannah itself. The American general Robert Howe with 850 soldiers marched to meet the threat, but the British found a track through swampland and Campbell attacked the American front and rear. Routed, the Americans lost 83 killed or drowned, 453 captured, 50 guns and 23 mortars. British casualties, 13. Campbell occupied Savannah. *See* Charleston I; Port Royal Island.

Savannah II (*American Revolution***)** *16 September–9 October 1799.* Savannah was held by a garrison of 3,200 British regulars and American Loyalists (General Prevost). The city was besieged by an allied force of 3,500 French soldiers, 1,350 Americans and the 200-strong legion of Count Pulaski, The overall American commander, Benjamin Lincoln, could make little progress. He followed a 5-day bombardment with an infantry attack, 9 October, but lost 244 killed and 584 wounded and was beaten back. British casualties, 155. The French troops re-embarked for France and the Americans raised the siege. *See* Briar Creek; Charleston II.

Savannah III (*American Civil War***)** *November–December 1864.* This was William Sherman's famous "march to the sea"; the label of "the battle of Savannah" is misleading. Sherman, with 62,000 troops, left Atlanta on 15 November for Savannah, 225 miles away. He systematically destroyed all railroads and resources along a marching front of 60 miles. Despite harassing flank and rear attacks by Confederate cavalry (Wheeler) Sherman reached Savannah 10 December. The city (Hardee) refused to surrender, but Confederate troops abandoned it when Sherman brought in siege guns from the Federal fleet. *See* Atlanta.

Savo Island (*World War II*). *See* Guadalcanal.

Saxa Rubra (*Revolt of Maxentius*) 28 October 312. Between the Roman Imperial troops, under Emperor Constantine, and the rebel legions of Maxentius, pretender to the throne of the Roman Empire. Maxentius' cavalry on the wings was routed by Constantine's cavalry; the infantry, left unsupported, fled. Only Maxentius' guard resisted and died where they stood. *See* Heraclea.

Scarlet Beach, *New Guinea (World War II)* **22 December–9 October 1943.** An almost continuous and bitter 18-day battle between Australian (Wootten) and Japanese (Katagiri) troops. The Australians captured Finschhafen, 2 October, but the Japanese launched a violent counter-attack against Scarlet Beach, where the Australians had landed. They were eventually driven off into the forested hills, having lost 1,000 men. *See* Finschafen; Lae; Wau.

Scarpheia (*War of the Achaean League*) 146 BC. Between the Romans (Metellus) and the Achaeans (Critolaus). The Greeks were defeated with heavy loss, Critolaus being killed.

Scheveningen (*First English–Dutch War*) 31 July 1653. A narrow victory for the English fleet of 75 ships (Monck and Graves) over the 100 Dutch ships (Marten Tromp). Tromp was killed and Evertzen, assuming command, drew off in the darkness after losing ten ships. *See* Beachy Head; Kentish Knock; Portland.

Schoneveldt (*Third English–Dutch War*) 7 June and 14 June 1673. An English fleet of 54 ships (Prince Rupert of the Rhine) combined with a French one of 27 ships (Comte d'Estrées) to destroy the Dutch fleet and permit a landing. Off Schoneveldt the Dutch — 55 ships under

the great de Ruyter — checked the allied force in two separate engagements, forcing the English and French to return for refits. *See* Southwold Bay; Texel II.

Schwechat (*Hungarian Rising against the Austrians*) 30 October 1848. A rebel force, led by General Moga, marched on Vienna. In the suburb of Schwechat they stood up bravely but ineffectually to Austrian regulars and suffered heavy casualties. General Windischgrätz, having defeated these levies, next day bombed into submission the revolutionaries who had erected barricades. *See* Kopolná.

Scio (*or Chios*) Island, Aegean (*Turkish–Russian Wars*) 5 July 1769. Having stalked each other for weeks, a Russian fleet of ten ships (Admiral Spiritov) and seventeen Turkish ships under Grand Admiral, came to battle. Both flagships blew up, but Russian seamanship was good and the Turks were forced into the bay of Ceşme. Two days later Russian fire-ships destroyed the enemy fleet.

Sebastopol (*Crimean War*) 17 October 1854–11 September 1855. Victorious at the Alma River (q.v.) the British (Raglan) and French (St. Arnaud) laid siege to the great fortress of Sebastopol. With too few men for encirclement, the allies opened an artillery bombardment that continued for nearly a year. The Russian commander, Menshikov, was ably assisted by the able military engineer, Todleben. Throughout the bitter winter the allied armies suffered great losses through exposure and hunger and from lack of co-operation between British and French commanders. Canrobert succeeded St. Arnaud, then Pelissier commanded the French. His attack on the Malakoff, a key fortification, failed on 18 June, as did the British assault on the Redan, but the allied bombardment inflicted terrible losses on the Russians. Raglan died and was succeeded by Simpson. On 8 September the French stormed and held the Malakoff, though the second British assault on the Redan failed. But the loss of the Malakoff made Sebastopol untenable and Prince Mikhail Gorchakov abandoned it, thus virtually ending the war. Russian losses, about 75,000; British, 11,000; French, 12,000. *See* Alma; Balaclava; Inkerman.

Sebastopol (*World War II*) *May–July 1942*. On 8 May the Germans launched a major offensive to capture the Kerch peninsula and Sebastopol, the only Russian centres holding out in the Crimea. Repeated dive-bomber attacks broke Russian resistance at Kerch and 100,000 men surrendered. The Russian commander in Sebastopol, General Vlasov, went on the offensive outside the Sebastopol defences, but after 5 days' fighting his troops were encircled and captured. Sebastopol held out until General Manstein's Eleventh Army captured it, on 5 July, after a months' incessant fighting. The Russians suffered 80,000 battle casualties. *See* Caucasus; Crimea.

Sebastopolis (*or Phasis*) (*Muslim invasions*) *692*. After the Byzantine naval victories against the Muslims, the Arabs agreed in 679 to keep the peace for 30 years. In 692 they provoked the land battle of Sebastopolis in which the fast-moving Arabs routed the steadier but less adaptable Byzantines. The Muslim victory gave the Arabs Armenia and the last remaining Byzantine strongholds east of the Taurus River. *See* Constantinople III; Cyzicus.

Secchia, *The* (*War of Polish Throne*) *14 September 1734*. The Austrian Imperialists, under Count Königsegg, surprised the camp of the French army (de Broglie), capturing 5,000 prisoners, 100 guns and all stores, baggage and ammunition. *See* Parma; Philippsburg.

Secessionville (*American Civil War*) *15 June 1862*. 6,000 Federals (Benham) attacked the strong position of Secessionville, blocking the road to Charleston, held by 2,000 Confederates (Evans). The Federals were repulsed. Casualties: Federals, 600; Confederates, 200. *See* Seven Days Battle.

Secunderbagh (*Indian Mutiny against the British*) *16 November 1857*. An action during the second relief of Lucknow, by Sir Colin Campbell. The Secunderbagh, a walled enclosure, was held by rebels. After a bombardment it was taken by storm by Scottish and loyalist Indian troops. *See* Cawnpore.

Sedan (*French–Prussian War*) *1 September 1870*. After Marshal Bazaine had withdrawn 170,000 French troops into Metz, where the Prussians bottled them up, the only French field army was that of MacMahon. Napoleon III took command of this army of 130,000 and marched to relieve Metz. On 29 August a Prussian manoeuvre deflected the French who moved into Sedan, a border fortress. Here the Prussians, directed by Moltke, trapped them, with armies converging from north and south. Crown Prince Frederick William with the Prussian Third Army was recalled from a march on Paris to aid in the encirclement. On 1 September the French tried violently to break out, inflicting 9,000 casualties on the Prussians. But the enemy grip was relentless; the French lost 3,000 killed, 14,000 wounded and 20,000 prisoners. Napoleon and MacMahon surrendered and next day the surviving 82,000 French troops gave in. This overwhelming defeat opened the way to Paris. *See* Metz; Paris II.

Sedgemoor (*Monmouth's Rebellion against James II*) *5 July 1685*. Between the Royal troops (Earl of Faversham) and the rebels, under James, Duke of Monmouth. Monmouth attempted a night attack on Faversham's camp, but Royal troops, led by John Churchill (later Duke of Marlborough), put Monmouth's cavalry to flight. His infantry fought stubbornly, but they were overpowered and routed with heavy loss. This defeat ended the rebellion. Monmouth was executed. Sedgemoor was the last military ground action in England. *See* Bothwell Bridge; Londonderry.

Segesvár (*Hungarian Rising against Austria*) *31 July 1849*. The Russians, who were allies of the Austrians, joined in the onslaught against the rebellious patriotic Hungarians. General Josef Bem, a Pole in Hungarian service, had done well, but now he and his Hungarians were defeated by a converging Austrian army (General Haynau) and a Russian army (General Paskiewich). The rising was coming to an end. *See* Temesvár.

Segikahara, *Japan* (*Mitsunori Rebellion*) *16 September 1600*. 80,000 troops of the Shogun Tokugawa Tyeyasa routed 130,000 rebels under Mitsunori, who was among the dead.

Seine Mouth (*Hundred Years' War*) *15 August 1416*. The English fleet (Bedford) sailed into the Seine to supply Harfleur, which the French were besieging. The blockading force of eight large carracks and smaller vessels attacked the English fleet. After 6 hours' hard fighting the French were defeated, losing ten ships.

Selby, Yorkshire (*English Civil War*) *11 April 1644*. The Marquis of Newcastle, acting for Charles I, sent Lord Belasyse to block the northward approach of a Roundhead army under Lord Fairfax and his son, Sir Thomas. The Roundhead leaders attacked first, at Selby south of York, and the incompetent Belasyse lost more than 1,000 men and all his artillery and baggage. *See* Adwalton Moor; Marston Moor.

Selinus (*Second Carthaginian invasion of Sicily*) *409 BC*. This city was besieged by 100,000 Carthaginians under Hannibal (not the Punic Wars Hannibal). A relief attempt by the Syracusans, under Diocles, came too late. After resisting stubbornly for 9 days, the garrison, hopelessly outnumbered, was overpowered. The place was stormed and sacked. All the survivors were sold as slaves. *See* Himera; Syracuse II.

Sellasia, *Sparta* (*Wars of the Hellenistic Monarchies*) *221 BC*. The leader of the Achaean League — twelve cities of the northern Peloponnese — appealed to Macedonia for help against the Spartan king, Cleomenes III. The 10,000-strong Macedonian phalanx, with Achaean troops, defeated the hard-fighting Spartans and Cleomenese fled. But Antigonus of Macedonia then occupied the Pelopponese and formed the Hellenic League.

Seminara (*French–Spanish Wars in Italy*) *October 1495*. 6,000 Spaniards and Neapolitans (Gonsalvo de Cordova and Ferdinand of Naples) attacked a much larger French army (D'Aubigny). The Neapolitans fled and though the Spaniards fought well they were overpowered and routed. Only Cordova with 400 Spanish cavalry made an orderly retreat. *See* Cerignola; Garigliano.

Sempach (*Swiss–Swabian War*) *9 July 1386*. One of the most interesting battles of history. Leopold III of Swabia, leading 6,000 Austrians, anticipated a victory over 1,600 Swiss pikemen. The Austrian heavy cavalry, several times bloodily defeated by Swiss pikemen when charging, dismounted and advanced across the mountain fields as armoured pikemen. The Swiss drew the heavily clad Austrians on, tiring them. When gaps appeared in the line, the Swiss counterattacked. Leopold's army disintegrated. (According to legend, Arnold Winkelried created the first gap by grasping several Austrian pikes and plunging them into his breast. His comrades then darted through the gap.) *See* Laupen; Morgarten; Nafëls.

Seneffe, *near Nivelles* (*Dutch War of Louis XIV*) *8 August 1674*. An army of 45,000 French (Condé) stood firm against 60,000 Flemings and Spaniards under

William, Prince of Orange (later William III of England). William, finding Condé's position too strong to attack, began a retreat towards Le Quesnay, exposing his flank. Condé took instant advantage of this error and scattered the enemy vanguard. William now took up a strong position at Seneffe, from which Condé was unable to dislodge him. The conflict ended in a drawn battle after 17 hours' hard fighting in which one-sixth of the troops involved were killed. *See* Enzheim; Sinsheim.

Senegal (*Napoleonic Wars*) *13 July 1809*. The French garrison surrendered to a British force of three warships with some transports carrying troops, under Captain G. H. Columbine.

Senekal (*Second British–Boer War*) *29 May 1900*. A Boer force was in strong positions on the Biddulphsberg as a British column led by General Rundle approached. To protect themselves still further, the Boers started vast bush fires through which the British had to pass. The attack failed. Rundle had 7 officers and 177 men killed or wounded; many wounded were burnt to death. *See* Sanna's Post; Vaalkrantz.

Senlac. *See* Hastings.

Senta, *Tisza River, 80 miles from Belgrade* (*Austrian–Turkish Wars*) *11 September 1697*. Emperor Leopold I of the Holy Roman Empire, alarmed by growing Turkish strength, sent Eugene, Prince of Savoy, and a veteran army to check the Turks. In a great battle the Austrian Imperials crushed the Turks, who suffered 20,000 casualties. Turkey had to cede territory to Austria, Poland and Venice. *See* Azov; Peterwardein.

Sentinum, *Umbria* (*Third Samnite War*) *295* BC. Five Roman legions (Fabius Maximus and Publius Decius) attacked the allied Samnites and Gauls (Gellus Equatius). The Gauls' chariots broke the Roman left, but Decius rallied

the legionaries at the cost of his life. On the right the Samnites were routed, leaving the Gauls' flank exposed; Fabius at once attacked and broke the Gauls. Meanwhile the Samnite camp was attacked and Equatius slain. Roman casualties, 8,200; Gauls and Samnites, 25,000 killed and 8,000 prisoners. Samnium accepted peace terms. *See* Camerinum; Lake Vadimonis.

Sepeia (*Argos War*) *494* BC. Between the Spartans (Cleomenes) and the Argives in the Pelopponese mountains. The Spartans, by a ruse, surprised the Argives while the soldiers were dining, and routed them. The defeat deprived Argos of leadership in the Pelopponese and put Sparta on the road to power.

Serbia (*World War I*) *6 October–4 December 1915*. Field Marshal von Mackensen commanded German, Austrian and Bulgarian armies — 300,000 — in a new effort to conquer Serbia. (Having been repulsed in the Battle of Rudnik Ridges.) The Serbian commander, Putnik, had 200,000 men. As the battle commenced, the Austrians crossed the Save River, the Germans the Danube and Belgrade fell, 9 October. The Serbs, though desperately courageous, were poorly armed. Bulgarian forces cut the railroad from Salonika and prevented Allied support for the Serbs. The Serbs could soon only surrender or retreat to the coast; 100,000 of them, after a remarkable retreat through wintry mountains, reached the Adriatic. But another 100,000 had been killed, wounded or captured. *See* Salonika II; Rudnik Ridges.

Seringapatam I (*Second British–Mysore War*) *5–16 February 1792*. The city was besieged by 22,000 British and native troops with 86 guns (Lord Cornwallis) and defended by a Mysori garrison (Tippu Sahib). On 6 February redoubts commanding the city were captured and on the approach of British reinforcements (Abercromby), 16 February, Tippu agreed to peace terms.

Seringapatam II (*Fourth British–Mysore War*) 6 April–3 May 1799. Tippu Sahib had started yet another war against the British and General Harris was sent with 6,000 British and Indian troops to besiege Tippu's capital. On 3 May engineers blew holes in the walls and the fort was stormed on 4 May. During the two days' fighting, Tippu and 8,500 Mysore soldiers were killed. British losses, 1,464. *See* Sidassir.

Seringham, *India* (*Carnatic War*) 2 April 1753. Between 1,000 British troops (Major Lawrence) and the French, with Mahratta and Mysori allies (Astruc). The French attacked an isolated post, held by 200 Sepoys, and carried it before Major Lawrence could come up. Lawrence then attacked, captured the position and drove off the French and Mahrattas. *See* Madras II.

Seta, *Japan* (*Yoshinaka's Rebellion*) 1183. The army of the ruler Yoritomo, under his brothers Noriyori and Yoshitsune, defeated that of Yoshinaka who was killed.

Seven Days (*American Civil War*) 25 June–1 July 1862. A series of actions fought by General Lee with 100,000 Confederates against the Federal commander, McClellan, with 95,000 men. Lee's object was to take pressure off Richmond, the Southern capital. The Federals made only one attack — that of Hooker at Oak Grove; it was repulsed. Major features of the battle:

26 June: About 16,500 Confederates (A. P. Hill) were bloodily repulsed in trying to cross Beaver Dam Creek against Porter's corps.

27 June: Lee renewed the attack against Porter, who fell back across the Chickahominy that night.

26 June: With McClellan withdrawing to new positions, Lee sent in another attack, but poor co-ordination made his assault abortive; Stonewall Jackson had not made his attack on time.

30 June: An attack by Longstreet and A. P. Hill swamped McCall's Federal division and made penetration, but McClellan manoeuvred his entire army onto Malvern Hill, a strong position.

1 July: Lee twice attacked the Federal lines but broke off under the weight of Federal artillery fire. McClellan continued his retreat next day and Lee retired on Richmond.

Casualties: Confederates, 20,000; Federals, 16,000. *See* Cedar Mountain; Fair Oaks.

Sevenoaks, *Kent* (*Cade's Rebellion*) 18 June 1450. The rebels, under Jack Cade, ambushed the Royal troops (Stafford). The force under Stafford was inadequate and was routed, Stafford being killed.

Seven Weeks' War. *See* map.

Seven Years' War. *See* List of Battles.

Shaggy Ridge, *New Guinea* (*World War II*) December 1943–23 January 1944. Capture of this ridge, 5,600 ft high, was one of the most arduous operations in Australian military history. Units of the Australian 7th Division (Vasey) dug Japanese out of foxholes on the very peak of the ridge. *See* Finschafen; Lae; Wau.

Shahjehan (*Mongol invasion of Central Asia*) 1221. This city was besieged by the Mongols (Tuli Khan) and was bravely defended by the garrison under the Turkish general Bugha. On 21 successive days the besiegers sent in assaults and all were repulsed. Finally the inhabitants made terms with Tuli Khan and opened the gates. *See* Kharismia; Samarkand.

Shaho River (*Russian–Japanese War*) 14 October–28 November 1904. The Russian army of Kuropatkin, retreating towards Mukden, turned to

```
AUSTRIAN-PRUSSIAN
WAR—1866
```
Baltic Sea

North Sea

HOLSTEIN

HANOVER
Hanover •

R. Oder

R. Elbe

Berlin •

R. Neisse

• Brussels

R. Rhine

SAXONY • Görlitz

Breslau •

Dresden •

SILESIA

Gitschen • Trautenau
Nachod

Sadowa •

Prague •

• Chalons-sur-Marne

R. Danube

Landeshut •

Vienna •

give battle to the pursuing Japanese (Oyama). Along a 40-mile front several fierce actions were fought until autumn rains and then winter snows ended the battle. *See* Liaoyang; Mukden I.

Shaldiran (*Turkish–Persian War*) 24 August 1514. Between 120,000 Turks (Selim I) and about 80,000 Persians (Shah Ismael). The wing led by the Shah was victorious, but the Persian left was routed. Trying to restore order on that side, Ismael was wounded; his army panicked and fled.

H.M.S. *Shannon* vs U.S.S. *Chesapeake* (*British–American War*) 29 May 1813. One of the most remarkable single-ship naval actions. Captain Sir Philip Broke of H.M.S. *Shannon*, probably the most efficient ship in the Royal Navy, challenged Captain James Lawrence to bring the new U.S.S. *Chesapeake* out of Boston and fight. Lawrence accepted, though his crew had only just been raised. Both ships had 38 guns. Within a few minutes Shannon's gunners

had killed or wounded one-third of Chesapeake's crew, including Lawrence. Broke then grappled and boarded. In all, there were 146 American and 83 British casualties. Broke took *Chesapeake* into Halifax as a prize.

Sharqat, *Mesopotamia* (*World War I*) 29 October 1918. A mainly mounted British–Indian Corps (General Cobbe) had pressed back the Turkish Sixth Army (Hakki) until they made a stand at Sharqat. Cobbe's attack was so vigorous that he took 11,300 prisoners and 51 guns; next day Hakki surrendered another 7,000. British casualties, 1,886. This battle ended the fighting in Mesopotamia, during which nearly 29,000 British and Indian troops had been killed or had died of disease. *See* Kut-al-Amara.

Sheerness (*Second British–Dutch War*) 7 June 1667. The Dutch fleet under de Ruyter sailed up the Medway River as far as Upnor Castle and destroyed seven British warships without loss to the Dutch. *See* The Downs.

Sheriffmuir (*Jacobite Rebellion of 1715*) *13 November 1715*. About 3,500 royal troops (Duke of Argyle) did battle with 9,000 Highlanders (Earl of Mar) near Perth. Argyle's left wing was routed by the Macdonalds, and his left and centre, after a stubborn fight, retired. Argyle retreated to Stirling. *See* Preston II.

Shijo Nawate (*War of the Emperors*) *1339*. Japan comprised a Northern and a Southern Empire. The army of the Northern Emperor, under Takaugi and Tadayoshi, and the troops of the Southern Emperor, under Masatsura, met in decisive combat. Masatsura was attacked at Yoshino, the Imperial residence. Being too weak to defend it, Masatsura marched out to meet his enemy and fell fighting. Within a year Japan was united under Northern rule.

Shiloh (*or Pittsburgh Landing*) (*American Civil War*) *6–7 April 1862*. Between 43,000 Confederates (Johnston) and 42,000 Federals (Grant). The Confederates surprised Grant's position on the west of the Tennessee River and drove back the first line in confusion. By nightfall, Grant was practically defeated, but Johnston failed to take advantage of his opportunity. Grant was reinforced by 20,000 men during the night and went on the offensive next day. Johnston was killed and after severe fighting his successor, Beauregard, ordered a retreat. Casualties: Federals, 13,087 including 1,754 killed; Confederates, 10,697, including 1,723 killed. *See* New Orleans II.

Shinowara (*Yoshinaka's Rebellion*) *April 1183*. Between the troops of the rebel Daimio Yoshinaka and the Japanese Imperial army, consisting of 100,000 horsemen, under Taira-no-Kore. The Imperial troops were defeated with a loss of 20,000 killed.

Shipka Pass (*Russian–Turkish War*) *21 August 1877–9 January 1878*. About 7,000 Russians (Radetsky), moving on the Turks through the Bulgarian Balkans, were attacked by a vastly stronger Turkish army (Suleiman). As reinforcements arrived, Radetsky recovered lost ground, but in 5 days the Turks lost 8,000 and the Russians 4,000. On 10 December the Russians captured Plevna and rushed more men to Shipka Pass; the new commander, Gurko, soon had 50,000. On 9 January, in a furious no-quarter battle, the Russians crushed the Turks, who lost 4,000 killed or wounded and 36,000 prisoners. *See* Kars II; Plevna; Plovdiv.

Shirogawa, *Japan* (*Satsuma Rebellion*) *24 September 1876*. The last remnants of the rebels, under Saigo, were defeated by the Imperial army (Prince Taruhito). The rebels were practically annihilated, and most of their leaders killed. Saigo committed hari-kiri on the field.

Shköder I, *Albania* (*Turkish Wars in the Mediterranean*) *May–August 1474 and June–8 September 1478*. (The place is better known as Scutari, but this is confusing because of the famous Scutari on the Black Sea.) Shköder was held by a Venetian garrison led by Antonio Loredano against a Turkish siege. The Turks lifted that siege, but 4 years later Muhammad II again besieged Shköder. Under Antonio di Lezze, the Venetians held out against all odds. Muhammad retired, but left Shköder blockaded. When a peace was signed — giving Shköder to the Turks — only 600 Venetians remained alive. Turkish losses in the two sieges were 30,000.

Shköder II (*First Balkan War*) *22 April 1913*. Montenegrin troops had besieged the Turkish-held city. While the siege was in progress, Bulgaria and Serbia, Montenegro's allies, made peace with Turkey and Schköder was given to Albania. However, the Montenegrins took the city by storm in a sharp battle. Austria now intervened and Nicholas I of

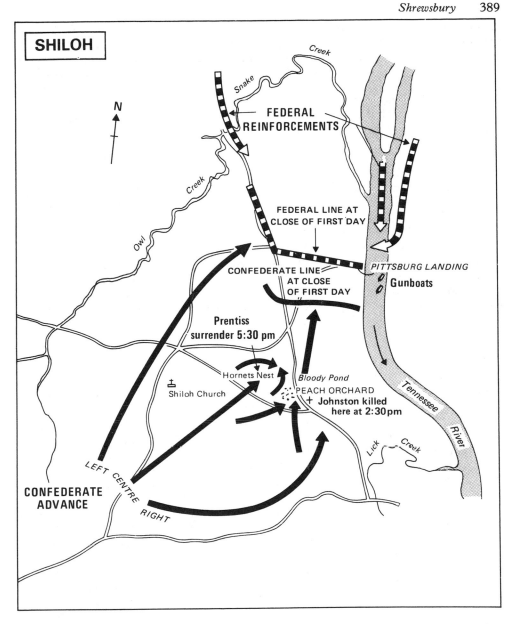

Montenegro grudgingly ceded Shköder to Albania. *See* Ioannina; Luleburgaz.

Sholinghar (*Second British–Mysore War*) *27 September 1781*. Having beaten Hyder Ali at Porto Novo on 1 June and at Pollilur on 27 August, General Eyre Coote led his 10,000 British troops into action against Hyder Ali's army of 80,000 at Sholinghar. With his guns at risk, the Mysore leader made several cavalry charges to save them, but he lost 5,000 men in the process and in the retreat that followed. The British lost 100. *See* Alighar.

Shrewsbury (*Percy's Rebellion*) *21 July 1403*. The Percy family rebelled against King Henry IV. Harry Hotspur, the younger Percy, joined Welsh insurgents led by Owen Glendower and the Scots of the Earl of Douglas. The king's

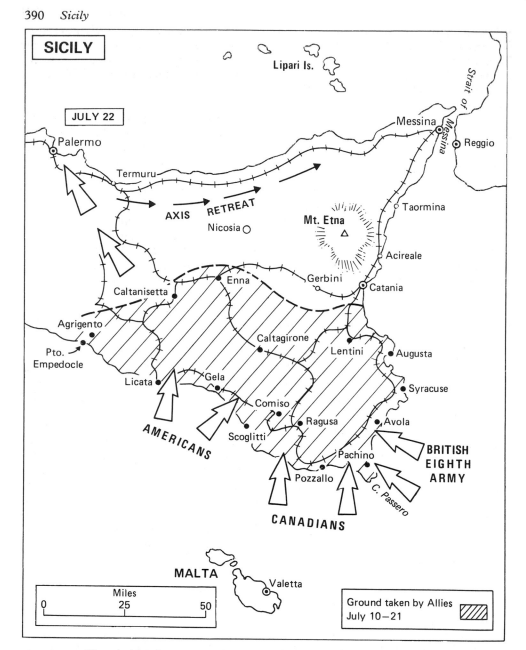

young son, Henry (the future Henry V), was at Shrewsbury with a small army where his father joined him. North of Shrewsbury Hotspur positioned his 10,000 men against the royal army of 12,000. Bowmen on both sides caused casualties. As Hotspur and Douglas led an attack to cut down the king, Hal turned and attacked Hotspur in the rear. An arrow killed Hotspur and the rebels fled. *See* Bramham Moor; Homildon Hill.

Shropshire (*Roman Conquest of Britain*) 50. Caractacus waged guerrilla warfare against the Roman legions until Ostorius Scapula trapped him on a Shropshire hill near the Welsh border. In a pitched battle the Romans routed the Britons, but Caractacus escaped. The

Brigantes tribe to whom he fled for protection handed him over to the Romans who took him and his family to Rome and paraded them in chains through the streets. *See* Medway River; Verulamium II.

Sicily, *Operation Husky* (*World War II*) *9 July–17 August 1943*. Eisenhower directed this massive first assault on the Axis homeland. Sicily was held by 350,000 German and Italian troops, all under General Guzzoni, an Italian. The British and Americans heavily bombed enemy defences, then 3,000 ships and landing craft ferried in 160,000 men (Alexander) with their 600 tanks, 14,000 vehicles, 1,800 guns. The landing took place along 100 miles of southern beaches, principally under Montgomery (British Eighth Army) and Patton (U.S. Seventh Army).

The Eighth Army captured Syracuse on 12 July, Augusta on 14 July. The Seventh Army took Licata on 9 July, Palermo on 22 July. Near Mount Etna the advance was halted and resistance became stiffer as German reinforcements arrived; German Hube was sent to command the German divisions. American pressure near Etna enabled the British to take Catania on 5 August. Bradley's Americans captured Troina on 6 August, Randazzo on 13 August. British and Americans reached the key port of Messina on 17 August.

The Axis evacuated 40,000 Germans and 60,000 Italians into Germany, but they had lost 178,000 in killed, wounded and captured. Allied casualties, 31,158, including 11,923 American. The Allies now hoped for rapid conquest of Italy, but the Germans built up their strength too quickly and too strongly. *See* Anzio; Salerno.

Sidassir (*Third British–Mysore War*) *6 March 1799*. Between a British advance guard of three regiments (Colonel Montresor) and 12,000 Mysoris (Tippu Sahib). Montresor's small force faced the Mysore attack for over 6

hours, and were nearly out of ammunition when General Stuart arrived with the main army and drove back the enemy with a loss of 2,000 men. British losses, 143.

Sidi Barrani, *Egypt* (*World War II*) *9–11 December 1940*. The Italians held a series of strongly fortified posts and manned by 75,000 troops (Graziani). From the British base of Mersa Matruh 36,000 men of the Western Desert Force (later the Eighth Army) under O'Connor made an enterprising march and attacked the Italians from their right flank and rear. At a cost of only 600 casualties, O'Connor captured 38,000 Italians. The threat to the Suez Canal was averted. Principal British units were the 7th Armoured Division and 4th Indian Infantry. *See* Bardia; Libya; Sidi-Rezegh; Sollum; Tobruk.

Sidi-Rezegh, *Operation Crusader* (*World War II*) *18 November 1940–6 January 1941*. Auchinleck masterminded and Alan Cunningham (victor of East Africa) led this operation, aimed at forging a link with the Australians in besieged Tobruk. They had 118,000 troops of the Eighth Army and confronted Rommel with 100,000 — three German Divisions (Afrika Korps) and eight Italian divisions. British armour reached Sidi-Rezegh on 19 November, but the Germans checked this thrust, counterattacked and reached the Egyptian frontier — in the rear of the British. The situation was confused and Cunningham wanted to fall back; Auchinleck replaced him with Ritchie.

British units over a wide area fought to link up and on 29 November they opened a corridor to Tobruk. Unable to supply his own scattered forces, Rommel began to fall back westwards, 7 December. The British took Gazala on 17 December, Benghazi on 15 December and El Agheila on 6 January. By then the battle had ended. The victory was decisively British, but they had no reinforcements to exploit it — all available troops had been sent to

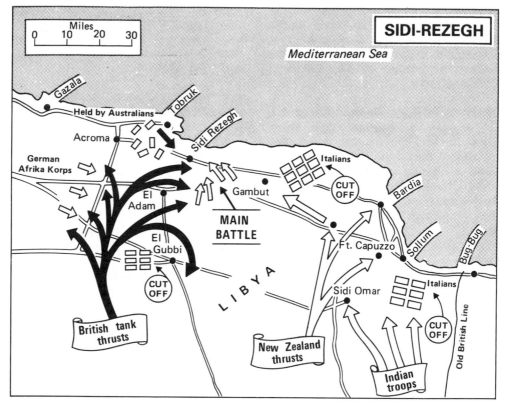

SIDI-REZEGH

Miles
0 10 20 30

Mediterranean Sea

Gazala

Tobruk

Held by Australians

Sidi Rezegh

Acroma

German
Afrika Korps

Italians

CUT OFF

Bardia

El
Adam

Gambut

MAIN
BATTLE

Ft. Capuzzo

Sollum

Bug Bug

El
Gubbi

LIBYA

Sidi Omar

Italians

CUT OFF

CUT OFF

British tank
thrusts

New Zealand
thrusts

Indian
troops

Old British Line

the Far East. Rommel, however, was getting men and material from Italy. Casualties: Axis, 33,850; British, 17,730. *See* Gazala, Libya; Sollum; Tobruk III.

Siegfried Line (*World War II*) *1944*. Advancing across France, Belgium and Luxembourg, the Allied armies reached the Siegfried Line; Eisenhower, supreme commander, then had seven armies reaching from the North Sea to the Swiss border. The German commander, Field Marshal Rundstedt, had six armies. Throughout September–November much bitter fighting occurred.

In the north the Germans halted the Allied Operation Market Garden — the attempt to flank the northern end of the German lines by establishing a bridgehead over the Rhine. This involved the airborne landing at Arnhem (q.v.). The Canadian army (Crerar) fought hard to take South Beveland, 30 October, and Walcheren, 3 November. By 9 November they controlled the key supply port of

Antwerp and had captured 12,500 Germans. But the effort caused 27,633 Canadian casualties.

The American First and Ninth Armies became involved in particularly heavy fighting at Aachen and in Hürtgen Forest. The Third Army beat off a powerful counter-attack by German armour and infantry near Metz. Meanwhile, the U.S. Seventh Army in the Vosges seized the vital Saverne Gap and took Strasbourg, 23 November. The French First Army (Lattre de Tassigny) pressed through opposition to the Rhine at the Swiss border, though the German Nineteenth Army held a powerful salient near Colmar. On the whole the Allied gains in territory were meagre, but they had taken 75,000 prisoners. German battle casualties are unknown; the Americans suffered 85,000 during September–November. *See* Aachen; Ardennes II; Arnhem.

Sierra Maestra (*Castro Revolt in Cuba*) *28–29 June; 11–21 July; 28*

July–3 August 1958. The Castro brothers, Fidel and Raúl, with the Argentinian Guevara and 300 men, fought as guerrillas in the Sierre Maestra hills. The government commander, Cantillo, with 1,000 picked men, made three assaults against the rebel hideout, but Fidel Castro repulsed each one. He then took the offensive. *See* Moncada Fortress; Santa Clara-Santiago.

Sievershausen, *near Hanover (Wars of the German Reformation)* 9 July 1553. Between the Germans (Maurice, Elector of Saxony) and the Brandenburgers (Margrave Albert). The Brandenburgers were defeated, but Maurice was mortally wounded. The Saxon victory brought the Protestant princes of Germany territorial rights and religious toleration. *See* Mühlberg.

Siffin, *Arabia (Muslim Civil Wars)* 656. A series of running desert encounters between the Muslims of caliph Ali and the followers of Moawiyeh, who claimed the Caliphate. Ali lost 25,000 and Moawiyeh 45,000 men, but Moawiyeh was undefeated. The dispute was referred to arbitration, but the "final solution" came in 661 when Ali was assassinated. Moawiyeh became the first Omayyad caliph. *See* Kerbela.

Sikajoki (*Russian–Swedish War*) 18 April 1808. Between the Swedes (Klingspor) and the Russians (Buxhowden). The Russians tried to outflank the Swedes by moving on to the ice at the mouth of the Sikajoki River, at the same time attacking frontally. Both attacks were repulsed, and after 8 hours' fighting, Klingspor took the offensive and drove off the Russians.

Silistra (*Crimean War*) 1854. The fortress was besieged by the Russians on 20 March 1854 and was defended by a Turkish garrison assisted by two English officers, Captain Buller and Lieutenant Nasmyth. Many assaults were repulsed and the garrison held out until 22 June. The Russians raised the siege, having lost over 12,000 men. *See* Alma; Sinope.

Silpia. *See* Elinga.

Simancas, *Spain (Spanish–Muslim Wars)* October 934. A victory for King Ramiro II of Leon over the Muslims of the Caliph Abd-er-Rahman III. The armoured Leonese cavalry won the first Christian victory over the Muslims south of the Pyrenees since 718. It was hailed all over Christian Europe. *See* Zamora.

Simnitza, *Romania (Russian–Turkish War)* 26 June 1877. Between the Russians (Grand Duke Nicholas) and the Turkish garrison of Sistova. By night the Russian advance guard, 15,000-strong, under Dragomiroff, crossed the Danube in boats, and then, under Skobelev, drove the Turks from their positions. *See* Kars; Plevna.

Sinai Peninsula–Suez (*Israeli–Egyptian War*) 29 October–November 1956. Egypt had taken over the Suez Canal on 26 July. On 29 October the small but highly efficient Israeli army (Dayan) raced across the Egyptian border and quickly overcame larger forces of Egyptians in the Sinai. On 31 October British and French aircraft began to bomb Egyptian airfields as a preliminary to dropping airborne troops, 4 November, to seize Port Fuad and Port Said at the northern end of the canal. The same day the Israeli offensive stopped, for by then the Israelis had captured the entire peninsula. They had suffered 1,000 casualties including 172 killed, but had taken great numbers of prisoners, tanks, guns and trucks. Under political attack by the United States and the United Nations, Britain and France called off their offensive and withdrew their troops in December. In March the Israelis left Sinai and a U.N. peace-keeping force took over. *See* Israel–Arab Wars; Israel War of Independence; October War.

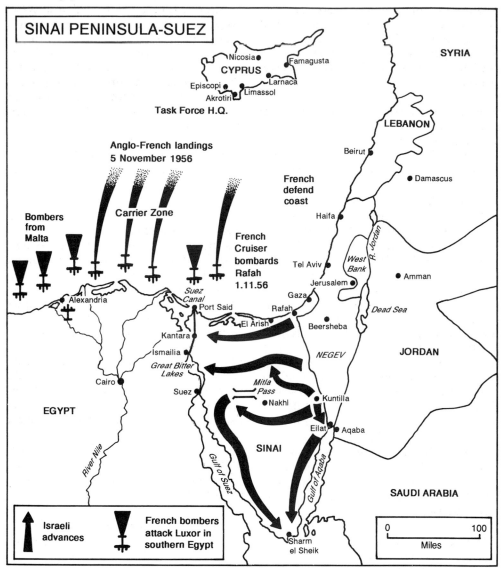

SINAI PENINSULA-SUEZ

SYRIA

Nicosia●
●Famagusta
CYPRUS
Episcopi ●
●Larnaca
Akrotiri ●
●Limassol
Task Force H.Q.

LEBANON

Beirut ●

Anglo-French landings
5 November 1956

French
defend
coast

● Damascus

Carrier Zone

Bombers
from
Malta

Haifa ●

French
Cruiser
bombards
Rafah
1.11.56

Tel Aviv ●
West
Bank
R. Jordan

● Amman

● Alexandria
Suez
Canal
● Port Said
Jerusalem ●
Gaza ●
Rafah ●
Beersheba ●
Dead Sea

Kantara ●
El Arish

Ismailia ●
NEGEV
JORDAN

Great Bitter
Lakes

Cairo ●
Suez ●
Mitla
Pass
● Nakhl
● Kuntilla

EGYPT

Eilat ● Aqaba

SINAI

River Nile
Gulf of Suez
Gulf of Aqaba
SAUDI ARABIA

Israeli
advances
French bombers
attack Luxor in
southern Egypt

0   100
Miles

Sharm
el Sheik

Singapore (*World War II*) *31 January 1941–15 February 1942*. The battle for Singapore began as the battle of Malaya ended. The British (Percival) had 85,000 troops — British, Indian, Australian (Bennett) — but only 50,000 were fighting soldiers. With them he had to defend a perimeter of 30 miles and an area of 220 square miles against strong Japanese forces (Yamashita). Singapore was supposed to be impregnable, but its great guns were designed to repel naval attack, not land-based attacks. Heavy siege guns opened fire on Singapore on 5 February. On the nights of 8 and 9 February about 5,000 Japanese crossed Johore Straits from Malaya and quickly repaired the damaged causeway linking island and mainland. The defensive line shrank and crumbled; water, food and ammunition were soon depleted. Percival then surrendered Singapore, with 32,000 Indian, 16,000 British and 14,000 Australian soldiers. Japanese casualties, 9,800.

Thousands of civilians who had left Singapore before surrender were killed or captured in their small boats. More than 50 per cent of the military captives died in captivity. *See* East Indies; Java; Malaya.

Singara I, *Persia* **(***Persian Wars of the Roman Empire***)** *348*. The most renowned of the nine major battles fought between Constantius and the Persian king, Shapur II, between the years 337 and 350. Constantius was successful at first and captured the Persian camp, but the Roman legionaries had become exhausted from chasing the more lightly clad Persians and the whole army fell asleep that night. Shapur's army stealthily approached and butchered most of the Romans. *See* Amida; Nisibis.

Singara II (*Persian Wars of the Roman Empire***)** *360*. Having regained control of Singara after their defeat in 348, the Romans built a fortress. Shapur II and his Persian army besieged the place, captured and then dismantled it. The garrison became slaves. *See* Amida; Nisibis.

Sinnaca, *Syria* **(***Parthian War***)** *53* BC. The army of Crassus, after the Battle of Carrhae the previous year, surrendered to the Parthians, after another bloody fight. *See* Carrhae.

Sinnigallia (*Roman–Gothic War***)** *551*. Off the Adriatic coast the Romans closed with and boarded the ships of the Goths' leader, Totila, capturing most of them. Many Goths drowned. The Gothic tactics were notably inferior to those of the Romans.

Sinope, *Black Sea* **(***Crimean War***)** *30 November 1853*. The Russian fleet attacked nine Turkish ships lying in the harbour of Sinope. No quarter was given and the Turkish fleet was destroyed. Only 400 Turks, almost all wounded, escaped the massacre. *See* Oltenite; Silistra.

Sinsheim (*Dutch War of Louis XIV***)** *16 June 1674*. Leopold I of the Holy Roman Empire sent an Austrian army of 100,000 under Charles V of Loraine to help the Dutch in their war against the French. The great French commander, Turenne, took 100,000 troops across the Rhine and surprised the Austrian force, routing them and inflicting 30,000 casualties. Turenne laid waste to the region to destroy his enemy's source of supply and withdrew across the Rhine. *See* Enzheim; Maastricht II; Seneffe.

Sitabaldi (*Third British–Mahratta War***)** *24 November 1817*. A unit of Madras native troops and some Bengal cavalry, about 1,300 men in all, under Colonel Scott faced 18,000 troops of Nappa Sahib, Rajah of Nagpur, who also had 36 guns. The sepoys held their ground for 18 hours, until relieved, at a cost of about 300 men. *See* Kirkee.

Skalitz (*Seven Weeks' War***)** *28 June 1866*. While not as significant as the main battles in this war — Langensalza, Munchengratz and Sadowa, q.v. — that of Skalitz was another devastating defeat for the Austrians. With one Prussian Corps, Steinmetz attacked two Austrian Corps (Ramming), captured 4,000 prisoners and eleven heavy guns and occupied Skalitz fortress and city.

Slankamen (*Austrian–Turkish Wars***)** *19 August 1691*. The Austrians of the Holy Roman Empire of Leopold I had made great inroads into Turkish Europe; then the Turks surged into a counter-offensive. To meet this new threat the Austrians put together an army of 20,000 under Lous William I of Baden-Baden. Near the confluence of the Danube and Tisza he routed the Turkish army of 40,000 and the enemy commander, Vizier Mustafa Kuprili, was killed. *See* Fleurus II; Harkany.

Slivnitza (*or Slivnica, near Sofia***) (***Serbian–Bulgarian War***)** *17–19 November 1885*. King Milan I personally led 25,000 troops when they invaded Bulgaria. The Bulgarians could oppose the Serbians with only 15,000 troops under Prince Alexander and General Stambolov. Alexander attacked and was himself attacked, but the Bulgarian lines held and the Serbs retreated, having lost 3,000 men to the Bulgarians 2,000. *See* Pirot.

Sluys (*or L'Ecluse, Holland*) (*Hundred years' War*) 24 June 1340. The English fleet of 250 ships (Morley and Fitzalan) attacked the French fleet of about 200 (Quiéret) at anchor in Sluys Harbour. Practically the whole of the French fleet was captured or destroyed, and Quiéret was killed. The French lost 25,000 men. The English 4,000.

Smolensk I (*Great Northern War*) 22 September 1708. Charles XII of Sweden, with 4,000 infantry and six regiments of cavalry, attacked a force of 16,000 Cossacks and Tartars. After heavy fighting and a narrow escape from capture, Charles routed the Cossacks, but he was now embarking on a winter war in the depths of Russia. *See* Poltava.

Smolensk II (*Napoleonic Wars*) 17 August 1812. Massive armies were manoeuvring around Smolensk — 175,000 French, under Napoleon, and 130,000 Russians (Bagration). About 50,000 and 60,000, respectively, were engaged in the battle for the city. Bagration's corps held the place which Napoleon attacked and captured two of the suburbs. During the night the Russians fired Smolensk and evacuated it. Casualties: Russian, 10,000; French, 9,000. *See* Borodino; Mogilev.

Smolensk III (*World War II*) 16 July–6 August 1941. This great battle of encirclement took place as the Germans invaded Russia. The Russians made many counter-attacks in efforts to encircle the invaders, but these efforts lost cohesion under the combined assault of

German infantry in front, under General Hoth, with Guderian's tanks in the rear. A panzer thrust to Vyazma, 27 June, cut Russian communications. The Germans claimed the capture of 310,000 troops, 3,205 tanks, 3,120 guns and 1,098 aircraft. It seems more likely that 100,000 Russians were killed or captured.* Many formations withdrew, and 140,000 of the 160,000 civil population reached safety. The bold and skilfully executed advance to and beyond Smolensk was one of the most remarkable tank operations of World War II. Credit lies with the tank general Guderian. *See* Kiev; Moscow.

Sobraon (*First British–Sikh War*) 10 February 1846. The British had already defeated the Sikhs in three battles. Now their commander, Ranjur Singh, entrenched his 26,000 troops on a bend of the River Sutlej; he considered the position impregnable. With his army of 15,000, General Gough feinted at the Sikh right and then rolled up their line from the left and towards the river. More than 8,000 were killed or drowned. British casualties, 2,383. *See* Aliwal.

Soczawa (*Polish–Turkish Wars*) 11 May 1676. The Poles were making valiant attempts to throw out the swarms of Turkish invaders, led by Ibrahim Pasha. At Soczawa the Poles of John Sobieski were reinforced by Lithuanians and mercenaries and they routed the Turks, despite their greater numbers, on the open field. They retreated to Kaminiec, the only fortress they now held in Poland. *See* Zurakow.

Sofia (*Byzantine–Bulgarian Wars*) 981. The Byzantine Emperor Basil II, threatened by the growing power of the Bulgars under Tsar Samuel, marched from Constantinople to smash the Bulgars. His army was large enough, but Samuel's generalship was better and near Sofia Basil was soundly defeated and forced back to his capital. *See* Adrianople III; Balathista.

---

*The Halder Diaries say 185,475 between 3 July and 25 July.

Sohr (*or Soor, Bohemia*) (*War of Austrian Succession*) *30 September 1745*. Insisting on reclaiming Silesia from Frederick the Great of Prussia, Maria Theresa of the Holy Roman Empire sent Prince Charles of Lorraine with 30,000 Austrians. Frederick had only 18,000 men, but they were veterans, superior in musketry and discipline to the Austrians. Prince Charles lost 6,000 in killed, wounded and captured and had to retreat. Maria Theresa then ordered another attack towards Berlin. *See* Hennersdorf; Hohenfriedeberg.

Soissons (*Founding of Merovingian Dynasty*) *486*. Notable as the first military exploit of Clovis, the founder of the French monarchy. He defeated Syagrius, Count of Soissons, annexed his dominions and made Paris his new capital. Clovis united his conquests from the Romans, Germans and Goths, laying the foundations of modern France.

Sole Bay (*English–Dutch Wars*) *28 May 1672*. The allied French and English fleets, about 140 ships under the Comte d'Estrées and the Duke of York, were surprised at anchor by a Dutch fleet of 115 ships (de Ruyter). The French were first attacked, but soon edged out of the fight and the battle was left to the English. The conflict was indecisive, but the allied fleet was too crippled to take the offensive for over a month. *See* Schoneveldt; Texel.

Solferino, *North Italy* (*French–Austrian War or Italian Wars of Independence*) *24 June 1859*. An army of 150,000 Austrians, under the Emperor Franz Josef with Generals Wimpffen and Schlick, fought a major battle against the French and Piedmontese, under Napoleon III and Victor Emmanuel, with MacMahon, Niel and d'Hilliers in command. The French attacked the Austrian position on the heights round Solferino, which were held by Schlick, and after hard fighting captured them. Meanwhile Wimpffen, with three corps, attacked the

French left, but was held at bay throughout the day by Niel's corps. When night fell, the Austrian centre had been broken and Franz Josef retreated. Casualties: Austrian, 22,000; Allies, 18,000. Napoleon III, sickened by the slaughter, signed a truce with Austria, a defection which gave a setback to Italian hopes for independence from Austria.

Sollum–Halfaya Pass, *Operation Battleaxe* (*World War II*) *15–17 June 1941*. The Germans had been overwhelmingly successful (apart from their failure to take Tobruk) and Churchill induced Wavell to mount a counter-offensive. A double attack, on the coast at Sollum and inland at Halfaya (Hellfire) Pass, it was decisively beaten back. The British suffered 1,000 casualties and lost 100 tanks, half their armoured strength. *See* Sidi-Rezegh.

Solomon Islands (*World War II*) *1942–4*. The Japanese occupied the Solomons — seven large and many small islands — early in the Pacific war. The Americans retook Guadalcanal between 7 August 1942 and 21 February 1943, then, successively, Russell Island, Rendova, New Georgia, Kolombangara and Vella Lavella. Seeking to reinforce and supply their troops, the Japanese precipitated a naval battle in Kula Gulf, 6 July and 12–13 July. By now the Japanese had lost 10,000 men; the Americans, Australians and New Zealanders lost 1,150 killed and 4,100 wounded. The principal battle was that for Bougainville, invaded on 1 November. Savage Japanese counter-attacks were staved off, but the U.S. 3rd Marine Division lost 423 killed and 1,418 wounded in destroying 4,000 Japanese. The final Japanese offensive came between 8 and 25 March 1944. In fanatical charges the Japanese lost 5,000 men while inflicting 263 American casualties. With another naval defeat, 25 November, between Buka and Rabaul, the Japanese could no longer supply the remaining army elements. In any case, the Allied offensive had already moved hundreds of

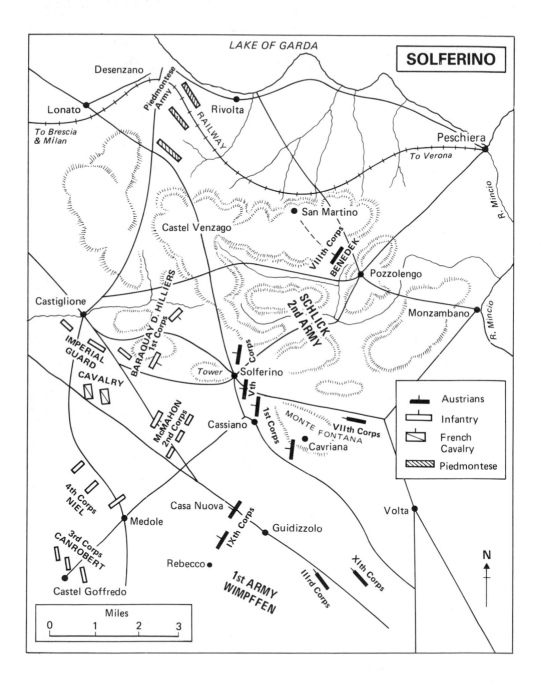

LAKE OF GARDA

SOLFERINO

Desenzano

Lonato

Rivolta

Peschiera

To Brescia
& Milan

To Verona

Castel Venzago

San Martino

VIIIth Corps

BENEDEK

Pozzolengo

Castiglione

SCHLICK
2nd ARMY

Monzambano

IMPERIAL
GUARD

BARAQUAY D'HILLIERS
1st Corps

CAVALRY

Tower

Solferino

Vth Corps

Austrians

Infantry

McMAHON
2nd Corps

Cassiano

1st Corps

MONTE
FONTANA

VIIth Corps

French
Cavalry

Cavriana

Piedmontese

4th Corps
NIEL

Casa Nuova

Volta

IXth Corps

Guidizzolo

3rd Corps
CANROBERT

Medole

Rebecco

XIth Corps

N

Castel Goffredo

1st ARMY
WIMPFFEN

IIIrd Corps

Miles

0   1   2   3

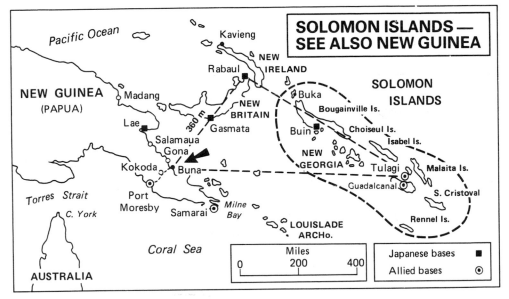

miles north and west. *See* New Guinea;
Rabaul.

Solway Moss, *Cumberland (English–Scottish Wars)* **24 November
1542.** James V's Scottish invading army
of 10,000 (Oliver Sinclair) was blocked by
a band of 500 English borderers (Thomas
Dacre and John Musgrave). Because of
poor leadership, the Scots were defeated
and many important nobles were captured. Shock of the defeat hastened the
death of James V and brought to the
throne Mary Stuart, Queen of Scots. *See*
Flodden.

Somme River I *(World War I)* **24
June–18 November 1916.** One of the
bloodiest and most futile battles of
history. After a week of artillery bombardment the Allies — British, British
Commonwealth, French — launched a
massive infantry attack. Under General
Haig, the British were trying to capture
Bapaume; Foch's French troops, on a 10-
mile front, were aiming for Peronne. In
the south the French Sixth Army
(Fayolle) made immediate gains, but in
the north the British Fourth Army
(Rawlinson) was cut down by concentrated machine-gun fire and in one
day, 1 July, suffered 57,450 casualties
including 20,000 dead. This is the
heaviest British one-day loss in warfare.

At this time the Germans were led by
Falkenhayn north of the Somme and
Gallwitz south of the river. As the
Allies continued to make small but
terribly costly gains, the Germans
brought in Field Marshal Hindenburg
with Ludendorff as his chief-of-staff.
Haig, on 15 September, used tanks for the
first time in war (at Flers), but only
eighteen of the thirty-six tanks func-
tioned. The fighting deteriorated into a
battle of attrition and, in cold, drenching
weather, Haig called it off on 18 November. The Allies had gained a mere 125
square miles at a cost of 420,000 British
and 195,000 French casualties. Senior
planning and leadership had been grossly
inadequate. German losses, 650,000. *See*
Arras II.

Somme River II, *Kaiserschlacht
(Emperor battle),* **to the Germans**
(World War I) **21 March–4 April
1918.** The Germans had to secure a major
victory on the Western Front before the
Allies were stiffened by large numbers of
Americans, following the U.S. entry into
the war in 1917. Ludendorff brought

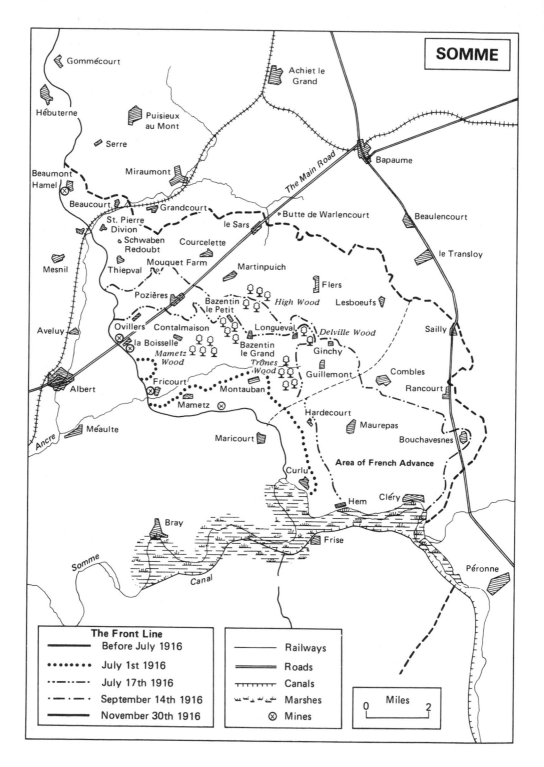

SOMME

Gommécourt

Achiet le Grand

Bapaume

Hébuterne

Puisieux au Mont

Serre

Miraumont

Beaumont Hamel

Beaucourt

Grandcourt

Butte de Warlencourt

le Sars

Beaulencourt

St. Pierre Divion

Schwaben Redoubt

Courcelette

le Transloy

Mesnil

Thiepval

Mouquet Farm

Martinpuich

Flers

Pozières

Bazentin le Petit

High Wood

Lesboeufs

Aveluy

Ovillers

Contalmaison

Longueval

Delville Wood

Sailly

la Boisselle

Mametz Wood

Bazentin le Grand

Ginchy

Trônes Wood

Guillemont

Combles

Fricourt

Montauban

Rancourt

Mametz

Hardecourt

Maurepas

Bouchavesnes

Méaulte

Maricourt

Area of French Advance

Ancre

Curlu

Hem

Cléry

Bray

Frise

Somme

Péronne

Canal

The Front Line
— Before July 1916
•••••• July 1st 1916
—·—·— July 17th 1916
—··—··— September 14th 1916
——— November 30th 1916

——— Railways
═══ Roads
⊥⊥⊥ Canals
Marshes
⊗ Mines

Miles
0   2

powerful reinforcements from the quiet Russian front and after careful planning launched a massive assault against the British lines. After a bombardment by 6,000 guns and a gas attack, three German armies — seventy-one divisions — jumped off along a 50-mile front south of Arras. They were: Seventeenth (Below), Second (Marwitz), and Eighteenth (Hutier).

This onslaught was devastating and the British Fourth Army (Gough) of only fifteen divisions gave way; next day Gough ordered his army back behind the Somme. As a result on his right the Third Army (Byng) pulled back. In 4 days the Germans took 14 miles. Ludendorff now threw his weight into Hutier's attack south of the Somme. Montdidier fell, 27 March, despite combined English–French (Fayolle) efforts to hold it. The situation was so desperate that Marshal Foch was brought in as chief co-ordinator of defence and General Rawlinson replaced Gough, some of whose troops had broken in panic.

After a gain of 40 miles, exhaustion and slowness of supplies brought the Germans to a halt. They had split the French and British and they nearly captured Amiens. Casualties: Allies, 160,000 battle casualties, 70,000 prisoners; German, 150,000 killed or wounded. *See* Cambrai, Lys River; Somme River I; Ypres.

Somnath (*Mahmud's Twelfth invasion of India*) *1024*. This city, one of the holy places of the Hindus, was captured by the Afghans, under Sultan Mahmud of Ghazni. He destroyed the temple's phallic idol and killed 50,000 Hindus.

Son-Tai *Indo-China* (*French–Tonkin War*) *14–16 December 1883*. Defended by a garrison of 25,000 Chinese, including 10,000 "Black Flags" under Lin Yung Ku, the fortress was attacked by the French (Admiral Courbet) with eight river gun-boats and force of 7,000 men. The outer defences were captured and the garrison was driven into the citadel. On 16 December the French stormed the citadel. In the 3 days they lost 92 officers and 318 men killed or wounded. Chinese losses, about 1,000.

Sorata (*Inca Rising Against Spain*) *July 1780*. The city was besieged by the rebelling Peruvians under Andres. They diverted mountain streams against the walls and opened a large breach. Storming the city, they massacred the garrison and inhabitants of 20,000.

South African Wars. *See* List of Battles.

Southern France, *invasion of* (*Operation Anvil, later Dragoon*) *15 August 1944*. Four U.S. and three French divisions made sea and airborne landings. The eight divisions of the German Nineteenth Army retreated except at Toulouse and Marseilles, which were captured 28 August. The operation had little strategic value. *See* D-Day.

South Mountain (*American Civil War*) *14–15 September 1862*. The opening action in the larger Battle of Antietam. The Federal right forced its way through Turner's Gap, but 15,000 Confederates (D. Hill) on South Mountain had delayed the Federals long enough to ensure their capture of Harper's Ferry. *See* Antietam.

Southern Philippines (*World War II*) *28 February–15 August 1945*. A series of 38 American assaults (Eichelberger) against the 450,000 Japanese holding the islands of Palawan, Panay, Negros, Cebu, Bohol and Mindanao. All the central islands were secure by the end of May. Mindanao, second largest of the Philippines, was invaded 10 March at Zamboanga and landings continued until July. At the time of the surrender, 15 August, about 100,000 troops were still holding out, principally the Thirty-Fifth Army in eastern Mindanao. In these complex, exhausting operations the Americans suffered 13,700 killed and 58,000 other casualties. *See* Borneo; Leyte; Luzon.

Southwark (*Jack Cade's Rebellion*) 5 July 1450. Cade and his rebels were raiding across the Thames to loot and destroy in London. Matthew Gough and thousands of armed citizens held London Bridge and set fire to the central draw-bridge, but Cade's men forced them back. Gough was among the many Londoners killed.

South-West Africa (*Namibia*) Guerrilla War 1966–1986. Guerrillas from South-West Africa People's Association (SWAPO) began a war against occupying South African troops in 1966. Most SWAPO fighters operate from Angola, which borders Namibia. In combined air-land operations South Africans claimed to have killed 3,000 SWAPO fighters by 1985. The South African forces have lost 33 killed and 240 wounded.

Southwold Bay (*Dutch Wars*) 14 August 1665. Fought between the English fleet (Duke of York) and the Dutch fleet (Admiral Opdam). The English were victorious, the Dutch losing 18 ships and 7,000 men. The English lost only one ship.

Soviet Union, *Operation Barbarossa* (*World War II*). The German assault on Russia was the greatest ground offensive in history — 138 divisions in three army groups. The Russian resistance, initially with 148 divisions, gave history its greatest land battle. Several of the independent battles are described in various alphabetical sections.

Army Group C (Leeb) smashed through the Baltic States towards Leningrad: B Group (Bock) moved towards Moscow north of the Pripet Marshes. A Group (Rundstedt) was to take the Ukraine in the south. All along the line the Russian commanders — Voroshilov, Timoshenko and Budenny — fell back. The biggest Russian reverse was in the Kiev area where German armour performed a gigantic pincers movement and killed or trapped 600,000 Russians of Budenny's command.

When winter stopped this enormous over-battle — along a front of 1,500 miles — the Germans had penetrated 550 miles and occupied more than 500,000 miles of Russian territory, and had inflicted 2,500,000 casualties and taken 1,000,000 prisoners. German losses were at least 775,000 and possibly as many as 1,000,000. The principal features of the succeeding years are these:

1942: Major offensive on the southern front in the Caucasus. The Germans took the Crimea but were blocked at Stalingrad (q.v.). That year they suffered 1,200,000 casualties to the Russians' 1,000,000.

1943: Gaining strength, the Russians recovered the Ukraine. The Germans fought desperately to take the Kursk salient, but the Russians (Rokossovski and Vatutin) destroyed about 42 per cent of the enemy armour. The Germans (Kluge) were forced to abandon Orel (q.v.), and though they resisted fiercely they continued to lose ground.

1944: Russian armies reoccupied the Crimea, Ukraine, White Russia, Bessarabia. By the end of August the Germans held only the Baltic States, but large German pockets held out until March 1945. Possibly 7,000,000 Russians and 2,000,000 Germans and their Allies — Italians, Rumanians, Hungarians — were killed in this vast conflict. *See* Crimea; Kursk; Leningrad; Moscow; Sebastopol; Smolensk; Stalingrad.

Spanish Armada (*English–Spanish Wars*) 21 July–29 July 1588. The Spanish "Invincible Armada" of 130 ships was to seize control of the English Channel so that Spanish troops could invade the country. Under the command of Duke of Medina-Sidonia, the armada included 20 galleons and 44 armed merchantmen armed with 2,500 guns and carrying 10,000 sailors and 20,000 soldiers. The opposing British fleet, under Lord Howard, assisted by Drake, Hawkins and Frobisher, had 34 ships with 6,000 men. Another 163 private vessels supported, but most were too weak to help effec-

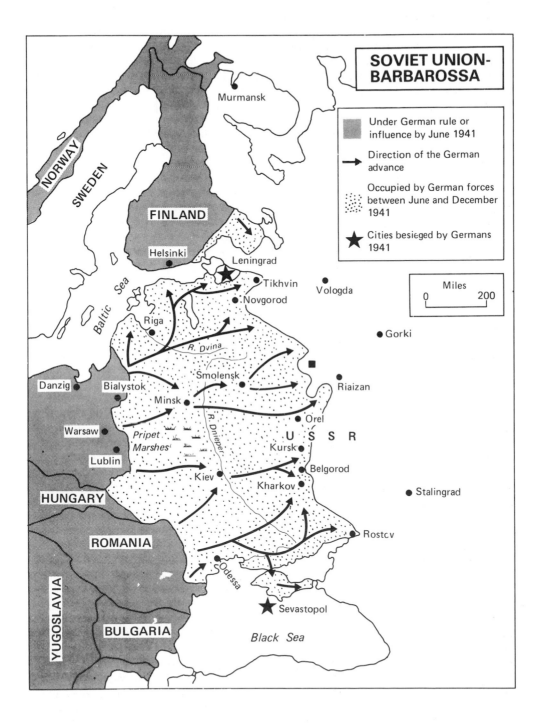

SOVIET UNION-BARBAROSSA

Under German rule or influence by June 1941

Direction of the German advance

Occupied by German forces between June and December 1941

Cities besieged by Germans 1941

Miles
0   200

NORWAY

SWEDEN

FINLAND

Helsinki

Murmansk

Leningrad

Tikhvin

Vologda

Novgorod

Baltic Sea

Riga

R. Dvina

Gorki

Smolensk

Riaizan

Danzig

Bialystok

Minsk

Orel

Warsaw

Pripet Marshes

R. Dnieper

U S S R

Kursk

Lublin

Belgorod

Kiev

Kharkov

HUNGARY

Stalingrad

ROMANIA

Rostov

YUGOSLAVIA

Odessa

Sevastopol

BULGARIA

Black Sea

SOVIET UNION- RUSSIAN FRONT

Miles
0   180

Orel

Kursk

Kiev   Voronezh

Lebedin

Bielgorod

Poltava   Kharkov

Dnieper   *R. Don*

Izyum

Pavlograd   Lisichansk

Dniepropetrisk   Voroshilovg'd   Stalingrad

Krasnoarmisk   *R. Donetz*

R. Volga

Taganroo   Rostov

CRIMEA   *Sea of Azov*   270 m   Nov. 1942

Kerch

R. Kuban   Krasnodar

Novorossisk

Tuapse   Mozdok

Grozny

Batum   Tiflis

Ground retaken by Russians
by end of February, 1943

Caucasus Mts.

tively. On 21 July British gunnery began the battle against the Spanish 7-mile crescent-shaped line and intermittently for a week attacked the larger Spanish ships. On 28 July Medina took many of his ships into the shelter of Calais, where eight British fireships caused great damage. At Gravelines, 29 July, in an 8-hour battle three Spanish ships were sunk and five sent aground on fire. The Spaniards took advantage of a wind and English shortage of ammunition and sailed north around Scotland. Many ships were wrecked. By the end of October fewer than half the armada ships were safely back in Spain. England's victory won her a reputation as a leading naval power. *See* Cadiz; Flores.

Spanish Succession War. *See* List of Battles.

Sphacteria. *See* Pylos.

Spicheren (or Forbach) (French–Prussian War) 6 August 1870. Between 27,000 Germans (Steinmetz) and 24,000 French (Frossard). In a confused battle the French were driven from all their positions and compelled to retreat on Metz. The Germans lost 223 officers and 4,648 men, the French 4,000. *See* Colombey; Wörth.

Spion Kop (Second British-Boer War) 19–23 January 1900. Buller's second attempt to break through the Boer lines on the Tugela River and relieve Ladysmith. On 19 January a British division (Warren) turned the Boer right, and gradually drove them from ridge to ridge till the evening of 22 January when Spion Kop, the centre of the position, was taken. It was impossible to drag artillery up the steep slopes and the brigade holding the hill lost about a third of their strength during 23 January. A Boer counter-attack (Botha) retook the hill and next day Buller retreated across the Tugela.

Spira (or Speyer, South Germany) **(War of Spanish Succession) 15 November 1703.** The French (Tallard) and the Austrian Imperialists (Prince of Hesse) were each about 20,000 strong. By superior generalship, the Austrians were overpowered by the French cavalry, and defeated with a loss of 6,000 killed, wounded or missing. The Prince of Hesse was captured. The Austrians had now been thrown out of the Bavarian Palatinate. *See* Hochstädt.

Splitter (Swedish invasion of Brandenburg) 18 January 1679. Between 16,000 Swedes (Horn) and 10,000 Brandenburgers, (Elector Frederick William). The Swedes were routed, Horn being taken prisoner. Only 1,500 Swedes reached Riga to embark for home. It was a major reverse for Charles X. *See* Fehrbellin; Kiöge.

Spotsylvania (American Civil War) 10–12 May 1864. Following the stalemate of the Battle of the Wilderness, the Federal army of 101,000 (Grant and Meade) moved towards a key road junction on the way to the Confederate capital of Richmond. The Army of Northern Virginia — 56,000 men under Lee — blocked the way. The Federals made two fierce but futile frontal assaults, though 1,000 prisoners were taken. Early on 12 May Grant struck hard at Bloody Angle, trying to eliminate a salient. He took 2,000 Confederate prisoners. For almost a week the Federals probed the Confederate flanks, but found no weakness and the battle petered out, 20 May. The fighting had been bloody. Casualties: Federal, 17,400; Confederates, about 9,600. *See* Drewry's Bluff; New Market; Wilderness.

Spurs. *See* Courtrai and Guinegate.

Stadtlohn, Westphalia (Thirty Years' War) 9 August 1623. The army of the Protestant Princes of Germany, about 22,000 strong, under the reckless Duke Christian of Brunswick gave battle to the army of the Catholic League

(Tilly). Christian, with 15,000 troops, had marched into Lower Saxony, where he was threatened and then pursued by Tilly's well-trained army of Bavarians. On a hill at Stadtlohn Christian turned to fight. Enemy pressure broke his cavalry wings and his infantry panicked. Cut off by a bog, they were overwhelmed by the Bavarians, who killed 6,000 Protestants and captured 4,000, as well as all Christian's artillery and baggage. Christian and 2,000 cavalrymen reached the Dutch border and safety. Christian never again held military command. *See* Breda; Dessau Bridge; Fleurus I.

Staffarda, *Upper Po River* (*War of the Grand Alliance*) *18 August 1690*. Louis XIV sent a French army (Catinat) to crush opposition in the Duchy of Savoy. Duke Victor Amadeus II gave battle at Staffarda, but was overwhelmed. *See* Fleurus II; Leuze; Marsaglia.

Stainmore, *Westmoreland* (*Rise of England*) *954*. A victory for the Saxons over Norsemen led by Eric Bloodaxe, exiled King of Norway. Eric was killed and the Viking kingdom of York came to an end.

Stalingrad (*World War II*) *23 August 1942–2 February 1943*. The Germans reached Stalingrad's western suburbs with aggressive speed, 24 August, but then encountered stubborn opposition from the Sixty-Second Russian army (Chuikov) and Stalingrad civilians. Shelling the city to rubble, the Germans fought their way to the city's centre, 22 September. All this time the Russians were preparing two powerful drives above and below the city. On 19 November the northern assault (Rossokovski) punched a corridor through the German line and Vatutin passed troops through it to rout the Third Romanian, Eighth Italian and Second Hungarian armies. Next day Yeremenko broke through on the south, crushed the Fourth Romanian Army and took 65,000 prisoners. While the Russians now hastened to snap the

pincers behind the Germans in Stalingrad, Hitler refused to allow his Sixth Army (Paulus) to withdraw. By 23 November no fewer than 300,000 Germans and their allies were trapped in a pocket 25 miles long and 12 miles deep.

Manstein, 12 December, began an attempt to link with Paulus and made ground steadily until 21 December when Russian resistance halted his effort. The Luftwaffe was unable to strafe the Russians effectively and could not drop adequate supplies. Their surrender invitation refused, the Russians, 10 January, began heavy shelling; by 16 January the pocket had shrunk to 15 by 9 miles. Russian armour then split the pocket, and then divided one of these. On 1 January one section surrendered. Under the savage Russian assault scores of thousands of German soldiers had died and on 3 January Paulus surrendered 23 generals, 2,000 other officers, 90,000 soldiers, 40,000 non-combatant soldiers and civilians. Only 5,000 ever returned to Germany.

Hitler's refusal to permit an earlier surrender had one advantage for the Germans. So much Russian strength was held at Stalingrad that German Army Group B (Kleist) was just able to extricate itself from a similar situation in the Caucasus. Apart from casualties and captives, the Germans had lost 2,000 tanks, 4,000 guns and 500 transport aircraft. A major offensive was now impossible. *See* Caucasus; Soviet Union; Ukraine.

Stamford Bridge I (*Rise of England*) *25 September 1066*. King Harold had been in London waiting for a Norman invasion in the south and a Norwegian one in the north. After the English defeat at Fulford he led his Danish household troops rapidly to York, taking by surprise the invaders, under Harald Hardrada, camped at Stamford Bridge. Harold charged, then lured the Norsemen into a counter-attack; turning on his enemies Harold hit them hard. When Hardrada was killed Harold offered peace to his half-brother, Tostig, who had gone over to the Norsemen. The offer was refused, so Harold sent his infantry in once again. Few Norsemen survived to reach their ships. In the moment of his victory Harold learned that the Norman duke, William, had landed on the south coast. *See* Hastings.

Stamford Bridge II (*Wars of the Roses*) *August 1453*. A mere encounter between the retainers of Sir Thomas Neville of the Warwick family and those of Lord Egremont developed into a pitched battle. It was an indecisive conflict, but is considered one of the beginnings of the Wars of the Roses. Neville was a follower of the House of York (white rose), Egremont of Lancaster (red rose). *See* St. Albans.

Standard, The (*English–Scottish Wars*) *22 August 1138*. Fought at Cowton Moor, near Northallerton, between the invading Scots (David I, King of Scotland) and the English (Thurstan, Archbishop of York, and Raoul, Bishop of Durham). The Scots were routed, and fled in disorder. The banners of St. Cuthbert of Durham, St. Peter of York, and those of other saints were carried in a wagon in the midst of the English army, hence the name of the battle. *See* Lincoln I.

Stara Zagora (*or Berrhoe, Balkan Mountains*) (*Byzantine–Bulgarian Wars*) *September 1189*. The Byzantine Emperor Isaac II took an army from Constantinople to put down a rebellion by the Bulgars, who had sought the help of the Cumans, a Turkish race. However, the Bulgars won the battle, thus establishing the Second Bulgarian Empire. *See* Adrianople IV; Balathista.

Stavuchany *or* Khotin (*Russian–Turkish War*) *28 August 1739*. Between 68,000 Russians (Münnich) and the Turkish army (Veli) which was 90,000 strong. The Russians stormed the Turkish entrenched camp and drove the Turks into the Danube where thousands drowned. Seizing Jassy, he prepared to move on Constantinople. *See* Choczim.

Steenkerke *or* Steinkirk (*War of the Grand Alliance*) *8 August 1692*. Between the English (William III) and the French (Duke of Luxembourg). The English attacked the French camp at daybreak, inflicting heavy casualties. The capable Luxembourg rallied his troops, and after a stubborn close-quarter fight repulsed the English attack, and by noon the Alliance army was in full retreat. William, who should have won the battle, lost 8,000 men, half of them English. *See* Leuze; Neerwinden I.

Stiklestad (*King Olaf's Return*) *Summer 1030*. King Olaf II of Norway, exiled by his Danish and Swedish enemies, landed near Trondheim in an attempt to regain Norway. His force was defeated and Olaf killed by Danes and rebellious Norwegians. On his canonisation in 1164 Olaf became Norway's patron saint. *See* Swold; Viborg.

Stirling Bridge (*English–Scottish Wars*) *11 September 1297*. Between the Scots, under Sir William Wallace, and 50,000 English under the Earl of Surrey acting for Edward I of England, who had proclaimed himself King of Scotland. Wallace attacked the English army as it was crossing a narrow bridge over the Forth, and annihilated its vanguard of 5,000 men. This conflict is also called the Battle of Cambuskenneth. *See* Dunbar I; Falkirk I.

Stockach I, Baden (*French Revolutionary Wars*) *25 March 1799*. Between 40,000 French (Jourdan) and 60,000 Austrians (Archduke Charles). The French were defeated and driven back on the Rhine. Jourdan, losing 5,000 men, gave his command to Massena. The Austrians, part of the Second Coalition against France, were also at war with the French in Italy. *See* Magnano.

Stockach II *or* Moskirck (*French

Revolutionary Wars) 3 May 1800. Their defeat at Stockach the previous year had angered the French. The Army of the Rhine, 50,000 men under Moreau, crossed the Rhine to move into the Black Mountains. About 60,000 Austrians (Krajowa) manoeuvred to block the French. In a violent battle the French captured 5,000 Austrians and forced the rest to fall back. Each side had 2,000 battle casualties. *See* Höchstädt II.

Stoke, *Nottinghamshire* (*Wars of the Roses: Lambert Simnel's Rebellion*) *16 June 1487.* The Earl of Lincoln had taken a 10-year-old boy, Lambert Simnel, and trained him to take the part of the Earl of Warwick, who was actually in the Tower of London as a prisoner of Henry VII. Proclaiming Lambert Simnel king, Lincoln raised an army of Englishmen, Irishmen and German merecenaries. The consequent battle went badly for the Royalist troops (Earl of Oxford) under German crossbow fire, but reinforcements came up and Lincoln's Irish contingent broke. The Germans and others fought for 3 hours until overwhelmed. Most of the rebel leaders were killed. Henry VII made Simnel a kitchen scullion in the palace. This battle, and not Bosworth, was the real ending of the Wars of the Roses. Warwick, the last male Yorkist with a claim to the throne, was executed in 1499.

Stollhofen (*War of Spanish Succession*) *22 May 1707.* Louis XIV's French empire had nearly collapsed after his defeat at Ramillies, 1706, but he gained some initiative when able to prevent an attempt to put Archduke Charles of Austria on the Spanish throne. He sent an army (Villars) against the supposedly impregnable Lines of Stollhofen, stretching from Strasbourg to Karlsruhe. Villars led forty-five French battalions in a spirited storming of the lines, breaking them and taking fifty guns. German territory was now vulnerable to further French attack. *See* Almansa; Ramillies.

Stones River (*or Murfreesboro*) (*American Civil War*) *31 December 1862–3 January 1863.* A costly fight between 45,000 Federals (Rosecrans) and 35,000 Confederates (Bragg, Hardee and Polk). Both sides, 31 December, attacked the opponent's right flank, the day ending with the Federal army tightly compressed against Stones River, but with the Confederates losing heavily in piecemeal attacks. Each side made a strong attack, 2 January, but it was Bragg who broke first, withdrawing on 3 January. Casualties: Federals, 12,906; Confederates, 11,739. *See* Chickamauga; Perryville.

Stonington, *Connecticut* (*Pequot War*) *5 June 1637.* Colonists attacked and burnt a large stockaded Indian village, driving off troublesome Pequot Indians. The survivors, fleeing west, were intercepted and slaughtered, 13 July.

Stono Ferry (*American Revolution*) *20 June 1779.* The British general, Prevost, withdrawing to James Island, Charleston, left a rearguard of 900 on the mainland at Stono Ferry. Here they were attacked by 1,200 American militia (Moultrie). Superior in discipline and training, the British regulars repulsed the attack at a cost of 301 American casualties. British losses, 189. *See* Briar Creek; Savanna II.

Stony Creek, *Lake Ontario* (*British-American War of 1812*) *9 May 1813.* An American force of 2,500 under General Dearborn and naval captain Chauncey had been harassing British positions, and had forced 700 British (Vincent) to withdraw from Fort George. Making a stand, the British inflicted a sharp defeat on the Americans; two generals were among the captured. *See* Chrysler's Farm; Lake Erie; Sackets Harbour.

Stony Point (*American Revolution*) *15–16 July 1779.* A British expeditionary force from New York had captured a part-built American fort on the Hudson River. They strengthened it, then manned it with 700 troops (Lieutenant Colonel Johnson). Washington sent 1,350 men (Anthony Wayne) to retake the place, which they did with a night bayonet attack. In the fierce fight the Americans killed 63 British, wounded 70 and captured 543. Wayne had 95 casualties. The fort was dismantled. *See* Monmouth; Paulus Hook.

Stormberg (*Second British–Boer War*) *10 December 1899*. General Gatacre, with 3,000 men, made a night march to attack a Boer position. Misled by his guides, he was ambushed. Under heavy Boer fire Gatacre was forced to retire, with a loss of 89 killed or wounded and 633 prisoners. *See* Colenso; Magersfontein; Modder River.

Stow-on-the-Wold (*English Civil War*) *26 March 1646*. The Parliamentarians and their New Model Army had all but conquered England and Scotland until only one Royalist force remained — a cavalier army of 1,500 under Lord Astley. Trapped at Stow-on-the-Wold, Astley surrendered after a brief fight. Charles I surrendered on 5 May. The so-called Second Civil War broke out 2 years later. *See* Langport; Philiphaugh; Preston I.

Stralsund I (*Thirty Years' War*) *20 February–4 August 1628*. Ferdinand II of the Holy Roman Empire wanted to make a "Hapsburg Line" across General Europe and needed the Hanseatic city of Stralsund as a key point. The Austrians besieged the place, which had a small garrison of Swedes and Scottish mercenaries. Gustavus Adolphus of Sweden sent aid by ship and when the city held out Ferdinand's army commander, Wallenstein, travelled to Stralsund and supervised assaults on 8 and 9 July. Beaten back and having by now suffered 12,000 casualties, Wallenstein withdrew his troops. *See* Lutter am Barenberge; Wolgast.

Stralsund II (*Great Northern War*) *June–October 1715*. The town was besieged by 36,000 Prussians and Danes under Frederick William III of Prussia and Frederick IV of Denmark, and was defended by a Swedish garrison under Charles XII. The besiegers seized the island of Rügen, which commanded the town. Charles's attempt to retake it ended disastrously. He escaped, but was severely wounded, while the whole of his force was killed or captured. By 20 October Stralsund was no longer defensible and Charles left for Sweden on the last remaining ship. The garrison then surrendered. *See* Ahvenanmaa; Fredrikshald.

Stratton, Cornwall (*English Civil War*) *16 May 1643*. Parliamentarians, under General Chudleigh, held a hill in predominantly Royalist Cornwall. Sir Ralph Hopton led a Cavalier army in a charge up the hill and the Cornishmen were so spirited that after fierce fighting they overwhelmed the Roundheads; 1,700 were taken prisoner, including Chudleigh, and they lost all their artillery and baggage. *See* Lansdowne.

Stromboli Island (*Dutch War of Louis XIV*) *8 January 1676*. This battle between twenty warships and six fireships (Diquesne) and twenty-two Dutch ships (De Ruyter) was fought over the sovereignty of Sicily. The Dutch disorganised the French fleet, but the battle was indecisive and the French still held Sicily. *See* Augusta; Sasbach.

Sudan Civil War *1955–72*. This political-religious war was fought between the Muslim Arabs of the north and the Christian negroes of the south, following Sudanese independence from British rule. The worst fighting occurred between November 1958 and October 1964 during the military regime of General Ibrahim Abboud. In 1963 the southerners, who had been brutally oppressed by the Arab army from the north, formed the Anya-Nya ("venom of the viper") guerrilla army under General Joseph Lagu. When

General Gaafer Nimeiri came to power in a coup, the Soviet Union gave him military aid and Russian bombers flown by Russian pilots bombed Anya-Nya strongholds. Following peace efforts by the World Council of Churches and Emperor Haile Selassie of Ethiopia, the war ended in March 1972.

Suddusain (*Second British–Sikh War*) *1 July 1848*. A force of 18,000 Bhawalpuris and British (Lieutenant Edwardes) encountered 12,000 Sikhs (Malraj). The Sikhs attacked, but were beaten off, largely because of superior British artillery. *See* Gujerat.

Sudley Springs (*American Civil War*) *29 August 1862*. This action, part of the second Battle of Bull Run, was brought on by Federal General Pope when he was hunting for General Thomas Jackson's troops, who had been harassing him. Jackson deliberately invited attack to distract Pope from a larger Confederate force which was moving up. Pope's troops were beaten back and suffered 5,000 casualties. *See* Bull Run; Cedar Mountain.

Sudoner (*Hussite Wars*) *1419*. John Ziska was leading the Hussites as they left hostile Prague for their fortified mountain at Tabor, near Usti. Pursued by the Catholic troops, Ziska turned his troops sharply against them and routed them, causing many casualties. It was this action which caused Pope Martin V to declare a "Bohemian Crusade" against the Hussites. *See* Prague I.

Suero River, *Spain* (*Civil War of Sertorius*) *75 BC*. Between the rebels (Sertorius) and the Roman Army (Pompey). The Roman right, led by Pompey himself, was broken and defeated, but Afranius captured the Sertorian Camp, routing and dispersing the rebel army. Sertorius was not conquered, however, and died under assassin's knives in 73 BC.

Sugar-Loaf Rock, *Trichinopoly* (*Second Carnatic War*) *2 October 1753*. General Astruc and a 34,000-strong French-Indian army were besieging Trichinopoly, a main feature of which was Sugar-Loaf Rock. Major Stringer Lawrence was sent with a British-Indian force of less than 6,000 to break the siege. Under the spirited British attack, the French lost 100 killed or wounded and fled. General Astruc was taken prisoner. British casualties were less than 40.

Sungari River (*Chinese Civil War*) *6–19 January: 21–25 February; 8–15 March 1947*. The Chinese People's Liberation Army (Communist) made three major attacks across the ice-solid Sungari River against Chiang Kai-shek's Nationalist army. All were bloodily repulsed, but at the end the Nationalists held only a small north-bank bridgehead. On 4 May the PLA sent 270,000 men across the Sungari 150 miles into Manchuria where, in more bitter fighting, the offensive stopped, 28 June. However, the Nationalists had paid so heavily for their past-victory that the PLA was able to take the initiative. *See* Chinese Chinese Civil War; Mukden II; Szepingkai.

Süntelberg (*Charlemagne's Campaigns*) *782*. Charlemagne sent an army of Franks to arrest the pagan Saxon chief, Witukind. The Saxons were waiting for them atop a slope in modern Hannover and the Franks were almost wiped out as they charged up hill. On the Aller River Charlemagne, in revenge, had 4,000 Saxon prisoners slaughtered when they refused to betray Witukind. Three years later Witukind surrendered and was baptised. *See* Roncesvalles; Trisza River.

Surinam (*Napoleonic Wars*) *5 May 1804*. This West Indian stronghold, held by a Dutch garrison, was captured by a British squadron (Commander Hood) supported by 2,000 troops (Sir Charles Green).

Sursuti, The I (*Muhammad Ghori's invasion of India*) 1191. Between the Afghans (Muhammad Ghori) and the Hindus (King of Delhi), who reportedly had 200,000 cavalry and 300 elephants. The greatly outnumbered Afghans were surrounded and routed. Ghori escaped on an elephant.

Sursuti, The II (*Muhammad Ghori's invasion of India*) 1192. Returning to the field where he had suffered defeat the previous year, Ghori gave battle to the Rajputs and Delhi armies under the Rajah of Ajmir. With an army of 120,000 Afghans he routed the Rajputs and captured the rajah. He now campaigned to conquer Hindustan.

Sveaborg, *Finland (Russia–Swedish War*) February–3 May 1808. Sveaborg was defended by a garrison of 7,000 Swedes and Finns led by Admiral Kronstedt when it was besieged by General Suchtelen. Napoleon and Alexander of Russia, as allies, were invading Finland, which was Swedish territory, because Sweden would not declare war on England. In bitter winter weather the Russians could not bring up heavy guns. But neither could supplies reach Kronstedt so he offered to surrender if at least five Swedish warships did not relieve Sveaborg by 3 May. On that day he handed over to the Russians the town, 200 guns, two frigates and nineteen transports. The inconclusive war lasted just one year.

Sveaborg II (*Crimean War*) 9–11 August 1855. The town, which had become an important Russian arsenal, was bombarded by a British fleet (Admiral Dundas). With the arsenal and storehouses destroyed Dundas withdrew.

Svenskund, *Baltic (Swedish–Russian War*) 9 July 1790. After his victory at Viborg, the Prince of Nassau did not exploit his opportunity but waited until 9 July, birthday of his sovereign, Catherine the Great, to do battle with King Gustavus III, who had sheltered his fleet of galleys behind low rocks in Svenskund Fiord. Advancing into the fiord without thought for tactics or safety, the Russian ships came under deadly, concentrated fire that destroyed a third of their number and caused 9,500 casualties. Gustavus, with fewer than 300 casualties, and having restored the balance of the war, signed an advantageous peace treaty. This was the last real battle of oared ships. *See* Viborg.

Svištov (*Russian–Turkish War*) 26–27 June 1877. Russia declared war on Turkey in support of Serbia, and the Army of the Danube moved south to the Danube, objective Nicopol. An advance force of 15,000 (Dragomirov) crossed the Danube by night and surprised the Turkish fortress of Svistov. Next day the main Russian army (Skobelev) took the place by storm with few casualties to the attackers. Nicopol fell 16 July, Plevna was to be the next target. *See* Plevna.

Swold Island, *Baltic (Scandinavian Wars*) August 1000. Olaf I of Norway and his fleet was defeated in a great but semi-legendary battle by the Viking Sweyn I Forkbeard and the Swede Olaf Skutkonung.

Sybota, *Epirus (Corinthian–Corcyrean War*) 433 BC. Fought between a Corinthian fleet of 150 galleys and a Corcyrean fleet of 110, aided by ten Athenian triremes. Both sides claimed victory, but the advantage lay with the Corinthians, who captured several ships.

Syracuse I, *Sicily (Great Peloponnese War*) 415–413 BC. Athens sent 134 galleys with troops to attack the city-state of Syracuse. By the time the siege began two of the three Athenian generals were no longer available and command fell to Nicias, an indecisive man. Construction of the siege works was so slow that Gylippus, with 2,000 Spartans, arrived to join Hermocrates, commanding in Syracuse. Athens sent the veteran Demosthenes, with 70 galleys and 5,000 soldiers, to support Nicias. A land attack against the Syracusans and Spartans failed early in 413 and the Athenians lost ship after ship to audacious Syracusan raids. Demosthenes and Nicias, now without their navy, led their army inland. The Syracusans and Spartans destroyed it in flank attacks. The Athenians lost 34,000 men in the disastrous campaign, including 6,000 sold as slaves. Demosthenes and Nicias were beheaded and Athens was finished as an imperial power. *See* Amphipolis; Cumae; Cynossema.

Syracuse II (*Second Carthaginian invasion of Sicily*) *387 BC*. Having won a naval victory off Catania, Himilco the Carthaginian threw 50,000 troops into a siege of Syracuse, where Dionysus the Elder, a vigorous and clever general, commanded the garrison. The Carthaginians lost 10,000 men in an epidemic, then Dionysus sent Leptinus to attack the Carthaginian fleet in harbour; he destroyed every ship. At the same time Dionysus' troops attacked the enemy lines and routed the Carthaginians. Himilco fled and committed suicide, but Dionysus was unable to push the Carthaginians from territory they had captured in western Sicily. *See* Acragas; Crimisus.

Syracuse III (*Second Punic War*) *214–212 BC*. Syracuse, in the hands of the pro-Carthaginian faction (Hippocrates), was besieged by 25,000 Romans (Marcellus) and a fleet (Appius Claudius). The great inventor and physicist Archimedes was present in Syracuse and his military catapults, slings and other devices played an important part in the defence. Other Sicilian towns rebelled and drew off some of the besiegers, but taking advantage of a festival in Syracuse Marcellus' Romans captured part of the town. A Carthaginian relieving force was repulsed and the rest of the city was captured with much slaughter; Archimedes was among the victims. *See* Capua; Nola.

Syria (*World War II*) *June–July*

***1941*.** An Allied victory over Axis and Vichy French forces. The strength of each Allied national contingent was: Australian, 18,000; U.K., 9,000; Indian, 2,000; Free French, 5,000. Vichy strength (Dentz) was about 35,000, including Foreign Legion and Algerian troops. The Allied commander was at first the British general, Wilson, then the Australian Lavarack. In the arudous 5-week campaign the Vichy French troops fought hard and skilfully. The crossing of the Litani River was stubbornly contested, Australian artillery driving off Vichy warships which had come inshore to shell Australian positions. British aircraft won control of the skies. Other principal actions were Djezine, Mardjayoun, Damour and Mezze. The battle for Mardjayoun was of great significance. By holding a pass in a long and costly battle, the Australians denied enemy access to Palestine; this could have had disastrous consequences.

Allied victory meant that the Axis powers could not now control the eastern Mediterranean and so threaten the Suez Canal from the north. Casualties: British and Indian, 1,800 including 1,200 taken prisoner; Free French, 1,300, including 1,100 taken prisoner; Australian, 1,600 killed or wounded, 3,150 sick, no prisoners; Vichy French, 3,348 killed or wounded, 3,000 prisoners.

Szentgotthárd, *Hungary (Austrian–Turkish Wars*) *1 August 1664*. The Austrians (Montecuccoli), aided by some French (Charles of Lorraine), took up strong positions behind the Raba River to block a massive invasion by the Turks (The Grand Vizier, Ahmed Kuprili). An able general, Montecuccoli, defeated the Turks in a fierce, protracted fight which so demoralised them that they signed a peace treaty a few weeks later. *See* Candia II; Khotin II.

Szepingkai, *north of Mukden (Chinese Civil War*) *16 April–20 May 1946*. At a key railway junction on the South Manchuria Railway 115,000 troops of the

People's Liberation Army (Communist) of Mao Tse-tung blocked the Nationalist First Army (Sun Li-jen) advancing from Mukden. In a pitched battle of remarkable ferocity the Nationalists were victorious. This was the first major battle of the war.

Szigetvár, *Hungary* (*Turkish invasion of Europe*) *5 August–7 September 1566.* The fortress of Szigetvár was manned by 3,000 troops under a Croatian noble, Zriny I, when attacked by Suleiman I, the Magnificent, and his Turkish army. Suleiman, now aged 72 and probably the most powerful ruler in the world, died of natural causes, but his death was kept secret in case it should demoralise the Turkish troops. They were told of the sultan's death only after they had stormed the city. Few of the garrison survived. *See* Astrakhan II; Vienna I.

Tabraca, *west of Carthage* (*Gildo's African Revolt*) *398*. Mascazel led 5,000 handpicked Roman legionaries against Gildo and his 70,000 rebellious Africans and some Roman soldiers. The legionaries routed the superior enemy and Gildo committed suicide in prison.

Tacna (*Peruvian-Chilean War*) *26 May 1880*. Chile had gone to war with Peru and Bolivia over the rich nitrate deposits in the Bolivian littoral; at that time Bolivia had a Pacific coastline. At Tacna the Chileans (Baquedano) decisively defeated the allies under the Bolivian president, Campero. After a five-year war of manoeuvre and intrigue Bolivia lost access to the Pacific, Peru ceded its own nitrate province and Chile became the dominant power in western South America. *See* Tarapaca.

Tacubaya (*Mexican Liberal Rising*) *11 April 1859*. The Government troops (Marquez) decisively defeated the Liberals (Degollado) who lost all their artillery and stores. The rising collapsed. *See* Calpulalpam.

Taginae (*or Tadinum*) (*Wars of the Byzantine Empire*) *July 552*. Emperor Justinian I of the Byzantine Empire sent the able eunuch General Narses with 20,000 men to reconquer Italy from the Ostrogoths. In the Apennines near the Flaminian Way Narses confronted King Totila and a strong Ostrogoth army. By cleverly co-ordinated use of archers and pikemen Narses routed the Ostrogoths, 6,000 of whom, including Totila, were killed. Narses then crushed all Gothic power in Italy. *See* Casilnum; Rome IV.

Tagliacozzo, *central Italy* (*German invasion of Italy*) *23 August 1268*. A German army of the Holy Roman Empire, led by Conradin, aged 16, and son of the late Conrad IV — and by Frederick, Duke of Austria — invaded Italy to threaten Charles of Anjou who held southern Italy and Sicily. Charles was too good a general for his enemies and he encircled and routed them. He executed Conradin and Frederick. *See* Benevento; Messina II.

Taierchwang (*Chinese–Japanese War*) *31 March–9 April 1938*. The first major Chinese victory over the invading Japanese in the protracted conflict that preceded World War II. They claimed to have killed 7,000 Japanese. *See* Nanking.

Taiken Gate (*Japanese Hogen Insurrection*) *1157*. The Imperial troops (Bifukumonia and Tadamichi) defeated the rebels (Shitoku) in this decisive battle of a bloody civil war.

Taillebourg, *northern France* (*English–French Wars*) *April 1242*. Louis IX of France defeated Henry III of England who was leading a mixed force of

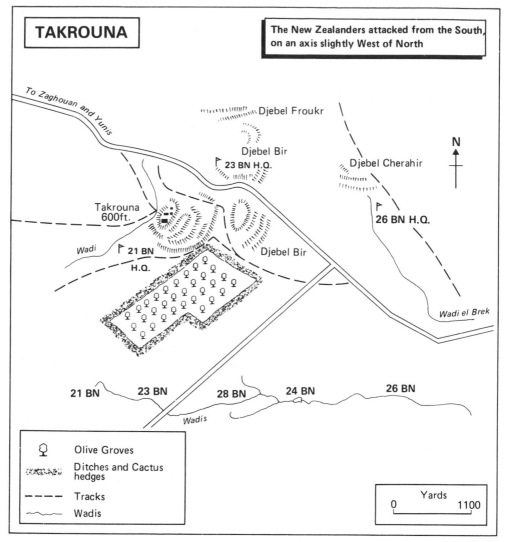

TAKROUNA

The New Zealanders attacked from the South, on an axis slightly West of North

To Zaghouan and Yunis

Djebel Froukr

Djebel Bir

23 BN H.Q.

Djebel Cherahir

26 BN H.Q.

Takrouna
600ft.

Wadi

21 BN
H.Q.

Djebel Bir

Wadi el Brek

21 BN   23 BN   28 BN   24 BN   26 BN

Wadis

Olive Groves
Ditches and Cactus hedges
Tracks
Wadis

Yards
0   1100

English troops and French rebels. Defeated, Henry was driven from France.

Takashima (*Chinese invasion of Japan*) *1281* A Chinese invasion fleet had been wrecked and the survivors (Chang Pak) took refuge on the island of Takashima. Attacked by Kyushu troops (Kagesuke), the Chinese were virtually wiped out.

Takrouna (*World War II*) *19–21 April 1943.* The most severe key action in the larger battle for Enfidaville, Tunisia, q.v. Takrouna was a rocky 600-ft outcrop held by the Italian Trieste Division (La Ferla). It was taken with great gallantry by 1,062 New Zealanders (Kippenberger). Suffering 50 per cent casualties, the New Zealanders killed many enemy and took 732 prisoners and much material. Takrouna has been called "the most gallant feat of arms of World War II". (Lieutenant General Horrocks). *See* Mareth Line.

Taku Forts (*Second British-Chinese War*) *25 June 1859 and 21 August*

1860. The forts guarded the entrance to the Hai River, leading to Tientsin. Britain and other Western powers wanted to enforce trade with China, but had first to break through militarily. The Chinese repulsed a naval-marine attack. Then a British–French army of 17,000 under Sir James Hope stormed and took the forts after heavy naval bombardment. Tientsin was opened to trade. *See* Peking III.

Talana Hill (*or Dundee*) (*Second British-Boer War*) *20 October 1899.* The Boers (Meyer) holding the heights of Dundee were dislodged, but the British lost their commander (Symons) among their 162 casualties and 331 prisoners. The Boer thrust to Ladysmith was unimpeded. *See* Ladysmith.

Talas (*Chinese Imperial Wars*) *751.* In an unlikely alliance, the Muslim Arabs and the Tibetans blocked the Chinese army of General Kao Hsien-Chih, who surprised them with an astonishing march across the Pamir Mountains. He then threatened to take Tashkent whose prince called on the Arabs for assistance. Their furious battle tactics decisively defeated Kao at the Battle of Talas, in Kirghiz. Chinese control west of the Pamirs came to an end.

Talavera, *south-west of Madrid* (*Napoleonic Wars*) *28 July 1809.* 20,000 British troops under Wellesley (later Duke of Wellington) aided by 20,000 Spaniards (General Cuesta) marched up the Tagus Valley and encountered 50,000 French (Marshal Victor). Without waiting for Soult, who was moving from the north with another French army, Victor attacked. The Spaniards soon broke, leaving 16,000 British facing 30,000 French (combat strength). In a savage battle Victor lost 7,300 men and twenty guns and fell back. Wellesley, with 5,400 casualties, had won a notable victory but was not strong enough to pursue Victor or confront Soult and retired into Portugal. *See* Busaco: Oporto.

Talikhan (*Mongol invasion of Khorassan*) *1221.* Genghis Khan captured the fortesss after a 7-month siege in which tens of thousands of people died. *See* Samarkand.

Talikota, *Bombay province* (*Mogul–Hindu Wars*) *May 1565.* Muslim sultans from the Indian Deccan led a vast confederated army to crush the Hindu kingdom of Vijanyanagar, which was blocking the advance of Muhammadans from the north. Their victory destroyed the Hindu kingdom, thus uniting Muslims from north and south. *See* Panipat II.

Talladega, *Alabama* (*American–Creek Indian War*) *9 November 1813.* General Andrew Jackson, with a force of Tennessee militia, surrounded a Creek War party and killed 500 at slight loss to himself. *See* Fort Mims; Horseshoe Bend.

Talneer, *India* (*Third British–Mahratta War*) *17 February 1818.* Sir Thomas Hislip's British column had arrived to take possession of a fortress ceded to them by treaty. The commandant refused to hand it over, but after a bombardment surrendered. The garrison of 300 then cut down two British officers and their sepoy escort who had been sent to accept the surrender. The enraged British and Indian troops then stormed the place, killing every man of the garrison; the commandant was hanged. *See* Kirkee.

Tamai (*British Sudan Campaigns*) *13 March 1884.* 4,000 British troops (Graham) in two squares attacked and destroyed the camp of the Mahdist rebels of Osman and Digna. Casualties: British, 214; Mahdists, 2,200 killed. *See* Khartoum; Omdurman.

Tanagra-Oenophyta (*First Peloponnesian War*) *457 BC.* A Spartan army marched across the Corinth Isthmus to check further Athenian aggression. At Tanagra, with some Theban allies, the Spartans attacked 14,000 Athenians and

6,000 Thessalians; the latter deserted and the Spartans were tactically victorious, but they had suffered grievous casualties. At Oenophyta 2 months later the Athenians, rallying under Myronides, defeated the Spartans and Thebans, thus regaining control over central Greece. *See* Aegina; Coronea I.

Tananarive (*French Conquest of Madagascar*) *24 February–30 September 1895.* Frustrated for nearly 300 years in their attempts to conquer Madagascar, the French sent a major expedition of 15,000 troops (General Duchesne). After an arduous campaign, Duchesne bombarded the capital, Tananarive, and Queen Ranavalona III surrendered.

Tangier (*Portuguese invasion of Africa*) *April 1437.* A disastrous repulse for King Edward of Portugal at the hands of the Moors. He left his brother Frederick as proof of his intention to evacuate Ceuta, 25 miles away. He did not keep his promise and Frederick died in captivity 5 years later. Edward's son, Alfonso V, occupied Tangier in 1471. *See* Ceuta; Toro.

Tanjore I (*Seven Years' War*) *12–17 August 1758.* Unable to break into the Indian-held fort and now short of artillery ammunition, the French commander, Lally-Tollendahl, was about to retire. Hearing of this, the Indian commander, Monacji, attacked and surprised the French camp. Beaten off, he nevertheless captured all the French siege guns. *See* Madras II.

Tanjore II (*First British–Mysore War*) *11 August–20 September 1773.* Having held the fort against the French in 1758, Monacji now lost it to the British — 20,000 men under General Joseph Smith. Having earlier breached the walls, Smith sent his troops in at midday while the garrison was having its usual siesta. Smith reported — "Victory was immediate."

Tannenberg I (*War of the Teutonic Knights*) *15 July 1410.* An overwhelming victory for the Polish King Ladislas II, aided by Jan Ziska and his Bohemian mercenaries as well as by Russians and Lithuanians, over the hitherto almost invincible Teutonic Knights. Their Order lost its power after this reverse.

Tannenberg II (*World War I*) *26–30 August 1914.* One of the great military disasters. The Russian First Army (Rennenkampf) had been victorious over the Germans at Gumbinnen, but did not exploit the victory. The new commander of the German Eighth Army, Hindenburg, and his chief-of-staff, Ludendorff, had time to prepare to meet the Russian Second Army (Samsonov) moving from the south. Deploying 300,000 men against 300,000 men, Hindenburg and Ludendorff organised a gigantic double envelopment on right and left flanks. The Germans knew, by listening to Russian radio messages sent in clear, that Samsonov was attacking on a 70-mile front, while Samsonov had no idea of his critical position. As the pincer-grip tightened, he ordered further attacks. He was badly mauled on his right by Mackensen and Below and on his left suffered a tremendous artillery bombardment from François' I Corps. On 28 August François turned the Russian left flank while the right wing broke under pressure. Given no help by Rennenkampf and the Russian First Army, Samsonov lost control of the situation, ordered a retreat and committed suicide. The pincers closed and the Russians had lost 30,000 killed or wounded, 92,000 taken prisoner, 400 of their 600 guns. German casualties, 13,000 killed or wounded. *See* Gumbinnen; Masurian Lakes I.

Tansara Saka (*Japanese Satsuma Rebellion*) *4 October 1876.* Prince Taruhito attacked rebels in a strong position and defeated them but lost heavily in the process.

Taormina (*Muslim conquest of Sicily*)

902. The Byzantines held Sicily with such an iron grip that the Muslims, invading the island in 827, did not take Syracuse until 878. Even then the garrison of Taormina held out until 902. Stormed once more, the fortress fell and was burned. *See* Apulia; Erzurum.

Tara (*Irish Rebellion*) *26 May 1798*. About 400 British Royalist troops defeated 4,000 insurgent Irish, killing 500 of them.

Taranto, *southern Italy* (*World War II*) *11 November 1940*. Admiral Andrew Cunningham sent twenty-seven aircraft from H.M.S. *Illustrious* to attack the Italian fleet "safe" in the harbour of Taranto. Aerial torpedoes crippled three Italian battleships and two cruisers and sank two other ships. Half the Italian battle fleet was disabled for several months. The British lost two aircraft. *See* Matapan.

Taraori (*Muslim invasion of India*). The Muslim (Persian) Sultan Muhammad of Ghor, after a reverse in 1188, brought a highly trained army of mounted archers and crushed the Hindus, whose armies were already fragmented by friction and lack of overall control. Muhammad overran practically all of north-west India, but was himself displaced by the Mongols. *See* Indus River; Somnath.

Tarapaca (*Peruvian–Chilean War*) *17 November 1879*. A disaster for the Peruvians under the onslaught of superior numbers of Chileans. *See* Tacna.

Tarawa-Makin (*World War II*) *20–23 November 1943*. The Japanese (Admiral Shibasaki) had heavily fortified the Tarawa atolls, in the Gilbert Islands. The Americans heavily blasted key sites with air and naval strikes, then 5,000 of their V Amphibious Corps (Holland Smith) landed on Betio. They ran into deadly fire from 4,800 Japanese marines and in securing two small beaches 1,500 Americans were killed or wounded. They

took Tarawa, but in the savage 4-day fight lost 991 dead and 2,311 wounded. Few Japanese survived. The action at Makin, same period, cost the Americans another sixty-six dead and 152 wounded, with 440 Japanese killed. During this battle the carrier *Liscome Bay* was torpedoed with the loss of 650 men. Possession of these islands gave the Americans air bases from which to attack the Marshall Islands. *See* Kwajalein-Eniwetok; Rabaul.

Tarento (*Spanish Campaigns in Italy*) *August 1501–1 March 1502*. Gonsalvo de Cordova, with 5,000 Spaniards, invested the Neopolitan fortress (Potenza) but had not the strength for a sustained siege or a major assault. The north front of the fort, facing a lake, was unfortified. With great effort, the Spaniards carried smaller ships overland from the Bay of Tarento, launched them on the lake and so took the fort on its undefended side. The feat was typical of Cordova's inventiveness.

Tarragona (*Peninsular War*) *May 1811–28 June 1811*. Tarragona was held by a Spanish garrison when besieged by 45,000 French (Suchet). The French took key posts one by one and finally stormed the higher part of the town. Casualties: French, 6,000; Spanish, about 12,000 plus 8,000 survivors taken prisoner. *See* Albuhera; Ciudad Rodrigo.

Tarsus (*First Crusade*) *1097*. Tancred, a Norman lord from Italy, reached Tarsus with only 100 knights and 200 infantry. The confident Turks left their fort to attack the Crusaders and were cut to pieces. But the Crusaders lacked unity and Baldwin of Boulogne, arriving to find Tancred holding Tarsus, used his superior force to order Tancred to move on eastwards and fight the Turks. Then he refused to allow into the fort another 300 Normans from Italy who had come to reinforce Tancred. That night the Turks crept up and massacred the Normans camped outside the walls. *See* Antioch I; Dorylaeum I.

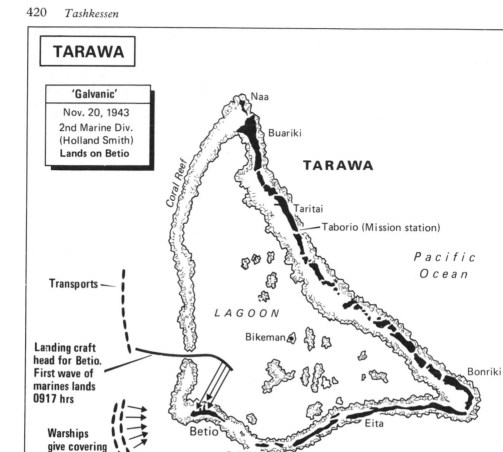

TARAWA

'Galvanic'

Nov. 20, 1943
2nd Marine Div.
(Holland Smith)
Lands on Betio

Naa

Buariki

TARAWA

Coral Reef

Taritai

Taborio (Mission station)

Pacific Ocean

Transports —

LAGOON

Bikeman

Landing craft
head for Betio.
First wave of
marines lands
0917 hrs

Bonriki

Warships
give covering
fire

Betio

Eita

Bairiki

Firm ground   Coral

Miles
0   5

Tashkessen (*Russian–Turkish War*) *28 December 1877*. Between 2,000 Turks, under an English general in Turkish service, Valentine Baker, and a Russian division (Kourlov). Covering the retirement of a larger Turkish army, Baker held firm against several Russian onslaughts. He lost 800 men but inflicted 1,100 casualties on his enemy. *See* Kars; Plevna.

Tassaforonga (*World War II*). *See* Guadalcanal.

Tauris (*Civil War of Caesar and Pompey*) *47 BC*. The Caesarian fleet (Vitinius), though inferior in number and quality, attacked the Pompeian fleet (Marcus Octavius) scattered it, and forced Octavius out of the Adriatic. *See* Pharsalus.

Taus (*Hussite Wars*) *14 August 1431*. A victory for the Hussites — followers of a creed established by the martyred John Huss — under Jan Ziska over the Bohemians led by Emperor Sigismund. *See* Aussig; Český-Brod.

Tayeizan (*Japanese Revolution*) *1 November 1868*. The followers of the Shogun or Generalissimo made their last stand in Tokyo at the Tayeizan temple. The emperor's troops defeated and massacred them and took control of the Shogun's capital. *See* Shirogawa.

Tchernaya River (*Crimean War*) *16 August 1855*. The Russians (Gortschakov) attacked positions held by three French and one Sardinian division (Marmora) and after severe fighting were repulsed. Casualties: Russian, 5,000; Allies, 1,200. *See* Alma; Balaclava; Kars.

"Tearless Battle" (*or Laconia*) (*Greek City-state Wars*) *368 BC*. A force of Arcadians was trying to cut off a Spartan army (Archidamus), but in a narrow defile in Laconia the Arcadians were themselves ambushed. The Spartans, who lost not a man, called the fight the "Tearless Battle". The Arcadians suffered heavily.

Tegea (*Greek City-state Wars*) *473 BC*. The Spartans had reached Tegea and were about to attack it when they were attacked by the combined forces of the Arcadian League and the Argives. Though victorious, the Spartans were now too weak to take Tegea.

Tegyra (*Boeotian War*) *375 BC*. Pelopidas, with the Sacred Band of 300 Thebans, routed a large force of Spartans in a narrow pass near Orchomenus, killing 600 including their two generals. (Gorgidos formed this picked band of Theban shock troops in 378 BC. It consisted of 300 men traditionally grouped as pairs of lovers. Pelopidas kept the band together and fostered their esprit de corps. They were said to have remained undefeated until their heroic annihilation at Chaeronea, 338 BC.) *See* Leuctra.

Telamon (*Conquest of Cisalpine Gaul*) *225 BC*. Having wiped out a Roman army at Clusiam, q.v., the Cisalpine Gauls (or Po Valley Celts) reached the Italian coast west of Rome. Here they were caught between two Roman armies and after desperate fighting were destroyed. *See* Clastidium.

Tel-el-Kebir (*Egyptian Rebellion or Arabi's Revolt*) *13 September 1882*. Arabi's Egyptian army, 22,000 strong, waited in the desert near Zagazig to block the approaching British army of 17,000 (Wolseley). Making a night march, the British attack surprised the rebels who suffered heavy casualties and were routed. British casualties, 339. *See* Alexandria IV.

Tel-el-Mahuta (*Egyptian Rebellion or Arabi's Revolt*) *24 August 1882*. The British (Graham), marching to Kassassian, q.v., drove off a force of Egyptian rebels which tried to block them. *See* Tel-el-Kebir.

Tel-Li-Ssu (*Russian–Japanese War*) *14–15 June 1904*. Between 35,000 Russians (Stakelberg) and 40,000 Japanese (Oku). The Russians withstood several frontal attacks, but on the second day the Japanese turned the enemy flank and forced a disorderly retreat. Casualties: Russian, about 10,000; Japanese 1,163. *See* Liaoyang.

Tellicherry (*First British-Mysore War*) *14 June 1780–18 January 1782*. Held by a small British garrison, Tellicherry was besieged by Mysore troops under Ali Khan. Despite many attacks, the garrison held firm until Major Abington arrived with reinforcements 18 months later. Abington then stormed the Mysore trenches, capturing all sixty enemy cannon and 1,200 prisoners, including Ali Khan. *See* Porto Novo.

Temesvar (*Hungarian Rising Against Austria*) *9 August 1849*. The Austrians (Haynau) defeated the Hungarians (Dembinski) in their last stand on the war. On 12 August the Hungarian leader, Gorgéy, surrendered his army of 22,000 to the Russians — allies of Austria. General Haynau then brutally dealt with any still resisting groups of patriots and hanged eleven Hungarian generals. Hungary was absorbed into the Austrian empire. *See* Kapolna; Segesvár.

Tempsford, *near Bedford* (*Rise of England*) *918*. Edward the Elder, son of Alfred the Great, in his systematic campaign against the invading Danes, stormed and took the Danish fortress of Tempsford. The Danish leader, Guthrum II, was killed and Danish resistance in East Anglia was broken. *See* Brunanburh; Tettenhall.

Tenchebrai (*or Tinchebray*) *28 September 1106*. Henry I of England and his army decisively defeated his brother, Robert of Normandy, and made him prisoner — for 28 years until his death. He annexed Normandy to the crown of England.

Tenochtitlán, *now Mexico City* (*Spanish Conquest of Mexico*) *30 June 1520 and 13 August 1521*. The Spanish conquistador, Cortez, entered Tenochtitlán with his 600 troops, 8 November 1519, and found the Aztecs friendly. Nevertheless, he held their emperor, Montezuma, as hostage. Under Guamemotzin, the Aztecs revolted and Cortez fought his way out of the city, 30 June 1520. He suffered heavy losses on his Spanish "night of sadness" (*la noche triste*). Montezuma was killed in the fighting. Cortez defeated a large Indian army at Otumba, q.v., then returned to Tenochtitlán, which he took by storm, 13 August 1521, and destroyed it. With the capture and murder of Guamemotzin, who had become emperor, the Spanish ended Aztec resistance.

Tergoes (*Netherlands War of Independence*) *16 August 1572–20 October 1572*. Held by a small Spanish garrison, Tergoes was besieged by 7,000 Dutch patriots (Zeraerts). Colonel Mondragon, with 3,000 Spanish veterans crossed flooded ground and broke the siege, the Dutch being demoralised by the unexpected attack. *See* Brielle; Haarlem.

Tertry (*or Testry, Somme*) (*Rise of France*) *687*. A victory for the Austrasians (Pepin II) over the Neustrians (Thierry III). Then he conquered the Frisians, Allemanni and Burgundians. Pepin's victories brought more unity to the Frankish kingdom than it had known for nearly 200 years.

Teruel (*Spanish Civil War*) *15 December 1937*. The Republican (Government) armies of the East (Sarabia) and of the Levante (Menendez) launched a joint offensive against the Nationalist garrison of Teruel, commanded by Colonel d'Harcourt. The place held under heavy attack and in bitter weather. Nationalist commander Franco sent in a counter-offensive (Varela and Aranda), but the Republican lines held. However, d'Harcourt could no longer sustain resistance and surrendered. The Republicans, occupying Teruel, were themselves besieged and fierce fighting continued. Nationalist cavalry struck so hard north of the city, 7 February, that the Republicans suffered 15,000 casualties and lost 7,000 troops as prisoners. Nationalist Moroccan troops (Yague) then cut off Teruel from the north, leaving only the Valencia road open. Sarabia had no option but to withdraw his Republicans, but he left 10,000 dead in the city and another 14,500 in enemy hands. *See* Gijon; Saragossa III; Vinaroz.

Tettenhall, *Staffordshire* (*Rise of England*) *910*. A decisive victory for Edward, King of Wessex and son of Alfred the Great, over the Northumbrian Danes. He soon ruled as far north as the Humber River. *See* Brunanburh; Tempsford.

Tetuan (*Spanish–Moroccan War*) *4 February 1860*. The city, held by 40,000 Moors was stormed and taken by 30,000 Spaniards (O'Donnell). Casualties were heavy.

Teutoburger Wald, *Westphalia* (*Germanic Wars of the Roman*

Empire) AD *9*. Accepted as one of the decisive battles of history. From his base in Westphalia, the Roman leader Varus marched east with 20,000 legionaries to put down an insurrection. In wild country between the Ems and Weser rivers the Roman legions were ambushed by a large force of Germans, then half-wild tribesmen, under Arminius. Though the Legions held firm, they could not come to grips with the spear-throwing Germans. Next day Varus mistakenly ordered his cavalry to break through, but the horsed units were badly disorganised by the rough country and the Germans slaughtered them. On the third day the Germans swamped the surviving Roman infantry. Varus committed suicide to avoid capture. Emperor Augustus was forced to accept that the Roman Empire could not extend north of the Rhine. *See* Lippe River.

Tewkesbury (*Wars of the Roses*) *4 May 1471*. Edward IV led his Yorkish (white rose) army west to cut off the Lancastrians (Duke of Somerset) marching north from Weymouth to recruit along the Welsh border. At Tewkesbury the Lancastrians had a strong line, but Somerset, seeing a weakness in the Yorkist line, left his position to attack. Edward's spearmen drove Somerset's men back in disorder. With the Lancastrian flank now unguarded, the Yorkist infantry rushed to the attack. The Lancastrian forces fell to pieces. Edward, the young Prince of Wales, was killed, Somerset was beheaded and their figurehead, Queen Margaret, wife of Henry VI, surrendered. Henry himself died mysteriously leaving Henry Tudor the only Lancastrian claimant to the throne. *See* Barnet; Bosworth Field.

Texel I (*First English–Dutch War*) *30–31 July 1653*. An English fleet (Monck, later Duke of Albemarle) crossed the Channel and gave battle to the Dutch (Maarten Tromp) off Texel island. The first day was indecisive; Monck was then reinforced and defeated the Dutch.

Tromp, killed in the battle, lost twenty of his hundred ships. The English loss was also considerable. This was the last battle of the war. *See* Lowestoft; North Foreland I.

Texel II (*Third English–Dutch War*) *20 August 1673*. Sixty English ships (Prince Rupert) and thirty French ships (d'Estrées) were to land troops to support the overland invasion of the Netherlands by Louis XIV. They were blocked by seventy Dutch warships under de Ruyter who manoeuvred so skilfully that the allies could not use their superior numbers. After a day-long battle de Ruyter withdrew, having prevented the allied invasion. *See* Maastricht II; Schooneveldt.

Thala, *North Africa* (*Numidian Revolt Against the Romans*) AD *22*. A large force of Numidians (Tacfarinas) attacked this fortress held by no more than 500 legionaries. The Romans sallied out and inflicted so severe a defeat on Tacfarinas that he could never again assemble an army.

Thames River, *south-east Ontario* (*American–British War of 1812*) *5 October 1813*. A victory for 4,500 Americans (William Harrison) over the British (Proctor) and their Indian allies. The death in action of the Shawnee chief Tecumseh — who had protested about Proctor's tactics — ended the Indian alliance with Britain. Casualties: American, 45; British and Indian, 48 killed or wounded; 477 prisoners. *See* Chateaugay River; Lake Erie.

Thapsus, *now in Tunisia* (*War of First Triumvirate*) *46 BC*. With ten legions Julius Caesar gave battle to the fourteen legions of his allied enemies, chief of whom were Sextus Pompey, son of the late Pompey the Great, Titus Labienus, a former lieutenant of Caesar's, Metellus Scipio, defeated at Marsalus and Juba I of Numidia. Caesar's tactics and the steadiness of his veterans defeated the coalition, two of whom committed suicide. The Roman senate now appointed Caesar dictator for 10 years. *See* Munda; Ruspina.

Thebes (*Alexander's Macedonian Conquests***) *355* BC.** The Thebans, mistakenly believing Alexander to be dead, revolted and surrounded the Macedonian force of occupation in the acropolis, known as the Cadmea. Alexander then arrived with a relief force, one of whom, a captain, Perdiccas, courageously gained entry to the city and led the first assault. Taking the city, Alexander had 6,000 inhabitants executed and destroyed the city, leaving only one building intact — the home of Pindar, the poet. *See* Granicus River.

Thermopylae I (*Persian–Greek Wars***) *480* BC.** In the pass of Thermopylae 5,000 Greeks took up strong positions to block the sweeping advance of Xerxes and his 100,000 Persians. The Greeks held for 3 days, then a traitor showed the Persians a flanking route through another pass. Leonidas I of Sparta with 300 men fought a valiant rearguard action which allowed the other Greeks to escape, but all 300 Spartans fell. Xerxes continued his successes until his defeat in the great naval battle of Salamis, q.v. *See* Marathon.

Thermopylae II (*Wars of Hellenistic Monarchies***) *191* BC.** Antiochus III, the Great, invaded Greece with his Syrian army, but the Romans, who also wanted Greece, landed an army (Manius Glabrio and Marcus Cato) and drove the Syrians back to Thermopylae. Here the 40,000 disciplined Romans were too much for the Syrians. Capturing a Syrian post protecting the flank, the Romans inflicted a disastrous defeat on the enemy army. Only Antiochus and 500 men returned to Asia. *See* Cynoscephalae; Magnesia; Panion.

Thetford (*Danish invasion of England***) *870*.** A victory for the Danish invaders over the East Anglians led by Edward. *See* Brunanburh; Tempsford; Tettenhall.

Thirty Years' War. *See* List of Battles.

Thorn (*or Torun***) (***Great Northern War***) *May–22 September 1703*.** Charles XII with 10,000 troops besieged the powerful fortress of Thorn on the Vistula. Its garrison of 5,000 resisted stubbornly, but the place fell to the besiegers and Charles controlled all Poland. Charles threw back a Russian relief army and Augustus II finally renounced his claim to the Polish crown. *See* Holowczyn; Pultusk I.

Thurii, *near Sybari, Italy* (*Roman–Lucanian War***) *282* BC.** A Roman army (Caius Fabricius) routed the Lucanians and Bruttians who were besieging Thuril and its Roman garrison.

Tiberias (*Crusader–Turkish Wars***) *1 July 1187*.** Saladin threw 60,000 men around the Crusader fortress of Tiberias, western Lake Galilee. In Acre the Frankish crusaders assembled 10,000 infantry, 1,200 mounted knights and 2,000 light cavalry under Reynald of Chatillon, Raymond III of Tripoli and King Guy of Jerusalem and marched towards Tiberias. On 3 July, in great heat and short of water, Guy halted the army at Hattin, 3 miles from the lake. Here, at dawn next day, Saladin attacked. The crusader infantry, ordered to stand firm under the hail of arrows, rushed towards the lake. Surrounded on a hill — the Horns of Hattin — they suffered heavy casualties and many from thirst before surrendering. The horsemen were also surrounded and only about forty escaped. A few wealthy knights were ransomed; others including Reynald were executed. Tiberias surrendered on 5 July. This defeat led to a series of other reverses for the crusaders. *See* Jerusalem VIII; Ramleh II.

Ticinus River, *northern Italy* (*Second Punic War***) *218* BC.** 26,000 Carthaginians (Hannibal) clashed with 25,000 Romans (Scipio the Elder). The Romans were defeated with heavy loss,

Scipio being severely wounded. *See* Cannae; Trasimeno Lake; Trebbia River.

Ticonderoga I (*Seven Years' War or French and Indian War*) 8 July 1758. General Montcalm, with 3,600 French and Canadians, was strongly entrenched on a ridge in front of Fort Ticonderoga. The British General Abercromby had 15,000 men, including 6,000 regulars. Without waiting for his guns to come up and making no attempt to outflank Montcalm, Abercromby ordered a succession of six frontal assaults. The position could not be taken by such crude generalship and Abercromby lost 1,944 killed or wounded to Montcalm's 377 casualties. *See* Trout Brook.

Ticonderoga II (*Seven Years' War*) 22–26 July 1759. The fort was now held by Bourlamaque with 3,500 French and Canadians, and was attacked by 11,000 British under Amherst. On 23 July Bourlamaque withdrew to Isle-aux-Noix, in Lake Champlain, leaving only 400 men (Colonel Hebécourt) to check Amherst as long as possible. Before being driven out, 26 July, Hebécourt blew up the magazine.

Ticonderoga III (*American Revolution*) 22 June–5 July 1777. The British (Burgoyne) invested the fort, defended by 5,000 Americans (St. Clair). The Americans evacuated the place under Bougoyne's pressure — specifically from two 12-pounder guns. *See* Bennington; Valcour Island.

Tiflis (*Mongol invasion of the Caucasus*) 1386. As Tamerlane and his Mongols approached Tiflis, the Queen of Georgia, who ruled the Caucasian tribes, led her soldiers out and offered battle. They were no match for the fierce, veteran Mongols and were cut to pieces.

Tigranocerta I, *capital of Armenia* (*Third Mithridatic War*) 69 BC. Lucullus led his Roman army of 10,000 in pursuit of Mithridates I and besieged him in Tigranocerta, held by Mithridates' son-in-law Tigranes. Tigranes assembled no fewer than 100,000 Armenian and Pontic troops to attack the Romans. The veteran Romans, under Lucullus' calm and brilliant leadership, manoeuvred to high ground behind Tigranes and charged his cavalry. With this dispersed they then routed the enemy infantry. Lucullus was unable to press further into Armenia because his men were reluctant to enter the mountains. *See* Cyzicus II; Nicopolis.

Tigranocerta II (*Roman Empire's Parthian Wars*) AD 59. The Romans (Corbulo) drove Tiridates I out of Artaxata and then pursued him. Despite constant Parthian harassing actions, Corbulo reached and took Tigranocerta, where he placed a puppet on the throne for Rome. *See* Arsanias River; Artaxata.

Tigris River (*Roman Empire's Persian Wars*) April 363. The Emperor Julian led an army on Syria to repel the Persians (Shapur II) who had been capturing Roman outposts. Forcing the passage of the Tigris, Julian manoeuvred to attack the Persian army. While the Romans were on the move, the Persians attacked. Julian, mortally wounded, died in camp. The legionaries selected a general, Jovian, as their new emperor; Jovian made peace with the Persians, but died in the field. *See* Amida I; Argentoratum.

Timor (*World War II*) February 1942–February 1943. Australian troops and commandos fought the Japanese invaders in Portuguese Timor and Dutch Timor. In Portuguese Timor, after inflicting heavy casualties, the Australian 2/40th Battalion surrendered. In Dutch Timor commandos of the 2/2nd Independent Company opposed a Japanese force of 1,000, later increased to 16,000. In 13 months the Australians killed 1,500 Japanese for the loss of 40 of their own men. The 2/2nd were the only troops (apart from those in Papua) who did not surrender to the Japanese during their invasion. The unit was withdrawn in January 1943 and replaced with another commando unit. The Commanding Officer of 2/2nd was first Major A. Spence, later Major B.J. Callinan. *See* New Guinea.

Timosoara   (Hungarian   Rising Against Austria). This is identical with Temesvar, q.v.

Tinian Island, *Pacific (World War II) 24–31 July 1944.* Taking the Japanese garrison of 9,000 by surprise, the American 2nd and 4th Marine Divisions established a beach-head and killed 1,200 Japanese when they made a counter-attack. In a week's fighting, the Americans lost 327 killed and 1,771 wounded; the Japanese were killed almost to a man. *See* Mariana Islands.

Tippencanoe   Creek   (*Tecumseh's Confederacy*) 7 November 1811. A victory for 1,000 Americans led by W. H. Harrison, Governor of Indiana, and an army captain, over the Shawnee tribe led by Tenskwatawa, brother of Tecumseh. After a furious battle, the Americans burnt the Indian village and retired. Indian resistance in the American northwest, though aided by the Canadian British, was now broken.

Tippermuir, *Scotland (English Civil War) 1 Septembre 1644.* The Earl of Montrose (James Graham) rallied the Highland clans to the Royalist cause and gave battle to Lord Elcho's army of 5,000 Covenanters (men who had taken the "covenant" to oppose Charles I). Montrose was greatly outnumbered, but inflicted an overwhelming defeat on his enemy; 2,000 Covenanters were killed. Montrose then occupied Perth and Aberdeen. *See* Inverlochy; Marston Moor.

Tisza (Theiss) River (*Conquests of Charlemagne*)   September   796. Charlemagne sent troops from Bavaria

and Italy to crush the barbarian Avar tribes who had been raiding into western Europe for 200 years. Eric of Friuli led the charge which drove the Avars from their great earthwork-protected settlement on the Tisza, a tributary of the Danube. The Avars were destroyed as a people and never again menaced Europe. Pope Leo III crowned Charlemagne Emperor of the West.

Toba (*Japanese Revolution*) 1 May 1868. The Shogun Yoshinobum, invading Satsuma, was decisively defeated by the Imperial army and soon surrendered. The rebellion then petered out. *See* Tansara Saka; Tayeizan.

Tobruk I, *Libya (World War II) 7–22 Janunary 1941.* This natural fortress town was held by 32,000 Italians (Manella) when besieged by the British XIII Corps (O'Connor), 7 January. The place was captured, 21–22 January, by the Australian 6th Division and British 7th Armoured Division. They took 25,000 Italian prisoners. *See* Bardia.

Tobruk   II   (*World   War   II*)   10 April–29 November 1941. After its capture from the Italians, Tobruk had been garrisoned chiefly by the Australian 9th Division (Morshead). Meanwhile the Germans (Rommel) had mounted an offensive, 24 March, at Agheila. Moving rapidly forward, Rommel made strong attacks on Tobruk, 10–14 April and on 30 April, but all were beaten back. Rommel reached the Egyptian frontier on 28 April, but despite repeated attacks and continual dive-bombing the Tobruk garrison held out for 240 days, making frequent aggressive raids into Axis territory. On 29 November the British Eighth Army, victorious at Sidi-Rezegh, relieved Tobruk. The defence is one of history's greatest. *See* Sidi-Rezegh.

Tobruk III (*World War II*) 20–21 June 1942. Rommel, beginning his second offensive, smashed through the British defences at Gazala, 26 May–14

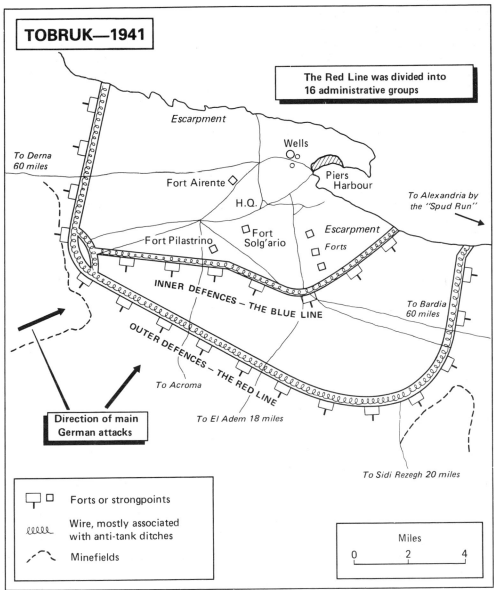

TOBRUK—1941

The Red Line was divided into
16 administrative groups

Escarpment

Wells

*To Derna
60 miles*

Fort Airente ◇

H.Q.

Piers
Harbour

*To Alexandria by
the "Spud Run"*

Fort Pilastrino □

□ Fort
Solg'ario

□ *Escarpment*

□ *Forts*
□
□

INNER DEFENCES – THE BLUE LINE

*To Bardia
60 miles*

OUTER DEFENCES – THE RED LINE

To Acroma

To El Adem 18 miles

Direction of main
German attacks

To Sidi Rezegh 20 miles

⊔ □   Forts or strongpoints

ℓℓℓℓℓ   Wire, mostly associated
with anti-tank ditches

‿‿   Minefields

Miles

0   2   4

June, and forced the British Eighth Army (Ritchie) into full retreat. Ritchie left 35,000 troops in Tobruk, chiefly the 2nd South African Division (Klopper), while withdrawing his main body still further east. Capturing the key point of Sidi-Rezegh, 17 June, Rommel attacked Tobruk with his 15th and 21st Panzer Divisions. After a 2-day battle, 20–21 June, Klopper unaccountably surrendered Tobruk, 33,000 men and an enor-mous quantity of stores. Ritchie was replaced by Montgomery. During this offensive the British lost 80,000 men, including prisoners. *See* Alamein; Bir Hacheim; Gazala.

Tofrek (*British Sudan Campaigns*) *22 March 1885*. About 5,000 Mahdists, followers of the rebellious Osman Digna, attacked 2,000 British and Indian troops (McNeill) in their desert zariba — an impromptu fortification of thorn bush. They broke through but were repulsed and in a fierce 20-minute fight lost 1,500 killed. British casualties, 470. *See* Abu Klea.

Tolbiacum, *near Cologne (Rise of France) 496.* The Merovingian king, Clovis I, gave battle to the savage Allamanni tribe again invading Frankish territory. Allemanni spears and arrows were winning the fierce battle against the Franks' axes when Clovis personally led a charge which routed the barbarians. They did not cross the Rhine again. *See* Soissons; Vouille.

Toledo I (*Spanish–Muslim Wars*) *May 1085.* Alfonso VI, the Valiant, of Leon and Castile, captured the Moorish stronghold of Toledo which remained a Christian bastion for the duration of the wars to drive out the Moors — another 400 years. *See* Zallaka; Zamora.

Toledo II (*Spanish Civil War*) *20 July–27 September 1936.* Toledo fell to Republican (Government) troops on 20 July, but a scratch Nationalist garrison of only 1,300 (Colonel Moscardo) held the Alcazar, the commandingly situated palace-fortress. About 15,000 Republicans, unable to take the place by storm, settled down to siege. In August Colonel Varela led two Nationalist columns up the Tagus and on 26 September cut the road to Madrid, and attacked the Republican besiegers. Varela's troops, including Moroccans, were better trained and they routed the Republicans. After the relief of the Alcazar all suspected Republicans in the city were massacred. *See* Madrid; Malaga III.

Tolentino, *north-east of Rome* (*Napoleon's "Hundred Days"*) *3 May 1815.* With Napoleon escaped from Elba, Marshal Murat, his brother-in-law and former King of Naples, raised an Italian army of about 45,000 to fight for Murat's lost kingdom. Against Napoleon's advice, Murat gave battle to an Austrian army of 60,000 (Bianchi) and were badly beaten. Murat fled to France, but after Napoleon's defeat at Waterloo was captured and executed. *See* Ligny; Waterloo.

Tolenus (*Roman Civil Wars*) 90 BC. The rebellious Marsians attacked the Roman legions of Lupus as they were crossing the Tolenus River and routed them with a loss of 8,000. *See* Asculum II.

Tondeman's Woods (*Second Carnatic War*) *14 February 1754.* 12,000 Mysore and Mahratta troops (Hyder Ali) ambushed and captured a large convoy of supplies escorted by 180 British and 800 Indian troops, en route to besieged Trichinopoly, q.v. *See* Seringham; Sugar-Loaf Rock.

Tongres, *modern Belgium* (*Gallic Wars*) *winter 54 BC.* The Eburonian (Gallic) chief Ambiorix attacked an isolated Roman post at Tongres. When the assault failed, Ambiorix offered the 9,000 Romans safe passage to their base camp at Namur, 50 miles away. The Roman leader, Sabinus, accepted the offer, but on the march the horde of Eburones overwhelmed the Romans and slaughtered every man. Ambiorix then besieged Namur, but Julius Caesar led a relief force to drive off the Eburones. *See* Avaricum.

Toplica River (*Turkish–Serbian War*) *September 1387.* Murad I and his Turkish army, after many conquests, took Nish from the north Serbs. King Lazar Hrebeljanovich formed a Pan-Serbian league and won a great victory over the Turks on the banks of the Toplica River. This brought Croats, Albanians, Poles and Hungarians to Lazar's standard. Turkish steps to crush this coalition led to the battle of Kossovo, q.v.

Torgau, *Elbe River* (*Seven Years' War*) *3 November 1760.* About 65,000 Austrian and other troops of the Holy

Roman Empire under Count Daun held a massive fortified camp near Torgau, which Frederick the Great attacked with 44,000 men. The plan was for the Prussian cavalry under Zieten to charge the enemy front while Frederick circled west and attacked the enemy rear. Zieten was unable to attack by the appointed time. Not knowing this, Frederick made his assault against an unweakened line, which included 400 cannon. In the first attack 5,400 of 6,000 Prussians fell. With attack after attack and Zieten's eventual piercing of the Austrian lines, Frederick forced Duan to retreat and took Torgau. But his tactics had cost him 13,120 casualties. Austrian casualties, 4,200 killed or wounded, 7,000 prisoners. *See* Burkersdorf; Liegnitz II.

Toro (*War of Castilian Succession*) *1 March 1476.* The Castilian crown was claimed by Isabella I (sister of the dead king, Henry IV) and by Henry's widow, Queen Juana of Portugal, for her daughter Juana. Alfonso V of Portugal, with 8,000 Portuguese and Castilian troops held Toro for Juana. Ferdinand V, Isabella's husband, led an army which routed Alfonso's army, thus ensuring Isabella's succession. *See* Alhama de Grabada.

Toronto (*Canadian Rebellion against Britain*) *5 December 1837.* The defeat of 800 insurgents, led by William Mackenzie, at the hands of a force of regulars under the Lieutenant Governor of Toronto, Sir John Colborne. Nevertheless, the insurrection led to dominion status for Canada. *See* Batoche.

Toulon I (*War of Spanish Succession*) *17 July 1707.* A combined attack by troops of the Holy Roman Empire and of Britain against the great French port. Prince Eugene and the army of the Holy Roman Empire under Victor Amadeus II, Duke of Savoy, marched on Toulon along the Mediterranean coast. They were supported by a powerful British fleet under Admiral Shovell, who landed guns and reinforcements for the

attack. The French fought well, but it was lack of co-ordination and initiative which stopped the allied assault and the attackers withdrew. Shovell burned some French ships. *See* Turin.

Toulon II (*War of Austrian Succession*) *21 February 1744.* A confused, ill-conducted battle between twenty-nine British ships (Matthews) and twenty-seven French and Spanish ships (De Court). The allied fleet inflicted the greater damage and broke the British blockade of Toulon. Matthews and some of his captains were court-martialed and cashiered. *See* Cape Finisterre I; Velletri.

Toulon III (*French Revolutionary Wars*) *19 August–18 December 1793.* France was suffering from several reverses when the worst of all happened: The great naval base of Toulon opened its gates to a force of British, Spanish and French Royalists under Lord Mulgrave, who garrisoned the place against attack. A French army (Dugommier) besieged Toulon and gradually ate into the allied defences; Napoleon Bonaparte, then an artillery captain, played a major part in the assault. Mulgrave evacuated his force by sea. *See* Hondschoote; Neerwinden II.

Toulouse I (*Muslim invasion of France*) *721.* Muslims, invading from Spain, had captured Toulouse in 718 and Narbonne in 719, and were ready for more aggression. Duke Eudes of Aquitaine rallied a Frankish army and gave battle to the Muslims of Samh ibn-Malik. The swinging axes of his infantry overcame the Muslim horsemen, who were badly beaten and lost their leader. *See* Covadonga; Tours.

Toulouse II (*Napoleonic Wars*) *10 April 1814.* The Duke of Wellington, with 25,000 British and Spanish troops, having forced the French out of Spain, brought to bay at Toulouse Soult's army of 30,000. The French easily repulsed a premature Spanish assault, but the British, led by Beresford, drove the

French out of the city. Casualties: French, 3,000; British, 2,600; Spanish, 2,000. This was the last battle of the Peninsular War. Napoleon had already surrendered in Paris, and on 11 April accepted exile on Elba. *See* Ligny; Paris I; Tolentino; Vittoria.

Tou Morang (*Vietnam War*) 7–13 June 1966. A fierce battle between allied American and South Vietnamese troops holding a key position in the central highlands and North Vietnamese attackers. In 7 days and nights of heavy jungle fighting the allied troops were supported by massive artillery fire and many air attacks and won a major victory. Casualties: North Vietnamese, about 1,500; Allies, 320. *See* Vietnam.

Tourcoing, *near Lille* (*French Revolutionary Wars*) 18 May 1794. An encounter battle between an allied army — Austrians, British and Hanoverians — led by the Prince of Saxe-Coburg, and the French army of General Pichegru, temporarily under the command of General Souham. Saxe-Coburg divided his command into five columns but only the two centre ones made any progress; they were thus isolated and suffered 5,500 casualties. Hit hard, the allied army could not prevent Souham from taking Charleroi. *See* Fleurus III; Watignies.

Tournai I *Schelde River* (*Netherlands War of Independence*) 1 October–30 November 1581. Spanish troops, under Alexander of Parma, besieged Tournai, bravely defended by Princess Espinay. Capitulating on 30 November, she was permitted to march out her garrison with all the honours of war. *See* Antwerp I; Maastricht I.

Tournai II (*War of Spanish Succession*) 27 June–3 September 1709. Marlborough, unable to bypass with safety the powerful fortifications of Tournai on his way to Paris, invested the place. The garrison commander, de Villars, had 90,000 French troops, but Marlborough, with the help of Prince Eugene of Savoy, had assembled 100,000 English, Dutch and German troops. Having suffered 3,000 casualties and with no hope of relief, de Villars surrendered. *See* Lille; Malplaquet.

Tournai III (*French Revolutionary Wars*) 22 May 1794. The British, Austrian and Hanoverian allies held good positions on the Scheldt River when attacked at 5 a.m. by 62,000 French. Heavy fighting went on all day and the key village of Pont-a-Chin changed hands four times. The French, under General Jacques Macdonald, were holding it when General Henry Fox stormed it with three fine British regiments. The whole French army fled, could not rally again and the battle ended at 10 p.m. Casualties: French, 6,000; Allies, 4,000. The performance was particularly impressive. *See* Fleurus III; Tourcoing.

Tours (*Muslim invasion of France*) 732. A powerful force of 65,000 Muslim horsemen, led by Abd-er-Rahman, was moving from Spain towards the Loire and central France. The danger was critical as Charles Martel (the Hammer) hurriedly assembled enough Frankish infantry to form into a solid block to check the Muslim army. The horsemen attacked ferociously, wave after wave riding straight into the Frankish square and slashing with their swords. The Franks stood firm, wielding axes and swords. Arab records say the battle lasted 2 days, but Frankish accounts say 7 days. Finally, the death of Abd-er-Rahman himself sapped the Muslim fervor. The invaders withdrew and by 759 were all back south of the Pyrenees. Tours was a decisive battle of history. *See* Covadonga; Toulouse I.

Towton, *Yorkshire* (*Wars of the Roses*) 29 March 1461. This battle followed the Lancastrian (red rose) defeat at Ferrybridge, q.v., the previous day. Now the 30,000 Royalist Lancastrians (Henry VI, Northumberland, Somerset,

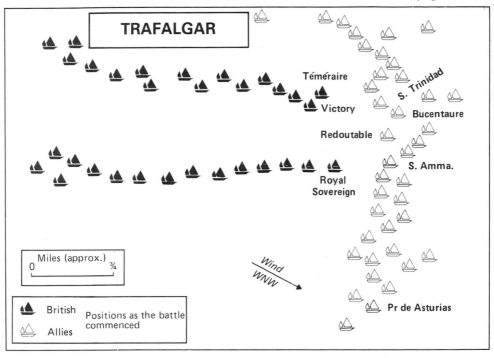

TRAFALGAR

Téméraire

Victory

S. Trinidad

Bucentaure

Redoutable

S. Amma.

Royal
Sovereign

Miles (approx.)
0   ¾

Wind
WNW

Pr de Asturias

British
Allies
Positions as the battle
commenced

Lord Dacres) held a slope at Towton, with their right flank on Cock River. The Yorkists (Warwick) had two great advantages: in heavy snow blowing towards the Lancastrians, their spearmen could advance unobserved, and the wind gave the Yorkist archers a longer range than the Lancastrian archers. The Lancastrians were goaded into charging downhill against the Yorkists and a savage hand-to-hand fight took place. It went on for 6 hours until Yorkist reinforcements under the Duke of Mowbray came up and attacked the Lancastrian left flank, breaking Henry's army. Hundreds of armoured knights drowned in the flooded Cock River. The casualties in this, the largest battle of the Wars of the Roses, were very great. The Yorkist King Edward said there were 28,000. The Lancastrians lost the flower of their chivalry. Henry VI was soon captured and imprisoned in the Tower; Queen Margaret and her son fled to France. While the battle ensured the rule of Edward IV, it did not end the Wars of the Roses. *See* Ferrybridge; Hedgley Moor; Saint Albans II.

Toyotomi Castle, *Osaka (Conquest by Tokugawa Shogunate) 1614–15.* General Iyeyasu, victorious at Sekigahara, controlled all Japan except this one castle held by Hideyori, only surviving son of Toyotomi Hideyoshi. His garrison resisted with remarkable will and courage for a year, when privations forced surrender. Iyeyasu put the entire garrison to death. *See* Hara Castle; Sekigahara.

Trafalgar *(Napoleonic Wars) 21 October 1805.* Eighteen French and fifteen Spanish ships (Villeneuve), sailing from Cadiz towards the Straits of Gibraltar, encountered the British fleet of twenty-seven ships (Nelson) 10 miles off Cape Trafalgar. Villeneuve turned north in a single line; Nelson in two lines attacked at right angles from the west. With his flagship, *Victory*, and eleven other ships, Nelson drove at the enemy van while Collingwood attacked the rear of Villeneuve's line. These tactics, aided by accurate gunnery, decided the battle; eighteen allied ships surrendered, four others were taken latter off Corunna. No

British ship was lost, but Nelson was mortally wounded and 1,500 British seamen were killed or wounded. Allied casualties, 14,000. The decisive victory ended France's naval power and made Britain mistress of the seas for a century. *See* Cape Finisterre III.

Trasimeno Lake (*Second Punic War*) 217 BC. The Romans intended to trap Hannibal and his 35,000 strong Carthaginian army between two armies, 40,000 men in all, under Flaminius and Geminus. Hannibal's intelligence was good, his tactical ability even better. At Lake Trasimeno he hid most of his troops in mist-shrouded hills. On a mid-summer morning, as Flaminius led his 40,000 legionaries in a long column along the lake road, Hannibal struck. His Africans, Spaniards and Gauls swooped down on the Romans and killed or captured the entire Roman army, for a cost of 2,500 casualties of their own. Hannibal then met and wiped out the 4,000 legionaries of Geminus. Hannibal marched south along the Adriatic coast while the Romans frantically rebuilt their armies. *See* Cannae; Trebbia River I.

Trautenau (*Seven Weeks' War*) 27 June 1966. Between the Prussians (Bonin) and Austrians (Gablenz). The Prussians at first drove back the Austrians, but Gablenz advanced a mass of reinforcements and the Prussians, weary after a long march, retreated. The tactical victors, the Austrians, suffered 5,742 casualties because of the accuracy of the Prussian rifle; Prussian casualties, 1,227. *See* Langensalza; Münchengratz; Sadowa.

Travancore (*Second British–Mysore War*) 28 December 1789. About 15,000 Mysore troops (Tippoo) made a night attack on a British fort. Successful at first, they were repulsed by a shock charge of defenders and then routed, losing 2,000 men. *See* Seringapatam.

Trebbia River I (*Second Punic War*)

218 BC. Having made his remarkable winter crossing of the Alps, Hannibal reached the Po Valley with about 30,000 troops who had survived the crossing and Roman attacks. The first clash — an indecisive cavalry skirmish — occurred on the Ticino River. Against good advice, Sempronious then took 40,000 legionaries across the Trebbia to attack Hannibal, though a snowstorm was raging. Hannibal used his cavalry to bend back both Roman wings, then his younger brother circled to the Roman rear and led a furious charge. After a day's desperate fighting about 20,000 legionaries struggled back to their camp. An associated disaster for Rome was that 10,000 Gallic warriors now joined Hannibal's army. *See* Saguntum; Trasimeno Lake.

Trebbia River II (*French Revolutionary Wars*) 21–22 June 1799. Count Suvorov and Baron Melas, with their 25,000-strong army of Russians and Austrians, were aware that Moreau, with an army of 25,000 French, and Macdonald, with another 35,000, were manoeuvring to crack the smaller allied army between them, or to unite and overwhelm it. Suvorov took the initiative by turning to meet Macdonald on the Trebbia. In what was largely a "soldiers' battle" — the generals playing little part — fought without mercy in and out of the river, Macdonald lost 4,000 killed and another 12,000 wounded or captured. Then he pulled back. The Russians and Austrians had 6,000 casualties. (Napoleon was in Egypt.) *See* Cassano d'Adda II; Novi Ligure.

Trebizond (*End of Roman Byzantine Empires*) October 1461. After the fall of Constantinople the surviving members of the House of Comnenus fled to Trebizond, which Muhammad II besieged. The Turks captured the city and the old "Empire of the East" faded from history 8 years after the Turks captured Constantinople, q.v.

Treves I (*Triet*) (*Caesar's Gallic*)

Wars) *55 BC.* The Germanic Asipete tribe, said to be 300,000 strong, made a raid into Gaul. Somewhere near Treves, on the Moselle River, Caesar, with 50,000 legionaries, inflicted such a severe defeat that few Asipete warriors recrossed the Rhine. *See* Cremona II.

Treves II (*Gallic Revolt Against Rome*) *AD 71.* The campaign is misnamed, as the revolt involved more than the Gallic and Germanic tribes, such as the Batavi, Triveri and Lingones. The separatist uprisings of the Batavian auxiliaries spread to legions and auxiliary units in north-eastern Gaul and the Roman areas of Germany, under the leadership of Claudius Civilis. Petillius Cerialis, with six veteran legions, was sent to restore order. He routed the Batavi at Treves and generally crushed the other mutineers. Not for a long time were other separatist movements successful. See Cremona I.

Trevilian Station (*American Civil War*) *11–12 June 1864.* Two Confederate cavalry divisions (Hampton and Fitzhugh Lee) were moving towards the Federal cavalry division of Philip Sheridan when another Federal cavalry brigade (George Custer) rode between them. Defeating Custer, the Confederates then dug in against Sheridan, who attacked next day, only to be repulsed. Casualties: Federals, 735; Confederates, 900. *See* Cold Harbour.

Tricameron, *near Carthage* (*Wars of Byzantine Empire*) *November 533.* Between the Romans (Belisarius) and the Vandals (Gelimer and Zano). The Vandal defeat, with a loss of 3,000, ended all Vandal domination in Africa. *See* Carthage II.

Trichinopoly (*Indian Tribal Wars*) *26 March 1741.* The Mahrattas besieged the town and fort, held by a chief named Chunda, who held enormous stocks of food. The Mahrattas feigned a retreat of about 150 miles, on which Chunda, an avaricious man, sold most of

the grain he had in store. The Mahrattas, anticipating this, returned to the siege and quickly starved the garrison into submission, taking the fort on 26 March.

Trifanum, *mouth of Liri River, Italy* (*Rome's Latin League Wars*) *338 BC.* A decisive victory for the Romans (Torquatus) over the troops of the combined Latium cities of what is better known as the Campagna region. The Latin League cities had been Rome's allies, but after Trifanum Rome annexed all of Latium to its growing empire. *See* Caudine Forks.

Trincomalee I (*Seven Years' War*) *10 August 1759.* A victory for a British squadron of twelve ships (Pococke) over fourteen French ships (d'Ache), though the French lost no ships. *See* Madras II.

Trincomalee II (*First British–Mysore War*) *3 September 1767 and 26 September 1767.* A British force (Colonel Smith) beat off the Mysore army of Hyder Ali, who lost 2,000 men. Later that month Smith, with 12,000 British and Indian troops, unexpectedly encountered the combined armies of Mysore and Hyderabad, 60,000 men under Hyder Ali. The British recovered first from the surprise meeting and their superior discipline enabled them to rout the enemy army, which lost 4,000 men and 64 cannon. British casualties, 160. *See* Porto Novo.

Trincomalee III (*War of the American Revolution*) *12 April 1782.* A French fleet of twelve ships (de Suffren) intercepted the eleven-ship British fleet of Edward Hughes, making for Trincomalee. It was a victory for the French, who crippled two British ships, but British maritime power was unimpaired. *See* Cuddalore I; Madras III.

Trincomalee IV (*War of the American Revolution*) *26 August–3 September 1782.* The fourteen-ship

French fleet (de Suffren) anchored off the British-held port, and landed troops and marines who took the place from the small garrison. When the British fleet of twelve ships (Hughes) appeared on the horizon, de Suffren sailed out for his fourth fight with Hughes. British gunnery was good and the French lost ninety killed and 252 wounded, but de Suffren's tactics prevented Hughes from retaking Trincomalee. *See* Cuddalore I and II.

Trinidad *(French Revolutionary Wars) 17 February 1797.* A British naval-military operation (Admiral Harvey and General R. Abercrombie) captured the island from the French.

Tripoli I *(Muslim Conquest of Africa) 643.* The city was defended by a strong army of Byzantine troops and African levies under Gregory when a Muslim column under Abdullah ibn-Sa'd reached it after over-running much of Cyrenaica. The garrison greatly outnumbered the Muslims, but the Arabs' aggression demoralized them. Abdullah's troops stormed the city and captured it, inflicting heavy casualties. *See* Alexandria II; Carthage III.

Tripoli II *(U.S. War with Tripoli) 31 October 1803 and 16 February 1804.* The pirates of the Barbary States — Tunis, Tripoli, Morocco, Algiers — had declared war on American shipping, and the United States (President Jefferson) sent warships into the Mediterranean to protect American merchantmen. One fleet (Captain Preble) blockaded Tripoli. On 31 October the frigate *Philadelphia* ran aground in Tripoli Harbour. Capturing it, the pirates turned its thirty-six guns against the blockading fleet. On the night of 26 February 1804, seventy-four men under Lieutenant Decatur slipped into the harbour and burnt the ship. Tripoli sued for peace in 1805.

Tripoli, *Lebanon (Crusader–Turkish Wars) February–26 April 1289.* A Mameluke army besieged the great fortress city, held by the Christians for 280 years, and now nominally ruled by Lucy, Countess of Tripoli. As the walls crumbled under the bombardment of great stones the Venetians and Genoese inhabitants sailed away. The climax came on 26 April, when the Mamelukes stormed the fortress. Lucy and many lords hurried to their ships and safety. The victorious Mamelukes killed all male Christians and sold the women and children as slaves. Tripoli was virtually destroyed. *See* Acre II; Antioch III; Tunis II.

Trivadi, *Mysore (Seven Years' War) August 1760.* Major Moore, with 230 British and 2,700 Indian troops, tried to prevent Hyder Ali, with 6,000 Mysore troops, from linking with a French force. He was overwhelmed and his troops scattered.

Trnovo *(Bulgarian Civil Wars) July 1217–18.* The Bulgarian King Boril had been weakened by defeat at Philippolis. Now his cousin, Ivan Asan, sought Russian help and led a revolt in northern Bulgaria. He besieged the capital, Trnovo, then took it by storm. The captured Boril had his eyes put out. *See* Klokotnitsa; Philippolis II.

Trout Brook *(Seven Years' War) 6 July 1758.* The advance guard of a British army (Abercromby) proceeding to Ticonderoga gave battle to a French scouting column, which was virtually wiped out. Lord Howe, the brain behind the incredibly inept Abercromby was killed in the fight. Without Howe, Abercromby was to wage the ruinous battle of Ticonderoga, q.v.

Troy *(Trojan War) 1204–1194 BC.* Fact and legend are inextricably mingled. The Achaeans, a Greek army led by Agamemnon, besieged Troy, near the Dardanelles, supposedly in vengeance for the abduction of the Greek Princess Helen by Paris, son of the Trojan king. In the 10th year of the siege Hector, Paris's brother, was killed by the Greek hero Archilles, who was in turn slain by Paris. The Greeks then built their wooden horse by which a small party was able to enter the city and open the gates for the main army. The Trojans were defeated and Helen was rescued. It is quite likely that such a battle-war did take place, but parts of the legend are unconfirmed.

Truceia, *Gaul* (*Neustrian–Austrasian War*) *593*. Queen Fredegond led her Neustrians to victory over the Austrasians of Childebert II.

Truk, *Carolina Islands* (*World War II*) *17–18 February and 28–29 April 1944*. Truk was known as Japan's "Gibraltar of the Pacific". In the first battle the American Fifth Fleet (Spruance) and Task Force 58 (Mitscher) by naval bombardment and aerial attack destroyed two Japanese light cruisers, four destroyers, nine other naval vessels, twenty-five merchantmen and about 350 aircraft. The Americans lost twenty-five aircraft and had one carrier damaged. In the second battle waves of bombers and fighters from Task Force 58 sank about forty enemy ships — not one remained afloat — and ninety-three aircraft. The Americans lost forty-six aircraft but saved twenty-five pilots. *See* Kwajalein-Eniwetok; Mariana Islands; Tarawa-Makin.

Tsinan (*Chinese Civil War*) *14–23 September 1948*. The north-eastern city of Tsinan was held by 80,000 Nationalists for Chiang Kai-shek when attacked by a People's Liberation Army for Mao Tse-tung. Casualties for the 10-day conflict were heavy before the defence crumbled. Many of the garrison survivors changed sides. By now the Nationalists were losing the war. *See* Chinese Civil War; Hwai-hai; Kaifeng; Mukden II.

Tsingtao (*World War I*) *18 September–8 November 1914*. Joining the Allies in the war against Germany, Japan sent 23,000 troops to take the German-controlled Chinese city of Tsingtao, held

by 4,000 marines. On 23 September 5,000 British troops landed. Under cover of naval artillery bombardment, the Allies prepared for an assault, made on the night of 6–7 November. The Germans surrendered next morning. Casualties: German, 700; Japanese, 1,800; British, 70.

Tsushima Strait I (*Mongol invasion of Japan*) *1419*. Japanese ships, under several barons of Kyushu, decisively defeated the invasion fleet of Chinese and Korean ships. No further invasion was attempted after this debacle.

Tsushima Strait II (*Russian–Japanese War*) *27–28 May 1905*. The greatest sea battle since Trafalgar. A Japanese fleet of about forty-five ships (Togo) intercepted the comparable Russian fleet (Rozhdestvenski) sent from the Baltic to attempt to break Japanese domination of the China Seas. The Japanese ships were faster and had better firepower and Togo used both to the full. First, with an angled approach to the Russian fleet, which was sailing in line-ahead, he cut off the van and in the first duel sank one battleship, crippled a second and scattered the Russian fleet. Before dark he sank three more enemy battleships, Rozhdestvenski hurried by night towards the Russian port of Vladivostok, but Japanese destroyers and torpedo boats caught him and that night and next morning sank, captured or drove ashore twenty-eight Russian ships. Rozhdestvenski was captured and only twelve of his fleet reached safety. Japanese losses, three torpedo boats. Russia was soon willing to accept peace terms. *See* Mukden I; Port Arthur II.

Tunis I (*First Punic War*) *255 BC*. The Romans sent Marcus Atilius Regulus, with 17,500 infantry and about 2,000 cavalry, to capture Carthage. Carthage had relied on its fleet for protection; it was defeated in 256 BC and had no walls. But it had imported the Spartan general, Xanthippus, to organise and command its army. He had a fine force of 100 elephants, 12,000 infantry and 4,000 cavalry. To counter the charge by elephants, Regulus arranged his legions in columns and the elephants simply ran through the Romans to the rear where they were useless.

Xanthippus saw his opportunity and sent his cavalry through the open lanes. Attacking the legionaries from flank and rear, the Carthaginian cavalry was soon supported by their infantry in front. In the debacle only 2,500 Romans got away in their ships. Captured, Regulus was paroled to negotiate peace terms. Failing to achieve this, he kept his word to return to Carthage — and certain death. *See* Ecnomus; Panormus.

Tunis II (*Eighth Crusade*) July 1270. Louis IX of France landed with a strong force of French and Sicilian knights, expecting to be welcomed by the Emir of Tunis, supposedly ready to become a Christian. But the Emir gave battle and Louis besieged the city. Plague broke out and when Louis died Charles of Anjou and Philip III, the new French king, evacuated the survivors. *See* Antioch III.

Tunis III (*Invasion by Holy Roman Empire*) June–July 1535. Charles V, Holy Roman Emperor, sent Andrea Doria of Genoa with 600 ships to stop the Mediterranean ravages of Barbarossa II, the Barbary pirate appointed by Suleiman the Magnificent as supreme commander of the Turkish fleet. Off Tunis Doria scattered the Turkish ships, then landed troops to capture Turkish-held Tunis. *See* Baghdad III; Preveza; Vienna I.

Tunisia (*World War II*) 1942–43. Rommel was retreating towards Tunisia after his defeat at Alamein; British, American and Free French forces (Eisenhower) had landed in French north-west Africa, 11 November. The Germans and Italians quickly seized Tunisia, to protect Rommel's rear and to thwart Allied ambitions in North Africa. The German von Arnim and the nominal

Axis commander in Tunisia, the Italian General Messe, soon had powerful forces.

The British and Americans made good initial progress, the understrength British First Army (Anderson) reaching Tebourba, only 12 miles from Tunis, 28 November. But efficient Axis counter-attacks drove them back 20 miles in 7 days. By 24 December Eisenhower settled for defensive positions in front of the Axis line. Early in February 1943 Rommel and his Afrika Korps retreated behind the powerful Mareth Line, where he re-equipped. On 14 February he sent his Panzers against the inexperienced Americans at Kasserine Pass, smashing them back more than 20 miles in 9 days and inflicting 5,275 casualties, including prisoners.

An imminent breakthrough was stopped by Allied air support and a British counter-attack; by 22 February Rommel was pulling back. On 26 March the British Eighth Army (Montgomery) breached the Mareth Line and by mid-April Allied forces from west and east had linked, with Alexander now commanding all ground forces (under the Supremo, Eisenhower). The Axis defences were now squeezed tighter. On the east coast of Tunisia, the Eighth Army took Sfax on 10 April; Sousse, 12 April; Enfidaville, 13 April. On the north, Bradley's American XI Corps took Mateur on 3 May, Bizerte, 7 May. The same day Montgomery's 7th Armoured Division captured Tunis.

Their movements restricted by Allied air superiority, Axis ground formations were pocketed — three divisions between Bizerte and Tunis, several more on the now isolated Cape Bon peninsula. The battle ended on 13 May. Casualties: Axis, 40,000 dead or wounded, 267,000 prisoners, including the redoubtable Afrika Korps with its commander, von Arnim, the Fifth Panzer Army and the First Italian Army; British, 33,000; American, 18,558. Axis losses in material were immense: 250 tanks, 2,330 aircraft, 232 ships. Demoralised by naval and air bombardment, the Axis garrisons of islands off the Tunisian coast surrendered between 30 May and 13 June. The fighting in North Africa was now over and the Allies could attack the enemy in Sicily. *See* Mareth Line: North-west Africa; Sicily; Takrouna.

Tupelo, *Mississippi* *(American Civil War)* *14–15 July 1864.* The Confederate cavalry leader, Nathan Forrest, had been a serious military embarrassment to the Federals, who sent 14,000 troops (Andrew Smith) against him. They took up strong positions at Tupelo, which the Confederates (Stephen Lee) attacked, chiefly using Forrest's cavalry. On the night of 14 July Forrest probed to the rear of the Federal position and was beaten off, as was another attack on 15 July. Smith withdrew, having suffered 674 casualties. But he had inflicted a sharp defect on Forrest, who lost 210 killed and 1,116 wounded. *See* Brices Cross Roads.

Turbigo, *north Italy* *(French–Austrian War)* *3 June 1859.* The Austrians (Clam-Gallas) attacked the advance guard of Macmohon's corps, while another 4,000 Austrians attacked the main French army as it was crossing a bridge over the Ticino canal. Both assaults failed, and the Austrians lost 4,200 men. *See* Solferino.

Turckheim *(Second Dutch War of Louis XIV)* *5 January 1675.* The French army (Turenne) and that of Leopold I's Holy Roman Empire (Montecuccoli) were ready to go into winter quarters in Alsace. But Turenne made a brilliant southwards march under cover of the Vosges Mountains and near Colmar fell on the completely unsuspecting army of his old enemy, Montecuccoli. Routing the Austrians, he pursued to the Rhine. By this clever manoeuvre — winter fighting was most unorthodox in this era — Turenne recovered the whole of Alsace. *See* Enzheim; Sasbach.

Turin I *(Revolt of Maxentius)* *312.* Between the legions of Gaul, 40,000 men under Constantine, and the considerably stronger army of Maxentius. Maxentius counted on his heavy cavalry to break the Gallic lines, but it was repulsed and Maxentius was driven into Turin with great loss. *See* Verona.

Turin II *(War of Spanish Succession)* *7 September 1706.* About 10,000 French, under Duke of Orleans and Count of Marsin, besieged Turin, 26 May, held by the Austrians of the Holy Roman Empire. Prince Eugene of Savoy collected Austrian troops from parts of Lombardy and joined by Victor Amadeus II, Duke of Savoy — he had escaped from Turin to raise a relief force — attacked the French. Without efficient leadership the French army was destroyed, 6,000 troops being captured. Eugene had relatively light casualties — 1,500 — but 5,000 of the Turin garrison had died during the siege. The French abandoned attempts to capture northern Italy. *See* Cassano d'Adda.

Turnhout *(Netherlands War of Independence against Spain)* *22 August 1597.* Prince Maurice of Nassau, an able commander, had already liberated much of The Netherlands from Spanish control. Now he made a spectacular forced march, overtook the army led by Albert, Archduke of Austria, and inflicted 3,000 casualties at small cost to himself. *See* Nieuwpoort; Zutphen.

Tuttlingen *(or Teuttingen)* *(Thirty Years' War)* *24 November 1643.* The Bavarians (de Mercy and Werth) surprised the French camp of de Rantzau and routed his troops. Rantzau, his staff and all his artillery and supplies were captured. This French defeat liberated Rottweil. With Rantzau a prisoner, French command devolved on Turenne, who would become one of the greatest of generals. *See* Breitenfeld II; Freiburg.

Tyre I *(Babylonian–Phoenician War)* *585–573 BC.* Nebuchadnezzar II attacked Tyre, the great Phoenician commercial centre, held by Ittobaal II. The attack failed and the Babylonians laid siege to the island-city which, supplied from the sea, resisted for 13 years. The Babylonians then raised the siege. *See* Jerusalem.

Tyre II (*Alexander's Asiatic campaigns*) *February–August 332* BC. Alexander had captured all of Phoenicia except Tyre, which was on an island half a mile offshore. Alexander's first attempts to build a causeway from the shore were frustrated by Tyrian galleys which attacked the Macedonian engineers. Alexander countered by bringing up a fleet of his own, which bombarded Tyre with great stones and fire spears. In August Alexander led an assault along the causeway, breached the walls and took the city. The garrison had lost 8,000 during the siege; another 30,000 were now sold as slaves. *See* Gaza I; Issus.

Tyrnavos (*Greek–Turkish War*) *21–23 April 1897.* Launching an assault with 58,000 men, the Ottoman General Edhem quickly drove back the 45,000 Greek troops of Crown Prince Constantine. They made a stubborn stand near Tyrnavos, Thessaly, but when the Turks lapped around both flanks the Greeks retreated. The retreat became a route and the Turks occupied place after place until the European powers intervened to end the war. *See* Plovdiv.

Tzeki (*Taiping Rebellion*) *20 August 1862.* In the final phase of the war Chinese merchants from Shanghai financed an army of liberation against the Taiping rebel regime. Its leader was Frederick Townsend Ward, an American ship's captain and soldier of fortune. His eleven victories in four months won him a commission as general in the Imperial Chinese Forces and his force was known as the "Ever Victorious Army". He attacked the walled city of Tzeki, but was mortally wounded while directing the successful assault. He was succeeded by Captain Charles G. Gordon, then known as "Chinese Gordon", later as "Gordon of Khartoum".

**Ualual (*Abyssinian–Italian War*) 5
December 1934.** The war did not officially begin until 3 October 1935, but the
clash at Ualual precipitated it. Italian and
Abyssinian (Ethiopian) forces fought in a
disputed zone on the Italian Somaliland
border. About a hundred Abyssianians
and thirty Italians were killed. The
Abyssinian government demanded that
the League of Nations investigate the
incident and the Italians demanded
reparation and apology.

**Ucles (*Muslim conquest of Spain*)
1109.** The Moors heavily defeated the
Spaniards under Don Sancho of Castile,
who was among the killed. The Christians
could not mount another offensive for 50
years. *See* Alarcos.

Uji (*Taira War*) 1180. A victory for the
Taira Clan (Shigehera) in crushing the
rebellion against their domination at the
Court of the Emperor Antoku. The
princes who had led the revolt, Yukiiye
and Yorimassa, were killed.

**Ukraine (*World War II*) 23 July
1943–27 July 1944.** Having won major
victories at Stalingrad and in the
Caucasus, the Russians mounted a big
offensive to drive south-west on a 500-
mile front between the Pripet Marshes on
the north and the Black Sea on the south.
Principal forces were the First Ukrainian
Army (Zhukov) and Second Ukrainian
Army (Konev).

In 1943 the most important action was

the battle for Kharkov, former capital of
the Ukraine Republic, and a vital communications centre. The Germans had
twice taken the city and now Hitler had
ordered that it must be held at all costs.
Enveloped on three sides, it fell on 23
August. On 15 September, after hammering at the Germans in Novorosisk for a
year, the Russians broke through. The
principal German commanders, Kluge
and Manstein, struggled to hold a firm
front.

Konev struck south-west towards
Romania, overwhelmed fourteen German
divisions, captured their bases at Uman
and crossed the middle Bug on 15 March.
The Russians rolled on 60 miles to the
Dniester, forced a crossing at Mogilev
into Bessarabia and advanced to the
Pruth, 26 March. The Russian arrival at
the Pruth marked their recovery for the
first time of what Stalin called the "Soviet
State frontier". In 18 months they had
come 900 miles from Stalingrad and
reconquered all but 60,000 square miles
of their pre-1930 territory.

On a front of 100 miles west of Kiev,
Zhukov pounded the Germans with the
usual overwhelming massed artillery barrages, then raced 40 miles south-west in 3
days to cut the Lwow–Odessa railroad.
The rail junctions of Vinnitsa (Hitler's
former headquarters in the Ukraine) and
Proskurov, key strongpoints of western
Ukraine, were captured on 30 March, and
held against heavy enemy counterattacks. Before the Russians could force
Jablonica Pass, Carpathians, to reach the

Hungarian Plain, Hitler seized Hungary. A German counter-attack (Model) from Lvov gave the Germans 2 weeks' breathing space until 27 July when the Russians captured Lvov; the battle for the Ukraine was over. Casualties for this great and complex battle can only be estimated. Russian, 150,000; German, 200,000. *See* Caucasus; Crimea; Stalingrad; Soviet Union.

Ulm (*Napoleonic Wars: Danube campaign*) *7–20 October 1805*. An Austrian army of 75,000 (Archduke Ferdinand but effectively under Leiberich) was sent into Bavaria to join a Russian army (Kutusov) moving up the Danube Valley to block Napoleon, who was expected to appear with his army through the Black Forest. Ferdinand formed his positions around Ulm, then learned, 7 October, that Napoleon was crossing the Danube in his rear. Frantic at being cut off from Vienna, Leiberich tried to cut his way out of the French trap. He was too late; Napoleon now had 150,000 men behind him. Also, Ney had captured Elchingen, 14 October, enabling Napoleon to get 50,000 more troops across the Danube. Some battered Austrian divisions got through the net, but Leiberich and the major part of the army fell back on Ulm. Here he surrendered 20,000 men rather than have them slaughtered. In all, the Austrians lost more than 50,000 men, mostly prisoners. Napoleon now turned to deal with Kutusov. *See* Oberhollabrunn.

Ulundi, *north-east of Durban* (*British–Zulu War*) *4 July 1879*. Ulundi was the base of Cetawayo, the Zulu chief, who had 20,000 warriors. He was attacked by 5,000 British led by Wolseley and Chelmsford and in a fierce fight lost 1,500 warriors killed. The defeat broke his tribe. Cetawayo himself was captured the following month. British casualties, 15 killed, 78 wounded. *See* Isandhlwana; Rorke's Drift.

United States–British War. *See* List of Battles.

United States–Mexican War. *See* List of Battles.

Upsala I (*Danish–Swedish War*) *May 1520*. A strong force of Danes (Otho of Krumpen) was entrenched at Upsala, Sweden, when vigorously attacked by the Swedes led by Christina Gyllenstierna, widow of Sten Sture. After severe fighting the Danes' greater numbers won the battle for them.

Upsala II (*Danish–Swedish Wars*) *June 1521*. The Swede, Gustavus Vass, with 3,000 troops, defeated the troops of the Bishop of Upsala, who backed the Danes and held Upsala for them. Gustavus occupied Upsala. The Bishop was executed as a traitor.

Urosan (*First Korean War*) *August 1595*. Urosan, held by a Japanese garrison (Kiyomasa), was besieged by Chinese and Koreans (Tik Ho). Starving, the garrison was saved by the approach of a relief force (Hideaki and Hidemoto). While withdrawing, the Chinese and Koreans besiegers were attacked, routed and butchered.

Ushant I, *Brittany Peninsula* (*War of the American Revolution*) *27 July 1778*. The first major naval battle of the war, between thirty British ships (Keppel) and thirty French ships (d'Orvilliers). While moving in opposite but parallel directions, the two fleets opened fire — and left the battle at that. Keppel, returning to Portsmouth, was court-martialled but acquitted. *See* Newport.

Ushant II (or, "*The Glorious First of June*) (*War of the French Revolution*) *1 July 1794*. A French fleet of twenty-six ships (Joyeuse) was escorting a merchant convoy across the Atlantic to America when intercepted by the British fleet of Lord Howe. After 4 days of manoeuvres, Howe struck decisively, capturing six French warships and sinking one; 3,000 French sailors died. But the French fleet had given enough cover for the merchant ships to reach Brest in safety. *See* Saint Vincent II.

Ustí Nad Labem (*Hussite Wars*). *See* Aussig.

Utica I (*Second Punic War*) 203 BC. The young but brilliant Roman general, Scipio, had conquered Spain, but the Senate would not allow him to invade Spain. So Scipio went to Sicily, and on his own initiative, raised an army of Romans and Syrucusans, plus two legions which had been banished to Sicily after their defeat at Cannae. The Senate relented and sent Scipio with this force to Africa. Scipio got his troops ashore 20 miles from Carthage, but was at once penned by Carthaginians led by Hasdrubal (son of Gisco) and Numidians (King Syphax). Building up a strong defence, Scipio drove back his enemies. Undefeated, they moved to the Great Plains of the interior to reorganize. They were too slow. Scipio took 16,000 men, made a rapid 5-day march and surprised the Carthaginian army. Routing it, Scipio then moved on Carthage itself. *See* Ilipa; Zama.

Utica II (*Wars of First Triumvirate*) 49 BC. Julius Caesar, occupied in Spain, sent two legions under Curio to take over North Africa from the Pompeian army led by Varro. Varro made the mistake of leaving his trenches to attack Curio and was routed. His way open, Curio moved inland. *See* Bagradas River; Ilerda.

Utica III (*Muslim conquest of Africa*) 694. A large force of Greeks and Goths held Carthage and much of what is now modern Tunisia for the Holy Roman (Austrian) Empire. A Muslim invading force of 40,000 led by Hassan el Dhaba overcame the defenders at Utica and drove the Imperialists out of Africa. Hassan destroyed Carthage, which ceased to exist other than as a remote settlement without interest to Europe.

Utsonomiya, *Honshu* (*Japanese Revolution*) 2 May 1868. The Royalist troops under Takamori defeated the forces of the Shogun, led by Keisuke; the Emperor had triumphed over the Generalissimo, his chief-of-staff in modern terms.

Vaal Krantz (*British–Boer War*) 6 February 1900. Making a third attempt to relieve besieged Ladysmith, General Buller with 20,000 troops took Vaal Krantz, held it for 2 days against Boer attacks under Botha, then again retired behind the Tugela River. British casualties, 374. *See* Ladysmith; Paardeberg; Spion Kop.

Vadimonian Lake, *near Rome (Rise of Rome)* 283 BC. Trying to extend its northern borders, Rome was constantly harassed by Gauls and Etruscans. North of Rome a Roman legion under Publius Dolabella got between the Gallic and Etruscan forces. Dolabella caught the Etruscan army as it was crossing the Tiber and annihilated it. Then he routed the Gauls. Neither race again troubled the Romans in central Italy. *See* Heraclea; Sentinum.

Valcour Island (*American Revolution*) 11 October 1776. A small British army (Carleton) was sent to the northern end of Lake Champlain with twenty-nine lake ships, total armament eighty-seven guns, in support. To block this threat Colonel Benedict Arnold had thrown together a fleet of sixteen ships of eighty-three guns. In a 7-hour fight near Valcour Island, Carleton's ships crippled the American fleet. Next day Carleton's vigorous pursuit forced the Americans to abandon their surviving ships. *See* Quebec III; Ticonderoga III.

Valenciennes I (*Netherlands War of Independence against Spain*) December 1566–24 March 1567. Spanish and German mercenaries (Noircarmes) besieged the city but could not bring their batteries to bear for nearly 4 months. The garrison surrendered the second day of the bombardment; this untypical rapid surrender has been attributed to treachery.

Valenciennes II (*Spanish–French War*) 18 May–16 July 1656. The Spanish (Manesses) held Valenciennes when besieged by the French under Turenne. Vigorously prosecuted, the siege soon wore down the defenders to the point of surrender. Then, 16 July, the Great Condé, the able Frenchman then in Spanish service, attacked Turenne's siege lines on both banks of the Schelde River, inflicted about 4,000 casualties and routed the French. This was a rare defeat for Turenne. *See* Arras I; Dunes.

Val-'es-Dunes (*Rise of Normandy*) June 1047. William of Normandy (later the Conqueror), with help from Henry I of France, thoroughly defeated the Norman barons who had revolted against his rule. Secure in Normandy, William began to build a formidable army. *See* Hastings.

Valetta (*French Revolution*) 18 September 1798–5 September 1800. The French held the capital of Malta with 60,000 troops (Vaubois) when a British–

443

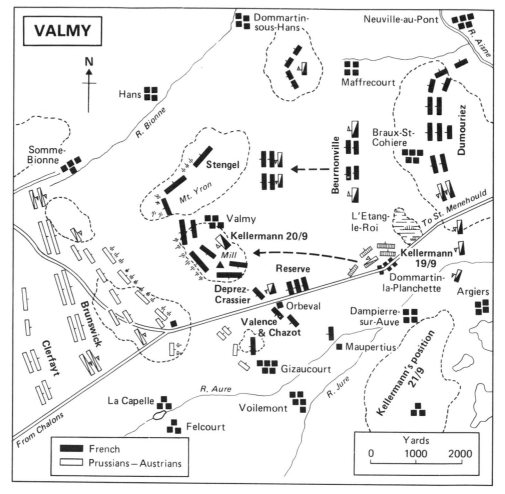

Maltese force led by Sir Alexander Ball besieged it. Famine killed about 20,000 French and so forced surrender. The Maltese are said to have lost 20,000 also.

Valmy, *100 miles east of Paris (French Revolution or War of the First Coalition) 20 September 1792.* The Prussians and Austrians had been successful in their campaigns against the disorganised French Revolutionary armies in north-west France, and had pushed them steadily back. At Valmy, Generals Dumouriez and Kellermann the Elder formed 36,000 troops into a resistance block. Then followed the "cannonade of Valmy" — a 7-hour artillery duel in fog at a range of 1,300 yards. Prussian infantry advanced, but most turned back before coming into French musket range. Casualties were about 300 on either side, but the Prussians (Duke of Brunswick) soon retreated across the Rhine. The battle was decisive in that it inspired the French to take the offensive in their new-found revolutionary fervour. *See* Jemappes.

Valparaiso *(Spanish Argentinian Campaign) 31 March 1866.* Classed as a battle, though almost entirely one-sided. A Spanish fleet (Nunez) bombarded the open and undefended city and destroyed it.

Valutino (*Napoleonic Wars: Moscow campaign*) *19 August 1812*. At Smolensk and nearby Valutino, Napoleon concentrated 120,000 men and prepared a trap for the Russians. Largely because of errors by French Marshals Junot and Murat, the Russians escaped the trap, though they lost 15,000 men to the French 10,000. *See* Borodino; Smolensk.

Van Tuong Peninsula — *Operation Starlight* (*Vietnam War*) *30–31 August 1965*. About 2,200 Viet Cong troops had penetrated to the peninsula south of a major American air base at Chu Lai. The Americans (Walt) sealed off the base of the peninsula then air-landed other troops to trap the Viet Cong against the sea; 5,000 Americans in all were involved. In a continuous 2-day fight all Viet Cong resistance was overcome. Casualties: American, 50 dead, 150 wounded; Viet Cong, 1,000 killed. *See* Vietnam.

Varaville (*Rise of Normandy*) *1058*. A victory for the Normans (William, later the Conqueror) over the French and Angevins led by Henry I of France. William's cavalry were immensely superior. *See* Hastings; Val-'es-Dunes.

Varese (*or Maltese*) (*Italian Wars of Independence: Garibaldi's Rising*) *25 May 1859*. With 3,000 patriots, Garibaldi repulsed 5,000 Austrians (Urban). The victory was surprising but not decisive. *See* Velletri II.

Varmas, *Colombia* (*Colombian War of Independence*) *March 1813*. An early victory for Bolivar and his Colombian patriots over the Spanish Royalists. *See* Boyacá; Carobobo; Junin.

Varna I, *Black Sea* (*Crusade Against Ottoman Turks*) *10 November 1444*. Inspired by Pope Eugene IV, János Hunyadi of Transylvania raised an army of Bosnians, Hungarians, Poles, Serbians and Wallachians and with the kings of Poland and Hungary under his command Hunyadi marched to Varna, to fight the Turks. The Venetian fleet, whose support he had been promised, remained at Gallipoli. The Turkish sultan, Murad II, who had supposed he was at peace with the European powers, hurried his army to Varna. Hunyadi made a frontal assault, which the Turks repulsed; then they routed and massacred the crusaders, including the two kings. *See* Kossovo II; Nicopolis; Salonika I.

Varna II (*Russian–Turkish War*) *5 August–12 October 1828*. During the Russian advance into Turkish territory one of the principal blocking actions occurred at Varna, besieged on 19 July by 15,000 Russians (Diebitsch). After a spirited defence of 3 months the garrison surrendered, having forced the Russians to end their campaign for that year. *See* Kulevcha; Navarino.

Vasaq (*Turkish–Hungarian War*) *September 1442*. At least 80,000 Turks (Shiabeddin) attacked strong positions held by only 15,000 Hungarians (Janos Hunyadi). They were repulsed with a loss of 20,000 killed or wounded. Hunyadi would not be so fortunate 2 years later. *See* Varna I.

Veii, *near Rome* (*Rise of Rome*) *405–396 BC*. The Romans, in conflict with various Italian kingdoms, laid siege to the Etruscan stronghold of Veii. For 11 years the siege persisted ruinously for both sides until a new Roman commander, Camillus, led a violent assault and captured Veii. The victory gave the Romans much greater prestige.

Veleneze (*Hungarian Rising Against Austria*) *29 September 1848*. An indecisive conflict between the Hungarians (Moga) and the Croats under Jellachich, Governor of Croatia. The Hungarians were in revolt against the Austrian Empire of Ferdinand I, whom Jellachich served. *See* Schwechat.

Velestinos, *Thessaly (Greek–Turkish War)* 5 *May* 1897. 9,000 Greeks (Colonel Smolenski) held strong positions under attack by a Turkish force (Hakki) and fought well all day. With the Turks threatening his line of retreat, that night Smolenski withdrew to Vole and embarked his troops. The war ended a few days later.

Vella Lavella (*World War II*). *See* Solomon Islands.

Velletri I, *south-west of Rome (War of Austrian Succession)* 11 *August* 1744. An Austrian army (Lobkowitz) was seriously threatening Naples, then held by the Spaniards. Charles IV of the Two Sicilies quickly forged his army and that of the Spaniards into a combined force which defeated the Austrians and drove them back. *See* Cuneo; Toulon II.

Velletri II (*Italian Wars of Independence: Garibaldi's Rising*) 19 *May* 1859. Between 10,000 Garibaldians under Roselli and 10,000 Neopolitans under Ferdinand, King of Naples. By night, the patriots' advance guard, under Garibaldi, attacked the town of Velletri and drove out the Neopolitans. *See* Varese.

Venice (*Italian Wars of Independence*) 20 *July–28 August* 1849. Venice, rebelling against Austrian rule, had proclaimed itself the Republic of St. Mark (under Daniele Manin). After the Austrian crushing of similar rebellions in Lombardy, Rome and Sicily, Venice now stood alone. A greater Austrian army (Radetsky) besieged Venice and bombarded it. Ill-prepared for siege and with cholera raging in a hot summer, the Venetians surrendered. *See* Novara II.

Vera Cruz I (*French Expedition Against Mexico*) 27 *November* 1838. French nationals had suffered heavy losses during a Mexican army mutiny. Unable to obtain reparations, the French sent a fleet (Baudin) of sixteen ships using new explosive shells, which heavily bombarded Vera Cruz and its great fortress of San Juan d'Ulloa for 5 hours. The effect was devastating, and by 5 p.m. the Mexicans had ceased firing, and their government paid up.

Vera Cruz II (*U.S.–Mexican War*) 21–27 *March* 1847. Vera Cruz, held by a garrison of 5,000 (Morales), was reputedly the strongest fortress in the Western Hemisphere. The American aim was to take it and then proceed to Mexico City. The fleet landed 13,000 troops (Winfield Scott), and then bombarded the forts for 6 days and forced its surrender. Casualties: Mexican, 180; American, 82. *See* Buena Vista; Cerro Gordo.

Vercellae (*Cimbric invasion of Italy*) 101 *BC*. The Cimbri (Boiorix), a fierce Gallic people, had crossed the Alps for an attack on Rome, but near Milan ran into the legions of Gaius Marius, already victorious over the Teutones on the Rhone. With help from the legions of Catalus, Marius defeated and massacred the enemy. There was no further Gallic invasion of Italy. *See* Aquae Sextiae.

Verdun (*World War I*) 21 *February– 18 December* 1916. The greatest battle of attrition in history, famous for the French pledge of *Ils ne passeront pas!* The vast fortress area of Verdun was held initially by 500,000 men when the German chief-of-staff, Falkenhayn, organised 1,000,000 men of the Fifth Army (Crown Prince Wilhelm) for a massive attack. On 21 February, 1,400 guns bombarded an 8-mile front for 12 hours. The first German infantry attacks captured key positions — Fort Douaument, 25 February; Hill 295 (Le Mort Homme) and Vaux, 29 May; Fort de Vaux, 6 June. Two other violent attacks to gain vital heights were repulsed, 23 June and 11 July. By now the French had suffered 315,000 casualties, the Germans, 280,000. Principal French commander until 1 May had been Petain. He had been replaced by Nivelle who launched a

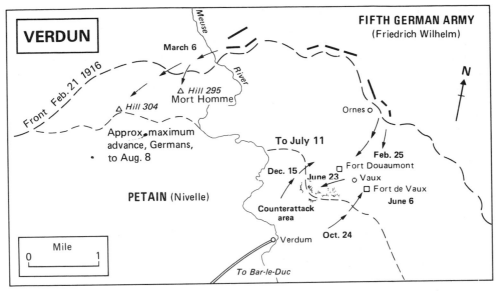

VERDUN

March 6

Meuse

River

Front Feb. 21 1916

△ Hill 295
Mort Homme

△ Hill 304

Approx. maximum
advance, Germans,
• to Aug. 8

PETAIN (Nivelle)

To July 11

Dec. 15

June 23

Counterattack
area

Ornes o

Feb. 25

☐ Fort Douaumont

o Vaux

☐ Fort de Vaux

June 6

Oct. 24

☐ Verdum

To Bar-le-Duc

FIFTH GERMAN ARMY
(Friedrich Wilhelm)

N

Mile

0   1

counter-offensive, 24 October, which, largely under Mangin's generalship, won back much lost ground, including Forts Douaumont and de Vaux. Fighting ended on 18 December 1916, although intermittent activity continued, with neither side any further forward. Between them the French and Germans fired 40 million shells into Verdun. Casualties: German, 434,000; French, 543,000.

Verneuil (*Hundred Years' War*) *17 August 1424*. The French, already severely mauled by the English army (Duke of Bedford) and their Burgundian allies, decided on an all-out assault against their English enemies. They put together an army of 10,000 Orleanists, led by the Scottish Constable of France who was also the Earl of Buchan, and 5,000 Scots, led by the Earl of Douglas, Buchan's father-in-law. Bedford had only 9,000 men, but armed with the deadly longbow — range 250 yards — and protected by a line of pointed stakes, they held off the French–Scottish charges. The Duke of Alencon tried a flanking attack, but was captured. After losing 7,000 men the allied survivors fled across the Loire. Douglas and Buchan were among the many Scottish dead. Eclipsed only by Agincourt, Verneuil was a vivid

example of English military skill of the period. *See* Cravant; Orleans.

Verona (*Roman Empire's Civil Wars*) *March 312*. Several generals contended for the Roman throne; one, Constantine, marched from Gaul into Italy with 50,000 soldiers, at Turin pushed aside the army of his rival Maxentius, then besieged Verona, held by Pompeianus, an aide of Maxentius. Pompeianus slipped through the siege lines and returned with an army to break the siege, but Constantine defeated this attempt. Pompeianus was killed and Verona surrendered. *See* Carrhae II, Saxa Rubra.

Verrières Ridge. *See* p. 455

Verulamium I (*Caesar's invasion of Britain*) *54 BC*. When Caesar landed five legions near Dover and marched inland, the Briton chief Cassivellaunus retreated before Caesar and harried his rear and flanks. At Verulamium (St. Albans) he agreed to Caesar's peace terms. Caesar withdrew from Britain, having paved the way for future Roman influence. *See* Medway River.

Verulamium II (*Roman Conquest of Britain*) *61*. Under Roman provocation, the Iceni people of East Anglia rallied to their widow queen, Boadicea. At Camulodunum (Colchester) they killed Roman settlers and British collaborators. Then they overwhelmed the Ninth Legion hurrying from Lincoln. Postumus, commanding the Second Legion in Gloucester, would not move from his fortifications, but Paulinus set out from Wales with 10,000 men of the Fourteenth and Twentieth Legions. The Iceni burned Londinium, then Verulamium, massacring tens of thousands. With astute generalship, Paulinus now attacked Boadicea's great army and reportedly killed 80,000 of them, including women and children in the column. Roman casualties, 400 dead, 750 wounded. Boadicea took poison, the hesitant general Postumus stabbed himself to death. *See* Mons Graupius.

Veseris, *near Vesuvius* (*Rome's Latin War*) *339 BC*. The Latin army was at first successful against the Roman legions of Torquatus and Decius Mus. Mus, to permit the withdrawal of the remainder of the army, deliberately sacrificed himself in a forlorn hope attack. Torquatus then exploited the opportunity with his more veteran troops. The Latins lost three-quarters of their force. *See* Caudine Forks.

Vesontio, *now Besançon* (*Gallic Wars*) *Autumn 58 BC*. With six legions, Julius Caesar occupied the main fortress of the Sequani Gauls. Marching north, Caesar made camp near Mulhouse, where seven tribes of Gauls under Ariovistus attacked them. Despite their overwhelming numbers, the Gauls could make little impression against the disciplined, veteran legionaries. Since the more important action took place 2 days' march from Vesontio, the battle is rather misnamed. *See* Bibracte; Sambre River.

Viborg, *Denmark* (*Danish Dynastic War*). Between the armies of the rival Houses of Sweyn III and relatives of Canute V, who had been assassinated. Sweyn's army was routed and he himself overtaken and killed. Waldemar, the victor, became Waldemar I and later was known as "the Great". *See* Reval; Stiklesrad.

Vicksburg (*American Civil War*) *7 May–4 July 1863*. Vicksburg was a Confederate fortress blocking Federal attempts to control the Mississippi River. The Federal commander, Grant, had already made five attempts to take Vicksburg which had a garrison of about 25,000 (Pemberton). On 17 April 1863 Grant sent a cavalry force to create a diversion and then moved his army down the west side of the river. The battle had several phases.

7 May: Crossing the Mississippi with his corps, Sherman brought Grant's strength to 41,000. By manoeuvring, Grant divided two Confederate armies standing ready to defend Vicksburg.

14 May: Grant attacked and captured Jackson, capital of Mississippi State, then turned north and confronted Pemberton and his army which had been advancing to help Jackson.

16–19 May: A major clash at Champion's Hill, between Grant's 29,000 men and Pemberton's 22,000. The Confederates lost 3,851 casualties to the Federals' 2,441, and a Confederate division was cut off and forced to leave the area. The Federals (Sherman) them overwhelmed the rearguard Pemberton had left to cover his retreat to Vicksburg; he thus lost another 1,700 men.

19 May–4 July: With 30,000 men, Pemberton was besieged by a Federal force which soon grew to 75,000, spread around 9 miles of good defences. Grant's one major assault, 22 May, cost him 3,200 casualties. He then waited for constant shelling, hunger and disease to do their work. On 4 July, with half the garrison dead, wounded or sick Pemberton surrendered. Total Federal casualties, 9,362.

Vicksburg was decisive. It split the Confederacy geographically; it enabled

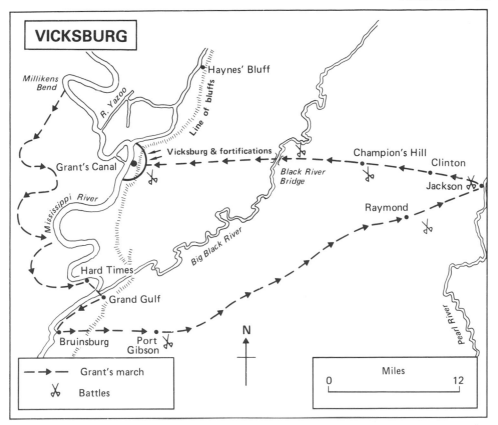

VICKSBURG

Millikens Bend

Haynes' Bluff

R. Yazoo

Line of bluffs

Grant's Canal

Vicksburg & fortifications

Champion's Hill

Clinton

Black River Bridge

Jackson

Mississippi River

Raymond

Big Black River

Hard Times

Grand Gulf

Pearl River

Bruinsburg

Port Gibson

N

- → - Grant's march

Battles

Miles

0   12

the Federals to use large forces against other objectives. Combined with the Confederate reverse at Gettysburg, it robbed the South of any chance of victory. *See* Chickasaw Bluffs; Gettysburg; Port Hudson.

Vienna I (*Turkish invasion of the Danube*) *26 September–16 October 1529.* Suleiman I of Turkey, challenged in Hungary, led 100,000 troops up the Danube to Vienna, held by 20,000 men — including Spanish and German mercenaries hurriedly sent in by Holy Roman Emperor Charles V — under Salm-Reifferscheidt. The Turks repeatedly attacked the city's walls and were as repeatedly harassed by the garrison's sorties through the gates. Recognising failure, Suleiman withdrew, losing many soldiers to Christian cavalry attacks. Had Vienna fallen, the Turkish–Muslim empire

would have stretched much further into Europe. *See* Mohács; Tunis III.

Vienna II (*Austrian–Turkish Wars*) *17 July–13 September 1683.* Emperor Leopold I fled from Vienna under the new Turkish threat — an army of 75,000 led by Mustafa, the Grand Vizier. Unable to breach or climb the walls under the spirited defence led by Starhemberg, the Turks began to mine them. The defenders' situation was critical when Charles V of Lorraine and John III Sobieski of Poland reached Vienna with a relief force of 20,000. They routed the Turks and Mustafa withdrew his army. His emperor, Muhammad IV, beheaded him. *See* Harkány; Khotin II.

Vienna III (*World War II*) *2–13 April 1945.* The Russian advance had gathered momentum on both sides of the Danube as Ukrainian armies (Tolbukhin) took

Sopron, Nagykanizsa and Bratislava. The battle for the Austrian capital was one of fierce street-fighting, with the German defenders holding the Russians out of the southern sector until 7 April. But the Russians took the east, south and west railway stations on 8 April and the following day they held the centre of the city. The battle ended on 13 April. *See* Budapest.

Vietnam War (*or Second Indo-China War*) *1959–75*. On 8 July 1959 the Viet Cong (Vietnamese Communists) attacked the South Vietnamese army or Arvn for the first time — at Bien Hoa, near Saigon. On 20 December 1960 the National Front for the Liberation of South Vietnam (NLA) was formed in North Vietnam to organise the take-over of the South. Arvn was beaten by the Viet Cong in the battle of Ap Dac on 2 January 1963 and it was clear that South Vietnam needed help if it were to remain free. That year the NLA's strength in South Vietnam was built up to 25,000 soldiers and 80,000 militia. At the request of President Diem the United States sent more military "advisers"; 17,000 were on duty during 1973.

The "Americanization" of the war by President Johnson took place by stages between August 1964 and June 1965. The first American combat unit of 3,500 marines landed at Da Nang on 8 March 1965. At the end of that year 165,700 American servicemen, under General William Westmoreland, were in South Vietnam.

The Americans undertook massive search-and-destroy operations with helicopters, artillery and armoured vehicles. Operation Cedar Falls north of Saigon (January 1967) and Operation Junction City (February) were successful. At the end of 1967 more than 500,000 Americans were in Vietnam and American bombers were flying 200 sorties a day over North Vietnam.

On 30 January 1968, during the truce which marked the Tet Buddhist new year festival, the Viet Cong began a major offensive against towns in the north and coastal provinces and the central highlands. On 31 January 5,000 Viet Cong, who had infiltrated into Saigon, attacked selected targets, including the Presidential Palace and the American Embassy. The Americans and Arvn forces fought back effectively. At the end of the unsuccessful Tet offensive the Viet Cong had lost 46,000 dead and 9,000 wounded, against 2,788 killed and 8,886 wounded for the Arvn and 1,536 killed and 7,775 wounded for American and allied forces. The Communists losses in the Tet Offensive exceeded those of the Americans for the entire war.

At the end of 1968 American military strength in South Vietnam reached a peak of 549,000. General Creighton Abrams, replacing Westmoreland as Commander-in-Chief, employed mobile forces in helicopters to hit Viet Cong concentrations.

The Viet Cong launched offensives in February, May and August 1969. Increasingly American troops were withdrawn from the combat areas and on 1 September 1969 the South Vietnamese were made responsible for the entire Mekong Delta. Gradually too the number of Americans in Vietnam was reduced — down to 171,000 in 1971. The reduction was forced by powerful American public opinion against the war.

On 30 March 1972, after heavy bombardment, 15,000 North Vietnamese troops with 120 Soviet tanks attacked into Quang Tri province. They broke through the defences and in a period of 3 days Arvn suffered 25,000 casualties.

The United States retaliated against a series of enemy offensives by heavily increased aerial bombing of the north. On 11 August 1972 the last U.S. combat unit was withdrawn from South Vietnam, though 43,000 air force personnel remained. For the United States the end of the conflict came on 27 January when a peace treaty was signed. Casualties: Between 1 January 1961 and 27 January 1972 the American forces had lost 45,941 men killed and 300,635 wounded. Australian involvement in Vietnam began

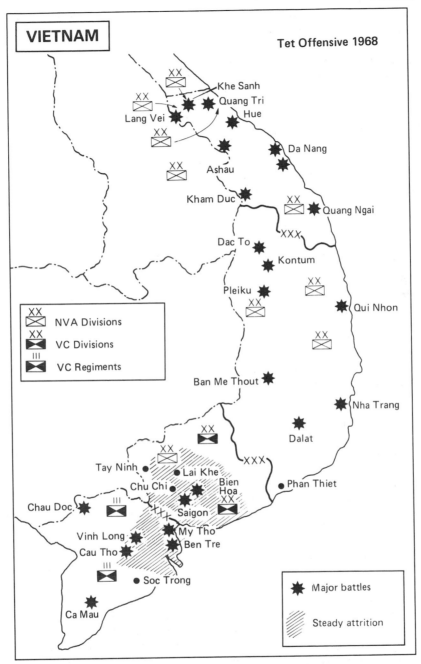

VIETNAM

Tet Offensive 1968

Khe Sanh
Quang Tri
Hue
Lang Vei
Da Nang
Ashau
Kham Duc
Quang Ngai
Dac To
Kontum
Pleiku
Qui Nhon
Ban Me Thout
Nha Trang
Dalat
Tay Ninh
Lai Khe
Chu Chi
Bien Hoa
Phan Thiet
Chau Doc
Saigon
Vinh Long
My Tho
Cau Tho
Ben Tre
Soc Trong
Ca Mau

NVA Divisions

VC Divisions

VC Regiments

Major battles

Steady attrition

in 1962 and 2 years later three battalions with supporting troops were on service in Phuoc Tuy province. About 47,000 soldiers served during the war with a strength of 8,000 at the peak of commitment. The most important Australian battle was that of Long Tan, August 1966, when 108 men advanced into a Viet Cong trap of 2,500 men. After 3 hours the Viet Cong ran, leaving behind 245 dead. Australian casualties were 17 dead, 21 wounded.

Throughout 1973 and 1974 the Communist build-up intensified and many cease-fire violations occurred. During March and April 1975 Communist attacks broke the Arvn forces and the government surrendered to the Communists on 30 April. In 16 years of war more than 150,000 South Vietnamese troops were killed and 400,000 wounded. Unofficial casualty figures for North Vietnam and Viet Cong troops are 100,000 killed, 300,000 wounded.

The war is sometimes said to have started in 1961; demonstrably, hostilities began in 1959 though direct U.S. military aid to South Vietnam commenced in December 1961. *See* An Lao; A Shau; Dien Bien Phu; Nam Dong; Van Tuong.

Vigo Bay, "Battle of the Spanish Galleons" (War of Spanish Succession) 12 October 1702. Forcing their way into Vigo harbour, thirty British and twenty Dutch ships (Admiral Rooke and Duke of Ormonde) destroyed eleven French and Spanish warships, captured ten and took eleven merchantmen loaded with treasure, mostly silver. The victory atoned for the defeat of the English–Dutch fleet at Cadiz in August. *See* Gibraltar I.

Villach (Austrian–Turkish Wars) August 1492. Between the Turks (Ali) and a Christian army (Duke Maximilian). The battle was going badly for the Austrians when 15,000 soldiers held prisoner in the Turkish camp broke out and attacked the Turkish rear. This led to a Turkish defeat; they lost 10,000 killed and 7,000 prisoners. *See* Guinegate.

Villa Viciosa (War of Spanish Succession) 10 December 1710. About 13,000 Austrians (Starhemberg) were retreating into Catalonia when attacked by 20,000 French (Vendôme). The action swivelled, the Austrian left wing being cut to pieces while the right and centre made ground, driving back the French with heavy loss. Starhemberg was too weak to exploit his partial success. *See* Brihuega; Denain.

Villers-Bretonneux I (World War I) Somme, 30 March–5 April 1918. In this action the Australian 9th Brigade saved the entire British line from collapsing during the last great German offensive of the war. The Australians lost thirty officers and 635 men from a total of 2,200. *See* Somme.

Villers-Bretonneux II (World War I) 24–27 April 1918. This Australian counter-attack by night across difficult and unknown ground to retake Villers-Bretonneux is often cited as the most impressive operation of its kind on the Western Front. The 13th Brigade (Brigadier Elliott) and the 15th Brigade (Brigadier Glasgow) suffered 1,000 and 455 casualties respectively. *See* Somme.

Villeta, Venezuela (War of the Triple Alliance or Lopez War) 11 December 1868. The armies of Brazil, Uruguay and Argentina were far too strong numerically for the Paraguayan army (Lopez) and were beaten back to their entrenched camp at Angostura. *See* Aquidaban; Parana.

Villiers (French–Prussian War) 30 November–3 December 1870. General Ducrot led a determined large-scale sortie from beleaguered Paris against the Wurtembergers of the Prussian Army. After initial success the French were repulsed with the great loss of 424 officers and 9,053 men. Prussian casualties, 156 officers, 3,373 men. *See* Paris.

Vimiero (Peninsula War) 21 August 1808. Wellesley (Wellington), having landed with his expeditionary force the previous month, was marching towards Lisbon. At Vimiero, 32 miles north-west of the city, he ran into 14,000 French (Junot) who had marched out to stop him. The French lost 1,800 men and thirteen guns in the attempt and were thrown back. British casualties, 720. The French agreed to evacuate Portugal if transported back to France in British ships. This remarkable and short-sighted arrangement gave Napoleon 26,000 veteran troops to use again against the British. *See* Corunna.

Viminacium, *in modern Yugoslavia (Wars of Byzantine Empire)* 601. The Avars, a barbarian Mongol tribe, had penetrated deep into south-west Europe. Byzantine emperor Mauricius sent an army (Priscus) to repel them, which he began at Viminacium and completed with a cavalry sweep almost to the Danube. He killed 20,000 barbarians, bringing peace for 18 years. *See* Constantinople II.

Vimy Ridge *(World War I)* 9 April 1917. The Canadian Corps of the British First Army captured this dominant ridge from the Germans as part of the second Battle of Arras.

Vimy Ridge was the strongest German defensive position in north-western France and it had withstood repeated attacks for 3 years. More than 130,000 French soldiers were killed or wounded in 1915 in trying to take the ridge. No Allied operation on the Western Front received a more thorough preparation than did the attack on Vimy; the preparations included miles of tunnels to enable attacking troops to reach their starting point without being shelled. After heavy British shelling, the Canadian attack took one objective after another with remarkable precision. Canadian casualties were 10,600, including 3,000 dead. The Germans lost 20,000 men. The Canadian capture of Vimy with the Australian capture of Mont St. Quentin, q.v., were the two most competent British operations on the Western Front. *See* Arras.

Vinaroz *(Spanish Civil War)* 9 March–15 April 1938. Vinaroz, a fishing village on Spain's Mediterranean coast, was merely the finishing point of a much larger battle. With great superiority in artillery and air support, a large Nationalist army (Davila) attacked the Republican (Government) troops covering Catalonia, and forced them back as much as 10 miles a day. When a Navarrese division (Vega) took Vinaroz, General Franco had succeeded in cutting Republican Spain in two. *See* Ebro River; Teruel.

Vindalium *(Roman–Gallic Wars)* 21 BC. The Romans (Maximus) defeated the Gallic Arverni tribe (Bituitus) in central France (Auvergne). Seventy years later Vercingetorix, son of an Arverni king, led the Gallic revolt against Caesar.

Vincennes, *Indiana (American Revolution*) 23–25 February 1779. The British lieutenant governor in Detroit, Lieutenant Colonel Hamilton, with 100 men, occupied Vincennes and its strongpoint, Fort Sackville. Making a march of 180 miles in freezing weather, the American Colonel Clark with 127 men took the position after 2 days' fighting. Though a small-scale action, Vincennes gave the Americans control of all Illinois until the end of the war.

Vincy, *near Cambrai (Austrasian–Neustrian Wars)* 717. The Austrasians under Charles Martel defeated the Neustrians (Chilperic II) at Vincy and at Ambleve. He was building up his power base before he challenged the insurgent Muslims. *See* Tours.

Vinegar Hill, *Wexford (Irish Rebellion Against England)* 21 June 1798. Father John Murphy had collected a strong rebel force of 16,000 in camp at Vinegar Hill, where he was attacked by British regulars (Lake). The Irish were routed with 4,000 killed or wounded and the rebellion was virtually ended.

Vis. *See* Lissa.

Vistula River *(World War I)* 28 September–31 October 1914. The Russians (Ivanov) were overwhelming the Austrians in Galicia. Hindenburg, then commanding on the Eastern Front, sent the German Ninth Army (Mackensen) to bolster them and to attack with the

Austrians east to the Vistula River. By 9 October the Germans are within 12 miles of Warsaw, but weak, slow attacks by the Austrians on their part of the front allowed the Russians (General Russki) to concentrate strength against the German advance. On 17 October Hindenburg ordered a retreat. Having lost 42,000 men, the Germans and Austrians were back to their starting line by 31 October. *See* Galicia; Lodz.

Vittoria,   north-central   Spain (*Peninsular War*) 21 June 1813. Napoleon's brother Joseph, King of Spain, had evacuated Madrid and fled north, covered by an army of 66,000 under Jourdan. Wellington, with 80,000 British, Portuguese and Spanish troops, outflanked Jourdan by crossing the Ebro and routed the French with powerful assaults at three different points. The French lost 8,000 men and nearly all their artillery (151 guns, 450 wagons of ammunition) and transport. Allied casualties, 5,000. Napoleon's Spanish adventure was now nearly over, as Wellington prepared to push the French from Spain. *See* Salamanca; San Sebastian; Toulouse III.

Vittorio   Veneto   (*World   War   I*) 24 October–4 November 1918. For his final offensive against the Austrians on the Piave River, the Allied commander in Italy, Armando Diaz, had fifty-seven divisions, including British, French and American units and 7,700 guns to oppose the Austrians' fifty-eight divisions and 6,000 guns. The first 4 days were tough and slow, but three Italian armies established small footholds on the north bank of the Piave. The fiercest fighting occurred in the Monte Grappa area where the Italian Fourth Army was trying to split two Austrian armies. As the bridgeheads expanded and came together the offensive picked up speed and Vittorio Veneto was taken, 30 October. On 1 November the Italians forced a crossing of the Livenza River at Sacile. Suddenly, Austrian resis-

tance collapsed and by 4 November, when fighting ended, 500,000 Austrians were prisoners. The Italian casualties of 38,000 brought their war total to 650,000 killed and about 1,000,000 wounded. The magnitude of the Italian losses in World War I are little known among the other Allies. *See* Caporetto; Piave River.

Vögelinseck (*Appenzel–Schwyz Rebellion*) 15 May 1402. 5,000 troops from various Swiss Confederated towns defeated about 1,000 rebels from the eastern regions of Appenzel and Schwyz.

Volconda,   India   (*British–French Wars in India*) 21 April 1751. About 1,600 British (Captain Gingen) and 5,600 Indian troops (Abdul Wahab) gave battle to 17,000 troops of Chunda Sahib, supported by a French battalion. Gingen insisted on attacking, despite disparity of numbers, and was forced to retreat with heavy loss. Volconda preceded the capture and siege of Arcot, q.v.

Volturno I (*Italian Wars of Independence: Garibaldi's Rising*) 1 October 1860. Garibaldi, in positions in front of Capua with 20,000 men, was attacked by 40,000 Neopolitans (de Riva). After a full day's fighting he defeated the demoralised Neopolitans who lost 2,070 prisoners. Garibaldi, who had suffered 2,023 casualties, advanced on Gaeta, q.v. *See* Varese; Velletri II.

Volturno II (*World War II*) 12–16 October 1943. The British and American allies, after the landing at Salerno, q.v., found Field Marshal Kesselring's troops ready to delay them on the Volturno River. The U.S. Fifth Army, which included a British corps, and the British Eighth Army pounded the German positions with artillery fire and made an amphibious attack, 12–13 October, on the Tyrrhenean coast. Bridgeheads were established across the Volturno. On 14 October Capua, in the centre, changed hands several times in tank and infantry fighting. But by 16 October the Germans, their flanks pushed back 3 miles, were compelled to withdraw from delaying positions north of the Volturno. Even then the American Fifth Army fought several fierce actions with German rearguard forces in the mountains at the head of the Volturno Valley. *See* Anzio; Cassino; Salerno.

Vouillé (*or Vougle, near Poitiers*) (*Rise of France*) *May 507*. Clovis I, King of the Franks, intent on driving the Visigoths from France, sought out their army under Alaric II. With their deadly axes, the Franks routed the Visigoths, killing Alaric, whose people abandoned Toulouse, their capital, and retreated into Spain. *See* Tertry; Tolbiacum.

Vyazma–Bryansk (*World War II*) *5–20 October 1941*. The Third and Thirty-second Soviet Armies were the last Russian armies holding out against the German onslaught, Operation Barbarossa. They held the line Vyazma–Bryansk against Panzer army groups led by Generals Strauss and Kluge. The German attack split the defenders into two pockets in which more than 650,000 Russian troops were trapped. Fighting was fierce but the Soviet Third Army at Vyazma surrendered on 14 October and the Thirty-second at Bryansk on 20 October. *See* Moscow; Soviet Union.

Vyborg I, "*the Baltic Battle of Trafalgar*" (*Swedish–Russian War*) *3 July 1790*. The Swedes had a large fleet of twenty-two warships and twelve frigates under Prince Carl while Gustavus III had an oar-powered fleet of nineteen transports, twenty-seven galleys and 236 gunboats. Gustavus put his troops ashore at Vyborg. Meanwhile, Prince Carl had been attacked by seventeen Russian warships and seven frigates (Kruse). When Tchitchagoff joined Kruse with another twenty-four ships, Carl was blockaded in Vyborg, with all the Russian ships, under Prince of Nassau-Siegen. Short of food, the Swedes tried to break the blockade by sending down a fireship; currents carried it back into the Swedish fleet where two ships caught fire and blew up. In the great confusion which followed Swedish ships fired on one another and others came under the Russian guns. The Swedish sailing fleet was practically wiped out but Gustavus managed to extricate his great fleet of galleys. *See* Svenskund.

Vyborg II (*Russian–Finnish War*) *29 April 1918*. The Russian civil war had spread into Finland, which had proclaimed its freedom in 1917. Mannerheim organised a Finnish White Army and gained the help of a German corps (Goltz) to drive out the Bolsheviks and Finnish Communists. The pitched battle at Vyborg achieved this and Finland became a republic.

Addendum

Verrières Ridge (*World War II*) *25 July 1944*. The Black Watch of Canada was repeatedly ordered to attack German entrenched positions on this ridge in Normandy, following the Allied landing on 6 June. Advancing across open ground, without air support and unaided by tanks and artillery, the regiment suffered 400 dead and 1,500 wounded and, of course, failed to capture the enemy positions. The defeat reflected badly on the entire British and Canadian leadership; in particular the reputation of Canadian Major General Guy Simmonds was seriously damaged. The Germans suffered few casualties. The disaster was hushed up until 1994.

Wagram (*Napoleonic Wars*) *5–7 July 1809*. Determined to strike a crushing blow against the Austrians, Napoleon had assembled 190,000 men and 488 guns along the Danube's right bank. On the night of 3–4 July he ferried most of this force onto Löbau Island, near the left bank, and the next night struck from Löbau at the Austrians on the bank. He pushed them back, expanded his bridgehead and soon after noon, 5 July, his troops were in conflict with the 139,000-man 446-gun army of Archduke Charles Louis. On 6 July heavy fighting with artillery attacks occurred along the 5-mile front. To that date, the gunfire may have been the heaviest in any war. The decisive blow came at noon that day when Napoleon sent Macdonald with 8,000 men in a hollow rectangle to hit the Austrian right centre. The French took heavy casualties but they broke the enemy line. The Austrian army fell back and their belated attempt to attack the French rear was beaten off. Casualties: Austrian, 43,000; French, 34,000. Napoleon now had Europe almost where he wanted it. *See* Aspern-Essling; Mogilev; Raab.

Waizan (*Hungarian Rising against Austria*) *10 April 1849*. About 7,000 Hungarians (Damjanics) defeated two Austrian brigades (Götz) and drove them out of Waizan. *See* Kapolná; Segesvár; Temesvár.

Wakamatsu (*Japanese Revolution*) *22 September 1868*. The Shogun's* followers made their last stand at the castle of Wakamatsu, which the Imperialists stormed. This ended resistance to the royal regime.

Wakefield, *Yorkshire* (*Wars of the Roses*) *30 December 1460*. Richard of York (white rose) had arrived at Sandal Castle, Wakefield, with 5,000 troops and decided to remain there until reinforcements arrived. Meanwhile, Queen Margaret approached from York with 18,000 men. Placing a detachment in full view of the castle, she hid the greater part, under Lord Clifford, out of sight of the castle. Against the advice of other Yorkish leaders, the Duke of York rode out with his army to attack the Lancastrians — to be hopelessly trapped and defeated. The Duke, his 18-year-old son, the Duke of Salisbury, and 2,900 Yorkists lost their lives. *See* Blore Heath; Mortimer's Cross; Northampton II.

Wake Island (*World War II*) *8 December–23 December 1941*. About 2,000 miles from Hawaii, Wake was defended by 524 U.S. servicemen and 1,216 civilian construction workers under Commander Cunningham. They survived an air raid, 8 December, and beat off a landing, 11 December. On 23 December 2,000 Japanese marines overwhelmed the

---

*The Shogun was the Japanese hereditary commander-in-chief and virtual ruler for some centuries until the office was abolished after the revolution of 1868.

garrison. Casualties: American, 120 killed, the rest captured; Japanese, 820 killed, 355 wounded. *See* Guam I; Pearl Harbour.

Walcheren I (*Netherlands War of Independence against Spain*) 29 January 1574. A Spanish fleet (Romero) was sent to the Schelde Estuary to hunt and exterminate the "Sea Beggars" — the Dutch privateer navy. But the Sea Beggars (de Boisoit) — brilliant seamen and hard fighters — virtually destroyed the Spanish fleet. *See* Alkmaar I; Leyden; Mookerheide.

Walcheren II (*Napoleonic Wars*) August–October 1809. The British sent an expedition of thirty-four warships and 200 transports to capture Antwerp from the French and based the 40,000 troops on malaria-infested Walcheren Island. Under an incapable naval commander (Richard Strachan) and an equally incapable general (Lord Chatham), the campaign never did get properly started. In 8 weeks the British commanders lost 217 men in action, 7,000 dead from illness and another 14,000 seriously ill. *See* Flushing.

Walcourt (*War of the Grand Alliance*) 25 August 1689. The first land battle of the war. The French had the most powerful army in Europe and part of that army, under Duke Louis d'Humiéres and Duke de Villars, confronted a smaller German–English army of 35,000 in Flanders. The British contingent of 8,000 was led by John Churchill, Duke of Marlborough. Prince George Frederick of Waldeck, commanding the allies, used the English as shock troops and broke the French, who suffered heavy casualties. Marshal Francois de Luxembourg replaced d'Humiéres. *See* Fleurus II.

Wallingford (*The English "Anarchy"*) January 1153. A brief conflict, in bitter winter weather, between Henry Plantaganet leading the forces of his mother Queen Maud (Matilda), claimant to the throne, and Stephen of Blois. Winter helped both sides to agree to peace terms. *See* Alnwick II; Winchester.

Waltersdorf (*Napoleonic Wars: Friedland — Poland Campaign*) 5 February 1807. In this "preliminary" battle a French corps (Ney) decisively defeated a Prussian army (Lestocq) which suffered 3,000 casualties. *See* Eylau; Friedland; Heilsberg.

Wandiwash I (*Seven Years' War*) 22 January 1760. Colonel Coote, with 1,900 British and 3,350 Indian troops, defeated Lally-Tollendal's 3,900 French and Indian troops, mainly because 3,000 Mahratta cavalry, allies of the French, did not join in the battle. *See* Madras; Pondicherry.

Wandiwash II (*First British–Mysore War*) December 1780–22 January 1781. A small Indian garrison under a single British officer, Lieutenant Flint, held out under a massive siege by the Mysore army of Hyder Ali. When the approach of a relief column forced the Mysoris to raise the siege, Flint had only enough ammunition for another hour's fighting. *See* Porto Novo.

Warburg (*Seven Years' War*) 31 July 1760. The French, 30,000 troops under Chevelier du Muy, made a thrust against the Prussians towards Hanover. They were blocked by an allied Prussian–British force under the Duke of Brunswick. The honours of the battle went to the British cavalry commander, Marquis of Granby, whose brilliant tactics against the French flanks forced their retreat. They lost 3,000 in killed, wounded or captured. *See* Liegnitz II; Minden II.

Wargaom, *near Poona, India* (*First British–Mahratta War*) 12 January 1779. A Mahratta army (Mahadaji) attacked a British column of 2,600 (Colonel Cockburn) on the march. The British beat off the attack and made a stand in the village of Wargaom, though they lost fifteen officers and 350 men. Under a truce the column was then allowed to retire unmolested. *See* Alighar.

Warsaw I (*First Northern War*) *28–30 July 1656*. Charles X of Sweden, to extend Swedish control of the southern Baltic coast, invaded Poland. In 2 days' furious fighting the Swedes defeated the Poles at Warsaw. Only support for Poland by Russia, Denmark and Austria saved Poland from complete Swedish domination. *See* Febrbellin.

Warsaw II (*Polish Rising against Russia*) *6–8 September 1831*. A garrison of 30,000 (Dembinski) held the city against 60,000 Russians (Paskevich), who had been sent to quell the rebellion. During the heroic defence 9,000 Poles were killed; in the Wola redoubt, defended by 3,000 troops, only ten remained alive. Dembinski surrendered. Paskevich, who had lost 3,000 killed and 7,500 wounded, became governor of the subdued Poland. *See* Grochow; Ostroleka.

Warsaw III (*World War I*) *1914–15*. Part of the battle of the Vistula, q.v.

Warsaw IV (*Polish–Russian War*) *1920*. Part of the Battle of Poland I, q.v.

Warsaw V (*World War II*) *1939*. The final part of the Battle of Poland II, q.v.

Warsaw VI (*World War II*) *31 July–3 October 1944*. The spearhead of the liberating Soviet armies (Marshal Budenny) reached the Vistula and the suburbs of Warsaw. General Bor-Komorowski, leader of the Polish Home Army and the Polish government-in-exile in London, together decided that the German Army was beaten and decided to defend Warsaw so that the Russians and the Polish Communist Party could not take the city. The Germans were not yet beaten, and Hitler ordered that the Warsaw rising be crushed not by conventional military units but by the S.S., the Kaminski Brigade (Russian prisoners who had gone over to the Germans) and Dirlewanger Brigade (German civil convicts turned soldier). All were under the command of the notoriously ruthless S.S. General Bach-Zelewski.

About 42,500 Polish Home Army fighters, armed civilians and the Communist People's Army attacked the Germans and in less than a day captured two-thirds of Warsaw. The S.S. counter-attack, beginning on 4 August, was crushing; by 10 August the Poles were isolated into three small areas, where they were dive-bombed and shelled. The British and Americans air-dropped supplies to agents outside the city who then took them through the sewer system to the defenders. Under desperate conditions, the Polish leaders said that unless they had massive help from the Red Army they could not hold out beyond 1 October. The Russians had established two bridgeheads across the Vistula but sent only token help. On 3 October Bor-Komorowski signed an armistice with the Germans. Casualties: Polish, 15,000 fighters and 200,000 civilians killed; Germans, 10,000 killed, 7,000 missing (mostly killed), 9,000 wounded.

Wartemberg, *Prussia* (*Napoleonic Wars: Leipzig Campaign*) *3 October 1813*. Blucher, with 60,000 Prussians, defeated 16,000 French (Bertrand). The French were in a strong position protected by a dyke and swamps and held out for nearly 5 hours before Blucher turned their flank. Casualties: Prussian, 5,000; French, 500. *See* Dennewitz.

Washita River, *Oklahoma* (*Cheyenne and Arapahoe Wars*) *27 November 1868*. The U.S. 7th Cavalry (Lieutenant-Colonel Custer) made a sudden attack on an Indian camp and killed more than a hundred warriors including Chief Black Kettle. Custer lost sixteen men killed. *See* Beecher Island; Salt River.

Waterloo (*Napoleon's Hundred Days*) *18 June 1815*. At Ligny and Quatre Bras, Napoleon had been success-

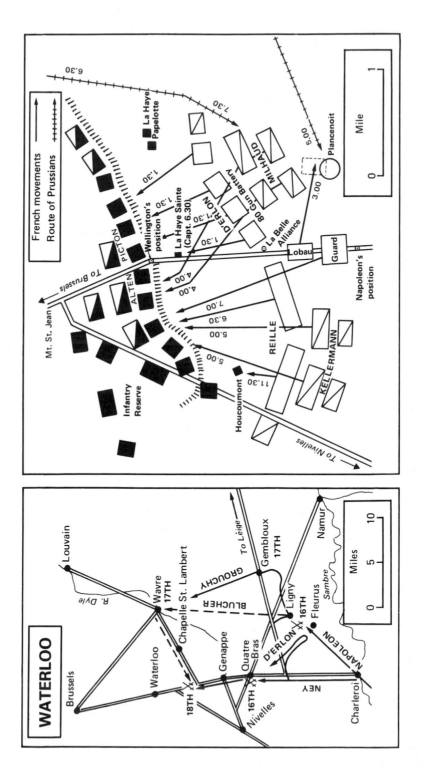

ful in splitting the Prussian army (Blucher) from the English–Dutch army (Wellington). Now he planned to drive the wedge deeper. Wellington had 67,661 troops — 24,000 British, the rest Dutch, Belgians and Germans — and 156 guns along the narrow ridge of Mont Saint Jean. Napoleon placed the greater part of his 71,947 men and 246 guns at La Belle Alliance to confront Wellington and sent de Grouchy with another 33,000 to threaten Blucher and his Prussians. The whole front was no more than 4 miles long, but effectively less than that.

The key points in Wellington's defences were the great Chateau de Goumont, better known to history as Hougoumont, and the farmhouse of La Haye-Sainte. Taking the initiative, Napoleon attacked at 11.20 a.m., and fierce battles developed at the strongpoints and in around the squares of British infantry. Ney, leading the French cavalry, took La Haye-Sainte and at Hougoumont French troops got a footing at great cost.

Napoleon now had to handle a crisis on his right flank, where the Prussians (Counts Zieten and Dennewitz) with 31,000 troops took the village of Plancenoit. Napoleon threw in reserves who retook the village with the bayonet but now, at 7 p.m., he had to turn back to the main battle. He brought up nine battalions of his veteran Old Guard infantry, and Ney led them in yet another assault. The British line held firm. Wellington now counter-attacked, as did the Prussians at Plancenoit. The French began to retreat and the battle was decided by 8 p.m. Prussians troops pursued, but the most élite French units' discipline was good enough to withstand being ridden down and annihilated. The Grenadiers of the Old Guard were never broken and marched out in perfect order. The rest of Napoleon's army became leaderless fugitives.

The troops on both sides had suffered grievously. Most had started the battle drenched and exhausted after a sleepless night in heavy rain. British dead and wounded numbered 15,000, Prussians 7,000. The usual estimate of French casualties is 25,000, plus 8,000 prisoners and 220 guns. Napoleon abdicated (for the second time) on 22 June and was sent to St. Helena. *See* Ligny; Quatre Bras; Wavre.

Watigaon (*First British–Burmese War*) *15 November 1825*. A large army of Burmese (Maha Nemyo) repulsed Indian troops of the British army, whose leader, McDonnell, had made the mistake of advancing in three widely separately columns. *See* Kemendine.

Watrelots (*Netherlands War of Independence against Spain*) *18 January 1567*. About 1,200 Flemish Protestants (Teriel) gave battle to 600 veteran Spanish troops (Rassinghem). Defeated, 600 of the Protestants took up positions in an old graveyard where they died to a man under Spanish attack. This was the first fight of the 53-year war. *See* Brielle.

Wattignies (*War of the French Revolution*) *15–16 October 1793*. About 26,000 troops, mostly Austrian under Prince of Saxe-Coburg, were besieging the fortress of Maubeuge, which covered Paris. Jourdan was sent with 50,000 French to break the siege by attacking the Austrians on Wattignies Plateau. The attack was decisively beaten back, but that night Jourdan transferred about 10,000 men to his right flank, overlapping the Austrian left flank. When Jourdan attacked early next morning he simply rolled up the Austrian line. Saxe-Coburg not only fell back hurriedly but abandoned the siege of Maubeuge. Casualties: About 3,000 on each side. *See* Hondschoote; Tourcoing.

Wau, *New Guinea (World War II)* *27 January–4 February 1943*. The Japanese strongly attacked Wau and the small Australian force there was hurriedly reinforced, many troops landing at the airstrip under fire. The Japanese were halted and driven back in a week, but there followed a 7-month campaign of bitter fighting in the mountains between Wau and Salamaua. *See* Finschafen; New Guinea; Wewak.

Wavre (*Napoleon's Hundred Days*) *18–19 June 1815*. At Ligny, 16 June, Napoleon had defeated Blucher who fell back to Wavre, 10 miles from Waterloo. Napoleon sent de Grouchy with 33,000 troops to keep the Prussians away while he dealt with Wellington at Waterloo. Grouchy found the Prussians holding Wavre in force, but he attacked them. Blucher manoeuvred most of his men out of the way towards Waterloo, leaving only 15,000 troops (Thielmann) to occupy Grouchy. Instead of closely pursuing Blucher, Grouchy pounded away at Wavre. Next morning he forced Thielmann out of his positions — 12 hours after Napoleon's defeat at Waterloo, where 33,000 more French troops might well have won the battle for Napoleon. *See* Ligny; Waterloo.

Waxham Creek (*American Revolution*) *29 May 1780*. About 425 American infantrymen (Colonel Buford) were retreating towards North Carolina and Colonel Tarleton led a British cavalry force of 500 in pursuit. It is claimed that Buford waved a white flag in surrender, but that Tarleton's men rode down the Americans. Certainly, 113 Americans were killed, 150 gravely wounded and others less seriously wounded. *See* Charleston II.

Wednesfield, *east central England* (*Danish–English Wars*) *911*. Edward the Elder had succeeded Alfred the Great. The lands of Edward's sister, Ethelfleda, were attacked by Danes from the Danelaw (the southern part of England occupied by the Danes). With Edward's help, Ethelfleda — "The Lady of the Mercians" — made war on the Danes. It was Edward with an army of West Saxons who won the battle of Wednesfield. *See* Ashdown; Reading.

Weihaiwei, *Shantung Peninsula* (*Chinese–Japanese War*) *4–12 February 1895*. The Japanese cut the boom protecting the harbour of Weihaiwei and in a series of raids by torpedo boats sank several Chinese warships. When the Japanese brought land batteries to bear on the bottled-up Chinese fleet the commander, Ting, surrendered and committed suicide. The seizure of Weihaiwei ended the war. *See* Port Arthur I.

Weissenburg (*or Wissembourg*) (*French–Prussian War*) *4 August 1870*. The opening battle of the war. 25,000 troops of the German Third Army (Crown Prince Wilhelm) attacked and carried the French positions covering the town of Weissenburg. Casualties: Prussian, 1,551; French, 2,300, including their commander, Douay, out of the 4,000 defenders. *See* Spicheren; Worth.

Wepener, *Orange Free State* (*Second British–Boer War*) *9–25 April 1900*. The Boers (De Wet) invested this town, held by 1,700 British South Africans (Colonel Dalgety). The Boers shelled Wepener and made several infantry attacks, but the garrison, suffering 300 casualties, held out until relieved. *See* Ladysmith; Vaal Krantz.

Werben (*or Havelberg*) (*Thirty Years' War*) *22 July 1631*. Gustavus Adolphus of Sweden and his 16,000 troops built up strong positions in readiness for the attack by 22,000 Bavarians (Tilly) of the Holy Roman (Austrian) Empire. Heavy artillery and musket fire stopped Tilly's first attack. Regrouping, Tilly vainly tried again on 28 July. With 6,000 casualties, he broke off and marched south, with the Swedes in pursuit. *See* Breitenfeld I; Magdeburg.

Wertingzen, *Austria* (*Napoleonic Wars: Austerlitz Campaign*) *11 October 1805*. French cavalry (Murat) charged and defeated nine Austrian infantry battalions entrenched around

Wertingzen. The French took 2,000 prisoners and several guns.

Western Front (*World War I*) *1915–18*.

The label applied to the *German* Western Front to distinguish it from the Russian or eastern Front. However, the term was quickly and generally used by the French and British allies. It refers to the battle line which stretched, by 1915, in an unbroken line of 400 miles from the Belgian coast, near Ostend, to the Swiss border near Belfort. From Ostend to about Noyon the Western Front ran on a north–south line; from Noyon to Verdun it ran west–east and from Verdun to Belfort south–east. The Belgian army held the far left (north) of the line, the British and British Empire troops the north central sector and the French the rest; tactical requirements sometimes meant variations of these divisions. Because of the complex trench systems, deeply protected by barbed wire, neither side achieved a decisive breakthrough until March–April 1918. Hundreds of battles, large and small, occurred along the Western Front. The majority were initiated by the British and French and all resulted in heavy casualties. These were the principal offensives and battles:

1915

Allied offensive in Artois and Champagne 1 January–30 March.

Battle of the Wöevre 6–15 April. Repeated French assaults against the north side of the St. Mihiel salient were repulsed with heavy losses.

Second Battle of Ypres 22 April–25 May.

Battles of Festubert and Souchez (Second Battle of Artois) May–June.

Renewed offensives in Artois and Champagne 25 September–6 November. The main battle was at Loos.

1916

Battle of Verdun 21 February–18 December.

First Battle of the Somme 1 July–13 November.

1917

Battle of Arras 9–15 April. Capture of Vimy Ridge.

Nivelle Offensive (Second Battle of the Aisne, Third Battle of Champagne) 16–20 April.

British offensive in Flanders June–July. Messines captured.

Third Battle of Ypres (Passchendale) 31 July–10 November.

Battle of Cambrai 20 November–3 December.

1918

German Somme offensive 21 March–5 April.

German Lys offensive 9 April–8 May.

German Aisne offensive 27–30 May.

First American offensive; Battle of Cantigny 28 May.

Battles of Chateau Thierry and Belleau Wood 30 May–17 June.

German Noyon–Montdidier offensive 9–13 June.

German Champagne–Marne offensive and Second Battle of the Marne 15–19 July.

Allied counter-offensive, Aisne–Marne, 18 July–5 August.

Allied Amiens offensive 8–11 August; 21 August–4 September.

Allied Meuse–Argonne offensive 26 September–11 November.

Hindenburg Line offensive 27 September–17 October.

British–Belgian final Flanders offensive 28 September–14 October.

Allied Sambre–Scheldt offensive 17 October–11 November.

Casualties on the Western Front: German and Austrian 1,500,000 killed, 3,500,000 wounded; French, 1,250,000 killed, 4,000,000 wounded; British Empire, 850,000 killed, 2,000,000 wounded; Belgium, 13,745 killed, 44,686 wounded.

Western Sahara War *1975–* .

Morocco and Mauritania both claimed the former Spanish territory of Spanish Sahara while the Popular Front for the Liberation of Saguia el Hamra and Rio de oro (the Polisario Front) wanted an independent state. Algeria backs Polisario. Two wars have been fought concurrently

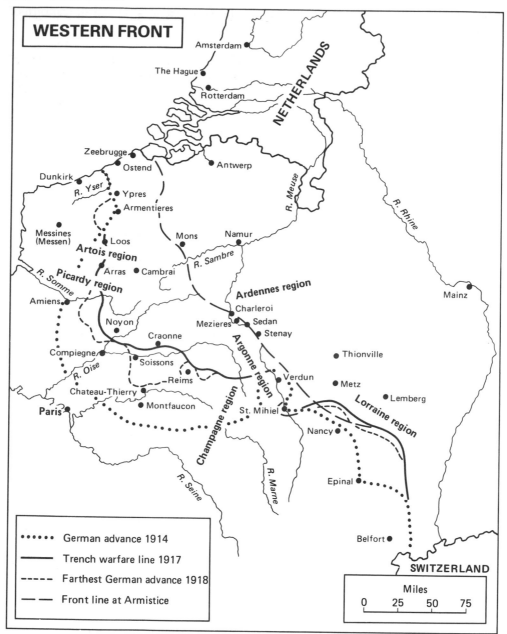

WESTERN FRONT

Amsterdam

The Hague

Rotterdam

NETHERLANDS

R. Meuse

R. Rhine

Zeebrugge

Ostend

Antwerp

Dunkirk

R. Yser

Ypres

Armentieres

Messines
(Messen)

Loos

Mons

Namur

Artois region

R. Sambre

Arras   Cambrai

Picardy region

Ardennes region

Mainz

R. Somme

Amiens

Charleroi

Noyon

Mezieres   Sedan

Thionville

Craonne

Stenay

Compiegne

Soissons

Verdun

Metz

R. Oise

Reims

Argonne region

Lemberg

Chateau-Thierry

Montfaucon

St. Mihiel

Lorraine region

Paris

Champagne region

Nancy

R. Seine

R. Marne

Epinal

Belfort

SWITZERLAND

••••• German advance 1914

——— Trench warfare line 1917

----- Farthest German advance 1918

— — Front line at Armistice

Miles

0   25   50   75

— Morocco against Mauritania and Polisario against both countries. On 7 June 1976 Polisario attacked the Mauritanian capital, Nouakchott, and in April the following year claimed to have killed 14,200 Moroccan and Mauritanian troops and to have shot down thirty-two aircraft for a loss of 200 Polisario soldiers. In July 1977 Polisario again attacked Nouakchott. On 5 August 1979 Mauritanian and Polisario signed a peace treaty. Polisario was now able to give all its attention to Morocco and on 28 January 1979 attacked Tan-Tan, inside Morocco. In November King Hassan sent against Polisario what many military experts regarded as the strongest desert fighting force since the days of Montgomery and Rommel. Nevertheless, it was outmanoeuvred by Polisario, which had some major victories in southern Morocco. On 13 October 1981 the biggest fight of the war took place at Guelta Zemmour: the Moroccan garrison was wiped out by 3,000 Polisario fighters equipped with tanks. Between November 1980 and May 1982 Morocco built a 200-mile "Berlin Wall" between Cap Bojador and Jebel Qarksis, to keep Polisario in the desert. It was not effective and in 1985 the war seemed endless.

Wexford, *Ireland (English Civil War) 11 October 1649*. A garrison of Irish and English Royalists tried to hold Wexford against Cromwell and his 10,000 Roundheads. These veterans broke through, massacred the defenders and sacked the city as they had earlier done at Drogheda. *See* Carbiesdale; Drogheda.

White Mountain (*Thirty Years' War*) *8 November 1620*. The Bohemian Protestant forces of Christian I of Anhalt and the soldiers of the Hungarian Bethlen Gabor, camped on White Mountain, hoped to protect Prague, the Bohemian capital, against the advancing army of the Catholic League under Tilly. They had 15,000 men to face Tilly's 25,000. Tilly bombarded White Mountain, then, under cover of heavy mist, attacked with his cavalry and infantry. Anhalt lost 5,000 men killed or captured and the rest fled. Prague fell to Tilly without resistance. *See* Sablat; Wiesloch.

White Plains (*American Revolution*) *28 October 1776*. The first action occurred, 16 September, when the British (Howe) probed the American positions on Harlem Heights, Manhattan Island. Howe then moved most of his 20,000 men up East River and landed behind Washington's lines at Pell's Point, forcing the Americans to retreat to White Plains. The British flanking assault, 28 October, captured heights dominating White Plains village and Washington again retreated.

Casualties: About 300 on either side. *See* Long Island.

White Russia — *Byelorussia (World War II) 22 June–13 July 1944*. Using four armies on a 350-mile front, the Russians struck hard at the German Central Army Group (Busch). Almost at once key centres and their garrisons fell. Vitebsk (five divisions) was taken 27 June, Mogilev (five divisions) 28 June, Bobruisk 33,000 Germans) 29 June. On 3 July 50,000 Germans were trapped in Minsk, a key communications centre. By 5 July the Germans had lost the Pripet Marshes region to Rokossovski. With the capture of centres in Lithuania and Latvia, 13 July, the German front was split into the Upper Baltic area and the East-Prussia–Poland sector. The Russians now held all White Russia and in 24 days had either annihilated or eliminated as effective forces twenty-five German divisions. *See* Leningrad; Ukraine.

Wiazma (*Napoleonic Wars: Moscow Campaign*) *3 November 1812*. During the French retreat from Moscow the corps led by Eugene Beauharnais and Davout tried to make a stand at Wiazma, but the Russians (Kutusov) drove them out, inflicting 2,000 casualties. *See* Berezina; Krasnadi.

Wiesloch, *near Heidelberg (Thirty Years' War) 22 April 1622*. A mercenary army (Count Mansfeld) employed by the Bohemian Protestant ruler Frederick V joined another Protestant army under George, Margrave of Baden-Durlach. Together they hoped to prevent the army of the Catholic League, under Tilly, from linking with the 20,000-strong Spanish army under Córdoba. Tilly attacked first and knocked back the Protestant advance guard, but was himself sharply checked by the main enemy army. Had Mansfeld advanced he could have now prevented the Bavarians from joining the Spaniards, but when he stayed put Tilly marched wide around the Protestant forces and linked with Córdoba. *See* White Mountain; Wimpfen.

Wilderness, *Virginia (American Civil War) 4–8 May 1864*. The Federals, under their supreme commander, Grant, and Meade, commander of the Army of the Potomac, mustered nearly 120,000 men and had 316 guns. The Confederates (Lee) had only 64,000 men and 274 guns. Both sides were committed to action in wild and difficult terrain. Several fierce actions took place, most of them ending because of exhaustion. A Confederate encircling attack engineered by Longstreet succeeded, but when he tried to support it with a frontal assault he was seriously wounded by fire from his own men. The Federal right wing was nevertheless driven back on confusion. Both sides spent a whole day, 7 May, straightening out their positions but that night Grant withdrew north-east. Casualties proved that the Confederates had the better of the involved and often bitter fighting. Federals, 17,666 (2,246 killed, 12,073 wounded); Confederates, 7,750. In all, five generals were killed, six wounded and two captured. *See* Bristoe Station; Spotsylvania.

Wilhelmstahl (*Seven Years' War*) 24 *June 1762*. Following the Treaty of Hamburg between Prussia and Sweden, Frederick the Great could now deal with the Austrians while Ferdinand the Duke of Brunswick held the French. At Wilhelmstahl in Westphalia Ferdinand manoeuvred the French onto a plain, pinned them down with his Prussian infantry and sent in the British cavalry. This charge was led by the highly competent Lieutenant-General Sir John Granby. The French were routed and suffered 4,000 casualties. In October Ferdinand drove the French back across the Rhine. *See* Burkersdorf; Freiberg.

Williamsburg (*American Civil War*) 5 *May 1862*. The Confederates had strongly positioned 32,000 men, under Longstreet and Daniel Hill, to block the

Federal army of 40,000 (Sumner) pursuing them after their evacuation from Yorktown, Virginia. Having inflicted 2,239 casualties on the Federals at much less cost to himself, Longstreet withdrew further by night. *See* Fair Oaks; Yorktown II.

Wilson's Creek, *Missouri (American Civil War) 10 August 1861*. Between 5,600 Federals (Lyon) and 11,800 Confederates (McCulloch). The Federal attack was partly successful. The Confederates, holding the initiative, then made three abortive charges against Federal positions on Oak Hill. Lyon was killed and his successor, Brigadier Sturgis, made the puzzling decision to withdraw. Casualties: Federals, 1,236; Confederates, 1,095. *See* Belmont.

Wilton, *Wiltshire (Danish invasion of Britain) 871*. The West Saxons under Alfred gave battle to the invading Danes and could not be broken. The Danes then feigned a retreat, drew the Saxons after them and then turned about in an overwhelming counter-attack. Alfred made peace with the Danes and paid them the tribute they demanded — the Danegeld — to withdraw to London. This gave him time to rebuild an army. *See* Chippenham; Reading.

Wimpfen, *central southern Germany (Thirty Years' War) 6 May 1622*. After the Battle of Wiesloch, q.v., the Catholic League armies under Córdoba and Tilly had joined. The Protestant army leaders, Mansfeld with his veteran mercenaries and Prince George with his Baden troops, now needed to link with Prince Christian of Brunswick. Moving separately, Mansfeld and George hoped to induce Tilly and Córdoba to divide *their* forces. Instead, Tilly and Córdoba together concentrated against George, who, with 14,000 men, found himself facing 45,000. Nevertheless, his cavalry successfully charged the enemy guns while his own artillery kept the Catholics at bay. Then a Spanish cannon ball exploded George's magazine. The enemy at once charged and the Protestant army was broken. Few survived, but George escaped. *See* Höchst.

Winchelsea (*Hundred years' War*) 29 August 1350. A Spanish fleet (la Carda) entered the English Channel to support the French. Off the southern English coast the English navy grappled the enemy ships, boarded them and practically destroyed the Spanish fleet. *See* Calais I.

Winchester I, *Virginia* (*American Civil War*) 26 May 1863. A force of 17,000 Confederates (Stonewall Jackson) attacked Federal-held Winchester from three sides in a cleverly co-ordinated operation that inflicted 2,000 casualties for a cost of 300. Chasing the retreating Federals (Banks), Jackson again manoeuvred to escape a trap being set for him. His activities tied up many Federal troops. *See* Cross Keys; Front Royal; Port Republic.

Winchester II (*American Civil War*) 14–15 June 1863. The Federal commander in the Winchester area, Milroy, had left it too late to obey orders to withdraw under Confederate pressure. Cut off and pursued by a full corps of Confederates (Ewell), Milroy lost 3,358 men captured and another 1,000 killed or wounded and all his guns and supplies. Ewell had only 269 casualties. *See* Brandy Station; Gettysburg.

Winchester III (*American Civil War*) 19 September 1864. The Confederates now held Winchester, controlling the vital Shenandoah Valley with 12,000 men (Early). The Federals put 38,000 men into the attack under Philip Sheridan. Attacked on two sides by such overwhelming numbers, the Confederates gave ground and by dark could no longer hold Winchester. The Federals bought their victory dearly — about 900 killed and 3,983 wounded. Confederate casual-ties, 276 killed, 1,827 wounded. *See* Kernstown II.

Winchester, *England* (*The English "Anarchy"*) 1141. Maud, having captured Stephen of Blois, her rival for the English crown, was in a strong position, but Stephen's troops held Wolvesey Castle, besieged by Maud's soldiers under her half-brother Robert of Gloucester. Yet another Blois force broke the siege and captured Robert and to save him Maud had to exchange Stephen. *See* Lincoln I; Wallingford.

Windhoek (*World War I*) 12 May 1915. Windhoek, capital of German south-west Africa, was held by a garrison of about 7,000. A South African force under Louis Botha stormed and captured the place, then cleaned up other pockets of resistance. *See* East Africa; Rufiji River.

Winkova (*Napoleonic Wars: Moscow Campaign*) 18 October 1812. Murat was leading the French advance guard during the retreat from Moscow when attacked by Russian cavalry (Count Dennizov). Murat quickly took up positions, but the Russians drove him out. Murat lost 2,000 killed, 3,000 prisoners and all his guns and equipment. *See* Berezina.

Winnington Bridge, *Cheshire* (*Royalist Rising*) 19 August 1659. Oliver Cromwell was dead, his son Richard had resigned and there was a resurgence of sympathy for the Royalist cause. Sir George Booth raised a cavalry force, but in a sharp battle 5,000 Parliamentary troops under General Lambert defeated and scattered Booth's army. Booth's effort was unnecessary; the next year Charles II was given the throne.

Winwaed, *near Leeds* (*Teutonic Conquest of Britain*) 655. King Penda of Mercia now controlled much of Britain. Oswiv, brother of Oswald of Northumbria, who had been defeated by Penda, led the Bernicians of Northumbria in a successful battle against Penda, though Penda had been supported by East Angles and Britons. Penda's defeat did not mean the end of Mercia. *See* Ellandun; Heavenfield; Maserfield; Nechtansmere.

Wisby, *Baltic* (*Danish–Swedish War*) *1613*. A 3-day battle between the Swedish fleet of Gustavus Adolphus and the Danish one of Christian IV. Both fleets were crippled and neither could claim victory.

Wittenweier (*Thirty Years' War*) *30 July 1638*. Breisach, q.v., key to the Rhine and gateway to Germany, was under siege by Bernard of Saxe-Weimar — an ally of France and Sweden in their war against the Austrians. The Austrians sent an army under the Bavarian general, Goetz, to break this siege, but Bernard defeated him decisively at Wittenweier. The French (Turenne) joined the siege and Breisach's position became hopeless. *See* Rheinfelden.

Wittstock, *north-west of Berlin* (*Thirty Years' War*) *4 October 1636*. The Catholic Austrian and Spanish forces had been successful along the Rhine and in central and southern Germany. The Swedish army under Banér was in an exposed position in Brandenburg and John George I of Saxony with 30,000 Bavarian, Austrian and Saxon troops, took up positions to prevent the Swedes from reaching the Baltic and safety. Banér had only 22,000 men, mostly Swedes and Scots in Swedish service, so unable to use weight, he used strategem. With part of his army he advanced to the foot of the slope held by his enemy and sent the Scottish generals James King and Alexander Leslie with the bulk of the army on a wide encircling movement. The over-confident Allies left their trenches to attack the small Swedish force. King and Leslie then hit their exposed flank and rear. The trapped Catholics fought back, but defeat was inevitable, and they lost 12,000 killed or

wounded and 8,000 captured. Swedish casualties, 5,000. Protestant hopes were again high. *See* Nordlingen; Rheinfelden.

Wolf Mountain, *Montana* (*Sioux War*) *7 January 1877*. An American column of 476 (Miles) with two field guns trapped 1,000 Sioux warriors — some of those who had taken part in the massacre of U.S. cavalry at Little Bighorn River — and routed them. *See* Little Bighorn; Wounded Knee Creek.

Wolgast, *south Baltic coast* (*Thirty Years' War*) *2 September 1628*. Christian IV of Denmark and Norway landed an army at Wolgast to march south and invade the Holy Roman (Austrian) Empire. But nearby, besieging Stralsund, was an enemy army, under Wallenstein, who abandoned the siege and attacked Christian's army as it marched from Wolgast. Few Danes survived to reach their ships and safety. Christian asked Ferdinand II for peace terms. *See* Frankfort-on-the-Oder; Stralsund.

Worcester (*English Civil War*) *3 September 1651*. Charles II, invading England while Cromwell was invading Scotland, reached Worcester at the head of 16,000 Scottish Royalists. His retreat cut off by Cromwell and unable to bring English Royalists to his side, Charles could only make a stand. Cromwell had 20,000 veterans of the Parliamentary New Model Army and 10,000 militia. Also, he had built a bridge of boats across the Severn River and could move his troops at will.

At one point in the 5-hour battle there was a good chance for Charles. He noticed that Cromwell had left the isolated right wing, which was thus leaderless. Charles gathered all the troops he could and charged out of Worcester's east gate in an attack that sent the Roundheads reeling. A cavalry charge would have routed them, but Charles's cavalry commander, David Leslie, would not move and despite Charles's pleas the Scottish horse fled north. Cromwell reappeared on the right wing and his regiment forced the Royalists back into the town where many were killed in the narrow streets. Few Scots survived the battle, but Charles escaped to the Continent. This was the last battle of the Civil War. *See* Dunbar II.

Wörth (*French–Prussian War*) 6 August 1870. In north-east France the French had placed about 38,000 men under MacMahon to block the Prussian invasion at that point. Crown Prince Frederick William had an army of 77,000 and great superiority in quality and quantity of artillery. That the French managed to hold off the enemy for 8 hours was due to their chassepot rifles and their mitrailleuse machine-guns. But weight of numbers told; MacMahon, having lost 12,000 men, retreated behind the Vosges Mountains. The Prussians had almost as many casualties. *See* Colombey; Spicheren; Weissenburg.

Wounded Knee Creek (*"Ghost Dance War"*) 28 December 1890. The war was so called because of a wild religion then influencing Indian tribes and which included a "ghost dance". An armed Indian tribe caused trouble in South Dakota. While they were being disarmed by the U.S. 7th Cavalry (Colonel Forsythe) the warriors opened fire. A long hunt-and-kill battle followed. Casualties: Indian, 145 killed, 33 wounded; American, 30 killed, 34 wounded. *See* Wolf Mountain.

Wrotham Heath, *Kent* (*Wyatt's Insurrection*) 18 January 1554. Sir Thomas Wyatt raised a force of 4,000 to fight the proposed marriage of Queen Mary to a Spanish prince. At Wrotham Heath his Kentish "troops" under Sir Henry Isley were routed by Lord Abergavenny and Royalist troops.

Würzburg (*French Revolution Wars*)

3 September 1796. The French army of the Sambre-and-Meuse (Jourdan) defeated at Amberg, q.v., was still 40,000-strong and retreated to Würzburg. But here the Archduke Charles Louis of Austria again attacked him with 45,000 Austrians. Losing 2,000 men and some cannon, Jourdan retreated west of the Rhine. This retrograde move took the teeth out of the overall French invasion of Austria. *See* Caliano.

Würtzchen, *near Dresden* (*Napoleonic Wars: Leipzig Campaign*) 21 May 1813. The Allied Russian (Sayn-Wittgenstein) and Prussian armies (Blucher) were defeated by the French, under Napoleon personally, in a battle noted for its carnage. The allies retreated east across the Oder River. Each side had about 100,000 troops and each suffered 20,000 casualties. *See* Leipzig.

Wynandael, *northern France* (*War of Spanish Succession*) 28 September 1708. An Allied army of British and Prussians were besieging Lille. A French force of forty battalions of infantry and forty squadrons of cavalry (Motte) intercepted a great convoy of supplies, but in the pitched battle which developed they lost 7,000 men under the determined attack of a much smaller British force (Webb). *See* Lille; Oudenarde.

Wyoming Valley, *Philadelphia* (*American Revolution*) 3 July 1778. A British raiding party of 900 (Major John Butler) made an expedition to attack the settlement of Wyoming Valley, which was defended by 360 Americans led by Colonel Zebulon Butler. The British–Indian party made their headquarters at Wintermoort Fort. Colonel Butler decided to attack first, but his Americans' were quickly beaten. Only sixty of them escaped and John Butler said that his Indians took 277 scalps but "only of men carrying arms". *See* Monmouth.

Xanten (*Reign of Otto I, "The Great"*) *940*. During his early years Otto I, creator of a new Holy Roman Empire, fought two civil wars to ensure his succession. The first was against his half-brother, 938–9. The second was against a group of rebellious nobles. Supported by Louis IV of France, Otto won the Battle of Xanten by using his horsemen to drive the enemy soldiers against his own infantry. The following year he won the Battle of Anderbach; Lorraine came under his control.

Xaquixaguana (*Spanish Conquest of Chile*) *1548*. Spanish royal authority was under threat in Peru where Gonzalez Pizarro, younger brother of the great explorer–soldier Francisco, was treating Peru as his own preserve. Charles V of Spain appointed Pedro de la Gasca as his viceroy. With the help of the loyalist Pedro de Valdivia, Gasca defeated Pizarro in the battle of Xaquixaguana, a battle fought almost entirely with swords.

Xeres (*Spanish–Muslim Wars*) *19–26 July 711*. Intent on conquering Spain, where they already had bases, the Muslims from north Africa pitted a Muslim army of 12,000 and tens of thousands of African auxiliaries, all under Tarik Ali, against about 85,000 Spanish Christians led by King Roderic. On the fourth day of fighting the Muslims were outflanked and the Spanish killed 16,000 of them. They might have broken, but Count Julian and his followers then deserted the Spanish ranks. The rest of Roderic's army was routed and he himself drowned in the Guadalquiver River. The Muslims had begun a long series of victories.

Xiengkhouang (*Viet Minh invasion of Laos*) *20 April 1953*. Seizing a base abandoned by the French army at Samneua, the Viet Minh pro-Communist forces advanced towards the capital Luang Prabang. Supported by rebel Laotians, they captured Xiengkhouang in a fierce encircling battle. Laos mobilized and the United States rushed military aid. French troops retook Xiengkhouang early in May. *See* Dien Bien Phu; Laos; Vietnam.

Yalu River I, *Korea* **(***Chinese–Japanese War***)** *17 September 1894*. The Japanese admiral Yugo Ito took ten cruisers and two gunboats to the mouth of the Yalu River where he attacked a Chinese fleet of two battleships and eight cruisers (Ting). Circling the Chinese ships, Ito badly damaged four of them by gunfire. The battle continued until sundown, when Ito took his fleet to the open sea. The battered Chinese ships retired to Port Aurthur. *See* Port Arthur I; Pyongyang.

Yalu River II (*Russian–Japanese War***)** *1 May 1904*. With the Russian fleet blockaded in Port Arthur, the Japanese landed 40,000 troops (Kuroki) at Jinsen for a drive north against the Russian army at Liaoyang, Manchuria. The Russian supreme commander sent 7,000 troops under Zasulich to hold the Yalu River. The Japanese crushed this force, killing or wounding 2,500 Russians. *See* Liaoyang; Port Arthur II.

Yalu River III. *See* Korea.

Yamazuki (*Japanese Taira War***)** *May 1814*. Between the followers of the Taira family and the forces of the rebellious Yoshitsune. The Taira army was defeated.

Yarmuk River, *Jordan Valley* **(***Muslim Conquest of Syria***)** *20 August 636*. The Byzantine Emperor Heraclius sent 50,000 troops under Theodorus Trithurius to push the aggressive Muslim army of Khalid ibn-al-Walid out of Syria. Khalid had only 25,000 troops, but they were hardened warriors. Their first charges were beaten back, but regrouping they came in time and again, slashing with their swords. The Byzantines' Asiatic auxiliaries broke first, and a general collapse followed. Few Byzantine soldiers survived and 4,000 Muslims were killed. Byzantine power vanished from Palestine and southern Syria and Islam appeared to be invincible. *See* Aleppo; Damascus I; Jerusalem VI.

Yawata (*War of the Japanese Emperors***)** *January 1353*. Between the armies of the Northern and Southern Emperors of Japan. The southern army, under Moroushi, won decisively, leading to national amalgamation.

Yeavering (*or Geteringe***) (***English–Scottish Wars***)** *May 1415*. A Scottish force of 4,000 (Sir Robert Umfraville) invaded northern England but were defeated by only 430 English troops (Earl of Westmorland).

Yellow Ford, *near Armagh, Northern Ireland* **(***Tyrone's Rebellion***)** *14 August 1598*. The Earl of Tyrone and Hugh O'Donnell, with 5,000 Irish troops, were besieging Blackwater Fort. They turned against the approaching English relief force (Bagenal) and overwhelmingly defeated it at a ford on the Callan River, 2,000 English being killed. Blackwater

Fort then surrendered. This was the worst disaster ever suffered by English troops in Ireland. The rebellion was quelled in 1604.

Yellow River (*Mongol invasion of Western Hsai*) *1226*. From his base in Mongolia, Genghis led an army of 180,000 south in a campaign against the Tangut emperor. The emperor's Hsai army numbered more than 300,000 when it confronted the Mongols on the banks of the frozen Yellow River. By feigning confusion, Genghis enticed the Tangut cavalry to charge across the ice. Mongol dismounted archers harassed them and as the enemy cavalry lost cohesion Mongol horsemen charged them. While this was going on Genghis sent his well-disciplined infantry to bypass the battle on the ice and attack the Hsai infantry on the other river bank. It is said that the Mongols counted 300,000 enemy dead. Genghis died during the return to Mongolia. *See* Kalka River.

Yellow Sea (*Russian–Japanese War*) *10 August 1904*. The Russian fleet, trapped in Port Arthur and under artillery fire from land batteries, fought to reach the open sea. The Japanese fleet (Togo) blocked the Russian ships and forced them back into the harbour where they could be destroyed. *See* Port Arthur II.

Yellow Tavern (*American Civil War*) *11 May 1864*. 10,000 Federal cavalry (Sheridan) struck towards Richmond, the Confederate capital. The Confederate cavalry commander, J. E. B. Stuart, had only 4,500 troopers, but he divided his force. One, under James Gordon, followed Sheridan; with the other Stuart rode to intercept Sheridan. In the subsequent clash Sheridan had a double victory, driving off both Confederate forces and killing both Confederate generals. Stuart's death was a sharp blow to the Confederate strength. Federal casualties, 625. *See* Wilderness.

Yelna, *near Smolensk* (*World War II*) *2–30 August 1941*. This relatively small battle is of great significance to the Russians as the first victory of the Red Army over the Germans. After the capture of Smolensk the Germans had taken Yelna and other places, forming a salient of about 150 square miles. The Russians drove them out with heavy loss of life on both sides. In October the Russians in Yelna were encircled during the German offensive and crushed into submission. *See* Smolensk; Soviet Union.

Yemen War *1962–9*. On 18 September 1962 the Iman Ahmed of Yemen died and was succeeded by his son, al Badr, who was displaced by a coup organized by Brigadier Abdullah Sallal. Al Badr fled to the north to rally his Royalist supporters while an occupying Egyptian army of 30,000 moved in to support Sallal. With total air control, the Egyptians bombed Royalist centres indiscriminately and used poison gas against their enemy. Royalist resistance was so spirited that President Nasser increased his army occupation to 70,000. Saudi Arabia supported the Royalists, the Soviet Union supplied the Republicans. Sallal was overthrown in 1967 after the Egyptians withdrew (a result of their defeat in the Six-Day war), but the military stalemate continued until Saudi Arabian mediation produced a peace in 1969. In this ferocious war 130,000 combatants were killed but only the Egyptian figures are in any way precise — 9,000 killed, 21,000 wounded.

Yenan (*Chinese Communists "Long March"*) *16 October 1934–30 October 1935*. This is the name of convenience sometimes given to the fighting march of the 90,000 Communist troops who evacuated Kiangsi Province under Nationalist pressure and set off for Yenan, Shensi, 6,000 miles away. The Communists fought blocking Nationalist armies and several equally strong provincial armies and they crossed eighteen mountain ranges and twenty-four rivers.

The commander-in-chief, Chu Teh, and his political commissar, Mao Tse-tung, got through with 20,000 men. Yenan became the Communist capital.

Yenikale Gulf, *Black Sea (Turkish–Russian Wars)* 14 July 1790. A closely fought but indecisive battle between the Turkish fleet (Osman) and the Russian fleet (Onschakov). Both fleets lost fourteen ships. *See* Rimnitz (Rimnik).

York (*Danish invasions of Britain*) 867. The Danish chieftain Ivan the Boneless laid siege to the Saxon stronghold of York, seeking battle to avenge the killing of his father in Northumbria. The two kings of Northumbria united and penned the Danes against the walls of York; the garrison then attacked from the other side. The Danes, who excelled in close-quarter fighting overwhelmed and annihilated the Saxons, who lost all power in northern Britain. *See* Aclea, Hoxne.

Yorktown I (*American Revolution*) 6–19 October 1781. Yorktown, on the York River of Virginia, was held by Lord Cornwallis with 7,500 men. On the opposite bank his troops also held Gloucester. Washington, with 8,845 American troops, and Rochambeau, with 7,800 French, established siege lines around the fortified town on 6 October. The Allied heavy siege guns caused great damage. On 14 October British advanced redoubts were stormed and the Allied guns were moved closer. With the French navy blockading Yorktown, Cornwallis had no hope of reinforcement and he surrendered the city and his army. Casualties: British, 156 killed, 326 wounded; American, 20 killed, 56 wounded; French, 52 killed, 134 wounded. The battle ended the fighting in America. *See* Chesapeake Cape.

Yorktown II (*American Civil War*) 4 April 1862. Striking towards Richmond, the Confederate capital, a Federal army of 45,000 (McClellan) found the route blocked by entrenched Confederates.

There were, in fact, only 12,000 of them under Magruder, but McClellan was apparently unaware of the weakness of his enemy for he laid a regular siege to Yorktown, using many heavy guns. They opened fire 1 May but on 3 May Magruder successfully withdrew and disengaged. He had done his job of tying up the Federal army to permit Confederate defence of Richmond. *See* Ball's Bluff; Williamsburg.

Youghiogany (*Seven Years' War*) 27 May 1754. Forty Virginians (George Washington) surprised a detachment of French (Jumonville) on reconnaissance from Fort Duquesne; all the French were killed or captured. This mere skirmish is important historically as one of the causes of the Seven Years' War, known in America as the French and Indian War. It broke out two years later.

Ypres I, *Belgium (World War I)* 14 October–11 November 1914. Ypres — in West Flanders — and the slightly higher ground to its east was a key point in the Allied Western Front, with the Belgian army holding the line from Ypres to the sea and the British from Ypres south to La Bassée. The German chief-of-staff, Falkenhayn, attacked with the German Fourth and Sixth Armies, 14 October. The Belgians could hold their front only by opening sea sluice gates and flooding it. The French rushed in massive reinforcements during the 9-day German offensive, then Foch launched a great but vain counter-attack, 20–28 October. The British had held on to a salient that poked 6 miles into the German front, and could not be dislodged before heavy rain and snow ended the battle. The frontal assaults and massed artillery and machine-gun fire caused enormous casualties. German, 130,000; French, 50,000; British, 2,368 officers and 55,787 men; Belgian, 32,000. *See* Aisne River I; Champagne I; Flanders; Ypres II.

Ypres II (*World War I*) 22 April–25 May 1915. Using poison gas (chlorine)

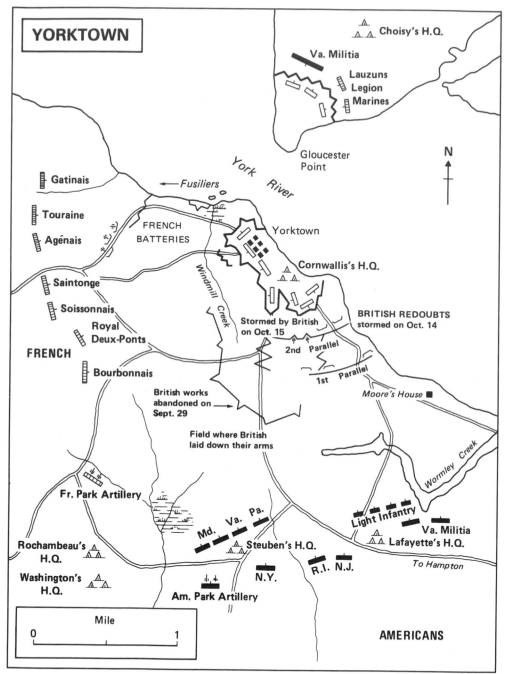

YORKTOWN

Choisy's H.Q.

Va. Militia

Lauzuns
Legion

Marines

Gloucester
Point

N

Gatinais

← Fusiliers

York River

Touraine

Agénais

FRENCH
BATTERIES

Yorktown

Saintonge

Cornwallis's H.Q.

Soissonnais

Royal
Deux-Ponts

Stormed by British
on Oct. 15

BRITISH REDOUBTS
stormed on Oct. 14

FRENCH

Windmill Creek

2nd Parallel

Bourbonnais

1st Parallel

British works
abandoned on →
Sept. 29

Moore's House ■

Field where British
laid down their arms

Wormley Creek

Fr. Park Artillery

Light Infantry

Va. Militia

Rochambeau's
H.Q.

Md. Va. Pa.

Steuben's H.Q.

Lafayette's H.Q.

Washington's
H.Q.

R.I. N.J.

To Hampton

N.Y.

Am. Park Artillery

Mile

0   1

AMERICANS

for the first time, the Germans quickly forced a 4-mile gap in the British Second Army line of the Allied front. With the Germans slow to take advantage of their breakthrough — the gas had been an experiment and its success surprised them — the Second Army commander (Smith-Dorrien) rushed Canadian troops into the gap. They managed to hold on during a second gas attack, 24 April. British counter-attacks were terribly costly in life without much gain, and

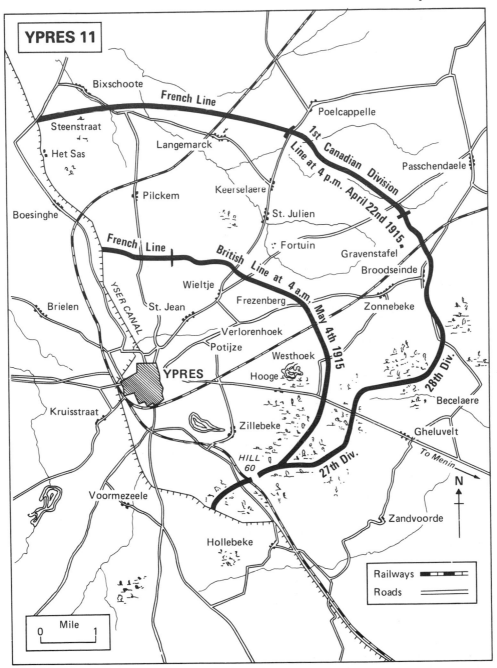

YPRES 11

Bixschoote
French Line
Poelcappelle
Steenstraat
1st Canadian Division
Langemarck
Line at 4 p.m. April 22nd 1915
Het Sas
Passchendaele
Keerselaere
Pilckem
Boesinghe
St. Julien
French Line
Fortuin
Gravenstafel
British Line at 4 a.m.
Broodseinde
Wieltje
May 4th 1915
Brielen
St. Jean
Frezenberg
Zonnebeke
Verlorenhoek
Potijze
Westhoek
YPRES
Hooge
28th Div.
Kruisstraat
Becelaere
Zillebeke
Gheluvelt
To Menin
HILL 60
27th Div.
N
Voormezeele
Zandvoorde
Hollebeke

Railways
Roads

Mile
0   1

YSER CANAL

Smith-Dorrien ordered a withdrawal to the edge of Ypres itself. His chief, Field Marshal French, replaced him with Plumer. On 1 May Plumer carried out Smith-Dorrien's plans to withdraw. The Germans attacked many times, but after give and take the Allied line held and the battle petered out on 25 May. Allied casualties were 60,000 to the Germans 35,000. German use of gas was a tactical error; the prevailing winds of the area are westerlies, so that when the British and

French replied in kind the Germans suffered more heavily from gas than did the Allies. *See* Artois II; Flanders; Neuve Chapelle.

Ypres III (*World War I*) 21 July–6 November 1917. After heavy bombardment for 10 days Haig had planned a major offensive for 1917 and on 21 June his artillery opened a massive 10-day bombardment on German Fourth Army front (Armin). On 31 July the Fifth Army (Gough) attacked out of the Ypres salient, supported by British Second Army (Plumer) on its right and French First Army on the left. A few miles of ground and 6,000 German prisoners were taken that day. Then heavy rain filling the thousands of shell-holes and soaking into the torn fields created a massive bog. Fighting resumed on 16 August when Langemarck was taken, but Gough could make little progress. On 20 September Plumer gained another mile, taking Menin Road Ridge, despite German use of mustard (blister) gas. German tactics had changed. They relied on small machine-gun parties in shell-holes, supported by small concrete block-houses impervious to artillery fire. Covered by these, the Germans delivered mass counter-attacks before the British could consolidate the ground gained. The final action occurred on 6 November when Canadian troops stormed and held Passchendaele, 7 miles from Ypres. British casualties of 400,000 hardly compensated for the mere 9,000 prisoners they had taken. Estimated German casualties, 65,000. However, the British effort had taken pressure from the French. *See* Broodseinde; Flanders; Messines; Passchendaele.

Yugoslavia (*World War II*) 6–17 April 1941. An outstanding example of a great victory won at little cost to the aggressors. On 6 April German troops — twenty-seven divisions in all — invaded Yugoslavia from four neighbouring countries, while Hungary and Italy also moved columns into the country. Yugoslavia had forty divisions on paper, but the troops were ill equipped and German fragmentation of the country prevented co-ordinated military resistance. Five German divisions blocked any attempt by Yugoslavian forces to link with their Greek allies. For total casualties of 558, the Germans inflicted 50,000 (including 17,000 civilians in air attacks on Belgrade) and took prisoner 6,000 officers and 335,000 men.

Yungay, *Chile* (*Peru–Bolivia–Chile War*) 20 January 1839. The Confederation of Peru and Bolivia threatened to dominate much of South America, and Chile rapidly built up a strong army (General Manuel Bulnes) to protect itself. When the Confederation forces invaded Chile, Bulnes' army decisively beat them. This led to political reverses which destroyed the confederation.

Yser River (*World War I*) 18 October–30 November 1914, then 1915–18. The Yser River formed the northernmost part of the Allied lines on the Westrn Front and for most of the war the river line was held by the Belgians; on their right were the British. The first battle stopped the German advance to the sea. A battle of attrition then continued for the rest of the war. The Germans held the east side of the river, the Belgians the west side; the distances were short, there was little cover and casualties were heavy. *See* Flanders; Western Front; Ypres.

Zab River I, *Tigris tributary (Bahram's Revolt against Chosroes) 591.* An able Persian general, Bahram Chobin, won a great victory against the Turks at the Battle of the Hyrcanian Rock in 588. He then turned against the Romans, in 589, beating them at Martyrpolis. Defeated at Araxes, Bahram refused to accept the rule of the young Chosroes, deposed him and took the Persian throne. Supporting Chosroes, a 30,000-strong Roman army under General Narses was sent into Persia to restore Chosroes. Other Roman forces moved into Media. Bahram, with 40,000 troops, tried to halt the invasion at the Zab River. Narses now had 60,000 men and decisively defeated Bahram in a battle of brute force. Bahram sought refuge with the Turks and was killed. *See* Nineveh.

Zab River II (*Muslim Civil Wars***)** *January 750.* The rebel force of Abbasids gave battle to the army of the Ommiad caliph, Marwan II. The fight is said to have lasted 11 days and it ended with the rout of the Ommiads. Abu-al-Abbas became the first Abbasid caliph. *See* Heraclea; Kerbela; Pontica.

Zallaka (*Spanish–Muslim Wars***)** *23 October 1086.* The victories of Alfonso VI of Castile and Leon had alarmed the Muslim chiefs in Spain. They sent to Africa for Yusuf ibn-Tashfin and his Berbers to deal with Alfonso. After a swift march from Algeciras, ibn-Tashfin came upon the much larger Spanish army of mounted knights and infantry, rigid in ranks. The savage Berber horsemen cut the Spanish force to pieces, though Alfonso escaped. Ibn-Tashfin became ruler of most of southern Spain.

**Zama, *near Carthage (Second Punic War) 202 BC.* Carthage was in great danger from threat of Roman attack and the great leaders Hannibal and his brother Mago, campaigning in Italy, were hastily recalled to defend their city. Hannibal put together a force of 37,000, including his own 12,000 veterans from Italy, and eighty elephants. The Roman commander, the capable Scipio, had about the same number of men, but his Numidian cavalry and his Roman legionaries were more highly trained than his enemy. Hannibal's elephants failed to demoralize the Romans, then the Roman cavalry chased the Carthaginian cavalry into the desert.

The Roman legions now attacked Hannibal's three separate lines of defence. Their steady, disciplined thrust crushed two of the lines, but they had suffered casualties and were weary. Scipio regrouped them for the final attack — this time against veterans under Hannibal himself. At the critical moment the Roman cavalry returned to the battle, attacking the Carthaginians in the rear. The battle ended with 20,000 Carthaginians dead and the rest captured, though Hannibal escaped. The Romans lost 1,500 killed, but gained the Carthaginian empire. Scipio was awarded the

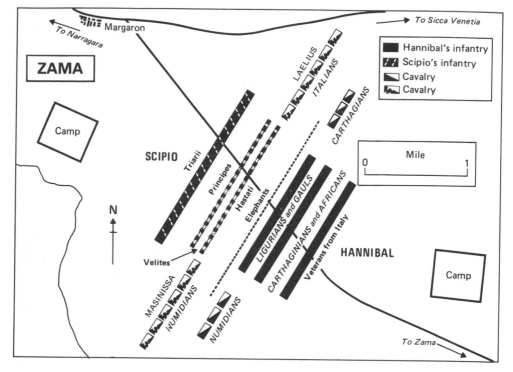

surname Africanus as a tribute to his victory. *See* Carthage I; Magnesia; Utica I.

Zamora I (*Spanish–Muslim Wars*) 901. A pitched battle, north-west of Madrid, between the Spaniards under Alfonso, King of Asturias, and the Moors of Abdullah, King of Cordova. The Moors were defeated with heavy loss and Alfonso extended his kingdom as far as the Guadiana River. *See* Zamora II.

Zamora II (*Spanish–Muslim Wars*) 939. The Muslims (Abd-er-Rahman III), besieging Zamora, were routed by the relief army of King Ramiro II of Leon, but Moorish rule in Spain was no weaker by the defeat. *See* Zallaka; Zamora I.

Zeebrugge (*World War I*) 23 April 1918. German submarines, though contained by the Allied convoy system, were still a meance to the Allies in 1918. U-boats operated from bases at Zeebrugge and Ostend and from the shelter of the canal port of Bruges, Belgium. British Admiral R. J. B. Keyes organized a raid against the bases, with seventy-five ships taking part. The light cruiser *Vindictive* dashed into Zeebrugge with destroyer and submarine escort. The ship drew alongside the mole or central breakwater and demolition parties disembarked. A British submarine loaded with high explosive was blown up against the lock gates and two blockships were also sunk. The base was not entirely blocked. In another raid on 9 May the *Vindictive* was deliberately sunk against the lock gates. Forty destroyers and submarines were unable to get out for many weeks. British killed or wounded were 635. *See* Atlantic I.

Zeim (*Russian–Turkish War*) 20 April 1877. The Russians (Melikov) attacked the Turks (Mukhtar) in strongly entrenched positions and were beaten off. *See* Kars II; Plevna; Sistov.

Zela I, *north-central Turkey (Third Mithridatic War) 67 BC*. The Pontic army of King Mithridates attacked the Roman camp and practically annihilated the legions under Triarus. *See* Zela II.

Zela II *(Wars of the First Triumvirate) August 47 BC*. Julius Caesar, with seven legions, had gone to northern Turkey to put down a threat by Pharnaces, son of Mithridates II. Pharnaces and his troops attacked the legionaries by surprise while they were making camp. The disciplined Romans quickly took up combat formation and annihilated their enemy. It was after this battle that Caesar sent his famous message to Rome — *Veni, vidi, vici.* I came, I saw, I conquered. *See* Zela I.

Zendecan *(Turkish–Afghan War) 1039*. The Seljuk Turks (Mohgrul Beg) defeated the Afghans (Musrud, Sultan of Ghuzni). Musrud retreated to Kabul, which the Turks were unable to capture. They maintained a siege for 6 years.

Zenta, *Theiss River (Turkish–Hungarian Wars) 11 September 1697*. (Often erroneously shown as having taken place in 1679.) Prince Eugene of Savoy marched to oppose a great Turkish invasion of Hungary from Belgrade under the personal command of Sultan Mustafa II. Eugene waited until the Turks were crossing a temporary bridge over the Theiss River. When the cavalry was across Eugene cut the bridge in two and drove the infantry into the river. About 30,000 Turks perished and the Austrians suffered only 500 casualties. This was the last serious Turkish threat to Hungary. *See* Vienna II.

Zeugminium, *northern Greece (Greek–Hungarian War) 1168*. The Greeks of Manuel I, Emperor of Constantinople, defeated the Hungarian invaders. The battle ended the 5-year war and the Hungarians were back beyond their frontiers.

Ziezicksee *(French–Flemish War) June 1302*. Philip IV of France, unable to defeat the Flemish fleet on his own, hired the Genoese captains Grimaldi and Rieti and the Genoese galley fleet. They destroyed the Flemish fleet on the Netherlands coast.

Zlotsow, *Bulgaria (Polish–Turkish Wars) August 1676*. A victory for the Poles (John Sobieski) over the 20,000 Turks and Tartars led by Muhammad IV. Muhammad lost half his army. *See* Zurakow.

Znaim *(Napoleonic Wars: Wagram Campaign) 14 July 1809*. After Wagram, Marshal Masséna's 8,000 French troops came under attack by the Prince of Reuss with 30,000 Austrians. As the Austrians moved forward at deliberate pace, Masséna ordered his much smaller force to charge. The startled Austrians were driven back through Znaim with heavy loss; the French took 800 prisoners. *See* Wagram.

Zorndorf, *Brandenburg (Seven Years' War) 25 August 1758*. A Russian army of 42,000 (Count William of Fermor) invaded Brandenburg and plundered some cities while Frederick the Great was campaigning against the Austrians to the south. Hurrying north, Frederick combined his own 15,000 men with another 21,500 retreating before the Russians. Forming into three great squares, the Russians waited for Frederick's offensive. Frederick attacked one square at a time, relying heavily on his cavalry under Seydlitz. The fighting was particularly ruthless all day; the Russians had 21,000 casualties, the Prussians 13,800. Fermor withdrew his battered army next day. *See* Hochkirk; Kay; Olmütz.

Zuider Zee *(Netherlands War of Independence against Spain) 11 October 1573*. Between thirty Spanish ships (Bossu) and twenty-five Dutch ships (Dirkzoon). The Spanish lost five ships and all but the flagship fled. After a remarkably brave fight Bossu and his battered ship were captured. *See* Alkmaar I; Brielle; Haarlem.

Zusmarshausen, *near Augsburg, Bavaria* **(***Thirty Years' War***)** *17 May 1648*. An uneasy coalition army of Swedes (Wrangel) and French (Turenne) surprised the joint Bavarian–Holy Roman Empire army under Groensfeld and Melander — though Montecuccoli was its driving force. Impeded by an intolerable train of camp followers outnumbering his 30,000 fighting men by four to one, Melander tried to get the artillery and baggage away, leaving Montecuccoli to defend the rear. The courageous and capable Italian general retreated from ridge to ridge, using his cavalry to beat off the attacking force while the infantry withdrew. With Melander mortally wounded, Montecuccoli fell back on Landsberg with the loss of Bavaria and everything except the bulk of his troops. The Swedes and French ravaged Bavaria to the River Inn, where the reorganized Austrians, under the able General Piccolomini, halted them. *See* Nördlingen II; Prague II.

Zurakow, *Poland* **(***Turkish–Polish Wars***)** *April–November 1676*. John Sobieski, with 100,000 Poles, was besieged in Zurakow by 200,000 Turks and Mongols (Shaitan). The Poles were well supplied and under Sobieski's aggressive leadership made numerous sorties against the besiegers, inflicting heavy losses and returning to the safety of the city's walls. With his army wasting away and unable to make any impression on the defences, Shaitan agreed to withdraw from Poland if the Poles would not harass his retreat. The Poles had lost only 3,000 men to the Turks estimated 80,000, but agreed to the terms. *See* Zlotsow.

Zutphen (*Netherlands War of Independence against Spain***)** *22 September 1586*. The Spaniards (Duke of Parma) held Zutphen against the newly proclaimed nation, the Union of Utrecht, which had rebelled against Spanish domination. Queen Elizabeth of England sent an English army under the Earl of Leicester to help the Dutch besiege Zutphen. The Battle of Zutphen occurred when the Spaniards made a major attempt to break the siege. Leicester intercepted the Spanish column but was beaten off, and had to abandon the siege. Among the English killed was Sir Philip Sidney. The Spaniards lost Zutphen 5 years later. *See* Antwerp I; Turnhout.

Update Supplement: Conflicts Since 1986

Afghanistan War *1979*. The Mujihadeen or 'holy war warriors' fought with such determination and skill against the combined Soviet–Afghan forces that by 1985 the government controlled only 35 per cent of the country. The Soviet Union replaced Babrak Karmal with Dr Muhammad Najibullah but the Resistance continued to be successful. By 1987–1988 the guerrillas were shooting down an average of one Soviet aircraft every day. Following the Geneva Agreement of 14 April 1988 the Soviets agreed to withdraw from Afghanistan and did so on 15 February 1989. In effect, the Soviet Union had lost the war, with combat casualties of 13,833, but it continued to support Najibullah.

A new phase of the war was then fought between the 'Democratic Republic of Afghanistan' (DRA) and the Mujihadeen Resistance, made up of seven rebel groups. Abandoning guerrilla tactics, the Resistance besieged Jalalabad on 6 March 1989, and lost 500 men killed and 1,500 wounded in the unsuccessful operation. In 1990 a coup against Najibullah failed because of his use of air power. He regained the initiative and brought in a national reconciliation policy. By 1990 the Mujihadeen leaders in exile had forfeited the good opinion of their backers, notably the Pakistan government. By now 40,000 foreign Muslims from 40 different countries were fighting for the Mujihadeen Resistance and the real struggle was that between Afghan nationalists and fundamentalists.

In 1991 the Resistance won the war against the government and Najibullah went into hiding. Predictably, the Resistance itself then split. On one side were the forces of the new president, Barhannudin Rabbani, and Ahmed Shah Massoud, on the other the prime minister, Gulbuddin Hekmatyar, backed by General Abdul Rashid Dostum. Both sides were well supplied with weapons. Between 1 January 1994 and mid-year more than 4,000 people had been killed in Kabul alone, and 40,000 wounded. More than half the city was destroyed. The war that had begun in 1979 was still going on, fuelled by weapons supplied by the original principals in the dispute, the Soviet Union, the United States, and Pakistan. *See* Koran: Khost; main entry.

Angola Civil War. *See* Cuito Cuanavale

Bangladesh Guerrilla War *1971–*. The newly created nation of Bangladesh (formerly East Pakistan) began in 1971 to drive out the Buddhist tribes living in the Chittagong Hill Tracts and to give their lands to Muslim settlers from Bengal. The Buddhists formed a 'self defence association', the Jana Sanghati Samity (JSS). The largest tribe, the Chakmas, created a military wing, the Shanti Bahini. These guerrillas were so successful in fighting the Bangladeshi occupation that after 13 years of frustration the Bangladeshi government ordered Major General Noor Uddin Khan to 'find a permanent solution to the Hill Tracts Problem'. His solution was terrorism, expulsion and genocide. The Shanti Bahini held out, even though aid from India and the Soviet Union dried up. The government brought in gangs of armed and vicious Muslims to help the army hunt the rebels, but still the Chakmas held out, though their only outside support came from publicity given to their cause by Amnesty International and the Anti-Slavery Association. When the president of Bangladesh, General Hussein Ershad, was replaced by a woman president, the Chakmas hoped for peace and justice but this has not been forthcoming. *See* main entry.

Burma Guerrilla War *1949–*. The Karen National Liberation Army (KNLA) began to fight for a homeland in 1949 and was aided by guerrillas from the Kachin, Kayan, Shan, Arakan, Mon, Naga, Kerreni and other tribes. The Karens, who total three million, are by far the largest group but the KNLA numbers only 5,000. The Burmese armed forces consist of 200,000 men, supported by a police force of 40,000 and a People's Militia of 35,000. During 1988 the Burmese Army called its operations against the Karens the 'Campaign of the Four Cuts'. They proposed to cut off the Karens' trade routes, to cut off outside aid, to cut off one rebel group from another and to cut off rebels' heads. The oppressive military regime was defeated in elections in 1990 by the National League of Democracy (Aung San Suu Kyi), but refused to accept the result. The Karens continued their war of liberation in the eastern hill and jungle region. Their base is Manerplaw, near which 1,000 soldiers of the Democratic Alliance (a collection of ethnic minority groups) were killed in bitter fighting during the period June 1989–June 1990.

It was clear in 1994 that the government was slowly winning a war of attrition against the Karens and their allies, who now included about 3,000 students who had fled from Rangoon and other cities. Even so, the resistance mounted by the guerrillas is one of the most remarkable in the history of irregular warfare. The KNLA had by then endured for 45 years, under only one leader, the legendary General By Mya.

Cambodia Civil War *1986–*. When President Heng Samrin put Cambodia's army under Vietnamese command, the opposition groups took to the jungle. Apart from the Khmer Rouge (Pol Pot's barbarous party) they comprised Son Kann's Khmer People's Liberation Front (KPLNF) and Prince Sihanouk's Armée Nationale Sihanoukienne (ANS), both non-Communist. Under Vietnamese pressure, the KPLNF and the ANS lost all their bases and the Khmer Rouge lost its mountain stronghold, Phnom Malai. Retreating into Thailand, the resistance fighters established bases and refugee camps. The Vietnamese Army then tried to seal off the 450-mile border against guerrilla incursion. Fighting became severe and by 1989 the Vietnamese army had lost 25,000 men in Cambodia, Vietnam was in political isolation and President Gorbachev told the Vietnamese president, Nguyen Co Thach, that the Soviet Union could no longer pay $3 million a day to support Vietnam's campaign in Cambodia. In July 1988, Vietnam undertook to withdraw its troops by 1990, and this promise was kept.

The US and its allies were so intent on driving out the Vietnamese and supporting 'democracy' that they ignored the possibility that the Khmer Rouge might return. All along, the Khmer Rouge leadership foresaw the possibility that it could regain power by a 'coalition' with the less barbaric resistance groups of Prince Sihanouk and Son Sann. Khmer Rouge guerrillas and the village militia skirmished throughout 1988 and 1989. The Khmer Rouge assumed the title 'Party of Democratic Cambodia' and claimed it was no longer waging a revolutionary war but a people's war to 'liberate' the country. The character of the war changed: the combat was no longer confined to sporadic fighting in the Thai border region and, with the Vietnamese troops gone, the Khmer Rouge and the Resistance generally was no longer tied down there. General fighting erupted again in August 1990, even as powerful countries were trying to promote a peace settlement. The government forces, the Cambodian People's Armed Forces (CPAF), lost the strategically important town of Staung. The aim of the Khmer Rouge was to cut railways and highways in order to close in on Phnom Penh and to demonstrate its power.

The UN created the United Nations Transitional authority (UNTAC) to supervise what was hoped would be 'post-war transition.' UNTAC consisted of 20,000 troops drawn from several countries, including Australia, Austria, Canada and Sweden, all under the command of Lieutenant General John Sanderson, an Australian. But even after fair and democratic elections the Khmer Rouge continued to be a threat. A government thrust under General Long Sopheap, in January 1994, captured a major Khmer Rouge base at Pailin, but the army could not penetrate certain parts of the country and could not prevent the Khmer Rouge from attacking settlements and trains. In July 1994 the Khmer Rouge captured three foreign tourists, a Briton, an Australian and a Frenchman, demanded a ransom for them, and eventually killed them. The Western Powers' inability to gain the freedom of their nationals demonstrated, yet again, the Khmer Rouge's domination over Cambodia without its being in government. At the end of 1994 it remained too strong to be crushed. Much of its power came from its being able to terrify ordinary Cambodians rather than from the number of ruthless fighters in its ranks.

Chad–Libya War *1986–8.* When Goukouni Queddei's Gouvernement d'Union Nationale Transition (GUNT) disintegrated in 1986 the Chad conflict changed from being a civil war into a war between Libya and Chad. At the end of 1986 Chadian forces routed the Libyans at Bardai and, in January 1987, at Fada and Zouar. Gaddafi was forced out of the Aouzou Strip. The Chad military leader was Idriss Deby, a flight lieutenant in the Chad Air Force who had been appointed Commander-in-Chief. Deby planned an anti-government coup but was betrayed; 800 of his followers were killed in fighting. Nevertheless, Deby captured the town of Tina in November, and on 20 November ambushed and wiped out a large government force at Guerada; a week later he captured Abeche. On 2 December, Deby's forces occupied Ndjamena and President Habre fled to Cameroon. Deby released 600 Libyan prisoners of war, but made it clear that he would fight to keep the Aouzou strip out of Gaddafi's hands.

Russia–Chechnya War *December 1994–1995.* The minor and tiny republic of Chechnya, which borders on Russia and Georgia, broke away from Russian control on 11 December 1994. The Chechen president, General Jolkhar Dudayev, leading only a few thousand irregularas, defied the Russian President, Boris Yeltsin, and the Defence Minister, General Pavel Grachev, who sent in a Russian force of 20,000. It was humiliated by the ill-armed Chechens. In one report the rebels claimed to have put out of action 100 Russian tanks and to have killed 600 Russian troops. The Russian leaders attacked the Chechen capital, Grozny, from the air but made the bizarre mistake of not surrounding the city before they assaulted it, on 31 December. Russian tanks and infantry became separated and the Chechen fighters took a heavy toll of both. Before a major assault early in January 1995 General Alexander Lebed, the most popular Russian general, announced that he would not allow any of his units to operate in Chechnya because 'it is absolutely unclear why we are killing people'. Most Western foreign ministers, though critical of Russia's brutal methods, favoured the overthrow of General Dudayev, said to be 'another Saddam Hussein'. When Russian troops captured the palace in Grozny on 18 January President Yeltsin announced that the war was 'effectively over'. However, neither side controlled the devastated centre of the capital or the outlying districts, and the war raged on. The conflict was remarkable for the way in which the Chechen fighters,

486

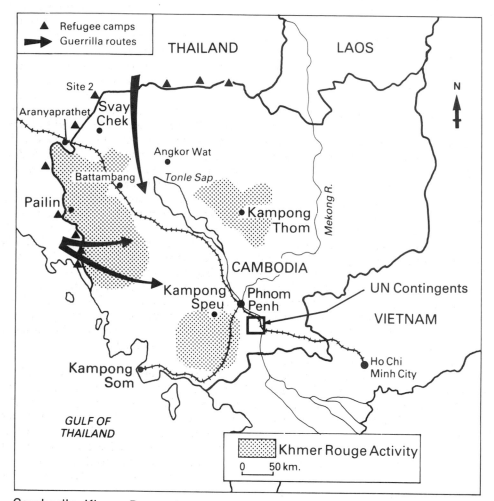

Cambodia: Khmer Rouge Activity Continues Despite Peace Efforts

armed with nothing more than tank-killing rocket-propelled grenades and AK-47 rifles, held out against the Russian army. The Russians suffered 3,500 casualties in the war and the Chechen irregulars an estimated 1,000. Civilian casualties greatly exceeded both.

Colombia Civil War *1958–92*. The war in Colombia began as a struggle between liberals and conservatives, but various armed groups then came into being. The main ones at the beginning were Colombian Armed Forces (FARC), the military wing of the Communist Party; 19th April Movement, known as M-19 and the most powerful force until displaced by the Army of National Liberation (ELN). The multiple wars, which were actual fighting wars, were made even more complex by the activities of the private armies owned by the narcotics barons. The most notorious of them was Pablo Escobar, who declared 'total war' against President Virgilio Barco. In 1988 the rule of law broke down but in 1990 M-19 and FARC disbanded under government military pressure. The government's Elite Force, under General Miguel Antonio Gomez, was trained by the British SAS and its successes were dramatic. In 1990 US military drug counter-narcotics experts set up an operation centre in Panama to co-ordinate policies in Latin America. The bloody war ended in 1994 when Pablo Escobar was killed by security forces. In the period 1985–94 the military's casualties were 3,200 killed, 5,600 wounded.

Cuito Cuanavale (*Angola Civil War*) *December 1987–March 1988*. One of the largest battles in Africa during the 20th century, other than those of World War II in North Africa, Cuito Cuanavale was the climax to earlier operations between the South African Defence Force (SADF) and National Union for the Total Liberation of Angola (UNITA) on one side and the Cuban Army backed by the Angolan government army on the other. Fighting had begun in August 1987 when the Angolans launched an offensive in the country's south with about 50,000 men. Between 9–16 November the SADF heavily supported UNITA on the Hube River, where the Angolan army lost 525 men killed. On 15 December the SADF fought a two-hour battle against the Angolan 21st Brigade as part of Operation Hooper. Operation Hooper ended South Africa's attempt to show that its aid for UNITA was marginal. More than 9,000 troops of the SADF were operating 400 miles deep in Angola, with tanks and heavy artillery. The SADF and UNITA began their siege of Cuito Cuanavale in December 1987, an operation that neither side could afford to lose. The Angolans, in deep bunkers, survived sustained SADF shelling. In January the South Africans mounted a large-scale assault, but it was blocked by Angolan–Cuban aircraft while Cuban Rangers reinforced the garrison. Further SADF attacks captured the town in March 1988, strengthening the SADF's position as the protector of UNITA and proving that South Africa was a regional power to be taken into account during any peace talks. The SADF lost 31 men killed and 90 wounded during the operations, UNITA 35 and the Angolan–Cuban allies about 1,500. *See* main entry for Angola.

East Timor Resistance War *1975–*. The Portuguese abandoned East Timor (also known as Timor-Dili) in 1975 after 500 years of colonialist rule. The civil war that followed was won by Frente Revolucionara de Timor-Leste, known as Fretelin. Fretelin declared independence on 3 November 1975. A few days later Indonesia, which already possessed West Timor, annexed East Timor. Within 10 years the Indonesian army had massacred 200,000 of the 1975 population of 688,000. The Minority Rights Group, London, reported: 'East Timor has incurred, in percentage terms, greater suffering from the Indonesian invasion than almost any other victim of invasion this century.' From their bases in the mountains and in forests, guerrillas, led by Xanana Gusmao, raid Indonesian army bases and posts and ambush patrols.

488

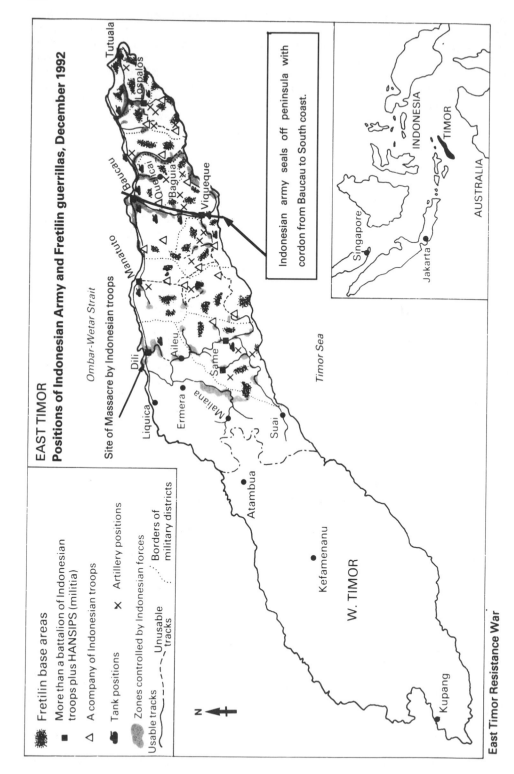

EAST TIMOR
Positions of Indonesian Army and Fretilin guerrillas, December 1992

Site of Massacre by Indonesian troops

Indonesian army seals off peninsula with cordon from Baucau to South coast.

Tutuala
Lospalos
Baucau
Quelicai
Baguia
Viqueque
Manatuto
Ombar-Wetar Strait
Dili
Aileu
Same
Maliana
Liquica
Ermera
Suai
Timor Sea
Atambua

W. TIMOR
Kefamenanu
Kupang

SINGAPORE
INDONESIA
Jakarta
TIMOR
AUSTRALIA

N

Fretilin base areas
More than a battalion of Indonesian troops plus HANSIPS (militia)
A company of Indonesian troops
Tank positions
Artillery positions
Zones controlled by Indonesian forces
Borders of military districts
Usable tracks
Unusable tracks

East Timor Resistance War

Fretelin's fighters are organised into units of 500 and their strategy is to surround various large settlements on a random basis, leading the Indonesians to ring each town with military posts. Having forced the occupation force to react, the Fretelin units moved on to another town. The Indonesian Army command structure changed in 1989 and in 1990 the Resistance reorganised because it was accepting more non-Fretelin members. It was now a smoothly functioning organisation of trained fighting men and women.

On 12 November 1991 Indonesian troops opened fire on several hundred Timorese in a Dili cemetery, peacefully attending a memorial mass for a resistance fighter shot the previous month. More than 90 people died in the massacre and others later died of their wounds. In January 1992 the Indonesian Army had another 'triumph', capturing Fretelin's deputy chief, Jose de Costa; a few weeks later they caught Xanana Gusmao, Fretelin's commander. Nino Kotis Santana took over and in 1993 claimed 'effective control' of East Timor.

Elephant Pass (*Sri Lanka Civil War*) *10 July–4 August 1991*. About 3,000 Tamil troops of the Liberation Tigers of Tamil Eelam (LTTE) including 500 women soldiers, attacked a Sri Lankan army stronghold at the head of Elephant Pass. This narrow stretch of dunes and marshes connects the Sri Lanka mainland with Jaffna Peninsula, which the Tamils claim as their own. The army garrison of 1,000 held out but after some days the Tamils were clearly winning their first excursion into open warfare. The Sri Lankan High Command landed 8,000 troops and marines, under Brigadier Vijaya Wimalaratne, on a beach six miles from the beleagured base, but against Tamil suicide attacks they progressed only 300 yards a day. After 24 days the relief column broke the siege. Having lost 564 fighters killed the LTTE leader, Vilupillai Prabhakaran, ordered a withdrawal. The army lost 200 men killed. The LTTE appeared to be unaffected by the reverse.

El Salvador *1980–94*. The regime of Jose Napoleon Duarte was ruthlessly oppressive and his death squads killed more than 60,000 people up to 1988. The Salvadorean army, at first no more than 12,000 unruly killers, became a US-trained counter-revolutionary army of 57,000 but it could still not crush the 8,000 guerrillas. In the period 1989–90 there were two major developments. One was the army's 'hearts and minds' campaign to woo the peasants away from their support for the guerrillas. The other was the biggest rebel offensive of the war when 3,500 guerrillas entered the capital, San Salvador, in a massive raid. The humiliated army countered with death squad massacres. Again reorganised and equipped with the latest American weapons, the army's chain of command was still so cumbersome that 'immediate reaction' battalions could not, in fact, react quickly. In 1990 the rebels, under Joaquin Villalobos, agreed to peace talks, but only if they could negotiate with the military as equals. Colonel Mauricio Vargas, the military's negotiator, said that this demand was an 'insurmountable obstacle'. At no time did hostilities cease but in 1993–4 a degree of stability reached El Salvador, largely because aid from outside was drying up, for both government and insurgents. In fraudulent elections held on 24 April 1994, ARENA, the government party, was victorious but the rebels, now a legal party, emerged as the second political force. *See* main entry.

Georgia Civil War *1993*. Abkhazia, a part of Georgia demanding independence, privately obtained weapons and munitions from Russian generals, and overwhelmed the national army of Eduard Shevardnadze, which retreated to Tbilisi. The Russian leader, Boris Yeltsin, then supplied arms to Shevardnadze enabling him to put down the Abkhazis. Much damage was done during this strange war, which indicated Russia's total control over Georgia.

Guatemala Guerrilla War *1980–*. Unrest continued in Guatemala after the upheaval of 1954 with guerrilla groups fighting the government over land reform and wealth distribution. The government's main response was to massacre civilians suspected of providing the guerrillas with shelter and food. In 1990 Amnesty International reported that 130,000 civilians had been killed since 1960. The four groups of revolutionaries remained in collaboration under the title Guatemalan National Revolutionary Unity, but in 1994 probably numbered no more than 2,000 fighting men. Their strength in the field was more formidable than this low number of men might suggest and in 1991 the army rushed Special Forces to three provinces. The rebels sank a naval patrol boat in Puerto Quetzal naval base. The Guatemalan military was outstandingly unsuccessful against the guerrillas, who were led by Rodrigo Asturias.

The Gulf War 1990–1. On 2 August 1990 Iraq invaded its neighbour Kuwait and thus precipitated a great international reaction and a destructive war. Control of Kuwait's coastline would give Iraq greater and more convenient access to the Persian (or Arabian) Gulf. Iraq's leader, Saddam Hussein, also demanded rights to the Rumailah oilfields on the Kuwait–Iraq border. Poor intelligence left the West at a great strategic and psychological disadvantage in the first weeks of the confrontation. The UN Security Council condemned Iraq's invasion, urged a ceasefire and demanded a withdrawal. Saddam Hussein strengthened his hold over Kuwait and the UN mounted Operation DESERT SHIELD to prevent any further Iraqi aggression. For Britain it was Operation GRANBY and for the French, Operation DAGUET. Commander-in-Chief was American Lieutenant General H Norman Schwartzkopf. By 30 August the American commitment in the Gulf and Saudi Arabia had risen to 260,000 men. Arab–Islamic forces totalled nearly 200,000 from 13 countries. Iraq moved 550,000 troops and 4,200 tanks into the Kuwaiti theatre.

DESERT SHIELD was succeeded on 16 January 1991 by DESERT STORM, the code-name for the UN campaign to eject Iraqi forces from Kuwait. The Iraqi forces had supposedly been on maximum alert for several days, but UN air and missile attack achieved almost complete surprise. Allied aircraft pounded targets in Iraq and Kuwait almost round-the-clock, targeting in particular *Scud* and other missile sites, command posts and communications, troop concentrations and artillery emplacements. The Iraqis fired *Scuds* against Israel and Saudi Arabia. On 24 February Schwartzkopf commenced the ground war; the US 1st Marine Division led Egyptian, Saudi and Kuwaiti units into Kuwait and reoccupied Kuwait City. The British 1st Armoured Division and US formations attacked through southern Iraq, defeating Republican Guard tank divisions and moving on Basra.

Trapped by the Allies' encircling movements, the Iraqi armies were defeated in detail in 100 days. Only two divisions out of 42 in the southern sector remained operational. A ceasefire came into effect on 28 February 1991. Allied losses: American, 389 killed, some of them accidentally, and 457 wounded. Other Allied casualties, 77 killed 830 wounded. Iraqi casualties: 100,000 killed, 300,000 wounded (US Defence Intelligence Agency); 30,000 killed, 100,000 wounded (British Ministry of Defence). At the ceasefire the Western Allies had nearly 500,000 men in the theatre; the US had 100 ships, Britain 18 and France 10, with 14 other nations contributing a total of 46 ships. In addition, the US was using another 250 ships to supply its army.

India–Pakistan War 1947–. The war, with its occasional flare-ups ranging in intensity from skirmishes to battles, is over Kashmir. India claims two-thirds while Pakistan claims the entire region on the grounds that the majority of the population is Muslim. The permanent presence of UN observers in Kashmir does not prevent fighting: it merely ensures that it is

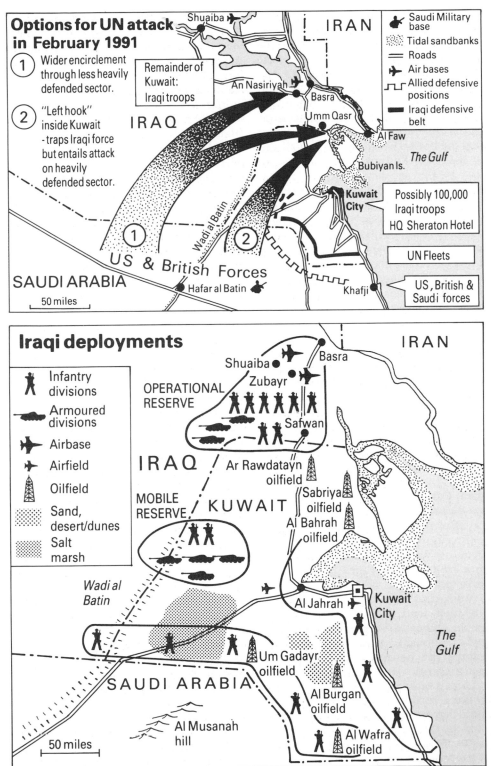

Options for UN attack in February 1991

① Wider encirclement through less heavily defended sector.

② "Left hook" inside Kuwait - traps Iraqi force but entails attack on heavily defended sector.

Remainder of Kuwait: Iraqi troops

IRAN

Shuaiba

An Nasiriyah

IRAQ

Basra

Umm Qasr

Al Faw

The Gulf

Bubiyan Is.

Kuwait City

Possibly 100,000 Iraqi troops HQ Sheraton Hotel

UN Fleets

US, British & Saudi forces

SAUDI ARABIA

US & British Forces

Hafar al Batin

Khafji

Wadi al Batin

50 miles

- Saudi Military base
- Tidal sandbanks
- Roads
- Air bases
- Allied defensive positions
- Iraqi defensive belt

Iraqi deployments

- Infantry divisions
- Armoured divisions
- Airbase
- Airfield
- Oilfield
- Sand, desert/dunes
- Salt marsh

IRAN

Shuaiba

Basra

Zubayr

OPERATIONAL RESERVE

Safwan

IRAQ

Ar Rawdatayn oilfield

MOBILE RESERVE

KUWAIT

Sabriya oilfield

Al Bahrah oilfield

Wadi al Batin

Al Jahrah

Kuwait City

The Gulf

Um Gadayr oilfield

SAUDI ARABIA

Al Burgan oilfield

Al Musanah hill

Al Wafra oilfield

50 miles

The Iraq War

reported. Territory has changed hands. For instance, India's Siachen Glacier operations pushed Pakistan back from the Nubra Valley, while Pakistan took over the provinces of Gilgit and Baltistan. The conflict intensified to dangerous levels in 1990 and even in winter, when the battlefront is normally quiet, the tensions often erupt into violence. The hostilities along the border between Indian Kashmir and Pakistani Kashmir have, since 1990, been merely incidental to the greater struggle being waged inside Kashmir. This conflict takes place in the great Kashmir Valley and especially in Srinigar, between militants, both Hindu and Muslim, wanting total independence for Kashmir. Uprisings lead to clashes between Indian troops and Kashmiri Muslim fighters. Indian troops rape and torture Muslim women, a deliberate part of Indian army policy. The wars of 1962, 1965 and 1971 resulted in total Indian fatalities of only 6,000, but another war would involve destruction to civilian centres on a great scale. China would not allow India to break Pakistan, which would also be backed by the entire Muslim world. The conflict could lead to the first use of a nuclear bomb since 1945, as both sides possess such a bomb. During 1994 there were threats of war by both sides.

Jaffna Fort (*Sri Lankan Civil War*) *June–September 1990*.

An old Dutch fort, Jaffna was held by Sri Lankan forces, an affront to the Tamils of Liberation Tigers of Tamil Eelam (LTTE) since Jaffna itself was the Tamil 'capital'. The Tamils made several vain attempts to scale the walls and attacked several military installations and two naval bases in the area. In August a Sri Lankan helicopter gunship ambushed 200 Tigers cycling to reinforce the besiegers of the fort and wiped them out. After a siege of 96 days the Sri Lanka defence forces broke through the Tamil cordon to relieve the garrison. On 26 September the government abandoned the fort and the LTTE claimed that this was a victory for them. Casualties were heavy on both sides.

Battle to relieve Khost (*Afghanistan War*) *December 1987–January 1988*.

The Afghan Army, backed by Soviet forces, garrisoned Khost in 1981 with 8,000 troops. Khost commands the mouth of a frontier pass close to the Pakistan border and the Mujihadeen laid siege to it. In December 1987 the Soviet–Afghan allies used armour, artillery and air support to protect a large convoy of trucks in an operation to relieve the great fortress. Having only light guns and multi-barrel short-range rocket launchers the guerrillas could not reach the targets on the plain, but themselves came under fire from heavy artillery. Soviet SU-25 warplanes dropped 1,000 lb bombs on the Mujihadeen positions. The action to relieve Khost was successful, but it cost the Soviet–Afghan force 150 dead and left the guerrillas still holding the heights, and as many as 10,000 guerrillas continued to ambush Soviet convoys on the road from Gardez to Khost. The troops who forced their way through to Khost had to run the gauntlet of Mujihadeen fire when they took the trucks out of Khost. The end situation was that while the operation enabled the garrison to hold Khost, the siege was not broken and it continued until the war ended. Mujihadeen casualties were probably about 150 dead and 250 wounded.

Battle of Koran (*Afghanistan War*) *December 1987*.

Small though it was, this battle showed the tactical skill and fighting ability of the Mujihadeen Resistance. The plan to attack Koran, a garrison town north-east of Kabul, was the work of Ahmad Shah Massoud, who built a scale model of the defences. In the hills above Kabul he placed troops armed with Stinger anti-aircraft missiles to protect his assault force of 550 men from Soviet and Afghan government jets and helicopter gunships. Massoud's surprise attack at dawn was successful, though he said that his casualties of 14 killed and 11 wounded were 'unacceptably high'. The Army lost 29 killed, 60 wounded and more than 350 captured.

Kurdish War of Independence 1975–.

Following World War I, Allied forces and the defeated Turkey drew up the Treaty of Sévres, which recognised the right of the Kurds to create their own state. The treaty was never ratified. The Kurds occupy a region which straddles the borders of Iraq, Iran, Syria, Turkey and the former Soviet Union, all of which oppose the idea of a separate Kurdish state. The Kurds, members of one 'Front' or another or a 'Liberation Army', have fought a guerrilla war since 1975. Saddam Hussein turned against his own Kurds in March 1988 when he began a campaign of unrestricted chemical warfare against them. Following the UN War against Saddam in 1990 the British and French created a 'safe haven' for the Kurds in northern Iraq.

During 1990–2 the main focus of the Kurds' fight for independence moved to Turkey. The Kurdish Workers Party (PKK), with a fighting strength estimated at 8,000, waged an armed struggle across south-eastern Turkey. The People's Liberation Army of Kurdistan (ARGK) was similarly active and its operations reached the proportions of a fullscale insurrection. Some 'battles' lasted for four days. Simultaneously, Iran's 8,000,000 Kurds are locked in a bloody struggle with the Islamic Revolutionary Guards. In 1994 the Kurds were still under attack by Iran, Iraq and Turkey though these countries did not have a concerted military approach to the 'Kurdish problem'.

Vastly experienced guerrilla fighters, the Kurds are capable of sustained operations, as the Battle of Kuarkouk showed. On 19 July 1988, 500 peshmerga (guerrillas) held a strategic position close to where the Iraqi, Iranian and Turkish frontiers meet. In command of the Kurds was Jamil Goran, a former colonel in the Iraqi army, who placed his men in shallow trenches behind sangars. The Iraqi High Command parachuted the crack 68th Commando Brigade of 1,800 men into what it supposed was the Kurds' rear. In fact, Goran's force had no rear and caused the Iraqis such heavy casualties that the

Brigade ceased to function. On 27 July fresh Iraqi units made no impression on the Kurds' defences. After a week the Kurds withdrew in good order towards the Turkish border and further Iraqi units could not halt this movement. On 2 September the Iraqi Air Force dropped gas bombs, an action that continued until Turkish protests to Saddam Hussein put an end to it. On 5 September Jamil Goran crossed the frontier. He had lost 28 fighters; Iraqi casualties, according to Turkish estimates, were 2,000.

Liberia Civil War December 1989–.

Troops of the National Patriotic Forces of Liberia (NDPL) invaded Liberia from Ivory Coast to overthrow President Samuel Doe. The NDPL army of 10,000, under Charles Taylor, overran most of the country but broke into two tribal groups, the other being led by Yarmie Johnson. The savage fighting and mounting casualties brought into being a West African Peace-Keeping Force (WAPF) consisting of troops from Nigeria, Ghana, Guinea, Sierra Leone and Gambia which deployed in Liberia in September 1990. In the first 10 months of the war, as Taylor and Johnson fought for control, 60,000 people were killed, apart from combatants. The war degenerated into one of tribal hatreds and all groups sought vengeance on others. The conflict was continuing into 1994.

Massawa (Eritrean War of Independence), January 1990.

Ethiopian government troops began a three-pronged offensive against the Eritrean People's Democratic Revolutionary Front (EPDRF) on 14 January 1990. The EPDRF lured a large force deep into its territory and attacked on the flanks, killing 3,000 Ethiopians and wounding 4,000. The Ethiopians suffered further losses on the Debre Tabor front in battles on 18 and 19 January and in the battle of Gondor on 20 January. The Eritrean People's Liberation Front (EPLF) launched a surprise attack at Massawa to blunt the Ethiopian build-up for an

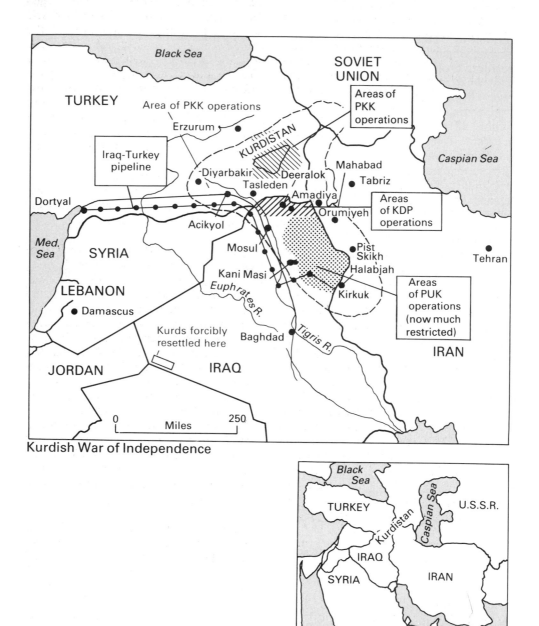

Kurdish War of Independence

offensive on the Keren front. The EPLF put 35,000 Ethiopian soldiers out of action in capturing Massawa and in subsequent fighting on the Ghinda front. It captured 80 tanks, 8 B-21 rocket launchers and 20,000 light weapons. The guerrillas also destroyed most of the navy's speedboats and captured the naval facilities at Massawa. The battle of Massawa was one of the largest battles in Africa since 1943.

Morocco–Polisario War *1976–92*. Following Spain's withdrawal from its former colony of Western Sahara in 1976, Morocco and Mauretania partitioned the country, not reckoning with the Popular Front for the Liberation of Saguia al-Jamra and Rio de Oro (Polisario). Polisario went to war to achieve independence and defeated a Mauritanian force. Morocco claimed the entire area but, unable to occupy the territory in the face of Polisario harassment, its army built the 1,000-mile Hassan Wall, a system of fortified defences. Despite the Wall, its garrison of 110,000 and advanced surveillance systems, the Moroccan Army was unable to restrict Polisario's operations. In a major operation on 7 October 1989, Polisario attacked the Hassan Wall in the Guelta Zammour area, breaching 10 miles of defences and killing 200 Moroccan troops. Four 'battles' took place between December 1989–March 1990. Under UN supervision a referendum was held at the end of 1993. The result showed a majority of Sahrawis in favour of union with Morocco. Hostilities lessened but the garrison of the Hassan Wall was not reduced in 1994.

Mozambique Civil War *1982–94*. Following Mozambique's war of independence against Portugal the Mozambique National Resistance (MNR, or Renamo) came into being to oppose the Mozambique Liberation Front (FRELIMO). In 1982 South Africa entered the conflict and supported Renamo to ensure that Mozambique could not become a threat to South African security. Portugal, Morocco, Saudi Arabia and Zaire also aided Renamo. Armed conflict raged throughout the country. 'Two ill-fed and ill-equipped armies stagger around the countryside like punch-drunk boxers in a hopeless military stalemate,' wrote a Western journalist in 1990. Following the collapse of European communism, the governments of Eastern Europe, once so generous with their help for the government, were no longer able to provide aid. Following peace talks in Rome during 1991 the fighting became less intense and widespread and the war officially ended in December 1993. During 1994 intermittent fighting took place, with Frelimo receiving military supplies from China.

Nagorny-Karabakh War of Independence *1988–*. Nagorny-Karabakh is an enclave, peopled mostly by Christian Armenians, within the republic of Azerbaijan whose population consists mostly of Muslim Azeris. When the Nagorny-Karabakh Armenians sought to become part of autonomous Soviet Armenia they were attacked by the Azeris and widespread fighting occurred in 1988–9. President Gorbachev demanded that both the militias hand over their weapons to the Soviet Army but they ignored the order. The Azeri militia cut all road and rail routes linking the Armenian region to the outside world and the Armenians became dependent on air supply. Fighting continued into 1994.

Nicaragua Civil War *1979–88*. The 'Contra War' ground to a halt in late 1988 when the US Congress cut off military aid to the insurgents. The Bush administration reluctantly endorsed the Congressional decision, which had been influenced by the Arias Accord of 1987. This was named for President Arias of Costa Rica, who won the Nobel Peace Prize for his efforts to 'further the peace process' in Central America. Officially the Contra War was over but the Contras refused to disband, and on 1 November 1989 President Daniel Ortega of the Sandanista Party declared a new offensive against them. Mrs Violette Chamorro and her 14-party coalition won the national elections, an unexpected reverse for the ruling Sandanistas. An immediate ceasefire was arranged and on 25 April 1990 the rebels began to surrender their weapons. They were disarmed and demobilised by June 1990. In December that year 70 armed former Contras seized a police post and gave battle to Sandanista soldiers at Jalapa, 125 miles north of Managua. In 1994 Nicaragua was in a state of uneasy tension and a renewal of the war seemed possible. *See* main entry.

Northern Ireland Terrorist War *1984–94*. The war intensified in 1984–5 and by mid-1987 the British Army had 10,200 men in Northern Ireland in an attempt to keep the peace. The IRA's policy was to provoke the British government and army to introduce punitive measures so harsh that the IRA propagandists could claim 'repression.' Overall, the strategy was 'diversification,' meaning indiscriminate attacks on 'soft' targets. Attacks took place in Germany, Holland and on the British mainland. During the first four months of 1990 the IRA made 43 attacks in Northern Ireland. Secure caches of arms and Semtex explosives imported from Libya gave the IRA all the material it would need for a decade. At the end of May 1990 the IRA murdered two young Australians on holiday in Holland, believing them to be British soldiers on leave from Germany. More incidents took place in 1990 than in any year since 1974. In 1993 the IRA exploded bombs in the Lancashire city of Warrington and in London, killing civilians and causing widespread damage. In March 1994 the IRA fired mortar bombs into Heathrow Airport, London. Nobody was injured but the attack indicated that the IRA felt able to operate in Britain with impunity. On 31 August 1994 Sinn Fein/IRA announced an end to violence but refused to say whether the end was permanent, despite the British government's insistence that it do so. Loyalist (Unionist) paramilitary violence continued. Many military analysts and Northern Ireland experts believed that the

IRA's 'peace' was a tactical manoeuvre, but Sinn Fein's leader Gerry Adams was hailed in the United States as a peacemaker. On 14 October 1994 the Loyalist paramilitary organisations declared an end to violence and the peace became complete, though many people remained doubtful about its durability. *See* main entry.

Peru's 'Shining Path' War *1980–*. In 1980 Abimael Guzman, a professor of philosophy, founded the Communist Party of Peru, which became known as Sendero Luminoso (Shining Path), from the movement's slogan. Sendero Luminoso declared war against the Peruvian state and attacked the army, police and their 'collaborators', while the forces of law and order committed atrocities against 'collaborators' of Shining Path. In 1988 the Rodrigo Franco Command (CRF) made its appearance. Encouraged by senior government officials, it killed academics and others who showed sympathy for Sendero Luminoso and other rebel movements that emerged in its wake, such as Tupac Amaru Revolutionary Movement (MRTA). Desperate peasants formed village defence groups against Sendero Luminoso. Deaths from the general anarchy had reached 30,000 in 1992, the year in which Abimael Guzman was captured in Lima. Tried and sentenced to life imprisonment, Guzman was incarcerated in an island underground prison, but his supporters maintained their war.

Philippines' 'People's War' *1969–94*. The Communist Party of the Philippines (CPP) and its military wing, the National People's Army (NPA) began a 'People's War' against the corrupt President Marcos in 1969. After many minor successes, by 1984 the NPA was active in 60 of the 73 provinces. Its strategic centre was on Samar Island. Other armed rebel groups included the Bagsa Moro army, the Moro Islamic Liberation Front (MILF) and the Cordillera People's Liberation Army

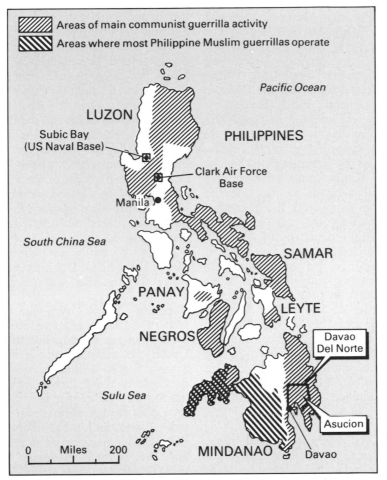

Legend:
- Areas of main communist guerrilla activity
- Areas where most Philippine Muslim guerrillas operate

Pacific Ocean

LUZON

PHILIPPINES

Subic Bay
(US Naval Base)

Clark Air Force
Base

Manila

South China Sea

SAMAR

PANAY

LEYTE

NEGROS

Davao
Del Norte

Sulu Sea

Asucion

0   Miles   200

MINDANAO   Davao

Philippines Guerrilla War

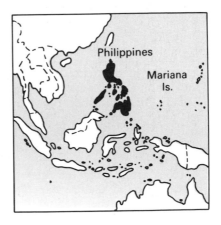

Philippines

Mariana
Is.

(CPLA). The war continued even after the deposing of President Marcos in 1986 and losses were heavy on both sides. For instance, in 1988, 1,913 guerrillas, 912 members of the security forces and probably 2,000 civilians died. Under President Cory Aquino and the Defence Secretary, General Fidel Ramos, a new strategy was adopted in 1989. The old search-and-destroy methods, whose success was measured in body counts, were replaced by seven-person Special Operations Teams using political and psychological methods to dissuade the peasants from supporting the guerrillas. President Aquino and her supporters crushed an army rebellion in 1989. In 1990 Rodolfo Aguinaldo, the governor of Cagayan Province, led an uprising but in the consequent campaign most of his men were killed. In 1992 General Ramos succeeded Mrs Aquino as president and reformed the army. He also succeeded in cutting off most of the arms and supplies reaching the rebels and in 1994 the People's War simmered down, though several 'armies' remained undefeated in the mountains and jungles of the Philippines islands.

Rwanda Civil Wars *1990* and *1994*. Ninety per cent of the Rwandan population of 6.5 million were Hutu peasant farmers, but the Tutsi tribe developed a system of feudal overlordship, enforcing their political will through their superior wealth. They also had a monopoly on military organisation. During 1963 and 1964 Tutsi guerrillas made many raids against the Hutus, who in turn waged war against the Tutsis. On 1 October 1990 a Tutsi rebel force calling itself the Rwandan Patriotic Army (RPA) invaded Rwanda from Uganda. The rebels were anxious to present themselves as a national rather than a rebel army. Most of the fighting took place around Gabiro barracks, 60 miles from the capital, Kigali. At the joint request of President Habyarimana of Rwanda and President Musaveni of Uganda, France and Belgium sent peace-keeping troops. The brief war was over within the month but diplomats in Kigali said that further fighting was inevitable.

They were right. On 6 April 1994 the presidents of Rwanda and Burundi were killed when a missile brought down the aircraft in which they were travelling. The Hutus blamed the Tutsis for Habyarimana's death and the Hutu–Tutsi hatreds flared up again. As the Hutus began to slaughter the Tutsis, the Rwanda Patriotic Front (RPF) of the Tutsi tribe attacked the barracks of the Hutu-dominated presidential guard in the capital city, Kigali. In the tribal madness that followed more than one million people were massacred, according to UN estimates. Virtually the entire population was displaced and a major UN humanitarian and peace-keeping effort was necessary.

Somalia Wars *1974–94*. In 1969 Major General Siyad Barre seized power in a coup, and in 1970 turned to the Soviet Union for aid and advice. When the Soviets armed Ethiopian troops during the Ogaden crisis, Somalia cut all ties with the Soviets. From that time Somali and Ethiopian troops were at war until May 1988. Barre and the Ethiopian leader, Colonel Mengistu, negotiated a pull-back but the Somali National Movement (SNM) began a major attack on northern Somalia, hoping to overthrow Barre. The war was fought on mainly tribal lines. The large Ogadeni tribe made up much of the army, together with some of the Darode clan. The Isaq and Hawich tribes opposed the government. By mid-1990 almost incessant fighting had reduced Somalia to chaos. More than 50,000 people died in what was known as 'the Northern War'. The fighting reached a climax in January 1991. The guerrillas mounted forays and the Government replied with sweep-up operations. Neither side could knock the other out. Barre fled from Mogadishu on 27 January. Casualties during the final two weeks of the war amounted to 1,500 dead and 'several thousand' wounded. Unrest continued unabated and the UN was drawn into the conflict. The main military responsibility fell to the US whose troops landed near Mogadishu in December 1992. Pakistan, Australia and Nigeria also supplied troops, and later Ethiopia and Eritrea, in what was intended basically as a humanitarian mission. The followers of Somali warlord General Muhammad Aidid opposed the UN operation and attempts to capture him proved fruitless. In Operation Quickdraw, 31 March 1994, the Americans withdrew from Somalia, where conflict and disorder continued.

Sri Lanka Civil War *1983-*. Open fighting between the Buddhist Sinhalese and the Hindu Tamils began in 1983 when the Tamils turned to violence in order to obtain a separate state in the north, to be called Eelam. Several guerrilla groups were created, notably the Liberation Tigers of Tamil Eelam (LTTE). Heavily armed by the Tamils of India, the Sri Lankan Tamils developed the structure of a regular army so that when the Sri Lankan forces attacked their bases on the Jaffna Peninsula in February 1987, the Tamils survived. Prime Minister of India Rajiv Gandhi sent an Indian Peace-Keeping Force (IPKF) in 1986 but during its Operation PAWAN the IPKF suffered 2,500 casualties and its 70,000 troops were withdrawn at the end of September 1989.

A new threat to law and order developed in southern Sri Lanka. The Janata Vimukti Paramuna (JVP) a Maoist group, declared war against the central government, which supported right-wing death squads to overcome JVP. In the end the JVP was overwhelmed by government security forces. But there was no defeating the Tigers, under their leader, Vilupillai Probhakaran. Having fought the security forces for seven years the Tamils declared an indefinite ceasefire on 31 December 1990. On 2 March the Minister for Defence, Ranjan Wijeratne, was killed by a car bomb and the following month the security forces launched an offensive against the rebels. The Tamils counter-attacked at once and atrocities committed by one side matched those of the other. The government began Operation THUNDERBOLT, a security operation involving the random check of many vehicles in Colombo for explosives and weapons. On 21 June 1991 a Tamil suicide bomber planted a car bomb near military headquarters; it killed 80 people and wounded 200.

The army's Operation LIGHTNING STRIKE against Tamil strongholds in the Mullaittavu jungle of northern Sri Lanka was largely successful, but while the Tamils of Tamil Nadu — the Tamil state in southern India — continued to help the Sri Lankan Tamils the total defeat of the LTTE and its allies seemed remote.

In September 1993 Sri Lankan forces attacked rebel-held areas in the north in the biggest offensive for more than a year. The army destroyed a well-fortified women's camp and attempted to seal off Kilali lagoon. The Tigers, piloting explosive-laden boats in suicide attacks, rammed naval boats. The offensive ground to a halt and was continued in a desultory but always savage manner into 1994. *See* Elephant Pass, Jaffna Fort.

Second Sudan Civil War *1982-*. When President Gaafer Nimieri was overthrown in a coup in 1985, the embattled Sudan People's Liberation Army (SPLA) hoped for peace overtures from his successor, Sadiq al-Mahdi, but al-Mahdi maintained the harsh Islamic law of the *sharia* and Colonel John Garang, leader of the SPLA, prepared for a long war. He went on the offensive in 1988, moved northwards and achieved some victories, but overwhelming force and air power forced him back to the Christian south. Iraq provided the government's forces with the bombs used in attacks on Christian-held towns. On 30 June 1989 Brigadier Oman Hassan al-Bashir overthrew the al-Mahdi government and set up an even more repressive regime of Islamic militants. Colonel Gaddafi of Libya lent al-Bashir MiG-23 jets to bomb SPLA positions. In the period 1990-4 much of the war was fought along roads where army convoys on their way to relieve besieged garrisons came under SPLA guns. The main sufferers through-

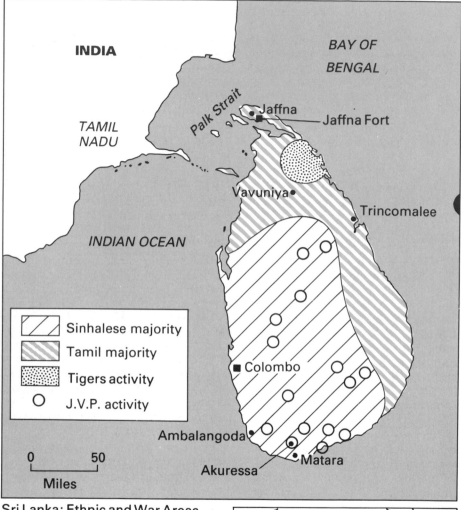

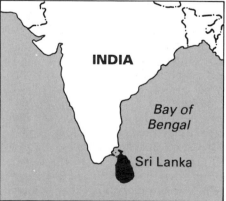

Sri Lanka: Ethnic and War Areas

out the war, unfinished in 1994, were the Christian civilians of the south.

Yugoslav Civil Wars *1990–*. The nation of Yugoslavia consisted in 1945 of six republics: Serbia, Slovenia, Croatia, Bosnia-Herzegovina, Montenegro and Macedonia. Despite their tensions, these republics may have gone on living in peace but for the break-up of Eastern Europe during 1989–90. On 25 June Slovenia declared its independence from the rest of Yugoslavia and the first clash of the war that followed occurred at Velika Bas on 30 June. As other republics demanded independence the Yugoslav army faced war on several fronts and ancient hatreds erupted, for instance those between the Serb-Orthodox Christians in Bosnia and the majority Muslims in Bosnia and that between Serbs and Croats. The Serbs shelled Dubrovnik, 'the jewel of the Adriatic', and a place without military significance, for no better reason than that it was peopled by Croats.

Croatia and Slovenia gained their independence and in April 1992 the European Community and the United States recognised the independence of Bosnia-Herzegovina. Confused and constant fighting took place between the Yugoslav Army and its allied Serb militants on one side and the allied Muslims and Croats on the other. Serb strategy was to pick off one town after another and engage in 'ethnic cleansing' — this meant the murder and expulsion of Muslims. The Muslims were the main sufferers in 1993–4 and Bosnia was the main battlefield. Over and over again the West and the UN promised to help the Muslim victims and threatened reprisals against the Bosnian Serbs but did little beyond declaring six areas to be 'safe zones', a meaningless label. One of these was the capital, Sarajevo, which was relentlessly shelled by Serb guns on heights surrounding the city. On the morning of 12 February 1993 a mortar shell burst killing 68 people queueing for bread in Sarajevo's central market. NATO threatened to use its air power against the Serbs but did not insist that the Serbs lift their siege of the city, and snipers were not forbidden to fire into the city.

The Serbs turned their attention to Gorazde, which they regarded as a strategic prize. At the request of the UN commander in Bosnia, Lieut.-General Sir Michael Rose, on 11 April 1994 NATO made its first attack against ground forces since the Alliance was formed in 1950. Serb shelling stopped soon after the bombing but before long some of the most bitter fighting of the Bosnian war took place. Later NATO air strikes did nothing to lessen the Serb's brutality and militancy. Seizure of their heavy weapons reduced the shelling of Sarajevo, but frequently they showed their contempt for foreign intervention by taking back some of the weapons and by operating tanks in areas where they had agreed not to go. At one time, when NATO threatened to use force to lift the siege of Sarajevo, Russia sent its own troops to take up positions around the capital, ostensibly to aid NATO. It was clear that the West could not make air strikes or engage in ground action against the Serbs without consulting Russia. The American initiative to stop the fighting between the Muslim government forces and the HVO, the Bosnian Croat militia, was more successful.

Meanwhile the UN embargo on supplies reaching Serbia itself continued. In mid-summer 1994 its leader, Slobodan Milosevic, ordered the Bosnian Serbs to comply with UN resolutions and when they failed to do so he cut off supplies to them. This merely made them more obdurate and from time to time they stopped UN columns from reaching besieged enclaves with humanitarian aid, and they took UN observers hostage. The defiance of the Bosnian Serbs was a possibly fatal blow to Western hopes of containing the conflict with limited military action. It was also a severe political and military humiliation. The US had to turn to Russia to use its considerable influence with the Serbs and made desperate efforts to restart negotiations to end the conflict. The wars in

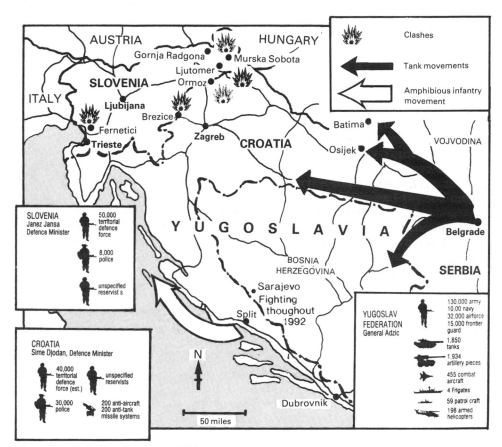

Yugoslav Civil War (August 1991)

ex-Yugoslavia repeatedly showed the very difficult problems for miliary commanders when they were not given freedom of action or the firepower they need. The political leader of the Bosnian Serbs, Radovan Karadic, and the military commander, General Radko Mladic, were totally without compromise — except as a tactic to secure a military advantage — and were the major obstacles in the search for peace. At the end of 1994 the wars in former Yugoslavia had cost 400,000 lives, the majority being Muslims; many more had been injured and two million people had been displaced (UN estimates).

Zulu–ANC War *1990–4*. The open and ferocious violence between the Zulu Inkatha movement, led by Chief Mangosuthu Buthelezi, and fighters of the African National Congress (ANC), has few equals in any contemporary war, other than that in Rwanda in 1994 and parts of former Yugoslavia in 1990–4. In its goal to control all South Africa through a central government, the ANC knew that it must break Zulu power in Natal Province. The leaders of the 7,000,000 Zulus had quite different policies from the ANC. Whole villages fled in terror as Zulu impis swarmed towards them behind feather-topped shields and waving spears and pangas. The bloodshed of August 1990 was the most concentrated upsurge of violence seen in South Africa in the 20th century, until the massacres in Rwanda in 1994. In two weeks of fighting more than 600 people were killed and 3,500 injured. Neither Chief Buthelezei nor ANC leader Nelson Mandela were able to stop the fighting, but it died down in 1994 after the first democratic elections held in South Africa brought the ANC to power. The Zulus also won seats in the new parliament.